THE BBC SYMPHONY ORCHESTRA

THE
BBC SYMPHONY ORCHESTRA

The first fifty years

1930-1980

Nicholas Kenyon

BRITISH BROADCASTING CORPORATION

Published by the
British Broadcasting Corporation
35 Marylebone High Street
London W1M 4AA

ISBN 0 563 17617 2

First published 1981
© British Broadcasting Corporation 1981

Filmset by August Filmsetting, Stockport, Cheshire
Printed in England
by William Clowes (Beccles) Ltd

Contents

Foreword by Sir Adrian Boult ix

Introduction x

Acknowledgments xiii

1 'In the air': to 1930 1

2 Boult's Great Orchestra: 1930–35 49

3 International Fame: 1935–39 110

4 Keeping Music Alive: 1939–45 155

5 Renewals and Replacements: 1945–50 192

6 The Sargent/Schwarz Era: 1950–1962 230

7 Winds of Change: 1959–71 289

8 A French Revolution? 1971–75 358

9 From Kempe to Rozhdestvensky: 1973–80 396

Bibliography 436

Appendices

A Personalia 439

B First performances by the BBC Symphony Orchestra,
22 October 1930–22 October 1980 447

C The concerts of contemporary music:
complete programmes 1931–39 488

D The BBC Symphony Orchestra: a discography 499

E The fiftieth anniversary season, 1980–81 509

F The BBC Symphony Chorus 1928–80 513

General Index 518

Index of Composers and Works 533

List of Illustrations

Between pages 114–15
BBC string orchestra rehearsing under Percy Pitt in the 1920s (BBC); Percy Pitt; Roger Eckersley (© Tim Eckersley); BBC Symphony Orchestra with Adrian Boult in the Queen's Hall, 1930 (BBC); Adrian Boult in 1934 (BBC); Serge Koussevitzky rehearsing in 1935 (BBC); Willem Mengelberg (EA); Bruno Walter (Exclusive New Agency, Roehampton); Toscanini in 1935 (BBC); The Symphony Orchestra's first Continental tour, 1936 (© Tim Eckersley); The tour leaves Vienna for Budapest; Toscanini and his wife, 1938 (BBC Hulton Picture Library); Cecil Graves, Roger Eckersley and Sir John Reith in 1935 (© Tim Eckersley); William Walton conducting the Symphony Orchestra, Bedford 1941 (BBC).

Between pages 178–9
BBC Symphony Orchestra in 1942 (all BBC): First Violins, leader Paul Beard; Cellos, principal Ambrose Gauntlett (left); Flutes, principal Gerald Jackson; Clarinets, principal Frederick Thurston; Bassoons, principal Archie Camden; Trumpets, principal Ernest Hall. An ENSA concert in 1943, the audience and the 'overflow' audience; Boys of Bedford School listen in the gallery to a rehearsal from the School Hall by Boult and the Symphony Orchestra, June 1944 (BBC); Yehudi Menuhin rehearsing with Boult, October 1944 (BBC Hulton Picture Library); Michael Tippett in 1945 (BBC Hulton Picture Library); BBC Symphony Orchestra in the newly-restored Studio 1 at Maida Vale, April 1947 (BBC); Rafael Kukelik (CB); Sir John Barbirolli (EA).

Between pages 242–3
Sir Adrian Boult with Paul Beard (Popperfoto); Boult's last concert as Chief Conductor of the Symphony Orchestra, Royal Albert Hall, 20 April 1950 (BBC Hulton Picture Library); Sir Malcolm Sargent at the Last Night of the Proms, 1961 (GM); Sir Adrian Boult, Michael Tippett and Paul Beard

(EA); Sir Adrian Boult, Michael Tippett and Ralph and Ursula Vaughan Williams (EA); Bruno Walter rehearsing with the Symphony Orchestra, Maida Vale, 1955 (BBC); Sir Thomas Beecham (GM); Rudolf Schwarz, Chief Conductor of the Symphony Orchestra, 1957–62 (GM); Igor Stravinsky (EA); William Glock, Controller of Music, in 1959 (EA); Leopold Stokowski (BBC); Norman Del Mar (GM); Hugh Maguire with Antal Dorati (EA); William and Anne Glock with Hugh Maguire on the Symphony Orchestra's tour of the USA, 1965 (EA); Antal Dorati conducting the Orchestra in Carnegie Hall (EA); Antal Dorati in 1963 (GM).

Between pages 306–7
Sidonie Goossens in 1926 (© Sidonie Goossens); Sidonie Goossens with Igor Stravinsky, Maida Vale, December 1958 (EA); Colin Davis with Victoria Postnikova, October 1967 (Popperfoto); Colin Davis, 1961 (GM); Pierre Boulez (GM); Preparations at Maida Vale Studio 1 for a rehearsal of Boulez's *Pli selon pli*, performed May 1969 (BBC); Diego Masson and Pierre Boulez working with engineers on Boulez's *explosante-fixe* at the Proms, 1973 (CS); Karlheinz Stockhausen (CS); Peter Maxwell Davies (CS); Malcolm Arnold (CS); Lennox Berkeley (CS); Engraving of the Engine House, Camden Town; Pierre Boulez in the Round House during rehearsals, 1974 (BBC); Stockhausen's *Carré* for four orchestral groups (CS); William Glock (BBC); Robert Ponsonby (EA); Rudolf Kempe (BBC); Kempe conducting the Symphony Orchestra at a Promenade Concert, 1975 (BBC).

Between pages 370–1
Colin Davis, 1976 (CS); Andrew Davis (GM); John Pritchard, Chief Guest Conductor from 1978 (CB); John Pritchard, chief guest conductor from 1978 (CB); Rozhdestvensky rehearsing at Maida Vale, 1980 (CB); Rozhdestvensky with Rodney Friend, 1980 (CB); Charles Mackerras (BBC); Gennadi Rozhdestvensky with his wife Victoria Postnikova (BBC); The BBC Symphony Orchestra 1980 (all CB): Violins, co-leader Rodney Friend; Horns, co-principal Alan Civil, right; Cellos, principal Ross Pople; Brass, tuba principal, Jim Gourlay; Rodney Friend; Colin Bradbury, principal clarinet and Geoffrey Gambold, principal bassoon; Sidonie Goossens, principal harp; John Wilbraham, principal trumpet until 1980. The Royal Albert Hall (Camera Press); The Orchestra at the Royal Festival Hall; Sir Adrian Boult (GM).

CS = photo Chris Samuelson; CB = photo Clive Barda; EA = photo Erich Auerbach; GM = photo G. MacDomnic.

Foreword by Sir Adrian Boult

It is indeed an honour to have been asked to write a foreword to this history of the BBC Symphony Orchestra. Great symphony orchestras do not grow on every tree, and a comparison of the London orchestral climate in 1930 with the glittering landscape of 1980 will show something of the confidence which Lord Reith reposed in us as musicians, also his belief in broadcasting in all its aspects.

I am indebted to Lord Reith for giving me the great opportunity of working with such a fine body of players, who became not only my colleagues but also my friends. My admiration for Miss Sidonie Goossens, who was with us at the first concert in 1930, and who graces the platform at nearly every concert still, is unbounded and I would like to send her my special congratulations.

Every good wish to everyone, and many more years of brilliant success.

Adrian C. Boult

Introduction

This is not primarily a book of reminiscence. Many volumes have been written about what it feels like to play in a great orchestra, about the sort of lives orchestral players and conductors lead, or about the broader issues of the structure and organisation of orchestras. (A recent lively example is the collection of interviews published as *Orchestra*, edited by André Previn, which includes some comments by past and present members of the BBC Symphony Orchestra.) This book attempts instead to provide a comprehensive record of the BBC Symphony Orchestra's achievement in the first fifty years of its existence. The unique character of the Orchestra resides in its combination of roles: it is both a broadcasting orchestra and a public concert-giving orchestra. The primary reason for its existence is its broadcasting function: it provides programmes of orchestral music of the highest quality for BBC programmes, which can reach far larger audiences than any live concert. But since its inauguration, the focus of the Orchestra's work has been its annual season of public concerts and its contribution to the summer season of Henry Wood Promenade Concerts, both promoted by the BBC. To this has been added an increasing number of other appearances in Britain, and tours as far afield as the United States of America, Russia and Japan.

The most remarkable result of this dual role has been the BBC Symphony Orchestra's breadth of repertoire. There can be no other orchestra in this country – and few in the western world – which has played so wide a range of music at such a high level, which has so consistently performed so much of the twentieth-century orchestral repertoire, and which has introduced so many important new works to concert and radio audiences. For most of its history, the BBC Symphony Orchestra has been free of the economic constraints which limit and conventionalise so many orchestral programmes in London. The Orchestra has been, and is, guided by administrators and conductors who believe in leading and stimulating public taste. As a result, the Orchestra has maintained an adventurousness in its repertoire which the list of a thousand-and-more premières in Appendix B amply demonstrates. It is on this aspect of the Orchestra's work, the one by which it has most profoundly affected musical life in this country, that I have chosen to concentrate. This has necessitated a large amount of documentation in the text. There are many prosaic lists of programmes and dates, accounts of composers' new and unfamiliar works, samples of critical reactions. I hope that readers who are interested in the narrative of the Orchestra's life will return to these factual sections as points of reference.

I have attempted to sketch in two general backgrounds to this account of the Orchestra's work. First is the changing pattern of orchestral life in London, a subject that has so far been very little treated in print – a new batch of postwar memoirs from musical administrators would be welcome. Second is the development of music broadcasting in this period: a subject which has been better documented, at least in outline as far as 1955, by the valuable work of Professor Asa Briggs – a history of all the BBC's musical activities remains to be written. There is too little in this book about the Orchestra's contributions to each season of the Henry Wood Promenade Concerts: I have tried to avoid duplicating the material in David Cox's comprehensive survey, *The Henry Wood Proms* (BBC Publications, 1980).

I have had the opportunity to write in some detail about the administrative decisions which have guided the BBC Symphony Orchestra's development. The BBC, it is said, has lived by the memo and may yet perish by it. The enormous amount of paperwork generated by the Corporation's structure is a blessing (albeit in disguise) to any historian, for it means that much is recorded on paper which in a smaller organisation would have been spoken, or merely thought. I have been given complete freedom by the BBC to use the relevant documents and to quote from them (the only exceptions, as always, are the personal files of staff employees) and I would like to stress that the opinions I express and the conclusions I draw are mine alone. One other note is perhaps necessary: I have not written this history from the background of fifty years' experience of its subject. I was educated, orchestrally, by the Hallé in Manchester; my own live experiences of the BBC Symphony Orchestra go back scarcely ten years. The rest is new research.

It seems to me that the tensions and problems of the BBC Symphony Orchestra's existence have remained fairly constant through the fifty years of its life. What should be the balance between the Orchestra's broadcasting activities and its public concert-giving role? Should the Orchestra concentrate primarily on excellence of performance, or on quantity of output for the broadcast services? What is the relationship between the BBC's administrators, who make the licence-payers' money available to the Orchestra, and those who guide its musical fortunes? Among the latter, who should set the Orchestra's artistic policy: its Chief Conductor, or the BBC's Music Division? Can the BBC justify to itself the promotion of concerts which, because of their adventurous repertoire, inevitably draw small audiences? Indeed, is the BBC justified in spending its income from the licence fee to run a first-rate orchestra when there are now many other active orchestras among whom the necessary broadcasting work could, perhaps, be shared out? All these questions acquired greater force in June and July 1980 when the members of the BBC Symphony Orchestra were, in common with all members of the Musicians' Union, on strike against the BBC as a result of BBC proposals to reduce significantly the number of salaried musicians employed by the Corporation. For the only time in the history of the Henry Wood Promenade Concerts, the first night of the season was cancelled. Although this dispute did not directly threaten the existence of the BBC Symphony Orchestra, the Orchestra will enter its second half-century acutely conscious of its relationship with the BBC. I have always had at the back of my mind Sir Walter Raleigh's famous words: 'Whosoever, in writing a modern history, shall follow truth too near the heels, it may haply strike out his teeth.'

N.K.
New York/London
1980

Acknowledgments

Robert Ponsonby, the BBC's Controller, Music, asked me if I would write this book at a time when I was working in the BBC's Music Division. I thank him, Stephen Plaistow and Guy Protheroe, who arranged for me to be given leave of absence in order to carry out the research. The later stages of writing coincided with my leaving the BBC for New York; I thank all those concerned, especially Anthony Kingsford of BBC Publications, for their forbearance during this period and their help in producing the book.

Many people have given indispensable assistance. Sir Adrian Boult initiated me with patience and great kindness into the early history of the Orchestra, and agreed to write a foreword. Sidonie Goossens, who has been principal harpist of the Orchestra for all its fifty years of existence, told me much about the first years that I would not have discovered in the archives. I have had many enjoyable conversations with players and administrators past and present: I would particularly like to thank Pierre Boulez, Antal Dorati and Sir Colin Davis, former Chief Conductors; Sir William Glock and Eric Warr, formerly Controller of Music and Head of Music Programmes of the BBC; Ernest Hall and Colin Bradbury, past chairmen of the orchestral players' committee; and members of the Orchestra during the 1930s and after, especially Bernard Shore, Harry Danks and Kathleen Washbourne. A large number of colleagues have provided memories of the Orchestra at various points in its history; I had very detailed impressions from Felix Aprahamian and Howard Hartog. The whole manuscript has been read by Robert Ponsonby, Lionel Salter and Peter Tanner; sections have been read by Sir William Glock, Colin Bradbury, Sidonie Goossens and Eric Warr. The proofs were read by Julian Budden and Paul Inwood. All of them have made most helpful corrections and suggestions.

For making the BBC's material on its Symphony Orchestra available, I thank Jacqueline Kavanagh and the staff of the BBC Written Archives Centre, Caversham; the staff of the BBC Central Registry, in The Langham;

Nicholas Ratcliffe and the staff of Music Registry, Yalding House; Angela
Dainton of the BBC Reference Library, The Langham; Left Staff Registry,
in The Langham; News Information in Broadcasting House; Barrie Hall of
Radio 3 publicity; all the staff of the BBC Music Library in Yalding House;
and the BBC Symphony Orchestra Unit at the Maida Vale Studios. Material
was also kindly made available from the Royal Philharmonic Society's archives by Mrs Sylvia East, and from Sir John Barbirolli's records by Michael
Kennedy. John Douglas Todd's Radio 3 series of 1972, 'Four Glorious
Decades', provided useful material, as did Bernard Shore's book *The
Orchestra Speaks*. David Cox generously allowed me to read the typescript of
his book *The Henry Wood Proms*; we disagree on some points of interpretation, but his book and this are intended to be complementary. I am grateful
to Mrs Gwendolen Beckett, Sir Adrian Boult's secretary for nearly fifty
years, both for documentation and for illuminating background information.

It would be unduly formal to thank my friends in the BBC's Concerts
Management department, especially Freda Grove (who recently retired as
Concerts Organiser), Christopher Samuelson and Daphne Smith: we have
chatted endlessly over the past few years, and without them this book would
have been either never started, or else finished much sooner. I owe a special
debt to the past and present General Managers of the Symphony Orchestra,
Paul Huband and William Relton, who have provided much detailed
information and have both read the second half of the book. Records of the
Symphony Orchestra's public concerts are maintained – corrected down to
the last detail – in Yalding House; though she would not wish me to mention
the fact, it is entirely due to the work of Dorothy Wood, who worked in
Concerts Management from the orchestra's foundation until 1963, that
these and other accurate archives exist.

I am very grateful to those who undertook the daunting task of assembling
the appendices. They have been compiled especially for this book and are all
based only on the material which the BBC could make available; errors and
omissions will have occurred, and we would be grateful to learn of these.
Appendix A, which lists members of the Orchestra since 1930, was compiled
by Jane Chapman from information provided by BBC Programme Contracts Department, supplemented by orchestral lists in the published concert programmes; a period of enforced inactivity during the Musicians'
Union strike enabled Elizabeth Williams and her colleagues in Orchestral
Management to check and correct this list: one tiny benefit from an unhappy
period. Appendix B, which lists first performances given by the Orchestra,
was compiled in two parts: Ross Lorraine drew the list for 1930–1939 from
Radio Times and the BBC's Programme Index; Cecile Latham-Koenig drew

the list for 1939–1980 from the Symphony Orchestra's records held at Maida Vale Studios (which have now been transferred to the BBC's Written Archives Centre). I also acknowledge information from *A Dictionary of Twentieth Century Composers* by Kenneth Thompson (Faber); and from a selective list of first performances for the years 1930–1934 published by the BBC in its Annual for 1935. Appendix D, the Discography, is based on the card index maintained by the BBC Gramophone Library; my thanks to Derek Lewis for making the information available. Appendix F is a revised version of an article I wrote for the programme of the BBC Symphony Chorus's fiftieth anniversary concert in 1978.

My thanks also go to Margaret Gallaway, Caroline Wilkinson, Elizabeth Sherman, Rob Tiller and Sally Berkeley, for typing the manuscript; and finally to Ghislaine and Anna, for making it all worthwhile.

'And those musicians that shall play to you,
Hang in the air, a thousand leagues from hence.
And straight they shall be here. Sit and attend.'

Henry IV, Part I. William Shakespeare.

1

'In the air' to 1930

Music broadcasting begins

A *Punch* cartoon of a hundred years ago depicts a vision of the future: a lady stands with her pageboy in front of a huge oven-like structure, hung with curtains and displaying large portholes with taps, labelled 'Bayreuth', 'Covent Garden', 'Westminster Abbey'. She instructs the boy: 'Now, recollect, Robert, at a quarter to nine turn on "Voi che sapete" from Covent Garden; at ten let in the Stringed Quartette from St James's Hall; and at eleven turn the last Quartette from "Rigoletto" full on. But mind you close one tap before opening the other!'

It was to be some time before the art of music broadcasting reached such a height of sophistication. The first attempts to relay musical events took place in the last decades of the nineteenth century – but through the medium of the telephone, not the wireless. At the Electrical Exhibition in Crystal Palace during 1892, performances from the Lyric Theatre in London and concerts in Birmingham, Liverpool and Manchester were relayed by telephone with considerable success. It was not until 1919, when the Marconi Company installed its first experimental transmitter at Ballybunion, Ireland, that wireless became established. The next year, when the Company opened a transmitter in Chelmsford, musical items were broadcast by a group of engineers playing cornet, oboe, one-string fiddle and piano. When it became clear that these first experiments were rousing considerable public interest, the *Daily Mail* decided to promote a major musical event. On 15 June 1920 Dame Nellie Melba travelled to Chelmsford and broadcast a group of songs which were relayed all over Europe and were heard as far away as Newfoundland. It was a most successful exercise. The *Daily Mail* described the broadcast as 'a wonderful half-hour' in which 'Art and Science joined hands'.

By 1922 regular broadcasts had been established from two stations: first a tiny establishment at Writtle, and then from Marconi's Wireless Telegraph

Company in the Strand, London. Small-scale music was a vital part of both organisations' output, though their resources were ludicrously small. From Writtle, the effervescent P.P. Eckersley (later Chief Engineer of the BBC) provided entire evenings of music single-handed. A 'night of grand opera' consisted of his singing a series of arias with mock-interruptions; his signing-off number ran

> Dearest, the concert's ended, sad wails the heterodyne.
> You must switch your valves off, I must soon switch off mine.

From Marconi's station, known as 2LO, a great variety of songs and chamber music was broadcast with a professionalism which grew slowly. The service began on 11 May 1922 with speech only, but on 24 June the first concert was broadcast with the singer Charles Knowles, the cellist Beatrice Eveline and the pianist Ethel Walker. By the autumn of that year, 2LO had some 30,000 licensed listeners, with a total audience of perhaps 50,000. From the summer the musical output of the station was directed by L. Stanton Jeffries. The early musical broadcasts were by no means free from problems. There were technical problems of balance and difficulties caused by human fallibility: inexperienced artists all too often tripped over micro-phone leads, disconnecting broadcasts before they had begun, or else enquired anxiously about the standard of their performance over the air before the microphone had been switched off.

By the middle of 1922, with the advent of broadcasts from Metropolitan Vickers in Manchester and Western Electric in Birmingham, and with many smaller firms in operation, it was clear that some coordination was necessary, and in October after lengthy negotiations the British Broadcasting Company was formed around the operations of 2LO. J.C.W. Reith, who had been managing director of an engineering firm, was the new General Manager, A.R. Burrows was Director of Programmes, and Stanton Jeffries, who had worked on the business side of the Marconi Company, was London Station Director. The Company's first official broadcast was on the night of 14 November. The election results were broadcast: results which brought the Conservatives to power for a period which the new Prime Minister, Bonar Law, hoped would bring 'tranquillity, and freedom from adventures and commitments both at home and abroad'.

If British politics was about to enter a period of weary somnolence, quite the opposite was true of British broadcasting: it was just beginning both adventure and commitment. Opposition to the newfangled techniques was quick to arise. It was most fiercely expressed by those who placed radio together with the emergent cinema and the outbreak of popular jazz and dance music, and characterised them all as forces working for the dilution of great culture, producing an age of the second-rate and the passive in entertainment. D.H. Lawrence screamed:

'For God's sake, let us be men
not monkeys minding machines
or sitting with our tails curled
while the machine amuses us, the radio or film or gramophone.

Monkeys with a bland grin on our faces.'

Few at this point saw the creative possibilities of the medium, and were unwilling to accept the implications of its ability to reach large numbers of people. Some expected it simply to reinforce the cultural values of a prewar élite; they were likely to be shocked, for the world had changed – radio was a reflector of change, not its only instigator. As one historian of the period (L.C.B. Seaman in *Post-Victorian Britain*) has written:

Much that was disseminated by the new processes was ephemeral or bad; but the hostility to mass culture so frequently expressed from the 1920s onwards was often the result of a narrow educational system, a too early hardening of the spiritual arteries, and, above all, of an ingrained distaste for the masses as such.

Policies and priorities

Within the British Broadcasting Company, the first faltering steps were being taken towards what might be characterised as a musical policy; on 29 November 1922 A.R. Burrows wrote to Stanton Jeffries, suggesting some priorities in their song broadcasts, and showing that he was quite well aware of the nature of the Company's audience:

Now that we are commencing to pay artistes nominal fees I am satisfied that the time has come when we should dictate to them, in a diplomatic way, what style of song it is in the interests of all that they should sing . . . their vast audience . . . has but a low proportion of persons who habitually attend the Albert, Queen's and Wigmore Halls and such other places of high class musical entertainment. Until we have got the public so interested in wireless that we can lift them above their present standard of musical appreciation we must use as the foundation for all our musical programmes a large proportion of items of a really popular character . . . I am satisfied that our programmes will be appreciated still more than they are today if you can introduce a bigger percentage of instrumental music.

That larger percentage of instrumental music was not slow to materialise. By 23 December a group of eight players had been gathered to provide regular broadcasts of music from Marconi House in the Strand, and London's activities were linked with those of Birmingham, Manchester and Newcastle, where the opening broadcast on Christmas Eve 1922 came from a lorry parked in a stableyard.

But the provision of orchestral music took longer to become established. Indeed, the BBC was broadcasting complete operas from Covent Garden long before it presented a symphony concert. This circumstance was due entirely to the suspicion with which concert promoters regarded broadcasting; they were convinced that it would lower receipts in the halls and cause the death of live music-making. The only organisation which cooperated with the BBC was the British National Opera Company, whose opera season at Covent Garden in January 1923 provided an early opportunity to expand the scope of broadcast music. A keen amateur transmitter, who was also a consultant engineer to Covent Garden, suggested to A.R. Burrows that performances from that season might be relayed. In great haste, an underground line was installed between Covent Garden and Marconi House (about a quarter of a mile away in the Strand), and Mozart's *The Magic Flute* was heard in January 1923. 'It was the first time that Grand Opera had come under the ever-growing magic of wireless', wrote the *Daily Express* (9 January), 'and no theatrical manager could have wished for a more wonderfully successful first night'. The opera was relayed complete, as was Humperdinck's *Hansel und Gretel*; excerpts from nine operas were broadcast during the season, culminating in Melba's appearance in *La Bohème*. An announcer stationed in the prompter's box outlined the plot and announced entrances and exits. Such announcements had to be made over the music; a letter arrived at the BBC threatening death to anyone who spoke during the excerpts from Wagner's *Die Walküre*. 'As our days were already lively enough without any shooting incident,' recalled Burrows, the opera 'passed uninterrupted.'

The enthusiastic support of the British National Opera Company for broadcasting, and the success of those first operatic relays, had one important influence on the future course of the BBC's orchestral policy. It was decided to ask that Company's musical director, Percy Pitt, to become Music Adviser to the BBC, a part-time post which he accepted and took up on 1 May 1923. Unlike many distinguished figures Reith might have chosen for the post (several of whom were subsequently involved with the BBC through its Music Advisory Committee) Pitt did not belong to the professional ring of academics who dominated English music after the war. He had been edu-

cated in France and Germany, where he had been in touch with the most
adventurous musical developments – currents of thought which were
regarded with profound suspicion by many English musicians of the post-
Stanford generation, with the notable exception of Henry Wood (with whom
Pitt became associated on his return to London). Pitt was never a well-
known public figure, nor even an outstanding conductor; but whether
through knowledge or instinct Reith chose someone who was innovative,
unrestricted in his outlook, who helped to shape the BBC's musical direction
and turn its eyes and ears towards the Continent. He was in touch with
important musicians abroad (he used to irritate his BBC superiors by
corresponding with these foreigners in their own language, without keeping
file copies of his letters) and the fruits of his contacts can clearly be seen
in the BBC's concert and broadcast programmes of the 1920s.

Orchestras at Savoy Hill

Pitt joined the Company on the day its headquarters moved to premises in
the Institute of Electrical Engineers at No. 2 Savoy Hill. 'Savoy Hill', as it
became universally known, provided little office and studio space, but at the
time they seemed adequate. Pitt was able to expand the eight-piece studio
band by the addition of a celesta, cornet, trombone and more instruments
until there was a nucleus of eighteen, expanded to thirty-seven for special
occasions. On 21 June 1923, Pitt conducted the first broadcast symphony
concert with an augmented orchestra, and followed it later in the year with
an ambitious all-Wagner programme on 26 November. He was joined in the
conducting of this, the BBC's first orchestra, by Stanton Jeffries and Kneale
Kelley (a violinist, who also led the 18-piece band). Jeffries now assisted Pitt
with the music output; Rex Palmer took over as London Station Director.

Meanwhile, Pitt gathered around him the nucleus of the BBC's musical
staff. One person whom he immediately invited to join the Company was a
vital influence over the coming years: Edward Clark. He worked first as
Music Director in Newcastle, where he programmed such ambitious works
as Mahler's Fourth Symphony and even planned a British première of
Schoenberg's *Gurrelieder* (a project he was later to realise in London), and
then from 1926 as a programme planner in London. Clark, like Pitt, had been
trained abroad; he had studied with Schoenberg. As a conductor, his skills
were unremarkable, but his friendship with virtually every important continental composer of the time was to prove of inestimable value to the BBC's
musical activities. Kenneth Wright, trained as an engineer but loving music
above all else (he had intended to take up a musical career after university,
but was swept into the earliest days of broadcasting and became Manchester

Station Director), arrived in London and worked as Pitt's assistant, with a secretary, Dorothy Wood. Stanford Robinson arrived in 1924 to share their office in Savoy Hill, next to that of Rex Palmer, who directed the London Station. Robinson recalls his first day in the office as supremely inactive, until about 5.30 when, just as he was despairing of any work in the organisation, Dorothy Wood asked him if he would be so kind as to ring up Charing Cross Station on Kenneth Wright's behalf and ask the price of a season ticket to Richmond. Robinson was soon diverted into busy activity with the foundation of the London Wireless Chorus in October 1924, but he remained connected with the BBC's orchestral music throughout a long career.

To the close partnership of Wright and Clark were added, in 1927, two other important figures: Julian Herbage, who quickly became Clark's indispensable companion in the planning of programmes; and W.W. Thompson, universally known as 'Tommy', who was Henry Wood's concerts manager, and joined the BBC when the Proms were taken over. Herbage remained a member of staff until 1946, but then retained both an important part in the planning of the Proms (until 1960) and a central role in the programme *Music Magazine* which he co-founded with Anna Instone. Thompson managed all the BBC's public concerts from 1927 until 1954, a remarkable span of service. In the early days the planning nucleus seems to have consisted of Clark, Herbage and Wright for the symphony concerts, and Clark, Herbage and Thompson for the Proms – responsible primarily to Pitt (and then Boult) for the former, and to Wood for the latter. When asked how they planned the Proms, Thompson used to recall that he and Clark would spend the first day sharpening pencils and then retire to a local hostelry for a bottle of Châteauneuf-du-Pape.

Another recruit to the BBC's administration in 1924 was to influence considerably the course of its musical affairs. This was Roger Eckersley, who became first assistant to Cecil Lewis, the organiser of programmes, on 11 February 1924, and very soon succeeded him as Director of Programmes in the new Corporation. Roger Eckersley was typical of the amiable inexperience of the early staff of the BBC. His brother Peter had become Chief Engineer of the BBC after his operatic successes broadcasting from Writtle, and had suggested to Roger that he might find a post in the Company. Roger Eckersley, educated at Charterhouse, failed at the law, ran two golf clubs and then started a chicken farm in Buckinghamshire which lost money; he was happy to consider such an offer. His gentlemanly bearing and easy manner were to facilitate numerous contacts: among his earliest friends in London was Landon Ronald, who, Eckersley recalled, 'amused himself by sitting down at the piano and singing to his own accompaniment . . . But what he really liked was sitting down to a game of poker . . .'

It was towards the end of 1923 that Reith and Pitt, still faced by objections from the major musical promoters in London, in particular William Boosey of Queen's Hall, to the broadcasting of symphonic music, made a decision that the BBC should attempt to put on its own series of public concerts. The Board meeting of 13 December agreed that the only way for the BBC to show that concert organisations were mistaken in their attitudes to broadcasting would be for the BBC 'to go out into their own field and show them what we can do if we like'. After much suspicion and caution, the Trustees of the Central Hall, Westminster, agreed to let the hall to the BBC for a series of six concerts from February 1924, and the first took place on 22 February. The BBC gathered such orchestras as were prepared to perform, and the roll-call of conductors almost exhausts those who were in sympathy with broadcasting: Pitt himself, and Jeffries; Landon Ronald, an eager supporter of the medium; Hamilton Harty, conductor of the Hallé Orchestra in Manchester; Eugene Goossens (then well known for his advocacy of 'advanced' music in London); and the distinguished figure of Sir Edward Elgar. Programmes were frankly popular, and audience figures were very high; but the acoustics of the hall did not help the broadcasters, and the results over the air were thought to be unsatisfactory.

In the studio, the 2LO Wireless Orchestra, as the Savoy Hill ensemble became known, gradually began to establish itself during 1924. But the personnel was constantly changing; players had many different commitments, and it was impossible to ensure regular attendance. The position was strengthened first by the appointment of a full-time conductor, Dan Godfrey (who was brought from the Manchester Station in May 1924), and by the issuing of the first orchestral contracts in August to 22 players. These contracts covered six performances a week by the orchestra. There were a large number of broadcasting hours to be filled, for throughout these early years music made up a very large proportion of the broadcast output: around three-fifths of an average day in November 1923; almost two-thirds in 1926, (though the increase was largely in the popular field). These first contracts did not give the BBC any real hold over its musicians. The Company was not providing them with full-time employment and security, and the best musicians had almost constant calls on their services from other ensembles, opera houses, and theatres, none of which could afford properly constituted orchestras, and all of which relied to a greater or lesser extent on *ad hoc* personnel.

The most pressing difficulty in establishing permanent ensembles was what Ernest Newman, the trenchant music critic of *The Sunday Times*, described as 'that wild absurdity and immorality', the deputy system. The system was indeed absurd, but in the economic conditions of London music-making in the 1920s, before orchestral players were offered any sort of full-time employment, the practice could scarcely be described as immoral. The deputy system meant simply that if you were asked to play in a concert, and found anything more lucrative to do on that date or the days of any rehearsals, you sent someone else without reference to the management. Or as one weary administrator, Mewburn Levien, Secretary of the Royal Philharmonic Society, once put it: 'A, whom you want, signs; he sends B (whom you don't mind) to the first rehearsal; B, without your knowledge or consent, sends C to the second rehearsal, who, not being able to play at the concert, sends D, whom you would have paid five shillings to stay away.' (Only two qualifications need to be added to this formulation as regards the 1920s: first, there was little signing, and second, it was unlikely that there would be as many as two rehearsals.)

Towards a permanent orchestra

So that when the BBC entered the field of public symphonic concert-giving in 1924, it was competing in a very depressed market. The costs of concert promotion had risen steeply since the war; too many London organisations were chasing an audience with unrehearsed popular programmes; there was no stimulus to increased standards among orchestral musicians, whose aim had to be to earn a living wage as effectively as possible. The complaints of those years were consistent; the *Annual Register* records bleakly the situation during the first years of the decade.

1921: 'The orchestral position was as parlous as ever . . . complaints were rife that the historic old [Royal Philharmonic] Society owed not a little of its more or less doubtful position to its own lack of initiative – which in its turn, was due to paucity of funds. This vicious circle, however, was not the sole prerogative of the RPS. . . .'

1922: 'The conditions under which orchestras existed and still exist precluded the probability of any great exhibition of enterprise in the orchestral concert world.'

1923: '. . . there was a vast deal more of quantity than of quality . . .'

1924: '. . . the same weary round of concerts . . . a general level of mediocrity, and the changes were rung on much the same programmes.'

Nor was any of the London orchestras providing an individually adequate standard. The London Symphony Orchestra was still based on a prewar nucleus of players, but the great orchestra which Nikisch and Richter had created had to be slowly reconstructed after 1919 under the direction of Albert Coates. Ernest Newman returned from a visit to America in 1925 to declare sarcastically (*The Sunday Times* 29 March 1925):

> I was afraid that after the splendid American orchestras our own would sound very poor, but I was agreeably disappointed. The LSO, I suppose, ranks as our premier orchestra; and I am glad to be able to record that at its concert last Monday it compared not unfavourably with the orchestras in some of the New York picture houses.

Sir Henry Wood reformed his Queen's Hall Orchestra, adding the prefix 'New' to its title, and continued to be the fiercest disciplinarian in London, ensuring considerable loyalty among his players. The quality of the novelties he was able to introduce was severely limited. The list for the 1918 season makes depressing reading – works by Converse, Rimsky-Korsakov, Glazunov, Roger-Ducasse, Kasanli, Florent Schmitt's *Le Palais Hanté* and Samazeuilh's *Le Sommeil de Canope*. Wood, too, suffered from financial difficulties, as did the senior concert-giving organisation in London, the Royal Philharmonic Society. That Society continued to give significant first performances: Holst's *Hymn of Jesus* in 1920, Bax's Viola Concerto and Vaughan Williams' Pastoral Symphony in 1922 all met with some success, but the strain on its slender financial resources was very great, and there were fears that it might have to discontinue its activities. Other orchestras came and went in London: Landon Ronald's Sunday concerts in the Albert Hall continued, and a young Malcolm Sargent conducted a British Women's Symphony Orchestra. By 1925 new works were reduced to a trickle: only Holst's Choral Symphony had any success, while after Herbert Howells's new Piano Concerto at a Royal Philharmonic Society concert in Queen's Hall a well-known member of the audience shouted from the balcony: 'And *I* say, thank God it's over.' The LSO had to be content with a new Symphonic Concerto for piano by Baron Frédéric d'Erlanger, who happened to be one of its three chief patrons; the Hallé played the Irish Symphony by their own conductor, Hamilton Harty.

It was to this latter orchestra, the Hallé, and to the other provincial orchestras, that sensitive musicians had to look for any evidence that orchestral standards were being maintained in the country. Unaffected by the flurry for metropolitan work which created the deputy system, these organisations had a fairer chance of success. Adrian Boult had considerable success reviving the fortunes of the City of Birmingham Orchestra; with typical modesty, however, he remarked that if ever he wanted to hear a good concert, he took the train to Manchester.

In London, such displays of initiative as took place were chiefly confined to the field of chamber orchestral and small-scale music. Exceptional series were mounted by Edward Clark and Anthony Bernard in 1921, with Schoenberg's Chamber Symphony in the Aeolian Hall, and by Eugene Goossens in 1924, when the Schoenberg Second Quartet and Stravinsky's *The Soldier's Tale* were introduced to London. The impetus of these adventures proved impossible to maintain through the economic conditions of the twenties.

The BBC, however, was beginning to possess an economic security denied to other concert promoters. The expansion of broadcasting was taking place at an astonishing rate: by the end of 1924, Percy Pitt's role as part-time Music Adviser was expanded into that of full-time Director of Music (he began to work in that capacity on 25 November), and it was resolved to mount a new series of symphony concerts, this time featuring the Wireless Players, augmented to form a Wireless Symphony Orchestra. In the 1924–5 season Pitt arranged for a short series of four monthly concerts to be broadcast from Covent Garden Opera House. The conductors were altogether more distinguished than those of the previous season: Bruno Walter, whose Wagner *Ring* cycle of that year at the opera house is remembered as the highlight of the 1920s by orchestral players who took part, conducted one on 12 February 1925; Ernest Ansermet came from Paris for what was the first of many visits to the BBC on 15 January; and Pierre Monteux directed the first of the series on 10 December 1924. A strange première formed the most ambitious concert of the season: Joseph Lewis came to conduct the British première of Edgar Stillman Kelley's oratorio, *The Pilgrim's Progress*; the Wireless Orchestra was augmented by the Birmingham Symphony Orchestra, and two choirs were also imported for the concert. Once again the artistic success of the season was mixed.

1925 saw the expansion of the Orchestra's organisation with the appointment of an orchestral secretary, the contra-bassoon player T.J. Dickie; and in 1926 there was a change of regular conductor when Dan Godfrey left in April, to be replaced in June by John Ansell, conductor at the Winter Garden Theatre, London. Expansion of playing work in the studio took the place of public concerts during the following season, and there was no special 1925–6 series. However, one major musical event of 1926 was the broadcast on 30 March of Rimsky-Korsakov's opera *Kitezh*, which was given its first performance in England in a concert performance at Covent Garden directed by Albert Coates. A 'Broadcasting Symphony Orchestra' played, and this opened the way to a substantial collaboration between the Covent Garden orchestra and the Wireless Orchestra later in the year.

Committees

There was an administrative development in this year which was to bring
mixed blessings on the BBC: in an effort to increase its public accountability,
Reith formed a Music Advisory Committee, under the chairmanship of Sir
Hugh Allen, Professor of Music at Oxford and Principal of the Royal
College of Music. Reith's friends Sir Walford Davies and Sir Landon
Ronald were also on the Committee, together with such figures as John
McEwen of the Royal Academy and Professor Donald Tovey from Edinburgh. If Reith thought, as Kenneth Wright reported, that the function of
this Committee was 'to agree and confirm what I've already decided to do',
he was in for a shock. The Committee represented established interests, at
the opposite pole from those of Reith's Music Department, and in the years
to come it would attempt to interfere in artistic decisions, claiming that
the BBC should support only British music and musicians at a time when
Pitt and Clark were at their most adventurously continental. The conflicts
were to reach a peak in 1929 when the Committee was nearly disbanded, and
were to reassert themselves throughout the liveliest years of the Symphony
Orchestra.

Throughout 1925 and 1926 the BBC was undergoing the difficult
transition from Company to Corporation, and after its experimental years
was opening itself to an onslaught of objections to its activity in the evidence
presented to the Crawford Committee, which met in 1925. William Boosey
of Chappell's had presented his case against the medium, saying that 'broadcasting affects the sale of popular sheet music, because a large number of
people who listen to Broadcasting absolutely neglect the piano to do so,
having neither time nor inclination for both occupations'. Artists under his
direction, Boosey continued, were not allowed to broadcast. (But as the
BBC noted in its rejoinder to the evidence, 'the fact remains that most of
them do so regularly'.) Boosey's evidence was not rooted in reality: from the
beginnings of broadcasting there had been many reports of a sudden rise in
sales for sheet music when a song had just been broadcast, and concert
audiences were undoubtedly increasing as a result of broadcasting. A far-
seeing writer like Percy Scholes had prophesied as early as 1923 that 'in five
years' time the general musical public of these islands will be treble or quad-
ruple its present size'.

The publication of the Crawford Committee's report took place in March
1926, and the British Broadcasting Company was established as a Corporation on 1 January 1927. The title of Reith's post was changed to Director-
General, and he was knighted. For the 1926–7 season, it was decided to

mount a full-scale series of symphony concerts, the most ambitious yet. For these concerts Pitt had the collaboration of the Covent Garden Orchestra, which under its leader Wynn Reeves amalgamated with the Wireless Orchestra to form a 'National Orchestra' of around 150 players.

The first-rate programmes for these concerts clearly bear the stamp of the combined enthusiasms of Percy Pitt and Edward Clark. There was a considerable emphasis on continental music and conductors. Honegger came to conduct his oratorio *King David*, and his virtuoso orchestral piece *Pacific 231*. Richard Strauss directed his Alpine Symphony; other German conductors included the Director of the Leipzig Opera, Gustav Brecher, and the young Hermann Scherchen, who brought, no doubt with Clark's encouragement, Schoenberg's *Verklärte Nacht*. From Italy there was Bernardino Molinari with music by Casella and Respighi; from France, Ansermet again, conducting Ravel as well as Balakirev and music by Ethel Smyth. English conductors were Hamilton Harty (who began the series on 30 September and also conducted the massive Berlioz *Grande Messe des Morts*), Albert Coates, Landon Ronald, and Elgar. Gustav Holst conducted the first performance of what must be one of the earliest BBC musical commissions: his choral dance *The Morning of the Year*. The series was rounded off by a Wagner programme under Siegfried Wagner.

Though the interest generated by these concerts was great, there was nevertheless continued criticism of the standard of orchestral playing which they displayed. The string playing was particularly poor because of constantly changing personnel. It was decided within the BBC that an effort must be made to introduce a strong no-deputy clause into the contracts of the orchestral musicians. At the end of the 1926–7 season some players were replaced, and an attempt at restriction on deputies was introduced into the orchestral contract. But loose administration and the impossibility of enforcement in the prevailing orchestral conditions largely negated its effectiveness.

In the summer of 1927 a most important development of the BBC's musical activities took place. Following pessimistic rumours from William Boosey that Chappell's were about to turn the Queen's Hall into a picture palace, the Corporation agreed to cooperate with Henry Wood in the running of his famous Promenade Concerts. The BBC's agreement with Wood in May 1927 covered not only the Proms, but also a three-year period during which he would conduct twenty-five concerts for the BBC in the studio or in public *per annum*, and 'give us your general help either in an advisory capacity directly or indirectly'. The BBC, interestingly enough, attempted to make Wood agree not to conduct outside organisations 'where it is agreed between us that the organisers are taking such a hostile attitude towards broadcasting as to be inimical to the cause', but Wood unsurprisingly would not accept such a restriction. However, William Boosey, who had previously taken the most hostile attitude of all to broadcasting, saw the opportunity of preserving his concert hall in association with the Corporation, and so allowed the BBC to promote its own series of concerts there in the 1927–8 season.

The 1927 Proms and the experiences of the remainder of that year brought together all strands of opinion in London which favoured the formation of some kind of permanent orchestra for the capital. An incident during the BBC's first Prom season (for which Wood's own orchestra continued to play) brought into the clearest possible focus the inadequacy of the orchestral system then in operation. A young visiting violinist, Daisy Kennedy, broke down during her performance of the Brahms Violin Concerto during the Prom on 24 August, and claimed to the Press afterwards that the trouble had been that the performance was unrehearsed. Wood issued a sharp rejoinder: 'No work with which I am connected is ever performed in public unrehearsed.' An anonymous BBC spokesman was less discreet: 'All new and difficult works are rehearsed . . . The Brahms Concerto has been performed by the Queen's Hall orchestra about 150 times, so I really do not see that a rehearsal is necessary.' That satisfied no one, and more detailed enquiries were made. It emerged that the violinist had been able to play through the work at a private rehearsal with Wood at the piano, and then to play 'some passages' with the orchestra on the day. This inspired Ernest Newman to a waspish article (28 August). He suggested an advertisement to foreign players: 'Do not be afraid to come to England to play your concertos. . . . Take it from us that you and the orchestra will rehearse – *though perhaps not together*.'

In his previous week's article (21 August), Newman had been more constructive, and had summed up informed opinion about the London orchestral scene: 'So long as only the critics lament the shocking condition of orchestral music in London they are accused of ignorance or malevolence. Shall we never get rid of our lazy national habit of trusting to muddling through? . . . Obviously what we need is not three or four second- or third-rate orchestras but one first-rate London orchestra.'

The events of the new concert season corroborated this view. The BBC launched its first series of public concerts at the Queen's Hall, again forming a National Symphony Orchestra in collaboration with Covent Garden. But it also took the adventurous step of inviting the Hallé Orchestra from Manchester under Sir Hamilton Harty to present two of the concerts in the series (13 January and 23 March). The Hallé, a comparatively stable organisation which had been working with a permanent conductor, upstaged all the London orchestras. It provided ample proof that English musicians could play in a disciplined manner, if they were only given the resources and stable framework within which to do so.

In the most important concert of this season, Edward Clark persuaded Schoenberg to come to England in person for the première in this country on 27 January 1928 of his *Gurrelieder*. 'It is only the BBC which can afford to pay for the orchestra [the work] requires', commented *The Times* on 28 January. But those who knew the piece were able to confirm Newman's judgement that 'the performance mostly failed to do it justice'; the BBC's enterprise was spoiled by inadequate performance. Other premières during the season (all conducted by Wood in his share of the concerts) were Janáček's *Sinfonietta*, Respighi's *Church Windows*, and Bloch's Israel Symphony.

Meanwhile, at the end of December one external impulse towards the formation of a permanent orchestra had come with the visit to this country of the Berlin Philharmonic, under Wilhelm Furtwängler. The magnificent sound of this orchestra was unparalleled in the memory of Londoners, at least since the visit of the New York Philharmonic under Walter Damrosch in the early twenties. The Berlin orchestra provided great, perfectly co-ordinated music-making. As the *Annual Register* reported, its 'remarkable dexterity' 'set the town aflame'; Frank Howes, then music critic of *The Times*, recalled in his autobiography that 'the British public . . . was electrified when it heard the disciplined precision. . . . This was apparently how an orchestra could, and, therefore, ought to sound.'

As for the BBC, the critics were marshalling their weightiest phrases against the poor playing of its orchestra. Writing of a concert in the Queen's Hall series conducted by Sir Landon Ronald, the *Musical Times* said in January 1928 that the BBC

> has been censured on a variety of trifling points, but never for the one heinous offence it has committed and goes on committing: for this corporation with all its assumed and conspicuous wealth, has given and is giving us the worst orchestral performances ever heard in London . . . This year at Queen's Hall they have assembled an orchestra which sounds as if it were composed in great part of 'substitutes'.

Radical change was clearly necessary. Both Percy Pitt and Roger Eckersley recognised the need for a permanent orchestra within the BBC, and were beginning to explore the basis on which it might be run. It may have been at this time that Pitt, with his extensive knowledge of the continental scene, took Eckersley on a tour of some important broadcasting organisations abroad. Eckersley recalled the visit in his autobiography, without giving a date for it.

> Our destinations were Berlin and Vienna, with Buda Pest as an afterthought. We paid several visits to the headquarters of the Berlin Philharmonic. We sat in on rehearsals, we had discussions with the authorities about musicians' contracts, pay, hours worked and so on . . . In Vienna . . . I spent some time with Herr Kraus, then conductor-in-chief of the Vienna Philharmonic, who gave us a lot of advice on the administrative management of the orchestras . . . We had not really much excuse for going to Buda Pest but I did want to see some broadcasting studios which were supposed to be more up-to-date in some respects than any others on the Continent . . . an experiment was being tried out whereby the conductor led his orchestra from a glass-proofed box, and judged his results by what came back to him over the air on the headphones.

But this visit may well have taken place at a later date during the negotiations, for the first stimulus towards a permanent orchestra came not from within the BBC Music Department, but from the circle of musicians around Sir John Reith.

Two of Sir John Reith's closest musical advisers, Sir Walford Davies and Sir Landon Ronald, may take the credit for having opened the discussions which led to the first proposals for a permanent orchestra under the aegis of the BBC. Sir Walford Davies had approached the officials of the Royal Philharmonic Society as early as February 1927, with a view to bringing about some collaboration between the Society's own orchestra and the BBC's Wireless Orchestra during the forthcoming season. When he attended an RPS meeting on 15 February 1927 (after discussing the matter informally at the ISM Conference in Felixstowe) the aim was to open discussions for co-operation 'so that the Society's orchestra could become a really permanent body'. Reith and Eckersley met RPS officials on 23 February 1927, and various schemes of joint concerts were discussed; eventually, however the BBC decided simply to pay for the broadcasting of some RPS concerts. Amalgamation of the Wireless and RPS orchestras would have solved little, for both were of a low standard.

'Fairly straight sailing'?

If a date and an occasion had to be named when the first notion of the BBC Symphony Orchestra was conceived then it might be 12 March 1928, at the lunch which Sir Landon Ronald and Sir Thomas Beecham had together on that day. Ronald had himself suffered from the poor quality of the BBC's orchestra and knew of the Corporation's anxious efforts to improve it. Always a keen mediator, Ronald saw the opportunity to bring about a reconciliation between broadcasting and one of its most vigorously outspoken opponents. For Sir Thomas Beecham had poured fun and scorn on broadcast music from the beginning. Music on the wireless, he had said, 'is the most abominable row that ever stunned and cursed the human ear, a horrible gibbering, chortling and shrieking of devils and goblins'. He did not need the wireless. But he did want a good orchestra in London, and at the beginning of 1928, having just returned from a tour of America, he was in the mood to create one. Since the end of 1927 rumours had been current that Beecham intended to give London a permanent opera company with an associated permanent orchestra. If the BBC had the resources and the desire to create a permanent orchestra too, so much the better. They could provide precisely the framework Beecham needed on which to build a grand union of interests which would dominate London music: a gramophone company, the Royal Philharmonic Society, perhaps a couple of existing orchestras. Against this, his opposition to broadcasting was a small battle to lose.

So Landon Ronald could write excitedly the next day to Roger Eckersley, now the BBC's Director of Programmes: 'It is practically certain that I am going to ask you and Sir John Reith to come and dine with me alone with Sir Thomas Beecham, when we shall have very big and important things to speak to you both about. I think I may go so far as to say that I have, at last, entirely broken Beecham's opposition to broadcasting . . .' This optimistic letter was the prelude to some intense negotiations and more lunches, during which it became plain that both Beecham and the BBC wanted a permanent orchestra in London; whether they wanted it for the same reasons was not explored in any detail. Beecham was already expounding his plan to other interested parties, and on 1 April he met representatives of the Royal Philharmonic Society at the Hyde Park Hotel; he outlined the basis of his proposals, without mentioning the involvement of the BBC.

Just over a month after Ronald's lunch with Beecham, the first formal proposal for a London contract orchestra came to Roger Eckersley's desk. It came, not from Beecham himself, but from his agent, the impresario Lionel Powell. This marked another surprising change of heart on the part of a firm anti-broadcaster: as early as 1924, Powell had suggested to the board of the London Symphony Orchestra that conductors who broadcast on the BBC should not be invited to direct LSO concerts, in case this had an adverse effect on ticket sales; he had criticised the BBC to the Crawford Committee (see above).

In the following years, however, Powell had come to know Roger Eckersley well, and they had often discussed the question of whether he should allow his concerts to be broadcast and his artists to be heard on the BBC. According to Eckersley 'he used to tell me that he had spent his life finding, publicising and building up these artists, who were his exclusive property in this country. Why should he let the Corporation use them unless we made it worth his while? He was perfectly friendly and perfectly frank, and thoroughly businesslike.' Beecham also saw Eckersley frequently over lunch, and it was on 23 April 1928 that Powell unveiled, with a flourish, a plan which had clearly been talked about informally between himself, Beecham and Eckersley during the previous month:

> Referring to our conversation the other day, you know that in every other country in the world, and in practically every town of importance, there exists a first-class permanent orchestra, with the exception of London. Sir Thomas Beecham returned from America three months ago, after conducting the
>
> NEW YORK PHILHARMONIC ORCHESTRA
> PHILADELPHIA ORCHESTRA
> BOSTON SYMPHONY ORCHESTRA
>
> and he has decided, realising the importance of such an Orchestra to the community and the country, to form at any cost, an ORCHESTRA in LONDON equal to these Orchestras in America.

Powell's extremely nebulous proposal was that the musicians (number unspecified) would be on a three-year contract. He claimed to be 'at present in negotiation with several famous Conductors, in different parts of the world, who have refused to visit England on account of not being able to obtain satisfactory rehearsals with a permanent Orchestra'. He undertook to make the orchestra available from the beginning of October to the end of March each year. Powell's plans clearly envisaged an orchestra which would provide his own public concerts, and which would tour the country under his agency. There was one problem: 'you know Sir Thomas Beecham's antipathy to Broadcasting, and it is not going to be an easy matter to persuade him to broadcast'. Powell's plan was to persuade Beecham not of the desirability, but rather of the profitability of broadcasting, in view of the 'enormous cost of such an Orchestra'. Powell hoped to clinch his argument with the BBC by stating that the 'very heavy loss . . . has been guaranteed by a Syndicate'.

Who these guarantors of the proposed scheme were remained unclear; they were apparently close to Beecham and Powell, and the BBC never questioned their existence in any detail. Powell followed up his letter with a first specific proposal, which was to cost £57,860, providing eighty-five musicians for a 26-week period, giving seventy-eight concerts. The orchestra would play five times a week and rehearse six times; with repeated programmes, the aim would be to average three rehearsals per concert. Powell believed he could earn £51,000, including £4,000 if agreement could be reached with Columbia to record the orchestra. Without that £4,000, some £10,000 was left as a deficit which would be 'provided annually for a period of three years by 100 guarantors'. Apart from such small matters as the fact that Powell's scheme completely overlooked the cost of conductors and solo artists for the concerts, the outline was not bold enough for the BBC. The Corporation wanted something much more in the nature of a full-time orchestra; its own first detailed scheme drawn up in reply to Powell was for an orchestra playing for forty-four weeks in London, touring for four weeks, and having a four-week holiday. This, it was thought, would cost £107,795; even allowing for the saving on concerts which would no longer be promoted by the BBC, and savings by reducing some of the regional orchestras, the deficit could well be £18,000.

On 10 May 1928 Roger Eckersley summed up the situation to Director-General Reith. There were three possibilities: either the BBC could attempt to control the proposed scheme; it could form a partnership with Beecham, providing a guarantee; or it could simply come in as a customer, buying the services of the new orchestra. Eckersley thought that a deficit of at least £20,000 on a first season should be allowed for. It was decided to go ahead on the basis of the second option. Beecham would have the responsibility of engaging the orchestra, and also the task (which was likely to be a troublesome one) of negotiating with the Musicians' Union: 'I think it would be a good thing if we were not in on this as it matters less if Beecham quarrels with the MU than ourselves.' The orchestra would be engaged for twelve months of the year, and the BBC would take it over for the Proms on the understanding that Henry Wood would continue to conduct that series. The BBC would contribute £10,000 to the deficit annually, as would Beecham's guarantors. This was the state of the scheme when on 14 May Beecham met Reith, with Sir Landon Ronald. Beecham's charm and Ronald's enthusiasm appear to have carried the day with Reith; the scheme came back to Eckersley's desk for him to carry on with the plans. Beecham kept in touch with the Philharmonic Society, but insisted that nothing was said at their Spring General Meeting on 24 May, because the BBC wished to complete the negotiations.

But negotiating in any detail with Sir Thomas Beecham was a difficult task. Throughout the discussions he displayed a great reluctance (justified in the event) to commit himself to any undertaking, or indeed to put anything down on paper about his side of the scheme. Following his meeting with

Reith, Beecham retired to France, and on 19 June sent this blandly reassuring message to Eckersley:

> ... this particular enterprise seems fairly straight sailing ... what is wanted generally in these matters is a single scheme and the steady goodwill of all parties involved to see it through. I have carried it a little further with the Columbia Graphophone Co. who have submitted to me a fairly concrete proposal into which I can go when I see you.

On 19 July, the RPS reaffirmed to Beecham their support for the principles of the scheme, without knowing any more details.

Little more was achieved by way of discussion, before the startled officials of the BBC read in the *Daily Mail* of 27 July:

> We are able to announce today a new scheme of Sir Thomas Beecham's which will be of immense importance and of the most stimulating effect to English music. Sir Thomas – one of the finest musical minds this country has produced, and a conductor of a brilliance nowhere surpassed in the world today – has interested himself in providing London with an absolutely first-class orchestra.

There followed an interview with Beecham, in which he detailed the proposed salaries and conditions of service of the orchestra members. He referred to the BBC in passing as one of the supporters of the scheme. Beecham said:

> The new orchestra will give a weekly symphony concert at Queen's Hall. This will be the musical event of the week in London. There will be concerts of well-studied performances of the classics and important novel productions ...
>
> They will go on from October to March. When the orchestra gets into its stride it will be second to none in the world, and these Queen's Hall concerts will have a European importance. In time it will probably be very difficult to obtain admission – just as at certain famous symphony concerts on the Continent, where subscription seats are family heirlooms.
>
> Then there will be a weekly concert in one or another of the London suburbs – suburbs, some of them, where a first-class orchestra is as yet unknown ...
>
> Then there will be regular Sunday afternoon concerts of a more or less 'popular' kind at the Albert Hall with operatic extracts and so on. And then, thirdly, the provincial concerts (about 32 in the season), corresponding to the Lionel Powell concerts in which I have toured with the LSO in recent years.

The winter concerts at Queen's and Albert Halls, in the suburbs and the provinces, will number in all about 110. About a quarter of these I shall conduct. Perhaps one in six of the Queen's Hall concerts will be choral. There are masses of fine things waiting to be produced . . .

The effect of this article was not enhanced when, the next day, provincial papers, presumably wishing to comment on the article but stuck for copy, printed an old piece by Beecham, entitled 'Why I dislike the wireless', in which he ran through some of his former prejudices about the medium: 'There has been committed against the unfortunate art of music every imaginable sin of commission and omission, but all previous crimes and stupidities pale before the latest attack on its fair name – broadcasting it by means of wireless.' This was scarcely likely to sooth ruffled nerves at the BBC. Beecham, in a letter dated 27/28 July, wrote to Reith:

> The Daily Mail informed me two days ago that having obtained some information concerning the proposed new orchestra from certain influential but indiscreet guarantors of the scheme, it was printing the same at once. I formed the opinion that as they would publish *in any case*, it would be advisable for me to edit the statement – if necessary – with vigour. I tried to get you on the phone twice yesterday but without success . . . I do not think there is anything in today's article to embarrass you or your Corporation. The sentence about the BBC is a qualified utterance. I suggest we leave it at that for the time being . . .
>
> I have two articles from Provincial journals purporting to be interviews with me on the subject of Radio. I never gave such interviews. The articles are a re-hash of many isolated remarks made on a different occasion two years ago . . . I have threatened the agency which supplied the copy with legal proceedings.

Tempers were calmed; Eckersley sent the text of a brief BBC announcement to Beecham, saying that their negotiations would be resumed in November. But over the summer, Press interest in the scheme grew. From the point of view of the BBC, nothing was settled: but the Press jumped to conclusions, particularly in view of the future plans for Henry Wood's Prom concerts.

Roger Eckersley had suddenly suggested to Wood in May that the Wireless Orchestra should take the place of Wood's own orchestra in the 1928 Proms; the reason was that its personnel might form the basis of the intended new permanent orchestra. Wood was extremely annoyed that the BBC had made no hint of this possible move when agreeing the terms for the 1928 season. He made so many detailed demands for changes in the Wireless

Orchestra if they were to undertake the Prom season that Eckersley had to back down: Wood's demands (made on 8 May 1928) show that he had an unrivalled knowledge of London players, their abilities and habits – apart from changes of personnel, he insisted that two particular players 'must agree not to constantly fidget in and out during the progress of any rehearsals upon business missions, but will devote themselves to the music in hand'. So Sir Henry Wood's Symphony Orchestra played – but at the end of the season, Wood spoke in dark and guarded terms to his players about the BBC's plans. He refused to make a Press statement, but it was reported that he had declared to the Orchestra: 'This will be a farewell season, and I have had to fight with the BBC to get them to keep this orchestra for this year.' He was implying only that he might not be able to choose his players personally in 1929, but the Press misunderstood. 'LAST OF THE PROMS?' asked the *Evening News*.

Two days later the *Daily Chronicle* revealed 'The Truth about the Crisis': it was not centred on the Proms; the news was that the 'BBC PLAN A GREAT NEW ORCHESTRA'.

> ... While there is some truth in the rumours, the matter is one that affects the constitution of the orchestra alone.
>
> It is the intention of the BBC sooner or later to create an orchestra comparable with that of the Berlin State Opera, the Philadelphia Symphony Orchestra, and other of the world's leading orchestras.
>
> While the new organisation must necessarily contain a large sprinkling of members of the Queen's Hall orchestra, the scheme will involve dispensing with the services of some people.
>
> It is probable that a beginning will be made before the 1929 season of 'Proms', and that the orchestra which will then be used will form the nucleus, together with members of the Wireless Symphony Orchestra, of the more ambitious organisation which the BBC has in mind, but which may take several years to complete ...

A BBC statement was more cautious: 'The arrangements for the Promenade Concerts of 1929 are not yet complete, but the BBC hopes that Sir Henry Wood will find it possible again to conduct.'

In fact, the BBC was fully intending to create its new orchestra by 1929, and to persuade Wood to work with it in the Prom season. But Beecham, not Wood, was to have the major say in its personnel: a fruitful source of conflict. Beecham returned to London to conduct the opening concert of the BBC's new Queen's Hall series on 12 October, and continued to treat the scheme as his personal property. To the *Daily Mail* he declared: 'The economic basis is assured. The details are settled . . . It will probably be called the London Philharmonic Orchestra [*sic*]. The concerts will absorb those of the Royal Philharmonic Society. . . . There will be daily rehearsals. Rank-and-file players will be paid £10 or £12 a week, and the leaders of the different sections about double.' Reith wrote the same day to Eckersley: 'Beecham in today's *Daily Mail*. This discussion of salaries is very indiscreet. Do you think he could be induced to stick to the artistic side of things, or is it useless?' Eckersley wrote a quick note to Beecham: '. . . forgive my interference, but . . . keep away from the subject of the salaries paid to musicians.' On the more controversial issues of the orchestra's name and the participation of the Royal Philharmonic Society, no warnings were given to Beecham. Beecham's only action was to write an apologetic note to Eckersley:

> The *Daily Mail* should not have said a word about players or salaries. It was not an interview, and the conversation was private. I can only account for the indiscretion by remembering that the gentleman (it was the critic) had two bottles of hock . . . Do your best to come to supper tonight after the concert to Lady Cunard . . . She wants you to bring Sir J. Reith also.

By this time the Royal Philharmonic Society had the impression from Beecham of a definite scheme of collaboration. There were to be twenty concerts 'under the control of the Society' to take the place of the Society's usual series; 'the Society to be guaranteed against loss on these concerts by the management of the Orchestra'. Columbia would assure forty recording sessions (a piece of wild optimism), and there would be Albert Hall Sunday afternoon concerts, concerts in the suburbs, and so on. But this was all purely Beecham's intention as in April 1928, before the collaboration began; it did not represent any agreed scheme of action. Moreover, Beecham now assured the RPS (in a letter read at their 18 October meeting) that 'the scheme is in its penultimate state of organisation' and that the completed scheme would be ready by December. Such was not the impression at the BBC.

Eckersley was anxious to finalise some financial details of the negotiations as soon as possible. The BBC Governors had approved the scheme in principle. The BBC's Contracts Department had also been at work, and had produced new figures which showed a loss of £67,332 on an experimental season. Eckersley wrote to Beecham on 19 October 'I do hope you'll be able to lunch with me, and give me a little time afterwards to get down to a few business details . . .' They saw each other on 23 October and at last Beecham had some financial facts. Eckersley to Reith:

I lunched with Beecham on Tuesday and brought him back here afterwards and discussed matters with him for at least an hour and a half. I did not show him any of our figures . . . Beecham has a very businesslike grip of values in the concert world, and it was very interesting to find that his figures were not on the whole very much different from our own.

There was one radical difference, however, which was that Beecham estimated huge box-office receipts for the concerts, while the BBC (in line with their experience in recent seasons) had been more cautious. Hence Beecham's estimated deficit for the full-time scheme came to £40,000, while the BBC's stood at £70,000. Reith and Eckersley agreed that between £50,000 and £60,000 would be a reasonable figure to work on: the BBC would then contribute £30,000; Beecham's guarantors would rise to £20,000. If this loss were exceeded, the cost would be met 50–50 by the BBC and Beecham.

Eckersley met Beecham again in November 1928 and put an arrangement to him during 'an hour's most friendly discussion':

I suggested that the actual organisation of the concerts should be handled departmentally within the Corporation, and that a small (Business) committee to meet here would be appointed . . . There would further be an Artistic Committee at which Beecham would chair . . . he suggested Landon Ronald, Geoffrey Toye, Filson Young, and of course the Musical Director of the Corporation.

Beecham replied on 13 December, agreeing the basic financial proposition, but objecting to any possible further liability above £60,000: 'Some of my most influential supporters decline to enter into a contingent undertaking where the liability is apparently unlimited.' He suggested insuring against this possible extra loss. Eckersley thought this impracticable, and insisted that Beecham raise his contribution. He wrote on 27 December: 'Let us hope that 1929 will see the fulfilment of our mutual desire in regard to the orchestra.' The desire was there, but the edifice of the new orchestra was being built on what increasingly looked to be shaky ground.

The Ideal Orchestra?

Meanwhile, at the turn of the year, the BBC's supposed plans were occupying a large amount of space in the Press. Almost every paper knew more about the plans than the Corporation did, and pontificated accordingly. *The Times* had already declared (13 October 1928) that 'The Ideal Orchestra' was 'an illusion':

. . . the BBC seems to offer a kind of convenient back door to State-aided music. Let it with the funds at its disposal take into its service the best players, wherever they are to be found, and the thing will be done.

But there is a fallacy there, and one which ought to be evident to people so given to the formation of teams as the English are . . . Great orchestral playing requires a far more subtle combination of individual faculties than does rowing. Suppose, what is by no means certain, that this country contains orchestral players in each department who man for man are as fine execu-tants as their opposite members in either the Berlin or Philadelphia or-chestras . . .

The BBC is the biggest purveyor of music in the country, and the whole essence of its contract with its servants is that they should be available to supply all sorts of music at all sorts of hours of the day and night. Not for it or its clients is the unified style of playing or even, except on the rarest oc-casions, the fully rehearsed programme. General utility and versatility must be the object of any body of performers which the BBC may engage. It is not to be supposed that its orchestra should meet every morning for rehearsal under its own conductor with the prospect of giving at most two perform-ances of one programme at the end of the week. This was the method by which Mr Stokowski built up the reputation of his Philadelphia players, and it is the normal one where perfection is the aim. An eminent musician invented a motto for the BBC's music, which ran, 'Very good, very cheap, and very often.' No doubt he meant 'good' as regards the quality of the works chosen and 'cheap' as regards the cost to the listeners. With these readings it is an excellent motto for a musical mission to the masses, but it is the 'very often' which precludes the 'very good' as regards style in performance. The ideal orchestra must of necessity be very expensive to somebody and comparatively infrequent in its benefits to anybody.

We may conclude, then, that there is no strong likelihood of London acquiring this perfect engine of music either through the BBC or anyone else, and that conclusion need not be unduly depressing.

Musical Opinion (November 1928) saw too that such an orchestra as the BBC planned

can only be achieved in terms of cash. In Germany and Austria, the cost of the orchestra is never once discussed: national pride forbids it, for music is considered necessary to the nation's salvation. In America it is different: the utmost publicity is given to the financial upkeep of their orchestras. The famous Philadelphia Orchestra has an endowment fund of £400,000. This immense reserve explains exceptional qualities. If London also is to have such an exceptional orchestra, then the BBC alone can establish it, for its resources are national and almost inexhaustible . . . The position at the moment is that if the BBC is to form an exceptional orchestra for England, who is to decide its composition and who shall direct it?

Sir Landon Ronald was optimistic on the first day of the new year in the *Daily Herald*: 'I consider the outlook most hopeful, and I am convinced that the schemes initiated by Sir Thomas Beecham . . . the foundation of a first-class permanent symphony orchestra in conjunction with the BBC . . . will become accomplished facts in 1929 . . .' Then on 5 January Beecham released further mythical details to the *Daily Mail*:

The roles of the two partners are clearly defined. The BBC with its great organisation and powerful publicity, undertakes the business side. The artistic responsibilities devolve on me.

I shall choose the players who will constitute the orchestra; I shall be responsible for the framing of the programmes and for the selection of soloists. . . .

A strange spirit has moved some to begin already to disparage the players. I smile; for at present none is engaged. I have three leaders in my mind, but I have not chosen yet.

As for the title, I can tell you it will not be 'The BBC Orchestra'. Probably it will be the 'Royal Philharmonic'. An invitation was some time ago extended to the Philharmonic Society (which is in low water) to come into the new scheme. Amicable negotiations are in progress; and now, subject to some few outstanding details, there is, I can say today, every prospect of an harmonious union.

This provoked the BBC into making its own uninformative announcement of the scheme. The *Daily News* reported:

The long-expected announcement with regard to the promised permanent orchestra for London has at last been made by the BBC. We learn that the BBC negotiations with Sir Thomas Beecham have come to a satisfactory end . . .

It had been generally expected that there would be some mention of the Royal Philharmonic Society in the announcement, but this is not so.

There are several other things in the document which we had hoped to see, as, for instance, what the strength of the new orchestra is to be, how many concerts there are to be in London, and whether there are to be any concerts outside London.

By far the most important thing, however – and this is passed over in silence – is how far the orchestra will answer to the definition of a 'permanent' orchestra – that is, how many times in the year it will be conducted by Sir Thomas Beecham, and, if he is not to conduct all the concerts, who is to do so?

The irrepressible Philip Page of the *Evening Standard*, a constant critic of the BBC, concluded in the terms of the popular limerick that 'the BBC have returned from the ride with Sir Thomas Beecham inside, and I imagine there is a smile on the face of the tiger'. This led the *Daily Express* to ask (9 January):

> Has Sir Thomas Beecham surrendered to the BBC? Or has the BBC surrendered to Sir Thomas? In short, stand the hopes of British orchestral musicians where they should in 1929?
>
> Sir Thomas Beecham, swathed in a crème-de-menthe dressing gown, discussed yesterday with a representative of the 'Daily Express' the suggestion that his proposed partnership with the BBC in forming a permanent national orchestra represented a bowing, on his part, to superior odds.
>
> The first thing Sir Thomas said, waving his long-stemmed pipe with the precision of a baton, was 'No surrender!'
>
> 'As if I, of all men, would surrender myself to the BBC!
>
> 'No. It is a mutual arrangement on a fifty–fifty basis. The orchestra will be the finest that England has ever heard. . . .
>
> 'For the first time, the governing body of the BBC – who have hitherto considered themselves as universal purveyors and censors of entertainment – will have no say, except in a business way.
>
> 'I shall not allow the percentage of foreign guest conductors to creep above the 25 per cent level. At present it is more than twice that. Similarly, I shall devote a good deal of my time to developing native talent.'

This was pure fiction: or at least, pure imagination on Beecham's part. The interview ended with a revealing little exchange:

> 'One other thing: it is quite true that I cancelled my American tour because of illness.'
>
> He slapped his chest delicately.
>
> 'You will doubtless rejoice to hear that I am now in the best of health again.'
>
> And Sir Thomas winked.

As well he might have. Eckersley took the revelations calmly, as his essential belief in Beecham's good faith implied: 'You've seen this of course', he wrote. 'He goes a little far. But it doesn't matter! Let's get an orchestra whatever is said in the Press and ignore everything else!'

There were many problems. Who exactly were Beecham's guarantors? The question does not seem to have occurred to Roger Eckersley before 7 January 1929: 'I mentioned [to Beecham] that the next step was some agreement legally binding on the guarantors, whose ability to guarantee we must be satisfied about.' Their representative was to be a Colonel Martin, a director of Hambros Bank: no other name was ever mentioned in writing. Moreover, the intentions of Beecham and the BBC with regard to the scheme appeared still to diverge considerably. Beecham's first aim was to build an all-inclusive scheme, involving the Royal Philharmonic Society and the gramophone companies, removing competition in London and ensuring financial support. The BBC was more concerned to consolidate its place at the centre of the enterprise, and was prepared to give enough financial support to guarantee it a controlling interest. To Beecham, the BBC was a peripheral factor in his project: if success could be achieved without the assistance of the Corporation, that was fine.

Indeed, he was still, in January 1929, discussing his plans with the Royal Philharmonic Society, on the basis of his April 1928 scheme. He assured the Society on 19 January that 'the whole of the series of 35–40 [London] concerts shall be the concerts of the RPS ... the proposed new orchestra is hereinafter to be known as the Royal Philharmonic Orchestra'. The RPS was anxious to maintain artistic control of its concerts. Beecham told them that this could only be arranged through his agency. He 'had been given absolute control of the artistic side' by the BBC. Not surprisingly, Beecham was anxious to keep the RPS and the BBC officials apart: 'Sir Thomas wished to have the Society as partners in a dual arrangement. He must have the Society on his side of the fence during any negotiations that might ensue ...' His fiercest warning to the RPS was that 'if the Society went directly to the BBC and made arrangements and this came to his ears ... then he would withdraw ...'

A rival scheme

Beecham was now working on several fronts. His plans for a permanent orchestra had become known as early as July 1928 to the orchestra with which (through Lionel Powell) he had been most closely associated, the London Symphony. The LSO had, not unsurprisingly, been extremely worried by the proposal, and had attempted to extract a convoluted assurance from Beecham that he would 'endeavour to formulate a means whereby the members of the London Symphony Orchestra should be at liberty to perform at the usual series of symphony concerts so that the LSO as such should be thus enabled to carry on their policy, business and traditions.' But when it became clear that Beecham's negotiations with the BBC were proceeding apace, the LSO decided to move on its own. It had to protect itself against the possibility of a permanent orchestra destroying its character and attracting its best players. So it set about working out a limited scheme of guaranteed work – with some irony, along the lines of the original plan which had been suggested to the BBC by Lionel Powell. Powell brought together the Opera Company at Covent Garden, the Gramophone Company (HMV), and his own touring promotions, to guarantee 151 concerts a year for an orchestra of seventy-five contracted players.

How far Beecham was kept informed of the LSO scheme remains unclear. But he was likely to have known through Powell of the orchestra's activities, and the LSO's grouping of interests was a great threat to Beecham's idea of the scheme – greater than it was to the BBC's plan. The BBC would be prepared to compete with such an orchestra, whereas that was precisely what Beecham sought to avoid. It surely was not a coincidence that, when Beecham lunched again with Eckersley on 24 January 1929, he suggested putting off the full scheme until 1930. There would still be an experimental scheme from the autumn of 1929, but Beecham would then have time to develop new ideas – including the ambitious notion of a new central London concert hall which would be the permanent orchestra's home. Beecham agreed to a one-third share in the deficit of the experimental season; the managing director of the Beecham family's pill business was now to be his financial right-hand man in the enterprise. This agreement, such as it was, was formulated by Eckersley on 6 February: twenty-two Fridays were booked at the Queen's Hall for 1929–30, and the future, he wrote to Beecham, 'depends on the creation of a hall. This is, of course, in your hands.' Meanwhile Beecham kept all his options open. He negotiated with the Royal Philharmonic Society about the use of their concerts and their name, without informing the BBC. And he doubtless kept himself informed about the progress of the LSO's scheme.

By March 1929 Eckersley was becoming anxious about Beecham's lack of activity with regard to the experimental season: 'I am really rather worried about the future and little time we have to get everything ready for the autumn,' he wrote on 4 March. Meanwhile, news of the LSO's new plans was reaching the BBC, and it became necessary to act quickly. A two-pronged attack was launched, confirming the BBC's outline scheme in the Press and simultaneously setting in motion the auditions procedure for the new orchestra. On 6 March Reith wrote firmly to Beecham enclosing the BBC's press statement, and saying that 'communications with the Press will be limited as herein described, it being understood that you will restrict your observations in the same way'. On 8 March the *Daily Express* announced that 'Negotiations between Sir Thomas and the BBC have reached a satisfactory conclusion, and auditions will be held in the next few weeks . . .' The Press statement of 15 March said:

> In the autumn of 1929 the BBC proposes, with the co-operation of Sir Thomas Beecham, to inaugurate a trial season with a view to the establishment twelve months later of a permanent symphony orchestra. As at present planned this orchestra will consist of about ninety players selected from the best talent available. Public concerts will be given for eleven months in the year, mostly in London but also in the provinces. Musicians will be engaged on a full time non-deputising basis. The name of the new orchestra has not yet been determined. There will be equal opportunities for women.

But on 11 March Beecham had confused matters still further by proposing to Eckersley a quite new scheme for financial co-operation based around his new concert hall. Perhaps this was because he wished to sidestep the formal agreement which the BBC's solicitors had drawn up for the consideration of his guarantors. He eventually agreed that the document should be submitted to his solicitors for consideration. Meanwhile the BBC was being deluged with enquiries about the new orchestra: a further press release had to be issued, and the Music Department complained that, because it knew absolutely no details of the scheme, 'we have no knowledge or instructions with which to reply to the many outside enquiries'. The situation was almost farcical.

Meanwhile, Roger Eckersley was having to make a difficult decision. He knew that announcement of the LSO–Powell scheme was imminent: should he at once invite key players to join the BBC Orchestra, without any assurance that the BBC's own scheme would be settled? He wrote a note to Reith explaining the rival scheme, and said:

> I think we may however have quickly to make up our minds definitely to write to some of the players we know we shall want, and give some kind of definite assurance for the future. Am I justified in so doing? remembering that the final scheme has always a long odd chance of not coming off . . . certain gambles have to be taken in schemes of this kind . . . it means the abandonment of the principle of auditions for all.

At the news of the LSO scheme, Reith exploded. 'Surely the situation is very serious [he wrote on 18 March] . . . it would cut right across our ideas altogether . . . I cannot conceive that there is room for two permanent orchestras in London . . .' Reith thought that the BBC's negotiations with the gramophone companies had been badly handled, and that if the BBC had held out promises of recordings for both major record companies, HMV would not have committed itself to the LSO. But Eckersley managed to convince Reith that the situation was not as bad as it seemed (20 March):

> The other scheme cannot, because of Powell's provincial and operatic commitments, provide more than a very modified permanency and does not go very far on the road to creating a national gallery of music, which is our aim. The LSO players, I understand, are not to be engaged on a permanent basis, but merely per performance. This means that they will get little more rehearsal than is the case in outside concerts at the moment. The essence of our own scheme is the daily rehearsal.

Eckersley's ambivalence with regard to his dealings with Beecham are very clearly expressed in this letter to Reith. Concluding, he sounds a note of wise caution: 'I must repeat once more that all my suggestions are dependent upon Beecham's guarantees in regard to the new hall, and his own guarantors. I have his word in regard to these, but nothing more.' Later the same day, however, Eckersley talked again to Beecham, and fired with new enthusiasm, added a postscript: 'He does not think the HMV scheme will interfere with ours at all . . . the hall matter is practically settled – it is in Chesham Place. His guarantors are also in it. He thinks it will be very profitable . . . I really believe one could see a fairly clear road ahead on the lines suggested above.' Eckersley's words echo Beecham's a year earlier: 'fairly straight sailing . . . a fairly concrete proposal'; such generalities were unlikely to produce results, but Beecham had the knack of painting rosy horizons so that immediate problems were overlooked.

Meanwhile Beecham was still hankering after collaboration with the Royal Philharmonic Society, because their name would bring lustre to the proceedings, and (more important) because their connection with the Columbia record company would guarantee some recordings. The BBC was still anxious to acquire the RPS's name for its concerts, and at a meeting in late January had discussed possible privileges for RPS members as well as the constitution of an artistic committee. Little progress was made, for the RPS demanded a controlling voice on the artistic committee which Reith was not prepared to concede. The BBC let the matter rest, but Beecham did not. On 27 March he alerted the RPS to what might happen if both the BBC and LSO went ahead with their plans: 'It is not inconceivable that the RPS may soon find itself in a position of embarrassment in respect of competent players.' He proposed that the RPS engage his new orchestra, and through April carried on negotiations. On 26 April he told the RPS with sublime confidence: 'The BBC have left to me the settlement of reasonable terms. I am a sort of plenipotentiary.' And he went so far as to discuss a proposed list of players in detail.

A surprised Eckersley reported to Reith on 15 May: 'It is necessary to say that during the past fortnight Beecham has been interviewing these people with a view to close collaboration during the forthcoming season . . . the line he has been taking presents certain new factors . . .' The RPS was even more surprised when they learnt that there were objections from the BBC: 'Sir Thomas Beecham stated that he was acting as plenipotentiary on your behalf', they wrote to Eckersley at the end of May. Beecham's explanation for wanting to co-operate in the forthcoming season (as he put it to Eckersley in a letter of 2 May) was naïve: 'I find much virtue in the idea . . . to give the concerts in the name of the RPS. At the expiration of a year the Society will be faced with the alternative of coming into the scheme or remaining out of it. After a year's glory as it will enjoy during 1929–30 it will not willingly return to its more modest condition.'

In fact Beecham had seen several ways out of his problems: the RPS orchestra would provide him with a ready-made band of players around the BBC nucleus; Columbia would provide recordings; the RPS would provide a ready-made concert series. In return, of course, the RPS wanted special privileges and facilities for their members, and made their demands to the BBC. 'I am quite against giving them nearly as many facilities as they demand,' Reith wrote gruffly on 13 May. It was clear that Beecham's idea of his orchestra was still diverging from the BBC's, and that the RPS was caught between the two parties in the disagreement. Eckersley met with RPS officials on 15 May and suggested postponing the agreement for a season. On 23 May Reith noted: 'I have agreed to do without RPS.' The same day, the RPS secretary was writing a pained letter to Eckersley, mentioning 'certain difficulties of which we know nothing . . . what are the obstacles to a complete agreement?'

At this point Beecham vanished, writing to the RPS that he was 'bitterly disappointed', and suggesting that the Society negotiate directly with the BBC as he was 'much too busy to take any future part in discussions'. Eckersley met the RPS officials on 10 June and explained frankly that negotiations between Columbia and the BBC had not in fact taken place, and pointed out that recordings were a crucial factor for Beecham. The forthcoming season would be 'for the purposes of trying out our musicians' and collaboration should be deferred. At this meeting Beecham was not present. He too had

discovered the flaw in the plan. He wrote an unusually formal typed letter to
Eckersley:

> ... I very much regret being unable to be present at the Conference today ...
> I learn that the matter is far from being settled so far as Columbia is con-
> cerned, and that it is possible this Company may not enter the scheme in the
> way originally indicated. This, of course, may involve a complete regrouping
> of the different interests concerned, with the result that while I still want
> Columbia in the project, I may have to leave them out of it. This readjusted
> situation is going to increase rather than lessen the delicacy of the situation
> with regard to the Royal Philharmonic Society.

The BBC decided to postpone the idea of collaboration with the RPS, to
abandon the idea of using their name for the orchestra, and to pursue a policy
of non-exclusivity with regard to recording the orchestra.

Since Beecham's last reassurance to Eckersley in March, little had happened to give the BBC any confidence in Beecham's collaboration. The vital
step of approaching players and holding auditions was now a top priority,
before the HMV/LSO scheme attracted the best talent. Under the direction
of Percy Pitt, an auditions procedure for the rank-and-file was arranged.
Whereas principals would be approached personally, rank-and-file players
were to be auditioned on the widest possible basis around the country. As
much of the orchestra as possible had to be ready for the autumn of 1929 for
the experimental season. So experienced string players such as Albert Sammons and Lionel Tertis were asked to travel around the country listening to
new talent at some 1000 individual auditions arranged in the BBC's regional
centres. Beecham did not take part in the preliminary auditions, and only by
May did he agree the list of twenty-seven prominent players who should be
approached for their services without undergoing auditions. But he did, it
seems, take part in the final auditions for the rank-and-file strings. Kathleen
Washbourne, an original member of the 1929 orchestra, remembers being
auditioned 'from behind a screen' in London by a panel which turned out,
when the audition was over, to include Beecham. So his effect on the new
orchestra's personnel was not completely absent.

Beecham bows out

As far as final agreement went, Beecham and the BBC were still far apart.
The draft of the contract between the BBC and Beecham's solicitors was still
circulating: a draft was presented on 30 April, revised on 18 May; a new draft
prepared on 2 July; comments were not received from Beecham's side, and
the final document was sent by the BBC to Beecham's solicitors only on 13

August. On 10 July Eckersley noticed that he had not received Beecham's agreement to bear one third of the deficit on the experimental 1929–30 season in writing. He wrote to Beecham, wishing to discuss 'one or two urgent matters', and was met by a reply from Beecham's secretary. It was perhaps at this point that Eckersley's powerful confidence in Beecham began to disintegrate. He was unable to contact Beecham personally. There is a new tone in his letter of 30 August, written a fortnight after the final agreement had been submitted to Beecham's solicitors:

> Now that you are back in London it will perhaps be possible for us to meet shortly and discuss the immediate future of the Orchestral Scheme . . . I have not heard from you regarding the proposed hall . . . This and other points as yet undecided affect the financial outlook very much and I am sure you will understand how necessary it is to clear up the present uncertainty . . .
>
> I understand that nothing has come from your solicitors . . . It is impossible for me to proceed with any certainty in regard to the engagement of musicians and other points until our relations have been officially established on a business basis . . .
>
> I hope I do not give the impression of being too importunate, but time is getting comparatively short and there is a great deal more to be done.

The reply to this was a letter from Beecham's secretary saying that he would be in London again in the middle of September. Beecham and Eckersley did not meet again until the beginning of October. Beecham's solicitors finally came to life, saying they had no copy of the draft agreement; a new copy was sent on 26 October. Further discussions revealed that Beecham had given no view to his solicitors about the document, but assured Reith and Eckersley categorically that it would be signed by Christmas. It was stated that he was to meet his guarantors on 9 December to ensure that all was settled. On 14 December the BBC solicitors reported that there had been no progress. Beecham was asked to contact his solicitors, and on the last day of 1929 this letter from his solicitors arrived at the BBC's solicitors:

> We have had the opportunity of interviewing certain of the proposed Guarantors of the orchestral scheme. After several prolonged discussions which we understand have taken place between them, we regret to inform you that the terms of the draft contract submitted to us for their approval are unacceptable to them. For the satisfaction of your Clients we enclose a memorandum which we understand contains the summarised opinions of the group of which Sir Thomas Beecham has hitherto been the representative.

The enclosed memorandum gave some radical reasons for the guarantors' disagreement, but at no time was any mention of the guarantors' names made. The points of argument were summarised under five headings:

1. When the orchestral scheme was first laid before the Guarantors in 1928 it was represented to them that it was an inclusive and not an exclusive scheme. In other words it was intended to make use of and absorb certain existing institutions such as the Royal Philharmonic Society, the London Symphony Orchestra and at least one of the Gramophone Companies . . .
2. This leaves in the concert world both of London and of the Provinces a lively and unrestricted competition which the Guarantors on their side are not prepared to face . . .
3. The figures originally laid before the guarantors by Sir Thomas Beecham were based upon . . . a very large number of concerts given by him and Mr Lionel Powell . . . they perceive an immediate discrepancy between these figures and those which the Broadcasting Corporation are able to produce in respect of their own concerts.
4. The Guarantors view with concern the right assumed by the Broadcasting Corporation to terminate the scheme . . .
5. The Guarantors are of the opinion that the scheme has been modified and moulded by the Broadcasting Corporation less with an eye to the visible than to the invisible audience . . . They are reluctantly forced to the conclusion that their aims and those of the Corporation are not identical.

The last point was true, and had been true from the beginning. The Beecham scheme was dead. Eckersley could protest vigorously (6 January 1930) that the Guarantors had either misunderstood the scheme, or had not been kept informed by Beecham, and that Beecham had misled the BBC and modified his own ideas without consultation – but the fact was that it was now impossible to reach agreement, and the BBC had to decide whether to go ahead on its own. Beecham withdrew rapidly from the scene: of his four engagements in the Queen's Hall series between January and March 1930, he fulfilled only one.

A comprehensive orchestral scheme

The abandonment of the Beecham scheme came as no surprise to anyone in the BBC, and indeed it was greeted with relief by members of the Music Department. Contingency plans had been afoot for several months before the end of 1929, and it was becoming increasingly obvious that these plans were better suited to the creation of an orchestra for broadcasting than were Beecham's proposals. In the middle of 1929, unable to delay any longer, the BBC had sent out invitations to twenty-seven key players, offering them posts in the new orchestra 'in the event of negotiations with Sir Thomas Beecham coming to a successful conclusion'. Was there perhaps a better way of using those players as a nucleus of a broadcasting orchestra than that which Beecham had proposed?

Members of the Music Department (who had been in the background while the Beecham scheme was developed by Reith, Eckersley and the contracts department) thought that a far more efficient plan for a broadcasting orchestra could be evolved. On 4 November 1929, when it seemed clear that Beecham's scheme was unlikely to survive, Edward Clark and Julian Herbage, with the support of Kenneth Wright, unveiled a radically new approach to the setting up of a permanent orchestra, which they had developed during 1929. Instead of one orchestra, reducing on occasions as needed to a smaller group (which was all that the Beecham scheme envisaged), Clark and Herbage presented an interlocking scheme for no less than five orchestras drawn from one group of players. 114 players could provide:

A A symphony orchestra of 114 to play full-size orchestral works.

B A symphony orchestra of 78 to play smaller symphonic works.

C A theatre orchestra of 36 to play dramatic programmes, musical comedy, etc.

D A light orchestra of 67 for light music and lighter symphony concerts.

E A popular orchestra of 47 for miscellaneous requirements.

Thus, ingeniously, orchestras *B* and *C* used all 114 players, as did the combination of orchestras *D* and *E*. It would be possible to schedule work for these two groups simultaneously, and the players would come together for the prestige events with the full symphony orchestra. The numerical details of the plan were as follows. The complete strength would be:

20 First Violins
16 Second Violins
14 Violas
12 Cellos
10 Double Basses
 4 Flutes (including Piccolos)
 4 Oboes (including Cor Anglais, Hecklephone, Bass Oboe, Oboe d'Amore, Oboe da Caccia)
 5 Clarinets (including E flat Clarinet, Bass Clarinet, Saxophone)
 4 Bassoons (including Double Bassoon)
 6 Horns (including Wagner Tubas)
 5 Trumpets (including Trumpet in D, Bass Trumpet, Cornets)

    5 Trombones (including Contrabass Trombone)
    2 Tubas (including Euphonium, Tenor Tuba)
    2 Harps
    5 Percussion players

    ___

    114 players

    ___

The sections would be divided as follows:

	A	B	C	D	E
First Violins	20	14	6	12	8
Second Violins	16	12	4	10	6
Violas	14	10	4	8	6
Cellos	12	8	4	7	5
Double Basses	10	7	3	6	4
Flutes	4	3	1	2	2
Oboes	4	3	1	2	2
Clarinets	5	3	2	3	2
Bassoons	4	3	1	2	2
Horns	6	4	2	4	2
Trumpets	5	3	2	3	2
Trombones	5	3	2	3	2
Tubas	2	1	1	1	1
Harps	2	1	1	1	1
Percussion	5	3	2	3	2
	114	78	36	67	47
		114		114	

This 'Comprehensive Orchestral Organisation', as Clark and Herbage called it, provided Eckersley with the confidence he needed to persevere with plans for a permanent orchestra after the demise of the Beecham scheme. Even before Beecham's guarantors had reported back, Eckersley was mentioning the scheme to Reith. 13 November 1929:

> There are many practical difficulties to be considered in regard to the scheme, such as the availability of the men for performance and rehearsal, the possible difficulty in regard to Beecham's guarantors, the artistic limitations of a scheme which forces players into what might be considered a certain amount of hack work, and the feeling that I still have in my mind that we

shall only get the best orchestra by having a complete entity which does not
chop and change, playing under a definite trainer . . . I will not go into any
greater detail about the scheme now and will put it to you with its pros and
cons when it is more crystallized . . .

In December, this plan had even been discussed in principle at a fruitless
meeting of the supposed Artistic Committee, with Beecham and RPS
officials present.

On 9 January 1930, Eckersley was in a position to present to Reith the
whole argument for continuing the formation of an orchestra without
Beecham. He set out the advantages of the BBC acting independently, and
concluded:

The new proposal of making the orchestra responsible for both studio and
outside work has, except for financial considerations, altered my original
conception of the scheme so much that were we discussing the matter today
for the first time, I would have attempted to put up a scheme to you whereby
the BBC would be the sole promoters. The proposition was in my opinion
entirely different when it stood as an outside concert-giving scheme alone.
We, as it were, were the amateurs needing professional help. Now, as so
large a proportion and importance of the work is studio broadcasting, the
position is altered.

There were also certain practical factors. The nucleus of twenty-seven
players had already been offered jobs. One thousand auditions had been held
for the rank-and-file places. Queen's Hall was booked for the autumn of
1930. It would be foolish to go back on all this.

Moreover, the experimental season of the new orchestra was by now in
full swing, and was receiving good notices for its work. A most impressive
series of programmes had included, rather ironically, a much-praised contribution to Beecham's Delius Festival (*A Mass of Life* on 1 November),
and Hindemith playing his own Viola Concerto (the *Kammermusik* No. 5)
under Wood on 22 November 1929. In the new year there was Bartók in his
own Piano Concerto No. 1; Ansermet in Stravinsky's *Le Chant du Rossignol*
and Honegger's *Rugby* (31 January); and Scherchen presenting the Toch
Piano Concerto (21 February) heard at the Frankfurt ISCM Festival in
1927. Wood conducted the world première of Bax's Third Symphony; and
the opportunity was taken to present the two prize string principals of the
future BBC Symphony Orchestra, Arthur Catterall and Lauri Kennedy, in
the Brahms Double Concerto on 7 March. The same concert presented one
of the most enduring orchestral works of which the BBC has given the British

première: Ravel's *Bolero*. Ernest Newman's review (*The Sunday Times* 9 March) was unprophetic but amusing:

> ... there is not much to it except the stunt, and it remains to be seen whether our audiences' interest in this will survive half a dozen repetitions of it. Someone, no doubt, will now write a similar piece constructed on one long decrescendo. The fun would then be to have the two works played simultaneously.

The climax of the season, on 15 April, was a concert postponed from the previous season, in which Henry Wood conducted the British première of Mahler's Eighth Symphony, a colossal undertaking which met with respect rather than enthusiasm from the critics.

Boult arrives

The other major development at the BBC while the Beecham scheme was collapsing was the appointment of a new musical director. If Percy Pitt's biographer is correct that he was born on 4 January 1869, then he would have reached Reith's enforced 'retiring age' of sixty at the start of 1929. Beecham had promised Pitt the musical directorship of his Imperial League of Opera (his other ambitious scheme of the later 1920s which never got off the ground). It was rumoured that Pitt offered to resign in order to devote himself to this work, and then withdrew his resignation when the post failed to materialise. Kenneth Wright, however, wrote that Reith callously got rid of Pitt and that Pitt 'read of his (own) resignation in the *Evening News*'. Certainly, Pitt's leaving the BBC – which took effect only at the end of 1929 – was an unhappy experience for him. He led a sad and difficult life before his death in November 1932, with great personal and financial worries; he left property valued at £31. But his achievement was considerable: his contribution to BBC music, his setting of its direction for the future, had been decisive; the success of his open-minded policy in the 1930s was his finest memorial.

Reith began to enquire of his advisers in early 1929 as to a possible successor to Pitt. A suggestion came from Walford Davies that Adrian Boult, conductor of the City of Birmingham Orchestra and a new member of the BBC's Music Advisory Committee, might be a suitable candidate. Sir Hugh Allen, who had known Boult at Oxford and had subsequently asked him to teach conducting after the war at the Royal College of Music, was in enthusiastic agreement. Boult's background fitted him admirably for the post. He had the advantage of a highly respectable background: Westminster School and Christ Church Oxford; teaching at the Royal College of Music, and a good reputation for the encouragement of English music. He had 'first caused *The Planets* to shine in public' (as Holst later put it) at the Queen's Hall on a Sunday morning in September 1918, and Elgar had praised a performance of his Second Symphony at the People's Palace in 1921 as 'one of the happiest events of my life'. But Boult also had a continental training: he had watched Nikisch at work, had been in contact with Reger, and had 'worshipped at the feet of Bruno Walter'. His musical tastes were very wide. Indeed he might well have worked abroad had not the Birmingham offer been made; when he moved there, he began to broaden the orchestra's programmes dramatically. The second British performance of Mahler's *Das Lied von der Erde* took place during these concerts, as well as one of Mahler's Fourth Symphony.

Boult was a candidate who could meet with the approval both of the Advisory Committee and of the Music Department: surely a unique position. (There was probably only one other conductor in the country who had a comparable breadth of interest, and that was Eugene Goossens – a close friend of Percy Pitt's, who would not have been tolerated by the Music Advisory Committee.) He did not need the job, for he was happy in Birmingham. He had an orchestra to build up; he had an aim in view, which was to extend the season from six to ten or eleven months; and he was planning to stay with the orchestra for at least ten years. But the offer of the Music Directorship of the BBC, particularly with the new permanent orchestra on the horizon, was one that could not be refused. In addition, Boult was not only a conductor; he felt himself to be an efficient administrator at a time when 'the best musicians in the country were quite hopeless administrators. My father had done pretty well in business: I knew I could do it. I realised it was my job to cope.' Encouraged by many musicians, including Henry Wood, Boult accepted the post of Music Director. It was not the post of Chief Conductor of the Symphony Orchestra – far from it, for in 1929, whatever the BBC's real expectations were, that post was formally to be Beecham's. Reith said to Boult firmly when they first met that Boult's job would be to direct the music, not to conduct it. 'He did not like sending for his Director of Music in the afternoon only to be told that he had gone home to rest as he was conducting that evening.' Of course, Boult realised that the Beecham scheme was foundering: he recalls Eckersley saying to him before an Advisory Committee in 1929 that the BBC was worried about Beecham's backers, and that the Corporation might have to go ahead with the scheme themselves.

It became publicly known in the middle of the year that Boult was to succeed Pitt. It was vital to involve him in the decision-making about the

new orchestra as quickly as possible. It was at first agreed that he would succeed Pitt on 1 January 1930, carrying on his Birmingham concerts to the end
of the season. But in the autumn of 1929 he discovered, as a Music Advisory
Committee member, that plans had already been made for the early period of
1930 when he would be officially in charge. He insisted that the date of his
appointment be postponed until May. This was the first example of a Boult-
ian firmness which was to characterise his dealings with the BBC through his
twenty-year career with them. As he wrote in his autobiography:

> The Corporation was not amused. I was interviewed by several most
> important people, but refused to budge. Finally, to my alarm and astonish-
> ment, I was tackled by Reith himself the moment the ladies had left a dinner
> table in Kensington . . . Reith refused to take the answer no. I already had an
> appointment to see him in a few days, I must come then, and tell him I had
> agreed to begin on the first of January. I went away horrified; if this was a
> sample of life at the BBC, I would stay in Birmingham, and I wrote and
> said so.

This letter was probably written on 22 November. That Boult was still furious may be guessed from a note of 26 November to Eckersley: 'I feel I owe
you an apology for today's invasion'.

Reith replied to Boult after he had seen him on 26 November, and covered
all the outstanding points Boult had made. He backed down on the question
of the starting date of Boult's appointment (which was now to be on 15 May
1930), and added that

> to such extent as is possible between the beginning of the year and then, you
> will come here, particularly in order to deal with any policy matters which
> have to be settled during that period, and generally to take up any special
> points you may wish to investigate. You will not be considered responsible
> for the Music Department, but on the other hand it will be arranged with Mr
> Eckersley that 'what you say goes'. I think this settles the whole matter . . .

And on the following day Boult was already active, making detailed comments on the proposed scheme of concert dates for the next season drawn up
by Kenneth Wright (who now had the title of Music Executive).

The appointment of Adrian Boult was a stroke of genius, with implications for the future which those who made the appointment cannot have
foreseen. His musical gifts, his administrative qualities, his unassuming
manner and meticulous approach to decision-making, his skill at delegation,
and perhaps above all his lack of desire for personal fame and attention, made
him an ideal man to take charge of the BBC's music at the start of 1930.

The situation which Boult inherited was one that any self-important conductor would not have stood for a moment. He found himself with an orchestra in which important orchestral members were already selected and auditioned; a scheme of organisation already under discussion; and almost total uncertainty as to whether any of the plans being mooted could go ahead in the following months. But Boult regarded it as his task to bring these plans to fruition; to create the best possible orchestra out of what was provided by the BBC. He set to work with a dedication and enthusiasm. There were still loose ends to be tied up over the Beecham proposals. 'Boult generally agrees', Eckersley appended to his 9 January memo; but it was not until 30 January that he could actually write to Boult outlining future plans.

For a start, Beecham had to be given a final ultimatum. On 20 January Eckersley wrote to him mentioning the 'unfortunate lack of understanding' between him and his guarantors, between him and the BBC. On 22 January the BBC's solicitors wrote to Beecham's solicitors again, saying that the BBC had presumed that Beecham had had the power to act for his guarantors. On 24 January Eckersley sent a note to Reith, 'Beecham has not replied and his time is up', and a note to Cecil Graves (who was now assuming an important role in the BBC administration as Assistant Controller), 'We must get on'. Graves replied on 27 January that no more had been heard from Beecham's solicitors. At this point a decision to abandon Beecham must have been made; Eckersley was able to write to Boult on 30 January:

> We are now in a position to take definite steps in regard to the appointment of the members of the permanent orchestra of 112 players. I should be glad to know what immediate steps you propose to take . . .
> 1. We are already committed to appointing certain members of our present Wireless Orchestra . . .
> 2. There may be other individuals to whom we have promised auditions . . .
> 3. Wright's suggestion that members of our present provincial orchestras should be given auditions . . . I think I told you that I spoke to Harty, asking him if he had any objections to our approaching members of the Hallé Orchestra, and he told me he would not mind our so doing . . .

This last statement was to prove unfounded. Eckersley also raised the questions of the salaries, negotiations with the Musicians' Union, and the continuing possibility of collaboration with the Royal Philharmonic Society. Boult's view on the latter point sums up well his approach to the whole task which faced him:

> I should have been willing to go to almost any lengths in order to cooperate

with the RPS . . . I am changing my mind . . . It is now recognised that the
work of a permanent orchestra has most to do with the perfection of ensemble
in an orchestra like the Berlin Philharmonic . . . I feel that we have no business to run Symphony Concerts at all if they are simply duplicating the
schemes of LSO, RPS, etc. Our only justification could be that our orchestra
is far finer than anything that can be heard elsewhere. If our opening series is
jeopardised by compromise control, we run a grave risk of losing our hold on
this ideal, and our justification for entering the market.

Boult's firmness carried conviction; control was henceforth to be entirely in
the hands of the BBC.

Recruiting an orchestra

The immediate problem in February 1930 was the orchestra's personnel,
and their contracts. It is necessary to go back to May 1929, when the nucleus
of twenty-seven players had been agreed between Beecham and Pitt, and
negotiations with the Musicians' Union about the form of contract had begun. The immediate challenge which arose was over terms. Graves reported
on 28 June to Eckersley the salaries that key members had already been
offered by the LSO/HMV partnership. Eckersley wrote to Reith: 'I dislike
having our hands forced in regard to salaries, but there are exceptional
cases . . . I would like to recommend that we offer these men the same terms
as HMV are suggesting . . . after all, HMV would not I imagine offer them
more than their market value.' The HMV challenge continued to be a worry,
however. Graves reported on 29 July: 'Gossip I heard a week ago was that
HMV were laughing about our permanent orchestra being now impracticable as they were getting all the men . . .' Over the summer of 1929 all the
players considered essential were approached, and on 20 August Owen Mase
of the Music Department reported to Percy Pitt that 'letters have been sent
hurrying up the recalcitrants . . . probably with violins we must fill these
places regardless of Sir Thomas's list'. He also referred for the first time to
the intended leader of the Orchestra: 'If you succeed in getting Catterall I
think it will smooth our way with the string players quite a lot.'

The greater permanence and stability offered by the BBC's scheme was
decisive with the players. Almost all those approached accepted. Several
negotiated better offers than had initially been made by the BBC. Fees for
section leaders and wind players were arrived at by a frank method of bar-
gaining. By October 1929 Arthur Catterall had accepted the post of leader of
the permanent orchestra (Charles Woodhouse was leading the experimental
orchestra of 1929–30).

By the start of 1930, the Orchestra already contained some of its outstanding figures. The highest-paid members, after Catterall, were the 'celebrity' figures: Aubrey Brain, principal horn; Lauri Kennedy, principal cello; Ernest Hall, principal trumpet; and Charles Woodhouse, the sub-leader. On equal terms after these special cases were the principal second violin and viola, the principal bass, principal flute, principal trombone, tuba and timpani.

But two problems remained. First, the remaining places had to be filled, including two vital principal posts, and this would involve approaching members of other orchestras. Second, undertakings had been made to certain members of the Wireless Orchestra that their services would be retained, and they were frankly not up to the required standard. Eckersley wrote to Reith on the first matter on 21 March.

> I am, perhaps wrongly, squeamish of robbing other orchestral organisations of their best players for our orchestra, at all events before acquainting the organisers of such other orchestras that we propose to do this. They say that all is fair in love and war, but I think the competitive spirit in matters of this kind is to be deprecated if carried too far. On the other hand we do want to get as good an orchestra as possible. Perhaps, therefore, I am being over-sensitive.

He wrote of approaching the leader of the RPS orchestra. Reith scribbled a pencilled note: 'I quite appreciate yr attitude but hardly think it applies especially here where there is nothing approaching a regular organisation, is there?' Public opinion was strongly to reinforce Eckersley's fears about the BBC 'poaching' talent.

The second problem, that of the undertakings, was more of an immediate worry. The original orchestral list had been agreed, presumably by Pitt and Beecham, in consultation with Kenneth Wright and Owen Mase. Henry Wood, who was to have an important part to play in the scheme as Chief Conductor of the Promenade Concerts, had not been consulted; nor, of course, had Boult. By March 1930 there was considerable agitation when the promises which had been made by Percy Pitt and Cecil Graves were discovered. Both Wood and Boult thought some changes of personnel were vital: with Eckersley and the new Concerts Manager, W. W. Thompson, they held a meeting to discuss the matter. But a month later (16 April) they were scarcely any further forward:

> The position is a difficult one, as the good faith of Mr Pitt and Mr Graves and the Corporation has been definitely engaged . . . we should naturally be most

unwilling to see the success of the orchestra prejudiced by the inclusion of
inferior players who will spoil the ensemble . . . the terms in which Mr Pitt
spoke to each of the men [were] 'so long as there was a wireless orchestra in
London they could always feel safe that they would be included in it' . . . we
shall have to negotiate some monetary compensation for them.

But it was urgent to arrange replacements, and Boult was adamant that the
players were unsatisfactory.

The details of the full-time contracts offered to all new players were bound
to be the subject of prolonged discussion. In spite of the three-year contract
offered under the LSO/HMV scheme, a contract covering fifty-two weeks
of the year was unheard of in the English musical world. The nearest approaching it was the Bournemouth Orchestra's plan of work, which was not
on the same scale as the BBC's. The year-round basis was the most revolutionary aspect of the whole BBC orchestral proposal, and would obviously be
watched closely by the Musicians' Union. The BBC's original plan was for a
contract which bound the players for 120 hours in every four weeks, and for
thirty-six hours every week during the Proms. This subsequently rose to
144 hours in every four weeks, including the Proms. The rank-and-file rate
was to be £11 per week, and only the principals and special cases were to be
offered three-year contracts. The salary catered for four weeks' holiday and
up to four weeks' sick leave. There was, of course, no arrangement at this
point for a pension scheme.

The Musicians' Union was quick to step in with a number of safeguards.
They stipulated that players should not be called for more than forty-five
hours in any one week; and that on not more than twelve days in any four-
week period could the players be called for three sessions (morning, afternoon and evening) on any one day. No session, however short, was to count
as less than two hours in computation. They also attempted to ensure one
free day every week, though this was modified to four free days in any four-
week period. Special circumstances for release were agreed, but as the no-
deputy undertaking was fundamental to the scheme, these conditions were
stringent. The MU also added a clause ensuring compensation in case of
dismissal. On the question of the basic rates there was more argument. The
MU insisted that £12 a week was a reasonable minimum, but Eckersley fore-
saw all principal rates increasing if this was agreed. Ironically, some rank-
and-file members of the Wireless Orchestra were receiving £12 a week, but
as none of them was to be engaged in the Symphony Orchestra, the question
of a drop in salary did not arise. But the MU still felt on 4 June 'a very uneasy
feeling that someone has badly blundered', and claimed that 'many of the old

servants are being very unfairly treated'. Eckersley had to reckon, not for the last time in the orchestra's history, with the breakdown of talks and the possibility of an MU strike, and set out the position to Reith on 6 June: 'Are we contracted?' he asked. The letter sent to prospective members says simply 'subject to the auditions of the contract which will shortly be sent to you being satisfactory'. As the BBC pointed out to the Union, before 1930 the BBC employed throughout the country some 166 musicians, paying them £74,360; after 1930 they would be employing 197 musicians at a cost of £112,840. The loss would be the players', and the MU, not the BBC, would have to accept the responsibility for wrecking an enlightened scheme of permanent employment. Fortunately, the Union realised how much was at stake for their members in this scheme, and agreed to a basic £11 a week on 16 June 1930. It was just a month before the disbandment of the Wireless Orchestra, and the immediate establishment of the new Symphony Orchestra.

By April 1930, in view of the cancellation of Beecham's appearances with the BBC Orchestra, rumours were appearing in the Press of the difficulties with the collaboration. The BBC commented tersely, 'The scheme for a National Orchestra is going forward. Its future does not depend upon the attitude of individual conductors.' Beecham blamed his cancellations on the BBC, saying they had changed his programmes at the last minute; while the BBC claimed simultaneously that Beecham's doctor had said he must withdraw. It was plain to the outside world that non-communication between the supposed partners in the new scheme had reached a high point.

The BBC held its peace until the end of May, when the formal notices had been sent out to the Wireless Orchestra members. It then felt able to announce the scheme. Boult talked to the *Evening News* on 29 May (he was introduced as 'the BBC's new musical director, who took up his duties at Savoy Hill only a few days ago'):

> Our plans for using [the orchestra] are, I think, unusual and interesting. The whole band will be used at least once a week for the BBC National Concerts, which will be held every Wednesday night throughout the winter. It will also be subdivided in two different ways . . . auditions of candidates are being held now . . . it sounds a very bold thing to say but we hope that the orchestra will be the best in England, and as good as any in the world.

The *Daily Chronicle* took up the story enthusiastically the next day: '£70,000 A YEAR ORCHESTRA. BBC'S 114 STAR MUSICIANS. AUTUMN START. FAMOUS CONDUCTORS FROM CONTINENT.'

A new Orchestral Manager, Richard Pratt, was appointed from 1 April, and W. W. Thompson was confirmed as Concerts Manager at the same time. On 7 July, Joseph Lewis came from Birmingham to replace John Ansell as the Orchestra's assistant conductor, in charge of the sectional light music sessions. It was felt important, says Boult, to give the orchestra a sense of identity before the 1930 Prom season, and so when their contracts began, at the end of July, the whole new Orchestra gathered for a week of rehearsals in the Central Hall, Westminster. Reith and Graves came to the first rehearsal; Wagner's Overture *The Flying Dutchman*, which was to open the first concert in October, was played through, and then Reith made a welcoming speech to the orchestra. Boult continued the rehearsal with Brahms's Fourth Symphony, and for the week they worked on the pieces in the first programme, with special emphasis on Ravel's *Daphnis and Chloe* Suite, which was new to the orchestra, and also rehearsed Elgar's Second Symphony. Then the members went their own ways, many to the section of the orchestra which played in the Proms, and which met for preliminary rehearsals immediately afterwards with Wood. The full orchestra was to reconvene in October to rehearse for the opening concert of the season.

The Promenade Concert season, which opened on Saturday 9 August, gave the London public a foretaste of the new Orchestra. There were only ninety members, and the leader was Charles Woodhouse, already contracted as sub-leader to Catterall in the full-size orchestra. But there was an immediate sense that this Orchestra was providing a new quality of performance: 'The tone in every section is improved beyond comparison. One had the impression of walking in a garden that had been thoroughly weeded . . . there is not the smallest doubt about it, the new orchestra is something in the nature of a glorious adventure for musical London,' wrote the *Manchester Guardian* on 11 August. The season was an exceptionally successful one, and the papers reported a frenzy of cheering for Henry Wood on the last night. A BBC spokesman felt able to pronounce that 'the orchestra for the Promenade Concerts had given many indications of the rich material to be employed by us in the coming season of Symphony Concerts which opens at the Queen's Hall on October 22'.

The Establishment closes ranks

But the project was not to be launched without more intense controversy. One of the finest boasts of the Prom orchestra was the new principal oboist, Alec Whittaker, who had joined the BBC from the Hallé Orchestra in Manchester. The BBC had also contracted their tuba player, Harry Barlow, and had approached their bassoonist, Archie Camden. The Orchestra had been informed of these approaches, but Sir Hamilton Harty made strong representations that Camden should not go to London, and the BBC desisted, 'a forbearance for which we earned no thanks', as a BBC official later commented. On 30 August, Harty took the occasion of his inaugural address as President of the Incorporated Society of Organists to deliver a fierce attack on the BBC's musical policies. Speaking in Torquay, he attacked music on radio as a 'debased and imperfect substitute for the real article', and then launched into the BBC's concert-giving policy:

> . . . it is morally wrong and quite indefensible for it to enter into direct competition with private musical interests. It was never meant that the BBC should have the trusteeship of large sums of public money in order to use this money to crush and imperil private enterprise. With sublime self-confidence and an almost infantile disregard of the problems and difficulties involved, the BBC has now developed into a huge concert-giving concern. I contend that it has absolutely no right to do so . . . The position has now become serious since the establishment by the BBC of a new Orchestra, great in numbers, upon which, according to newspaper reports, upwards of £100,000 a year is to be spent . . . With childlike innocence and trust they have believed that all they had to do was to bring together, by means of financial inducements impossible for anyone else to offer, the best players to be found – secure a goodly array of conductors, both English and foreign, and the thing was done. If certain players seemed to them to be desirable acquisitions, the fact that they were members of other orchestras was not allowed to stand in the way; make the financial inducements high enough and they were bound to come. It is no secret to anyone that these amiable bandits of Savoy Hill have raided as far north as Manchester . . .

The matter was raised again at the meeting of the Hallé Concerts Society in Manchester on 30 September. Harty concentrated on the poaching of players by the BBC and said: 'I should not be much of a friend to this Society if I did not warn it that its great orchestra is in serious danger . . . The Hallé Orchestra, which has gained the reputation of being the best orchestra in England, will certainly drop down to being a second or third rate organisation.' The BBC contented itself with pointing out the large amount of co-operation, help and financial subsidy it had provided for Hallé Orchestra broadcasts over the years, and looked forward to further collaboration. 'The formation of a National Orchestra has been welcomed by most of the musical interests of the country . . . It is obviously essential that the country should be combed for the best available talent.'

Meanwhile the massed forces of the London musical establishment were gathering strength against the BBC. In early October 1930 the LSO was seeking support for a concerted attack on the BBC's public concert-giving activities; but when the RPS revealed details to the Press the LSO withdrew. There were meetings between rival organisations brought together by the new threat throughout October; the Philharmonic Society drew up a document accusing the BBC of 'acting beyond the powers of its charter'. Its final alarmist cry was voiced in a document submitted to the ISM in November 1930: 'By mere force of circumstances the BBC will eventually come to control the entire musical activities in the country.' It was even suggested that it was the BBC's 'deliberate policy to do so . . . Music would thus become practically a Department of State . . .'

The BBC's case was perhaps best supported by Neville Cardus, writing in the *Manchester Guardian* on 6 September:

> For years musicians have deplored that in this country there has been no possibility of establishing orchestras as good and as permanent as those on the Continent, where the State comes forward with a subsidy. And now, when the BBC is able to put down the money and offer our best players engagements of good value and duration, the cry goes up about abuse of power and monopoly . . . we might as well get the fact into our heads once and for all that broadcast music is with us and has come to stay. The technique of it all is in its infancy, no doubt . . . It is inconceivable that in time a craving for good music and for real performances will not be stimulated in all sorts of out-of-the-way places, and that this craving will not lead to a new lease of life for a musical profession which a few years ago had little enough to live on in this country.

Cardus's words were prophetic. The Harty storm and the protestations of the musical profession had raised fundamental questions about the nature of the BBC's Orchestra which were to return many times in the future. Was it abusing its privileged position by giving public concerts in direct competition with private bodies? Should it confine its activities purely to the broadcasting studio? Should it attempt to rival, or simply be different from, other symphony orchestras in the country? Different answers have been given to these questions at different times in the Orchestra's fifty years' history, but the challenge to its policy has remained. It was perhaps appropriate that the questions should be raised so forcibly on the eve of the Orchestra's first public appearance.

2
Boult's Great Orchestra
1930-35

First Night

22 October 1930. At the north end of Regent Street, just where it curled round the Nash church of All Souls, Langham Place, into Portland Place, stood one of London's best-loved buildings. The Queen's Hall, its convex façade bending back from the east side of Regent Street into Riding House Street, harmoniously echoed the sweep of Nash's circular porch and spire of All Souls. It was a difficult building to see well: one had to cross the road and lean up against the massive bulk of the Langham Hotel on the west of the Place in order to appreciate the Hall's fine rhythmical façade of five entrances framed by six double columns, with a small pediment highlighting the central door. Set back between the columns, curiously heavy square windows with Greek-style caryatids opened on to small balconies; between each pair of columns stood the bust of a composer staring out variously towards the church, down Regent Street or, one might fancy, with raised eyebrows towards the huge bright white bulk of the BBC's new Broadcasting House, rising beyond Nash's church at the south end of Portland Place.

Difficult to imagine, from where one was standing, how large the Queen's Hall was. A walk round to the left of the façade, down Riding House Street, showed that it extended back almost as far as Great Portland Street; turn right into Great Portland Street, following the line of the back of the building, and take the first right. A cul-de-sac opposite Little Titchfield Street led up to No. 15 Door: the Artists' Entrance (which still survives today, bricked up, with the words 'QUEEN'S HALL' just visible at the end of the street, painted on the stonework at the top of the bricks). Retracing one's steps, and entering the hall, one had to descend a flight of steps round an oval vestibule to reach the stalls, for the auditorium was sited underground. It was not an over-attractive sight. When it was built in 1893, the architect T. E. Knightley had wanted it coloured grey and terracotta, but for ten years now it had been painted a weak blue-green-grey; the focus of attention

49

was the massive Hill organ above the curved stage, and above that, a row of large medallions framed by musical-looking gods and goddesses. To right and left, two balconies extended round the circular back of the hall and out along its sides: the lower one, steeply raked, with good visibility, the upper crowded with seats. The hall had been designed to accommodate an audience of 3000; but now, after alterations to ensure better sightlines from the lower circle, it held just 2400.

And on that evening every one of those seats was filled. Beecham had said of this (and any other) subscription concert series: 'They won't come: they'll send their servants!' And perhaps they did, but at least the hall was packed and enthusiastic with anticipation. In the cheaper seats, we may imagine ourselves alongside Mr Smeeth from J. B. Priestley's *Angel Pavement*:

> His seat was not very comfortable, high up too, but he liked the look of the place, with its bluey-green walls and gilded organ pipes and lights shining through holes in the roof like fierce sunlight, its little rows of chairs and music stands, all ready for business. It was fine. He did not buy a programme – they were asking a shilling for them, and a man must draw a line somewhere – but spent his time looking at the other people and listening to the snatches of their talk. They were a queer mixture . . .

Personalities and principals

To the keen observer of the London orchestral scene the view was of exceptional interest. For assembling on the platform that night was what he had been led to believe was the best collection of orchestral musicians in the country. Skimming through his programme (which had indeed cost him a shilling) he passed over the exhaustive analyses of the works to be performed (the programme, Mr Smeeth had noticed, looking at a nearby copy, 'seemed to be full of music itself') and the attractive advance notices of famous soloists who were appearing later in the series. He turned to the list of orchestral players. Who were they?

The Leader, Arthur Catterall, was perhaps the least familiar figure to metropolitan audiences: back in 1909 he had been Leader of Henry Wood's Promenade Concert Orchestra, appearing in the Queen's Hall, but then he had returned north to his home town of Manchester, where he became Leader of the Hallé Orchestra just before the First World War. He had led a distinguished career as a soloist and teacher as well as being the Hallé's leader; but in 1925 disagreements with Hamilton Harty led to his resignation from the Hallé post. Since that year he had devoted an increasing amount of time to his Catterall String Quartet, and to solo appearances; his being drawn to London, and back to orchestral leadership, was a major triumph for the BBC. Perhaps this was one of the unspoken reasons for Hamilton Harty's outburst against the BBC's new Orchestra.

At the head of the second violins (which Boult placed on the right of the stage) sat Barry Squire, an experienced leader of many of the *ad hoc* orchestras in London after the war. He too had played in Wood's Queen's Hall band, and went on to lead the orchestra for the seasons of Russian Ballet; he led at Covent Garden for the British National Opera Company in the twenties, playing under the BBC's former Director of Music, Percy Pitt. Principal viola was Bernard Shore, a player well known to the new Director of Music, Adrian Boult, since Shore had made his orchestral début in the British Symphony Orchestra under Boult only some nine years before. Though he had originally intended to be an organist, Shore was wounded in his right hand during the First War, and turned to the viola. He had studied with Lionel Tertis, and among younger players was one of the most active in the London freelance scene: he appeared with the Queen's Hall Orchestra and with the London Symphony Orchestra, and had also appeared as a soloist in the Proms and in BBC concerts. It is worth noting, perhaps, that like many of these central figures in the new orchestra he was by no means the most experienced player available – he had begun to work as a principal with the Queen's Hall Orchestra only the previous year. But the BBC's hope of success in creating a lively, vital orchestra depended on the use of young talent rather than on reliable experience alone.

In the centre of the stage were the twelve cellists. A major *coup* for the orchestra had been the attraction into its ranks of the principal cellist, Lauri Kennedy. Already a famous soloist in his own right, Kennedy had been absent from London orchestral platforms for some years. It was said that he had turned down offers from both the Philadelphia and the Chicago Orchestras: instead, he had preferred to tour in the International Celebrity Concerts. Born in Australia, Kennedy had made his début there at the age of eight, and had been encouraged by Melba. She sent him on a concert tour of America with John McCormack, and Kennedy subsequently appeared in London in 1921 with Chaliapin. His was one of the most glamorous names in the new orchestra.

Ranged on the amphitheatre-like terraces of the Queen's Hall were ten double basses under the leadership of Eugene Cruft. A central figure both in London orchestral life and of music broadcasting in the twenties, Cruft directed his own Octet. This was one of the most popular of the small musical groups which provided so much staple fare by way of light music broadcasts in the earliest years of the medium. Cruft had been particularly associated with the London Symphony Orchestra, which he had joined in January 1910, since his father had been a founder-member of their viola section. (His son John was to play in and subsequently administer that orchestra.) Cruft had also been a principal in the original Beecham Orchestra as well as with the London Chamber Orchestra, and had been frequently seen in the Royal Philharmonic and Royal Albert Hall Orchestras.

Centre stage, the principal wind players made an exceptionally impressive line-up. The only figure not well known in London was the first oboist, Alec Whittaker, who like Catterall had become a principal in Hamilton Harty's Hallé Orchestra. It was Whittaker around whom much of the controversy about the BBC Orchestra's poaching had centred. He was still under thirty, and had worked exclusively north of London. When he was thirteen he had been playing in the Opera House, Manchester; after much touring experience he became a principal in the City of Birmingham Orchestra in 1920. He joined the Hallé in 1924. Small wonder that Hamilton Harty thought that he would stay there for many years to come. But the attractiveness of the conditions offered by the BBC induced Whittaker to travel south, and he soon became one of the outstanding figures in the new orchestra.

Next to him sat Robert Murchie, first flute. His was the undisputed title of London's principal flautist; ever since he came to London from his native Scotland in 1906 to study at the Royal College of Music he had been prominent as a principal. Beecham had chosen Murchie to lead in his seasons of Covent Garden Opera, as well as for his appearances in Berlin. Murchie had played principal with the London Symphony, the Queen's Hall and the Royal Philharmonic Orchestras – few players managed to appear regularly with all three – and had founded two successful chamber groups, the London Wind Quintet and the London Flute Quartet. But then Murchie came from a musical background, and (like so many others in the orchestra) had begun to play at a very early age: when he was nine he was performing for ships' officers in Scotland, and at the age of sixteen played in the Scottish Orchestra under Richard Strauss.

Frederick Thurston, principal clarinet, exemplified a third strand of players in the orchestra: not so much the talented outsider, like Whittaker, or the experienced London freelancer, like Murchie, but rather a player who from the beginning of broadcasting had been associated with music on the BBC. He had, of course, appeared with the London orchestras, at Covent Garden and with the Royal Philharmonic, but his main work since 1922 had been as principal clarinet in the very first BBC studio ensemble. As this orchestra had grown in size over the years, Thurston had broadcast often as a soloist and a member of chamber music groups. He was the most experienced broadcaster among the wind players.

Another familiar figure on the London scene was the principal bassoonist Richard Newton. He had been Wood's principal in the New Queen's Hall Orchestra from 1924, and was one of the nucleus of the old Wireless Orchestra taken over into the Symphony Orchestra. It was no secret that the BBC had wanted to persuade Archie Camden, at that time principal of the Hallé, to join the orchestra, but had desisted from doing so. Not long after, Newton offered to step down so as to allow Camden to join the orchestra.

The eye wandered up the terraces to the back of the platform, to the brass section. Here the faces of the principals were immediately recognisable to even the most casual concert-goer. Aubrey Brain, first horn, was one of the country's best soloists on any instrument. Works had been written for him by several English composers including Ethel Smyth, and he had often played concertos in London. He had appeared with the Berlin Philharmonic under Bruno Walter, with the LSO in America under Nikisch, and as principal of numerous London orchestras. He had been associated with the BBC for two years and was an obvious choice for the post of principal horn, but it was felt to be a considerable triumph that he had been willing to be permanently contracted to the orchestra.

The principal trumpet was Ernest Hall, who was soon to assume a central role in the Orchestra's life, becoming chairman of its committee and remaining with it for twenty-two years. But to the audience in the Queen's Hall in October 1930 he was still one of the brightest of the younger men who dominated the London orchestral scene. Most familiar as principal of the LSO, he had also appeared as principal with the Royal Philharmonic and Covent Garden orchestras – in the latter he played in the first performances of Holst's *The Perfect Fool* – and sharp-eyed observers could have spotted him earlier in 1930 as the extra trumpet player when the New York Philharmonic visited London for their much-praised concerts under Toscanini. He too had been associated with broadcasting since the early days of studio orchestras in Savoy Hill.

And so the roll-call continued: Jesse Stamp, first trombone, who was only to survive, tragically, for less than two years. He was another Manchester player, but had been in London since 1909 and was a veteran of the scene – he had toured America with Nikisch, and Germany with Beecham. Harry Barlow, first tuba, was one of the leading figures of the brass band movement in the north of England. He played with the Hallé, and was the other serious loss besides Whittaker that the Hallé suffered in 1930. His 'Besses o' th' Barn' and 'Irwell Springs' bands were both famous throughout the country.

Charles Bender, principal timpanist, was one of the few remaining members
of Wood's original Promenade Concert orchestra: he had served twenty-
seven seasons. Most remarkable of all, though the audience in the Queen's
Hall could scarcely have imagined it at the time, was the harpist. Miss Sidonie
Goossens was one of the youngest members of this young orchestra: she had
been playing in London for just nine years, since she made her début in the
orchestra conducted by her father Eugene Goossens in 1921. She too had
been broadcasting since the first days, both in the 2LO Orchestra and in the
popular Wireless Quartet which then consisted of violin, cello, harp and
organ. Fifty years later, Sidonie Goossens would still be playing first harp in
the BBC Symphony Orchestra: an unrivalled record of uninterrupted service. She was the finest example of the success of the BBC's plan for its
orchestra in 1930: to attract the youngest, brightest talent in the hope of
nurturing and developing it in the years to come.

The expectations of that Queen's Hall audience could scarcely have been
higher. The BBC's declarations about its Orchestra had not been distinguished by their modesty; in an article (which before the year was out the
Corporation felt confident enough to include in its concert programmes) it
stated:

> It is the aim of the BBC that this Orchestra should set a standard for English
> orchestral playing, and should bear comparison with the finest orchestras in
> the world. With this object in view, not only have the best players obtainable
> been secured for the principal positions, but the choice of every rank-and-file
> player has been most carefully considered . . .

This last point would have made less impact on the 1930 audience than the
fame of the orchestra's principals, but it was equally important. For instead
of the collection of freelance string players, permutations of whom were
familiar from every orchestra in London, the rank-and-file players on the
platform were mainly unknown faces. They had come from all over England,
not just from London; the astuteness of the choices can be judged from the
fame some of the players achieved in later life: among the violins, there was
Marie Wilson, who was later to lead the orchestra at the Proms; Jessie
Hinchcliffe, who came from Huddersfield; Harry Blech, later to found and
conduct the London Mozart Players; and Sam Bor, later to lead the Scottish
National Orchestra. In the cellos, there was Ambrose Gauntlett, a much
loved figure from the Wireless Orchestra, and Alex Nifosi (for a long time
chairman of the orchestral players' committee). Then there were the unknown names who remained faithful to the orchestra for very many years:
like Kathleen Washbourne, among the first violins, who had been playing

and teaching in Bangor when she had applied to the orchestra and been summoned to audition at Savoy Hill. An enthusiast for contemporary music, she became one of the mainstays of the violin section, often playing at the first desk and occasionally deputising in later years for Thomas Peatfield as subleader and Paul Beard as leader. In the wind sections, there was the cor anglais player Terence McDonagh (who succeeded Whittaker as principal) and Anton Tschaikov among the clarinets (whose son Basil would become Chairman of the Philharmonia Orchestra).

No London audience could have known some of the young players whom the exhaustive country-wide auditions procedure had unearthed: second violins like Albert Hepton, from Bradford, and Joseph Young from Newcastle; cellists like Roger Briggs from Brighouse; the trumpeters Herbert Barr and Jack Mackintosh from Bradford and Sunderland. There was a good proportion of women: how ridiculous all the scaremongering in the press about the exclusion of women had been! Altogether the full strength of the new BBC Symphony Orchestra was 114 players.

Opening success

When Adrian Boult walked out onto the Queen's Hall platform just after the broadcast announcements were made at eight o'clock on 22 October, he was facing a musical public who knew little of his work, and who did not number him among their most popular conductors. Beecham and Wood were their favourites; Boult, who after his postwar appearances in London had been conducting in Birmingham since 1924, was an unknown quantity. But, as the *Morning Post* reported the next day:

> In the very sonority of *God Save the King*, which opened the first BBC Symphony Concert at the Queen's Hall last night, we felt that London now possessed the material of a first-class orchestra. And as the evening proceeded the feeling became a certainty . . . we had, from the technical point of view, the best English orchestral playing since the war . . . not to mention the admirable conducting of Adrian Boult, to whom . . . must go a very considerable share of credit for the triumphant success of the evening.

Every item in that remarkable concert was an unqualified success. The BBC, which had been severely criticised in many quarters for its actions in setting up the Orchestra, and Adrian Boult, whose claim to lead London's best orchestra was doubtful, to say the least, both triumphed. The programme was well designed to show off the Orchestra: Wagner's *Flying Dutchman* Overture started the evening; Suggia played the Saint-Saëns Cello Concerto; the Brahms Fourth Symphony opened the second half and

Ravel's *Daphnis and Chloe* Suite, the revelation of the evening, ended it. The newspaper reviews of the concert had a rare unanimity:

> . . . The permanent Orchestra of the BBC made its first appearance at full strength at the Queen's Hall last night under Mr Adrian Boult who has had the chief responsibility for its organization and training. The thoroughness of the preliminary work which has gone to the creation of an Orchestra out of a body of first-rate players was exemplified at once. . . . It was a welcome sight to see every bow in each section of the Strings moving as one and the resulting tone was more than welcome to the ear. The precision of the Wood-Band was no less admirable and the tone of the Brass magnificent. . . . The virtuosity of the Orchestra . . . wiped out any reproach Englishmen may feel in the face of visiting Orchestras from abroad.
>
> (*The Times*, 23 October 1930)

> So far as the sheer physical quality of the sound is concerned, the reputation of the new BBC Symphony Orchestra was made so soon as it had played the National Anthem at the beginning of last night's concert at Queen's Hall. The rich colouring almost tempted one to shout approval.
>
> (*Daily Mail*, 23 October)

> . . . If the BBC Orchestra continue as they have begun, we should have a combination second to none in Europe. . . . The fine individual playing in the Orchestra came to the fore, and passages which are often blurred, were secure and defined.   (*Daily Express*, 23 October)

> . . . The new Orchestra is certainly the finest in the country.
>
> (*The Sunday Times*, 26 October)

In some ways, the history of the BBC Symphony Orchestra has been the story of its effort to maintain the astonishingly high standard of performance and popularity set by its first concerts: concerts which challenged the achievement of the whole of the musical profession in the country. Morale in the new orchestra could scarcely have been higher; Edward Clark and his colleagues had planned a series of programmes which had both variety and substance, and Boult's reputation grew with every concert. 'No higher praise can be given to last night's BBC Symphony Concert at the Queen's Hall', wrote the *Morning Post* after the second concert on 29 October, 'than to say that it was every bit as good as the first.' *The Times* concurred: 'An instrument has been formed with which anything may be done, and Mr Boult is a conductor who gets the results he wants quite decisively and without fuss.' Arthur Rubinstein was the soloist, and there was again a packed audience who gave him a standing ovation for his performance of Tchaikovsky's First Piano Concerto.

In the third concert of the season on 5 November, which Boult also conducted, Adolf Busch gave the Beethoven Violin Concerto, 'an outstanding performance' (*The Times*), and the main work was *A Sea Symphony* by Vaughan Williams. Frank Howes, music critic of *The Times*, looking back to this period in his book *Full Orchestra*, judged that 'Boult's first three concerts with [the Orchestra] in the autumn of 1930 were a landmark not only in his personal career but in London's orchestral history'.

The successful impetus was being maintained in these public concerts, which rapidly became the fashionable centre of the London musical season. If subscribers had sent their servants to the first, they did so no longer; before the concerts, the players could look around the auditorium for famous faces – the sculptor Epstein was a regular visitor, as were many musicians. Beecham's social circle of supporters was not to be seen, of course, but there was only one serious rival for the BBC's audience in that season: the lively series of concerts organised by Lady Courtauld and conducted by the brilliant young Malcolm Sargent.

Behind the microphone

The life of the new BBC Symphony Orchestra, however, was not all glamorous public concert-giving. These events formed only the highlights of a busy round of studio concerts, for most of which the orchestra split into one or other of the two alternative section groupings of Edward Clark's and Julian Herbage's ingenious plan: a light orchestral concert under Joseph Lewis at Savoy Hill; a Bach cantata conducted by Stanford Robinson; or perhaps a chamber orchestral concert under Percy Pitt, who still made some appearances at the BBC. And then the climax of the regular week's studio work: the Sunday evening studio concert for the full orchestra. Kenneth Wright, who had devised the rehearsal scheme for the first season, had thought it essential to ensure a continuity of training and direction for the orchestra, especially because at this time it formally did not possess a Chief Conductor. He had therefore grouped the Symphony Concerts together into twos or threes, all directed by the same conductor. The Sunday evening studio concert was thus linked to the Wednesday evening symphony concert. But whereas the Wednesday concert took place in the Queen's Hall, there was no BBC studio at Savoy Hill large enough to accommodate the Sunday concert by the full 114 players, and it was necessary to find a larger venue within easy reach. After a protracted search, such a place was found – set back from the south bank of the Thames, just behind the future site of the National Theatre. A narrow flight of stone steps led down from Waterloo Bridge (near the present National Film Theatre) and a path led back under the bridge to the east.

Down the dark and dingy street which was then Commercial Road (reached by car from Stamford Street) stood an old disused brick building, the Red Lion Warehouse. Inside was a huge open space, which had been simply decorated. The brick walls were painted pale yellow; the iron girders which supported the roof, the woodwork and the carpet were all light green. Behind the conductor's back as he stood at the rostrum an exposed staircase led to an upper floor, where the librarians of the orchestra worked.

It was, at best, a primitive place to spend one's working life. Set near the river, the warehouse was inevitably damp. Smells, it was said, varied from *piano* to *fortissimo*. An all-too-familiar sight for the orchestral players was to see rats scuttering across the floor or up and down the wooden staircase – a circumstance which caused comment among the players which the conductor (whose back was turned to the rats) found it difficult to appreciate. But the acoustics were very satisfactory. A cloth was draped under the ceiling, about twenty feet from the ground. Bright white lights in plain fabric shades provided excellent illumination, and the studio ('No. 10') was made as inviting as possible in the rudimentary conditions. Around the sides of the orchestral area were a couple of rows of chairs and some settees for guests: the first home of that increasingly important BBC phenomenon, the studio audience. All concerts were given live, announced from the studio, and only gradually were problems of timing and co-ordination solved. But here, in these makeshift surroundings, many of the Orchestra's most memorable early experiences occurred – in which it was visited and conducted by Schoenberg and Webern, Stravinsky, Richard Strauss and Bruno Walter: concerts which made a deep impression both on the Orchestra and on the small studio audiences. 'No. 10' is remembered with much affection.

Henry Wood directed the Orchestra's work in November 1930: the Queen's Hall concerts were on 12 November, an all-Bach programme; on 19 November, Borodin's Second Symphony and Strauss's *Also sprach Zarathustra*, with arias by Mozart and Mahler sung by the superb Elisabeth Schumann; on 26 November a mixed programme featured the Bartók Rhapsody for piano and orchestra, Tchaikovsky's Fourth, and a second performance of Ravel's *Bolero*.

In the No. 10 studio, Wood came up against an early problem of priorities. The last work in one of his Sunday concerts was Delius's Dance Rhapsody, a fourteen-minute piece. But the preceding Mozart Concerto left a space of only ten minutes before the 10.30 Epilogue, whose timing had recently been declared as sacred as that of the Nine o'clock News. Stuart Hibberd, who was announcing, took the decision not to broadcast the Delius, and signed off, saying there would be a short pause before the epilogue. Wood was furious and, as Hibberd remembered, 'instead of closing the orchestra, he said to them in an angry tone of voice, "Now we will play the Dance Rhapsody". And play it they did – excellently too, to the small studio audience who had been invited.' Hibberd was strongly criticised the next day for his 'inept' decision, but this led to the agreement that the announcer should in future decide whether a programme should risk overrunning the Epilogue.

The distinguished succession of soloists in the Queen's Hall continued in the 3 December concert when Moiseiwitsch came to play the Beethoven Emperor Concerto in an all-Beethoven programme conducted by Landon Ronald. In the planning of the next programme the hand of Edward Clark can clearly be discerned: the conductor was Hermann Scherchen, who had visited the BBC before, in the late 1920s, and the evening featured the British première of Schoenberg's symphonic poem *Pelleas und Melisande* – a work from 1902–3, scarcely the most challenging of his scores, but enough to create the beginnings of a controversy which was to swirl around the BBC during the period when it espoused so-called 'advanced' composers. Scherchen stayed on to direct a Sunday studio concert which included a Purcell string fantasy, and another Queen's Hall concert, devoted to Beethoven's *Missa Solemnis* (the first of the concerts to feature the BBC's National Chorus, formed in 1928 and directed by Stanford Robinson – see Appendix F). And Schoenberg himself conducted the Orchestra (see p. 66).

The first season continues

At the start of 1931 another important foreign visitor directed the orchestra for a month. Ernest Ansermet of the Suisse Romande Orchestra was a convinced opponent of the twelve-note school of composition, and of all that it stood for. But the BBC was not in this period doctrinaire about its musical taste: there were too many different neglected avenues to explore. Ansermet's first two programmes at Queen's Hall featured French music: on 14 January he performed Debussy's *Ibéria* (and accompanied Solomon in Liszt's First Piano Concerto) and then on 21 January presented the British première of Poulenc's *Concert champêtre* for harpsichord, played by Wanda Landowska. The *Morning Post* dismissed this work as a 'concatenation of platitude', and Ansermet seems to have taken too much for granted with the Orchestra, which played below its best form. But the third of the concerts, on 28 January, was more exciting: it was entirely devoted to the music of Stravinsky, and presented the composer as soloist in his own Piano Concerto. Perhaps surprisingly, the hall was packed. Besides the Concerto, there was the Overture to *Mavra*, *Apollon Musagètes*, and then Ansermet conducted the first performance in England of the Four Studies for Orchestra (arranged from the Three Pieces for String Quartet and the Study for Pianola) which Stravinsky had dedicated to him: 'fugitive, freakish things that provided lighter relief', said the *Yorkshire Post*. The second half was devoted to *The Rite of Spring*. 'The work presents appalling problems for conductor and orchestra alike; but all these difficulties disappeared in tonight's performance and the astounding music of a pagan rite as conceived by Stravinsky so moved the large audience that, at its conclusion, there was tremendous enthusiasm' (*The Scotsman*, 29 January).

As well as playing the piano at Queen's Hall, Stravinsky conducted a Sunday studio concert – the first of several concerts he would direct across a period of thirty years with the Orchestra – and introduced the Eight Easy Pieces alongside suites from *Pulcinella* and *The Firebird*. He was the second distinguished composer to conduct the Orchestra; unlike some of Clark's other choices, he was also in demand in London outside the BBC, and would return to direct his *Symphony of Psalms* for the Courtauld Concerts.

Ansermet also conducted in the studio, and was deeply admired by the players. Here was a conductor who knew Ravel and Stravinsky personally, who had given the first performance of Ravel's *La Valse* and Stravinsky's *Pulcinella*, *Soldier's Tale*, *Renard* and *Les Noces*. Before Stravinsky's espousal of twelve-note methods caused a rift between them, Ansermet was the composer's most respected advocate. He had an enormous influence on the Symphony Orchestra in its early days – both as an interpreter and as a trainer. His copious blue pencil marks of dynamics and bowings were so respected as practical solutions to problems of performance that they remained in the orchestral parts for over twenty years. The cellist Alex Nifosi recalled in a conversation:

> From the orchestra it was interesting to watch the play of the opposite approaches in his personality, the analytical and the emotional. How first one and then the other took precedence, but were eventually reconciled in a performance that benefited from his ability to see a work from two angles at once. His Debussy and Ravel were clear – precise and transparent – but had all their essential warmth of feeling. But perhaps Stravinsky came off best from this ambivalence of Ansermet. . . .
>
> One of his pet habits at rehearsal, one that rather endeared him to orchestral musicians, was his way of indicating some tricky rhythm to the players. He would sing – well, sing is hardly the word – he would 'enunciate', faster than any singer, rather like machine-gun fire, using some made-up word or syllable sometimes beginning with a 'B' – often coming out as something quite unprintable.

Boult returned in February, and there was to have been a first performance in his concert on 4 February; *Morning Heroes*, the cantata by Arthur
Bliss. But this was postponed until the end of March; Szigeti in Mendelssohn's Violin Concerto, Bax's *November Woods* and Schumann's Fourth
Symphony took its place. *The Times* noted that the concert 'recalled the
players to certain first principles of ensemble playing which have rather been
lost sight of in recent programmes given under visiting conductors from
abroad', and found the Bax work 'a consummate piece of orchestral handling'. Boult followed this on 11 February with a hugely successful complete
performance of Holst's *The Planets*, with the composer present. 'One felt
glad for him,' enthused *The Observer*, 'that he should at last hear a first-rate
performance of his principal work, in which everything came out just as he
wrote it.' Once again the public realised what it had missed in orchestral
performances during the twenties. 'Under his [Boult's] direction a pianissimo is a pianissimo and a triplet has its exact value. Yet there is nothing
rigid or lifeless or merely finicking, because the detail is subordinated to the
main structural lines' (*The Times*). In addition, Wilhelm Backhaus played
Beethoven's Fourth Piano Concerto: 'a quite tremendous performance'
(*Observer*), 'played with the utmost skill and grace' (*Glasgow Herald*).

The succession of soloists in the season's programmes provided further
evidence that the BBC had spared no expense to ensure the concerts'
attractiveness. Following Backhaus on 18 February was the composer and
pianist Ernst von Dohnányi in Brahms's First Concerto under Boult; then
Albert Sammons in the Elgar Violin Concerto, Gieseking in the Brahms
Second Concerto, and Suggia again (deputising for Casals) in the Dvořák
Cello Concerto. The 18 February concert was notable for one of Boult's
specialities, Elgar's Second Symphony; and 25 February included an
Edward Clark novelty from Russia, *Factory: the Music of Machines* by
Alexander Mossolov. This was a late addition to a conservative programme
of Elgar, Beethoven (the Eroica) and Berlioz. 'The Russian composer's
freak piece took two minutes out of two hours of music by the BBC Orchestra
. . . That could do nobody any harm, and people were heard to say that they
liked it and that it was just like the noise that machines in a factory make.'
The *Manchester Guardian* thought that 'we might perhaps as well have had
the machinery on the concert platform . . . but, after all, it is easier to get an
orchestra there'. In the *New Statesman*, W. J. Turner dismissed the Mossolov as 'a mere musical photograph completely lacking in any psychological
expression or judgement'.

Turner concentrated instead on the account of the Eroica; he said it
represented 'a notable sign-post in the career of Mr Boult as a conductor . . .

the best [performance] I have ever heard of a Beethoven symphony under an English conductor'. His next observations were widely accepted inside as well as outside the BBC:

> The BBC's expensive and carefully selected orchestra can play very erratically; its standards of playing go up and down according to the exactness and ability of the musician that conducts it, and when I say that it plays better under Mr Boult than under any other of its conductors the credit must be given wholly to him. . . . Mr Boult is a strange figure; under a catholicity of taste which might have hidden a complete lack of real judgement there is apparently a very solid and definite musical character, for performances such as these cannot come by inspiration or accident during the concert.

Boult's reputation was growing: what the critics observed in his handling of the Orchestra was his attention to the shaping of phrases, and the moulding of each individual line. This was a subject to which Edwin Evans turned, in a considered appraisal for *Time and Tide* on 8 November, declaring that it had its drawbacks:

> Boult is giving practically all his attention to phrasing and tone. He moulds every inflection with loving care. The very movement of his left hand tempts one to think of his orchestra in terms of ceramics. But in doing so he sacrifices a great deal of the virtue that resides in impulse . . . one has the impression that the orchestra is being trained in the 'prunes and prisms' of musical speech. If that is a temporary stage in its process, well and good.

In a long leader, *The Times* singled out Boult's stylistic awareness for praise:

> For him, Mendelssohn, Bach, Beethoven, Tchaikovsky and Strauss are all very different people, saying very very different things . . . Compare the clear tart tones of the woodwind in the 'Hebrides' Overture with their mellifluousness in the Minuetto of Beethoven's Eighth Symphony, or the rhythmic hardness of the trumpets in Bach with their rich flow in 'Don Juan'. Imagination was brought to bear on each case, but clearly with the purpose of discovering what was the musical purpose underlying the writing . . .

Praise of Boult's subservience to the composer's intentions was to recur throughout his career. Appreciation of his precise stylistic characterisation was noted less often, but it was something that the orchestral players particularly valued: it was impossible to confuse, under his baton, the French and German and Italian styles, nineteenth- with twentieth-century music – each had its own life.

The next foreign visitor to the Symphony Orchestra was Oskar Fried, who became a regular guest. He directed Berlioz's *Symphonie fantastique* (11 March), and a Beethoven programme with the complete Ninth Symphony (another rarity, for Prom performances before the formation of the National Chorus had concluded with the third movement) on 18 March. Fritz Wolff directed a Wagner concert on 15 April, and Wood returned for two concerts. Boult's final contributions to the season included the delayed London première of *Morning Heroes* on 25 March. Bliss had written the work in memory of his brother, killed during the First World War, and it had been heard at the Norwich Festival in autumn 1930. Both work and performance were highly praised: 'The work is certainly the strongest that Mr Bliss has given us' (*News Chronicle*, 26 March). 'It was a wonderful performance for the sense of proportion maintained between instruments and voices . . .' (*The Times*, 26 March). Boult's other concert was the last of the season on 6 May; there was Weber, Vaughan Williams, Saint-Saëns – the Fourth Piano Concerto with Cortot – and Mahler: the *Lieder eines fahrenden Gesellen* with the famous Wagner singer Maria Olszewska.

The *Evening Standard* summed up the general reaction to the Orchestra's first season on 7 May:

> It has been a season on which those concerned can look back with satisfaction, in particular, Dr Adrian Boult, who has been largely responsible for the very high pitch of efficiency the orchestra has reached and maintained. This orchestra can now challenge comparison with the Philharmonic orchestras of Berlin and New York, and the money-no-object policy has at last been amply justified.

Some would be found to argue with the last statement, but about Boult's responsibility for the success of the first season there was no doubt.

A Chief Conductor

One important question remained in the mind of the critics: should such an orchestra have a permanent principal conductor? A. H. Fox-Strangways commented in *The Observer* (26 April 1931): 'What a conductor can do for an orchestra . . . is much; what they can do for him is more. Conductors are sometimes born, but more often made; made by their orchestras – whom they make.' A correspondent in the *Monthly Musical Record* (July 1931) took up the question of a chief conductor:

> I was talking with a distinguished foreign musician . . . a member of a leading Berlin orchestra . . . He had recently heard the BBC Symphony Orchestra

and he was emphatic that we had a collection of instrumentalists comparable
with any in Europe, if not in the world. He was at a loss to understand why
such a body of talented players [did not have] . . . at their head one man who
was capable of co-ordinating their destinies into some definite channel . . . It
is to be hoped that a British conductor would be found who would take on
the leadership in a full-time capacity.

Unknown at the time, a decision had already been made. Boult's success
with the Orchestra was well known to Reith, who had observed its progress
carefully. He spoke to Boult around Easter 1931: 'Now look here, everyone
tells me the orchestra plays better for you than for anyone else. Will you
become the permanent conductor? And do you want to remain Director of
Music as well?' Boult, anxious to pursue his first love, conducting, but eager
to oversee the whole enterprise of the BBC Music Department as well, took
on both jobs together. He became Chief Conductor on 15 May 1931. It was,
he recalled later, an almost impossible task. Decisions had to be made in
phone calls from the orchestral studio in the breaks of rehearsals; he had to
find sufficient time for the preparation of scores as well as the supervision of
the planning of the Music Department. He found that to take the afternoon
off, when there was a concert in the evening, was essential. The system could
not possibly have worked had it not been for Boult's skill in delegation,
attested to by those who worked in the Department during the 1930s.
Allocation of responsibilities was absolutely firm, and once fixed was adhered
to. Boult never interferred with his subordinates' work; he was always available for consultation when necessary, but confined his own responsibility to
policy decisions, the direction of the Orchestra, and the representation of the
Music Department within the BBC. He persevered (with increasing assistance from an Assistant and then a Deputy Director of Music) right through
the 1930s, finally relinquishing the Directorship only in 1942 when wartime
conditions made the combination of planning and conducting almost
impossible.
    Throughout the 1930s, much depended on the individual members of the
Music Department. The nucleus of the staff was that which Percy Pitt had
assembled in the mid-1920s. Kenneth Wright assumed many of the administrative duties of the department, and supported tirelessly the work of Clark
and Herbage. On them fell the main burden of programme planning for the
symphony concerts season; as before 1930, W. W. Thompson took part in
the planning of the Proms. The partnership of Clark and Herbage was very
close, and it was difficult to say who was responsible for what. Essentially, it
was Clark, with his unrivalled knowledge of European composers and of

contemporary music, who took the central role in originating programmes – the Friday evening series of new music, broadcast from the studio, was particularly his responsibility. To Clark's inspiration, encyclopaedic knowledge and close contact with important personalities, Herbage added the mind of a meticulous organiser with a command of broadcasting requirements, timings, and detailed planning. He made many contributions to the scheme of the Orchestra's work, which was generally overseen by Kenneth Wright. By now, Boult was able to rely on other figures as well. His secretary, Mrs Gwen Beckett, had worked first for Kenneth Wright; Walford Davies had suggested that she should move to be Boult's secretary – a post she was still fulfilling forty-nine years later. She kept his appointment diary and passed messages endlessly: in many ways she was the lynchpin of Music Department. To many outsiders she was an essential figure; she co-ordinated all the arrangements for audiences at studio concerts in 'No. 10' and later at Maida Vale Studios. Concerts Manager W. W. Thompson was now assisted by Dorothy Wood: together they did all the work of liaison with halls, arranging programme and poster printing, organising ticket sales and managing the concerts themselves – work which now occupies an entire department at the BBC.

Owen Mase, formerly an accompanist who now had the title Music Executive, dealt with artists and rehearsal arrangements, deputising on occasions for Boult. From 15 May 1931 Mase was designated Assistant Music Director, but in October 1935 he reverted to his former title when Aylmer Buesst – composer, conductor and husband of the singer May Blyth – was brought in for a short period as Assistant Music Director. Another familiar face in the Music Department was Victor Hely-Hutchinson, a quiet, unobtrusive figure who started an important broadcast series, 'Foundations of Music', which Julian Herbage also planned. Born in 1901 in Cape Town, Hely-Hutchinson left the BBC in 1934 to succeed Granville Bantock as Professor of Music at Birmingham University; but he returned after the war to hold the post of Director of Music for a short but crucial period before his untimely death in March 1947. And there was the popular figure of Walton O'Donnell, conductor of the BBC Military Band.

For the Orchestra it had been a most exhausting first season: its adventures in the studio had varied from Hindemith's *Konzertmusik* Op. 39 (6 March) to a jovial evening on 5 February spent under Stanford Robinson's direction, accompanying Sir Harry Lauder in his music-hall repertoire. (Lauder, when dissatisfied with the orchestra's tempi, would leave his microphone and beat time pugnaciously, regardless of Robinson.) On 3 March the famous singer Sir George Henschel, then eighty, conducted a concert which was a replica of one he had directed in Boston in 1881; in a rare gesture, the players stood at the end of the final item, Wagner's *Meistersinger* Overture, and cheered him. In April a special series of Russian music was given, under Albert Coates, including a repetition of Rimsky-Korsakov's *Kitezh* which had been such a broadcasting landmark in 1926. Pablo Casals conducted a classical Sunday concert on 20 March. There was opera too: typical of the adventurous policy of studio performances in which the Orchestra took part was the mounting of Debussy's *Pelléas et Mélisande* on 18 November 1930 with Tudor Davies and Maggie Teyte in the title roles – Percy Pitt conducted. In June 1931 Manuel de Falla visited the Orchestra, playing his Concerto for Harpsichord and five instruments, and directing his opera *Master Peter's Puppet Show*.

Clark's adventures

The greatest challenges came in the field of contemporary music. Edward Clark's advocacy of contemporary music in general and of the Second Viennese School in particular had already brought both Schoenberg and Webern to the BBC: they both returned that season. In the Friday evening series of contemporary concerts, Schoenberg returned on 9 January to introduce to this country his one-act drama *Erwartung*, as well as his orchestral transcription of Bach's 'St Anne' Prelude and Fugue. Webern directed the concert on 8 May in which the orchestral version of his Five Pieces for String Quartet was given its British première, alongside two pieces by Schoenberg: the *Music for a Film Scene* and the *Song of the Wood Dove* from *Gurrelieder*. In contrast, Webern conducted a concert on the national network the previous evening of Schubert's *Rosamunde* music, Wolf's *Italian Serenade* and Johann Strauss waltzes!

Then, in July, the Orchestra was subjected to its biggest challenge so far in the field of new music. The International Society for Contemporary Music had been meeting on the Continent for some eight seasons, and the British Section had never been able to invite the Society to a meeting in England for the simple reason that facilities were not available to perform the orchestral scores selected. Edward Clark and Kenneth Wright had visited the ISCM Festival in Liège in 1930, and there conceived the idea to bring the Festival to London in the next season; the new Symphony Orchestra could be made available to perform the new works. The inspiration and the enthusiasm for the project were Clark's, but as Wright later recalled, 'Needless to say I had to do all the paper pleading when we came home!' Boult attended a meeting of the ISCM jury in the house of E. J. Dent in Cambridge, with Berg, Koechlin, Casella and Gregor Fitelberg. The first

Festival in England was held in Oxford between 21 and 28 July 1931. A chamber orchestra of fifty-one players, drawn from the Symphony Orchestra, travelled to Oxford to give a concert of new works on the afternoon of 23 July, and then repeated the performances for broadcast the same evening in the Contemporary Music series. At the end of the period two concerts were promoted 'under the auspices of the BBC' in the Queen's Hall. The programmes deserve to be recorded in full. The first, on 27 July at 8.15 pm, presented *Muzyka Symfoniczna* by Roman Palester; the Symphony for small orchestra Op. 21 by Webern; *Rapsodia per Orchestra* by Virgilio Mortari; the Second Symphony by Vladimir Dukelsky; Constant Lambert's *Music for Orchestra*; and Gershwin's *An American in Paris*. The conductors were Alfredo Casella, Constant Lambert, Gregor Fitelberg and Hermann Scherchen. The following evening the Orchestra was joined by the London Select Choir and the National Chorus in Vaughan Williams' *Benedicite* and Roussel's *Psalm LXXX*. The choirs sang Szymanowski's *Chansons Polonaises*, and Ferencz Szabo's *Song of the Wolves*; and the Orchestra played *Tres Trozos Sinfónicos* by Juan José Castro; *Trois Mouvements Symphoniques* by Fernand Quinet; and *Zwei Etuden für Orchester* by Vladimir Vogel. Casella and Scherchen again conducted; they were joined by Arnold Fulton (for the choral pieces) and Boult. Half of each concert was broadcast live.

Where are they now?, one might reasonably ask of the many of the pieces included. Yet the significance of the concerts for the Orchestra's international reputation was important, as Edwin Evans later recalled:

The annual festivals of the ISCM attract critics from most European countries and from America . . . [these concerts] consisted entirely of new music of the most advanced character, such as would have taxed the efficiency of any orchestra in the world . . . the cosmopolitan audience of experts was loud in its praise. It was, so to speak, a baptism of fire. From that event onwards the Continental critics began to adopt a new tone towards us.

In another sense the date was historic. For some decades there had been no lack of new music, native and foreign, performed in London, but new music, especially of unorthodox character, requires ample rehearsal, which . . . it could rarely be given. . . . many a new work must have suffered lamentably in our esteem through no fault of our own. At this festival the BBC Orchestra created a new precedent . . . Considering the demands modern composers make upon orchestral players the change is as revolutionary as the music with which some of them have confronted our audiences. In this respect the BBC stoutly maintains its liberal policy, undeterred by the occasional protests of those who dislike having their aural habits disturbed. It has rightly regarded it as part of its duty to keep us in touch with contemporary musical thought, and it has performed that duty unflinchingly . . . The chief instrument of this liberal policy is the Orchestra . . .

Less taxing public appearances outside the Symphony Concert season included the Good Friday *Parsifal* under Henry Wood on 3 April; *The Dream of Gerontius* on 18 May under Stanford Robinson; and an appearance at the Canterbury Festival just before the Proms. The Proms were marked by the British première of Webern's *Passacaglia*, Op. 1, his first representation in the series.

Conspicuous expense

In spite of the artistic success of the new Orchestra, the BBC was by no means immune from criticism. 1931 was a bad year for the country economically; the apparent lavishness of the BBC's provision for its selected musicians was causing resentment among those whose futures were less secure; and the BBC's policy of promoting public concerts was under fire (not for the first and last time) from those whose interests were threatened by such activities. In February 1931 it was the Incorporated Society of Musicians who bore this particular grievance to Reith – though they were primarily representing the Royal Philharmonic Society, still smarting from Reith's abrupt withdrawal of co-operation after the failure of the Beecham scheme. In a long memorandum concerned with the need to preserve the historical continuity of the RPS, it was argued that the BBC had secured a monopoly of orchestral talent and was forcing the RPS out of business; that competition was taking place on unequal terms; and that the BBC should restrict its concert-giving activities. After unsatisfactory meetings, Reith was unwilling to give way at any point to the ISM, and sent a gruff letter which said that the BBC continued to support established musical organisations 'in general', and that it was unreasonable to bar the BBC's orchestra from public performance. In the summer of 1931 a smaller group of ISM members met Reith, and his irritation had clearly mellowed. Stronger co-operative links with the RPS were set up (which continue to this day). But it was not to be the end of the story of disagreement with the Royal Philharmonic Society, as events of 1933–4 were to show.

The BBC's concession to the ISM was formulated in somewhat pompous terms in the Corporation's *Year Book* published for 1932:

> The music profession, as everyone knows, is passing through times of difficulty . . . On the other hand, there are favourable influences at work,

such as broadcasting, the general effect of which is beneficial . . . the BBC is anxious to take immediate steps to help the musical profession in a time of difficulty. It has accordingly agreed that wherever possible it will employ professional musicians in preference to amateurs . . . There are some fine amateur performers in this country, and the BBC naturally cannot make any sacrifice of the best possible standards of performance in carrying out its undertaking. But the BBC feels that the distinction is a valid one . . .

Publicly, the argument against the BBC was summed up by the music critic of the *Daily Telegraph*, Ferruccio Bonavia: he was concerned with both the expense of the orchestra and its repertoire. 'National expenditure is undergoing strict scrutiny . . . and the economic policy of the BBC cannot expect to escape the general examination.' Rumours (without foundation, it appears) were rife at the time that the BBC could not afford to maintain the new Symphony Orchestra. Bonavia drew the parallel with the Hallé and the LSO: 'Neither of these is costing the Government a penny . . . there is ample justification for criticism.'

Bonavia also inveighed against the inclusion of newer works in the programmes and broadcasts. In a scarcely-disguised attack on the Clark–Scherchen–Schoenberg–Webern axis he wrote:

Has the BBC the right or the duty to pose as the prophet of the newest of new music? . . . as far as foreign works are concerned, the policy to be followed should be one of caution . . . Would it be too much to suggest that before the BBC invites the composer (who alone is supposed to know what he wants) to supervise rehearsals in person and present him with a handsome fee, there should be some guarantee that the work is worthwhile?

Fortunately the Corporation took no heed of this narrow-mindedness; and the readers of the *Daily Telegraph* were more eager to take up the BBC's injustice to orchestral musicians than its advocacy of new music. In letters printed in September 1931 correspondents suggested that the BBC should have given extra money to existing organisations for rehearsals; and that 'the BBC should confine its activities to its own sphere, which is broadcasting from its studios'. It is difficult to say how far the significantly anonymous letters represented resentment on the part of those freelance players who had not applied for, or had not been selected for, the new Orchestra. But at any rate, within a year, the prophecies of doom concerning the contraction of the London orchestral scene in the face of the BBC were to be decisively disproved.

Between seasons, some small modifications had been made to the or-

chestral scheme which provided for splitting the main orchestra to provide
different studio combinations. Not every aspect of this scheme had worked
well: there were problems with clashing rehearsals for different sectional
groups, and the extensive light music commitment of the smallest groups
proved unwelcome to the high-calibre players in the Orchestra. So changes
were made. The overall strength of the establishment was increased to 115,
mainly to provide an extra instrument for sections B and D. Instead of
referring to all sections as 'The BBC Orchestra', it was decided to name them
separately, to make clear its function. Only the full band would be known as
The BBC Symphony Orchestra. Sections B and D were both to be known as
The BBC Studio Symphony Orchestra, and Sections C and E as The BBC
Light Orchestra. In addition, for the regular Bach Cantata series, a new
combination of Section C strings with *ad hoc* wind was to be known as The
BBC Bach Orchestra. More significant was the decision to relieve the
orchestral scheme of responsibility for the lightest music altogether, and to
form a new BBC Theatre Orchestra which was to be independent of the 115
musicians. This was a group of twenty-five, under the direction of Leslie
Woodgate (soon to be the BBC's Choral Director): it played for the first
time in 'The Stage Revolves', a revue programme broadcast on 22 July 1931.

Second season

The 1931–2 season proceeded with something of the same mood of euphoria
as that which greeted the opening season. The Orchestra still had no rivals.
The London Symphony Orchestra, which appeared to be embarking on a
new and successful collaboration with Sir Thomas Beecham, was disrupted
in December 1931 by the death of its agent and promoter, Lionel Powell.
Financial crisis ensued, which was worsened by the cancellation of the
Covent Garden opera season in March. Beecham was once more talking
about forming a first-class orchestra of his own; when he was taken on to the
board of the LSO as a Member and shareholder in September 1931 it looked
as if the LSO was the obvious candidate. He suggested in November that
radical changes in personnel might be necessary; the directors promised to
consider any plan he might have to make the orchestra more stable. Hamilton
Harty offered his co-operation; Landon Ronald suggested an amalgamation
of the LSO, his own New Symphony Orchestra, and the orchestra of the
Royal Philharmonic Society. As 1932 wore on, however, it became clear that
the ideas of Beecham and of the LSO Directors as to the amount of change
necessary in the orchestra diverged considerably. As had happened two
years before with the BBC, the supposed collaborators drifted apart.
    Elsewhere, it was a lavish season whose musical extravagance contradicted

the prevailing economic gloom. Besides the series of the LSO and the BBC, there were the successful Courtauld concerts, directed by Malcolm Sargent, and recitals by Paderewski, Florence Austral, Kreisler, Supervia, Rachmaninov, McCormack and Robeson, and by the latest young prodigy, Yehudi Menuhin. But the BBC was sensitive to the accusations of extravagance levelled at its orchestral expenditure, and it revealed to the press that it was maintaining the standard of the Symphony Orchestra by cutting down on regional activities (a move which had in fact begun before the Orchestra's formation in 1930). In October 1931 the National Orchestra of Wales, for which local backing had been sought but not obtained, was disbanded. It was replaced by a smaller combination known as the Western Studio Orchestra.

The BBC's programmes for the 1931–2 season mixed the adventurous with the reliable with the same flair as in the previous year. As in 1930–31, the concerts were divided into four subscription series, each planned to attract a different audience. The prospectus solemnly explained the thinking behind the conception (perhaps one can discern the hand of Julian Herbage?):

> Those whose taste remains safely riveted to the accepted masterpieces will find satisfaction most continuously in Series A. True, there are some modern works in the programmes, but among them only Prokofiev's Violin Concerto stands out as something of an adventure . . . Series B should be the ideal scheme for those who pride themselves on catholicity of taste. It mixes the firmly established and the new about equally . . . The most venturesome music lovers, however, will probably prefer Series C, which it will be noticed, exhibits even the classics in comparatively little-known works. It includes, moreover, the greatest number of first performances and revivals of interesting modern works not frequently given . . . Series D differs externally from the others by havings its five concerts placed all together at weekly intervals in the spring, a plan that will be found convenient by those who are in town only for the London season . . . The modern French, Spanish and English programme gives both variety and allurement to this final series.

There were twenty-two programmes: Boult was to direct thirteen. After the opening concert, at which the Orchestra appeared for the first time in the series under Boult as its permanent conductor, the period was dominated by the visit of two important composers. The first was Richard Strauss: in No. 10 studio on 18 October he conducted his *Macbeth*, *Don Juan* and *Tod und Verklärung*, and in the second concert of the Queen's Hall series conducted the first hearing in England of his Hölderlin settings, Op. 71, with Margarete Teschemacher as soloist. Ernest Newman in *The Sunday Times*

(25 October) conjured up the composer's presence: 'A tall, spare man, for the most part, as it seemed to those immediately behind him, hardly moving his baton arm at all, but somehow or other getting very nearly its potential best out of the orchestra.' In the studio, Newman observed that

> he gave the minimum of time and attention to the niceties of detail about which most other conductors are so particular, and concentrated on the basic spirit . . . the results were remarkable; the works had an extraordinary inner life, as if they were coming straight from the central fire in the brain of the composer who created them. The orchestral playing was magnificent.

And the enthusiasm of the orchestra was again great: they stood to applaud for several minutes after the broadcast.

The stir created by Strauss's visit was as nothing, however, compared to the furore which greeted the return, in the second half of November, of Arnold Schoenberg. The *Manchester Guardian* wrote of 'the violent Schoenberg offensive which the BBC has been waging on all fronts during the last fortnight' (25 November). Three major works were heard, two broadcast from a contemporary music concert in No. 10 Studio, the third from Queen's Hall. Four songs were broadcast by Enid Cruickshank. The night chosen for the contemporary concert was, ominously, Friday the thirteenth; the programme juxtaposed the 1899 *Verklärte Nacht* with the British première of the more recent Variations for Orchestra, Op. 31, which Furtwängler had premièred with the Berlin Philharmonic on 2 December 1928. In the Queen's Hall concert, the Five Orchestral Pieces (which Wood had introduced back in 1912) provided a chronological link between these two pieces. The popular reaction was predictable; but one or two more thoughtful notices are of interest. In the *Sunday Referee*, Constant Lambert wrote that 'we should be unusually grateful to the BBC'. Comparing Schoenberg with Stravinsky (whose two most recent works had been heard at the Courtauld Concerts during the same week) he declared that 'Schoenberg's revolution in musical technique has been far more sweeping and consistent than Stravinsky's, and to my mind this last week has once again proved him to be the more powerful and interesting personality'. And then, comparing Schoenberg's musical methods with the literary techniques of James Joyce,

> I do not believe that as a method it will have the lasting influence of Joyce's literary style but I do believe that at one stage of his career Schoenberg alchemised it into an immensely subtle and resourceful medium, opening up a whole new world of emotional expression and beauty of sound . . . Schoenberg is, in fact, an impressionist in spite of himself.

In the Queen's Hall, Lambert noticed that

> the audience, apart from a few self-satisfied titterers, was obviously sym-
> pathetic but only half-convinced. A second performance might well create
> an entirely favourable impression. The orchestra under Dr Adrian Boult
> played the extremely difficult score remarkably well, though with a touch of
> the embarrassment and circumspection shown by a really polite Protestant
> who has found himself involved in a religious ceremony of some totally
> differing creed.

Lambert's remarks come strangely from the future author of *Music Ho!*;
and his praise of Schoenberg was at the expense of a stinging attack on
Stravinsky's *Symphony of Psalms* – a sentiment shared by the critic of the
Manchester Guardian. 'The ostentatious but quite unconvincing religiosity'
of the *Symphony of Psalms* was compared with 'the latent, potential creative
power and the immense technical mastery that . . . at once proclaim the
presence of a personality marked out for leadership' in Schoenberg's
Verklärte Nacht. Edwin Evans in *Time and Tide* wrote appreciatively of the
Variations, and castigated the BBC for not preparing its listeners: 'The
Variations were just sprung on them without an intimation of what kind of
music they were . . .' Schoenberg later wrote to Boult to thank him for the
'remarkably clear, beautiful and vital' performance.

It is a measure of how well the BBC avoided narrow-mindedness in its
programmes during the early 1930s that, the week after Schoenberg departed, the Symphony Concert presented a new work in a quite different
tradition which commanded universal enthusiasm. This was William
Walton's *Belshazzar's Feast*, previously heard under Sargent at the Leeds
Festival, but brought to London on 25 November for the first time. Boult
conducted. Even the grudging Philip Page of the *Evening Standard* (26
November) was roused to ecstasy:

> SMASHING RHYTHM. NEW WORK A TRIUMPH FOR BRITISH MUSIC.
> Last night's BBC concert will possibly come to be regarded as historic, for
> young Mr William Walton's *Belshazzar's Feast*, a work of immense sig-
> nificance, was being given for the first time in London . . . the vitality and
> vigour of the whole thing are amazing . . . the greatest achievement in
> British music for many years . . .

The *Daily Telegraph*: 'No work by a composer of the younger generation
has been more highly praised, and the consensus of first impressions suggests
that this is the most significant composition of its kind since *The Dream of
Gerontius*, of which it is a lineal descendant.' (A verdict which has held

good.) This superb concert also included a new work by Holst, *Hammer-smith*, arranged from his BBC commission for the Military Band ('not a superfluous note anywhere . . . one of the most brilliant pieces of orchestral writing which Holst has produced', said *The Times*), and a performance of the Mozart Sinfonia Concertante K364 by Albert Sammons and Lionel Tertis which people remember to this day.

The new year began with one of Boult's major triumphs – a complete performance of Act III of Wagner's *Siegfried*. Boult recalls the special re-hearsal arrangements made for this event: he thought that the particularly difficult string parts made an extra three-hour session essential, and sche-duled it; but found at the rehearsal that the young but experienced strings of the Symphony Orchestra could read through the music perfectly. The singers in the BBC's concert performance were Enid Cruickshank, Walter Widdop, and Robert Parker. The present music critic of *The Sunday Times*, Felix Aprahamian, who was there, says he was quite unable to recall how he got home that night, so overwhelmed was he by the music. Yet Boult was scarcely ever to conduct opera in our major opera houses during his career.

Igor Stravinsky was the next composer to appear with the Orchestra: on 27 January, Ernest Ansermet returned, and as in 1931 brought Stravinsky as soloist, this time in his own *Capriccio* for piano and orchestra; the *Sym-phony of Psalms* (recently conducted by the composer in the Courtauld Con-certs) was repeated. This performance, the critics agreed, was 'far better' than the first, but the *Glasgow Herald* still found it 'uncouth and irrelevant music'. The greatest personal success of the season, however, was scored by the visiting Russian conductor, Nicolai Malko. The gossip column of *The Star* reported that

> Malko, the conductor from Leningrad, swept even the reserved and severely critical audience which attends BBC Symphony Concerts off their feet. The little man runs to the platform, nods rather than bows to the audience, glints a second or two of menace at the players, and then dashes into the music. At the end, he cuts out all the graces of a conductor's acknowledgement, bows in a comical fashion, makes the orchestra stand up and runs off again.

His 3 February concert was a huge success: the programme was all-Russian, and it featured Szigeti in Prokofiev's First Violin Concerto.

Each of the following concerts had its special attraction: two premières, and a distinguished array of soloists. 10 February saw the British première of Bax's *Winter Legends*, for piano and orchestra, played by Harriet Cohen, which received a mixed reception: praised for its strange beauties but dis-liked for its predominant heaviness of scoring. The 17 February concert presented the British première, under Wood, of Hindemith's *Konzertmusik* for strings and brass. MORE HINDEMITH FUTILITIES, shouted the *Daily Telegraph*: 'of all the pretentious and bombastic things that have emanated from Central Europe in the last decade surely this misnamed Konzertmusik is the arch and ultimate type'. This concert also included Maggie Teyte singing Ravel's *Shéhérazade*. 24 February presented Cortot in Beethoven's Emperor Concerto, 9 March Elisabeth Schumann in Bach arias.

On 16 March, there was an all-Beethoven concert under an important new foreign visitor, Felix Weingartner. *The Times* provided the BBC with some admirable material for its fight against opponents of public appearances by its Orchestra: 'These readings of Beethoven are something worth broadcasting to the world; moreover, such a concert as this gives the complete answer to those who say that the BBC should confine itself to studio work, for only in the hall and before the audience there present can such delicate adjustment of musical values be fully realised.' Schubert's Ninth under Boult on 24 February argued the same case; and Bach's B minor Mass on 6 April impressed as a performance which, following 'many striking innovations due to Professor Tovey's scholarship', emerged as one in which 'every detail had been co-ordinated' (*The Times*). On 13 April Henry Wood conducted Elgar's First Symphony and Prokofiev played his own Third Piano Concerto 'in the rather stiff-wristed way that suits the style of writing', said Ernest Newman (*The Sunday Times*). Newman saved his venom for the famous orchestration of Bach's D minor Toccata and Fugue for organ, which Wood made under the pseudonym Klenovsky: 'Nothing quite so undesignedly hilarious as this monstrosity had been heard in the Queen's Hall for a long time . . . it aimed frenziedly at Michael Angelo, achieved only Michael Mouse.'

Boult's unstinting generosity in stepping down from the rostrum in favour of foreign conductors whom he believed would improve the Orchestra's standard was an important factor in the Orchestra's success. Weingartner had already made a great impact (in the studio on 20 March he had conducted one of his own pieces, a Symphonic Poem *The Spring*). In April came one of Boult's favourite colleagues, Bruno Walter, already well known to some orchestral members like Ernest Hall, Aubrey Brain and Ambrose Gauntlett from his *Ring* cycles at Covent Garden in the 1920s. Boult had met Walter in Munich in 1922, and had subsequently invited him to conduct the Birmingham Orchestra; he became a close friend during the 1930s. Boult's own testimony is simple and impressive: 'Bruno Walter has brought the beauty of music to me perhaps more than anyone else, certainly in later life . . .'

Alex Nifosi recalled that

Walter came onto the platform at rehearsal knowing that many of the orchestra already knew what he wanted. He rarely had to ask for something more than once . . .

Of course, we in the BBC Symphony Orchestra knew him to be a fine conductor and a great musician, but he never did or said anything that would have given anyone reason not to feel almost an equal. Often, he would say something that might well be a summary of all he stood for in music: 'Gentlemen – let us make music together'.

In rehearsal Walter had shown us what he expected from us. After that he would stand motionless, and with that faint, sad smile would let the music unfold. One of his most characteristic gestures was to stand with arms raised in front of him, with cupped hands, the palms turned towards him, as if gently encouraging the players.

After a good performance, one that had pleased him, his deep-set, dark eyes glowed, and sparkled a little more as he bowed – first to the orchestra and then to the audience. That was all.

Among the Sunday night concerts that the BBC Symphony Orchestra gave from the No. 10 Studio was one in which Bruno Walter conducted Strauss – Johann Strauss! I can still remember the style and spirit, and above all the sense of dedication he brought to this lovely music. It was almost as if he were showing off his beloved Vienna . . . There was certainly no hint in it that he was playing music of a quality any different from his normal symphonic repertoire. Instead, he carried us all with him . . . in his enthusiasm for Strauss's music . . .

In his first Queen's Hall concert with the BBC Orchestra [on 20 April] Bruno Walter conducted from the piano when playing Mozart's A major concerto. We always enjoyed this for it was as if we were taking part – with him – in a chamber music concert. I can still see him playing the A major, with the two outer movements sparkling like jewels and, best of all, his exquisite playing in the slow movement, especially the opening, which had everyone both audience and orchestra spellbound in wonder. When he conducted from the piano he was even more sparing in his gestures than usual – just starting off the orchestra in the tuttis. He relied on us to play as in chamber music with only occasional help from him. This was in complete contrast to most other pianist-conductors of that time – who stood up and gesticulated ferociously in the orchestral tuttis – continuing right up to the last moment before their solo entry.

Two concerts under Boult completed the season: in the first, on 27 April, it had been hoped that Manuel de Falla would play the piano in his own *Nights in the Gardens of Spain* (which Edward Clark had introduced to London in 1921), but instead the cellist Suggia returned to play Haydn, while interest centred on the première of a revised version of the *Colour Symphony* of Bliss. This four-movement portrayal of Purple, Red, Blue and Green was respectfully treated by the critics: the *Birmingham Post* (28 April) praised it for 'a freshness of invention that positively pounces on the ear; the orchestration is astonishingly telling and individual'. The last concert of the season featured Beethoven's Ninth Symphony, and it drew a salutary warning from the *Daily Telegraph* on a subject that was shortly to occupy much time at the BBC: 'BBC'S TIRED ORCHESTRA. CHORAL SYMPHONY UNDER-REHEARSED. Is the BBC Symphony Orchestra overworked? . . .'

As 1932 wore on, the tide seemed to be turning against the BBC: opposition to the Symphony Orchestra had previously been based on entrenched interests, and had been refuted by the quality of programming and performance. But now there was, occasionally, cause for complaint.

However, summing up the past season, Francis Toye in the *Morning Post* (12 May 1932) was a wholly favourable voice: he made the point that the concerts 'have attracted a special, and I believe new public of their own . . . I think there can be no doubt that we are here in the presence of a new body of music-lovers, whose interest in the art has been awakened by the radio . . .'

Out of the glare of public attention, the Orchestra had maintained its standards in the studio in many challenging works: contemporary concerts during the season had included a complete programme on 4 March 1932 of music by Clark's close friend Bartók (including his *Miraculous Mandarin* Suite). On 22 January 1932 a programme of music by Busoni had featured his Comedy Overture, Violin Concerto and *Turandot* Suite; a week later, Pfitzner's Piano Concerto was played. On 14 March a special programme was devoted to the music of Milhaud, conducted by the composer: *La Création du Monde*, the Violin Concerto and *Saudades de Brasil*. On 24 January the First Symphony by Honegger; on 5 February a Piano Concerto by the notorious composer of *Factory*, Mossolov, and – more significantly – the First Symphony of a little-known Russian, Dimitri Shostakovich.

Still without a home

In May 1932 Savoy Hill was closed, and the BBC's administration moved into the new Broadcasting House, 'within a stone's throw', someone said, of Queen's Hall, 'though it was not clear in which direction the stones might be thrown'. Logic would have suggested that the Orchestra would be housed in this grand new building, but in fact in almost every way it proved too small.

Immediately after the move, there was only one spare office on the third floor, and extra new premises had immediately to be sought. The Music Department was housed on the fifth floor, and Boult had a fine office with small waiting rooms (which soon became known as 'Boult holes'); the Music Library was housed on the same floor. But this lasted for less than four years: soon the number of administrative staff led to the Music Department's being transferred to offices in Marylebone High Street.

As for the new Broadcasting House's Concert Hall, it also was too small. The needs of the new Orchestra had not been considered: or, as it was defensively put in the BBC's official guide:

> It was never anticipated that the hall could be made big enough to seat the full BBC Symphony Orchestra of 114 players, which normally performs in the Queen's Hall. The BBC intended rather to use the hall for the smaller component orchestras, the largest of which, the 'B' Orchestra of 79 players, is not too big for the hall, and is able to play to the full audience of over 500 people. The volume of the hall is 125,000 cubic feet, which in the ordinary way would not be very big in relation to the numbers of the audience and performers, but the ventilating system, described more fully below, works so admirably that the usual effect of hot stale air is entirely absent.

This description is hard to square with the ecstatic description of the Concert Hall in the *Radio Times* on 3 April 1931, during the course of an extensive series of previews of the new Broadcasting House. A picture of the embryonic hall was captioned 'Where a Thousand People Will Hear Great Music' and the article enthused that this would be the home of the BBC Symphony Orchestra and one of London's larger concert halls. The sketch showed a far larger number of seats than was subsequently included in the hall.

The concert hall did serve for most smaller events in the years to come, especially for the contemporary concerts with studio audience, but the main Symphony Orchestra concerts remained in No. 10 Studio while a search for more permanent accommodation was made.

A rival orchestra

Meanwhile, in the outside world, Sir Thomas Beecham was active again. By May of 1932 he had abandoned the LSO in favour of a new orchestra which he was to form in collaboration with the agent Harold Holt, former partner of Lionel Powell. In spite of the LSO's efforts to save the situation, contact between them and Beecham was finally broken by July 1932: as an added annoyance to them, Sargent threw in his lot with the new Beecham scheme. Beecham gathered together players from his recent opera season at Covent Garden, took a few from the LSO (including a Director, whose resignation the LSO denounced as an action of 'a most traitorous nature, worthy of the strongest condemnation'), and finally succeeded in building the joint-enterprise edifice which had eluded him in the last four years. The Royal Philharmonic Society and the Courtauld–Sargent Concerts both engaged his new band (and the RPS's own orchestra ceased to exist). He acquired a recording contract. On 7 October 1932 the London Philharmonic Orchestra was born.

London had therefore the prospect of an unprecedented number of orchestral concerts in the 1932–3 season. The LSO soldiered on, bringing Hamilton Harty down from Manchester as chief conductor of their Monday-night series. The RPS series, featuring the new LPO, had some interesting programmes including the British première of Szymanowski's *Sinfonia Concertante*. The Courtauld–Sargent concerts were to give the London première of Bax's Fourth Symphony and a work by Kodály: such was their confidence in their following that each concert was to have two repeat performances instead of the usual one. In addition, such features as Schnabel's series of recitals of the complete Beethoven piano sonatas promised much for the season.

Against this background, the BBC announced programmes for the 1932–3 Symphony Concerts series (now organised into three series, A, B, and C, of six concerts each). The Piano Concerto by Vaughan Williams was to receive its first performance on 1 February 1933; there were few other premières, but the concerts included an amazingly advanced repertoire of twentieth-century music. Schoenberg's Variations for Orchestra were brought out of the studio on 8 February (to be conducted by the composer), and three fragments from Berg's opera *Wozzeck* were programmed under Wood on 8 March. A major undertaking of the season was the British première of Hindemith's *Das Unaufhörliche* on 22 March, under Henry Wood. Conductors were Boult (11 concerts), Wood (5), Landon Ronald and Ansermet (one each), with part-concert appearances by Schoenberg and Sir Edward Elgar. This latter visit was part of an ambitious scheme to celebrate Elgar's 75th birthday in three concerts during the season, at which *The Kingdom*, both symphonies, the Violin Concerto, the *Enigma Variations*, the *Introduction and Allegro* and the *Cockaigne* Overture would be heard.

It was an unfortunate coincidence that, long before the days of orchestral clash-lists, the main work in the London Philharmonic's inaugural concert was Strauss's *Ein Heldenleben*, which was repeated a month later by Wood and the BBC Orchestra in the second concert of the season. In the *Manchester Guardian*, Neville Cardus expressed his opinion forcefully:

> The difference between professional orchestras boils down to a matter of rehearsal – and conductor. The BBC Orchestra is sumptuous in tone and almost as finished in technique as the best Continental orchestras, but, alas this beautiful music machine is usually wasted for want of a great conductor . . . The new London Philharmonic is the best in the land, because it enjoys both a great conductor and a liberal measure of rehearsal. We could appreciate how great Beecham is by comparing tonight's reading of *Heldenleben* [by the BBC Orchestra] with the one given by the Philharmonic Orchestra . . .

That judgement was not universally shared, but the BBC had set up its orchestra as the best in the country, and it had to defend itself.

Matters looked up, however. The LPO, noted the BBC, was unsuccessful at filling its own Sunday series at the Queen's Hall. Its form was less reliable than that of the BBC. There were some signal successes in the BBC's Symphony Concerts season: a repeat of *Belshazzar's Feast* on 2 November; Ansermet back to conduct *The Rite of Spring* on 16 November; and Casals filling the hall for the Haydn D major Cello Concerto on 23 November. Then, in November and December, came the Elgar 75th birthday concerts, with Boult and Landon Ronald conducting music with which they were specially associated, and the composer making personal appearances. There was new enthusiasm and publicity for the Orchestra. In the *Daily Telegraph*, Richard Capell thought the performances 'nothing short of magnificent . . . the BBC Orchestra played better than ever in the two works which Dr Boult conducted, and which, in respect of tone quality, have never in all these years of countless performances sounded more beautiful'.

The Elgar commission

The Elgar Celebration Concerts brought to fruition one of the BBC's most famous unfulfilled plans. In the press reviews of the series there were many reflections on Elgar's lack of productivity during the previous twelve years. But the *Daily Mail* picked up a hint the composer had given during the Three Choirs Festival in Worcester that he was working on a Third Symphony which he was unlikely to finish 'since no one wanted his music now'. By the end of the Celebration Concerts the BBC was able to announce that it had commissioned this Third Symphony.

The tangled strands linking Elgar and the BBC in this project lead back to one man: not Sir Landon Ronald, who was to take the public credit for arranging the commission, but George Bernard Shaw. In 1932 he had written both to Elgar and to Reith. To Elgar: 'Why don't you make the BBC order a new symphony? It can afford it.' And to Reith, at the end of September: 'You could bring the Third Symphony into existence and obtain the performing rights for, say, ten years for a few thousand pounds. The kudos would be stupendous and the value for money ample: in fact if Elgar were a good man of business instead of a great artist, who throws his commercial opportunities about *en grand seigneur*, he would open his mouth much wider.' Reith then called in Landon Ronald, a close friend of Elgar's, who carried out the detailed negotiations with Elgar in order to secure an agreement to the commission. The project was finally settled during the Celebration Concerts. Elgar was delighted by Reith's 'kind and generous attitude in the inception of the idea' and called at Broadcasting House to sign 'the momentous agreement'. On 14 December he was present at the rehearsals for the final concert, Boult's performance of *The Kingdom*. He twice said to Boult, 'Don't let them go away, Adrian, I want to come and speak to them when you've finished.' He came on to the platform and gave what Boult described as 'a most moving and charming speech of thanks to them for their support and friendship all his life'.

The Third Symphony commission was announced the same day by the BBC, and Landon Ronald spoke at a dinner at the Guildhall School of Music in the evening.

> I consider this to be one of the most interesting events that has occurred in musical history since the Royal Philharmonic Society commissioned Beethoven to write a symphony for them in 1827, which resulted in his composing the immortal Ninth Symphony. My task was merely a labour of love, through my life-long friendship with Sir Edward Elgar, and the generous enthusiasm of Sir John Reith and the Governors of the BBC . . .

The *Daily Telegraph* (15 December) commented: 'The dedication of the symphony will be to the BBC – which must surely be the first corporation ever to be inscribed on the title page of a symphony.' It was stated then that the first performance was planned to take place in the following autumn. Writing to Elgar, Boult said pertinently: 'I had no idea until I saw the paper this morning that it was already so far advanced. It will indeed make next season a "peak".' George Bernard Shaw wrote to *The Times* (20 December):

> Sir, – I have occasionally remarked that the only entirely creditable incident in English history is the sending of £100 to Beethoven on his deathbed by the London Philharmonic Society; and it is the only one that historians never mention.

Thanks to Sir John Reith it is no longer unique. His action in commissioning a new symphony from Sir Edward Elgar, the first English composer to produce symphonies ranking with those of Beethoven, is a triumph for the BBC.

But is it not a pity that Sir Edward has had to wait so long for the advent of a public administrator capable of rising to the situation? The forthcoming symphony will be his third: it should be his ninth. It is true that we have loaded him with honours. I use the word loaded advisedly, as the honours have the effect of enabling us to exact much gratuitous work from him. He has given us a 'Land of Hope and Glory'; and we have handed him back the glory and kept all the hope for ourselves.

I suggest that we make a note not to wait until our next great composer is 70 before guaranteeing his bread and butter while he is scoring his Eroica.

Yours truly,

G. BERNARD SHAW

Dec. 16

Elgar was not so confident about the matter as either Shaw or Landon Ronald. In a letter to the record producer Fred Gaisberg (who had immediately proposed a recording) on 16 December Elgar did not refer to the work, except in a postscript: 'As to Symphony III – ?' Nevertheless, plans to perform the Symphony went ahead, and Owen Mase wrote to Elgar in April 1933 that the BBC hoped to include the work in the first concert of the 1933–4 season on 18 October. Elgar immediately vetoed that idea; by 2 May the intended performance had been put off until the projected London Music Festival of May 1934. When the preliminary BBC leaflet for the complete 1933–4 season appeared, that Festival was advertised, with no details except that the concerts would include three works – Elgar: Third Symphony (first performance); Walton: New Symphony; Hindemith: *Das Unaufhörliche*. That was the first and last announcement of the work. On 7 October Elgar wrote to Reith that he had to undergo an operation: 'Perhaps it will not be necessary to refer publicly to the Symphony in any way at present.' In November the composer had a stroke; on 23 February 1934 he died. The Third Symphony was nowhere near complete (see p. 98).

Schoenberg returns

During the first months of 1933 the Orchestra continued to be in the news. A purely classical programme with Huberman in the Mendelssohn Violin Concerto on 25 January was praised; the first performance of the Vaughan Williams Piano Concerto on 1 February passed without great enthusiasm

('he appears to handle the medium with some difficulty', said *The Times*).
Then the fun broke out again when Schoenberg came to conduct his Op. 31
Variations in public on 8 February. The popular press roused their weariest
clichés. Gordon Beckles of the *Daily Herald* went to a rehearsal: 'The great
BBC symphonic body was tuning up . . . "When are they beginning?"
I asked a musical official after two or three minutes. "Beginning?" he
whispered aghast. "Good heavens, they've been rehearsing since 2.15."
This is not a joke.' 'SCHOENBERG SHOCKS FOR LISTENERS,' warned the
News Chronicle on the day of the concert. The BBC, mindful of Edwin
Evans's criticisms when the work was broadcast from the studio in 1931,
arranged for Ernest Newman to provide a broadcast introduction to the
Variations: 'It will last for 20 minutes, and you may feel that you might be
better employed. I have studied the score very hard, every note of it. As
musical mathematics or musical chemistry, it is a marvel. You may get more
out of it than I imagine. I only hope so . . .' With this laconic persuasion, as a
correspondent to *The Star* reported, 'before he had finished I was quite
determined to enjoy it, and enjoy it I did, in a way.'

M. D. Calvocoressi contributed to the printed programme a thoughtful
article 'On tackling Schoenberg's music', and there was a long analysis of the
work itself by D. Millar Craig. Richard Capell wrote in the *Daily Telegraph*
that the piece 'is, no doubt, music of the torture chamber, but the listener is
not tortured . . . the result has for the listener a certain fascination.' J.A.
Forsyth in *The Sun* wondered not only if listeners understood the music but
'I wonder quite frankly and quite soberly if [Schoenberg] understands it
himself'. An unexpected corroboration of this reaction came from Sir John
Reith himself, who on the day following the concert happened to be speaking
to members of the Radio Manufacturers' Association. He was reported as
saying 'I am going to a meeting of the Music Advisory Committee over
which I preside two or three times a year. If you have any message to send
them concerning the Schoenberg music that was broadcast last night, I will
gladly take it. I shall certainly have some comments of my own to make.
Such music does not leave me cold – I wish it did – its effect is very much the
reverse.'

Nothing daunted, the Symphony Orchestra presented a month later the
Three Fragments from Berg's *Wozzeck*, previously heard in the studio (on
5 May 1932), which evoked a more favourable response. 'The music is
extraordinarily direct in expression, however strange and wilful its language
may be,' reported *The Times* (9 March). 'Of the performance', wrote Edwin
Evans in *Time and Tide*, 'one can only speak in glowing and grateful terms'.
If the BBC had needed encouragement to plan a complete performance of

the opera, Evans provided it in a lengthy plea that England should be allowed to hear the work in full.

The remainder of the season included piano concertos played by Schnabel (15 February), Lamond (22 February), Cortot (15 March) and Backhaus (29 March), but was dominated by the British première of Hindemith's *Das Unaufhörliche*, 'The Perpetual' (22 March), an ambitious setting of 'a philosophical poem dealing with such immensities as would have appalled Dante and left Goethe and Nietzsche gasping . . . It will not do. Hindemith is incapable of sustaining an argument which arraigns the cosmos' (*Manchester Guardian*, 23 March). 'On the whole, it was a trying experience . . . Presumably, this is Germany's idea of progress' (*News Chronicle*, 23 March).

At the start of 1933 there was a fortnight of Winter Promenade Concerts in which the Orchestra gave the British première of Hindemith's Philharmonic Concerto (written for the fiftieth anniversary of the Boston Symphony Orchestra in 1932). Percy Pitt had died on 25 November 1932, after conducting his last concert with the Symphony Orchestra only a week before: a memorial concert was given on 10 March. The Orchestra now numbered 119 players, its regular full strength until the War. To the original strength of 114 had been added a fifth flute, oboe and bassoon; a sixth trombone, and two extra horns; the brass section had been reduced by one tuba.

The London Music Festival: Koussevitsky

An innovation at the end of the 1933 season was the first series of what the BBC chose, in a somewhat inflated manner, to call 'The London Music Festival, organised by the BBC'. These six concerts in two weeks were chiefly a showcase for two groups of events: a series of three Brahms Centenary Concerts, conducted by Boult on 8, 10, 12 May; and a series of three concerts conducted by Serge Koussevitsky on 15, 17, 19 May. Koussevitsky had not appeared in London since 1925 when he had conducted the London Symphony Orchestra's twenty-fifth anniversary concert. Edward Clark had been anxious to invite him to the Orchestra since 1931, when the pianist Lilias MacKinnon intimated that he would be pleased to accept an invitation. Boult was unsure: 'Do you really think it is worth our while, I mean to the extent of arranging extra concerts for him?' he wrote to Clark on 30 January 1931. W. W. Thompson, the Concerts Manager, felt that Koussevitsky should be included on a list along with Toscanini, Furtwängler and Stokowski as being worth the special attention of the Orchestra. Koussevitsky was approached in May 1931, when Clark went to see him and invited him to London. Clark reminded Boult that the conductor had introduced Bax, Vaughan Williams, Walton and Lambert to audiences in Boston. After long negotiations, Koussevitsky agreed to come: but in the end there was only one substantial English work in the programmes, Bax's Second Symphony, plus Walton's *Portsmouth Point*.

Koussevitsky made alarming demands on the Orchestra, which on the whole they hugely resented. He insisted on 'sonority', which he pronounced with a long second syllable, and tore the Orchestra apart at rehearsal with his fierce demands. Bernard Shore wrote of his 'nervous intensity and fire, a tremendous energy that is tempered with charm and humour, and withal something of a tyrant, a tyrant who must be constantly beguiled by the finest playing if he is to be kept within bounds'. But the results were very fine indeed, as even those players who disliked him admitted – and he was invited to return for a 1935 Festival. In the *Radio Times* for 7 July, Koussevitsky wrote, 'Looking back on my past experiences, I can but welcome [sic] and congratulate the British Broadcasting Corporation on the marvellous achievements that it has accomplished within the comparatively short period of three years.'

Criticism

While the Orchestra's public life continued, inside the BBC concern was growing about the volume of public criticism directed towards the non-studio work of the Orchestra. Roger Eckersley, Director of Programmes, wrote to Reith (10 March 1933):

> Beecham told me the other day that this agitation against the BBC giving so many public concerts was very much in the air. He told me this quite unofficially and said we would be receiving official notification in due course. He mentioned Courtauld's name as one of those particularly interested in this matter, and I expect Holt is another. I do not at the moment see any reason why we should curtail our outside concert work.

Typically, Eckersley added a handwritten footnote to protect Beecham: 'I should add in fairness to Beecham that he does not necessarily agree with the agitation.'

Owen Mase, as Boult's Assistant Music Director, prepared a document setting out the BBC's reasons for public concert-giving, and sent it to Boult. 'I feel that in view of the loose talking and writing prevalent just now, a little clear thinking would not be out of place. Does the attached provide some?' The document presented the familiar arguments:

> No fine orchestra can develop or maintain its fullest artistic powers without the stimulus of considerable public performance . . . There is every reason to

believe that the broadcasting of music has genuinely increased the number of serious listeners who do want to hear music at first hand . . . it is quite noticeable that the public for the BBC Symphony Concerts is very largely a new one . . . The BBC pays a very large sum per annum into the pockets of the musical profession.

More radical was Mase's belief that a new, larger concert hall seating 5000 or 6000 people was necessary to accommodate the new audience created by broadcasting: 'Given careful educative publicity and a far-sighted planning of the best programmes and artists, over a period of a few years a public could be created that would fill such a hall . . .' He concluded somewhat rhetorically that the British people 'are not an unmusical race. They have never been given a chance.'

Boult sent this document to Reith, noting 'There are signs that this agitation is about to break out again, and it seems to me that the attached meets the arguments extremely well.' Reith (13 March) was more circumspect: 'I agree that it is desirable (as always) to be prepared. But what is it suggested should be done with the attached document? It certainly can't be issued to the Press in its present form . . . And is it proposed to issue it in advance of an attack, or as a reply to one?' There, for the moment, the matter rested.

The 1933–4 season boasted another first-class set of Edward Clark/Julian Herbage programmes, including two events of the utmost importance: the complete performance of Berg's *Wozzeck* planned for 14 March 1934, and the British première of Bartók's Second Piano Concerto, played by the composer, on 8 November 1933. But there was increased competition. The BBC, presenting an eighteen-concert Symphony Series, was up against the Royal Philharmonic Society, which was now presenting eighteen concerts (as against ten the previous season and only six in 1931–2). The RPS concerts took place on Thursdays, often in the same weeks in which the BBC played on Wednesdays. The three opening concerts of the BBC's season (18, 25 October and 1 November) were devoted to standard works; they came soon after the Proms and audiences suddenly dwindled, so that even for Carl Flesch performing the Beethoven Violin Concerto on 1 November the hall was only half-full.

On 13 November, the *Daily Herald* reported that 'a sudden falling-off in bookings for the BBC's weekly symphony concerts at the Queen's Hall has taken the BBC by surprise . . . Several critics have hinted during the present season that overwork is responsible for a certain flatness in the performances of the BBC Orchestra . . .'

A concerts management meeting at the BBC at the start of the season recognised that the Corporation's Symphony Season was losing against other ventures. The Proms audience was not coming to Symphony Concerts (a fact unchanged over fifty years); the 'social drive' of Lady Cunard and her associates was ensuring a fashionable audience for Beecham's concerts; the *Radio Times* was not being exploited as a vehicle for publicity; and the concerts were acquiring a reputation for presenting advanced music. The Bartók première on 8 November was generally disliked. Neville Cardus in the *Manchester Guardian* thought Bartók 'composes as though he owed the world of music a grudge . . . the piano snaps away like a spiteful maiden aunt. It is all tedious and crude.' Ernest Newman, however, found it 'an exhilarating racket', and all agreed that the Orchestra played well.

Then the seventy-year-old Felix Weingartner arrived to conduct the Orchestra on 15 November, and a programme of Brahms, Beethoven and the Berlioz *Symphonie fantastique* aroused enormous enthusiasm. 'Conductor Galvanises BBC Concert', ran the *Evening Standard* headline; 'Weingartner Brilliant at BBC Concert', said the *Daily Mail*. The next week, it was Sir Thomas Beecham's turn to make his first guest appearance with the Orchestra he had nearly founded. He conducted a miscellaneous programme of Mozart, Smetana, Tchaikovsky, Elgar and Delius, and the results were spectacular: 'One thing only can prevent this occasion standing out like a mountain on a vast plain; that is, many more appearances of the same conductor with this orchestra' (*News Chronicle*, 23 November). The comments only served to point up the less-than-satisfactory performances of the BBC Orchestra on other occasions. The following week, Schoenberg was unable to come to England and the projected first performance of his arrangement of a Handel Concerto Grosso was abandoned. Boult conducted the British première of the original version of Bruckner's Ninth Symphony, with three complete movements; it roused little enthusiasm among the critics.

It had been a more successful half-season than at first anticipated, but inside the BBC there was dissatisfaction. Eckersley asked for a report from Boult, which he sent on 6 November, with particular reference to lightening the work-load on the Orchestra. Boult thought the form of the Orchestra

quite satisfactory in comparison with their form of a year ago, though it is naturally not up to the high pitch which was reached during the May Festival under the direction of Koussevitsky . . . It is obvious that the Orchestra cannot keep up a continuous standard of super-efficiency . . . the amount of work that is generally done is not productive of over-strain, but is only just inside that limit . . . the first reform should be the avoidance of the three-session day . . . I feel it certainly desirable that some alteration be made in the working hours of the Orchestra, which I fear would reduce the hours in which the Orchestra is available for broadcasting.

Boult suggested sharing the Proms with other orchestras or cutting rehearsals in this period; possibly forming a second orchestra to deal with Saturday evening or Monday evening broadcast concerts; and creating a larger pause (with a week's holiday) between the end of the Proms and the start of the Queen's Hall season. He also asked that the Orchestra be given the stimulus of touring in England, 'or better still in one or two of the capitals abroad'.

Julian Herbage contributed to the discussion by suggesting revisions to the orchestral scheme. He felt strongly that tiredness in the Orchestra was caused not by symphony concert rehearsals, but by single rehearsals under inadequate conductors for studio concerts. He proposed that principals should only play three programmes a week, under reputable conductors; and that a small number of new conductors should be engaged under contract. 'The present system of Staff Conductors-cum-Programme Builders results in chaotic or rushed programme building and insufficiently prepared conducting. It has confused both issues to a quite indescribable extent.' Orchestral players of the 1930s corroborate the poor standard of direction of sections of the Orchestra by staff members who were not primarily conductors: Edward Clark, Victor Hely-Hutchinson and others were more active as conductors than their skills warranted. Ill-feeling among the smaller sections of the Orchestra was common.

Herbage stimulated Boult to add some general reflections on the state of the Orchestra, which provided a careful formulation of its achievement (Boult to Eckersley, 17 November):

The BBC Orchestra scheme was designed, first, to meet the needs of broadcasting . . . Incidentally (and I think this is the right adverb) it became one of the great orchestras of the world. I think we can fairly claim this as Weingartner, Walter and Koussevitsky, among many others, have all said so. . . . though the utmost care was taken about the selection of players, it was only incidental to the fulfilment of its broadcasting duties that this has happened. . . . I think it is clear that though our Orchestra is efficient and can remain so as it stands, it will sooner or later have to recede from the position it now holds in the concert world, unless its performing hours are somewhat reduced.

These few sentences isolate precisely the tensions which have underlaid the development of the BBC Symphony Orchestra since its foundation, and which have continued to dominate its policy through its fifty years' existence:

the conflicts between the demands of artistic excellence and the demands of efficient broadcasting, between hours produced to justify money expended, and the importance of a quality of performance which cannot be measured in output.

Boult later came down firmly in favour of a proposal to relieve the Symphony Orchestra of all its studio work between the Sunday evening concert and the Wednesday Queen's Hall concert, so that he could put into effect a scheme suggested to him by Lionel Tertis for sectional rehearsals 'under one roof in order that I may be present all the time in one or other of the rooms'. But he strongly opposed reducing the establishment strength of 119 in order to provide some personnel for these studio concerts: he supported Stanford Robinson's idea that the Theatre Orchestra should do these small concerts, and should be supplemented by a chamber group of twelve to fifteen players for the lightest repertoire.

Beecham again

Roger Eckersley, however, was thinking of reforming the Orchestra's public concerts along altogether broader lines, and suggested an astonishing re-grouping of musical interests in London. In a note to Controller, Programmes, on 28 February 1934, he attempted to link together the three questions which had been preoccupying the Music Department since the beginning of the 1933-4 season: the lack of support from the public for the Symphony Concerts; the large number of orchestral public concerts in London following the formation of the London Philharmonic Orchestra; and the problem of fatigue and overwork in the BBC Orchestra. On the last point he wrote:

> I would like to sound a note of warning regarding a too soft-hearted attitude towards the players . . . they are exceedingly well-paid and looked after, and have good holidays. I think it would generally be better to use the word stale-ness than fatigue, and, as far as the Proms are concerned, possibly boredom would not be the wrong word.

Then Eckersley dropped his bombshell: 'I will deal now with the new factor . . . that is the suggested scheme of collaboration with Sir Thomas Beecham.' Eckersley had once again been seeing Beecham socially, and (with the success of Beecham's recent concert) was once again persuaded that Beecham had a great deal to offer the BBC.

> This scheme, which was put forward by Beecham, and which was discussed quite non-committally between us at a recent interview, infers briefly the

joining together of the BBC and London Philharmonic Orchestras, alternating each week in a series of 24 concerts from October to April. Beecham
would conduct six of the concerts in which the BBC Orchestra was playing,
six in which the London Philharmonic Orchestra took part – 12 in all.
Dr Boult would conduct such proportion of the remaining 12 as was
mutually agreed, and which were not taken by guest conductors. As I see it,
Boult should have at least eight . . . The decision would turn upon whether
Beecham in a joint scheme such as is proposed, could be termed a guest
conductor.

Indeed it did. Beecham, with typical candour, in his formal memorandum
to the BBC suggesting the scheme, said, 'I am aware that in respect of this
joint series this would mean that I shall be occupying the position of conductor-in-chief of both orchestras'.

Eckersley summarised what he thought would be the advantages of the
scheme. First, there would be a closer identification with Sir Thomas
Beecham as a conductor: 'There is no question whatever but that Beecham
is one of the greatest conductors in the world. Many critics put him second
only to Toscanini . . .' Second, there would be closer co-operation in the
field of programme building generally, and the advantage of Beecham's
large following to the BBC's audience figures: 'The concerts would be
publicised as to present them as the one outstanding series of symphony
concerts to which all music lovers must go, and this would, it is felt, do away
with much of the present diffusion of audiences.' A curious aspect of the
scheme was that it was not to be formulated as a collaboration between the
BBC and the London Philharmonic Orchestra, but one between the BBC
and Royal Philharmonic Society (as promoter of the LPO concerts): a
reversion to the idea which had originated the whole idea of the BBC's Orchestra in 1927 and had come unstuck in 1930. Once again, however, Beecham had proposed the scheme without the knowledge of the directors of the
Royal Philharmonic Society: it was pure kite-flying.

Boult had given his cautious approval to the idea behind the scheme of
collaboration with the LPO, 'which in principle seems to be excellent'; but
on sight of Beecham's full plans he not unnaturally exploded. He wrote to
Eckersley on 5 March, with a copy to Reith:

> May I suggest that Sir Thomas Beecham who, two years ago, founded a new
> Orchestra in direct and obvious opposition to ours, would not now be
> approaching us if the scheme he brings were not very much to his advantage,
> in fact, as I have reason to believe, vital to the continued existence of the

London Philharmonic Orchestra . . . we cannot expect reliability from him;
he is often changing programmes, and cancelling engagements.

Boult compared the two orchestras in detail, and said that while he had
enjoyed conducting the LPO,

> it is not to the BBC's interest, and mine, that I should conduct the LPO
> much, unless I can undertake their training, which is out of the question.
> To the alternative possibility, Sir Thomas Beecham's frequent conducting of
> our orchestra, there are even graver objections. He gets magnificent results
> with them, but at such a cost that I shall feel called upon to insist on a drastic
> curtailment of the Orchestra's broadcasting hours in any week in which Sir
> Thomas Beecham is conducting. He usually arrives late for rehearsal, and
> keeps the Orchestra overtime.

After several such complaints, Boult concluded:

> I am afraid I have said very unpleasant things about Sir Thomas Beecham.
> No one admires him more as a conductor of certain schools of music, but I
> feel that the Corporation must be fully prepared before entering into any
> kind of undertaking with him. As a conductor of the occasional, carefully-
> chosen programme he has the greatest value for us . . .

Boult's objections were from someone very closely in touch with the day-
to-day work of the Orchestra, and they were supported by the whole of the
Music Department: he was not merely airing his individual views. In particular, it was felt that the proposed reduction in public appearances by the
BBC Orchestra from eighteen to twelve would have a disastrous effect on
morale, and 'would probably lead to many of our star players leaving us for
an orchestra which plays more frequently in public' (Herbage). But the BBC
and its Music Advisory Committee appeared determined to bring about this
reduction as a concession to the musical profession, whether or not collaboration ensued. It was extraordinary that Beecham's scheme should have been
promoted inside the BBC by Eckersley, the very man who had lived through
the débâcle of Beecham's negotiations with the BBC in 1928–30. Others in
the BBC had learned their lesson.

The scheme was discussed at a high level, in the meetings of the Programme Division, and in spite of what were termed 'reservations on the part
of the Music Department . . . it was thought advisable to write to Sir Thomas,
approving the scheme in principle and making it clear that the arrangement
must be experimental for one year . . .' A feeling of *déjà vu* must have affected
those who knew of the 1929–30 scheme. A copy of the letter was sent to the

Royal Philharmonic Society. By 23 March it was clear that collaboration in 1934–5 was impracticable; the Music Advisory Committee agreed, and a letter was sent to Beecham and the RPS explaining the situation. Beecham, it was then learnt, 'had been incensed' by what he termed the neglect of the BBC to implement their promises in regard to the scheme. The RPS and BBC officials met on 20 July, and the RPS displayed an extreme unwillingness to proceed with any scheme which could affect their identity; but they did not wish to tell Beecham this but rather to let the matter ride 'on the assumption that Sir Thomas would forget about it'.

Meanwhile, the matter had gone to Reith. In a closely argued note for Controller, Administration, Basil Nicolls (who had been closely involved with the administrative side of the Orchestra's first years of life, and was soon to become Controller, Programmes) put the case against the scheme:

> I submit that the suggestion for reducing our concerts is a fundamental rejection of our whole existing orchestral scheme, both economically and artistically. . . . It is incidental to the proposals, but none the less important, that they practically involve removing Dr Boult from his position as permanent conductor of the BBC Symphony Orchestra, and substituting someone who, on the face of it, has an allegiance to two orchestras. I am quite confident that in the long run the result would be disastrous . . . There is nothing wrong with our orchestra, which is the best in England, although at the beginning of the season it was tired as a result of the absence of a desirable break after the Promenade Season, which was particularly hard this year . . . I strongly recommend that booking [the Queen's Hall] for the next season should go ahead on the basis of eighteen concerts in the ordinary way.

How the matter ended remains unclear. Hearsay evidence is that Reith, having summoned a meeting, lost his temper and refused to have anything more to do with Beecham or his collaborative scheme. Certainly it vanished, never to reappear. But the proposal to reduce the Symphony Concert series from eighteen to twelve concerts in 1934–5 was implemented. What was gained from the BBC, however, was agreement to the principle that the Symphony Orchestra should tour: to the Provinces and to Brussels in 1934–5; perhaps to be followed by regular visits abroad. The only increase in public concert-giving in London was that the 1935 London Music Festival was to be increased from six to eight concerts. It was, from the point of view of the Orchestra's metropolitan musical reputation, a poor bargain.

British music

The beginning of 1934 was marked by a new venture: a series of six concerts of British music at the Queen's Hall between 1 and 12 January, conducted by Boult (four concerts), Beecham and Landon Ronald (one each). Throughout the three seasons in which it had given concerts the Orchestra had been criticised by the BBC's own Music Advisory Committee for its concentration on continental new music rather than on British works. The Committee, which, as noted, represented most of the established interests in British music-making, evidently believed that the BBC existed to support British music and British musicians. Ill-feeling about the Committee's activities was rife in the Music Department. It was to boil over in Boult's report to the Ullswater Committee in 1935 (see below, p. 112). Reith had nearly disbanded the Committee in 1929 because of its narrow-mindedness; but it was essential that the voice of the British musical establishment be heard within the BBC, and though Reith gave up chairing the meetings, the Committee continued to exist. A typical complaint came from Kenneth Wright to Boult in February 1933: 'There is hardly one member of our committee who has any real sympathy with, true understanding of, or live interest in present day musical developments. We get from them as a body almost exclusively negative criticism of our activities . . .'

On 24 May 1933 Boult reported that Owen Mase had made a suggestion which might help to defuse the situation where the Music Advisory Committee continually complained about the programmes and artists of the Symphony Concerts series. This was to programme a special series of six concerts exclusively devoted to British music, which could incorporate such features as a birthday concert for Ethel Smyth, and a considerable number of first performances. The scheme was immediately put up to Reith, who agreed. It cannot have been coincidence that a few days later, at the start of June, the Music Department was able to prepare a document defending itself against the charge of neglecting British music.

The range of composers represented in the concerts was wide, from the older generation of Elgar, Bax, Smyth, Delius and Mackenzie, to the more recently established figures of Walton, Lambert, Eric Fogg and Patrick Hadley. There were symphonies by Elgar, Bax (his Fourth), and Bliss (the *Colour Symphony* again) as well as the Sinfonietta by Eugene Goossens; there were miniatures by Roger Quilter, Cyril Scott, Rutland Boughton, Edgar Bainton and E. J. Moeran. It was difficult to please everyone: in the *Evening News* the 81-year-old Sir Frederic Cowen sounded a note of disappointment that Stanford, Parry and others, not to mention himself, found no place in the series. In the *New Statesman* the irascible W.J. Turner complained that 'there is not a single piece in the Festival that is by a totally unknown composer'.

It is clear that considerations of musical politics underlay many of the works selected. Constant Lambert viewed the series as a post-Christmas present for British composers (including himself), and commented in his *Sunday Referee* article (7 January):

> A little ruthlessness on the part of the BBC would certainly have improved the programmes . . . If a work is a bad one it should not be considered representative of British music merely because the composer has been writing long enough to know better. Unfortunately, the BBC has shown more consideration for the composers' feelings than for those of the audience . . . Either we can produce good music or we can't. If we can, then let it be played in company with the great masters.

Which was precisely the sentiment that lay behind the planning of the Symphony Concerts series by the BBC Music Department.

Another composer in the series, E. J. Moeran, replied to an article in the *Daily Telegraph* criticising the concerts:

> With one line of argument I distinctly do not agree, and that is the suggestion that the fact of a man's being professor at the RAM or the RCM entitles his work to a hearing at the Queen's Hall . . . It was a pity the opportunity was not found to include something by Jacob, and I should have liked to hear something by Finzi, Rubbra and Elizabeth Maconchy . . . Peter Warlock should have been given a place . . . I should have represented Cyril Scott by his Piano Concerto.

That was a most perspicacious list; but then these composers had little weight behind them in the musical establishment.

Reactions to the new works were predictable. The Symphony by R.O. Morris, a man far better known as a textbook harmonist than as a composer, was a mild disaster. Arthur Benjamin's Violin Concerto was praised by Ernest Newman, 'really masterly in its logical concision . . . I find the ideas refreshingly vital', while Frank Bridge's *Phantasm*, a Rhapsody for piano and orchestra, was thought 'for all its deliberate manner, to reach a high plane of imagination' (*Yorkshire Post*); Delius (in his *Fantastic Dance*) again gave 'cause for wonder at the never-failing beauty through which the stream of his creativity passes', while John Ireland's *Legend* for Piano and Orchestra meant, as usual, 'the facing of a new problem' (*Yorkshire Post*).

In fact, the most solid result of the series was the congratulatory letter which three members of the Music Advisory Committee (Allen, Landon Ronald, and McEwen) sent to *The Times* when it was over, praising themselves for their behind-the-scenes pressure:

> Would you permit us to express gratitude to the BBC for the generous treatment they have lately given to a large number of composers of this country at the Festival of British music with which the musical life of this New Year began?
>
> All must appreciate the great amount of thought, care, and labour such a festival entails; and many of the composers whose works were performed must have rejoiced in the opportunities provided for them. They and the musical world generally will realize that the BBC have made this gesture in a generous manner.

The sentiments of the letter corroborate to an uncomfortable extent Lambert's criticism that the series was designed for the composers, not for the audience. Not surprisingly, there were very thin houses for all the concerts save the last, at which *Belshazzar's Feast* was heard again.

Mahler and Berg

The 1933–4 Symphony Concerts went on while discussions about the shape of the next season continued within the BBC. Bruno Walter returned on 31 January to conduct Prokofiev playing the British première of his Fifth Piano Concerto. 'He gave the Orchestra no quarter and they responded as though glad of the treatment, with vigour, with brilliant tone . . .' (*Observer*, 4 February). On 7 February, Boult directed what was, incredibly, the first London performance of Mahler's Ninth Symphony. (Harty and the Hallé had given it in Manchester in February 1930.) This brought the tally of Mahler symphonies heard in London to only five: Henry Wood had given the First in 1903, the Fourth in 1905 and the Eighth in a famous BBC concert in 1930; and Bruno Walter had conducted No. 2, the 'Resurrection', with the Queen's Hall Orchestra in 1931. Boult had included the Fourth and *Das Lied von der Erde* in his Birmingham concerts, but the composer's reputation was by no means established by the time of this London première of the Ninth. *The Times* was moved to a substantial leader: 'MAHLER: THE LISTENER'S ORDEAL. The ghost of Gustav Mahler walks abroad; it hovers about the concert halls, haunts the brains of ambitious conductors, troubles the uneasy consciences of English audiences . . .' After detailing the full challenges the composer made to his audience, it concluded that the BBC 'sooner or later, in its own good time . . . will no doubt give us the complete series, one a week for ten weeks . . . It may be an ordeal for the listener, but no less extreme course will lay the spectre of a misprized genius.' As for the work, it was found to be strange, but undeniably great. *Musical Opinion*: 'No venture on the part of Adrian Boult and the BBC Orchestra has been more completely justified than the first performance in London of Mahler's Ninth Symphony . . . it is worth all the performances the BBC can give it.' Constant Lambert was typically astute (*Sunday Referee*, 11 February): '. . . here is that rare thing, a modern work which is genuinely difficult to understand. People should distinguish between music which is difficult to understand and music which is difficult to get used to . . . [the work reveals] a mind of remarkable originality.'

The remaining February 1934 concerts brought Busoni's remarkable Concerto for Piano, Male Voice Chorus and Orchestra, under Boult with Egon Petri, on 21 February. The most enthusiastic response to this piece came from the composer Sorabji, writing in the *New English Weekly*: 'Of a work in every way so stupendous, so absolutely original, so wholly *sui generis*, and of a performance so transcendental, so authentically inspired, it is hard to write clearly.' (And Sorabji indeed did not do so.) On 28 February Ansermet conducted a curious programme including Debussy's *La Mer* and Elgar's *Enigma Variations*; the last three concerts of the season brought Bax's First Symphony (under Wood, 21 March), Holst's Choral Symphony (under Boult, 11 April) and Walton's Viola Concerto (under Boult, 18 April, in which the principal viola of the Symphony Orchestra, Bernard Shore, stood in with great success for the indisposed Lionel Tertis). Fritz Busch visited the Orchestra, giving an outstanding studio concert on 4 March which included Mozart's *Linz* Symphony – a superb, flexible performance which was also issued on record.

The end of the season was dominated by the first complete performance in Britain, on 14 March, of Alban Berg's opera *Wozzeck*: the culmination of Edward Clark's work within the BBC on behalf of the Second Viennese School in this country, and one of the musical landmarks of the interwar period in Britain. Rehearsals occupied some three months; with the exception of Richard Bitterauf as Wozzeck, all the soloists were English: May Blyth sang the part of Marie; the cast also included Walter Widdop, Tudor Davies, Parry Jones and Mary Jarred. They were coached by Kurt Prerauer, a young répétiteur from Berlin, who had taken part in the production of the opera there. The orchestra had some eighteen three-hour rehearsals over a three-week period. In spite of this, Boult recalls being told by a friend from the Vienna Opera, to whom he showed the rehearsal schedule: 'My friend, I know your orchestra, I know you, I know *Wozzeck*. You will have to postpone your performance. It cannot be done.' But Boult went ahead, and it was done. In 1979 the letter which Berg wrote to Boult after the broadcast was published for the first time:

> I am longing to tell you how yesterday's *Wozzeck* performance delighted me . . . It equalled the finest stage performances with the work in the regular repertoire . . . The greatest happiness of all, perhaps, is the implied understanding with which this (one might say) up to then strange music was revealed. That is owing first of all to you, dear Mr Boult, and your strong shaping revealed through the whole performance; but then to your unique orchestra, and to the musically and vocally outstanding singers!

Only one matter concerned Berg: that the whole effort had been mounted for a single performance. In fact the BBC attempted to remedy this (and the widespread criticism that it was difficult to judge the work from a concert performance) by offering it complete and free of charge to Covent Garden. But the cost to Covent Garden of providing even scenery was prohibitive; the project failed.

Public opinion was generally favourable to the performance. There was a large audience in the hall. Though the *Daily Telegraph* publicised the complaint of a listener who rang up the BBC to enquire 'whether hyenas were loose', the paper received several appreciative letters, from Cyril Scott and, less expectedly, from Sir Richard Terry. An impressive tape of part of the performance survives in the BBC's sound archives; it corroborates the comments of the press:

> This performance was a remarkable achievement by all concerned, and most of all by Dr Boult and the BBC Orchestra, who played it with an assurance which made every moment musically clear. (*The Times*)
>
> The BBC Orchestra and Dr Adrian Boult as Conductor seemed to be playing the elaborate and difficult music as if they had known it for years. (*Glasgow Herald*)

London Music Festival 1934

The London Music Festival in May was shared between Boult (three concerts), Bruno Walter (two concerts) and Felix Weingartner (one concert). There was scarcely anything of festival importance in the programmes, and the press was quick to criticise the 'totally unnecessary and flamboyant title' (*Musical Opinion*). The *Musical Times* said it was 'in sober truth a series of six concerts of no more than average interest in respect of programmes but of more than average value as regards execution'. The main item of interest was a repeat of an earlier event. Hindemith's oratorio *Das Unaufhörliche* was mounted again, this time conducted by Boult.

To be fair, that the programmes were not more interesting was not entirely the BBC's fault. The original plan was to build the festival around two important British premières: that of Elgar's Third Symphony, and that of the new Symphony by William Walton. Elgar had died with his Symphony incomplete (see pp. 80–2): such fragments of the work as Elgar's friend W. H. Reed gathered together were handed over to the BBC by Elgar's daughter in November 1934. They were publicised by the BBC in a *Listener* supplement to commemorate Elgar, and in the same month were placed on indefinite loan in the British Museum. The composer Granville Bantock offered his services to Boult should it be decided to try and complete the Symphony posthumously. Walton's Symphony was also unfinished. The composer had many problems with finding a satisfactory conclusion to the work, and it was performed for the first time by Harty and the London Symphony Orchestra on 3 December of that year without its finale. The BBC was to give the first complete performance in the following season.

In the third concert on 9 May there was a modest novelty in the form of an overture by Cyril Scott which had won a competition organised by the *Daily Telegraph* and judged by Sir Henry Wood, Sir Hamilton Harty, Frank Bridge and Arthur Bliss. The Overtures were submitted anonymously: Cyril Scott's won first place over contributions by Frank Tapp and Arnold Cooke; among seven further commendations were pieces by William Alwyn, Grace Williams and Eric Fogg. This same concert also featured Vladimir Horowitz in an electrifying performance of the Tchaikovsky First Concerto: an occasion the pianist clearly enjoyed. He very probably communicated his enthusiasm about the Orchestra to his father-in-law, who in the following year was to become the Symphony Orchestra's most distinguished guest conductor: Arturo Toscanini.

The engagement of Bruno Walter for the Festival raised a problem that the BBC had not so far encountered, and it took them by surprise. The Corporation was accustomed to booking the services of the most distinguished soloists available, informing rather than seeking the permission of the conductor in question. For one of Walter's May concerts it secured the services of the famous German pianist Wilhelm Backhaus. Much to the BBC's consternation, Walter wrote in great agitation on 11 March that he could not possibly perform with Backhaus: 'He is a "Nazi" in a very decided and pronounced way, official favourite of Hitler . . .' The BBC attempted to persuade him to change his conscience, using the disarming phrase '. . . the political situation in Germany is not recognised in London music circles'. But Walter wrote back immediately: . . . 'there is remaining in myself a very strong resistance against a collaboration with a fellow-being in sympathy with the most anti-spiritual (and in consequence anti-artistic) system of our times.' The BBC must have tried again, for five days later, having had the difficulties of replacement explained to him, Walter wrote cautiously: 'It goes without saying that I would not make any difficulty, if it is unavoidable to have Backhaus in my concert.' But then the BBC agreed with Walter a compromise solution; he would not conduct the last concert of his three, the one in which Backhaus was to appear; Felix Weingartner would take it over. Walter gratefully accepted the idea, and wrote on 22 March to thank the BBC. On 4 April he thought it wise to add 'it is absolutely necessary that the reason of the cancellation of this concert must not transpire, or better, that it will be replaced by another one.'

It is curious that Walter, so close to Boult and so admired by the Orchestra, returned to the BBC so little in the years between 1934 and the war. Walter seemed resigned, but sad, and wrote to Boult in 1936, 'My standpoint in a question like this is the calmest in the world. If there is the wish to make use of my way of making music I will be asked and I do not wish to be asked if this wish is not strong enough. All my life I have felt in this way . . .' Boult did ask once more, in 1938 (see pp. 144–5), but narrow-minded BBC colleagues turned down his proposal.

Press enthusiasm during the Festival was saved as usual not for interesting music but for a 'great classical conductor', as the *Daily Telegraph* described Weingartner. 'No finer ending to the BBC's series . . . could have been planned', wrote *The Times*. Particular praise was lavished upon his 'classical and undistorted reading' of Beethoven's Fifth Symphony, which gave 'an impression of unswerving directness'.

1934–5

After the success of Weingartner's visit it must have seemed to the Music Department that there was pressure to make the Symphony Orchestra a glamorous competitor in the field of great performances of the classics rather than to develop its advocacy of new and neglected music. In the 1934–5 season Boult had five concerts, Hamilton Harty, Weingartner and Albert Coates one each, and Henry Wood had two. But each concert had its point and purpose, and there were two concerts of special interest: an all-Stravinsky evening at which the composer would appear; and one which included the British première of Berg's Symphonic Excerpts from his opera *Lulu*. There was one other major première in the season, Vaughan Williams' Symphony in F minor. Clark had built the programmes with his usual skill and care for balance: there were two nicely thematic evenings. One was on 31

October – Holst's *Planets*, Scriabin's *Prometheus*, and Strauss's *Also sprach Zarathustra*, quickly dubbed a 'Mystical Evening with the BBC Symphony Orchestra'. The other was on 23 January, a Russian programme – Borodin's Second Symphony, Tchaikovsky's Violin Concerto, and a novelty in the form of a Symphony by Yuri Shaporin (which had been written for the fifteenth anniversary of the Revolution, and sounded to many distinctly nostalgic for the Russia of Mussorgsky and Glazunov).

The opening concert on 24 September became a memorial to Delius who died on 10 June in a year which also saw the deaths of Elgar and Holst. Beecham was to conduct *A Mass of Life*. Though distinguished foreign soloists had been engaged to sing the Mass in German for once, and detailed annotations prepared, Beecham suddenly decided to revert to the English text: Astra Desmond and Roy Henderson replaced Olga Haley and Hermann Nissen. The Stravinsky evening drew a large audience to the Queen's Hall. The popular Fantasia *Fireworks* was added to a programme which already included the composer playing his *Capriccio* once again, and the *Firebird* Suite. But the major interest centred on the melodrama *Perséphone*, presented in concert performance with declamations by the dancer for whom the piece was intended, Ida Rubinstein. Once again, the BBC was criticised for going only half-way: those who failed to understand the music thought they might have been able to do so had Madame Rubinstein been allowed to dance.

Boult, who had been conducting in America, returned to the Queen's Hall on 6 February, and included in the concert a Scherzo by Gustav Holst. It had been sketched in 1933 and dictated to pupils at the end of his life; this was the first performance. The piece was enjoyed as a cheerful, untypical footnote to Holst's work. Beecham, who was busy with the Royal Philharmonic Society season, withdrew from his Handel concert on 20 February, and Boult conducted this 250th anniversary tribute, which included *Acis and Galatea* complete.

On 20 March, the extracts from Berg's *Lulu* were given a less than lukewarm welcome by an audience of composers, musicians and few others. But Neville Cardus in the *Manchester Guardian* rose to the occasion:

> . . . probably he is the most potent force we have known in music since Wagner . . . Nobody has put into music with Berg's stark horror the suggestion of the blood-red moon and the slow, hideous corruption of the soul and body . . . The rhythm of the closing scene of *Lulu*'s epilogue is simple and shattering . . . The BBC Orchestra played the score cleverly, but as though afraid it might explode at any moment . . .

This concert also included the first broadcast ever by Jascha Heifetz, in a Mozart concerto.

On 27 March Weingartner introduced to this country his completion of Schubert's Symphony in E, from the Royal College of Music's manuscript (which was once, it was said, lost on a suburban train and had turned up at Norwood Junction). Only recently had the Symphony's existence been acknowledged by renumbering the Great C major as No. 9. Finally, on 10 April under Boult, came the Vaughan Williams Fourth Symphony. Those expecting typically pastoral Vaughan Williams were to be severely shocked. The work turned out to be 'curiously unlike the music usually associated with his name. There is nothing vague and dreamy about it. On the contrary, it is essentially vigorous and precise, at times almost aggressively so' (Francis Toye in the *Morning Post*). There was widespread bafflement. Only Edwin Evans saw the piece for what it was: 'the strongest work its composer has so far given us . . . it established beyond all question his title to rank with the foremost composers in Europe today' (*Daily Mail*, 11 April). Neville Cardus was less prescient:

> I could not, for all my admiration of its parts, believe that it is likely to be listened to twenty years from today . . . The music fails to warm the senses or to enter the mind as an utterance of conviction . . . The symphony commands admiration at once, but not a reaction more enthusiastic . . . The playing of the BBC Orchestra and the conducting of Dr Adrian Boult in a strange score were beyond praise.

Vaughan Williams' tribute to Boult was generous: 'Adrian *created* the slow movement. I didn't know how it should go, but he did.'

To Maida Vale

The Symphony Orchestra had finally moved into its new home in Maida Vale at the start of the 1934–5 season. Broadcasting House had been too small for the BBC from the moment it was opened, and its Concert Hall could not accommodate the full Symphony Orchestra. So a search had begun for a site which would provide extensive studio space for orchestral music, and eventually a disused roller-skating rink was found in Delaware Road, in Maida Vale. In the rebuilding that followed, this was reduced to its shell – only the outer walls were left standing – and an entirely separate construction was built inside, providing five studios built on the most modern lines. Solid brickwork partitions gave sound-proofing between the studios, all of which were below ground level. The BBC said, carefully guarding its trade secrets, that 'in the construction of these new studios, the opportunity has been taken to try out some recent ideas in studio acoustics'. The main studio, Maida Vale I, has been, from that day to this, the chief home of the Orchestra. It has seen many changes in its plan – chorus rostra have appeared and disappeared, lighting, heating and air conditioning have been improved, an organ has been installed – and it has formed an indispensable part of the Orchestra's life, disliked by some, tolerated by many. When it was opened, however, it was a miracle of BBC science: the Corporation's largest London studio (220,000 cubic feet, twice the size of the Broadcasting House Concert Hall), with a sophisticated control room adjoining, so that the relay of broadcasts could be controlled directly. The Orchestra broadcast its first concert from the studios on 16 October 1934, immediately after the finishing touches had been put to the conversion and the recording equipment had been installed.

Around Britain and abroad

It was to be expected that the provincial visits undertaken by the Symphony Orchestra in the 1934–5 season would once again rouse the objections to the BBC's interference with local music-making and to unfair competition which had been heard since 1930. But not even the most pessimistic spirits within the Music Department were prepared for the reaction to the Orchestra's proposed concert in Manchester on 5 December 1934. Though the visit had been informally cleared with the Chairman of the Hallé Concerts Society, E.W. Grommé, there was opposition from the Hallé Committee, and ill-feeling was undoubtedly communicated to the regular Hallé audience. Matters were not helped by the close involvement of Beecham in the Hallé's affairs at the time: he used every opportunity to complain about the BBC, in spite of the fact that the Hallé administration was anxious not to prejudice the arrangement whereby Hallé members ensured a reasonable income for themselves by also playing in the BBC's Northern Orchestra. But the prominent local musicians of Manchester in the Hallé and the Manchester College of Music closed ranks. In spite of the appropriate presentation of Mancunian Arthur Catterall as a soloist, there was a tiny audience at the Free Trade Hall for the BBC's concert: on the morning of the concert there were rumours in the *Daily Express* of 'peaceful picketing by Manchester musicians', and the *Manchester Evening Chronicle* quoted a Hallé official as saying 'the public has a right to hear the orchestra, and we have no power to stop them'. The *Daily Dispatch* opened its columns to a long article by Boult, praising the Hallé's pre-eminence among the orchestras of the 1920s, and asking, 'May not the time have arrived when the spread of good music by radio has broken down any insularity in this matter of musical prowess?' But to no avail; on the night the orchestra was, said the *Evening Chronicle*, 'nearly as big as the audience'. The programme, a good concoction of largely twentieth-century music by living composers, included Strauss's *Ein Heldenleben*, Ireland's *Mai-Dun* Rhapsody, Hindemith's Philharmonic Concerto, and ended with Ravel's *Bolero*. From the local press there was unanimous, enthusiastic praise of the orchestra: '. . . for brilliance of execution it could hardly be excelled. The BBC tour certainly sets up a new example' (*Liverpool Post and Mercury*).

The affair of the Manchester visit was not over. Boult later commented to the Press: 'We enjoyed our visit to Manchester enormously; the audience was most intelligent and extremely interested, but we were decisively told in many quarters to keep off the Hallé orchestra's "grass" here' (*Daily Dispatch*, 9 October 1935). And a report that Boult had said the visit was a success brought this barbed response from R. J. Forbes, Principal of the Royal Manchester College of Music, in a letter to the *Daily Telegraph* on 13 February 1935:

> It would be interesting to know what criterion of success Dr Boult has adopted in arriving at that conclusion. It cannot be the box-office one . . . And in view of Dr Boult's expressed solicitude 'that there should be no suspicion of encroachment on local preserves', it would be interesting to know whether this new orientation of the BBC's public musical activities was considered and approved by the Corporation's Music Advisory Committee . . .

Sir Walford Davies replied with an elegant letter (18 February) which implied as deftly as possible that there had been an enormous argument about the matter in the Committee when it was discussed on 7 June 1934:

> I myself felt a paramount anxiety for the welfare of the centres visited, and I know this anxiety was vividly shared by Dr Boult. My colleagues, with far more experience than I of possible difficulties and dangers in the experiment, could not have felt less (though I find it hard to think they could feel more) solicitous about it than I did. In the case of Manchester, we were informed that the Chairman of the Hallé Society had been approached and had indicated his approval . . .

The second concert in the Colston Hall, Bristol, was far more successful: the programme was popular. A visit to Birmingham on 27 February was, as befitted the town where Boult conducted in the 1920s, a sell-out. The programme, another Clark/Herbage mixture, was out of the ordinary: Bach's 'St Anne' Fugue arranged by Schoenberg; the Brahms Fourth Symphony; Busoni's Two Studies for *Doktor Faust*; Delius's Dance Rhapsody No. 1, and Ravel's *Bolero* – some of which works had not been previously heard in Birmingham. Boult received especial praise for his conducting of the Delius.

The last of these provincial visits took the Orchestra to Dundee. Boult talked to the local press on the afternoon of the concert:

> . . . we do not seem to be wanted in Glasgow or Edinburgh . . . The idea seems to be that we would be doing harm to existing orchestras . . . I will leave it to other opinions to judge whether it is a sensible argument that a single visit to the BBC Symphony Orchestra to either of these cities in the course of a season would have the effect claimed.

Of the Caird Hall, Boult said: 'We could do with it in London, and that, I think, is the greatest praise I can give it.' Again local taste was considered in the programme: a Scottish Lament, *Coronach*, by the Dundee-born composer David Stephen (born 1869) was included. Wagner's *Flying Dutchman* Overture was also broadcast from the rehearsal during Scottish Children's Hour. The audience numbered 3000, including many, it was said, from Glasgow and Edinburgh.

To Brussels

For the Orchestra these visits were overshadowed by its first appearance abroad, on 12 March 1935, in the Grande Salle du Palais des Beaux-Arts, Brussels. The Orchestra travelled by train from Victoria on the afternoon of 11 March; their instruments were taken across in a four-ton lorry and a pantechnicon, travelling on the train ferry. The weather was extremely cold, but the orchestra played well and the concert was sold out. BBC diplomatic connections ensured a high-level audience for the concert. The King of the Belgians was represented by the Comte de Jonghe d'Ardoye. The Minister for Fine Arts, M. Herniaux, was there. The British Ambassador, Sir Esmond Ovey, and Lady Ovey were present, and held a reception for the Orchestra to meet Belgian musicians after the concert. The programme, once again, compels admiration as a model of its kind: framed by showpieces for the Orchestra (Weber's *Oberon* Overture and the favourite Ravel *Daphnis and Chloe* Suite No. 2) were two English works, the Vaughan Williams Fantasia on a theme of Thomas Tallis and Delius's *In a Summer Garden*; one classic, Beethoven's Seventh Symphony; and one Belgian work, *La Mer* by Paul Gilson. The Brussels Press was swept away by enthusiasm: Paul Tinel in *Le Soir* said the orchestra could compare with those of Berlin, Vienna and Amsterdam. Ernest Closson in the *Indépendance Belge* exclaimed, 'Superb in its ensemble, colour and shading!' and the British works were enjoyed even by one critic who was surprised to find that they 'showed not the least trace of that horrible jazz which passes for the only true English music'! The great success of this appearance confirmed enthusiasm in London among the Music Advisory Committee for full-scale Continental tour; and indeed, in a five year plan submitted to the Governors and accepted by them, a Continental tour was proposed for each of the years 1935 to 1940.

Toscanini

The culmination of the Orchestra's first five years of existence came in the 1935 London Music Festival, held between 10 May and 14 June. For the first time this season justified its title, bringing together three outstanding conductors, Boult, Koussevitsky, and – on his first appearance ever with a British orchestra, and only his second appearance ever in London (he had come in 1930 with the New York Philharmonic) – Arturo Toscanini.

Boult had arranged a special week's holiday over Easter for the Orchestra to prepare for the exceptional strain of the Festival. It began with Bach's B minor Mass under Boult, followed by three Koussevitsky concerts and four Toscanini concerts, all within a month. To say that apprehension was the main emotion of the members (and administrators) of the BBC Symphony Orchestra in the days before 3 June 1935 would be an understatement. They were terrified. Stories of Toscanini's violent behaviour had been common: it was reported that he frequently flew into rages, broke batons, threw scores on the ground, and in one famous legend was supposed to have broken a leader's violin over his head. The Orchestra was fully prepared; it expected the worst.

The tension was most effectively maintained by Koussevitsky, who at his rehearsals alluded repeatedly to the horrors supposedly in store for the Orchestra. But he worked relentlessly on his own programmes, raised the standards of the Orchestra, and wrought it into a height of responsiveness, which in fact prepared the ground ideally for Toscanini. Bernard Shore records Koussevitsky's phrases: 'Pianissimo must always have substance and arrive at the audience! Vibrato! Always vibrato in pianissimo!' 'Sing! Always sing your phrases! There is no music without singing!' In rehearsal, the first two chords of the Eroica Symphony were repeated insistently to attain the desired effect of rage and violence. In the concert, Koussevitsky's energy galvanised the audience. 'The Eroica was presented as a magnificently organic whole, robust and dignified and of noble proportions' (*Daily Telegraph*, 18 May). 'One of the finest performances of Sibelius's Second Symphony that we have yet heard . . . glowed with rare vitality' (*Morning Post*, 18 May). At the third concert 'Stravinsky's *The Rite of Spring* had its periodic try-out, to receive probably the best performance of its career . . .' (*Musical*

Times). He also included the Tchaikovsky Sixth Symphony and, surprisingly, two English works, the Vaughan Williams Fantasia on a theme of Thomas
Tallis, and Holst's Fugal Concerto. The *Musical Times* summed up the week
well: 'But for what followed, Koussevitsky's three concerts would have been
the outstanding memory of the 1935 season' (July 1935).

Toscanini's first concert was on 3 June. He arrived at Claridge's, where he
was looked after by Owen Mase of the Music Department, who was as a result to become a vital link in the chain that brought Toscanini back to England. Boult went to collect the conductor for his first rehearsal: 'I think we
all felt that Toscanini's coming was the culmination and goal of the BBC
Orchestra's career, and we felt it to be concentrated in his first rehearsal. I
was more nervous than I have ever been – even fetching him from Claridge's
was a nightmare because he too was always desperately nervous before meeting an orchestra for the first time.' Meanwhile the Orchestra gathered in
Queen's Hall, as their former chairman Alex Nifosi remembered: '. . . We
trooped on to the platform at Queen's Hall expecting almost anything . . .'

Toscanini began with Brahms's Fourth Symphony: a work that the Orchestra knew from countless performances under Boult. The work was
played with scarcely any interruption. The tension grew – stories were
recollected of a continental rehearsal of the Eroica which proceeded in silence
for the first two movements, only to end after the scherzo with an outburst
from Toscanini that he would not conduct unless five or six members of the
orchestra were replaced: the concert was postponed for a week while the
changes were made. Yet on this occasion, there were no outbursts. Boult
recalls that Toscanini said: '"*Bene, bene, bene*. Just three things." He then
found these three passages, put them right, and went straight on.'

Toscanini immediately won the Orchestra's admiration and respect, and
he found them better prepared than even he could have hoped. Alex Nifosi
says that

> a great factor in Toscanini's decision to come over to conduct the BBC
> Symphony Orchestra was his knowledge of our training under Sir Adrian.
> He knew that if he came to work for the BBC he would find an orchestra well
> used to an architectural approach to the classics . . . He and Sir Adrian have a
> similar feeling for the great architectural span of these big symphonies.
> They are different of course: Toscanini even in the great German classics
> imparts something of Mediterranean warmth into them, while Sir Adrian
> aims for a more restrained reading, but building up, also with meticulous
> adherence to the score, to a spacious but equally exciting climax.

The comparison is important. Toscanini had demanded twenty or more rehearsals with the Orchestra, but after his first experience of its readiness to meet his demands, he was able to shorten and drop rehearsals altogether from the schedule. The Orchestra's response was later eloquently described by Bernard Shore:

> In any orchestra accustomed to play under famous conductors there are players ready to criticise and make damaging comparisons. The spirits of Richter and Nikisch are called up in the last resort if the conductor under discussion cannot be belittled by comparison with a living colleague. But against Toscanini even those great names are powerless. Toscanini is the one living conductor whom every single member of the orchestra approves.
>
> Under Toscanini orchestral playing becomes a different art. He stimulates his men, refreshes their minds; and music that has become stale is revived in all its pristine beauty. Rehearsals are looked forward to. There is never a moment of dullness – everything is far too concentrated and vital – nor is there any vain repetition. The time-factor disappears. Sheer physical fatigue takes the place of the clock, which is so often watched hopefully when work is dull.
>
> After a stiff piece of detailed rehearsing Toscanini will say, 'Non va male! Bitte, da capo, from the beginning.' Such a demand from a boring conductor might bring a groan from the orchestra, which would suspect that the repetition was merely to afford him personal pleasure, or even just to fill up time. But with Toscanini there is no wasting a moment. Rehearsals finish as soon as he feels there is no more to be done. He is never satisfied, but he seems to have an exact picture of the utmost any orchestra can achieve. His continual striving for perfection is felt to apply to himself rather than to spring from dissatisfaction with the orchestra. If he cannot please himself he does not allow the players to feel they are to blame.
>
> Giving out an intense vitality himself, he expects no less in return, but he realises when the players are fatigued and he does not drive them harder than himself. When a sign of flagging shows he immediately breaks off and suggests a cigarette. Almost dead-beat himself at the end of two grilling hours over the *Pastoral* Symphony, he said: 'I am tired now, and I am sure you are, too. Let us rest.'

The first concert included Brahms's Fourth Symphony, Cherubini's *Anacreon* Overture, Siegfried's Death and Funeral March from Wagner's *Götterdämmerung*, and Elgar's *Enigma Variations*. In 1930 with the New York Philharmonic, Toscanini had given this last work, in a reading which – based entirely on the score rather than on English performance tradition – was thought strange. Now, with the BBC Orchestra, he gave a performance which impressed everyone for its authenticity and total conviction. The highest imprimatur was bestowed by Elgar's self-appointed defender, Sir Landon Ronald, in a letter to *The Times*:

> Sir: I have been constantly told that Elgar's music is so English in character and feeling that it could only be really understood and interpreted by one of his own countrymen. I have always strenuously denied this. Last Monday's magnificent performance of the *Enigma Variations* by Toscanini has, I lay claim, proved me to be correct. I maintain that Elgar did not write English music – whatever that may be; he wrote great music. On Monday at last a great foreign conductor proved this.

This encyclical was blessed by a long *Times* leader two days later, and a letter of agreement from Boult was published. Toscanini had united the establishment, the orchestral players, the critics and the concert-going public in a rare unanimity of praise. Neville Cardus in the *Manchester Guardian*:

> Tonight Toscanini has given his first concert with the BBC Orchestra, and it has been a musical experience of the rarest and finest kind – not, indeed, merely a concert but a revelation of the wonder and nobility of music and genius. . . . Here is the most powerful and personal, not to say tyrannical, conductor of them all, a man whose command over the orchestra is greater than that of all the virtuosi put together – and yet he is the one conductor in the world who is never an exhibitionist, never more concerned with Toscanini than with the masters whose works he serves like a priest . . .

'AN HISTORIC CONCERT', headlined the *Daily Telegraph*. Toscanini was quoted as saying afterwards: 'I am very very happy, very pleased and satisfied with everything. The people have been very charming.'

Toscanini's programmes were in two pairs of two. On 5 June the Wagner and Brahms were repeated, with the addition of Wagner's *Faust* Overture, the Good Friday Music and Prelude from *Parsifal*. On both 12 and 14 June he gave Beethoven's Seventh Symphony and Debussy's *La Mer*; the first concert was completed by a Geminiani Concerto Grosso and Rossini's *Semiramide* Overture; the second by Mozart's *Haffner* Symphony and Mendelssohn's *A Midsummer Night's Dream* Nocturne and Scherzo. Of the last concert, the *Daily Telegraph* proclaimed: 'TOSCANINI'S TRIUMPH. UNFORGETTABLE LAST CONCERT. A MATCHLESS ARTIST.' J.A. Westrup wrote that the conductor was 'an artist who has given London so rare an opportunity of understanding and appreciating all that music can mean – its riches and strengths.' In the *Manchester Guardian* on 7 June, Neville Cardus again powerfully summed up the universal praise:

> The concerts . . . are the most important events that have occurred for years
> in the orchestral life of this country. . . . Toscanini makes us believe in the
> objective reality of the score . . . he observes the markings diligently, and the
> effect we feel, if we know the score well, is that the performance is giving life
> and motion to a perfect photograph. . . . His understanding of style is know-
> ledge plus imagination . . . It is difficult to believe that he will not leave
> behind him a strong, lasting, influence on our standards.

In a rare press interview on the final day of his visit, Toscanini declared
himself delighted. 'It is one of the best orchestras I have ever conducted . . .
I like London audiences.' He praised the orchestra's discipline, its leader
Arthur Catterall, and (at the BBC's suggestion?) made a strong plea that the
Orchestra should continue to appear in public, because it would go stale if
confined to the studio. At the press conference Boult said that he hoped
Toscanini would return next year; the conductor replied: 'I would very
much like to if the BBC are willing.' Boult immediately said, 'We would be
very willing', and a provisional bargain was struck. Toscanini expressed the
wish to conduct a choral work, since he had heard so much about English
choral singing. And so ended a visit which had undoubtedly established the
position of the BBC Symphony Orchestra at the centre of Britain's musical
and orchestral life. It had been a triumph.

3

International Fame
1935-39

Ullswater

The success of the BBC Symphony Orchestra in the first four seasons did not make it immune from criticism. On the contrary, at the same time as the Orchestra reached its greatest achievements in 1935 with its first continental visit and its concerts under Toscanini, the whole organisation of the BBC Music Department and the Symphony Orchestra was exposed to extensive scrutiny. For at the end of 1936 the BBC's charter was due to expire. In 1935 the Ullswater Committee was set up to make a public inquiry into the BBC with a view to recommending 'the conditions under which the service, including broadcasting to the Empire, television broadcasting and the system of wireless exchanges should be conducted'. It was a comprehensive inquiry, and music as a major part of all broadcasting was clearly to constitute a substantial section of the investigation. What is more, it would clearly provide an opportunity for those interests in the country which felt they had been harmed by the growth of music broadcasting to state their case. This they did with some force, under the banner of the Incorporated Society of Musicians (which had led the opposition from the Royal Philharmonic Society and elsewhere to the public activities of the BBC Symphony Orchestra). As Asa Briggs has written:

> Behind much of the evidence, which at its best was evidence not against the BBC but against broadcasting, was a tacit assumption that all had been well with music before the advent of the BBC – a parody of the truth – and that there was a certain lump of musical activity which had to be fairly shared out between a number of existing interests. The BBC was an interloper, and what it did was to disturb the shares. . . . This was almost as wild a protectionist remark as the assertion that Children's Hour broadcasts had destroyed the sale of children's books.

The weight of unfavourable evidence against the BBC came from estab-

110

lished musical interests, and those interests were already fully represented within the BBC on its Music Advisory Committee. The tension between the Music Department, Reith and the Committee has already been described, and this had come to a head in the year preceding the Ullswater Committee.

Sir John McEwen protested in August 1934 that not enough was being done for British artists, and he drew a passionate defence of BBC policy from Kenneth Wright (in a memo to Roger Eckersley, 15 August), who wrote of 'our earnest desire to break away from this unoriginal, unenterprising system of building programmes in favour of an entirely new and undoubtedly financially risky policy of making the programmes of outstanding musical interest'. The planning had to be long-term, he said, and only the BBC could afford it. But the Committee returned to the attack in February 1935, trying to push through a policy statement that public concerts should aim at large audiences. Boult wrote with restrained bafflement to Reith: 'Out of context this document might equally well serve for a statement of policy of an out-and-out commercialist like Mr Harold Holt.' McEwen wrote an article in *The Music Journal* in February 1935 again pleading support for British artists, and wrote to Reith on 4 March in a tone which perfectly sums up the attitude of the Committee's members to the BBC: 'I do not have too much confidence in that vague and anonymous body, the Music Department, whose attitude inside the organisation and whose policy with regard to its public activities seem likely to bring neither credit nor betterment to the BBC.' (A good example of the sort of question which preoccupied the Music Advisory Committee may be read in the minutes of their 12 November 1936 meeting, when Landon Ronald 'expressed apprehension of the unfavourable effect in many quarters of the decision to include the pianos of foreign makes in the Corporation's equipment . . . After some dissension the Chairman read out the actual remarks of the judges [on the subcommittee who chose the pianos] to the various makes included in the tests.')

Boult patiently explained the BBC's policy once again to the Committee on 3 June, basing himself on Reith's famous formulation of 'giving the public something rather better than it thinks it wants': 'Our central aim remains in accordance with this maxim to guide musical opinion' – a view which cannot have found favour with the members of the Committee, who aimed to reflect opinion, not to guide it. Boult gave as the best possible example Henry Wood's Prom programmes, and said that

> we look on our public concerts as the apex of our work, concerts where we give our best performances, where we include the greatest artists, and where we give the public the great classics together with such novelties as we consider to be of first-class importance.

The BBC, he said, would prefer not to give public concerts rather than lower their standard. By August feeling was at its height. Eckersley wrote to Cecil Graves, now Controller of Programmes, with a strong plea to dissolve the Music Advisory Committee (21 August):

> I do not consider that they have ever helped us in a crisis . . . I have usually found them obstructive in their attitude, and the very fact of their presence has often held up urgent matters . . . I cannot think that their advice has always been disinterested.

At this, Boult drew back, and writing to Eckersley on 23 August agreed that

> the Music Advisory Committee is a source of friction which is very trying to all concerned, but I cannot help feeling that by their opposition they have occasionally helped us to modify a scheme and have therefore saved us from more public trouble. . . . The existence of the Music Advisory Committee is a safeguard . . .

This is typical of Boult's sane caution in the face of provocation. And Reith agreed with him, saying that Ullswater was anyway bound to recommend the Committee's retention.

In his report to the Ullswater Committee, however, Boult felt free to criticise the Committee fiercely:

> . . . I place a high value on the disinterested advice of the senior members of the music profession, but I seldom get that advice from the Music Advisory Committee, of which Sir Hugh Allen, Sir John McEwen, and Sir Landon Ronald are all members . . .

Boult's whole rejoinder to the music profession's evidence makes unusually powerful reading. It was fully supported by Reith, who had been horrified by the evidence which the Incorporated Society of Musicians submitted to Ullswater. He called it in his diary 'a monstrous document', and noted that 'I saw Walford Davies in the afternoon and he rang up the Secretary [of the ISM] to get a copy, but Eames refused to give it to him. This shows what a dirty game they are playing.' And in his autobiography *Into the Wind* Reith recalled his admiration for Boult, who went to the Committee and 'so flabbergasted them by saying at once that other witnesses had been telling lies, that they let it go at that'. Boult's written evidence shows he did just that:

> I am astonished at the inaccuracy of the statements of most of my colleagues in the musical profession who have given evidence before the Committee . . . they show an extraordinary lack of understanding of the primary purpose for

Early days: a BBC string orchestra rehearsing at Savoy Hill under Percy Pitt in the late 1920s

Percy Pitt, the BBC's first Director of Music, who retired in 1930

Roger Eckersley, who as the BBC's Controller of Programmes played a major part in the foundation of the BBC Symphony Orchestra

The BBC's new orchestra: a portrait of the BBC Symphony Orchestra with Dr Adrian Boult in the Queen's Hall, 1930. This publicity photograph must have been taken before the season began; Boult always placed the second violin section on the right of the stage and the cello section in the centre

Dr Adrian Boult, Director of Music and Chief Conductor of the BBC Symphony Orchestra, in 1934

Foreign visitors: three of the distinguished conductors Boult invited to conduct the Orchestra in the 1930s. Above: Serge Koussevitsky, rehearsing in Queen's Hall for the London Music Festival, May 1935. Below left, Willem Mengelberg; right, Bruno Walter

Arturo Toscanini conducts a British orchestra for the first time. A rehearsal with the BBC Symphony Orchestra for the London Music Festival, June 1935

A memorable farewell: as the BBC Symphony Orchestra leaves Vienna for Budapest on its first Continental tour in 1936, members of the Vienna Philharmonic gather on the platform to offer their thanks to Boult for the visit (above), and to play out the train with The Blue Danube *(below)*

Toscanini triumphs: after his BBC concerts in October 1938, Toscanini and his wife say farewell before sailing to the United States

Responsibilities of office: serious BBC officials in 1935. Cecil Graves, Controller (Programmes), Roger Eckersley, Controller (Entertainment), and (below) Sir John Reith, Director-General

Wartime in Bedford: the BBC Symphony Orchestra in William Walton's Violin Concerto, conducted by the composer with Henry Holst as soloist, November 1941

which the BBC exists, and they still appear to be phenomenally ill-informed
of the Corporation's musical activities.

The most serious charge levelled at the musicians who gave evidence was
that they simply wanted to increase employment in their own profession:

> I claim categorically that no substantial increase in employment can be
> given by the Corporation in the immediate future without lowering the
> standard of its programmes.

To accusations that the BBC had caused orchestral unemployment, Boult
was able to say that

> the Corporation is the greatest employer of musicians that this country has
> ever known. It gives permanent employment to 345 orchestral musicians,
> and this number is shortly to be increased. The latest figures show an average
> of 5500 engagements to British solo artists and 330 to foreign artists per
> annum . . .

Boult showed the large financial subsidies which broadcasting provided for
independent orchestral and other bodies. He pointed to the importance of
the BBC regional studio orchestras in providing employment for those who
formed the nucleus of the public orchestras, the Hallé, City of Birmingham
Symphony Orchestra, and the Belfast Philharmonic; he pointed out that
this cost the BBC £14,000 a year in each centre. It is hard not to hear an echo
of the Symphony Orchestra's visit to Manchester in the next sentence:

> It is amazing that Sir Thomas Beecham, President of the Hallé Society, and
> Mr R.J. Forbes, a member of that Society's Committee, should suppress this
> information when supplying evidence before the Committee.

A substantial part of Boult's document was devoted to refuting the view
that the BBC Symphony Orchestra should not give public concerts; it
covered familiar ground, but some of the stronger formulations are of interest – for these are considered statements to a Government committee, not
merely internal BBC communications:

> The suggestions that the Corporation's public concerts are damaging to
> others are not true, and can only be founded on jealousy. It is perhaps
> inevitable that certain members of the music profession, more particularly
> the prominent ones, should be jealous of the Corporation's undoubted
> achievements and should attempt to deny the value of those achievements,
> at the same time pretending that they are in some way damaging to the
> public interest. Sir Thomas Beecham is a case in point . . . [he has made]

many mis-statements in his evidence before the Committee.

In an important paragraph, Boult summed up what he felt to be the achievement of the BBC and its Symphony Orchestra:

As Music Director of the Corporation, it is a little difficult for me to give an opinion on the Corporation's contribution to the musical life of this country, but as the majority of those who have so far given evidence before the Committee have shown no appreciation of the value of the Corporation's work in this field, I feel it incumbent upon me to do so. Five years ago, prior to the formation of the Corporation's Symphony Orchestra, the reputation of British music and British musicianship abroad was extremely low. Our capital city contained but one orchestra, and that an inferior one. One of our provincial orchestras – the Hallé – was the best that this country could boast. The formation of the Corporation's Symphony Orchestra was the turning point. Symphonic musicians for the first time were offered whole-time contracts under reasonable and humane conditions. They for their parts were prohibited from accepting outside engagements and appointing deputies in their place, an evil system which had become traditional in this country. With this fine Orchestra working under admirable conditions, the Corporation was clearly capable of reaching a standard hitherto undreamt of in this country. At the time it was a matter for regret that the Corporation had to undertake this task independently, rather than in conjunction with existing musical interests; but having undertaken the task, the Corporation did it thoroughly. Five years of steady and patient work have elapsed, during which time a steadily improving standard has been set. Last season the Orchestra left London for the first time, and made four visits to provincial cities with the approval of the local societies, and scored great artistic successes. In March of this year, it made its first visit abroad, and gave one concert in Brussels, as a result of which the continental critics unanimously acclaimed it as the best orchestra in Europe, except for the Berlin Philharmonic Orchestra, with which they classed it. As a result of that one visit abroad, and the impression which it created, the Corporation has already received invitations for the Orchestra to take part in the official series next season in Vienna, Buda Pest and Zürich. Another invitation has come from Florence for a later date. The Orchestra was honoured in June of this year by being conducted by Toscanini, probably the greatest conductor who has ever lived. Toscanini's standard is so high that he will normally conduct none but the world's best orchestras, and his consent to conduct an orchestra is usually in itself a very high compliment indeed. After conducting the first concert, and finding what a highly efficient orchestra it was, he offered to change the final programme of the series so as to include some more difficult works, and even cancelled rehearsals that had already been arranged. After the final concert he expressed the hope that he would be invited again. These facts, and many others, go to show that the Corporation's musical policy, with which a certain number of public concerts are inseparable, is rapidly acquiring for this country a very high musical reputation. British professional musicians will ultimately benefit by it.

The BBC emerged unscathed from the investigation of the Ullswater Committee; its charter was renewed and its monopoly unaffected. But it was still felt to be insufficiently accountable for its actions towards the public: an accusation to which changes at the start of the 1935–6 concert season gave some weight. For the BBC planners had proposed to reduce broadcasts of the Symphony Concerts, confining them to the first hour only. Following a remark by Cecil Graves, Programme Controller, that broadcasts were on the whole too long, the suggestion that Symphony Concerts would be cut was leaked to the *Daily Telegraph*, which received a flood of letters protesting against the possible change.

> There is consternation among wireless licence-holders, and especially among those musicians who are prevented by age from attending concerts, at the BBC proposal. . . . We were under the impression that the BBC Orchestra existed for our benefit, to bring the best music into our homes. . . . Are we to be fobbed off by one grudging hour of symphony? (11 December).

The next day the BBC issued one of its most obfuscatory statements.

> Some of the concerts in the past have been on the long side and it has now been agreed that for Queen's Hall a good length to aim at would be an hour and a quarter...for the first half...and half an hour to three quarters of an hour for the second. But there are bound to be exceptions ... with new music especially the BBC is against cutting ... The time limits suggested above are not hard and fast rules . . .

Which left the question of broadcasts completely open. In fact the decision was not carried through – but a remnant of it can be seen in the fact that only half of each of the Continental tour concerts was broadcast, a fact which gave rise to much ill-feeling during 1936.

For the Orchestra, it was back to work as normal. Marie Wilson had led the Orchestra for the Prom season; Arthur Catterall was devoting an increasing amount of time to solo work. Edward Clark had gathered some fine new works for the Symphony Concerts 1935–6 series: Berg's Three Pieces from the Lyric Suite, to open the season on 23 October; and Bartók's *Cantata profana* (which was first heard in the studio during the Contemporary Series under Aylmer Buesst) to close it on 25 March. In between came two important new British works: Constant Lambert's *Summer's Last Will and Testament* on 29 January, and the first complete performance of the Walton Symphony under Hamilton Harty, who had directed the incomplete première with the London Symphony Orchestra. There was the usual distinguished list of soloists: Flesch, Petri, Hess, Szigeti, Hofmann, Casals, Busch and Tertis. The season was also to include 'Three Special Concerts', devoted to concert performances of stage works.

The series compared very favourably with anything offered by other orchestras in London during the year: the RPS had the première of Bax's Sixth Symphony (played by the London Philharmonic Orchestra), Rachmaninov playing his Paganini Rhapsody, Gordon Jacob's Oboe Concerto, and (perhaps in an attempt to climb on to the Second Viennese bandwagon) Schoenberg's transcription of a Cello Concerto by G. M. Monn – which was greeted with derision. The London Philharmonic Orchestra was content with Dunhill's Symphony in A minor; while the Courtauld–Sargent series premièred Donald Tovey's Cello Concerto (which was unwisely repeated in the BBC's concerts the following season). The question was again posed 'whether London contains a sufficient number of music enthusiasts to justify so many competing activities' (*Annual Register*).

The success of the first part of the season (besides the admirably prompt repeat of the Vaughan Williams' Fourth Symphony on 20 November) was Walton's complete Symphony. The finale was adjudged 'an exceedingly brilliant ending to the scheme' and the symphony as a whole 'has a remarkable eloquence from first to last' (*The Times*, 7 November). Richard Capell found it 'tremendously imposing', and Harty himself took the unusual step of declaring it the finest work of which he had ever given the première. The performance of Purcell's *King Arthur* on 11 December (first of the three special concerts) was much publicised beforehand for an innovation: the Queen's Hall was to be darkened, and the stage floodlit. 'Queen's Hall, when the BBC Music Department have finished with it, will resemble something between a greyhound racing track and a boxing ring,' wrote Jonah Barrington (formerly Cyril Dalmaine, the BBC's sacked Chorus Director of earlier in the 1930s) in the *Daily Express* (3 December). The work had been staged by Dennis Arundell and Cyril Rootham in Cambridge in 1928; the BBC's account, though complete, was in concert form. This project was the brainchild of Julian Herbage, who edited a new version of the score for the performance. Few were found to praise the work in this form; it was thought that the extraneous attractions of staging and dancing were necessary to endure the evening's music. Neville Cardus was perhaps unwisely direct: 'Frankly, the score contains much that few of us would relate to a composer of genius had we not been told by the scholars to do so.' It was to be several years before Herbage's work on behalf of pre-classical composers achieved the respect which it deserved.

The New Year of 1936 was darkened by the death of King George V, only a few months after his Silver Jubilee. The period of mourning coincided with a visit to the Symphony Orchestra by Paul Hindemith. He was to have played his *Der Schwanendreher* on 22 January, but the concert was quickly cancelled. Hindemith recalled the incident in a letter to Willy Strecker:

> There was great despair at the BBC. Boult and Clark wanted me to take part in the concert at all costs – it was held in the studio, not in the Queen's Hall. We debated for hours, but no suitable piece could be found, so we decided that I should write some funeral music myself. As I read yesterday in the newspaper, a studio was cleared for me, copyists were gradually stoked up, and from 11 to 5 I did some fairly hefty mourning. I turned out a nice piece, in the style of *Mathis* and *Schwanendreher* with a Bach chorale at the end (*Vor deinen Thron tret' ich hiermit* – very suitable for kings). It is a tune every child in England knows, though I did not find that out till later. Maybe you know it – they call it 'The Old Hundred' or something like that. We rehearsed it well all yesterday, and in the evening the orchestra played with great devoutness and feeling. It was very moving. Boult was, by English and his own personal standards, quite beside himself, and kept thanking me. I'm now going to specialise in deceased persons – maybe there'll be some more opportunities.

The piece was called *Trauermusik*, and Hindemith played the viola solo himself.

The following week's concert proceeded as planned, with the Constant Lambert première, conducted by the composer. This fifty-minute setting of songs by Thomas Nashe from a 1593 play was thought to be a disappointment after *The Rio Grande*. On 12 February Ansermet returned for Stravinsky's *Oedipus Rex*, juxtaposed with Mozart and Beethoven.

> The BBC is convinced that extremes meet, or at any rate that they ought to meet in programme building, so that when they have some provocative work by Schoenberg or, as last night, by Stravinsky, they put it into the same programme as Mozart and Beethoven, thus ensuring that half the audience is

bored for half the time and the conductor of the evening out of his proper
element for half the time.

Thus *The Times*, clearly in flippant mood; it dismissed *Oedipus* with the
sentence 'the work is monumental: monumental nonsense'. It is shocking to
look back and see that only Richard Capell wrote in favour of 'this curious,
barbaric, bare and enormously sophisticated score': otherwise the chorus of
derision was deafening. On 25 March the Bartók *Cantata profana* ended the
season and provoked another display of narrow-mindedness from *The
Times*: 'He is a fine scholar of his country's folksong and also a modern
composer with a highly elaborated technical style of his own. The main
themes are clearly based on the folk style, but they become sophisticated in
his handling so that the work as a whole sounds self-conscious and forced.'
The *Telegraph* concurred: 'His work has points of technical interest; it has
no humanity.'

The second of the special concerts (in which Darius Milhaud was to
conduct his opera *Christophe Colomb*) was postponed, but at the end of the
season there was a performance of Shostakovich's opera *Lady Macbeth of
Mtsensk*. Yet again the BBC earned the ingratitude of the critics for having
provided only a concert performance of an opera. Neville Cardus wrote:
'. . . the truth is that the idea is as silly as if a Russian public were expected to
enjoy a test match with the action confined to the stage of an opera house
with Bradman and Bowes in operatic costume.' The translation of the
libretto into English appears to have caused some mirth in the hall. Ernest
Newman was condescending: 'It really is rather deplorable that a work of
this kind, by a boy who at the best can be regarded as no more than promising,
should receive all this expensive boosting while the work of a genuine master
like Ernest Bloch, who is worth fifty Shostakovichs, should be almost
unknown in London.' His opposite number in *The Observer* disagreed:
'What struck one first and most was the certainty of touch: the designed
effect is achieved . . . the performance under Mr Albert Coates was brilliant.'

Into Europe

In April 1936 came the BBC Symphony Orchestra's first continental tour.
Four venues had been chosen, each an important centre of European music-
making: Paris, Vienna, Zürich and Budapest. At the end of 1935, it had been
proposed that Edward Clark should visit Europe to make advance plans for
the tour programmes, and this was reluctantly approved by the administration department. He was also to visit Monte Carlo in order to contact
Toscanini and establish with him the programmes for his appearance in the

1936 London Music Festival. Clark wanted to visit each city where the Orchestra was to appear, in order to discuss with all the appropriate people the likely success of his suggested programmes. But Basil Nicolls, Controller (Administration), felt that he should confine his visits to Paris and Monte Carlo, spending two days in each centre. He had to approve the visit on Christmas Eve. On that day, however, Alban Berg died, and Clark, a close friend and colleague, felt that he should go to Vienna (where he had in any case intended to discuss the tour programme) in order to attend the funeral. Kenneth Wright defended this decision to the administration department, arguing that Berg was one of the most important composers with whom the BBC had dealt, and that a representative should be sent to the funeral. The BBC even, again reluctantly, paid for a wreath. Clark, having attended the funeral, did not return to England until 11 January. He thus missed the 1935 season of Winter Proms (his return for which had been the original reason for approving the trip so quickly). And in what BBC administration saw as the major part of his task – contacting Toscanini in Monte Carlo – he had failed completely, adding to the problems which eventually caused the cancellation of the 1936 Music Festival. But Clark had planned some most impressive programmes for the tour, contacting Bartók in Hungary about the Budapest programme, and establishing (for example) that Schoenberg's Variations for Orchestra had never been heard publicly in Vienna. His scheme ensured that each concert should contain one work by a composer of the host country, one English work, one classic, and one showpiece. About the balance of these items there was fierce argument in the weeks after Clark returned to England, and his programmes were eventually altered without consulting him; this precipitated the last chapter of his BBC career (see below). The final shape of the programmes deserves to be shown in full:

Monday 20 April 1936
Paris, Salle Pleyel

Pour une fête de printemps .... *Roussel*
The Rio Grande, for Piano, Chorus &
   Orchestra (Clifford Curzon; Les Choeurs Russes
   Vlassov) .... *Lambert*
Symphony No. 8 .... *Beethoven*
The Rite of Spring .... *Stravinsky*

Tuesday 21 April 1936
Zürich, Tonhalle

Prelude, *Die Meistersinger* .... *Wagner*

Two Studies for *Doktor Faust*: Sarabande; Cortège .... *Busoni*
Viola Concerto (Lionel Tertis) .... *Walton*
Chant de Joie .... *Honegger*
Symphony No. 4 .... *Brahms*

Thursday 23 April 1936
Vienna, Konzerthaus

Tragic Overture .... *Brahms*
Variations for Orchestra, Op. 31 .... *Schoenberg*
Symphony No. 4 in F minor .... *Vaughan Williams*
Daphnis and Chloe (second suite) .... *Ravel*

Friday 24 April 1936
Budapest, Municipal Theatre

Introduction and Allegro, for String Quartet and
    String Orchestra .... *Elgar*
Four Orchestral Pieces .... *Bartók*
Tintagel .... *Bax*
Symphony No. 5 .... *Beethoven*

The administrative arrangements in Europe were made by an old
colleague of Boult's from his continental days, Dr Schiff, working with
W.W. Thompson, and in collaboration with Owen Mase in London; the
Orchestral Manager, Richard Pratt, and his assistant, Mr Tabb, looked after
the orchestra's immediate needs, while Bill Fussell, the orchestral porter,
dealt with instruments and seating layouts. As the tour was a major exercise
in international public relations, the Deputy Director General, Admiral
Carpendale, and Roger Eckersley both accompanied the party; Boult was
assisted by Kenneth Wright. The total number of the party was 130,
including the full strength of 119 musicians. Instructions to the players were
issued, down to the last detail – they were advised to take a tablet of soap with
them, told how to board a Continental train, and instructed to be polite to
foreign officials. Some 300 precise times of different activities in the six days
were included, including the tiniest excursion from hotel to restaurant.
One violinist was heard to comment: 'Knowing that most of us are past the
schoolboy stage, I think a little more tact might conveniently have been used
in telling us some of these details'.

The party set off from Victoria on Saturday afternoon, 19 April, and
arrived in Paris during Sunday. On the Monday morning there was a rehearsal in the Salle Pleyel ('a curious mixture of perfect clarity and an

impression of stuffiness and deadness caused by the curtains round and over the orchestra', Boult recorded); and a concert in the evening. Between the orchestra's morning rehearsal and the evening concert, another rehearsal and concert took place in the hall, necessitating rapid rearrangement of the platform. Tickets had not sold well – Parisian audiences were in the habit of waiting until reduced price seats were offered before starting to buy – but the house had been well papered, important musicians had been given tickets, and the hall was almost full. The British Ambassador, Sir George Clark, was present. It was a most successful occasion. Two encores were given (Wagner's *Meistersinger* Overture and *The Ride of the Valkyries*) and the press criticism was ecstatic. It was a reaction which would be matched in every city. Lambert's *The Rio Grande* scored a particular success; Roussel was in the audience to hear his *Pour une fête de printemps*, and praised the orchestra afterwards. *The Rite of Spring*, which had originally caused such a furore in Paris, was played; Boult, who had stood down in favour of other conductors when the work was performed in London, secured a trouble-free, precisely co-ordinated account which orchestra members recall as one of the most triumphantly secure in their whole history.

The following morning the Orchestra set off for Zürich on a special train, aiming to arrive at four in the afternoon for a short rehearsal before the concert. On this journey occurred the only incident of the tour which caught the imagination of the British press: as Adrian Boult sat in his railway carriage studying scores, his large and heavy suitcase fell off the rack on to his head. Temporarily, Boult seemed unharmed, but half an hour later he fainted, and was unwell throughout the journey. On arrival in Zürich, Carpendale insisted that he miss the short rehearsal before the concert and see a doctor. The doctor waived his fee in return for concert tickets; Carpendale made sure that the Zürich rostrum was safe in case of a recurrence of the fainting. The rehearsal started late, because the instruments were delayed by Customs until late afternoon, Arthur Catterall directing it from the leader's desk. As Eckersley remembered, '[Boult] was able to have a good dinner and subsequently gave one of the best performances of his life'. Again the concert was enthusiastically received. Afterwards a party was given at which the orchestral principals met their opposite numbers in Swiss orchestras: the celebrations lasted into the early hours of the morning.

At seven the next morning came the most memorable journey of the tour: the ride from Zürich to Vienna, through the Swiss mountains, over the Arlberg Pass. There was snow on the ground, and when the train stopped on the summit Eckersley recalls the 'disgraceful scene of our eminent conductor being unmercifully snowballed by various impenitent members of the

Orchestra'. After the long journey, Vienna was reached around ten in the evening. The next morning, Thursday, there was a rehearsal in the Grosses Konzerthaus ('very brilliant', said Boult of the acoustics; 'we found the hall easy and the quality particularly beautiful'). And in the afternoon a guided tour around the museums and monuments of Vienna was laid on, and a tea party given by members of the Vienna Philharmonic. There to greet Boult and the Orchestra was their old colleague Bruno Walter, as well as Professor Hugo Burghauser, President of the Orchestra. Here, as in Paris, the tickets had sold slowly for what was a very demanding programme. But there was an extensive number of guests, and the hall was well filled by an audience which greeted almost every work in the programme with great enthusiasm, and demanded encores. Wagner's *Ride of the Valkyries* and the *Meistersinger* Overture were again given. The concert was attended by the Federal President of Austria and by the British Ambassador, Sir Walford Selby. Boult was presented to the President in the interval, just after the first public performance in Vienna of the Schoenberg Variations for Orchestra; in an immortal statement of Viennese artistic conservatism, the President asked Boult, 'Who is this Schoenberg, anyway?'

The critics in Vienna were as unstinting in praise as those in Paris and Zürich; the Vaughan Williams Symphony was hailed as an important work, and the Orchestra was thanked in guarded terms for its presentation of the Schoenberg. The BBC Vienna Legation reported that 'most of the critics remarked with friendly interest on the presence of ladies in the orchestra'. On Friday morning, orchestra members arrived for their special train from Vienna to Budapest to see an unprecedented scene: members of the Vienna Philharmonic had gathered on the station platform with music stands and instruments, and proceeded to play a farewell to the BBC musicians in the form of Strauss waltzes and marches. The English musicians hung out of their carriage windows, amazed; Carpendale leapt up one of the carriage ladders on to the coach roof and directed the music from there. The *Radetsky March* and the *Blue Danube* featured among the selections. Eventually the train had to pull away, some minutes late, and the members of the BBC Orchestra were left to remember an extraordinary, spontaneous expression of friendship and good will. As Eckersley pondered: 'I can imagine the consternation on the faces of the station authorities at Victoria if such a thing happened in reverse.'

This Friday was the most exhausting day of the tour. Budapest was reached by the early afternoon. There was a rehearsal, a short break, and then the evening concert. In many ways it was the most difficult and unpredictable of the venues, but the Orchestra scored its largest popular success. Boult recorded of the Municipal Theatre, where the concert took place: 'A most uncomfortable place with built-out stage quite inadequate for our Orchestra. It was a triumph of arrangement that Fussell was able to pack them in at all, and many had not the full bowing room.' In Budapest the popular reaction to the programme was excellent, perhaps confirming the decision to include a very popular classic in the form of Beethoven's Fifth Symphony. Eighty per cent of the house was sold, a far larger proportion than in the other centres, and the rest was filled with guests: 2600 seats in all. The local agency said the success was much greater than they had dared to anticipate and was immediately anxious to arrange a second visit. The reception was tumultuous and the usual encores were played. Because official mourning for the death of King George was still being strictly observed in the Embassy in Budapest, the Minister and members of his staff did not attend, but Carpendale and Eckersley went to tea at the Budapest Legation to meet representatives of the broadcasting authorities and the Opera House.

After the concert the fun began. The staff, Boult and Catterall were entertained by the Hungarian broadcasting authorities: Boult made a short speech and then retired for the evening. Eckersley joined the Orchestra for its revels with the Hungarian musicians, who were evidently extremely hospitable. Sidonie Goossens recalls listening to folk bands and drinking apricot brandy through the night; Ernest Hall was encouraged by the Hungarians to play his trumpet on the table. With these wild celebrations, very few of the Orchestra retired to bed.

The return train was to leave at 6.30 am, and everyone arrived, exhausted. The train set off, with most of the Orchestra asleep in uncomfortable positions on their seats. Through Czechoslovakia to Prague, young soldiers guarded the line; they stood impassively as the train crossed the frontier into Hitler's Germany. At Dresden, the Orchestra changed into a red and chromium special train produced by the Nazis to take them to Calais. At Cologne they stopped for breakfast; a huge picture of the Führer dominated their view. On this train, 'the German authorities, with a clever eye to propaganda, served us with a champagne supper' (Eckersley). The boat train took them across the Channel, and on Sunday evening the party returned to Victoria.

In retrospect, the tour had been absurdly demanding. Boult recalled that Wright's dinners consisted usually of 'a cup of coffee while dressing'. W. W. Thompson 'seemed to be immersed in columns of figures with Dr Schiff at most uncomfortable times and places' (Boult) and 'all members of the staff who came had their hands more than full'. The success of the tour as international prestige was unquestioned: thanks to Carpendale's close connections with the broadcasting organisations and Eckersley's work with the consulates and embassies, excellent relations had been established in every centre visited. Musically, the decision to have difficult programmes had been vindicated.

Boult's major dissatisfaction concerned reaction at the English end. Very late in the day, London programme planners had decided to broadcast only half of each concert – on the face of it, an astonishing way to treat the greatest events in the history of the BBC's own Orchestra. Boult thought that if this decision had been known in advance, the classic works could have been repeated in more than one venue. But he was disappointed by the lack of representation of the tour on the air: 'I cannot help pointing out that from Vienna the applause was cut off several minutes before time in order to insert a boxing report, [whereas] from Zürich the whole concert including encores was heard in Vienna by Bruno Walter and others. Evidently either the Swiss or Austrian broadcasters thought it more important than we did – a flattering but not quite satisfactory attitude.' On the other hand, the tour programmes had been devised by Clark and approved by Music Department very late in the day: there were complaints from Thompson and Schiff that this made the advance promotion in Europe of the concerts exceptionally difficult. Cecil Graves disagreed with Boult on the question of broadcasting: 'It would have meant four full-length symphony concerts in one week, all of them built on rather the same lines, containing a fairly high proportion of music of minority appeal. We had to consider the interest of listeners as a whole . . .' And the Public Relations Controller answered the point in another way: 'Listeners here would have questioned the advantage of hearing, with the defects of long-distance transmission, an orchestra which they can, happily, hear not infrequently under better conditions on its home ground.'

Subordinate to this was the reaction of the English press, 'the least satisfactory part of the whole thing' (Boult). Apart from *The Observer*, which printed a substantial interview with Wright, reports were confined to diplomatic details, the occasional piece of extracted press criticism of the concerts, and the story of Boult's accident. But no one wished to complain about the overall success of the tour. It had been a magnificent exercise, had raised the Orchestra's morale, and won it an international reputation. It was one of the high points of the Orchestra's first decade.

Clark departs

The tour brought about the end of Edward Clark's association with the BBC. He felt very strongly that the programmes he had planned so carefully in consultation with the composers in each host country should not have been modified without consulting him. In particular, the balance of the Budapest programme was changed so that in place of a major English work (Bax's Third Symphony) and a major work by Bartók (agreed with the composer), there were instead small works by those two composers and a major classic (Beethoven's Fifth Symphony). The inclusion of Beethoven's Fifth infuriated Clark (as Kenneth Wright suggested in the memoir of Clark printed in Elisabeth Lutyens's autobiography *A Goldfish Bowl*); and he also felt he had made false assurances to Bartók. Elisabeth Lutyens, who married Clark after his departure from the BBC, wrote that 'rather than betray his old friend Bartók Edward had, no doubt precipitously and in a rage, tendered his resignation'. It is difficult to feel that 'betray' is an appropriate word in the circumstances: after all, Bartók was still represented in the programme. A change of balance in a concert programme is scarcely a matter for resignation. It is better to see the incident as the climax of a long history of tension between Clark and his BBC superiors, which his prolonged absence at the turn of 1935–6 must have exacerbated. Clark resigned in March 1936, writing in the strongest terms to Boult.

Not only was his resignation accepted; Clark was not even required to serve out his three months' notice. Music Department officials would have supported his stand, but the administration department would not persuade him to change his mind. Kenneth Wright, his chief intermediary and defender, was ill; there was an immense amount of activity over the preparation for the European tour. So at the end of March, before the tour that he had helped to plan had even taken place, the programme builder who had been primarily responsible for the success of the BBC Symphony Orchestra's concerts during its first six seasons left the BBC.

Paradoxically, though Clark disliked the BBC establishment and all it stood for, and though the BBC barely tolerated Clark's unbusinesslike methods, they were both indispensable to each other. Clark could never have achieved what he did – an open-minded assault on a narrow public taste comparable to that which William Glock was to undertake in the 1960s – without the administrative back-up of the BBC. The support of men like Herbage, Wright, Thompson, Wood, and most importantly the openness of Boult himself, were essential to the realisation of his ambitious schemes in all their demanding detail. But without Clark, the BBC in the early 1930s would have been an immeasurably poorer place. Stravinsky in his *Chronicle of My Life* summed up Clark's achievement: 'A few well-informed and cultured men, among them my friend of long standing, Edward Clark, have been able to form within this huge eclectic organisation [the BBC] a small

group which with praiseworthy energy pursues the propaganda of contemporary music, upholding its cause with invincible tenacity.'

Clark was a poor letter-writer; he frequently had to ask the help of
colleagues to put even the simplest proposal or request on paper. It is partly
because the documentation of Clark's activities is so scanty that due recognition of his achievement has been withheld in the past. But to read through
the opposite side of the correspondence is to realise what an easy, close
relationship he sustained with most of the important conductors and composers of the day. Letters survive to Clark from Ansermet ('Dear old boy'),
Bartók, Bax, Berg, Berkeley, Lord Berners, Britten, Casella, Coates,
Dallapiccola, Delius, Dent, van Dieren, Falla, Gerhard, Hindemith, Ireland,
Kodály, Koussevitsky, Lambert, Malipiero, Milhaud, Moeran, Nin,
Poulenc, Prokofiev, Schoenberg, Ethel Smyth, Sorabji, Stravinsky, Veres,
Walton and Webern: a roll-call of important musicians of the inter-war
years. (Among all the surviving letters to Clark there is only one unfriendly
example, from Rutland Boughton: 'The unfair treatment of my work by the
BBC is apparently becoming obvious . . . it will survive the rubbish you
chiefly have been instrumental in foisting on the London and wireless
public.' Boughton also wrote to express his pleasure at Clark's retirement
from the BBC.)

There was scarcely any internationally significant composer of the 1930s
whose work was not promoted in a discriminating manner by Clark. As a
programme builder he was unsurpassed. He was unreliable, disorganised,
and had a cavalier attitude to authority. He is the man Music Department
staff remember playing Santa Claus at Savoy Hill in the 1920s, or mocking a
BBC fire drill by appearing late from the building – carnation in buttonhole –
with umbrella unfurled, asking where the fire engines' hoses were. But he
had more than a touch of genius. His was one of those rare relationships
which the BBC uneasily sustains with creative talent. Clark's influence
survived in Music Department for some years; but there was to be a later
period when the BBC turned its back on the most adventurous of European
music and cultivated a narrower field.

Clark's last effort was to arrange a memorial concert for Berg. He invited
Webern to conduct, and Webern wrote to Wright suggesting the Violin
Concerto, with perhaps the addition of the Adagio from Mahler's Tenth
Symphony and his own Op. 6 Orchestral Pieces. The concert took place on 1
May in the Concert Hall of Broadcasting House, and the programme was an
all-Berg one, with two of the pieces from the Lyric Suite complementing the
British première of the Violin Concerto.

Summer 1936

The high point of the foreign tour should have been followed by the London Music Festival during May 1936, but there were problems. Koussevitsky, reportedly annoyed that his concerts in the 1935 Festival had been over-shadowed by Toscanini's, was unwilling to return. Moreover he was a strong supporter of Edward Clark (through whom he was first invited to the Symphony Orchestra) and had offered him a post as his Assistant Conductor; he was shocked to hear of Clark's departure from the Music Department. Toscanini, on the other hand, had expressed himself as anxious to return, and negotiations were in progress for a series of six concerts (plus one repeat) entirely conducted by him. However, the BBC's booking section did not show enough flexibility in dealing with Toscanini's financial requests and simply offered a direct proportion of his previous fee; correspondence abruptly ceased, much to the consternation of the Music Department. Rumours appeared in the Press that Toscanini did not wish to return to England for political reasons: these were angrily denied by his manager at the New York Philharmonic, Bruno Zirato, who claimed instead that Toscanini was tired and did not wish to travel. He was, however, to go to Salzburg at the end of his final New York season that summer, so that explanation was not entirely convincing. The BBC still held out and hoped to change his mind, but by March the Corporation had to admit that it had bungled the negotiations. On 17 March the 1936 London Music Festival was cancelled, and a notice issued to the Press saying that 'in the time available it was impossible to secure the services of any other conductor for this important task'.

Meanwhile, in the Music Department steps were being taken to make sure as soon as possible that Toscanini was signed up for 1937. Owen Mase was dispatched to Europe with a virtual *carte blanche* to track Toscanini down and negotiate a contract directly with him. This most unusual flexibility paid its rewards. At first Toscanini refused to see anyone, but Mase travelled to Paris on 18 June and established contact. He reported that Toscanini was, in principle, in favour of the engagement, provided that the concerts were not broadcast to Europe from the Daventry short-wave transmitter, whence he feared illegal recordings. Not until September, however, was an offer made to him, and Mase had to travel once again, this time to Stresa, to ensure that the negotiations remained on a personal level. As he reported back on 25 January 1937, all formal approaches had previously failed, and this was the only way to secure agreement. Small matters such as Toscanini's bringing his wife at the BBC's expense, and their stay at Claridge's, were readily

agreed. In the course of the discussions Owen Mase formed a close friendship with Toscanini: on subsequent visits to England Mase was to act almost
in the capacity of his agent – and did so directly after he left the BBC.

In 1935–6 the provincial tours of the Orchestra continued. On 31 October
the Orchestra visited Swansea with a popular programme; on 11 March it
visited Leicester: Weber's *Euryanthe* Overture, Beethoven's Pastoral, four
movements of Holst's *Planets*, and Ravel's *Pavane* and *Bolero*. 'It was a
brilliant and thrilling performance,' reported the local *Loughborough
Monitor*, 'holding the audience from first to last . . . superbly controlled
under the masterly hand of Dr Adrian Boult.' The visit made a paragraph in
The Star because the Orchestra arrived back in London at 12.30 am and were
not granted an overnight allowance: they were allowed to claim a taxi fare
home on production of a receipt from the taxi driver – a piece of paper doubtless as rare then as now. On 1 April it was the turn of Glasgow, which had
been denied a visit in the previous season because it had not made the
Orchestra welcome. 'Glasgow music lovers will welcome this news, in view
of Dr Boult's threat last year never to visit Glasgow or Edinburgh,' said the
Daily Express, which also ran a lively piece, 'Scots To Hear Music That
Caused Riot', introducing its readers to *The Rite of Spring*.

New faces

Without the London Music Festival, the Symphony Orchestra moved
straight from studio concerts into the Proms, which Marie Wilson once
again led. A major change took place in the Orchestra's personnel at the end
of the 1935–6 season. Arthur Catterall, who was increasingly in demand as a
soloist and quartet leader, resigned from the Orchestra on 19 July, six years
since his contract as leader had begun. It was a severe blow, for Catterall's
return to orchestral playing had been a major factor in the Orchestra's early
success. Although he had led the Orchestra only for the symphony concerts –
even the important studio concerts were frequently led by Laurance Turner
or Marie Wilson, and Catterall had never led at the Proms – he was an important and prestigious figurehead. His replacement was going to be hard to
find. The Press, naturally, tipped Marie Wilson to create a sensation by becoming the first permanent woman leader of an English orchestra. But Boult
knew very firmly whom he wanted. This was Paul Beard, who had led the
City of Birmingham Symphony Orchestra during Boult's time there. He had
not been thought eligible by Boult's predecessors for the Orchestra's leadership in 1930, although he had been an orchestral leader for ten years. He had
been playing the violin since the age of six, and had gained a scholarship to the
Royal Academy at the age of sixteen. But in 1932 Beard had been picked by

Beecham to lead his new London Philharmonic Orchestra, and there had increased his reputation considerably. Boult was anxious to attract his old colleague to the BBC Orchestra, and with the very favourable salary and conditions attached to the leader's post, in addition to the security which the London Philharmonic Orchestra could not provide, Beard accepted. He took over on 4 October 1936, at the start of the 1936–7 season.

There had been other changes in personnel in the Orchestra, though remarkably few. Lauri Kennedy, principal cellist, was succeeded in 1936 by his number two, the much-loved Ambrose Gauntlett (who died in 1978). The latter had been associated with broadcasting from the early days and was a member of the old Wireless Orchestra; he was also well known as one of the first revivers of the viola da gamba (his oft-repeated performance of the gamba obbligato in Bach's *St Matthew Passion* was universally known as 'Gauntlett's Gig'). At the principal bassoon desk, Archie Camden, no longer bound in faith to the Hallé after the departure of Harty, had succeeded Richard Newton, who stepped down to the second position. Camden was a nationally famous figure, particularly after his recording of the Mozart Bassoon Concerto, which did much to re-establish the instrument as a serious, lyrical member of the orchestra. He did not break his ties with Manchester, where he had been trained and spent much of his professional life: he was in demand to return there as a soloist, often to his old orchestra. As principal trombone, Sidney Langston had taken the place of Jesse Stamp, who died in 1932: he was one of the most experienced band players in the country, for he had belonged to the Harrogate Symphony Orchestra under Basil Cameron and the Wireless Military Band. Ernest Gillegin had succeeded Charles Bender as principal timpanist. Changes in the rank and file had been astonishingly few. Charles Woodhouse had departed, as had Harry Blech. There were five new first violins, and two promoted seconds; five new second violins; only two violas had been replaced; three new cellists. Gerald Jackson became first flute in succession to Robert Murchie in 1937, and later wrote entertainingly of his experiences in his book *First Flute*.

During 1936 there was also a major change in the Music Department. It was early in that year that Boult took action on a matter which had long troubled him: the burdens of the Directorship of Music and the Chief Conductorship were too great to be sensibly combined. Much of the weight of Boult's administrative duties had fallen first on Kenneth Wright and Owen Mase and then on Aylmer Buesst as his assistants, and though there were no complaints about their efficiency, the responsibilities were thought to be too onerous. The Music Department needed a resident representative who could speak with authority to the higher reaches of management.

The separation of the two jobs was discussed at the Music Advisory Committee, and agreed in principle on 17 February 1936; various solutions were proposed. On 16 March Walford Davies suggested to Reith that Sir Hugh Allen be nominated as 'Chief Musical Adviser', a move which would have caused the utmost consternation in the Music Department. Fortunately, Sir John McEwen threatened an internecine row on the Advisory Committee, so that idea was abandoned. It was then thought desirable by Allen, Ronald and McEwen to find someone of stature as a full-time Director of Music, and the search went on during 1936; but by the summer it became evident that there was no appropriate and available candidate. Instead, it was decided to formalise the post of Assistant Director of Music, and offer it to Dr Reginald Thatcher, the Director of Music at Harrow School. His appointment was confirmed by the Music Advisory Committee on 22 June 1936, and he took up his duties on 1 October. Boult remained *de jure* Director of Music, but his administrative commitments were eased considerably.

Thatcher's main responsibility, which Wright and Mase had not been able to assume, was in representing the Music Department to the upper levels of the Corporation: the increasing importance of the programme planners of the networks (both National and London Regional) meant that the Department was losing some of its autonomy with regard to programme selection. The demands of broadcasting began during these years to override the considerations of orchestral planning – a factor which was to become most important in the future.

At the same time the composition of the Music Advisory Committee was considerably enlarged. The three principals of the London music colleges still sat *ex officio*; added to them were the Chairmen of the Regional Music Advisory Committees, from Scotland, the Midlands and the North. The senior Inspector of Music in the Ministry of Education also sat, and he was joined by various distinguished non-specialist musicians. In 1937 the members were Sir Percy Puck, Sir Sidney Clive (a suggestion of the BBC, to represent 'the musically intelligent listener'), Dr Stanley Marchant, Sir Landon Ronald (who died on 13 October 1938), Dr G. T. Shaw, Lady Snowden (a *bête noire* of Reith's, who had made life extremely difficult for him as a Governor in the preceding decade), Dr George Dyson (appointed Director of the Royal College of Music in December 1937), Colonel Somerville (of the Ministry of Education), and Colonel Parminter. It was scarcely a less establishment body than that constituted earlier in the 1930s, but at least, Reith must have thought, criticism might well be diffused from such a large body.

1936–7

The 1936–7 Symphony Concert series, under the leadership of Paul Beard, adopted a revised plan. The twelve appearances of the previous season were increased to fifteen, and these were sold in three separate series as in the first seasons. The series was notable for the first appearance with the Orchestra of Willem Mengelberg; the public première of the Berg Violin Concerto under Henry Wood; the London première of Vaughan Williams' *Five Tudor Portraits*; and – most adventurous of all – the British première of Busoni's complete opera *Doktor Faust*. Boult was to conduct eight concerts, Wood two, Mengelberg, Ansermet, Harty and Beecham one each, plus an appearance by Leslie Heward. In fact Harty cancelled his concert and was replaced by Boult; he was also unable to appear as soloist in his own Piano Concerto.

Mengelberg's arrival caused a considerable stir. After Koussevitsky, Walter and Toscanini, what could the Amsterdam orchestra's conductor have to teach the BBC Orchestra? A good deal, it soon emerged. For Mengelberg was above all a trainer of orchestras: his special gift was for orchestral discipline, and his rehearsals were dominated by a relentless quest for precision. His programme consisted of a Vivaldi Concerto, Brahms's Piano Concerto No. 2 with Myra Hess, and Strauss's *Ein Heldenleben*. The latter piece was dedicated to him and he had first performed it with his Amsterdam orchestra some 37 years earlier. It also provided an admirable showcase for the talents of the BBC Orchestra's new leader, Paul Beard, as it had in past BBC performances for Catterall. At his first rehearsal, Mengelberg made several changes in the orchestra's seating arrangements, and spent a full twenty-five minutes tuning each section individually. After an extensive lecture on the need for perfect tuning, he spent the whole of the remaining first session on the beginning of *Ein Heldenleben* up to the entry of the solo violin. He made considerable alterations to the composer's articulation marks in the score. (His explanation, according to Bernard Shore, was: 'I have been a great friend of Richard Strauss since I was a boy, and I know just what he wants, and we will make some *changements* also!') He talked a great deal at rehearsal, and was often unpredictable: he was expected to rehearse his concert in running order at the final rehearsal, but wasted much of the time by having the harpsichord for the Vivaldi and the piano for the Brahms removed from the stage because he wanted to start with the Strauss. Bernard Shore described the impression Mengelberg made on the Orchestra:

> He looks robust and his face is young for his age, which he says is 'nearly eighty'; and his vitality throughout his rehearsals never flags for a moment,

though he drives himself hard the whole time. When it comes to the concert he becomes a geyser of energy. His eyes are then compelling – or repelling if he takes a dislike to any one, and he has the trick of taking in every player individually. His magnetism comes from the man's whole personality. He seems to increase in stature upon the rostrum. And his will is felt, rather than seen. His baton, which is often dispensed with (on account, as he says, of an irritating corn) is used as a time-beater only, and for indicating rhythmic impulse; it is quite independent of his left hand, which is responsible for the entire range of expression and for balance . . .

Such a wealth of detail is studied at rehearsal that he does not expect any trouble in balance at the concert. His hand then is generally concerned in directing the curve of the music and imbuing it with life and character. When a string passage is to be played with the utmost warmth and emotion he will curve his left arm up, as if he were a violinist at the great climax of a concerto holding his instrument as in ecstasy; and if it is a tune for any one of the three upper strings, he likes them to raise their instruments a little higher than is normal. 'Ysayeissimo,' he exclaims. In a great climax this gesture of extra effort is also required of the brass – horns, trumpets and trombones being directed to raise their instruments over the top of their stands.

Mengelberg's insistence paid off: the *Daily Telegraph* wrote of the 'wonderfully clarifying effect' of his conducting, and *The Times* said that 'the orchestra responded brilliantly to the demands made on them'.

The season continued with Casals in the Elgar Concerto: a performance almost universally held by the critics to have been unidiomatic. This stung the BBC into an unusual response: Ralph Hill was given space in the *Radio Times* to criticise the critics for their narrow-mindedness and lack of gratitude to a great artist. The appearance of Leslie Heward, conductor of the City of Birmingham Orchestra, on 25 November, was a considerable personal success. *The Times* praised his 'natural gift of leadership which is wholly free from self-assertion'. December saw the concert première of Berg's Violin Concerto under Wood (it had already been broadcast from the studio in the Berg memorial concert). Richard Capell was appreciative: describing it as a new 'Death and the Maiden' work, he praised its exquisite sounds and bold experiments, and said 'it will surely maintain a place of its own in music' (*Daily Telegraph*, 10 December). Ernest Newman was cynical: its dedication to a dead girl and the fact of Berg's death 'were bound to make it a good work; and if only Berg had had the foresight to die leaving it unfinished it would have automatically become a masterpiece'. Constant Lambert in the *Sunday Referee* came straight to the point and declared it 'in my opinion, the most beautiful and significant piece of music written since the War'.

Two important concerts in the BBC's studio contemporary music series brought Vaughan Williams' *Dona nobis pacem* to London for the first time (it had celebrated the centenary of the Huddersfield Choral Society in October) alongside Kodály's *Te Deum* on 13 November; and on 18 December Hindemith's opera *Cardillac* was conducted by Clarence Raybould, who had been appointed Chief Assistant Conductor of the Symphony Orchestra in May 1938. Over the following nine years Raybould did an enormous amount of work with the Orchestra. He had been born and educated in Birmingham, and established a modest reputation as a conductor and composer before the First World War. In the 1920s he had worked with the Beecham Opera Company, and later conducted for the British National Opera Company. He was perhaps best known as a widely-toured accompanist and solo pianist; he had a keen interest in young people's music-making, and was closely associated with orchestras at the Guildhall and Royal Academy, and after the Second World War with the National Youth Orchestra of Wales. Music for many films of the inter-war years was composed, arranged or conducted by him. Besides Hindemith's *Cardillac*, he also conducted for the BBC the first complete British performance of Hindemith's *Mathis der Maler*, Burkhard's oratorio *The Vision of Isaiah*, and many other smaller works; he conducted several of the Symphony Orchestra's outstanding wartime concerts and broadcasts.

At the beginning of 1937 orchestral music-making in London was continuing to grow at an almost alarming rate. Two or three orchestral concerts in a week had previously given cause for concern: but now there were concerts every night. During just one week in January, for example, on the Monday the Women's Symphony Orchestra appeared under Malcolm Sargent; on Tuesday the Patron's Fund concert at the Royal College of Music included Vaughan Williams' *Flos Campi* under Sydney Watson; on Wednesday the BBC gave its Symphony Concert; on Thursday Beecham conducted an all-Mozart programme for the Royal Philharmonic Society; on Friday Iris Lemare conducted a concert of choral works at Westminster School in connection with the Chelsea Festival; on Saturday morning Sargent conducted the Robert Mayer concert for children; and on Sunday afternoon there were orchestral concerts at both Queen's Hall and Covent Garden – at the latter, Beecham's London Philharmonic Orchestra appeared (having transferred its allegiance from the Queen's Hall), while at the former a new body under an old name, the Queen's Hall Orchestra, was conducted by Henry Wood.

Most of the adventurous programmes in London music-making were still to be found under the BBC's auspices: exceptions included Van Wyck's promotion of Nadia Boulanger conducting the Fauré *Requiem* and music by Schütz in November 1936, the appearances of the Dresden State Opera Orchestra under Strauss and Böhm in the same month, and the tour of the Vienna Symphony Orchestra under Weingartner and Kabasta (October 1936). Reflecting the beginnings of a new fashion, both these touring orchestras included Bruckner symphonies in their programmes (Dresden, the original version of the Fourth, and Vienna, the Seventh). Only the first British performance of Hindemith's Symphony from *Mathis der Maler* in a Courtauld–Sargent concert (under Fritz Stiedry from Leningrad) looks like a première the BBC ought to have given – but the BBC was soon to present the complete work. The Royal Philharmonic Society at the start of 1937 was content with novelties, of which the least unimportant were the Saxophone Concerto by Glazunov, the Rhapsody for Saxophone by Debussy, and the London première of the Piano Concerto by Pfitzner.

In the BBC series the new year opened with celebrations: Adrian Boult became Sir Adrian in the New Year's Honours. The Queen's Hall series continued with the two concerts at which Sir Hamilton Harty was to have appeared. On 27 January Harty was to have played the piano in the première of his own Second Piano Concerto; with his indisposition the opportunity was taken to introduce Vaughan Williams' *Five Tudor Portraits*, first performed at the Norwich Festival. 'Jolly Tudor Work', said the *News Chronicle*; it was enjoyed by audience and critics alike.

Beecham was enjoying a period of great success with the London Philharmonic Orchestra, and he was rapturously welcomed when he returned to the BBC Orchestra on 3 February at the Queen's Hall. His programme was typically mixed: Haydn's 97th Symphony, Delius's *Paris*, Grieg's Piano Concerto (with Gieseking) and Sibelius's *Swan of Tuonela* and *Return of Lemminkäinen*. The Delius, said Richard Capell in the *Daily Telegraph*, 'will remain in the memories of all who were there as a miracle of the conductor's art'. Bernard Shore records that 'the Haydn and Delius take up three-quarters of the time he spends on rehearsal. Both works he has played time and time again, but he tackles them with fresh outlook. Beecham sets out on a new journey each time.' At the end of *Paris*, the piccolo plays offstage. It goes wrong. 'Who did that?', says Beecham *sotto voce* to the violinist, and when the piccolo player complains that he cannot see the beat unless the stage door is held open, Beecham declares, 'My dear fellow, I will see that the entire staff of attendants at the Queen's Hall are put at your disposal tomorrow night, or if they cannot cope with the matter, I will personally break the door down!' Shore recalls: 'These rehearsals of Beecham's gather intensity, and there is nearly always a difficulty in finishing to time, for the more he gets inside a work the more there is to be done . . . He leaves the actual polish to the last moment.'

On 10 February Henry Wood revived Rachmaninov's *The Bells*, and Artur Rubinstein played John Ireland's Piano Concerto (which he had performed during the Proms) 'as if he thoroughly enjoyed it. It was a pleasure to hear this fine work again, with its tonic acerbities and its melting sweetness', wrote the *Daily Telegraph*. The next week Boult conducted Stravinsky's *The Rite of Spring* (which he had directed in Paris during the Continental Tour). There were two highlights in the rest of the season: Lionel Tertis celebrated his sixtieth birthday on 24 February by appearing in two huge works for solo viola: the Walton Concerto and Berlioz's *Harold in Italy*. These were programmed alongside a second English performance of the Symphony from Hindemith's *Mathis der Maler* which Ansermet conducted. There was a small, appreciative audience.

Without doubt, the most ambitious concert of the season, parallel in importance to the performance of Berg's *Wozzeck*, was the concert performance of Busoni's *Doktor Faust* on 17 March. The performance lasted from 8.15 until 11.30 pm. This venture, of a kind that only the BBC could attempt, split critical opinion. Ernest Newman had introduced the performance with three long articles in *The Sunday Times*, which considered the work but judged it a failure. The Sunday before the concert he wrote that 'dramatically, *Doktor Faust* falls between too many stools to be a success'; the Sunday after he added that 'for the greater part of the time *Doktor Faust* misses fire . . . the work for which [Busoni] ate his big heart out is only an ambitious failure'. Other critics were less sure in their judgements: the *Morning Post* was typical in calling it 'a work deserving the highest respect'. Edwin Evans said that it 'contains much fine music, but considered as opera it is strangely inconclusive . . .'; he added that 'the performance directed by Sir Adrian Boult was wholly admirable'. But *The Times* was decisively favourable: it 'left no doubt of its power as one of the few operas of modern times which can be spoken of as a great conception'. In the *London Mercury*, a young critic called Desmond Shawe-Taylor was completely convinced: 'A work of such originality and imaginative power that the memory of it must overshadow for some time the ordinary round of London musicmaking . . . the absolutely original and fertile intelligence of Busoni is always evident: cold, proud, ruthlessly intolerant of all gushing or insincerity.'

The 1936–7 season passed without any Winter Proms. These had been introduced in 1933, replaced by the Concerts of British Music in 1934, and revived with popular programmes in 1935 and 1936. The concerts were not unsuccessful, but they came at a time of year when there was already a glut of broadcast material. Unlike the summer season, the winter fortnight with its twelve concerts posed something of a headache to the programme builders. At a time when network planners were beginning to dictate to the concert planners (and not the reverse) they created a dilemma; the BBC felt it important not to promote concerts which were not broadcast. The decision to cancel the season, supported by the Music Advisory Committee, was conveyed to Wood informally in March 1936, and formally on 30 June. Wood was naturally dismayed, and replied from Lucerne: 'Such a back-sliding is a poor return from my own countrymen'; but he accepted the decision with resignation. By way of compensation, it was resolved to broad-cast a special series of six Symphony Concerts from the studio during January, in which Wood would feature prominently. He opened the series on 3 January with Vaughan Williams' London Symphony, and also contri-buted the 8 and 10 January concerts, which included D'Indy's *Symphonie Montagnarde*. Leslie Heward was given one; Sargent conducted one with the London Symphony Orchestra; and the final concert on 16 January was part of the contemporary music series – a studio performance broadcast from Maida Vale of the opera *Christophe Colomb* by Milhaud, conducted by the composer (which had been postponed from February 1936).

Throughout the winter, the studio series of concerts on Sunday evenings maintained a level of unusual interest: there were concerts under Clarence Raybould, Volkmar Andreae (who included a piece of his own, the Rhapsody for violin and orchestra), the irrepressible Nikolai Malko (who gave two pieces by Schechter), Fritz Reiner in a Wagner evening, and Lambert repeating the Walton Symphony. Boult presented a much-delayed per-formance of the Handel/Schoenberg Concerto Grosso with the Kolisch Quartet; Catterall returned for a Mozart concerto under Harty; and there was an appearance by a conductor who was nearly to become very important in the Symphony Orchestra's life, John Barbirolli. In the contemporary series a memorial concert to the composer van Dieren was mounted on 9 April under Constant Lambert: it presented the Overture *Anjou* and the *Symphony on Chinese texts* for five soloists, choir and orchestra. An English programme on 30 April brought Rubbra's First Symphony, the young Benjamin Britten's *Our Hunting Fathers*, and Leighton Lucas's *Sinfonia Brevis*, with Aubrey Brain as horn soloist.

Provincial tours continued during the season, to Hanley, Southampton, Edinburgh and Leeds. In Leeds long queues surrounded the Town Hall in the hope of obtaining last-minute tickets for the concert, but even standing room had been sold out. And on 11 April the Orchestra visited Dublin. Both in Edinburgh and Dublin, the Orchestra was welcomed with studious respect and enthusiasm by local officials anxious to dispel any doubts about the welcoming nature of the visit. There was a civic luncheon in Edinburgh, and the President and other ministers came in Dublin to what was the first public orchestral concert promoted there by Radio Athlone.

Toscanini returns

The climax of the season was provided by Toscanini's return to the Orchestra for the 1937 London Music Festival, an occasion which happily coincided with the Coronation of King George VI. Toscanini was welcomed by Boult in a letter reminding Toscanini that his 1935 Festival had been the Orchestra's 'summit of achievement in its five years of life'. Owen Mase took Toscanini, his wife and granddaughter aged three and a half, to watch the Coronation procession. Mase obtained them an excellent position near Westminster Abbey, and borrowed a pair of field glasses for close observation. They were stolen, but Mase had the cost refunded by the BBC: a nice illustration of the no-expense-spared policy which was maintained towards Toscanini.

After the success of 1935, the anticipation in London was considerable: everything was expected of Toscanini. The *Daily Express* gave him a half-page feature with treatment usually reserved for film stars: 'THEY PAY HIM £500 FOR CONDUCTING ONE CONCERT – and his wife cuts his hair for him', was the headline to an article by Spike Hughes. The *Daily Telegraph* photographed the maestro playing with his granddaughter. The concerts were sold out on the day booking opened, 12 April: 17,000 applications for tickets were received. The programmes were a little miscellaneous and rambling: certainly more Toscanini than BBC, they included only one English work, the Elgar *Introduction and Allegro*. The whole series was a galaxy of orchestral showpieces, with little rhyme and reason except that of sheer exuberance.

> There were extraordinary scenes at Queen's Hall last night when Signor Arturo Toscanini conducted the first of six concerts of the London Music Festival. When Toscanini stepped on the platform and the orchestra rose as usual, the majority of the audience followed its example. . . . Every work in the programme was followed by rapturous applause . . . an extraordinary spirit prevailed. It was a concert by a great orchestra that had for a week been rehearsing three hours a day under a conductor who unites passionate intellectual power with the gift of instantaneous physical expression of his mental intention.   (Edwin Evans, *Daily Mail*).

There was Corelli-Geminiani (*La Follia*), Busoni's *Rondo Arlecchinesco*, Beethoven's *Coriolan* Overture and Brahms's First Symphony. As for Ravel's *Daphnis and Chloe*, which the orchestra had played at its very first concert: 'The music had never sounded quite like this before' (Richard Capell); 'the playing of the BBC Orchestra in these pieces was the best I have heard in this country . . . tremendous and remarkable' (Neville Cardus, *Manchester Guardian*). The triumphant progress continued in the second concert (which contained the Elgar and Tommasini's *Il Carneval di Venezia*, plus a Cherubini Symphony, Berlioz's *Romeo and Juliet* extracts and Wagner's *Meistersinger* Overture), raising a note of bewilderment from the press. *The Times* headed its article: *The Conductor's Art*. 'When an artist has attained the exceptional, perhaps unique reputation of Signor Toscanini, there is some excuse for the hearer who goes to Queen's Hall with a little sceptism. But it could find nothing to justify such sceptism. Only the Tommasini piece came in for amused abuse: Bernard Shore recollects that Toscanini spent hours rehearsing it, 'and was like a boy with a toy as the orchestra exerted itself to read appalling passages at sight and to make the work sound like a masterpiece'.

The third and fourth concerts each included a Beethoven symphony: the Pastoral and the Eroica. The third was completed by a Rossini Overture, the Brahms/Haydn Variations and Strauss's *Tod und Verklärung*. According to Lauri Kennedy, former principal cello, Toscanini said at the start of the Pastoral Symphony: 'I want it pastoral – the whole thing so smooth.' And before the Eroica: 'Some say this is Napoleon, some Hitler, some Mussolini. For me it is simply Allegro con brio.' (Which sounds almost too good an illustration of Toscanini's famed objectivity to be true.) Of these two symphonies, Lambert wrote: 'I have never heard such astounding performances in all my life.' In the fourth concert there was a Vivaldi Concerto – and Shostakovich's First Symphony: 'the BBC Orchestra responded marvellously to Toscanini's ideas' (*Morning Post*); 'it will be remembered to Toscanini's honour what devotion and intensity he brought to the rendering of that clever, spirited composition.' (Capell).

As for the fifth concert, a collection of Mozart's Symphony No. 40, Debussy's *Iberia*, Bach/Respighi and Berlioz, it nearly exhausted the supply of superlatives: 'TOSCANINI AT HIS BEST' (*Daily Mail*); 'TOSCANINI'S GENIUS' (*Morning Post*); 'A GORGEOUS CONCERT' (*Telegraph*). The final evening was devoted to Wagner, and there followed the general assessments: 'We all know that the BBC Orchestra is a good one. Not one of us, and I include the orchestra itself, had the faintest idea it could play like that' (Lambert). Ernest Newman wrote two articles praising Toscanini's objectivity, his perfection as a faithful interpreter of the composer's wishes. And he concluded 'The player was not far wrong who said the other day when asked why it was that the orchestra thought so highly of Toscanini, "Because we feel we are being brought face to face with the truth".'

And so the Orchestra was left to recover. But not for long. So great was the success of the season, and so enthusiastic was Toscanini about the Orchestra, that by 17 June he had agreed with Mase to return not only for another Festival in 1938, but almost immediately for two concerts in the autumn season. In August Mase visited Toscanini in Salzburg to arrange the following May's programmes: the Verdi *Requiem* was agreed for two concerts. By October, a contract for these six concerts was ready: this time there would be no last-minute mistakes.

1937–8

The 1937–8 BBC season was sure to start in a glare of publicity. Not only were the second and third concerts to be conducted by Toscanini, but in the first concert there was to be the première of the previously unperformed Schumann Violin Concerto, a work whose claim to fame was that the composer had requested through a spirit medium that it should be disinterred for performance. That, however, was postponed until February 1938 (see p. 142).

Toscanini's two concerts took place on 30 October (exceptionally, a Saturday) and 3 November. Before the first of these, there occurred what the press had been waiting for but which had so far miraculously been avoided: an outburst. At the rehearsal of Beethoven's Ninth Symphony on 27 October Toscanini walked out after an hour, leaving a distinguished group of people attending the occasion – including Queen Eugénie of Spain, the Austrian Baron Franckenstein, Vaughan Williams and Cortot – somewhat at a loss. The *Daily Telegraph* more or less invented a story:

> Dissatisfied with the execution of a passage in the third movement he several times interrupted the rehearsal [*sic*: what could be worse than for a conductor to *interrupt* a rehearsal?] asking for a repetition of a passage which he considered the oboists were not playing correctly. When he could not obtain the desired result he threw his baton down and exclaimed that in the circumstances he did not intend to go on . . .

This was pure fabrication and the *Daily Telegraph* had to withdraw the story with specific reference to the oboists' not being to blame. In fact the first movement was being played at the time, and Toscanini had felt the orchestra were not giving of their best. Owen Mase commented: 'The incident was really very trivial; Toscanini thought it would be better to abandon the rehearsal after an hour, and so he stopped it and walked out . . . he told me he still thinks it is one of the finest orchestras there is.'

The Press self-perpetuatingly ensured that the displays of 'temperament' continued. At the end of the Brahms *Requiem*, in the first concert, Toscanini left the stage immediately because he had asked in the programme that there should be no applause in the hall (though a section of the audience did applaud). This was 'Toscanini in Concert "Incident"' in the *Sunday Dispatch*. The next morning, on the way to rehearsal Toscanini was photographed with a flash bulb on leaving his hotel, and struck out at the photographer; Toscanini's wife intervened and was accidentally hit by her husband. This was 'Drama on Way to Rehearsal' in *Reynolds News*. At the Beethoven concert, Toscanini had to postpone the start six minutes while Reith and the Prime Minister Neville Chamberlain took their seats next to the Duke of Kent. They had been delayed in the deep fog. Even this made news.

The concerts themselves were greeted with almost unrestrained ecstasy, and special praise was given to the participation of the BBC Chorus and Choral Society, for whose rehearsals the young Charles Groves had played; before visiting England for the first time Toscanini had been unwilling to work with amateur choral singers. Beethoven's Ninth, for almost the first time in all his concerts, raised purist eyebrows, for his tempi were exceptionally fast and the rhythms inexorably hammered out. 'A complete indifference to the music's usual emotional significance', said Neville Cardus (*Manchester Guardian*), '. . . a cosmic scheme which had no use for the nuance of merely mortal pathos'.

It must have been difficult for Boult and the Orchestra to follow this with four further concerts. The first, on 10 November, was notable for a fine account of Elgar's then neglected *Falstaff*. On 17 November came a repeat performance in London of the Cello Concerto by the musicologist Sir Donald Tovey, played by Pablo Casals. This hour-long work was by all accounts of a monumental dullness, and it stimulated Constant Lambert to a display of wit in his *Sunday Referee* notice:

> I am told by those who had the moral, physical and intellectual stamina to sit it out that Sir Donald Tovey's Cello Concerto lasts for over an hour. This I cannot vouch for as, like several other musicians, I was compelled to leave at the end of the first movement, which seemed to last as long as my first term at school. . . . His music is a vacuum and it is only natural to abhor it.

On 1 December the concert included the first public performance of John

Ireland's visionary choral work *These things shall be*, plus Walton's *Belshazzar's Feast* and Ireland's London Overture. Walton's *In Honour of the City of London* (conducted by the composer) completed a good British programme. This concert was attended by the Queen and the Duchess of Kent, with Osbert Sitwell and Sir John Reith. The BBC had little advance warning of the fact that royalty was to attend, and the audience was completely unaware of the fact until the National Anthem was played. Walton's City of London piece had been given at the Leeds Festival two months previously. It sets the familiar words of Dunbar, 'London, thou art of the flower of cities all'; Ernest Newman commented that 'the man who could believe that could believe anything . . .' but he thought that Walton had 'lavished all his virtuosity on the score, which is often exciting enough by its sheer volume and brilliance of sound'.

On 8 December Malcolm Sargent conducted the BBC Symphony Orchestra for the first time in their Symphony Concert series. He revived Bax's Fifth Symphony and performed Dvořák's Violin Concerto with Milstein; the performances were 'characteristically animated' (*Sunday Times*). An important contemporary concert on 8 October was devoted to the music of Szymanowski, who had died earlier in the year: British premières of his Overture Op. 12, Violin Concerto No. 2 (Antonio Brosa) and Ballet Music *Harnasie* were given, under Boult's direction. On 17 December Charles Munch conducted a group of works from the June 1937 ISCM festival in Paris, including Lars Erik Larsson's *Divertimento*, which has now become a repertory piece.

At the start of 1938, the Berlin Philharmonic visited London with Furtwängler. This quite overshadowed the BBC's concert with Mengelberg on 19 January, which was found disappointingly dry. On 26 January Prokofiev arrived to conduct a demanding half-programme of his own music, the Classical Symphony, Second Violin Concerto and *Romeo and Juliet* extracts (British première): awkwardly juxtaposed with Boult conducting Beethoven's Eroica Symphony.

On 9 February Mahler's Eighth Symphony, which Sir Henry Wood had conducted in 1930, was revived in Queen's Hall. This massive undertaking was cautiously welcomed: some thought it a fine work in a poor performance; others had no patience with the vastness of the piece: 'a pitiful contrast between noble aspirations and inadequate achievement', wrote J.A. Westrup in an intolerant notice in the *Daily Telegraph*.

Music of the Spheres

The next week brought the postponed première of the Schumann Violin

Concerto. This had been a long saga. The work had been disinterred by Jelly d'Aranyi, the soloist at the concert. *Psychic News* proclaimed in its lead story on 25 September 1937: 'BBC TO PLAY MUSIC TRACED AT SEANCES. Famous Violinist-Medium Will Broadcast Her Find.' It explained that Baron Erik Palmstierna, Swedish Minister in London, was wont to hold spiritualist meetings at his home, which were often attended by Miss d'Aranyi and her sister. At one of these meetings a spirit asked that a posthumous work of his for violin should be rediscovered and played by Miss d'Aranyi; when asked his name, he replied that it was Robert Schumann. In his book *Horizons of Immortality*, published to coincide with the intended first performance, Baron Palmstierna claimed that Miss d'Aranyi and the world at large was previously unaware of the concerto's existence. The BBC publicity department made the most of this: 'BBC ANNOUNCEMENT: Spirit Messages lead to Discovery of Lost Concerto': 'its existence was unknown until the other day to anyone except the curators of the Prussian State Library and one or two members of the Schumann and Joachim families.'

Unfortunately for the BBC and Miss d'Aranyi, the then current third edition of Grove's *Dictionary* was perfectly well aware of the concerto's existence, and devoted a substantial paragraph to it, even giving the tempo markings of each movement. The work had not been 'lost' but suppressed as unworthy: after Schumann's death, Clara Schumann, Joachim and Brahms agreed that the work should not be published. After the deaths of Clara in 1896 and Brahms in 1897, Joachim was the sole survivor of this vow; when he died in 1907 his son Johannes deposited the concerto along with his father's papers in the Berlin State Library, with instructions that the work should not be made public until 1956 (a hundred years after Schumann's death). Under the insistent pressure of Jelly d'Aranyi's spirit messages, Johannes Joachim yielded; when the pressure of the publishers Schott's was also added, the Berlin State Library agreed to release the manuscript. Jelly d'Aranyi was to give the first British performance, and Yehudi Menuhin the first American performance.

But Germany claimed the first world performance. And just before the BBC's intended première in October, Germany decided to postpone its performance until November, when it would be part of a Festival of Nazi Music. (This would have also ruled out participation in the performance by Johannes Joachim on the grounds that he was a Jew). Kenneth Wright was immediately dispatched to the office of Goebbels, Minister of Propaganda, to prove that the spirit messages to Miss d'Aranyi gave the Corporation an indisputable right to broadcast the work immediately. The main worry seemed to be that if performance were delayed, Menuhin would broadcast the work from America before the BBC's première.

Meanwhile, Elizabeth Joachim, 86-year-old daughter of the violinist, had cast doubt on Baron Palmstierna's account by writing a letter to *The Listener* (29 September) saying that 'there is no mystery in the matter at all . . . [the concerto's existence] was perfectly well known to many people besides ourselves . . . strange that spirits should have to take such a roundabout way to reveal what was not concealed.' This provoked a letter from Jelly d'Aranyi to *The Times* (1 October) in which she said she had never claimed that the work's existence was not known, simply that she did not know of it herself.

The performance had been prefaced by another impassioned outburst in *The Times* by Eugenie Schumann (15 January), in which she said it was Clara's decision not to publish the work, that Joachim had little part in the matter, and that he could not have committed a breach of faith and allowed the work to be performed. However, Johannes Joachim wrote to the *Daily Telegraph* that he thought that 'the course of events in the past 25 years rendered it unnecessary to maintain the term of prohibition originally laid down'. Adolf Busch said that he had seen the work and had agreed with Joachim, who had declared: 'the artist who loves Schumann will not play this work.' Menuhin (who gave the New York première in November) and Miss d'Aranyi did not agree. After all this build-up the performance was something of an anti-climax. Though the slow movement was consistently praised, the last movement was found disappointing, and the concerto as a whole was declared no more than moderately enjoyable. It did not establish itself in the repertory.

On 23 February Malipiero's Second Symphony was given its British première under Boult (it had been played at the ISCM Festival in Paris in June). It was found to be variously 'laconic' (*Daily Telegraph*), 'gloomy' (*Observer*), 'dry and stingy' (*Sunday Times*). The season closed with Bach's B minor Mass under Boult on 16 March, a performance praised for its clarity, which stimulated *The Times* to ask that the work should not be presented 'as a grand finale to a series of symphony concerts . . . it must abandon post-Handelian standards of volume once and for all' – a new edition of the work was, it said, necessary to replace Sullivan's 1886 version for the Leeds Festival, prepared in conformity with Bach's recently published autograph. A comment out of its time; the Sullivan version is still the basis of the standard English vocal score.

Studio concerts in the first part of 1938 included Nicolai Malko returning to conduct the British première of Miaskovsky's Symphony No. 14 (9 January), two concerts under Mengelberg (16 and 23 January), and Kodály's *Háry János* under Boult (30 January). Albert Coates conducted Scriabin's

Prometheus (20 March), and Boult repeated the Walton Symphony yet again (27 March). Wood had repeated the Vaughan Williams Fourth Symphony on 2 March in the Queen's Hall series: these two great English symphonies received splendid treatment from the BBC throughout the Thirties.

Contemporary concerts included the return of Hermann Scherchen, no better liked by the Orchestra than previously, for a complete account of Busoni's one-act opera *Arlecchino* (7 January); works by Igor Markevich, Christian Darnton, Elizabeth Maconchy (Viola Concerto) and Vladimir Vogel under Lambert (4 February); and the ambitious Piano Concerto of Alan Bush with the composer as soloist (4 March). Provincial concerts during the 1937–8 season were given in Newcastle, Nottingham, Aberdeen and Plymouth. British music was given in each concert, and Newcastle heard the first public performance of Hindemith's *Symphonic Dances*.

European tensions and BBC changes

Internationally, the situation during early 1938 became depressing. Hitler's advance, with little more than verbal protests from the rest of Europe, continued. One of his decisive steps might have had important consequences for the BBC Symphony Orchestra, had it not been for the continued little-England policy of the BBC's Music Advisory Committee.

On 12 March 1938 Germany invaded Austria, the day before a plebiscite ordered by the Austrian Chancellor in which the Austrian people would doubtless have reasserted their independence. The conductor of the Vienna Philharmonic Orchestra was Boult's friend and colleague Bruno Walter. Implacably opposed to the Nazis, as his refusal to appear with Backhaus had demonstrated to a surprised BBC some years earlier, Walter fled to Monte Carlo. Owen Mase spoke to him later in the month when Walter was conducting in the Hague, and Boult wrote to him in Monte Carlo. Walter replied on 21 March: 'I know that you feel with me and that you understand – better than anyone else – what besides my personal sufferances the death of Austria means to all of us.' Boult did not merely feel, however; he acted. (The incident was not, needless to say, reported in his autobiography.) He went to see Reith and immediately offered to step down as Chief Conductor of the Symphony Orchestra so that Walter could be invited to Britain to take over the post for as long or short a time as he wished. Boult would stay on the staff, of course, but the Orchestra would welcome Walter as they always had done, and the appointment would bring considerable lustre to the BBC, for Walter was already being approached by American orchestras. Reith agreed with the proposal, but felt the need to consult Allen as Chairman of the Music Advisory Committee. He turned it down at once, saying that it would be inappropriate to have any foreigner as conductor of a BBC Orchestra. And there the matter rested. Boult wrote to Walter, who replied on 12 June: 'I made up my mind to take a good rest . . . my season is "sold out" except March which I reserved for America . . . I would regret if I would not go . . .' Boult managed to persuade Walter to come to England again in 1939, and even after war was declared in September 1939 Walter was hoping to return in 1940. By then he was in America, and he kept in touch regularly with Boult.

A major change which did take place at the BBC in 1938 was the departure of Sir John Reith. For many years he had contemplated leaving the Corporation which he had done so much to create and to develop, and the possibility of a political post had always been attractive to him. When an offer came in 1938, it was less glamorous: the Chairmanship of Imperial Airways. But he felt impelled to accept, and announced to a stunned Board of Governors that he would leave at the end of June. The Governors mortally offended him by not involving him in their final choice of his successor. Reith would probably have picked Cecil Graves, then his Deputy; but the Governors chose Frederick Ogilvie, of Queen's University Belfast – an academic who, although he was said (by the *Evening Standard*, 20 July 1938) to have 'a passion for Bach fugues', was an unassertive figure with quite the wrong personality for guiding a large institution through the difficult years ahead. And so Reith, whose detailed involvement in the foundation of the BBC Symphony Orchestra, and whose trenchant support for the cultural content of his network, had done so much to create the exceptionally fertile soil in which the Orchestra flourished in its first decade, departed quietly. He made a last journey to the transmitter at Droitwich on the last day of the month, and on leaving at midnight signed the visitors' book 'J.C.W. Reith, late BBC'.

Toscanini again

In May 1938, the Orchestra braced itself once more for Toscanini's arrival. Owen Mase, who had been the BBC's chief link with Toscanini, had now left the Corporation to concentrate on his own activities as a promoter and agent, but he was retained to look after the conductor during his visit. As the *Annual Register* later recorded,

> In May and June the BBC Orchestra went through the refining fire of a Toscanini festival – as it was in effect, though it bore the title of London Music Festival. The programmes of the six concerts were typically mis-

cellaneous. Yet unity of effect arose from ever-present factors . . . of the conductor's musical vision and tremendous personality.

In retrospect the contents of the programmes were unsatisfactory: in the 19 May concert there was Mozart, Beethoven, Vaughan Williams, Weber– Berlioz and Smetana; on 23 May Bach, Beethoven and Strauss (*Don Quixote* with Feuermann and Bernard Shore). Then there was Rossini, Mozart, Brahms and Schubert on 3 June, and Scarlatti/Tommasini, Sibelius's Second Symphony, and Brahms's Second Symphony on 10 June. Undoubtedly the highlights of the series were the two performances on 27 and 30 May of Verdi's *Requiem*. No praise was found too high for these concerts: 'Supreme in conception and magnificent in execution, one by which standards may be corrected and others maybe judged.' Again the BBC Choral Society took part with great success, and the soloists were Zinka Milanov, Kerstin Thorborg, Helge Roswaenge and Nicola Moscona. Press comment may be summed up in a sentence by Neville Cardus: 'It is impossible to go on and on praising Toscanini; yet there is little else to do.'

Between Toscanini and the 1938 Proms, the Orchestra could not relax. The ISCM Festival was once again to be held in England, from 17 to 24 June; E. J. Dent was in his last season as President, and Edward Clark was Honorary Secretary. There were three orchestral concerts, beginning with Webern's cantata *Das Augenlicht* under Scherchen at the Queen's Hall. Elisabeth Lutyens later recalled:

> The work was received with bated breath and obvious emotion, the audience standing and cheering for minutes afterwards. It was an unforgettable experience and confirmed the earlier impression that here was a composer with a musical mind and an almost Mozartian ear that could only belong to a human being of utter integrity, and that Webern, who had convinced me from the very first note of his I had heard, would be a guiding spirit to all future music . . .

This of a composer whose music had only earlier that year provoked the cellist James Whitehead to bring to a halt the British première of Webern's String Trio; he walked off the platform declaring, 'Oh, I can't play this thing'.

The other orchestral concerts included scenes from Hindemith's *Mathis der Maler*, the *Danses pour orchestre* by Jean Binet, and excerpts (parts 1, 2 & 7) from the oratorio *The Vision of Isaiah* by the Swiss composer Willy Burkhard, which made a considerable impression. As a result, the complete work was broadcast in the BBC's contemporary series on 2 December. This

rare work was a modern reworking of the eighteenth-century German cantata plan, complete with narrative, arias and chorales, setting the story of
Isaiah from the Old Testament with texts from the psalms. Burkhard frequently used ecclesiastical modes: Edwin Evans called it 'an impressive
piece of devotional music in contrast to the quasi-sceptical cerebration of so
much other recent music'. Clarence Raybould conducted.

1938-9

The last Symphony Orchestra season before the Second World War was
planned on a lavish scale, not restricted by the increasingly gloomy state of
the country. Sixteen concerts (nearly back to the early 1930s ration of
eighteen) were included in two subscription series. Boult had nine, Walter
two. Henry Wood was to celebrate his jubilee as a conductor in the two concerts on 30 November and 7 December; Basil Cameron, Eugene Goossens
and Beecham each had one concert. The season was to culminate in the most
elaborate London Music Festival ever, planned independently under the
direction of Owen Mase, in which Toscanini concerts would be a centrepiece. The programmes were slightly disappointing; but though there was
only one première, and that a work by Eugene Goossens in his own concert,
each concert had its special point of interest.

The Times found nothing to complain about in the provision of orchestral
music in London, and reflected in an editorial on the mushrooming growth
of the art during the 1930s:

> The public which enjoys these amenities hardly realises that the habits of
> concert-going which they have made possible are the growth of no more than
> half a dozen years . . . London is well served with orchestral music and a
> practical example is given of the value of healthy competition and of how
> little desirable it is to create monopolies where art is concerned.

And the BBC's concerts, which included much twentieth-century music,
compared favourably with those of the London Symphony Orchestra, for
instance, which included music by only one living composer, Richard
Strauss. The Royal Philharmonic Society had more to offer, including the
European première of Bloch's Violin Concerto, and an all-Sibelius concert
to inaugurate the Sibelius Festival of six concerts at the end of October at
Queen's Hall in which Beecham conducted.

A prominent feature of the BBC's season was the generous provision of
choral works following the success of the BBC Chorus and Choral Society
under Toscanini. The Mozart *Requiem* and Beethoven's Ninth in Walter's
concerts, Holst's *Hymn of Jesus* and Honegger's *King David* under Boult, as

well as Handel's *Judas Maccabaeus* with the Philharmonic Choir. In the studio on Christmas Day Berlioz's *L'Enfance du Christ* was to be revived under Boult.

The season opened with an all-Brahms concert under Boult on 19 October; then Szigeti appeared in a rarity, the Busoni Violin Concerto: 'ingenious, resourceful and bristling with ideas,' said Capell in the *Daily Telegraph*; and the orchestra again repeated Walton's Symphony – a work increasingly respected by listeners and critics alike. Eugene Goossens on 9 November 'once again demonstrated the fact that he is easily the finest and best equipped of our younger school of conductors' (Neville Cardus). He had returned from America to direct his own *Nature Poems* (orchestrated from their piano version) and, by request, *The Rite of Spring*, of which he had given several performances in the 1920s. 'Has the famous "Rite" been better played? Never, we should say' (Richard Capell). Another temporary resident in America, Basil Cameron, was welcomed in his 16 November concert which included Bax's Fourth Symphony. Mahler's *Das Lied von der Erde* was revived by Boult for a rare performance on 23 November with Mary Jarred and Walter Widdop, sung in English as *The Song of the Earth*. The two Henry Wood jubilee concerts followed. *Judas Maccabaeus* on 30 November overran the 9.05 pm news bulletin by fifteen minutes, causing considerable protest and confusion. Wood's Handel was damned as usual, and his determination to give the oratorio uncut was taken as evidence of the work's dullness. The all-Elgar programme on 7 December was far better received: 'one of the most memorable concerts of Sir Henry Wood's jubilee year', said Bonavia in the *Daily Telegraph*.

4 November was an important day: Nadia Boulanger conducted in the studio the British première of a distinguished work – Stravinsky's *Dumbarton Oaks* – with Jean Françaix's Cantata *Le diable boîteux* for voices and orchestra, and pieces by Stanley Bate, Antoni Szalowski, and Leo Preger. The soloists included Hugues Cuénod. A new series of six special concerts began with Goossens conducting his oratorio *Judith* on 21 October; Monteux conducting a concert in memory of Ravel on 18 November, with an introduction by M. D. Calvocoressi; and a significant concert of new British music under Boult on 16 December with Britten playing his Piano Concerto, then the first performances of Herbert Howells' Concerto for String Orchestra and Rubbra's Second Symphony.

The start of 1939 was marked by Bruno Walter's return visit. On 11 January he was given a deeply sympathetic reception at the Queen's Hall, with prolonged cheers. Mozart's Symphony No. 40 and *Requiem* were welcomed – with surprise by Neville Cardus, who had often found Walter's conducting sentimental, at the opposite pole from Toscanini's objectivity. But he now said that 'Walter conducted with admirable simplicity and understanding – he was the perfect artist in all that he did. It was the conducting of a man for whom music is even more than an art – a way of life in fact.' The hall was again sold out for the Beethoven Ninth Symphony on 18 January (preceded by the Brahms Tragic Overture and *Song of Destiny*). Walter felt very deeply the affection and warmth shown him by the BBC Orchestra and Boult. Ironically, Boult was out of the country when he gave his concerts, and so did not meet him. Walter had decided to take French citizenship, and before leaving Claridge's at the end of his stay he sent this letter to Boult:

> I regret more than I can say that I have not seen you here, that I could not express viva voce what I have felt in these days of intense work with the institution that you have developed, educated and brought to the imposing form of today . . . I am sure not to exaggerate if I say that you help to make musical history in England. Culture in Central Europe has gone down; musical culture here is rising, by your merits and those of your excellent collaborators . . . go on as you have done until now . . .

In February Boult returned with the Berg fragments from *Wozzeck*, sung by May Blyth, and Honegger and Holst a week later. The first drew a small house; the second was interesting for its juxtaposition of two works each of which had caused a stir in the Twenties. Neville Cardus made the point that

> if it were not for the BBC, what would happen to work as fine in feeling, as austere in style as Holst's *Hymn of Jesus*? Our concerts have grown commercial to the extent that hardly any works are presented except those which the public knows more or less by heart . . . the standard repertory was established in a period when concerts were controlled mainly by a few wealthy patrons . . . How did the public ever come to know what it likes if it did not attend to a work for the first time?

The comment might stand as a tribute to the BBC's programmes in the Thirties – and today.

Beecham returned to the BBC not long after having vigorously denounced it again on 4 January at the dinner of the Incorporated Society of Musicians. His was a showy programme: Wagner, Berlioz and Tchaikovsky's Fifth, plus the obligatory Delius, *In a Summer Garden*. But Beecham carried all before him. 'He swayed and pawed the air and caressed it. He dived and crouched, he cajoled, implored and commanded. Sometimes he looked like a conjuror using his wand to draw a symphony out of a hat . . . For musical instinct pure and undefiled Sir Thomas has every other conductor of the present day easily beaten . . .' (Neville Cardus, *Manchester Guardian*). The next week, a concert by Boult was specially altered to include the return from a prolonged illness of Hamilton Harty, who conducted the first performance of his new work, *The Children of Lir*, composed in Antrim during his convalescence.

Boult conducted Bach, Debussy and Beethoven on 8 March in what was to have been the last concert of the season; but then the opportunity was taken to present on 15 March the first complete performance of Hindemith's opera *Mathis der Maler* – which had been heard in part at the ISCM Festival in 1937. Hindemith was present to supervise the rehearsals, and he was delighted with the orchestra's work. On the day of the concert he wrote an enthusiastic note to them: 'Far be from me the desire to make an impassioned speech to you like Napoleon before the battle. After yesterday's wonderful rehearsal that is not necessary. You sang and played my piece with such evident enthusiasm and with, as I trust, some liking for the music . . .' He considered the performance better than those he had heard in Germany. The press were uniformly unenthusiastic: 'SOME GRIM HOURS' was the *Daily Telegraph* headline.

Contemporary concerts were given under Boult, Ansermet and Scherchen; in the Special Concerts, Raybould repeated Busoni's *Arlecchino* complete on 27 January; Bliss conducted his *Morning Heroes* on 24 March, and Basil Cameron gave an American programme of Emerson Whithorne's Symphony No. 2, John Alden Carpenter's Concertino for piano and orchestra, and Anis Fuleihan's Suite, *Mediterranean*.

The last London Music Festival

In the spring of 1939, the London Music Festival suddenly acquired a variety and extravagance to match its name. In the last days of peace, a lavishness of entertainment and culture lightened the deepening worries about what was to come. The Festival was the brainchild of Owen Mase: though based round his now-close relationship with Toscanini, concerts by the BBC Symphony Orchestra and the conductor formed only the apex of a giant celebration. Mase had managed to unite the whole musical establishment on his council: Allen, Beecham, Boult, Walford Davies, Dyson, Cockerill, Harold Holt, Robert Mayer, and representatives of all the main London musical organisations. Religious bodies represented music in churches and cathedrals; bands were to play in the open air, and there was to be a giant firework display on Hampstead Heath to the strains of Handel's *Music for the Royal Fireworks*. The King and Queen consented to be patrons, and made the Great Hall at Hampton Court available for a concert. Plans were so far advanced by the end of 1938 that the event was announced as 'an organisation under Mr Owen Mase to bring under one management such music-making as shall go on in and around London between 23 April and 2 June next year'. The scheme brought to fruition an idea which Owen Mase had conceived and planned over five years. He worked in collaboration with Keith Douglas of the Royal Philharmonic Society, with the support of Sir Hugh Allen. There was a broadcast talk on the Festival by Sir Thomas Beecham. But George Barnes (later the first Controller of the Third Programme) reported brusquely: 'Script – Obvious, but lively towards the end: Delivery – Supercilious: Production – Nervous, Difficult.'

In the preface to the Festival handbook, Sir Walford Davies, then Master of the King's Musick, summed up the mood of the Festival:

> Never before has a musical event of such scope and comprehensive importance been planned for London . . . The Festival is an ideal piece of team work in its organisation. It is a give-and-take Festival. In a sense it is a five-weeks-long family party of musicians and music-lovers . . .

It was actually a last frenetic celebration before the coming of war; a final token of the explosion of music-making in London during the Thirties. Allen and Walford Davies would not survive the war; it would be a very different musical world which greeted London in 1946.

The BBC Symphony Orchestra's contribution to this gargantuan feast was especially designed by Mase to stand head and shoulders above the rest. In six Toscanini concerts between 6 May and 28 May, all nine Beethoven symphonies would be heard, plus two performances of the Mass in D. Boult would add two programmes of concertos in this period: Backhaus to play the Third and Fifth Piano Concertos; Solomon to play the Fourth alongside Busch (who had to be replaced by Szigeti) playing the Violin Concerto. It was a scheme likely to attract the greatest public attention. The contract for these concerts, incidentally, was signed between Toscanini and Owen Mase personally. Toscanini had some doubts about visiting England when the international situation was so uncertain – like many distinguished musicians, he had cancelled his engagements at the Salzburg Festival – but he was reassured that at any possible sign of trouble he could be whisked from the country by plane.

The King and Queen attended the opening concert of the series. Boult tells a delightful story of royal unpredictability in connection with this concert:

> The Director-General and I established ourselves by the Royal Entrance to

Queen's Hall in Riding House Street, with wives and other members of staff lurking in the Royal Reception Room outside the entrance to Block A. Luckily we were early because very soon a large car drove up, and to our intense astonishment out jumped the Duke of Kent, followed at a dignified interval by Queen Mary. We had had no notification of their coming, and the seats inside the hall had to be hastily re-arranged. Older readers will remember that, when Royalty was expected, Block A, just over the first violins, was cleared of its rows of seats and more suitable chairs, with a table for programmes, were placed on the second row level, with a discreet screen of palms between them and Block B. Queen Mary and the Duke had arrived some eight or ten minutes before time (it seemed like two or three hours) and Mr Ogilvie, then Director-General, engaged the Duke in conversation while I presented the wives and staff to Queen Mary. There was nothing else I could do. She knew none of them, but luckily Lady Bridgeman, wife of our Chairman, was there and they were able to carry on some conversation until Their Majesties arrived.

'Oh Mother, how nice; I had no idea you were coming,' said the Queen as she came in, and confirmed our feeling that Queen Mary's intentions had, for once, not been circulated as far as they should have been.

Toscanini was very unhappy about meeting the King and Queen, as Boult's story implies. On the day before the concert he insisted that he had had a sleepless night worrying about the possibility. So no pressure was brought to bear on him to see the monarchs during the interval, and he was allowed to rest. Comment on this point overshadowed musical criticism of the concert: to be begged to be excused meeting the King and Queen seemed to be the greatest testimony possible to the seriousness and singlemindedness of Toscanini's attitude to the music. Instead, Paul Beard represented the Orchestra. (He was delighted when the King asked whether, when one violinist stopped to turn the page, the other had to play twice as loud.)

Boult's first concert followed; Toscanini attended. Then came Toscanini's accounts of Beethoven's Fourth and Third Symphonies:

an experience that no one who was present will forget . . . [wrote Richard Capell] Toscanini does not allow that Beethoven ever felt Fate's grip upon him to relax . . . the orchestra played as though its life were at stake . . .

Toscanini's second Beethoven concert in the crowded Queen's Hall last night was, to use restrained and even guarded language, terrific. The great wheel of his right arm never ceased; on and on we were driven; the rhythm beat into the brain. It was as though we were listening to music in the teeth of a wind . . .

2

On 12 May followed the Fifth and Sixth Symphonies:

> Toscanini so despises exaggeration that his scheme of dynamics is extra-
> ordinarily economical . . . his scale of tone is jealously guarded; he gives us no
> extremities . . . The rare quality in Toscanini's interpretations. . . . is the way
> they seem to add to a composer's stature and genius; at each of these
> concerts we have been made aware that Beethoven's music is even greater
> than we have hitherto known . . . Toscanini's treatment of Beethoven is
> without doubt the most musically comprehensive of our time. But in fairness
> to other conductors, some protest should be made against the growing
> fashionable idea that Toscanini's idea of Beethoven is also the most poetically
> comprehensive. He is a great artist from his own point of view of music.
> Let us be content with that, and cherish him with some sense of proportion
> (Ernest Newman, *The Sunday Times*).

Then on 17 May, the Seventh and Eighth.

> As the procession of symphonies at Queen's Hall goes by, we are dazzled by
> the overwhelming technique of a conductor on whose brain is photo-
> graphed every detail of the score, who had considered all possible readings,
> and made his choice, and who sweeps his players onwards to an achievement
> they never believed possible (*Observer*).

> Seldom, even with Toscanini, has one had to such a degree the feeling that
> the conductor was simply the medium through which the composer was
> speaking . . . everything in the scores was made crystal-clear, every phrase
> sprang into being as if instantaneously cast in the finest metal, and passages
> that on other occasions have seemed to us a trifle weak or superfluous now
> become perfectly worthy and relevant parts of the total structure (*The
> Sunday Times*).

Then came Boult's second concert, and Toscanini's account of the Ninth
Symphony:

> As time goes on we shall forget this or that about it, but surely never the
> principles of this performance – which are, for that matter not exemplary
> principles, not imitable, for they belonged to a particular man's nature and
> vision . . . The supremely memorable thing about the evening was the whole-
> ness of the effect of Toscanini's performance – the grasp which made, as
> never before, the finale the goal and fulfilment of it all (Richard Capell, *Daily
> Telegraph*).

And finally, the *Missa Solemnis*, the performance of which, like the Ninth

had the supreme quality which endears all Toscanini's work to us – the greatness of the music being impressed upon us entirely from within the music
itself . . . Toscanini, while obviously accountable for the work sounding and
shaping as it does on a particular occasion, gives us the grateful and comfort-
ing and unfortunately rare experience that it is the composer himself who is
talking to us through an intermediary . . . [the performances] have been
stupendous, but stupendous in the composer's way in the first and last place.
The whole Festival, indeed, has taught many of us a great deal about
Beethoven that we did not know before . . . (Ernest Newman, *The Sunday
Times*).

And that may stand as the Symphony Orchestra's final tribute for the first
decade of its life. The end of that glorious decade came all too quickly. On 12
August the Proms began. War seemed imminent, and the BBC at last began
to plan seriously for its possibility. Out-of-London administration headquarters had already been purchased at Evesham; but the so-called 'Document C', setting out the BBC's plan of action if war should be declared, had
been issued internally in its final form only during August 1939. It was not a
moment too soon. In the early hours of 1 September Hitler invaded Poland.
This was the moment when war must surely have been declared: but it was
not. Chamberlain sent only an ultimatum to Hitler. All other wartime provisions, however, were put into effect at once. Director-General Ogilvie who
had succeeded Reith in 1938, went to the Queen's Hall that night. Henry
Wood was conducting a mainly Beethoven programme, with Harriet Cohen
as the soloist in the Second Concerto. At the conclusion of the Prom concert,
Wood spoke briefly to the audience, and Ogilvie addressed the Orchestra
announcing the suspension of the concerts. The Orchestra must be ready to
travel to Bristol at any moment; the signal was to be given on the Nine
o'clock News, when the phrase 'This is London' would replace the usual
'This is the BBC'. Orchestra members recall this as one of the most dispirit-
ing moments of their life. From Sir John Reith they would have expected a
fighting speech, a declaration of confidence in the future, a call to play their
part in the conflict. From his successor they received nothing but the looks of
a worried man, apologies, and a bald statement of fact. It was as if they had
lost the war already.

4
Keeping Music Alive
1939-45

Into the dark

When Director-General Frederick Ogilvie spoke to the Symphony Orchestra in negative and worried terms on the evening of 1 September 1939 about the coming war, he was doing no more than reflect the prevalent uncertainty within the BBC and the country at large about the course which the beginning of any war was likely to take. The emergency measures prepared for use on the declaration of war were designed to meet the possibility of immediate attack on large cities. They involved the evacuation of all schoolchildren and expectant mothers to rural areas and small towns; a nearly complete blackout after dark; restricted public transport services with blinds drawn and windows darkened. The BBC's own plans matched these radical moves. Major departments were to be removed from London immediately; in the case of the Symphony Orchestra, it was to be transferred to Bristol, along with other departments requiring substantial studio space. Bristol was chosen because, as the centre of the West Region broadcasting service, it had the best facilities to house a large organisation such as the Symphony Orchestra, and it was at least accessible from London. The part that Bristol might play in any German attack on England appears to have been discounted. As for the administrative side of Music Department, that was to go with the rest of the BBC's administration to Evesham in Worcestershire.

Through the unearthly limbo of Saturday 2 September the country waited for news, while the BBC behaved as if war had already begun. Emergency broadcast plans were put into operation: a diet of recorded light music with a minimum of comment filled the day. Only after Chamberlain had faced a hostile House of Commons was an ultimatum delivered to Hitler. The Nine o'clock News that evening on the BBC began 'This is London'. Evacuation was to begin.

As members of the Symphony Orchestra prepared to leave home on Sunday morning, they heard that war had been declared. At 11.15 am Neville

155

Chamberlain broadcast to the nation, in words which summed up the mood of bewilderment in which the country had lurched towards a war it did not want: 'You can imagine what a bitter blow it is to me that all my long struggle to win peace has failed.'

A few minutes after Chamberlain's broadcast finished there was a strange foretaste of drama: the air-raid sirens sounded, and many rushed to the underground shelters. But if anyone expected immediate conflict, they were to be disappointed. Evacuees made their way to the big city-centre stations, and there boarded the trains which took them into the country. Symphony Orchestra members arrived in Bristol on Sunday evening after dark to find it unlit and seemingly deserted. They stumbled through the streets in an effort to reach their base, the studios in Whiteladies Road; thence they were dispersed to billets. Only in the morning could they acquire their bearings in a strange city. They reported for work – but there was nothing to do.

Throughout the country, the emergency measures had included the cancellation of all public entertainment and the closing of theatres and concert halls. In retrospect, this was a disastrous move: like mass evacuation and the curtailment of the BBC's normal services, it was a response to a crisis which did not exist. But until Germany's intentions became clear, it was the only possible safe course. Between the BBC and the Government there was tension about the provision of official information, the avoidance of any public explanation for the BBC's hasty changes of programming, and a lack of co-ordinated planning. To the Government's prohibition of public entertainment, the BBC responded with a voluntary curtailment of almost all creative work. Between Saturday 2 and Tuesday 5 September, news, theatre organ music and records filled the day. On Wednesday 6 September a new phase began, with what Boult later described as 'homeopathic doses of everything, except variety . . . served out for nearly five weeks until a general outcry caused a hasty reshuffle . . .' As a *Radio Times* caption put it, with characteristic understatement: 'Sandy Macpherson is having a busy week at the BBC theatre organ.' One of the many problems was that broadcasting had now been reduced to a single network – there was no 'National' and 'London Regional' programme to accommodate a variety of serious music. This was to affect the programming of classical music even when it returned to the schedules.

Unemployed in Bristol

In Bristol, morale was very low. Throughout the country there was puzzlement, and in the press, anger. Asa Briggs records that the offensive against the BBC generally began on 17 September, but the previous Monday the *Bir-*

mingham Post had already launched an attack on the Corporation's musical policy:

> The makeshift resorted to during the days of suspense before the declaration of war will not be looked upon as any sort of basis for a future broadcasting policy . . . When we shall be hearing of people over half Europe suffering want, we shall not be satisfied with 'Tea for Two' and similar fare. Much great music will be required . . . and we shall look to the BBC almost alone to give it to us.

Ernest Newman, as so often, captured the mood of outrage in *The Sunday Times* (17 September):

> . . . The BBC pours out into the air day after day an endless stream of trivialities and sillinesses, apparently labouring under the delusion that in any time of crisis the British public becomes just one colossal moron, to whose sub-simian intelligence and taste it must indulgently play down.

The *Radio Times* was unwise enough to reply to this accusation during the following week, answering a minor point of Newman's that orchestral music was provided at unsocial hours: 'There, surely, you have your selfish music-lover rampant . . .' Newman did not let that pass; on 8 October he remarked grimly that 'too much association with enemy methods of propaganda is beginning to tell upon the virtue even of the BBC. A more flagrant misrepresentation of my complaint . . . could hardly be imagined . . .'. Newman was supported by many other papers. The *Musical Times* in October suspended its 'Wireless Notes' feature because there was no music to write about:

> . . . never was there a greater disappointment. The effect was as if a few harassed officials had fled to the country, snatching up a box or two of records and the band-parts of the first dozen light orchestral pieces that came to hand. No emergency could justify such programme poverty. What use might have been made of music of heroic mould!

Though the Press were unaware of the fact, this same viewpoint was being put forward with urgency within the BBC. Boult wrote in a memo of 25 October :

> If I had had my own way I should have been conducting the Beethoven C minor Symphony on September 6th, and I think I should have been right. Actually Berlin broadcast the 7th of Beethoven and the Haffner of Mozart from a Furtwängler Concert on September 17th before I had conducted a classical symphony.

But in Bristol Boult was remote from planning priorities, which demanded (for example) that news and announcements had to be made every half-hour, and that no programme should last longer than that length of time.

Though the attack on the BBC continued with unabated venom in the Press throughout September, changes were quickly made. The first fortnight for the Symphony Orchestra in Bristol was intensely depressing for all concerned, but gradually, the Orchestra crept back on to the air with music of the substance of Elgar's *Enigma Variations* and the Brahms *Academic Festival Overture* (12 September). Elgar, Franck, Beethoven and Dvořák followed during the week, and on the Sunday Newman launched his attack there was actually Delius, Sibelius, Elgar and even a little Wagner on the air. Director-General Ogilvie visited Bristol for the first time on 16 September, and agreed that the time allotted to serious music was inadequate and should be increased. On 28 September, the BBC capitulated to pressure and met a deputation of journalists in Broadcasting House, where, on behalf of the Director-General, Basil Nicolls, now Controller of Programmes, admitted that 'good music had been very badly hit, more even than the most extreme lowbrow would want'.

Concerts again

For the Symphony Orchestra's management the first priority was to restore the public concert-giving which had been so rudely interrupted when the Proms were abandoned on 1 September. The Concerts Manager, W. W. Thompson, who had travelled to Bristol with the Orchestra, wrote eagerly as soon as it became clear that the first period of emergency was over that all the machinery existed to begin public concerts again; they could be put on 'at a moment's notice'. Boult took up the request with Ogilvie on 16 September and wrote on 17 September: 'Musical culture cannot be allowed to lapse any longer now that the emergency period is over and that theatres, etc., are re-opening. The BBC should be early in the field with a weekly public symphony series.' On 24 September Nicolls agreed to the proposal. But there were some important provisions. Concerts could not be broadcast live if there was any danger of an air-raid, and the Ministry of Information had insisted that the origins of any live broadcast be censored. So the problems of advertising the concerts locally were likely to be great, and their stability could not be guaranteed. Nevertheless, the plan went ahead.

Bristol's most prominent agent, Charles Lockier, who ran the Bristol International Celebrity Subscription Concerts, was asked to promote the BBC events, and the first was planned for 1 November 1939 in the Colston Hall. Only the second half of each concert was to be broadcast, from 8 pm to

9 pm: on the printed programmes the Symphony Orchestra was stated to be on a 'Visit to the Colston Hall Bristol', and no details at all were given in the announcements. It was highly appropriate that the first concert included not only a British première of an English piece (*Five Variants on Dives and Lazarus* by Vaughan Williams, which Boult had premièred with the New York Philharmonic at the World's Fair the previous June), but also a concerto appearance by Myra Hess – who was to play such a vital role in wartime music-making through her establishment of the National Gallery Concerts in London. Within two months of the outbreak of war, the BBC had partly redeemed its blackened reputation, and began its championship of good music which was to continue throughout the war years.

With the resumption of symphony concerts, the question of the Orchestra's personnel became an urgent consideration. More than forty of the youngest members had been released for military service at the start of the war. This had been a heartbreaking decision for Boult to take, but it was unavoidable, and it had left the Orchestra reduced to some seventy members, undesirably small both for symphony concerts and for any split studio work. Rather late in the day, it was decided to attempt to grade orchestral personnel in terms of their indispensability, and to try and secure some agreement on the deferment of their military service from the government. Category A players were deemed 'impossible to replace'; Category B players' absence would lead to a lowering of standards in the string sections; and Category C players were less essential. The most important measure taken in November 1939 (and the only one that was possible) was to recall certain key players and regrade them in Category A, ensuring their availability for at least another year. Almost twenty players returned immediately, including two first violins, two seconds, two violas, two cellists, one bass, one flute, oboe, clarinet, bassoon, trumpet and two horns. They rejoined the Orchestra on 26 November, bringing it up to a strength of ninety players.

Players settled into their Bristol billets, and some struck out on their own. One adventurous enterprise which has become a famous part of Symphony Orchestra history was the partnership of harpist Sidonie Goossens and violinist Jessie Hinchliffe. Sidonie Goossens was married to Hyam Greenbaum, previously director of the Television Orchestra and now in Bristol as conductor of the Variety Orchestra; Jessie Hinchliffe was married to the composer Alan Rawsthorne. The four acquired the use of the Clifton Arts Club in Park Street. This splendid studio, complete with its small stage, became their home for the first year of the war. A large front room, overlooking Park St, housed the Rawsthornes; the Goossens lived in the main studio, retiring to a large divan on the curtained stage. This strange studio is remembered as a centre of the Orchestra's life in Bristol; it acquired its own legends, among which that of its resident ghost, the Little Grey Lady, persisted with unusual force. Life during that first six months, as 1940 began, was relatively trouble free. Supplies were easy to obtain: eggs from the local farms, meat from sympathetic butchers. There was eager support from the local population who recognised the Orchestra members' faces from their public appearances. Living the life of a small self-contained community, Orchestra members came to know the administrators and planners on a friendly basis almost for the first time. The lack of stuffiness of their hosts in Bristol, particularly G. C. Beadle, the West Region Controller, and Felix Felton, the Programme Director of the region, helped good relationships to flourish in the studios and canteen of the Whiteladies Road complex. The war seemed, for the moment, a long way away. It was a time of waiting.

The symphony concerts series continued; the only major restriction was the absence of international artists. But English guest conductors were still invited: Harty conducted the second concert (8 November) and Wood the third (15 November, including a typical novelty: *Sortilegi*, for piano and orchestra, by the Greek–Italian composer Pick-Mangiagalli). Boult at last managed to include Beethoven's Fifth on 22 November; Clarence Raybould was joined by Moiseiwitsch on 29 November. The last concert before Christmas inaugurated a notable period of co-operation with local societies: Boult conducted a chorus drawn from the Bristol Choral Society and Philharmonic Society in Elgar's *The Music Makers* and Wagner excerpts. Music was beginning to re-establish itself in the national consciousness. A second radio network was restored, to broadcast to the forces, thus relieving some of the pressure on broadcast time. And in Bristol Cathedral before Christmas, the Symphony Orchestra gave its services in aid of the Lord Mayor's Christmas Dinner Fund in a 'service of music' by Purcell, Schubert, Delius and Humperdinck, for which the Cathedral was packed. Under Trevor Harvey, Christmas carols were sung at the Embassy Cinema in Clifton for a united church celebration; Boult sang in the choir. The BBC musicians were becoming part of the local community.

Wartime policies

Press discontent, and the clear inadequacy of the BBC's plans for broadcasting in the war, led to a major internal investigation during November into the BBC's departmental policies. The main broadcast service was now called the Home Service. Two shortlived Home Broadcasting Committees were superseded by a Home Service Board, which requested detailed plans for wartime policy from Departmental Heads by mid-November. This request, at a time when programme activity was once more getting under way, caused some consternation. Boult wrote on 2 November to Basil Nicolls: 'I would like to say that we feel it is quite impossible to get our ideas on paper with anything like adequate detail and thoroughness by November 10th.' Nevertheless, Music Department produced its paper by 14 November, and its declarations of intent for the Symphony Orchestra's work were important. Boult wrote:

> In general, war conditions should in no way change the basis of the BBC's music policy . . . [though certain factors have] contributed to adjustments in proportions.
>
> The absence of an alternative programme has made it necessary for every concert to appeal to an infinitely wider audience . . . The widening of appeal must come through the shortening of programmes . . . and the rigorous ruling-out of the mediocre both as regards music and performance.
>
> . . . the tendency is towards an increased proportion of the great classics . . . a trend in this direction could easily go too far, and the importance of keeping abreast – if not in advance – of the musical world becomes even more necessary if music is to hold its place as a cultural force . . .
>
> We still feel that the Music Department's peace-time concert plans for the 1939/40 season remain an ideal scheme, and this scheme should now be reinterpreted . . .
>
> Soon, however, we must consider ways and means of bringing such conductors as Toscanini and Bruno Walter into our programmes again, as well as the leading international soloists . . . it becomes even more necessary that our programmes and policy should show no obvious signs of insularity.
>
> To sum up, in the first week of war . . . the musical world was temporarily paralysed, partly on account of our momentary failure to fulfil the needs of the music-loving public. It is necessary during the next few months, that every effort should be made for the BBC to regain its former role of leadership in musical England . . .

One point needs emphasis: Boult's declaration that insularity was to be avoided, and that programmes should have an international flavour. This policy was modified as the war progressed. Boult went on to detail the programme plans which would realise these aims. The Wednesday symphony concerts 'remain the backbone of our orchestral music policy', and would be broadcast from 8 to 9 pm. Sunday orchestral concerts, broadcast between 2.30 and 3.30 pm, would supplement this with some outside broadcasts and some further BBC studio events. During January and late March the Symphony Orchestra would be available to visit centres around Bristol. Boult

was especially anxious to include a weekly 'classical symphony' slot in programmes on Monday or Friday evenings, and had already planned Beethoven's Seventh and Brahms's Fourth for December.

Boult also proposed a series of 'special concerts':

> In order to keep alive and stimulate the interest in both modern musical
> developments and masterpieces of old music, we propose a series of monthly
> concerts. These concerts should be given before an invitation audience,
> probably in collaboration with some such body as Bristol University whose
> students (plus those evacuated from other universities) have already shown a
> most keen interest in our public symphony concerts . . .

His splendid paper was endorsed by Nicolls, though its detailed proposals
had to be qualified: in a covering note to the Home Service Board (16
November), he said that it 'should be regarded as an excellent statement of
aims and intentions in the field of music rather than as a programme scheme
which can be translated into action in its entirety at any given moment. It is
bound to be conditioned by general programme planning . . .' But Nicolls
agreed with Boult on one important point: 'I support the contention that we
should cater for minorities as reasonably as possible.'

The main features of the plan were put into effect almost immediately,
from 26 November. On the last day of 1939 Boult communicated the main
intentions of his policy to the public in a broadcast talk which did much to
reassure public opinion. The *Daily Telegraph* (6 January) said it showed 'a
welcome change of heart', and W. J. Turner in the *New Statesman* (13 January) wrote that 'another feature of Sir Adrian Boult's speech which is most
welcome is his declaration that he "hopes to get on with a monthly series of
some kind" of modern music. This is certainly most important . . .'

It was not until May 1940 that Winston Churchill became Prime Minister
and the war in Europe began in earnest. Before that month, conditions for
the Orchestra continued to be attractive in and around Bristol. In January it
made its first visits to other towns, led by Marie Wilson as Paul Beard was
temporarily indisposed. Cheltenham on 11 January (a pair of concerts on
Thursday afternoon and evening); Newport on 17 January, where Elgar,
Wagner and Tchaikovsky were broadcast, and Smetana, Handel and Beethoven's Eighth Symphony also included; in the Pavilion, Bath, on 24 January, Jelly d'Aranyi played Vaughan Williams' *The Lark Ascending*.

Meanwhile, in Bristol a new venture which was later to involve the
Symphony Orchestra was inaugurated: a series of lunchtime concerts
modelled on Myra Hess's outstanding National Gallery events. 'PAPER
BAG LUNCHES AT MUSEUM CONCERT', wrote the *Bristol Evening Post*

(10 January): '*Some of the Ladies Took Their Knitting, Too.*' These originated as chamber music performances, but such was the enthusiastic demand that their scope was soon extended. The Symphony Orchestra's new series of concerts in Bristol (without the now-ludicrous 'Visit to' tag) resumed on 31 January. The first concert boldly devoted its entire second part, which was broadcast, to extracts from Wagner's operas, with Eva Turner. A Bristol clergyman wrote to the *Evening Post*: 'May I express my surprise and regret that the BBC Symphony Concert from the Colston Hall today includes [music by Wagner] . . . These operas are the musical embodiment of German brutality and unprincipled domination, and are not fit for performance at the present time.' The paper's critic, however, disagreed: '. . . by their unstinted applause, the audience gave the lie to the fantastic myth that the music of Wagner cannot or should not be appreciated by civilised people at war with Germany.' Subsequent programmes were less provocative: Curzon playing Delius and Liszt piano works under Clarence Raybould (7 February); Tertis in *Harold in Italy*, conducted by Harty (14 February); Walton conducting his own Symphony (21 February); and Malcolm Sargent conducting Mozart, Strauss, Rachmaninov and Arthur Bliss's Music for Strings. Boult returned for the Vaughan Williams Pastoral Symphony.

Sir Henry Wood visited Bristol to direct *The Dream of Gerontius*, which was, unusually, broadcast in full on Sunday afternoon 17 March. Such was the success of the public concerts that plans to translate to Bristol a modified version of the intended London Festival in May were approved. It was a modest scheme, but suitably concentrated and skilfully planned. There were three full-scale symphony concerts: Harty conducting a Tchaikovsky Centenary Concert on 22 May with Moiseiwitsch; Albert Wolff in a mainly French programme including a suite from Rameau's opera *Castor et Pollux* and the César Franck Symphony (29 May); and Boult conducting the Eroica and the Bliss Piano Concerto with Solomon (5 June). Wolff's visit was a great success: he came *en route* from Paris (where he conducted the Opéra Comique) to South America, and 'electrified the audience and the BBC Symphony Orchestra, who played as Bristol has never yet heard them play . . . the great audience simply rose to him at the end of the programme and cheered . . .' (*Bristol Evening World*, 30 May).

In between these three Wednesdays came two Friday lunch-hour concerts, conducted by Basil Cameron and Julian Clifford, repeating some of the season's popular works; and two Popular Orchestral Concerts on Sunday evenings: Boult (26 May) with Constant Lambert's *The Rio Grande*, and Clarence Raybould (2 June) with a further Tchaikovsky Centenary event. At the first of these concerts, the broadcast half of the programme opened with the complete National Anthems of the Allies, newly orchestrated by Sir Granville Bantock. The French, Polish, Norwegian, Belgian, Dutch and Czechoslovak anthems were included, as well as 'God Save the King'. It was perhaps an appropriate moment for a display of solidarity, for Copenhagen, Oslo, The Hague and Brussels had already fallen into German hands by 17 May. Paris fell on 14 June.

New music continues

The first of Boult's intended special concerts of contemporary music took place before an invited audience on 12 April, and it had a very distinguished programme: the first broadcast performance of Benjamin Britten's *Les Illuminations* (sung by Sophie Wyss), Roussel's Fourth Symphony, Milhaud's *Suite Provençale*, and Kodály's *Dances of Galanta*. In the second concert on 17 May, Alan Rawsthorne – the BBC's resident Bristol composer – had his Symphonic Studies played here for the first time (they had been premièred at the 1939 ISCM Festival in Warsaw) and Bartók's Music for Strings, Percussion and Celesta received an early performance.

On 21 June the final concert of the series included the British première of Bax's Seventh Symphony (written for the 1939 New York World Fair), which was received with enthusiasm by a town which had never previously heard any of Bax's symphonies. On 11 June a new cantata by Alan Rawsthorne, *Kubla Khan*, was heard under Reginald Redman, and a few days before, on 6 June, a miniature by Britten, *A Canadian Kermesse*, was premièred.

For its pains in presenting the premières of works by Britten, Bax and others, the BBC was roundly attacked by a group of English musicians including Austin, Bantock, Dunhill, Ireland, Lambert, Martin Shaw, Ethel Smyth and Vaughan Williams in a letter to *Author* magazine during the summer of 1940: 'We consider that genuine [*sic*] music by British composers should be allotted a far bigger share of broadcasting time than it enjoys at present . . . a more whole-hearted recognition by a National institution of our own native composers would be of the greatest value to the progress of musical art in this country . . .' This cry, which was often to be made, especially in wartime, was fully rebutted by Boult, who provided figures to show that substantial amounts of British orchestral and chamber music were heard. But the correspondents replied: 'In the matter of broadcasting time devoted to British composers the astonishing admission is made that out of every twenty-two hours of serious music provided eighteen hours are given over to the foreigner!' Boult answered with typical understatement: '. . . what are the names of these "foreigners"? Here are some of them: Bach,

Handel, Mozart, Beethoven, Schubert . . .'

Musical life in London during the first months of the 1939–40 'phoney war' had been unsettling for the practitioners and unsatisfactory for the audiences. The livelihood of many musicians was put into jeopardy by the closure of concert halls: Beecham announced that the London Philharmonic Orchestra might not survive and appealed for funds. But the need for war-time music was soon recognised both by entrepreneurs and by grant-giving bodies. Jack Hylton offered the London Philharmonic Orchestra touring engagements in cinemas and town halls, thus inaugurating a pattern of activity for many orchestras during the war. This involved constant, much-appreciated tours to frequently unsuitable venues in acutely difficult con-ditions. The London Philharmonic Orchestra put itself under its own management, called Musical Culture Ltd. Two important private trusts, the Pilgrim Trust and the Carnegie Trust, both raised money for the arts which was matched by the Board of Education and the Treasury, totalling £100,000 in all. A Council for the Encouragement of Music and the Arts (CEMA) was set up under Lord Macmillan: its claim to be planning not only for wartime activity but for post-war reconstruction was realised in part in its own sur-vival to the present day under the title of the Arts Council of Great Britain.

With concert life reviving in the capital during early 1940 the musical world looked to the BBC to provide the usual series of Prom concerts at the Queen's Hall. But there were serious doubts as to whether this would be feasible with the orchestra in Bristol, and the BBC hesitated throughout January and February before deciding one way or the other. It had still not assured Sir Henry Wood of its decision by the end of March – by which time Chappell's had, not surprisingly, looked elsewhere for tenants of the Queen's Hall. The Royal Philharmonic Society, in the persons of Keith Douglas and Owen Mase, took on the season and engaged the London Symphony Or-chestra under Wood to provide the concerts. The suspicion of ill-feeling between Wood and the BBC was intensified by a press controversy and by the fact that the BBC subsequently did not broadcast any of the concerts. The lack of broadcasts was due, said Boult, to the BBC's financial proposal not being accepted; but according to Douglas and Mase, the BBC's offer was 'not an economic proposition'.

Guarding the home

In fact, by the beginning of June the whole complexion of the war had changed. Defeat in France and the massive evacuation from Dunkirk opened the way for the first bombardment of England by the Luftwaffe. Eden, the Secretary for War, announced on 14 May the formation of Local

Defence Volunteer forces throughout the country. Symphony Orchestra members in Bristol joined up: sixty-seven of the seventy-seven members eligible were enrolled in the first few weeks. In July the Local Defence Volunteers became the Home Guard. Boult himself was a member:

> We undertook many new, strange duties. From a broadcast we would rush to a parade, to a lecture, to a gas drill or to go on guard outside Broadcasting House [Bristol] where we would ground our rifles with an awe-inspiring clatter and demand of those entering the building 'Advance one and be recognised'. Though we lacked the uniform and equipment for a time, we did not lack enthusiasm, and those among us who were old soldiers were eager to help the 'rookies'. (Article in *Musical America*, 10 April 1945).

In June the air-raids over England began. Bristol was an important port, a suspected home of fifth-column activity following the fall of France, and within the Luftwaffe's restricted range of activity in the south of England. On 29 June 1940 the first attack was made; this was followed by many others: some 200 during the following year; more than one a day at the height of the attacks in the autumn of 1940. Life became increasingly difficult for the Orchestra: helmets had to be worn when walking home from the studio, and as the raids increased it became progressively more difficult to justify moving about at night. Concerts began to be recorded in the afternoons and broadcast by the engineers at night. 'The quality of war-time listening was very variable,' recalled Boult 'and we had to listen – from our shelters – to stuff which made us sometimes rather ashamed.'

There were some hair-raising incidents as the summer went on. The lights failed during a late-night attack, and candles and oil-lamps had to be brought into the studio while the Orchestra was still on the air, so that the broadcast could be finished. On another occasion, the Orchestra's leader, Paul Beard, had to contribute music to the Epilogue during a raid: he played the Air from Bach's Third Suite, kneeling on the ground beside the microphone under a table. Stuart Hibberd, next to him, read passages from the Bible. One night after a studio broadcast, before what looked likely to be a heavy raid, the orchestral porter, Bill Fussell, and his assistant decided that it was too risky to leave the van containing the orchestral instruments in its usual garage. They drove it, at considerable risk, far out of town on to the moors. The instruments survived, but the garage did not; in the morning it was found to have been bombed. Through all these incidents tragedy struck only once: during a bombing attack the double bass player Albert Cockerill and his wife were killed in their flat. This was the Symphony Orchestra's only loss during the Second World War. But this incident emphasised that the BBC would be irresponsible to leave its players in Bristol.

At the end of August 1940 Boult was in London, conducting the London Philharmonic Orchestra at the Central Hall, Westminster; later that evening air-raid warnings sounded and, walking up Regent Street, he happened to chance on one of the Proms' informal sing-ins with which the audience entertained themselves until nearly 4 am. Boult's recollections of the evening are hilarious and happy (*My Own Trumpet*, pp. 118–19), but at the time they prompted a protesting note from him to Nicolls about the 'cowardly, safety-first' policy of the BBC in not broadcasting more London concerts which were so obviously good for morale. Nicolls replied: 'The point is not the safety of our personnel but the danger of broadcasting sirens, as an indication to Germany that their raiders have reached London or wherever the programme is taking place, and the Ministry of Home Security objects strongly to the broadcasting of the noise of bombs.' Boult replied: '. . . the outsider like myself through ignorance gets very irritated by the two Ministries . . . exerting such annoying control over us at the present time . . .'

When the BBC resumed its symphony concerts series in the Colston Hall in October 1940, the main battle against the German air force seemed to have been won. But the raids continued, and a new notice appeared in the programmes for the concerts: 'In the event of an Air Raid Warning being received a notice will be displayed from the Organ Loft. The Concert will continue, but patrons wishing to leave may do so.' Nicolls' argument for as much discretion as possible was observed. The new series was to include lunchtime concerts as a regular feature; once again Myra Hess inaugurated the evening series on 2 October, with Beethoven's Fourth Concerto. Wood, Harty and Raybould continued the evening series, and the lunch-hour series on Fridays opened with the return of Arthur Catterall in Mozart and Moura Lympany in Ireland's Concerto under Julian Clifford.

Devastation

Throughout October and November conditions were becoming more and more intolerable in Bristol. The raids were severe, and Orchestra members had to pick their way through débris, avoiding fires, to reach the studios from their homes. On the night of 24 November the biggest raid of all occurred. Grabbing 'silly things, like an umbrella, haircutting scissors, and a blanket', Sidonie Goossens escaped the burning Clifton Arts Centre and retired to the shelters. She had overlooked many valuables, including all Alan Rawsthorne's manuscripts. It was the last she saw of the place she had made her home: by the morning it had been flattened. Goossens went with her husband and the Rawsthornes to shelter in the nearest pub. Constant Lambert and W. W.

Thompson were already there, helping to hose the wall next door, where a furniture shop was still burning. There was no fresh water, gas or electricity. In the early hours of the morning they walked together through the ruins down Park Street to the Llandoger Trow, the well-known pub opposite the Theatre Royal in King Street. There the proprietor and his wife cooked breakfast for them on an oil stove. They took stock of the appalling damage to the town: it was a scene of devastation to match that far more famous one inflicted on Coventry.

That was the turning point for the BBC in Bristol. The evening concerts planned for 27 November and 11 December were cancelled. Lunchtime events continued, with Leslie Heward, Clarence Raybould and Leslie Woodgate conducting. These included the first performance of Vaughan Williams' *Six Choral Songs for time of war*, postponed from a cancelled Prom concert.

But by the start of 1941, it was clear that it would be impossible to carry on in Bristol for much longer. The Variety Department moved to Bangor in April 1941 (it had arrived with twenty-two staff; it departed with 432 staff, seventeen dogs and a parrot), and urgent moves were made to see where the Symphony Orchestra and Music Department could be resettled. But there were many problems. 'The Corporation emissaries had a difficult time in their search. They went to eight or ten Mayors with the same question: "Can you produce two hundred and fifty beds, forty offices under one roof, ten studios of varying sizes, including two really big ones for orchestras?" ' (Boult, *My Own Trumpet*, p. 119).

The lunchtime concerts continued, but there was no attempt to re-establish the evening series. Only one other concert was given, a charity concert on Sunday 12 January. On 22 February a Saturday afternoon symphony concert was risked, with Ida Haendel playing the Tchaikovsky concerto under Wood. The next Friday lunchtime Walton conducted a concert of his own music (including his recently-orchestrated *Children's Pieces*). The series continued regularly through March, April and May, with appearances by Warwick Braithwaite, Herbert Menges, Basil Cameron, Constant Lambert and Boyd Neel; there were all-Wagner and all-Tchaikovsky concerts. On 6 April, Bach's *St Matthew Passion* was performed under Boult. Three special concerts were held, on 17 February, 17 March and 28 April. The first was heralded with fanfares by Eugene Goossens and Poulenc; it included Moeran's G minor Symphony, Stravinsky's *Capriccio* for piano and orchestra, and Ibert's *Escales*; Raybould conducted. In the second, Rubbra's recent Third Symphony was heard under Boult, with Roussel's *Pour une fête de printemps* and Khachaturian's Piano Concerto with Moura

Lympany. The third was the most notable: under Clarence Raybould, Benjamin Britten's Violin Concerto was given its first broadcast. Thomas Matthews was the soloist: he had premièred it at the Queen's Hall under Cameron in 1939. The programme notes warned: 'The music is of the percussive type, and it cannot be denied that it is stimulating.' The concert was completed by Honegger, Copland, Goossens and Martinů.

It is ironic that, just as arrangements were being finalised to transfer the Symphony Orchestra, the situation in Bristol eased. In June 1941, just before the transfer took place, it was found practicable to run a series of summer concerts: three symphony concerts, two smaller orchestral concerts, and two lunchtime events. The conductors were Wood, Boult, Raybould, Lambert and Cameron: choral forces from the town were involved in Mendelssohn's *Hymn of Praise* on 25 June.

From Bristol to Bedford

The BBC's time in Bristol ended with a flood of goodwill on both sides. The final musical events included the première of *Song of Faith* by the American, John Alden Carpenter, on Independence Day (4 July) under Leslie Woodgate; and a grand charity concert in aid of the Mayor's Hospital Fund on 6 July (all Beethoven, under Boult). There was a final lunch-hour 'Plebiscite Programme', in which the pieces were chosen from the Orchestra's repertoire by the votes of the audience. The selection may have interest as an indication of wartime taste: Wood's arrangement of the 'Purcell' Trumpet Voluntary, Mozart's Clarinet Concerto, Tchaikovsky's *Romeo and Juliet*, and Ravel's *Bolero* – this latter attracted the largest number of votes. 452 people also gave seventeen votes to pieces by Sibelius and Delius, nine to Walton, eight to Holst, seven to Vaughan Williams and three to Bax and Falla. One person requested 'Roll out the barrel'.

There were many expressions of regret that the BBC were leaving the town. Underwood of the Bristol Choral Society wrote to Boult: 'The BBC has created a new musical public in Bristol and we must put our heads together to do what we can to fill, however partially, the gap created by your departure.' There were rumours that the BBC might re-establish the Orchestra in Bristol after the war: Boult confined himself to hoping that 'everything should be done to give Bristol its own municipal orchestra ... the BBC would certainly give all possible support ...' Privately he had supported the idea of retaining Bristol as the Symphony Orchestra's centre, arguing that the financial gain would be considerable and that the Orchestra could move to London just for the Prom seasons.

By mid-July, the Orchestra was sorry to leave Bristol: there was only one more air-raid on the town after they left. But new accommodation had been found, in a town which was both safer and more convenient for possible visits to London. The Mayor of Bedford had offered to make facilities available, even though his town was already full of evacuees. W. W. Thompson's assistant, Dorothy Wood, was sent to Bedford for a week in July to examine what was available, and had reported favourably on the facilities at the Corn Exchange, Bedford School, and the churches and chapels which were to be made available for the Orchestra's use.

The Symphony Orchestra was due in Bedford on 30 July 1941. Most of the Orchestra travelled there by a special train (equipped with a dining car, soon to disappear from sight for the rest of the war) which went by a complicated cross-country route to avoid London. Boult, characteristically, decided to make the journey on his push-bike. 'I remember running into Mr Eshelby of Steinway's outside the British Restaurant in Aylesbury where I had been having lunch.' Through August, the Orchestra established itself in Bedford, giving just one concert before an invited audience in Billeton on 6 August. (Again, the Proms took place in London without the help of the BBC; but for the first time they took place in their now traditional home, the Royal Albert Hall, for the Queen's Hall had been destroyed by bombing on 11 May.)

Bedford proved to be an attractive place to work, and relationships with the townspeople, though inevitably less close than in war-torn Bristol, were excellent. There was always the danger of raids, and regular firewatching took place, but only twice did the planes come: once they passed over without incident, and the second time dropped only a few bombs out of range. On each occasion Orchestra members were treated as experts by the local population, for they were more experienced in the ways of air-raids. Stationed nearby were American servicemen, and a lively friendship grew up: Sidonie Goossens and Jessie Hinchliffe now moved into a flat on the embankment of the Ouse, which was frequently used as a local mess by the Canadian engineers, who were practising bridge-building over the river. Bedford provided office accommodation for the Music Department in two adjacent small hotels in an avenue leading down to the Ouse. Here the orchestral management was able to be reunited with the administrative personnel of Music Department under Dr Reginald Thatcher, who had previously been stationed with the rest of the BBC administration in Evesham.

Keeping together

With the escape from the difficult conditions of Bristol effected, it was possible to give sustained attention to a problem which had been causing an increasing amount of concern through 1941 : maintaining the standard of the Orchestra in the face of demands on its personnel by the armed forces. The BBC had hitherto been successful in maintaining a high level of performance in its concerts and broadcasts – a standard all the more noticeable because those orchestras which now spent much of their time travelling and giving troop concerts found it much more difficult to preserve their artistic standards. Touring brought important employment for hard-hit musicians, and it added immeasurably to the audiences for serious music throughout the country – the war may be said to have effected a revolution in that field – but as far as the highest quality of orchestral playing went, that responsibility remained firmly in the hands of the BBC.

Boult had noted in April 1941 that 'the Berlin Philharmonic is broadcasting at pre-war strength with pre-war personnel. We have got to stand up to this.' From Evesham on 28 April Thatcher urged that 'immediate and drastic steps be taken to safeguard the Symphony Orchestra'. He asked that indefinite deferment of service for all players be requested, and that it be asked whether a player's service in a military band, or such employment, would be 'comparable in any way with the value to the nation at this time of the Symphony Orchestra'. The matter thus raised was extended to all the BBC's orchestral musicians, for discussion at Control Board. In July it became known that Sir Hugh Allen was to be asked to chair a Ministry of Labour committee to advise on the deferment of service for musicians.

A temporary answer was needed quickly, and the one that arrived was unwelcome: indefinite deferment was impossible, and the Ministry could advocate only six months' temporary deferment subject to the recommendations of the Allen committee. Further deferment, it emerged, would be unlikely in the case of younger members. Deferment was granted for eleven important musicians in category A (indispensable), as well as for a group of category B strings. The call-up of two players from the Military Band and Variety Orchestra in November again alerted Thatcher to the problem; it was, he wrote, 'fundamental to get broadcasting treated by the Government as a function of the highest national importance'. In fact, the Symphony Orchestra lost very few players during the war. Apart from those who had left at the very beginning – some of whom, like Terence MacDonagh, Willem de Mont and Edward Chesterman, gained British Empire Medals for their services in the London blitz – the establishment remained remarkably intact. The morale and dedication of the Orchestra were sustained undamaged through the war years.

The reuniting of the Orchestra and the administration in the autumn of 1941 also led to thoughts about the future direction of control in the Music

Department. Boult was still Director of Music as well as Chief Conductor, though the separation of his two jobs had been agreed at the end of the 1930s. Yet in Evesham Reginald Thatcher had been in complete administrative control of the Music Department, while Boult had retained the direction of artistic programme planning in Bristol. Now the broadcasting situation was even more complicated. An entirely new branch of Music Department had been set up in 1940 to deal with the provision of music overseas. This had been run first by the indefatigable Kenneth Wright, but in 1941 the scope of the job had increased so much that Wright felt that a person of considerable status should be asked to undertake it.

At the very beginning of the war, the composer Arthur Bliss, who was living with his wife and family in Stockbridge, Massachusetts, had felt impelled to offer his services to the BBC, so as to make his contribution to the war effort. He had cabled his friend Boult and written to Thatcher, but in those early days of the war Thatcher had to reply with absolute truth that the staff of Music Department were under-employed with the small amounts of serious music being broadcast. Bliss's generous offer stood open, however, and in April 1941 he was asked if he would like to come and take charge of the Overseas Music Department. He accepted, in spite of the considerable upheaval which it caused him to leave his family and his teaching job. He soon settled in to work in London, first in an office in Bedford College, Regent's Park, and then at the BBC Marylebone High Street offices. By August he was already hankering for a more important part in the BBC's musical affairs, and feeling that he was under-used. In a letter of 31 August, he wrote to his wife:

> I have suggested to Adrian that I become Director of Music, and that he confines his duties to conductorship of the Orchestra; I want more power as I have a lot to give which my comparatively minor post does not allow me to use fully. I had an interview with Ogilvie, the Chief Pooh-Bah, but I doubt whether I rise to such eminence immediately.

Nevertheless, Bliss's commendably honest proposal for self-advancement clearly had much to recommend it. He was a figure of importance in the English musical world, but not an establishment figure. Boult had complete confidence in him, and for the first time felt that a possible candidate as Director of Music had been presented. Sir Hugh Allen, when approached with the proposal, was unsurprisingly sceptical. He doubted that 'a composer, conductor or other executant' should be Director of Music, and suggested a 'triumvirate'. But in January 1942 there was a change of Director-General: Ogilvie, whose period of office had not been altogether a success, gave way to two men who held the post jointly: R. W. Foot and Sir Cecil Graves. Perhaps this change helped Bliss, for Graves thought the idea of a triumvirate 'had little to recommend it' (5 March 1942) and supported the proposal that Bliss should be appointed. Bliss was confirmed as Director of Music in April 1942.

Philosophical digressions

The preliminary preparations for Bliss's appointment produced one fascinating period piece, a statement of the BBC's musical policy for his guidance, drawn up in December 1941 for Basil Nicolls as Controller of Programmes, and subsequently amended in discussion with Boult, Thatcher and Bliss. This primarily theoretical document could scarcely be more clear in its expression of wartime philosophy about the nature of art:

> Creative Principle: Music is an ennobling spiritual force, which should influence the life of every listener.
>
> Good broadcasting of music means:
> A. The observance of the artistic and technical limitations of the medium, in order to achieve –
> B. The best possible broadcast performance of all worthy music.
> C. Securing the maximum appreciation of such broadcasts by winning the largest possible audience, thereby continually raising public taste.

Expanding on points A and B, the paper discussed the relationship between the BBC and outside musical bodies, drawing an important distinction between those activities which lent themselves to being broadcast and those which did not. It was his development of point C, however, which is of special interest:

> C.   *The Maximum Audience*
> This consideration is the source of the great missionary element in Broadcasting. If the Creative Principle is accepted, the objective of carrying music to the greatest possible number of listeners is almost paramount. This objective may often appear to conflict with purely musical considerations and it may, in certain circumstances therefore, be repugnant to musicians. But although some programmes can be regarded as not pursuing this objective (e.g. the Contemporary Music concerts), it must be implicit in nearly all the musical activities of the BBC.

There, Nicolls for the first time formulated the professional broadcaster's point of view about the dissemination of serious music: that it was the size of audience that was primarily important, not what in a later decade was to be called 'the quality of listening'.

Bliss's response to this suggested policy was frank and sensible. To the suggested Creative Principle he responded with what he labelled a Truism:

> A sense of music is a primal thing in mankind, and a tremendous force, either for good or for evil.

He too added a peculiarly war-time view of the function of broadcast music, which was incorporated into the final document as a 'Practical Interpretation'.
Its purpose was:

1. Inexorably to continue and expand the principle of great music as an ultimate value, indeed a justification of life.
2. Faithfully to enrich leisure hours with entertainment.
3. Physically and mentally to stimulate tired bodies and worn nerves.

Then, under the heading 'Coaxing Caliban', he dealt with Nicolls' audience theory.

> The danger of the theory of the maximum audience for music is that it can so soon degenerate into wooing the lowest common denominator of that audience. We are apt to be a timid nation, aesthetically and intellectually, and a bit shamefaced when appealing to the finer instincts of people . . .

Bliss covered many other detailed points of policy – popular transcriptions of the classics, the use of 'fillers', condensed opera, the problem of 'crooners' – and concluded with what he headed 'A Fantasy':

> The ideal method of broadcasting throughout this country would be to have three separate channels. Available for all citizens that are worth fighting for would be two contrasted services, so that at any minute of the day he or she could draw on two of the three categories . . . For the Calibans, there would be a third service, 'the dirt track', a continual stream of noise and nonsense put on by untouchables with the use of records.

This blatantly elitist, if somewhat prophetic, formulation was unacceptable on two grounds: first, that it negated the idea of high standards in the light as well as the serious music output; and second, because it went against the fundamental Reithian concept that listeners could be led by a mixture of didacticism and enthusiasm to something different from that which they were used to. Bliss, on the other hand, was content to let those on 'the dirt track' remain there.

Nevertheless, the arguments of Bliss (and doubtless the comments of

Boult and Thatcher) ensured some modifications of Nicolls' views on maximum audiences. In the final circulated draft (6 March 1942) Section C was retitled

III   *The Audience*

If the Creative Principle is accepted, there follows the responsibility for broadcasting the maximum amount of fine music to all who need it. This maximum must in practice be determined by the competing claims of other types of programme; but the Creative Principle carries its own justification of programme time and expenditure.

There follows from it also the responsibility for spreading the appreciation of music as widely as possible. The BBC, in addition to its obligation as guardian of cultural values, must accept the duty of educating the public. It must therefore plan continually to add by worthy means to the number of those capable of enjoying fine music.

This compromise formulation still retains some of Nicolls' original pomposity. But in place of the 'paramount' importance of the 'maximum audience', there is a responsibility for spreading 'appreciation of music' (not merely ears near wireless sets). And audiences were to be increased 'by worthy means' – and whatever they were, they did not involve the dilution of classics by performance on theatre organs, military bands and nine-piece ensembles, such as had been envisaged in Nicolls' original draft.

This high-minded music policy did influence Bliss's decisions in the months following his appointment. But more important than such generalities was, as always, the exercise of personal taste in programme planning and programme building. Bliss's own conviction was that in wartime the BBC ought to give special support and encouragement to British and Empire composers; the period from 1942 on was one in which the new music heard on radio almost exclusively originated from countries allied to, or sympathetic to, the cause of Britain in the war. This significant shift in emphasis from Boult's 'policy unchanged' stance in the autumn of 1939 passed unremarked, or only favourably noticed, at the time. It is, however, possible to see here the roots of a policy which became debilitating to the BBC in the years ahead. Bliss's positive role, though, was to introduce an element of balance and design into a scheme of music programmes that had until then often looked random.

Bliss expressed his views in popular form in a lively interview printed in *Radio Times* (15 May) shortly after he took over. In answer to some pointed questions, he outlined his intentions. How did he propose to tackle the problem of modern music? 'There is no such thing as "modern" music, any more than there is a modern horse. No progressive country wants to live too much in the past.' Would British music receive special treatment? 'Yes. No other country in the world can show a finer school of composers than this country and naturally our audiences want to hear their works.' Had he any views on the fading-out of programmes? 'Yes, but they are unprintable! We are now coping with this technical difficulty.' (In January 1942 a broadcast of the Walton Violin Concerto was faded out before the end 'because part of the time allotted to it was taken up by an introduction to the work, read from the *Radio Times*', complained a letter to *The Times* on 9 January. And Elgar's daughter Carice Blake added her protest about the fading out of her father's Violin Concerto during the last movement cadenza on 25 January.)

Bliss was now established in the Marylebone High Street offices with Kenneth Wright and his department, including Julian Herbage (now designated Assistant Director of Music, London). Mid-week, on Tuesdays, Wednesdays and Thursdays, he travelled to Bedford to visit the main music department where some fifty staff altogether were stationed. Bliss wrote to one of his daughters (19 April):

> Your idea of a vast office, with me stalking up and down between rows of awestruck and adoring secretaries playing on their typewriters, must *immediately* be put into effect. At the moment I have only one secretary, neither awestruck or languishing for me, who performs on a machine so old and loud – like a tractor – that I have to beg her to stop whenever the telephone bell rings so that I can hear myself speak.

Bedford concerts

Concert-giving began in Bedford on 17 September 1941, at 7 pm. All major concerts were to be given in the Corn Exchange, a hall which proved to have good acoustics. 'A reasonably good studio, but a rather overpowering concert-hall', said Boult. It was situated in the centre of town, handy for the nearby Woolworths, where mid-morning refreshments could be obtained in the rehearsal break, and to which Boult recalls taking Laurence Olivier during sessions for some incidental music to a play. The first season's programmes, devised by Julian Herbage with the assistance of a young planner, Herbert Murrill, who was to become Head of Music for a short time, consisted of a high proportion of twentieth-century music – mostly of a nationalist, rather than an experimental nature. Boult included Bliss's Music for Strings in the opening concert, and Wood conducted an all-Russian programme (including Stravinsky's *Firebird*) on 1 October. Cameron conducted the Sibelius Seventh Symphony on 15 October, and Curzon repeated

The BBC Symphony Orchestra in 1942. Above: First Violins; Paul Beard, leader; Marie Wilson, sub-leader. Below: Cellos; Ambrose Gauntlett, principal (left)

Above: Flutes; Gerald Jackson, principal. Below: Clarinets; Frederick Thurston, principal

Above: Bassoons; Archie Camden, principal. Below: Trumpets; Ernest Hall, principal

Troop concerts: BBC Symphony Orchestra (top), audience (centre) and overflow audience (bottom) at ENSA music festival concerts conducted by Sir Adrian Boult at the Garrison Theatre, Aldershot, and the Royal Naval Barracks, Portsmouth, 1943

Wartime audiences: the boys of Bedford School lean from the gallery of the School Hall to listen to a rehearsal by Boult and the BBC Symphony Orchestra, June 1944

A young visitor: Yehudi Menuhin rehearses the Bartók Second Violin Concerto with Boult in October 1944; they gave the work's British première

Transported: Michael Tippett listens to a rehearsal of his oratorio A Child of Our Time, *conducted by Walter Goehr in the Corn Exchange, Bedford, in March 1945*

Back to London: the BBC Symphony Orchestra in the newly restored Studio 1 at Maida Vale, April 1947. Boult conducts, Paul Beard leads, and at the back of the platform are the orchestral porters, attendants and librarians, including Edgar Mays

A new Chief Conductor? Two possible choices for the successor to Sir Adrian Boult in 1950:
Rafael Kubelik (above); Sir John Barbirolli (below)

the Ireland Piano Concerto on 29 October under Leslie Heward.

The highlight of the season was undoubtedly the concert on 12 November, conducted by Boult and William Walton. Walton's Violin Concerto, previously heard in America and then at a Royal Philharmonic Society concert at the Albert Hall on 1 November (from which it had been broadcast), was given a second British performance under the composer's direction, with Henry Holst, the same soloist as at the première. Another of Walton's American works, the Comedy Overture *Scapino*, was given its first British performance. The Walton Concerto had drawn unfavourable comments after the Albert Hall performance. It was now praised by Ernest Newman in *The Sunday Times* and Dyneley Hussey in the *Spectator*, and several opinions declared it an advance on the Viola Concerto, a verdict which time has not yet sustained.

Russian music featured in the two following concerts: Khachaturian's Piano Concerto was played by Moura Lympany under Boult on 26 November, and Borodin's Second Symphony appeared in a mostly English programme under Malcolm Sargent on 10 December. Expression of solidarity with Russia reached its height on Sunday afternoon, 21 December, when a special Stalin birthday concert was held in the Corn Exchange 'before an invited audience of munition workers and members of the Russian Embassy'. The season was completed by five concerts in 1942: Boult revived Elgar's *Falstaff* and Vaughan Williams' London Symphony; Raybould's 18 February concert featured Cyril Smith in Falla's *Nights in the Gardens of Spain* and Franck's Symphonic Variations.

An extra concert was added to the end of the season at very short notice. Julian Herbage had heard a concert conducted by John Barbirolli with the London Symphony Orchestra in Cambridge in the middle of May, and had been so impressed that he tried to arrange a BBC engagement for him at once. Barbirolli had shown himself 'intensely keen to give a thoroughly rehearsed programme with our players', and they planned a Rossini, Vaughan Williams, Debussy and Brahms concert for 14 June. It was originally hoped to give this in conjunction with Harold Holt at the Albert Hall in London, but instead it was given in Bedford, with great success. It was the beginning of an important collaboration for the Orchestra.

There were also fortnightly Friday lunchtime concerts at 1.10 pm in the Corn Exchange, for which a small part of the back of the hall was devoted to promenading audiences. To keep the political balance even, the Stalin birthday concert was matched by one for President Roosevelt on 30 January, which included the *Suite fantastique* for piano and orchestra by Schelling with Moiseiwitch. Conductors in the series besides Boult and Raybould included Maurice Miles, Richard Austin, Herbert Menges, Julian Clifford and Constant Lambert.

These concerts perhaps lacked adventure. But that quality was supplied in full measure by a series of special concerts (the equivalent of those held in the studio during the Bristol stay) for which the Orchestra travelled to Cambridge and established a relationship with the Cambridge Arts Theatre Trust. These programmes provided a fine conspectus of twentieth-century music, though they never really touched on the 'advanced' repertoire which the Orchestra had promoted during the Thirties. The contents were miscellaneous, and were confused by the evident desire to include a British work in every programme. Each concert did, however, have a clear focus: in the first (22 October 1941) there was Roussel's Fourth Symphony under Boult; on 19 November Busoni's Violin Concerto was played by Jean Pougnet under Hyam Greenbaum; on 17 December a Bliss and Walton programme was conducted by the composers; it included the Bliss *A Colour Symphony* and Walton's Viola Concerto (played by Frederick Riddle). On 14 January 1942 Max Rostal gave the British première of the Khachaturian Violin Concerto and Raybould conducted Barber's *School for Scandal* Overture for the first time in this country; the British work was Rawsthorne's *Symphonic Studies*, which the composer conducted. On 11 February Constant Lambert conducted a group of the Orchestra in the first performance of Gerhard's Suite *Don Quixote*, plus his own Concerto for piano and chamber ensemble (with Louis Kentner as soloist). Finally on 11 March Boult conducted Vaughan Williams' Pastoral Symphony and Stravinsky's *Firebird*, plus Busoni and Bax.

Based in Bedford, the Orchestra found it easier to resume the tours of local towns which had been begun in Bristol: during the autumn of 1941 it gave Sunday concerts in Cheltenham, Luton, Kettering, and again in Cambridge. Extra events in Bedford included a charity concert which raised over £100 on 9 December. In the new year of 1942, Nottingham, Kettering again, and Rugby School followed. A troop concert was given before a massed invitation audience of khaki-clothed officers in the Sheldonian Theatre Oxford on 7 February, and three special schools programmes were given in Bedford on 31 January, 28 February and 26 March. Programmes were unremarkable; but the BBC was now beginning to play its part as a touring orchestra in wartime, where previously it had confined its role principally to that of a purveyor of broadcast music.

At the end of the season this was carried further by the first full-scale tour by the Orchestra since the war began: it visited five towns in South Wales poorly served by music, and between 18 and 22 June gave eight concerts under Boult. Such was the demand that afternoon and evening concerts were given in Newport, Swansea and Cardiff; there were single concerts in Aberdare and Treorchy. In Swansea the local Municipal Choir participated in Borodin's *Polovtsian Dances*. In Cardiff, half of one programme was given over to Welsh music: Boult conducted pieces by Grace Williams and Joseph Morgan, and Idris Lewis conducted works by Arwel Hughes and Maldwyn Price. In the second half, a massive combined choir from Cardiff, Newport, Rhondda Valley, Merthyr and Dowlais sang extracts from *Messiah*, *Elijah* and the *Hymn of Praise*; and Beethoven's Fifth Symphony completed what must have been a stirring occasion.

Back to London

The most important new development at the end of the 1941–2 season, however, was the Orchestra's visit to London for its first public concerts there since war broke out. It took part in the series of London summer concerts promoted 'Under the patronage of the Allied Governments and the British Council' by the Royal Philharmonic Society in collaboration with the BBC, the London Symphony Orchestra and Boosey and Hawkes. Julian Herbage represented the BBC on the planning committee; the secretary was Keith Douglas. The BBC's two contributions on 28 May and 4 June were planned to include major premières paying homage to two major allies: America, in the form of the British première of Roy Harris's Third Symphony; and Russia, with Shostakovich's Leningrad Symphony, whose wartime inspiration was thought to make it particularly suitable.

The Roy Harris première was given as planned, and the Orchestra's return to London was warmly greeted: *The Times* wrote that

> on the top of their form, they gave performances as memorable as those of the historic concerts with which Sir Adrian Boult launched the orchestra on its career . . . Here indeed was a reassertion of standards free from the defects of wireless transmission and war-time difficulties.

The Harris work was found to be a 'strong, closely wrought tissue of good musical logic in one movement'.

The material for the Shostakovich work did not arrive from Russia in time, and the première had to be postponed. The score eventually arrived from Russia on 900 slides of microfilm, and was broadcast from the studio not by the BBC Orchestra but by the London Philharmonic conducted by Henry Wood on 22 June (to mark the anniversary of Russia's entry into the war). The work had been written while the composer was working as an air-raid warden on the roof of the Leningrad Conservatory, and had been frequently played in Russia, said the publicity, 'as a call to arms'. The Russian Ambassador and his wife and Stafford Cripps were present. The *Annual Register* remarked tartly that

> it was therefore the symbol of a great emotional crisis by which the British people had been profoundly stirred, and came surrounded by an aura of romantic heroism and a considerable glare of publicity. . . . The musical verdict was that the stress under which the work had been brought to birth, so far from firing the composer's imagination, had stifled it.

Nevertheless the Symphony took a great hold in America, where it received sixty-two performances during the 1942–3 season alone.

In 1942 the BBC once more accepted its responsibility for the Promenade Concert season which had been abrogated in 1940 and 1941 – the only break between 1927 and the present day. An important development took place in the planning of the eight-week season: the concerts were shared between two orchestras. The London Philharmonic played from 27 June to 24 July, and the BBC Orchestra completed the season from 25 July to 22 August. Wood was joined by Basil Cameron in the first month, and by Boult in the second. Under the BBC's direction premières again assumed a significant place in the programmes; and the Orchestra introduced Rubbra's Fourth Symphony as well as works by Dunhill, Benjamin, Rowley, Demuth, Leighton Lucas, and introduced Aaron Copland's *Billy the Kid* to England.

This emphasis on new works was salutary in a concert-giving climate which increasingly paid little attention to any but the most familiar classics. The needs of troop concerts and hastily prepared London concerts (of which there had been an increasing number during 1942) necessarily restricted the repertoire. By the start of the 1942–3 season considerable dissatisfaction was being expressed with this state of affairs. Some were satisfied neither by the usual diet of symphonic classics nor by the BBC's provision of new works: 'everything was being performed for the first or the hundredth time' was the familiar cry. Nevertheless, the work of the BBC Symphony Orchestra, in the studio as well as in public, paradoxically assumed an even greater significance as the provision of orchestral music mushroomed during the 1942–3 season. There was one other main bulwark against falling standards: CEMA was now firmly established in its third season with a grant from the Treasury through the Board of Education. Under the new chairmanship of Maynard Keynes it established a Music Panel, which included Bliss, Myra Hess and Constant Lambert.

The BBC's 1942–3 season in Bedford followed the same pattern as the previous year's: twelve symphony concerts and twelve lunch-hour concerts.

Whether the influence of Bliss can be directly seen in the programmes is open to question, but they certainly contained a solid proportion of English music: Rawsthorne's Piano Concerto (7 October, Louis Kentner under Boult), Bax's First Symphony (4 November, Sargent, replaced in the event by Boult), Delius's *Brigg Fair* (18 November, Raybould), Vaughan Williams' Pastoral Symphony again (2 December, Boult) and Holst's Concerto for two violins (Paul Beard and Marie Wilson under Boult, 16 December). The pattern continued in the new year: Britten's *Sinfonia da Requiem* (Cameron, 27 January), Walton's Symphony (Raybould, 10 February), Bax's *Summer Music* (Wood, 10 March). There was twentieth-century European music too; plenty of Stravinsky, and Bartók's Divertimento for Strings. Szymanowski's First Violin Concerto was played by Eda Kersey. The Friday lunchtime series also had an English bias: Ian Whyte conducted Bliss, Vaughan Williams and Ireland on 16 October; subsequently there were works by Walton (the *Scapino* Overture, premièred the previous season), Herbert Murrill, Constant Lambert, Delius, Bax, Walton again, and John Ireland's *Legend*.

In the week of 12 October, a series of studio concerts celebrated Vaughan Williams' sixtieth birthday: the BBC Orchestra played under Boult on the 13th and Wood on the 14th, including the Piano Concerto and two symphonies.

The Orchestra devoted more time than ever during this season to its wartime touring activities. Under Bliss's direction, the Music Department was concentrating many of its more adventurous activities into studio concerts. The series in Cambridge, for example, which had been an important part of the 1941–2 season, was planned with a much more popular repertoire in 1942–3: the only living composers represented in the four concerts were Ibert, Ireland and Sibelius. Instead, contemporary music returned to the studio: there were no special concerts during the autumn, but four in early 1943, on 10 January, 7 February, 7 March and 18 April. These concerts launched the famous title 'Music of our Time', and to help with their programming Bliss sought the assistance of the man he knew had created the BBC's most forward-looking policies in the 1930s, Edward Clark. (In 1920 Clark had premièred two of Bliss's works in a concert series in London.) The resultant programmes look strongly like a mixture of Bliss, Clark and Herbage. Works included the Three Fragments from *Wozzeck* by Berg, Stravinsky's *The Rite of Spring*, and Hindemith's *Mathis der Maler* Symphony. But also included were Ireland's choral work *These things shall be*, Bax's Fourth Symphony, and Shostakovich's First. Maggie Teyte repeated her memorable *Shéhérezade*; Prokofiev, Milhaud, Sibelius and Busoni made up the programmes.

Bliss helped British composers by a large number of commissions, some of which were played by chamber-sized BBC groups: during 1943 Gordon Jacob, Armstrong Gibbs, Eric Chisholm, Montague Phillips, Chris Edmunds, Lennox Berkeley, Robin Milford and William Alwyn all contributed small-scale orchestral works. A special series of programmes was arranged 'in honour of Russia and France', and music played its full part in these. Such overtly political planning was especially noticeable in the overseas services; the *BBC Yearbook* noted that

> naturally, it was also the BBC's aim to present non-British listeners overseas with a vivid picture of our own musical life, which has been proving itself so very wide awake during the war . . . At least four good concerts of the 'Prom' type were broadcast weekly in each of the main overseas services . . . a music service was introduced in the BBC Eastern Service, with the special object of accustoming the Asiatic ear to western music in its best forms.

The Orchestra's work outside Bedford increased during the season. Besides the Cambridge series, there was a charity concert in the Albert Hall (Aid to China, 20 September 1942), a Luton schools concert (16 November), and an appearance by a section of the Orchestra at Myra Hess's National Gallery concerts on New Year's Day 1943, in the Christmas Story by Heinrich Schütz, a radical departure from the players' usual repertory.

Between 25 February and 4 March a 40-piece section, led by Marie Wilson, visited Aberdare for a short period 'in residence'. There were four concerts, two conventional and two unconventional: these latter consisted of one on St David's Day. The programme was advertised as *Adnabod Tir* by Grieg, *Cyn Toriad Dydd* by Delius, and *Caneuon y Llynges* by Stanford: later explained as *Recognition of Land*, *A Song before Sunrise*, and *Songs of the Fleet*. The Williamson Male Voice Choir joined the Orchestra for this occasion. On 3 March the Merthyr and District Philharmonic Choir participated in another unusual programme: Parry's *The Pied Piper of Hamelin*, and Vaughan Williams' *The Running Set* (Quodlibet of Traditional Dance Tunes). 'These were exciting nights,' Boult recalled. 'Each of the choral societies from the valleys . . . came over by coach with their own supporters.' In Leicester on 7 April the *Missa Solemnis* was performed, with the local Philharmonic Choir and BBC Singers.

Among broadcasts in 1943 which caught the attention were the first broadcast by the violinist Yehudi Menuhin, who was visiting England for war charities. The BBC made a special trip to London to record the Brahms Violin Concerto with him in the studio on 5 April, an occasion which has remained in many minds. He was immediately asked to return the following year.

Summer 1943

Conditions were once more favourable in London for a number of early summer concerts. This time the BBC promoted its own series of three: a solid series of well-known works under Boult's direction including Holst's *The Planets* on 19 May, both suites from Ravel's *Daphnis and Chloe* on 26 May, and Beethoven's Ninth Symphony on 2 June. Novelties were again left to the Proms, which began on the very early date of 19 June. Sir Henry Wood was by now unwell and was forced to take a rest after the concert on 21 June. Cameron conducted Wood's concerts, and Boult was also active: on 29 July he gave the British première of William Schuman's Third Symphony and Copland's *A Lincoln Portrait*. In August Boult took over a whole string of premières with the BBC Symphony Orchestra: Rubbra's *Sinfonia Concertante* with the composer at the piano (10th), William Busch's Cello Concerto (Florence Hooton, 13th), Arnold van Wyk's *Saudade* for violin and orchestra (14th), Kabalevsky's Suite from *Colas Breugnon* (17th), and Moeran's Rhapsody No. 3 for piano and orchestra (19th).

If this fare seems somewhat provincial, it must be recalled both that in wartime conditions there was little else available, and also that it contrasted very favourably with the continuing stereotypes of orchestral programmes being handed out by other orchestral bodies. That the Symphony Orchestra preserved such a record of first performances at this time is remarkable. Outside the influence of the BBC, ENSA and CEMA the scene was less bright. The strongly-worded attack of the *Annual Register* was typical:

> Full-sized professional orchestras were to be met up and down the country competing for box-office favour, often clashing with each other's dates, imposing their own haphazard time-table on local musical life, and hurling symphonies and concertos at a vast new population that had had no previous experience of that order of music. This sudden propagation of the masterpieces was no bad thing in itself: nobody wished to complain that Beethoven was being listened to by more people than ever before. It was the misdirection of the new industry that aroused misgivings. The new audience was being taught to believe that the highest musical ideal lay in the colourful, emotional, and impressive effect produced only by a large and varied body of instruments.
>
> Moreover, this one-sided view was being further narrowed by a limited choice of music. Travelling orchestras and their impresarios were more

concerned with box-office returns than with the spread of appreciation; so they fell into the easy habit of repeating the works that drew the biggest crowds, and the crowds fell into the easy habit of assembling for the works that were most often repeated. Thus the musical experience brought to vast numbers of people by this war-time movement ranged little beyond a few symphonies headed by Beethoven's fifth and seventh, and a few concertos headed by Rachmaninov's in C minor and Tchaikovsky's in B flat minor for piano. The vogue of the last-named work was carried to such a point that its title became a byword wherever musical affairs were responsibly discussed.

To make matters worse, the standard of performance went down. No orchestra could maintain an artistic level at a time when the chief factors in its working life were the scramble and discomfort of constant journeying and ill-rehearsed performances under a succession of different and, in some cases, inexperienced conductors. This indictment represents what was being said frequently and at length in musical journals and the musical columns of the daily press. Nobody deprecated the orchestral boom as such; but the course it was taking aroused widespread dissatisfaction.

The Symphony Orchestra's other major contribution to the war effort at the end of the 1942–3 season was to appear at a festival organised by ENSA (now officially called the Department of National Service Entertainment, but retaining its well-loved initials), first in Aldershot, and then in Southampton and Portsmouth. The energetic Walter Legge was attempting to increase the proportion of high-quality symphonic work in the ENSA programmes for troops, and had used a forces orchestra for a week's festival in January 1943. His approach to the BBC was cautiously accepted, and concerts were organised for May and June. The audiences were large and enthusiastic: in Aldershot's Garrison Theatre, Legge was able to tell the BBC Orchestra that they had beaten the takings at the Gracie Fields concert by one shilling and ninepence. At Portsmouth, where the hall used by the naval barracks had been decorated with bunting for the occasion, Legge came across a seaman who attended all the rehearsals, always standing in the same place. Legge asked him if he had always enjoyed music, to which the seaman replied: 'Music, sir? I didn't know what it was until this week, but it's fair got me, it has sir. It's worse than the drink.'

Such was the success of this tour that Legge immediately suggested more: he wanted the Orchestra to provide a fortnight in Yorkshire, Tyneside and Scotland in autumn 1943, a week's visit to the Southern Command at the end of the year, and a week around Leicester in February or March 1944. He also wanted a fortnightly series of concerts in suburbs around London. For the

BBC, Julian Herbage was enthusiastic, but thought that a monthly series (complementing two Wednesday symphony concerts and one Wednesday studio opera) would be as much as was possible. There was still considerable sensitivity to the question of public concert-giving within the BBC, and it was eventually decided only to undertake one ENSA tour in the autumn, to St Athan, where the orchestra performed at the huge RAF Station between 12 and 19 September.

Planning complexities

Increasingly, the Symphony Orchestra was returning to public prominence in London and national concert life. It was evident that it was maintaining its standards in wartime and was as equal to the demands of new works as it had ever been. Inside the BBC, however, a battle was taking place over the increased service demanded of the Symphony Orchestra. A particular problem had arisen over the requests made by the Overseas Service for the use of the Symphony Orchestra, since its ideas rarely coincided with those of the Home Service. Programme plans for the Home Service were often made far in advance, leaving Overseas very dissatisfied with the material they received. Moreover, Bliss was concerned with the poor standard of many studio broadcasts coming both from the Symphony Orchestra and from the regions, and in May had made a determined appeal for a tightening up on quality. Julian Herbage, however, thought that the fault lay in the organisation of the BBC orchestral system, which was no longer suitable for responding to so many varied demands by both Home and Overseas Services. In June 1943 he proposed that the Symphony Orchestra be augmented by two violinists, so that realistic splitting into section B and section C could be resumed; the smaller section C would form a 'classical symphony orchestra'. Herbage suggested that the BBC Scottish Orchestra should be augmented to a full symphony orchestra, and should alternate with section B in providing orchestral programmes for the networks. Then the full BBC Symphony Orchestra would remain as the prestige unit, while the BBC Northern Orchestra could supply much of the lighter music needed.

The situation was clearly unsatisfactory. Better planning, or the recording of concerts, or the acceptance of a greater number of repeats, should have been able to solve the problems of overlap between Home and Overseas services. Boult saw possible solutions clearly, and pleaded for more consideration of the Symphony Orchestra's special qualities (15 November):

> I would like to see the Orchestra taking part in three or four important programmes each week, and I cannot see that most of these cannot be placed

at times which Overseas can use, or, if not, the same programme be easily
repeated for this service . . .

I know something of the incredible complexity of the programme planning machine . . . May I repeat here that if planned reasonably well ahead,
the recent Northampton visit could have provided two good hours broadcasting in the afternoon, and an hour or more to Schools and Overseas in the
morning . . .

Why have we been only once to Rugby, Leicester, Oxford, Kettering in
our two years at Bedford; and wouldn't the cathedrals of Peterborough, Ely,
St Albans be glad to hear us?

However, even Herbage's modest proposal to increase the Orchestra's
strength by two violins caused a major upheaval. That the Symphony
Orchestra with a strength of ninety-three provided only thirty-six hours'
broadcasting a week was already thought by BBC executives to be uneconomic. It was not until over a year later, after endless discussion about
the overall orchestral needs of the BBC, that the proposal for two extra
violins for the Symphony Orchestra was discussed at a Director-General's
meeting, approved by the Ministry, submitted to the Treasury, and finally
approved in December 1944. E. J. Stratford and Enid Bailey joined the
Orchestra only at the start of 1945.

In the 1943–4 season at Bedford, the most significant new work was the
British première of Stravinsky's Symphony in C, given on 17 November
under Boult. The season was also notable for the first appearance in England
of the Portuguese conductor, Freitas Branco (20 October), whom the Orchestra thoroughly admired; he brought with him novelties by Lopes-
Graça and Artur Santos. Roy Harris's Symphony No. 3 was repeated (1
December) and the Three Fragments from *Wozzeck* performed again in
public (12 January 1944). John Barbirolli returned to conduct the Berlioz
Symphonie fantastique, Debussy, and an arrangement of his own, the
Elizabethan Suite. On 23 February Boult included Bax's new Violin Concerto with Eda Kersey. This had been first performed under Wood in the
studio the previous November, when Ernest Newman had been enthusiastic:
the piece 'will become, I think, the most popular of his works. Nowhere else
has his imagination taken such captivating forms, or worked at such consistently high pressure yet with such freedom of movement and certainty of
stroke.' Henry Wood gave his last BBC Symphony Concert on 8 March, including novelties to the end: this time there was d'Indy's *Symphonie
Montagnard*, with Eileen Joyce at the piano. In the final concert of the series
(22 March), the Orchestra played Vaughan Williams' Fifth Symphony

(premièred at the 1943 Proms under the composer's direction on 24 June).

The Bedford lunch-hour concerts which complemented these events were given by the section C of forty players, led by Marie Wilson. They were notable for the variety of conductors from around the country which they presented: Gideon Fagan (15 October), Edric Cundell (29 October), Kathleen Riddick (26 November), Mosco Carner (10 December), and Leslie Woodgate (24 December). Richard Austin (7 January), Harold Gray (21 January), Julian Clifford (4 February) and Reginald Redman (18 February) completed a series in which the BBC gave special recognition to the work of conductors with regional orchestras.

The Cambridge series continued, featuring English music in each programme: Ireland (30 October), Rawsthorne (15 January), Hadley (12 February), Bax and Bliss (6 May). The BBC presented its own return visits to Bristol in lunchtime and evening concerts on 17 March, taking with them the new Vaughan Williams Fifth Symphony (which was to be included in the Orchestra's fiftieth anniversary concert in October 1980).

Departure and death

In May the BBC again promoted a series of London concerts in the Albert Hall: the four programmes included Stravinsky's *The Rite of Spring* (10 May), Vaughan Williams' Fourth Symphony (12 May), Bliss's *Morning Heroes* (15 May), and Delius's *Sea Drift* preceding Beethoven's Ninth (19 May). The Bliss work formed a parting tribute to the BBC's Director of Music. Bliss had decided in the spring that the administrative burdens of the job outweighed its creative possibilities. With the added fact that his wife and family had been able to come to England, at the end of 1943, he felt that he should concentrate on composition and spend time with them. He left the BBC in the spring of 1944.

Who should succeed him? One amusing possibility had been suggested the previous year to Bliss, as he recalled. He had been telephoned by Lady Cunard, who had visited him in Marylebone High Street and offered to do all she could to reunite Bliss with his family in America. In return, Bliss was to give up his post in favour of – Sir Thomas Beecham, whom Lady Cunard wished to bring back to England. Bliss later wrote

> My first impulse was to laugh outright at the thought of Beecham sitting behind my desk, administering a large department, punctiliously answering memos, attending conferences, interviewing would-be broadcasters, etc etc, but this soon turned to anger at the unwarranted presumption behind this absurd deal and after advising her to write direct to the Director-General

herself, putting forward clearly all the reasons and facts, we parted very coldly. (Bliss, *As I remember*, p. 163.)

Instead, Bliss's successor was a familiar personality from the earliest days of broadcasting. Victor Hely-Hutchinson had in the late twenties been one of the backbones of Music Department: the educational series 'Foundations of Music' was his special responsibility, and he had frequently been heard giving piano recitals, or filling in during awkward moments on the air at Savoy Hill. In the thirties he had gone on to become Professor of Music at Birmingham University. It was perhaps appropriate that he should be invited to return, for he knew the administrative methods of the Corporation better than most. But it had been a much smaller organisation when he had worked for it, and during his tragically short tenure of office (cut off by his sudden illness and death), Hely-Hutchinson never succeeded in making an impact on the policy-making and musical direction of the Corporation. Always extremely moderate in his views, his declared intentions as to music policy were cautious and conservative (see Chapter Five). Under his direction, the unspoken bias of the BBC towards native music at the expense of continental new works was given a little more weight.

The summer of 1944 removed another great personality from the scene, whose service to the BBC and influence on the BBC's musical affairs over the previous fifteen years had been incalculable. (It had been little recognised inside the Corporation, except by Boult.) This was Sir Henry Wood, who that year celebrated his seventy-fifth birthday and the jubilee of his first Prom concert at the Queen's Hall. At the birthday concert, sponsored by the *Daily Telegraph*, the BBC Symphony Orchestra joined with the London Symphony and the London Philharmonic Orchestras under Boult, Cameron, Sargent and Wood himself in the Albert Hall on 25 March. Wood also gave a studio birthday concert with the Symphony Orchestra, including the Wagner *Rienzi* Overture which had opened his first Prom fifty years earlier. Bax wrote a tribute which was read by Stuart Hibberd. Characteristically, Wood's wish for his birthday pointed towards the future: he set up a subscription list for a new London concert hall to be named after him. He was also attempting to ensure the future of the Promenade Concerts with the BBC, but the Corporation was extremely reluctant to take on in perpetuity a commitment which was not well defined. After much argumentative correspondence the BBC agreed, and at a lunch in Claridge's during June Wood made over to the BBC the title 'Henry Wood Promenade Concerts' in perpetuity. Wood looked forward to his Jubilee Prom season with great enthusiasm. The welcome as he took his place on the first night, 10 June, was overwhelming.

But the Proms – and London music-making in general – had reckoned without the continuing dangers posed by the war. The gradual return to normal conditions of concert-giving was disrupted in mid-June. Hitler was losing the war in Europe, and in June 1944 launched his 'secret weapon' on England. The V1, a jet-propelled pilotless plane, was commonly known as the Doodlebug, or flying bomb; some 2000 were launched on London in the second half of June, and about half arrived, causing considerable damage. Suddenly conditions were back to those of 1940. The Proms were curtailed after 29 June before the BBC Symphony Orchestra had taken part, and disappointed audiences had instead to return to their radio sets. At least the BBC, learning from its previous experience, did not cancel the season altogether: Wood came to Bedford, and those parts of the Prom concerts which would have been broadcast were played by the Orchestra. Shostakovich's Eighth Symphony was given its British première on 13 July. On 28 July Wood gave a tremendous performance of Beethoven's Seventh Symphony with the Orchestra, broadcast on the Home Service; he then fell ill again. He was still in the throes of illness on 10 August, the last day of the season which would have been celebrated as his jubilee, and nine days later he died.

For the BBC Symphony Orchestra, Wood had been an indispensable companion since their foundation. In the first seasons he had shared the major load of the conducting with Boult; and he had directed the Proms single-handed. He had led the way to Boult in his open-minded advocacy of new works, and had continued to conduct many of them during the 1930s: it is easy to forget that the British première of Schoenberg's Five Orchestral Pieces was given by Wood back in 1912; with the BBC Symphony Orchestra he had given Webern's Passacaglia in the 1931 Proms and the first public performance here of Berg's Violin Concerto in the 1936 Proms. He was the ideal combination of the populariser and the educator: at the Proms, he would prove almost impossible to replace.

Wood had been a convinced supporter of broadcasting as a means of making music truly popular – the end that lay behind all his energetic life's activities:

With the whole-hearted support of broadcasting I feel that I am at last on the threshold of realising my life-long ambition of truly democratising the message of music and making its beneficent effect universal . . . I am quite convinced that not only in music, but generally, the medium of broadcasting, as utilised and developed in this country, is one of the few elements ordinarily associated with the progress of civilisation which I can heartily endorse.

It was a generous statement of support from a man who, by his own efforts alone, had achieved a quite remarkable popularisation of great music in the first half of the twentieth century.

Limbo

At the end of the 1944 Proms there was a strong move to return the Symphony Orchestra to London. Most other major BBC departments had returned to the capital by this time, and studio conditions in Bedford were becoming difficult – the resources demanded of a small town were as always very great. But logical though a move seemed, there was the question mark of Hitler's renewed attacks on the capital. The war in Europe was nearly won; yet at the start of September 1944 the first of the large V2 flying bombs was launched. The damage they wrought was very great, and the Government feared that ministerial departments would have to be evacuated once more. In fact, the bombs' effect was minimised because their action was not very precise, and they landed over a wide area.

During September Herbage was attempting to plan for the possibility of the Orchestra's return even before the impending season began; he suggested a season at the Albert Hall alongside engagements by the Royal Philharmonic Society and collaboration in a series of Sunday afternoon concerts with Harold Holt. In fact the Orchestra remained in Bedford, but took part in an increasing number of concerts in London, of which the Holt series was the most notable. These concerts had extremely popular programmes, with a preponderance of Beethoven and Tchaikovsky such as the BBC had successfully avoided earlier in the war. More important were two concerts for the Royal Philharmonic Society on 9 December 1944 and 17 March 1945; during the former, Boult was presented with the Gold Medal of the Royal Philharmonic Society. With typical modesty, he accepted it as a token of appreciation to the BBC Symphony Orchestra for its wartime work rather than as an award to him personally. There was a Wood memorial concert on 4 March, which reunited the three orchestras that had celebrated his seventy-fifth birthday only the previous year.

The Bedford symphony concerts continued, making one important addition: for the first time foreign guest conductors were invited. On 15 November, the first French visitor for four years was Charles Munch, conductor of the concerts at the Paris Conservatoire, with the young pianist Nicole Henriot. He included Roussel's Third Symphony as well as Britten's Frank Bridge Variations. More French visitors in February 1945 were Paul Paray and the pianist Yvonne Lefebvre, in Ravel, Dukas and Franck. Roger Desormière brought Ginette Neveu to play Brahms; Albert Ferber played

Rachmaninov's First Concerto in a Cameron concert (4 April). Other significant works included Holst's *Egdon Heath* (4 October, Boult), Mahler's Fourth Symphony (18 October, Cameron), and the British première of Eugene Goossens' Phantasy Concerto (1 November, Boult). Barbirolli returned for the first performance of Moeran's Sinfonietta (7 March) alongside Ravel and Brahms's Second Symphony. Piano Concertos by Bliss (2 May) and Rawsthorne (6 June) were heard, and the series ended with symphonies by Prokofiev, Sibelius and Beethoven on 20 June 1945.

Broadcast events during the season were headed by the return in September 1944 of Yehudi Menuhin who came across the Atlantic again to play for the Allied forces. This time he had a special prize with him: Bartók's Second Violin Concerto, of which he had given the first performance in America. He gave the first broadcast of the work, and followed it a fortnight later with a specially arranged concert on 20 September in which the public British première was given. (This is the better known of Bartók's violin concertos, and was the first to be heard here; No. 1, an early work, was not premièred until 1958.)

The alliance of the Western powers was celebrated at the start of 1944 when a new Soviet National Anthem was sent to Britain by Churchill, who had been given it by Stalin at their meeting in Teheran. This new anthem was to replace the *Internationale* and to be 'more suitable to the Socialist essence of the Soviet State'. It was written by A. V. Alexandrov, and immediately it arrived, one of the BBC's regular performers and arrangers, Augustus Franzel, was asked to orchestrate it. He did so within three days, and Boult and the Orchestra recorded it for broadcast before the Nine o'Clock News on Sunday 16 January 1945.

By the beginning of 1945 it was clear that a victory for the Allies in Europe was within sight. On Christmas Day 1944 the German offensive in the Battle of the Bulge had been halted. But only by March 1945 did the Allies cross the Rhine. Hitler hoped to be saved by the collision of American and Russian forces; in April his final hopes were destroyed by the shelling of Berlin, and on 30 April he committed suicide. Within a week all German armies in Europe had surrendered. The European war had ended.

The ending of the war as it affected music in the BBC did not, perhaps, take place until 27 June, when the Symphony Orchestra gave a special concert back in the Albert Hall with the cellist Pablo Casals. He gave unforgettable performances of the Schumann and Elgar Concertos. The BBC Symphony Orchestra, with an international soloist, playing in London to a crowded hall, felt that its life was back to normal. Yet that life was to change greatly in the following years.

5

Renewals and Replacements 1945-50

Back to London

Victory in Europe was celebrated on 8 May 1945. There still remained the horror of the atomic bomb and the surrender of the Japanese, but in England there was peace and the beginning of a painful return to normal life. Churchill called an election, which was held on 5 July; when the results were declared on 26 July (after a long delay due to voting by members of the forces overseas) Labour had one of the largest parliamentary majorities of the century. The country had voted for radical change; or rather, for the consolidation of the changes which the war had already brought about.

In musical life, it was impossible to foresee the economic conditions which would shape the developments of the immediate post-war years. But the BBC Symphony Orchestra began peacetime with an acute feeling that it was being taken for granted; though it had survived the war intact, had continued to provide first-rate music, and had set the standards by which the plethora of other orchestral music-making in the country was judged, it was immediately disregarded when the peace celebrations began. And with the benefit of hindsight one can judge that the first year of peace had a greater adverse effect on the Orchestra's future than any of the years of war.

V-Day and the next day passed without any major contribution by the Symphony Orchestra to the radio networks. Normal plans for broadcasting were of course disrupted, and with an insensitivity which had also marked the opening of the war, the programme planners left the classics of music off the air. The Symphony Orchestra was not heard on the Home Service until Day 3 of the celebrations, when Beethoven's Fifth Symphony, closely associated with victory in the minds of far more people than classical music-lovers, made an appearance. Boult felt a weary despair, and wrote from Bedford to the Director of Music, Victor Hely-Hutchinson: 'A number of things have cropped up in V-week which make it very clear to me that at any rate some people in the upper reaches of the BBC simply do not understand what the Orchestra is and what is stands for . . .'. In an unusually strong phrase, he referred to 'pathetic vacillation' over programme planning, and reflected bitterly on his experience in America, where the NBC Orchestra 'only play one programme a week, and although there are three and some-times four concerts a week, they always play the programme of the week or the programme of the week before, and so they have, if they wish it, six mornings on which to rehearse one programme'. Boult noted that 'in every case, of course, the concerts are presented as events of supreme importance'. He made a plea that the BBC should recognise the Orchestra's status: 'I think the time has come for us to assert that, though the Orchestra was founded for general broadcasting purposes, and has fulfilled them com-pletely, it may also, in fifteen years, be considered to have outgrown some of these requirements, and may claim some of the privileges of a thorough-bred.'

At the very beginning of peacetime, then, Boult was urging that there should be a look at the Orchestra's function within the BBC. He found a willing listener in Hely-Hutchinson, who had seen the Orchestra grow from its beginnings. But the elevated, impractical tone in which their discussions were carried on in the succeeding months was remote from the severely practical problem of ensuring the Orchestra's survival as a first-class en-semble: a problem which arose directly from post-war economic conditions in the London musical world. There was immediate conflict between the Orchestra and the BBC over its return to London, and Boult chose to take a moral stand on behalf of the Orchestra in justifiable but unfortunate circum-stances. Following the declaration of peace, Hely-Hutchinson had visited Bedford and discussed plans for the Orchestra's return. He had mentioned two possible dates: one before the 1945 Proms, one after. The question of the Symphony Orchestra's return to London had been raised as long ago as March 1943 by Bliss, who felt that accommodation difficulties in Bedford suggested the earliest possible return to the capital, but changes in the pattern of the war prevented this and the matter was postponed. With the likelihood of victory towards the end of 1944, however, a move was approved to bring the Symphony Orchestra back 'as soon as conditions were con-sidered suitable, and certainly immediately the war in Europe came to an end'. This statement was given to the Orchestra on 29 September and was assumed to be policy. But by the declaration of victory in May of the next year it was realised that studio accommodation in Maida Vale would not be ready in time for the Orchestra's return in the near future. Hely-Hutchinson conveyed the Orchestra's wish to return before the 1945 Proms, not after, but Richard Howgill of the Entertainment Department made a note on his memo 'i October earliest'. Boult wrote (17 May) to say that things were no better in Bedford: the situation as regards studios, 'always bad, is now deteriorating so fast that it has already become critical'. The next day Hely-Hutchinson reiterated to Howgill that whether or not Maida Vale was ready, the Orchestra must return after the Proms, on 24 September; all its members were keenly looking forward to the return to the capital. But the point was not taken. On 22 May Boult received instructions from Basil Nicolls and Hely-Hutchinson that, though they hoped to bring back the Orchestra in September, there was no guarantee that the studio accommodation at Maida Vale would be ready. Boult was accordingly told to instruct the Orchestra members to renew their tenancies in Bedford on a monthly basis from 24 September. They absolutely refused and, encouraged by what was clearly sympathy and agreement on the part of their Chief Conductor, they un-animously agreed that 'we definitely refuse to come back to Bedford after the Proms'.

Boult could have tried to negotiate this position with his superiors in London. Instead he simply reported it to Hely-Hutchinson, and added, 'I am afraid that I must associate myself completely with this decision, and ask that any disciplinary action that the Corporation sees fit to inflict on the Orchestra shall also fall on me. I know I need not give reasons to you, but if anyone wishes for them I can send them with pleasure.' Thus Boult, as so often in the past, identified himself completely with those under him in the hierarchy instead of those over him. Neither, however, did he attempt to act as a mediator. That task was left to Hely-Hutchinson, and it was not one to which he was well suited. He wrote a long memo about the problem to Assistant Controller (Programmes), but he cannot have seriously hoped that the matter would remain at that level. Within two days the Orchestra's action was being discussed by the Director-General, the Deputy Director-General, Senior Controller, and all the relevant Music Department officials.

Hely-Hutchinson summed up the situation: '1. The Orchestra are hold-ing a pistol to the head of the BBC; 2. They are perfectly capable of firing it off; 3. Is the BBC prepared to take the consequences if they do?' Of the three factors, the first was the only one which carried any weight at the time; but the second was by far the most important. BBC officials were perturbed by production of an ultimatum; what should have perturbed them more was the fact that most of the Orchestra seriously did not mind if their bluff was called and they were dismissed. The important sentence in Hely-Hutchinson's re-port was: 'Indeed, outside organisations have already angled for some of the most distinguished players . . .' He said that 'in nearly every case their loyalty to their own organisation, as well as their admiration and affection for Sir

Adrian Boult, has made them prefer to stay where they were' – but this was not to remain true in the following year. Hely-Hutchinson made the position quite clear: 'A very large majority of them are real experts who if they left the BBC Orchestra tomorrow could find elsewhere employment at least equally lucrative though not so secure, dignified or congenial . . . the threat – if it can be so described – is not an empty one, and the individuals concerned are perfectly able to put it into effect.' That such a situation was recognised in the first days of peacetime and then overlooked in the months that followed says much against the narrowmindedness of the BBC administration in this period.

It was clear that the BBC would have to reverse its decision, and so it did. The Orchestra was to be allowed back from 24 September, 'studio accommodation being risked'. But the new Director-General, William Haley (who had succeeded Cecil Graves in April 1944), was annoyed by the incident, and Boult felt it necessary to write to him and explain the Orchestra's position once more. Boult's letter (31 May) is justificatory rather than argumentative, and it perhaps missed the opportunity to warn Haley of the danger facing the Orchestra's existence. But he did say this:

> I want to assure you that there has never before been any sign of a desire for this kind of action, although they have had some considerable disappointments in their dealings with the Corporation through these fifteen years. Half of them know that they could earn far more money in the open market at present, but only two players have left us, one to fill a post that was offered him and the other to realise a pre-war ambition. Their conditions of work, taking repertoire into account, have always been twice as arduous as those of any other orchestra of like reputation in the world . . .

It was only the Orchestra's threat that remained in Haley's mind, however; in his reply (4 June) he wrote:

> . . . I can see that the Orchestra was feeling pretty desperate. . . . But you yourself get to the heart of the matter by admitting that no final appeal was made to the Management before the ultimatum was produced. It is a thoroughly bad thing when the first intimation a Director-General has of a crisis is the production of a pistol at his head. I can say the matter has still received dispassionate judgement on its merits, but that is not the best way to get it.

Haley concluded by expressing the wish that relations between the Orchestra and Corporation 'ought to be of a close and understanding nature'.

This minor but important incident did not work to the Orchestra's bene-

fit. In the minds of BBC management there may have been left behind the
impression of a body which was argumentative and demanding; possibly this
influenced those who had to make decisions about its future. At least that
may be one excuse for the lack of action to safeguard the Orchestra – a course
of events to which Boult's phrase 'pathetic vacillation' can readily be applied.

1945–6

The Orchestra was back in London. Studio accommodation in Maida Vale
was, as had been feared, not yet ready, so recordings took place in the
People's Palace in the East End – a building which was the successor to the
one which had seen many BBC symphony concerts in the years before 1930.
The opportunity was taken, at the suggestion of Julian Herbage, to promote
the Sunday afternoon symphony recordings there as public concerts, and so
the 1945–6 season began with two concurrent series. The Wednesday Symphony Concerts, displaced by the bombing of the Queen's Hall, took place in
the Albert Hall. The series was inaugurated on 17 October with the Dvořák
Cello Concerto played by Casals. The People's Palace series caused a mild
sensation in the East End: the first concert, at 2.30 pm on 21 October, was
sold out (capacity 1600) and hundreds of people were unable to obtain admission. Boult recalled that twenty years before, when the previous People's
Palace was used, he had been able to bathe in the nearby swimming pool after
conducting. The series continued with great success, and included a two-
part performance of Bach's *Christmas Oratorio* on 23 and 30 December. The
Albert Hall concerts included in November the first London performance of
Bartók's Second Violin Concerto played by Menuhin.

Among broadcast events the revival of the series *Music of our Time* stood
out: in the autumn of 1945 works by Rawsthorne, Stravinsky and Bartók
were included. On 7 November a cantata by the Russian composer Yuri
Shaporin was conducted by Albert Coates. *On the Field of Kullikorvo* received much attention in the press; the *News Chronicle* called it 'extraordinarily impressive' (8 November). 'Soviet composers believe in making
their music actual, and this is one of the most vivid and actual (*sic*) choral
works since 1900', quoth the *Daily Worker*. The Orchestra contributed to
the BBC's Purcell celebrations, with his ode *Hail, bright Cecilia* under Constant Lambert's direction on 22 November.

During the first part of 1946 Boult was given leave of absence to conduct
in Boston, and Julian Herbage took pains to suggest distinguished guest conductors to fill the gap. Two names of potential importance to the Orchestra
were introduced at this time. On 27 January the Czech conductor Rafael
Kubelik appeared at the People's Palace: Janáček's *Sinfonietta* had to be

omitted because all the necessary trumpets could not be found, but he directed Dvořák's Seventh Symphony (then called No. 2, in the old numbering) with 'fire and life', said the *Jewish Chronicle*. Though the Orchestra did not do him full justice, he was felt to have roused them. Herbage reported: 'His complete knowledge of the scores, his control over the orchestra, and his amazing vitality and enthusiasm are of a world-beating order, and when he achieves a little more poise (which need not detract from his intense driving quality) he will certainly rank among the world's greatest conductors.' Then on 20 February at the Albert Hall John Barbirolli, conductor of the Hallé Orchestra, 'scored a personal triumph in a beautifully balanced performance of Verdi's Requiem Mass' (*Daily Mail*). 'One of the most exciting performances within recent memory', said the *Daily Telegraph*. Herbage also enthused about Albert Wolff: his 'exquisite orchestral balance in Ravel; in the Mendelssohn Italian Symphony at the People's Palace, Wolff added to this exquisite balance a perfect sense of style and an irresistible élan which made this performance one of the most outstanding broadcasts to which I have ever listened'.

Boult returned from Boston and conducted his first Albert Hall concert in 1946 on 6 March; it included the British première of the Bartók Concerto for Orchestra, which was greeted with enthusiasm and a certain amount of relief. 'Not in the least problematical' (*The Times*); 'a masterpiece' (*Star*); 'this most lucid and human of all the Hungarian master's compositions' (*Daily Telegraph*). During the rest of the season two concerts were given for the Royal Philharmonic Society, and visits were made to Cambridge and Norwich. At a modest London Music Festival in June four concerts were given, one featuring the soprano Marjorie Lawrence and another repeating Barbirolli's Verdi *Requiem*.

On 7 and 14 July, the Orchestra contributed two concerts to the first postwar ISCM Festival, the twentieth. The activities of the Society had been carried on during the war in America, and it was felt necessary to reestablish links with Europe as closely as possible. Representatives from nearly twenty countries attended, and Covent Garden was booked for the two orchestral concerts. At the first, five different conductors directed five works by five composers of five different nationalities. The British representative was Elisabeth Lutyens's Three Symphonic Preludes conducted by Edward Clark. Robert de Koos played the solo part in his own Piano Concerto; Elsa Barraine's Second Symphony was heard ('full of delightful tunes', said the *Daily Mail*), and Richard Mohaupt's *Stadtpfeifermusik* was given. Fitelberg, van Lier and Rosenthal conducted these works. Finally, Boult conducted Prokofiev's *Ode to the End of the War*, which, Ralph Hill wrote, 'might just as well have been written as an ode to the beginning of the next war'. The second concert was more successful: it included two works already known – Bartók's Concerto for Orchestra and Rawsthorne's overture *Cortèges* – and included Roman Palester's Violin Concerto, played by Eugenia Uminska and conducted by Fitelberg, which was found attractive if insubstantial, plus a romantic Nocturne by the Frenchman Raymond Loucheur.

A Changed World

Outside the BBC, the musical world in London was changing rapidly. On 24 May 1946 *The Times* editorialised on the state of the capital's orchestral music-making. It declared that

> the same dilemma between planning and freedom as confronts the nation in other departments of social life now confronts London in the provision of symphonic music . . . the BBC Orchestra has from the nature of its organisation been most successful in maintaining its standards of performance, but also from the nature of its organisation can contribute least to the solution of London's problem, for its primary duty is to the wireless listener and its main habitation is the studio, not the public hall . . . we now have a multiplication of orchestras making a bid for public support for a policy, whose logical conclusion is the simultaneous performance in half a dozen theatres of the same few symphonies and concertos week in week out on Sunday afternoon . . . Art needs private enterprise, but 'enterprise' and not 'private' is the operative word.

Music was now basking in the warmth which the work of CEMA and ENSA and thousands of wartime concerts had kindled. It was a growth industry of an unprecedented kind, and it was a commercial business in which there was money to be made. Life was hard, rationing was increased in the wake of dire shortages in food supplies, but as the Labour Government's work took root employment ceased to be a problem. Indeed the experts pronounced that employment was 'over-full'; industry was no longer depressed. There were acute financial problems for the state, but few for the wage earner, though he could not even spend what money he had on food. Through all the hardships of the postwar period, a gradual determined increase in the standard of living took place.

The most striking result of orchestral expansion in London was the formation of a new orchestra. Walter Legge, who had had such success in providing wartime orchestral music through ENSA, was invited to bring together as many of London's outstanding players as he could into a full-size symphony orchestra. But the new ensemble was not primarily to be a public, concert-giving orchestra; its backing came from the Gramophone Company, and its purpose would be to provide fine recordings. At one time it seemed possible that Sir Thomas Beecham would be the orchestra's artistic director. When the Philharmonia, as it was called, made its first appearance in public at the Kingsway Hall on 27 October 1945, Beecham conducted – and asked for no more than a cigar as his fee. Legge was determined to retain control of the venture, and Beecham was unwilling to have his plans restricted. While the Philharmonia went on to become an outstanding orchestra – working with Herbert von Karajan, and becoming the only British orchestra besides the BBC's with which Toscanini would appear – Beecham set off on his own to create another new London orchestra, which would surface a year later as the Royal Philharmonic (see below).

The attraction of this newly lucrative freelance world to Orchestra members who had slaved through the war period with unstinting effort was very great. What would the BBC do to retain them? In June 1945 Hely-Hutchinson, who had been reflecting on the points in Boult's outburst about V-week, cautiously submitted a radical new scheme for the future work of the Symphony Orchestra – one which took account of Boult's views on its prestige. What he suggested was a reduction in the Orchestra's workload, a concentration on its public concert-giving activities, and the re-establishment of its pre-eminence in the musical world. The scheme would necessarily involve either

> 1. The formation of another BBC Orchestra in London to take over the routine work at present undertaken by the BBC Symphony Orchestra, whether complete or sectionally; or 2. The much more extensive booking of outside orchestras for studio work. The latter would probably be the better course (even if the players were at present available for the former, which they are not) as outside orchestras would be compensated by fairly regular studio bookings for the frequent appearances of the BBC Symphony Orchestra.

There was no attempt to estimate the cost of this proposal. Instead Hely-Hutchinson confined himself to familiar questions of policy:

> (i) Is it the BBC's business to maintain an orchestra whose functions would be as much public as broadcasting? and (ii) What degree of co-operation with (and hence forfeiture of independence to) any outside body is called for from the BBC so that the venture, if undertaken, may have an appropriate basis?

Hely-Hutchinson's covering note to his scheme was modest to the point of diffidence, and it is difficult to detect any note of urgency in his words:

I am not making a recommendation but simply submitting the matter to you for consideration. In any case nothing can be done at the moment; but it is a very large issue, and should it become advisable to do something along these lines, it would, I am sure, be helpful if we could all consider exactly what it would mean . . .

Restoring the Orchestra

The obvious reply to the proposal, which was made on 14 June by Richard Howgill (who was now Assistant Controller in charge of Entertainment), was that broadcasting considerations must always come first. The practical matter of the restitution of the Orchestra to its pre-war strength and the re-establishment of a pattern of work for it were the matters which needed immediate consideration. Indeed, in that same month the re-employment of players who had left to do military service was being considered, and those players placed at the end of 1939 in Category 'C' (i.e. those for whom no case could be made for not releasing them for military service) were invited to re-audition by Hely-Hutchinson. Boult and Clarence Raybould, who was later that year to retire as his assistant conductor, carried out these auditions; but there was still no clear end in view. What sort of orchestra was it planned to reconstruct? A meeting on 11 July within Music Department agreed with Howgill that augmentation back to the prewar total of 119 players was desirable. But that had to be referred to higher authority. It was not until 23 August that Basil Nicolls, the Senior Controller, agreed that the Orchestra should be restored to full strength; the matter was referred to the Director-General.

Haley was unsure of the wisdom of augmentation to full strength, for it was expensive. And was it necessary? He asked his Deputy to examine whether the proposal was a result of 'genuine pressure from programme and supply departments, or a painless way of resettling homecoming Category "C" musicians'. Moreover, the estimated cost of £49,000 p.a. would, he thought, be difficult to justify. He felt that 'the promise of extra use being got out of the big Symphony Orchestra by further augmentation will have to be much firmer and more explicit'. This, it must be noted, was a reaction to the restoration of the Orchestra to its pre-war strength – not to any radically new proposals.

Haley thus aligned himself with those who, throughout the Orchestra's history, have demanded of it economic productivity rather than a standard of excellence. In subsequent discussions he insisted on his point about extra use. Kenneth Wright noted: 'DG won't accept restitution unless the extra 20 players will give a guaranteed increase of two shows a week'. On 4 September he was able to report that these extra sessions had been agreed, but that the Orchestra would play as one group for half its weekly playing time. This was the situation when the Orchestra returned to work at the end of September, and Kenneth Wright kept a close eye on their duties in the succeeding months. He noted the hours put in during their first weeks back: 26; 28; 32; 24; 24; 24; 31. This did not include, for instance, travelling time to and from a provincial engagement in Coventry, and recording sessions with Casals. But they were enough for him to make the general point that a 36-hour-a-week contract, which had been suggested, was unnecessary to produce the required six broadcasts a week from the Orchestra. He suggested that 30 hours a week was reasonable, and added a general point: 'When an orchestra is playing, players are concentrating far more than non-musicians are likely to realise. All our players are expected to practise and keep themselves in good trim . . .'

These artistic matters were not deemed relevant, however. The financial case for augmentation had gone forward, but on 27 November Howgill wrote to Hely-Hutchinson that the proposed hours of work were not enough to convince the BBC authorities of the case. Seven broadcast sessions a week were necessary, not six. Boult once again said testily that the BBC could have far more hours of playing time if programme duplications were to be allowed. Not until the beginning of 1946 was this part of the question settled. There was a rearrangement of the orchestral duties so that the Theatre Orchestra played more of the necessary light music, while the Symphony Orchestra took over from that group the responsibility for studio opera. At the same time (11 January), Stanford Robinson was officially appointed Opera Director and Deputy Conductor of the Symphony Orchestra (the latter in succession to Raybould); and Walter Goehr succeeded him as conductor of the Theatre Orchestra.

Another consideration had arisen, however, which bore on the need for the Orchestra's augmentation to pre-war strength to be urgently agreed. In the autumn of 1946, it was proposed to inaugurate a new wavelength; originally referred to as Programme 'C', this became the Third Programme. Perhaps the most distinctive of all the BBC's post-war activities, it was to be a cultural channel concentrating on products of the highest quality. Preliminary plans by its first Controller, George Barnes, were made at the end of 1945. They indicated that the programme would require two concerts of symphonic music a week and one outside broadcast of a symphony concert. Hely-Hutchinson was quick to point out that 'this would only be practicable with the use of more recorded repeats, or by the augmentation of the Symphony Orchestra to pre-war strength, which, as you know, would, by

making available additional splitting of the full Orchestra, provide an additional two or three concerts a week. Even so it would be a tight fit . . .' As for
outside broadcasts: 'At present I am confident that the right sort of programmes in sufficient quantity are not available from outside sources . . .'
So the pressure on BBC house orchestras would be even greater.

In March 1946 the augmentation of the Symphony Orchestra to 119
players was finally agreed. There was a sense of urgency in the decision, for
it was conveyed to the BBC Governors only retrospectively, at their meeting
of 19 June; it was then described as an 'interim measure'. Boult was in no
mood to hail the decision as a triumph. Though he referred to it in a memo of
12 March to Hely-Hutchinson as 'indeed splendid news', he went on to say:

> It seems churlish to ask for more in the same breath, but I think I should say
> at once that I do hope that the use of the Orchestra in relation to its morale
> can be considered very soon . . . the Orchestra needs a change now, and if this
> kind of work [provincial visits, and perhaps a foreign tour] is known to be
> included in our year it will, I think, help our recruiting of such new players
> as we may need.

This is an interesting admission that it might be hard to find new players.
The recruitment of the succeeding months suggested just that: the BBC had
fallen behind the market. It was not, as it had been in 1930, easy to attract the
best players. Moreover, increasing numbers of Orchestral members were
disputing the salaries offered them under a new Musicians' Union agreement. A sub-principal violin refused £18 a week, and was supported by both
Paul Beard and Boult; a principal wind player was offered £23, but asked for
£28.

The strength of the market outside the BBC, and the new-found confidence of the Musicians' Union, was further reinforced by a Union demand
early in 1946 that the BBC should restrict the activities of all its orchestras to
the recording studio. In line with its demand to outside promoters that each
and every rehearsal should be paid separately, the Union suggested that the
BBC should be subject to these restrictions also. The BBC rebutted this
claim strongly, on the grounds that salaried musicians were entitled to be
asked to play whatever proportions of rehearsals and concerts their employ-
ers demanded. But the Union replied that 'in view of the definitely expressed
opinion of our members upon the unfair competition of BBC Orchestras
with other Symphony Orchestras [the BBC was asked to] amend the contracts of their Orchestras so that their work shall be confined to Studio
Broadcast'.

The only result of this extreme demand was that, in line with the Union's demands, the rank and file salaries were increased to £15 (as against £13.50 plus bonuses). This was not sufficient to stop the flow of players from the BBC. Payment for rehearsals outside the BBC ensured lower standards (because as a result fewer rehearsals took place!); but at least the musicians were well paid for what they did. The attractions of the 'security' offered by the BBC became less and less. Through 1946 the departures from the Orchestra assumed the nature of a crisis. They were recognised as such only after the Prom season of that year, which took place from 27 July to 21 September under the direction of Boult and Cameron, plus a new Associate Conductor, Constant Lambert: the London Symphony Orchestra and the BBC Symphony Orchestra played for four weeks each. The public enthusiasm for this, the first series of Proms since Wood's death, was enormous, and all attendance records were broken; but the artistic standard left much to be desired. It fell below that which was thought acceptable by both the BBC's Music Department and the press. A certain slackening of the standard was always thought inevitable during the pressures of the Prom season, but in this case there was no improvement with the start of the Symphony Concerts 1946–7 season. Performances became, if anything, more ragged.

Losing players

That the root cause of this poor standard was simply a loss of most of the best players in the Orchestra was something that Music Department was surprisingly slow to recognise. Discussion centred around problems of morale, choice of conductors, and the demands of the broadcast services. Then Richard Pratt, who was about to retire as Orchestral Manager at the end of 1946, specified the losses (in a document which Howgill described to Nicolls as 'enlightening'). Pratt spelled out the problem bluntly. In the single year since the end of the war, the Orchestra had lost:

Two sub-principal first violins
Two principal, two sub-principal, and one rank-and-file second violins
Two principal, one sub-principal and two rank-and-file violas (this *after* the loss of Bernard Shore, founder principal)
Three rank-and-file cellos
Two sub-principal double basses
Principal and two sub-principal flutes
Principal oboe
Principal and sub-principal bassoon
Principal clarinet
Two horns, including the principal, Aubrey Brain
Two sub-principal trumpets

One sub-principal trombone.

Thus all the important wind players, and many of the most distinguished string players had left in that one year. During the war the string sections had lost Marie Wilson, Laurance Turner, and then Bernard Shore. The total loss of players between 1939 and 1946 was forty out of an orchestra of around ninety.

It could be argued that the Symphony Orchestra when founded was an exceptionally young orchestra; that it was unreasonable to expect players who had given fifteen years' service to remain with the ensemble for ever; and that the rising generation of young players should be given an opportunity to join the organisation. But the best players were leaving the Orchestra only because its conditions of work and rates of pay were no longer attractive in comparison with those outside the BBC; and excellent players were not being recruited in their place. Following the agreement to augment to the Orchestra's former full strength in the spring of 1946, auditions were held. Of the twenty-three string players necessary to bring the total back to pre-war numbers, only eleven of adequate standard could be found; six firsts, four seconds, a viola and a cello were still needed by October that year. This should have alerted the BBC to the fact that the market was working against them, and that without a considerable increase in salaries (and perhaps special provisions of work for leaders and principals) there was little hope for maintaining the standard of the Orchestra.

Reporting on the poor standard of performance in the 1946 Proms (in a note of 21 September) Boult laid much of the blame on the system of continuous nightly performance which then obtained during that season. He himself thoroughly disliked conducting at the Proms, and was asking to be released from forthcoming seasons. His judgement was that the pre-war standard of the Orchestra could be recaptured, but only if working conditions were right:

> ... its work in the recent Promenade Season, though promising enough, was nowhere near the 1939 Festival level. On the present personnel (with perhaps one exception) I see no reason why the old level should not be recovered, provided that working conditions are right, and it is on this that I would ask for a prompt reply from a high level. Put bluntly, does the Corporation wish me to try and bring the Orchestra up to its 1939 standard or would it prefer to have a useful and efficient working body that will accede to all the demands of the various Services? There is naturally in planning circles a strong bias in the latter direction ... it might be simpler to yield to all planning demands, work our schedule on a minimum of rehearsal and a minimum of public

appearance, and give up inviting our Toscaninis and Menuhins, or at any rate acquiesce in their refusal to visit us when they discover what is happening. This is the decision I would ask immediately from those in charge of Corporation policy. There is no compromise . . .

This direct challenge fell on deaf ears. The only official sympathetic to Boult's view was Hely-Hutchinson, and his response to this urgent plea was to consider the matter for eight weeks. He then wrote in muted terms to Howgill (20 November): 'During the last two months I have been trying to discover the root causes of this falling off in standard, so that I could suggest a remedy . . .' In his long report he mentioned the complications of the planning procedures for the increased number of networks, the attractiveness of freelance work to musicians, the problems of guest conductors and of repertoire. His fundamental point was that 'in the past the Orchestra has had a feeling of *esprit de corps*. The feeling is not now so strong as it was, and one urgent function must be to prevent it from disappearing.' To this end he proposed that the splitting of the Orchestra into sections, which he felt reduced this *esprit*, should be ended; instead there should be 'two stable units (respectively about three-fifths and two-fifths of the present establishment) which often combine . . . The advantage of this scheme is that it provides the right psychological background for the players . . .' To this suggestion he added a sensible decision to restrict guest conductors to those of the highest quality. He then attempted to safeguard Music Department's control over programme planning in a way which shows that he had failed to grasp the changing nature of BBC radio and the special needs of the new networks: 'It is necessary for the orchestral resources to be allocated and the programmes built far more from the point of view of the Orchestra, and less from the point of view of the detailed, and sometimes conflicting, needs of the different Services . . .'

So Hely-Hutchinson's concluding recommendations were four:

1. Abolish the conception of the Symphony Orchestra as one single unit which frequently divides, and substitute the conception of two separate Orchestras which often combine.
2. Rigidly cut down the invitation of guest conductors and only invite them on grounds of outstanding eminence or specialised contributions to repertoire.
3. This [i.e. Music] Department to have independence of action as to choice of the detailed content of programmes.
4. A consistent policy must be pursued in relation to each Orchestra; this

can only be achieved if the allocation of orchestral resources, and the choice of conductors, is the exclusive responsibility of the Department.

This report was sound, in a cautious way, but it was also alarmingly out of touch with reality. It was remote both from the opinions of the players themselves, and from current thinking in the higher reaches of the BBC. Hely-Hutchinson's sweet reasonableness did not begin to convince George Barnes, Controller of the new Third Programme, who sent back a terse note with six points of dissent, including these three:

1. We have realised for some months that something has got to be done – and that immediately – about the Symphony Orchestra . . .
3. We regard the restoration of the Symphony Orchestra to its 1939 position in the world of music as essential . . . We cannot see that DM has in fact suggested a way of getting better and more contented players in the BBC Symphony Orchestra.
6. We cannot admit DM's points 3 and 4, since this is inconsistent with the position of Programme Heads as laid down in DG's memorandum on Sound Broadcasting of 24th July 1945.

Whether Music Department liked it or not, things had changed in the BBC, and if it continued to ignore these changes it could expect little attention and respect from Management. Meanwhile, standards were continuing to fall – concern was expressed at the playing in the Albert Hall concerts in November – and Boult was becoming more puzzled and distanced from the machinery of Broadcasting House: 'The conditions of work this autumn are most depressing,' he wrote wearily on 5 November, 'I don't understand the present planning machinery at all.'

A reduced Orchestra

The problems were discussed at a high level towards the end of November: the meeting brought together Basil Nicolls as Controller of Programmes, George Barnes of the Third Programme and Lindsay Wellington of the Home Service, with Howgill from Entertainment Division and other officials. By the middle of December there was a partial agreement with some points in Hely-Hutchinson's report: the splitting of the Symphony Orchestra was to be abolished, and a new establishment of ninety-six, including part-time players, was to be set up. Opera performances would be given back to the Theatre Orchestra and the Symphony Orchestra's output reduced to four performances a week, hopefully including some repeats. The reduced establishment solved the problem of recruiting new players in the easiest way possible – by not recruiting them. It was a defeatist move, but if there was to be no more money available, it was the only solution. In fact, the move reduced the annual cost of the Symphony Orchestra by some £20,000: if this had been redistributed in increased salaries to the ninety-six who remained, the BBC might well have attracted back into the Orchestra some of the recent departures. But such an increase would have had implications for all BBC orchestral salaries. Moreover, the shortfall in programmes created by the Symphony Orchestra's no longer splitting into sections had to be made up, and that too would cost money. In place of Hely-Hutchinson's proposal of a second Orchestra, the Theatre Orchestra was asked to supply more of the light classical repertoire. The light repertoire was to be supplemented by booking outside orchestras or *ad hoc* players.

During the autumn of 1946 the problems of the Orchestra and of the BBC's music policy in general had been aired at Board level by an active member of the Governors, Dr Ernest Whitfield. He had written on 14 September to the Chairman that he had come to the conclusion

> ... as a result of my attendance at Promenade Concerts, listening to musical broadcasts, and conversations with Sir Adrian Boult and other colleagues, that a reconsideration of our policy of music is essential ... We should have to decide whether we are anxious to provide music at the highest level; we are falling far short of this. None of the concerts I attended had been properly rehearsed. At the same time some of the orchestral performers seem to be tired ...

Whitfield raised many linked points: the programming of the Proms and the intensity of their demands on the Orchestra; the amount of orchestral music broadcast; the standard of the Symphony Orchestra; and the general direction of the BBC's music policy. The Board Meeting on 19 September asked for a report from the Director-General: it was not until they convened on 9 January 1947 that he was able to supply such a report, for it raised matters of fundamental importance. The answers provided to Dr Whitfield with regard to the Symphony Orchestra show the BBC's attitude to the acute problems of the post-war period.

> Since 1939, the Orchestra has lost 40 out of 119 players [40 out of 90 would have been a more accurate proportion], many of them principals of outstanding ability ... A few of the losses have been through ill-health, marriage, or other causes not connected with Orchestral conditions; but the majority of them can be attributed to players being tempted by outside market conditions. .... There are no doubt factors which cause players to yield to

temptation, and the decline in the quality of the Orchestra may be one of them.

The notion that a player who left the BBC Orchestra to earn more money, play in better conditions and lead a more rewarding life was 'yielding to temptation' is a revealing one. The paper continued by agreeing with Hely-Hutchinson's analysis that 'the deeper underlying causes of deterioration' lay in other matters. The reconstitution of the Orchestra as a body of ninety-six, and the new policy on guest conductors, were mentioned as agreed solutions. It was stated that the problems 'had been given the most serious consideration in conjunction with Sir Adrian Boult'.

Whitfield was not satisfied. After the Board Meeting, he wrote again to the Chairman on 13 January, querying several points. He knew that Boult was scarcely likely to have encouraged the reduction of the Orchestral establishment from 119 to ninety-six, and he considered that the problems of finding the right players had not been sufficiently well covered in the report. He laid great stress, rightly, on obtaining the best principals (especially in the wind section) regardless of cost. Nicolls had to advise the Director-General on the replies that should be given to Whitfield. They show that the essence of Boult's post-war appeal on the Orchestra's behalf had gone unheard.

> Boult naturally prefers conducting an orchestra which is about 20 players bigger than the standard orchestras of America and Europe, and in that sense he is sorry to see it cut down. He was, however, fully consulted . . . On attempting the restoration of numbers it proved difficult to get players of the requisite standard. . . . It is considered that there are only two places in which it would be desirable to obtain better principals. . . . There is no reason to suppose that the situation cannot be kept under control. . . . As Dr Whitfield knows better than most people the ensemble is more important within reasonable limits than the individual eminence of the players.

With this, the acceptance of a level of routine competence in the Symphony Orchestra (rather than the wish to spend money on obtaining the very highest standards of performance) became the policy of the day. There was always, as Nicolls put it, 'the prospect of securing an ensemble of the standard of 1938–9', but it remained only a prospect.

Launching the Third Programme 1946–7

The autumn of 1946 had seen the start of a new concert season, with more events in London than ever before. The Musicians' Union's regulation about payment of rehearsals made it on the one hand easier for unscrupulous promoters to put on profitable one-rehearsal concerts of all Beethoven and Tchaikovsky, filling halls; and on the other hand even more difficult for an organisation like the Royal Philharmonic Society to afford the necessary number of rehearsals for its more ambitious programmes. Sir Thomas Beecham, having returned from America, once more stepped into the entrepreneurial breach. Though his old orchestra, the London Philharmonic, was still active, organised by its players, Beecham decided to form a new semi-permanent orchestra in collaboration with the Royal Philharmonic Society, ensuring a degree of security through a recording contract with the Victor Company. Thus the Royal Philharmonic Orchestra came into being for the 1946–7 season. It appeared not only at the Society's concerts, but at Beecham's own events, and found a showcase in his Delius Festival in October and November 1946.

By the start of 1947, there was some feeling that the bubble was about to burst. Lionel Tertis wrote to the *Daily Telegraph* in January that 'the present-day mushroom growth of orchestras in London is ridiculous'. *The Observer* reported on 2 February that audiences were dwindling; the Royal Philharmonic Society was in financial difficulties; the new Royal Philharmonic had lost £700 on a concert in November; the National Symphony had been forced to cancel a concert in January; and the London Philharmonic Orchestra was losing £300 a concert at Covent Garden.

These factors were the result of increased costs – travel, subsistence and so on. In fact, during the rest of the season most concert-giving bodies found it just possible to survive. CEMA, now transformed into the Arts Council of Great Britain, supported three important regional orchestras, and in London it helped the London Philharmonic Orchestra and the New London Orchestra under Alec Sherman. In the 1946–7 season each of the four main London orchestras gave some 200 concerts; there were usually seven major concerts a week in London – with often four or five on a Sunday. In the absence of the Queen's Hall, this put extraordinary pressure on the Albert Hall. This in turn affected the BBC's ability to provide outside broadcasts of orchestral concerts, and Hely-Hutchinson went so far as to declare in an article in *BBC Quarterly* that the BBC's orchestral planning now depended on the availability or otherwise of the Albert Hall! A new concert hall was recognised as an urgent necessity, and the Gorell Committee, which was enquiring into the preservation of the Regent's Park Terraces, suggested a concert hall at the corner of the park, just east of a site previously favoured by Henry Wood. There were also proposals to rebuild Queen's Hall, but nothing was done because of the post-war building restrictions then in force.

The most important feature of the 1946–7 season in the BBC's broadcasting was the launching of the Third Programme. At the Maida Vale
studios on Sunday 29 September, Boult conducted the first performance of
the *Occasion   Overture* by Britten commissioned for the occasion, and other
English music by Handel (*Fireworks Music*), Purcell, Vaughan Williams and
Parry (*Blest Pair of Sirens*). Bliss conducted his own Music for Strings.
(Britten subsequently withdrew his work.) The musical declarations of
intent by the BBC about its new wavelength were impressive:

> a musician's choice . . . no need to exclude works because they are un-
> popular . . . standard works formerly excluded by their length to be given
> whole . . . major events repeated a day or two later . . . programmes built in
> series to afford study of a composer's output in a particular field . . . no
> attention to philistine complaints.

And the opening events of the network fulfilled the claims in full. On 24
October, repeated four days later, the BBC Symphony Orchestra played
under Beecham in a complete performance of Wagner's *Tristan und Isolde*,
with Marjorie Lawrence and Arthur Carron in the title roles. *Die Walküre*
under Beecham followed in December. Many other operas were broadcast
from home and abroad, including Benjamin Britten's *Peter Grimes* and *The
Rape of Lucretia* (the latter by the Glyndebourne Opera Company in the
studio).

The chief contribution of the BBC Symphony Orchestra to the networks
was redefined. The usual Albert Hall Symphony Concert on Wednesdays
was broadcast on the Home Service, and repeated in part on Thursdays in
the Third Programme. Then there was a Saturday concert from the People's
Palace, which was broadcast on the Third Programme and repeated in part
on Sunday in the Home Service. The combined results of these two series of
public concerts were most impressive in terms of repertoire. The 1946–7
series of Saturday evening concerts broadcast on the Third Programme
opened on 5 October with Kodály conducting his Concerto for Orchestra for
the first time in this country; Walton directed his Symphony in the second
part. Boult added Elgar and Mozart. This ultra-Third-Programme concert
was followed by several in similar vein. On 19 October Nikolai Malko returned to conduct Balakirev's Second Symphony. On 2 November Eugene
Goossens introduced his own Second Symphony; the piece was well received but the performance provoked several comments as to the unsteadi-
ness of the Orchestra. On 16 November Rafael Kubelik scored another
success with the British première of Martinů's Fourth Symphony: '. . . the
music tingled with life, and the sound seemed in an extraordinary way to

have both intensity and extensity', wrote *The Times*. 'Rafael Kubelik is a conductor who is temperamentally fitted to manage this kind of taut electrical discharge and give a taut and glowing performance of it.' Kubelik also introduced a little symphony by the eighteenth-century Czech composer František Mička, and finished with the Berlioz *Symphonie fantastique*. The opening four People's Palace concerts also included music by Purcell, Rawsthorne, Bartók, John Field and Liszt (*Dante* Symphony), all broadcast on the Third Programme. In this company, the Wednesday Home Service concerts were somewhat overshadowed; however, on 27 November Boult conducted the British première of Bartók's Third Piano Concerto (with Louis Kentner) at the Albert Hall.

The later part of the season saw a significant upward trend in both the morale and standard of the Orchestra. The decision about its organisation had, for better or worse, been taken, and the Orchestra was reconstituted as a 96-piece ensemble from April 1947. Most significant for morale, in June the Orchestra went on its second continental tour. Four concerts were arranged, in a more practical sequence than those in the mammoth 1936 tour: Paris was visited on 18 June, then Brussels on 23 June, Amsterdam on 25 June and nearby Scheveningen on 26 June. There were several other improvements on the previous tour's arrangements. Kenneth Adam, the BBC's Director of Public Relations, accompanied the Orchestra in order to deal with the press and publicity, and to play host to distinguished guests. Kenneth Wright led the administrative party, and Boult was therefore enabled to concentrate on conducting. In Paris Boult, Paul Beard and Kenneth Wright were all presented with honorary citizenship. The concert was a great success, with a standing ovation and encores – a member of the British Embassy staff said he had never seen such a display of enthusiasm by a Parisian audience since Bruno Walter's visit in 1938. Brussels followed, and then Amsterdam; at the concert in Scheveningen, Queen Wilhelmina of the Netherlands was present. The only mishap of the tour affected this concert: Paul Beard was stung on the wrist by a mosquito an hour before the concert. He insisted on playing, but he broke a string in his solo in *Ein Heldenleben*. The subprincipal took up the solo without a pause, and then during a rest lent Beard his violin to continue the solo.

The repertoire of the tour was most impressive. English works included Rawsthorne's Piano Concerto, Vaughan Williams' Concerto for two pianos, Britten's Violin Concerto, Elgar's *Enigma Variations*, Delius's *A Song before Sunrise*, and Walton's Violin Concerto. Dutch and French works were included. Much to Boult's approval, all the concerts were broadcast.

1947–50

In a state of some uncertainty, but with increasing cohesion and self-confidence, the Symphony Orchestra continued its activities through the years to its twentieth anniversary in 1950. Julian Herbage left the BBC staff in November 1946, but was retained on contract for the planning of the Promenade Concerts, and it is significant that during this period the Proms presented a far greater number of novelties, first performances and challenging works than did the Symphony Concert series. Nevertheless, the 1947–8 season included the first concert performance in this country of a work heard during the contemporary music series in the Maida Vale studios the previous April: Honegger's *Joan of Arc at the Stake*, conducted by Basil Cameron. This attracted less interest for its musical content than for the fact that it featured a new instrument, the Ondes Martenot, which was demonstrated by its inventor Maurice Martenot. Richard Strauss returned to the BBC to conduct his *Till Eulenspiegel* at the Albert Hall on 29 October in a concert which celebrated the fiftieth anniversary of his first appearance in this country, conducting the same work. 'The composer in old age can still exert control over an orchestra with a masterly economy of gesture . . .' (*The Times*). The other major event of the autumn was the celebration of the BBC's own silver jubilee: at the Albert Hall on 12 November 'the BBC threw in everything except the cash register', and brought the Northern and Scottish Symphony Orchestras to join the Symphony Orchestra on the stage. 'More than 200 musicians combined almost to blast us out of our seats. The echo worked overtime', reported the *Daily Express*. John Barbirolli and Boult shared the direction of the programme.

On 21 April came the major première of the season, in a concert which the BBC Orchestra gave for the Royal Philharmonic Society. This was Vaughan Williams' Sixth Symphony, which was universally admired by the critics: after the bitterness of the Fourth and resolution of the Fifth, *The Times* saw that 'he has started off once more on his travels and has begun to probe even greater mysteries'. 'A work that is intricate and far-ranging, high-flown and high-spirited, and at various times rousing, soothing, genial and formidable', wrote the *Glasgow Herald*.

The Orchestra once again performed Mahler's Eighth Symphony at the Albert Hall, for the newly formed Henry Wood Concert Society; the Society later promoted four Elgar concerts in June. A large number of provincial visits was made during the season, to Walthamstow, Brighton, Cambridge (where the Third Programme promoted a festival on February 26 and 28), Newcastle, Newport, Wolverhampton and Hanley. A new feature of the season was the increasing number of visits to provincial music festivals which had sprung up since the war. The Orchestra visited the Bath Festival on 25 April, and the Oxford Festival of British Music on 11 May: the all-English programme for the concert in the Sheldonian Theatre was an interesting one: Rubbra's *Festival Overture* and Butterworth's *The Banks of Green Willow* were followed by Stanford's Clarinet Concerto, played by the Orchestra's former principal Frederick Thurston. The academic *Oxford Times* critic noted that the Concerto's 'sole claim to permanency is in the fact that a few bars are quoted in Forsyth's treatise on orchestration'. But he enthused over the major work, a third performance of Vaughan Williams' new symphony.

The 1948-9 season began with the Orchestra's first visit to the recently-founded Edinburgh Festival. The Orchestra stood up well to competition which included the Amsterdam Concertgebouw Orchestra under Eduard van Beinum and Charles Munch, and the Augusteo Orchestra from Rome under Vittorio Gui and Carlo Zecchi. The Symphony Concerts season at the Albert Hall began on 13 October with a programme of Beethoven, Debussy, Ravel, and the Brahms D minor Concerto in an outstanding performance by Claudio Arrau. The King and Queen of Denmark attended the 27 October concert. On 14 November our own Queen's first child was born. The BBC, which had with great foresight already commissioned works from three leading composers, was able to broadcast a Festival March by Gordon Jacob immediately, and the following day repeated it on the Light Programme, adding Herbert Howells's *Corydon's Dance* on the Home, and Michael Tippett's *Birthday Suite*, played by the Symphony Orchestra, on the Third. At the start of 1949 another première was heard in the BBC Orchestra's contribution to the Royal Philharmonic Society's concerts, that of Rubbra's Fifth Symphony, which it was found difficult to like: *The Times* said that it 'marks a further stage in the progress of a sincere and determined thinker', but *Musical Opinion* admitted that the work 'as a whole seems under-vitalised and lacking in any purposeful drive'.

The BBC had more success with a linked series of broadcast and public concert performances of Stravinsky's music, which Ernest Ansermet came to conduct in February and March. On 16 February the ballet *Orpheus* was given a first British performance in an Albert Hall concert. 'The score abounds with imaginative touches of colour – it is as deftly constructed as anything Stravinsky has written in recent years – and to his technical mastery has been added an emotional depth that has sometimes seemed to be wanting' (*The Times*). On 19 February in the Maida Vale studios, players from the Symphony Orchestra joined the BBC Chorus for Stravinsky's new setting of the Mass. Two performances were given in the same concert on the Third, and the concert was repeated the next day on the Home: generous measure. The simple textures and stark style of the Mass were found puzzling but impressive: a positive analysis in the *Musical Times* (March 1949) 'found much of immediate and evident beauty . . . shot through with morning sunlight . . . a Byzantine richness [which] you do not fully perceive until you get the score to your piano desk . . .' It was a pity that the BBC did not give a public performance of this important new work.

In the 1949–50 season at the Albert Hall, Honegger's *Joan of Arc at the Stake* was repeated; Beecham conducted a Mozart and Strauss programme; Boult, Sargent and Kubelik all had programmes.

A new Head of Music

While the Symphony Orchestra had been carrying out its duties in the years 1947–50, the Music Department had been preoccupied with the Orchestra's future. The sudden death of Victor Hely-Hutchinson in March 1947 deprived the post-war reconstruction of the Orchestra of its continuity. It was a measure of how far the Orchestra members felt that the BBC's administrators were remote from their needs that they implored Boult to offer himself once more as Director of Music. But the BBC instead appointed Kenneth Wright as Acting Director of Music; and then in April 1948 a new man was found for the renamed post of Head of Music. This was Steuart Wilson. Knighted in the 1948 Birthday Honours, he was a well-known tenor who had been the BBC's Overseas Music Director for a time during the war, and had gone on to succeed Reginald Jacques as Music Director of the newly-established Arts Council in 1945. Wilson's vigour and forthrightness had made him a noted member of the music profession, inspiring strong admiration or dislike in turn. He was a frequent broadcaster, a famous Gerontius in Elgar's oratorio, but his relations with the BBC had not always been cordial. In 1937 *Radio Times* printed a letter which criticised Wilson for adding an aspirant 'h' before each note in a florid run during a Bach aria. Wilson, always quick to react, sued the BBC, and there followed an extraordinary legal case in which distinguished musicians debated the validity of this practice. Wilson won, and was awarded the considerable sum of £2000 damages. He used the money to mount performances of Rutland Boughton's opera *The Lady Maid* in Stroud and London, which he conducted himself. It should also be recalled (though it need not necessarily be thought relevant to what follows) that Wilson was divorced from his first wife, Ann Bowles, who in 1933 had become Mrs and subsequently Lady Boult.

Wilson arrived at the BBC with a ready-made solution to the problem of the BBC Symphony Orchestra: it needed a new Chief Conductor. Sir

Adrian Boult was to reach the BBC's retiring age in April 1949, and Wilson declared to the Director-General that his first priority when he arrived would be 'to plan for the future of the Symphony Orchestra, gradually re-placing Boult while looking for his successor within or without the present music staff' (26 May 1948). Wilson wrote later in the year: 'I made it clear on my appointment that I considered it my most important task to secure the succession to Sir Adrian Boult, and that it was not too soon to start at once' (memo of 6 December 1948 to Controller, Entertainment). Within two months of taking up his post, he had had discussions with Kenneth Wright (who now became Artists Manager) and with his Assistant Head of Music, Herbert Murrill. He formulated his plans. The Symphony Orchestra itself was given cursory attention. His reflections on the Orchestra as a performing body were based firmly on his Arts Council experience of outside orchestras, not on special knowledge of the BBC's situation. His solution to its problem was tantamount to suggesting the Orchestra's disbandment. He wrote on 26 May:

> When the Symphony Orchestra was formed in 1932 [sic] it was a pioneer step in England to have an orchestra on permanent contract ... since 1946 things have changed ... in normal conditions it would be reasonable to say that the BBC experiment had succeeded, that contract orchestras were now estab-lished, and that the BBC could retire from the field, leave its best players to be assimilated in the market, and would, from henceforth, hire the orchestras in planned rotation to serve the needs of broadcasting. In this way a far finer orchestra than at present could possibly be assembled on some temporary contract: it would vary in degree of excellence, but the ninety members of the Symphony Orchestra absorbed into other orchestras would undoubtedly raise the standard.

Whether Wilson expected this plan to be seriously considered is unclear; at any rate it went no further. His more important postscript also unfortunately passed unheeded:

> It [the above plan] would be an expensive and difficult piece of planning, raising very difficult problems of dates and fixed times, but if the BBC contemplates the retention of a House Orchestra of the 1932 [sic] standard, it must make up its mind quickly that conditions outside are not what they were in 1932 [sic] and our idea of rates of pay must rise.

Towards a new Chief Conductor

With this, Wilson's contribution to the overall problems of the Symphony

Orchestra began and ended. His consideration of conductors, however, was more fruitful. His plans could, if they had worked as he intended, have ensured a most successful new lease of life for the Orchestra. What, in 1948, was the possible field of successors to Boult? Wilson jotted down a list: a group of foreigners, starting with the distinguished candidates – Walter, Mitropoulos, Reiner, Eduard van Beinum (at that time in charge of the London Philharmonic), Eugene Goossens (in Australia), and the young Rafael Kubelik. Among those who had never yet conducted the BBC Orchestra was the youthful Herbert von Karajan, who made a great impression visiting London in 1948. Other foreigners might have been considered: Albert Wolff and Charles Munch of those who had close connections with the BBC Orchestra, Carl Schuricht and Sergiu Celibidache of those who had not. Of foreigners active in England, Wilson added Karl Rankl, Mosco Carner and Walter Susskind. But he focused his attention on the native English conductors whom he thought more likely to be possible choices; Wilson proposed initially that the selection among English names could be narrowed down to two, John Barbirolli and Malcolm Sargent: 'an ultimate choice between them for the Symphony Orchestra seems to be probable but not inevitable'. He wanted to postpone the final decision until the end of 1950, so that several conductors could be tried out; the new appointment would run only from the 1951–2 season. Boult would be gradually freed for outside work, and both Sargent and Barbirolli would be offered an increasing share of the time with the Orchestra. Staff conductors would also have a chance to prove themselves. Wilson wrote that 'Sir Adrian Boult could be retained as the Permanent Conductor provided that it was made quite clear to him that after the autumn of 1948 he would be free to accept outside engagements . . .' But there was the important qualification: 'If for any reason it was decided not to offer him or he would not accept such a suggestion . . .' – thus making it clear that the ending of Boult's appointment had not been discussed with him at this stage. It was a strange thought that Boult might not wish to continue in his post.

The question was aired at a meeting at 4 o'clock on Tuesday 22 June 1948 between Wilson, Nicolls (now designated Director of Home Broadcasting), Howgill (now Controller, Entertainment), and representatives of the Controllers of the Home Service and Third Programme. Wilson's plans were approved, but with several provisos: the period of trial for the various conductors should be shorter, so that a decision could be more quickly arrived at; the invitation to Barbirolli, Sargent and others should 'be on the basis of our having put the conductorship in commission for a couple of years rather than its being a trial period'; other guest conductors were to be invited as much as possible; an outside panel would be necessary to pass judgement on the 'candidates'. Finally, 'while the main trial is confined to Barbirolli and Sargent, it does not follow that we shall in the event offer the job to either of them'. Summarising the points, Nicolls also added 'It is understood that Sir Adrian Boult is agreeable to the proposals . . .' – but there was at this point no definite plan as to when they would take effect.

Reporting on the meeting to the Controller of the Third Programme, Christopher Sykes (a recent member of his staff, not concerned with the music output) mentioned that Nicolls had brought up the possibility of a foreign conductor several times, but

> this point was not pursued. This struck me as a pity, as of the younger generation we have no-one of continental standard and it is at least arguable that the finest service the BBC could do for British music would be to appoint a foreign conductor and let the challenge operate on British competitors. It did not seem proper, however, that as a newcomer I should propound this bold view . . .

Barbirolli?

Wilson subsequently decided that no conductor could take on the whole task alone. His first approach to Sargent in June confirmed this belief, for Sargent said that he would not want the full-time post, but would be very happy to co-operate with Barbirolli, leaving Barbirolli 'the responsibility for the Orchestra'; this did not sound promising. Wilson then contacted Barbirolli at the Cheltenham Festival at the end of June and made a detailed proposal to him. This included an invitation to conduct some of the 1949 Proms, and to take an increasing share of the Orchestra's work culminating in his taking on the Chief Conductorship. All negotiations were carried out through Barbirolli's personal manager, Kenneth Crickmore, and nothing was put on paper at this stage. After the Cheltenham Festival, Barbirolli went on holiday until just before the Edinburgh Festival at the end of August. At this point Crickmore was ill, and Wilson wrote directly to Barbirolli on 20 August clarifying certain points in the offer – in particular, trying to persuade him to take on part of the 1949 Proms as a separate task, not necessarily connected with the offer of the conductorship.

The proposed share of the work between Barbirolli and Sargent in the 1949–50 season at that point was as follows: they would share the two months of Proms; Barbirolli would in addition do six months' exclusive work in the season, and Sargent would do two months' exclusive work. 'Sargent is quite ready to come into such a scheme and it would remove at once any idea that we were "auditioning" conductors.' Wilson asked if he and his assistant Herbert Murrill could visit Barbirolli in Manchester at the end of August. Barbirolli's reply is worth pondering for the light it sheds on the assertion, which has been frequently made, that he merely used the offer of a BBC appointment to improve his conditions of work and standing with the Hallé Orchestra. He said he was unable to see Wilson as he would have started rehearsals for Edinburgh the previous day. He then stated

> as frankly and clearly as possible . . . that it is not possible for me to consider the 1949 Proms. . . . I cannot disassociate the Proms from the full appointment for two reasons, namely:
> 1.   If I undertook the Proms, and then for any reason we were unable to come to terms about the main appointment, it would have vitally disturbed the Hallé schedule to no purpose . . .
> 2.   It is virtually certain that conducting the Proms would cause my name to be linked with the BBC in such a way that a subsequent breakdown in negotiations would unquestionably be to the detriment of my own personal prestige . . .
>   I am honoured at the suggestion of 'taking full responsibility of the Symphony Orchestra' and I am most willing to give consideration to the scheme you suggest within any time limit you care to suggest. . . . I note with great pleasure Malcolm's willingness to enter into the scheme . . .

There are two possible interpretations of this letter: first, that Barbirolli shows himself so concerned with the possible breakdown of negotiations as to imply that this would be inevitable in the end; second, that he was being extremely honest in giving his real reasons for not wishing to conduct the 1949 Proms, when he could have simply declined on other grounds. Barbirolli probably deserves the benefit of the doubt; in spite of distancing himself from Wilson through his manager, and being available for meetings and discussions only with reluctance, there is every sign that he took the proposal seriously – if he was simply manoeuvring the BBC for his own 'personal prestige' he would scarcely have been likely to imply as much to Wilson.

Negotiations again lapsed, this time while Wilson went on holiday to Italy. When he returned Barbirolli was suffering the effects of a car accident and could not see him. Eventually a meeting was arranged in Sheffield on 18 October when Wilson, with the approval of Howgill, was able to make a detailed proposal to Barbirolli including financial terms. On 11 November Wilson attended a meeting of the BBC Board of Governors and gained their approval for a slightly revised scheme, in which Barbirolli would be engaged on the basis of six months' work, not including the Proms, and Sargent for two months plus half the Proms. If Barbirolli conducted the other half of the Proms that would be a separate matter – but it looked unlikely that he would do so. 'The responsibility for the Orchestra's personnel, discipline, training etc. to be solely Mr Barbirolli's.' And the starting date of such an arrangement was set for 1 October 1950.

At that point a complication unexpected by the BBC ensued: the offer became public knowledge. At their 18 October meeting Barbirolli and Wilson had agreed that the Hallé Society in Manchester should be informed: Wilson offered to do this, but Barbirolli said he preferred to do it himself. Shortly after this meeting, Wilson was telephoned by the Kemsley Press in London, asking him to confirm or deny a story that Barbirolli was to succeed Boult. He denied it. But the Press agency also rang Barbirolli's agent Crickmore, who seems to have been less discreet. Wilson said that the press statement then issued 'must be based on what is known only to Crickmore'. Moreover, Crickmore had apparently discussed the matter with Stanford Robinson in Manchester during October. All this put both the BBC and the Hallé in a difficult position – and incidentally infuriated the BBC's Controller, North Region, who felt that any approach to Barbirolli should have been made through him. On Saturday 27 November, the Hallé decided to confirm that the offer had been made 'because of the insistent rumours, and because it was felt that someone else had let the cat out of the bag' (as Wilson wrote). There was the expected outcry against Barbirolli's leaving Manchester, and local feeling rallied in his support. Probably this was what Crickmore, and possibly Barbirolli, had wanted. The Hallé realised what an asset they had and acted accordingly. They agreed to many of Barbirolli's requests concerning the orchestra.

In London there was annoyance and gloom. 'This Barbirolli affair seems to have run right off the rails', wrote a senior official, and Wilson ruminated on 6 December to Howgill:

> If, in these circumstances, Barbirolli declines the offer, it will be said that he used my conversations purely for his own purposes and that anyone in North Region could have told me that he would. With great respect I set no value on such *post factum* opinions. In the existing confusion only one good point remains, namely that there has been no concealment of the facts from Boult and Sargent, and that it is possible to leave the whole matter to die down until 1950.

Wilson seemed resigned to failure. The offer, approved by the Governors, had been made to Barbirolli with a time limit of the first day of 1949. On 28 December 1948 Barbirolli wrote to Wilson:

You were good enough to give me until 1 January to come to a decision. . . .
Please believe that I have given the most prolonged and careful consideration to all the factors concerned, all the time deeply conscious of the
honour you and your associates have paid me, and it is therefore with the
utmost regret that I find myself unable to accept.

May I, at the same time, tender to you and your associates my most sincere
thanks for all your kindness during this, for me, rather trying time. With my
warmest good wishes to you and your great orchestra.

Barbirolli gave no reasons, though there was no necessity for him to give any.
The first stage in the saga of the succession was over: but there was much
more to come.

Replacing Boult

The matter had been put to the BBC's Board of Governors in more general
terms by Nicolls, who drafted a note on 21 October 1948. Unlike Wilson's
considerations of the subject, this was based firmly on the unique nature of
Boult's achievement with the Orchestra. Yet it managed to invent some
specious reasons why Boult should be replaced:

BBC SYMPHONY ORCHESTRA: The Problem of the Conductor
Sir Adrian Boult has been Conductor of the BBC Symphony Orchestra for
twenty years. He reaches the staff retiring age of 60 on 8 April 1949. This and
the fact that he has asked to be excused from conducting the Orchestra in the
current Promenade Season, which constitutes an important fraction of the
year's output, make it necessary for the question of his successor to be considered. Sir Adrian did a magnificent job in the building up of the Orchestra
to the highest international standard before the war (Toscanini said on one
occasion that it was the best in the world), and the decline of the Orchestra
since 1939 is attributable to loss of players through military service and to
war conditions generally. [We have seen above that this explanation is
extremely misleading.] Sir Adrian must take most of the credit for the
marked improvement of the Orchestra in the present year.

Over the twenty years of his service as Conductor one of Sir Adrian's
indispensable qualifications for his post has been his absolute willingness to
conduct any music, classical or modern, which it has been desirable to
include in the programmes. It can be said with confidence that very few
conductors of international reputation would have been prepared to work for
years under such conditions of repertoire. This is mentioned partly as a
tribute to Sir Adrian, but chiefly as throwing light on an important aspect of
the problem of finding his successor.

The other main aspect of the problem is to find a conductor of actual or potential international standard who will be capable of improving the performance and esprit-de-corps of the Orchestra to an extent which will bring it back to its pre-war position as one of the finest orchestras in the world. 'Esprit-de-corps' is mentioned because in recent years the spirit of the Orchestra has not been of the best; it has, for instance, on occasion been resentful of the amount of rehearsal which conductors other than Sir Adrian require; and it should be the object of the new appointment to restore the Orchestra's morale as a step towards restoring its musical prestige.

A survey of the available British conductors who might deserve preliminary consideration for this post is sufficient in terms of (a) the repertoire obligation, and (b) the necessary standard of conducting, to raise the two following questions:-

(1) Can a foreign conductor be considered eligible?

(2) If it appears necessary in terms of repertoire to appoint two conductors, will this mean that the Orchestra can never attain the standard of performance which it would under one first-class conductor?

With regard to (1), it is suggested that a foreigner could only be appointed as sole conductor of the Orchestra if he were indisputably of the class of Toscanini, de Sabata, etc., although it is obvious that a foreigner could more easily be appointed as joint conductor.

With regard to (2), it is the opinion of Head of Music and others concerned that in principle the aim should be to find a single conductor who is ready to cope with the whole of the wide repertoire demanded by the BBC. He would have the help from time to time of guest conductors and specialists. It must here be emphasised that a conductor who was either limited or 'temperamental' in regard to repertoire could not possibly meet the demands of the BBC.

The last sentence was important, and was disregarded in the final solution. There was one other suggested proviso, which was that the new conductor or conductors should be appointed for periods of five years renewable by mutual agreement. The indefatigable Dr Whitfield also made his own contribution to the debate, writing to the Director-General with an excellent analysis of the problem of choosing between a conductor who could 'get through the simply frightful number of works expected of us' and one who 'will, on the whole, give us thrilling performances'. He suggested that a foreigner of 'unassailable' status might command approval, but drew attention to the recent outcry over the appointment of Rudolf Schwarz to the Bournemouth Orchestra.

From Barbirolli to Kubelik

Following the final refusal of Barbirolli, just before the end of 1948, Wilson acted fast in preparing alternative schemes. It had come to his notice during the summer that the Czech conductor Rafael Kubelik had decided not to return to Prague but to make his home in the West. He had first appeared with the BBC in 1938 when he was twenty-four, and had more recently scored great successes with them. At thirty-five Kubelik was young, but he was precisely the sort of personality the Orchestra needed, with a breadth of repertoire and vision that would be ideal. He was much in demand in England for concerts and recordings. But Kubelik had not so far been approached. How best to fit him into a possible scheme? On 31 December the possibility of approaching Bruno Walter on a short-term contract for three years was mooted, with Kubelik as an Assistant who, it was hoped, would succeed. Wilson's first firm proposal at this stage was for a shared scheme between Sargent, Kubelik and Boult, each doing short periods, with substantial use of guest conductors, including Walter.

This scheme was put up to Nicolls with a view to its being discussed at the Governors' meeting on 6 January 1949. He was not impressed. He wrote to Director-General Haley on 31 December: 'The basis proposed seems to me to amount too much to a "Balkanisation" of the post, and I feel the situation will not be satisfactory unless we have a predominant, more or less full-time conductor on, say, at least the recent Barbirolli basis.' He was more attracted to the idea that Bruno Walter might be persuaded to come for three years: then he felt Walter plus Kubelik as Assistant, with Boult as distinguished guest, would be an attractive possibility.

In all this hectic discussion, Boult's position was disgracefully ignored by the BBC. His formal retiring date was just three months away, on 8 April 1949, when he became sixty, and no definite proposal had yet been put to him. He knew of Wilson's moves to find a successor, but nothing of what might be required of him. Yet his services were taken for granted. When Boult was invited to conduct in America during the summer of 1949, Wilson went so far as to complain to Howgill (3 December 1948) that this would be inconvenient to his plans for the Proms. Yet this fell several months after Boult's supposed retirement. Boult was expected to be available when needed, and to leave when required. He was never asked whether he wanted to resign. In Nicolls' words to the Governors, only the fact that Boult was to reach staff retiring age and along with the scarcely relevant 'fact that he asked to be excused from conducting the Orchestra in the current Promenade Season' made it 'necessary for the question of his successor to be considered'. With complete disregard for Boult's need to plan his future, Wilson next suggested that Boult be offered two part-time contracts for 1949–50, excluding the Prom period which could be dealt with separately if Boult were available. This idea was fortunately rejected.

At the Governors' meeting on 6 January, the important decision was taken to approach Rafael Kubelik at once. No other scheme offered such a chance of immediate success. He would be asked to become Associate Conductor as soon as possible. Boult would be asked to continue as Principal Conductor for a year beyond his retiring age, until April 1950, and Kubelik would then be appointed Principal Conductor, 'if by that time he had proved suitable'. Sargent's role would be that of conductor of the Proms, both winter and summer seasons; he would also be offered studio dates. At the meeting, Nicolls and Barbara Ward spoke out strongly in favour of Bruno Walter, who could be invited from 1951, but it was felt that in two years' time Walter might well be too old to be reliable.

The results of this meeting were conveyed by Wilson to Boult in a curiously insensitive letter on 6 January. (Writing of Walter, for example, to whom Boult was devoted, Wilson said, 'Anyway, if he did come, we should have to reorganise our output entirely, so that he could lead a luxury life, in fact he would turn out to be an extremely expensive pet.') Wilson wrote with typical imprecision that it was agreed that 'you should continue on a staff contract for one year from 9 April, or whatever the precise date is . . . you should consider yourself free to take any engagements at all that may come your way in 1950, having regard to the fact that the BBC would certainly wish you to continue a considerable amount of conducting in that year, but no detailed proposition can be made now.' One of Wilson's more condescending remarks has an ironic ring in view of Boult's subsequent career: 'I feel we must make it clear that whatever you do for the BBC or stop doing for the BBC you have not retired from public conducting.'

Boult returned from conducting in Boston to find this letter, and replied on 27 January 1949 in measured terms:

Many thanks for your letter to which I have naturally given a good deal of thought. The three things that seem uppermost in my mind are these:

1. A real pleasure that Kubelik may take over – there is no one I would rather make way for.

2. Considerable disappointment that it is all to happen so soon. Quite frankly, I would much rather go on with the Orchestra I know, at any rate till

sixty-five, even if the Associate does more work than he has up to now. I had, too, hoped that I might still be with them during the special concerts of 1951, the twenty-first year of my work with them and the year in which I become sixty-two.

If anyone else is No. 1 Conductor at that time the position will be much more difficult – the retired headmaster is always a nuisance, and I cannot think that Kubelik, with the interest of his visits abroad, should mind being Associate Conductor at any rate until 1951; otherwise the position is at once more awkward for both of us.

3.   If I am once retired, I can't help feeling that to come back is going to be difficult and awkward. The conductor emeritus business does not appear to be working well in Boston, and I think it is a bad idea.

If I am really to begin looking for other work in a year's time I feel most reluctant to accept the position. The experiences of this last month, wonderful though they have been from many points of view, have only confirmed me once more in my feeling that I am no guest conductor; I want to work with a permanent body. Please let it be a BBC one.

But his requests were in vain: the reply was made that the extension of his contract should be for one year only, but that he would certainly be invited to play an important part in the 1951 Festival of Britain concerts.

During January Wilson saw Kubelik and outlined the BBC's offer to him. Personal considerations played an important part in Kubelik's reply, which was that he could not accept the post of Associate Conductor immediately, but would very much like to become Chief Conductor in April 1950. He was anxious at the start of 1949 to avoid any publicity which suggested that he would not return to Czechoslovakia, as he was attempting to ensure that his parents and his wife's parents were smuggled out of the country to the West; any idea that he had accepted a post with the BBC would make this the more difficult. He also had many commitments in the coming year, visits to Australia, America, Holland and Scandinavia, but said he would be able to fit in some fifteen engagements with the BBC in the twelve or thirteen months.

In spite of the uncertainty, Wilson felt increasingly sure that Kubelik would be an ideal successor to Boult, and recommended as much to the next Governors' meeting on 3 February.

The Board agreed with these suggestions and in particular that the Executive should be empowered to appoint Rafael Kubelik as Principal Conductor at the appropriate moment. Meanwhile it was noted that the strictest secrecy should be observed with regard to the intention to appoint Kubelik. With regard to Sir Adrian Boult, the Board asked for a press statement to be issued to the effect that he had consented to carry on as Principal Conductor beyond the retiring age of 60.

Press speculation had already been rife as to possible successors in the wake of the Barbirolli refusal. The *News Chronicle* claimed an 'authentic' list in January, which consisted of Stanford Robinson, Malcolm Sargent, Constant Lambert, Basil Cameron and George Weldon. It was typical of Wilson's bluff manner that when telephoned for a comment on the list, he suggested that they should add two names – Vic Oliver and Sidney Beer – and then they would have a wonderful vaudeville team.

Detailed proposals were put to Kubelik only in May 1949, shortly before he left England. It was agreed that he would spend a basic 26–30 weeks per annum exclusively with the Orchestra, including eight weeks of the Prom season. Both Nicolls and Boult were somewhat surprised by the shortness of this period: Boult wrote to Wilson saying that this seemed inadequate for a Chief Conductor, and Nicolls discussed the matter with Haley. He wrote to Howgill on 13 May that Haley 'thoroughly agrees with my feeling that the contract suggested does not really constitute Kubelik's being a successor to Boult in terms of what we mean by Conductor or Chief Conductor of the BBC Symphony Orchestra. D.G. feels that Kubelik should either cast his lot with us or not . . .' In reply, Wilson agreed to try and increase the period of work to thirty-five weeks per year, the periods of absence to be agreed a year in advance. This was the formal proposal which was put to Kubelik in August. Wilson wrote to him on 13 June and saw him in London on 25 August. The commitment was now strongly phrased: '. . . you agree to accept the post as a whole-time post with leave of absence for not more than three months in any one year during the orchestral season by arrangement with the BBC . . .'

At this meeting Kubelik was anxious to clarify the rights and responsibilities of the Chief Conductor in relation to the Music Department – an important area of policy which, as Wilson explained, had 'never been, to the best of my knowledge, set out before because they had themselves grown up with Sir Adrian Boult in his tenure of office and had varied themselves in accordance with the prevailing pattern of broadcasting'. He might have added that only since the separation of the Directorship of Music from the Chief Conductorship in 1942 had such clarification become necessary. Wilson's explanations were extremely woolly, but two extracts are worth quoting because of their implications for future policy. Under DIRECTION, Wilson wrote:

The Chief Conductor is a member of the Music Department working under the Head of Music. The general policy of music is laid down by the Head of Music; if the Conductor feels himself unable to carry out the plan for any reason . . . the Conductor makes his feelings known to Head of Music and discussion takes place, and a solution can only be reached with goodwill on each side.

This was scarcely likely to provide adequate machinery for the solution of possible conflicts; nor was a section headed RIGHTS:

If he [the Conductor] finds that he is unable to carry out the duties in the manner which he thinks best . . . or, if the assistance given him by Music Department is, in his view, insufficient . . . or he finds himself in disagreement with the programme policy . . . then he has the right to say that in the circumstances he cannot do his duty . . . Such a statement would be made in the first place to Head of Music, and if an agreement were not reached, the Controller of Entertainment and ultimately the Director of Home Broadcasting as the final authority.

None of Wilson's affable formulations covered the crucial point – the separate areas in which Conductor and Music Department could feel in control, and the possible overlap between them.

The contract letter was sent to Kubelik on 30 August 1949. At the beginning of September Boult was asked to speak to the Press about his experiences in America, and was asked whether he was about to retire; he said frankly that he was, in the following April. This was exactly what the BBC had wished to avoid, as it was now difficult to postpone the announcement of his successor. Wilson argued that the story should be allowed to die, because Kubelik was just leaving for America and Holland; but Howgill felt that an announcement should be made immediately. Nicolls was not worried about publicity: '. . . what we all want to aim for is Kubelik as full-time and full-allegiance Conductor of the BBC Symphony Orchestra' (note on Wilson's memo, 9 September). Meanwhile Wilson was once more altering Boult's proposed future, asking that while he should resign as Chief Conductor on 8 April, he should be retained for 'advice, consultation, and, if necessary, auditions', until the Orchestra went on leave in June 1950.

During September and October the necessary formalities with regard to Kubelik's employment were dealt with through the Home Office, and the question of his possible naturalisation as a British citizen arose. An interesting episode in Government–BBC relations was then enacted. On 4 November, Director-General Haley was approached informally after a meeting by Sir George Ismay, who said that the application for Kubelik's employment by the BBC had come into the Government machine because he was an alien, and the PMG was rather worried as to what would happen if he were asked in the House of Commons why the BBC had not appointed a British conductor. Ismay told me privately that he had already advised the PMG that he thought this was a matter for the Corporation, and it might be embarrassing to the PMG if he asked the BBC whether they had approached, say, Sir Malcolm Sargent . . .

Haley fully briefed Ismay off the record and suggested a formal line of reply to any questions about the appointment of a foreigner. Ismay seemed anxious to assure the Postmaster General that the BBC would be using several British conductors, and one in particular. But Haley insisted that he 'did not think it proper that the Corporation should disclose whom it had or had not approached in connection with the formal offer of the Conductorship' (Note by Haley, 7 November). Whether this incident had any connection with events which were to follow it is impossible to say; but a strongly expressed preference from Government quarters for a particular British conductor might well have had an effect within the BBC.

Kubelik departed to the United States, promising to return to sign and complete the agreement at Christmas. On 12 December, however, he telephoned Wilson in a state of great distress: his wife, who was in very poor health generally, and had undergone many operations on her leg, had sustained a bad fall. Kubelik's strong desire to settle in England had always been against the wishes of his wife, to whom he was devoted. She felt that the climate, security and ease of life in America would be preferable. Now Kubelik felt a strong obligation to accede to her wishes. Moreover, the opportunity to do so had presented itself in the form of a reopened offer from the Chicago Orchestra (which Kubelik had previously refused). Kubelik told Wilson on the phone that he thought that for the sake of his family he would have to accept that new offer. Wilson asked him to do nothing for a week, while he saw how his wife's injury healed.

Wilson knew that the pressures on Kubelik to accept the Chicago offer and remain in America would be very strong, and that the only personal influence on him outside his family would be his American agent. So he immediately cabled the BBC's representative in New York, Norman Luker, asking him to visit Kubelik in Pittsburgh as soon as possible to express his sympathy and ascertain the situation as regards the American offer. Initial enquiries by Luker suggested that Kubelik's decision had already been made. Wilson wrote in full to Luker explaining the BBC's problem and asking him again to pay Kubelik a personal visit. Meanwhile Kubelik and his wife had returned to New York. Wilson had cabled him to say that the offer remained open for 1951 if 1950 was impossible, and Kubelik had cabled Wilson to say that he would honour his engagements between May and September 1950.

On Christmas Day 1949 Luker visited Kubelik in New York. He sent an immediate cable to Wilson: 'AFTER LONG TALK KUBELIK TODAY AM CONVINCED NOTHING MORE CAN BE DONE WRITING LUKER.' The same day Luker typed a letter himself in his office:

> I saw Kubelik today and he told me the whole story in detail. I am quite sure that after an emotional struggle of real intensity he has now reached a final decision. The deciding factor is a medical one. . . . He was deeply touched by your new offer but it doesn't really help because the Chicago job is for at least two years. The season is from October to early April and he says that he would love to do any guest concerts for us in the intervening months though he was very diffident about it because he feels he has let you down so. . . . There is no doubt that he has come to decision with extreme reluctance.
>
> He was quite collected but very unhappy, almost as much over disappointing you as over his wife. I wish I could be writing to tell you I had overpersuaded him but the only solace I can offer is that I do not think any pressure or concessions would change him now. What particularly distresses him is the boundless affection for and sense of indebtedness to England, the BBC and you. He is grieved to have to go against all that.

Wilson had to accept the decision as final. Kubelik's appointment to Chicago would be announced immediately. A statement was prepared in case of questions to the BBC, but by a mistake its contents became public. A full explanation, over Steuart Wilson's name, of the failure to appoint Kubelik was given to *The Sunday Times*. Howgill was furious, as was Wilson, but there was nothing to be done. Wilson somewhat wearily summed up the possibilities at the end of the year. Kubelik could be approached again in two years but 'it would be safer to exclude him'; Barbirolli could not be approached again; 'the alternatives open are not attractive'. The deciding factor, though, was Wilson's view of the advisability of a foreign conductor. 'The appointment of Kubelik as a foreigner might have caused some comment, but his residence here and his popularity would have diminished that comment . . . But to appoint a non-resident foreigner would be a matter for such criticism that I should find it difficult to advise the Governors to accept the responsibility for the appointment.'

From Kubelik to Sargent

With that qualification, there was little room for manoeuvre. Only one English conductor had the status and experience for the post, and the willingness to undertake it, and that was Sir Malcolm Sargent. He had shown himself anxious to come into both the Barbirolli and Kubelik schemes as an Associate, and had already been approached to conduct in the summer and winter Prom seasons. Wilson thought him 'ideally suited as the Promenade Conductor', but realised that with 'so big a repertoire and in such "impersonal" conditions as studio performances' he might not be ideally fitted to the post. But there were many things to be said in favour of his appointment: his wide popularity, his large following among London concert audiences, and his vigorous methods. During January 1950 he was approached. Perhaps he realised that he was in a position to make his own terms; he replied as before, that he could not take on the post on a full-time basis. Nicolls reported to the Board of Governors on 26 January that 'Sir Malcolm has now been sounded, without commitment, and said that he is extremely interested in the appointment . . . It appears, subject to further detailed discussion, that he would be available for a minimum of 23 and a maximum of 35 weeks of the year . . .' Nicolls wrote: 'If a suitable conductor were available, a full-time conductor would be preferable. The market at home and abroad has been carefully surveyed and there is no other convincing candidate.' (This was not altogether true: the market abroad had been excluded as too risky to explore further.) '. . . The best course seems undoubtedly to be to contract Sir Malcolm Sargent on the above basis.'

It was in many ways an unsatisfactory conclusion to the protracted story. All along the BBC had been anxious to avoid anything resembling a part-time commitment on the part of the new conductor. Nicolls might also have recalled a sentence from his 1948 note to the Governors: 'A conductor who was either limited or "temperamental" in terms of repertoire could not possibly meet the demands of the BBC.'

It was too late for such considerations, however. The decision was made.

6
The Sargent/Schwarz Era
1950-1962

Planners and programmes

The BBC Symphony Orchestra which Sir Malcolm Sargent inherited in 1950 was a very different body from that which Boult first conducted in 1930. Even more significant, the BBC, its sponsor and nourisher, was a very different organisation from that which had founded the Orchestra. The relative simplicities of two broadcast networks, a National Programme and a London Regional Programme, had given way to the complex organisation of Home Services, Light and Third Programmes. Overseas broadcasts and the revived television channel (which before the war had had its own orchestra) added to the varied demands which were made on the BBC Symphony Orchestra as a purveyor of high-quality orchestral music. The administrators of the BBC had multiplied in number since 1930. A feeling of remoteness began to develop between the devisers of orchestral programmes and the organisers of the various 'services' which used these programmes. During the final part of the Boult era, as the new postwar structure of radio developed, there was a widespread notion that the planners of the Symphony Orchestra were no longer independent. Programme heads and service controllers 'requested' material from the Orchestra, and it was up to the orchestral planners to provide that material. Even public concerts were not entirely free of these pressures; for although they were in theory regarded as the prestige appearances of the Orchestra, when special repertoire was explored and the finest performances given, these concerts too were part of a plan of national broadcasting which was becoming increasingly sophisticated. Even the programmes of the Promenade Concerts, broadcast on different occasions in Home Service and Third Programme, could be criticised because they did not provide the right proportions of the 'established classics' in the half-concerts which the Home Service broadcast (a point made very strongly by Lindsay Wellington, Controller of that Service), nor the ideal balance of familiar and unfamiliar in the Third Programme's share.

Thus the Symphony Orchestra, which to an enviable extent in the 1930s had been its own master, was now increasingly the servant of the networks. Such a change was bound to affect the relationship between a fiercely individual Chief Conductor such as Malcolm Sargent and the BBC's Music Department. It was possible for Boult, Director of Music as well as Chief Conductor throughout the 1930s, to oversee the entire artistic side of the process by which orchestral music was put on the air – delegating programme planning, knowing the fixed points in the broadcast schedules, taking many of the rehearsals and concerts by the full Orchestra himself, and hearing the result on the two networks to which the Orchestra contributed. By 1950 a whole Music Department found it difficult enough to carry out the administrative side of such an operation; a new Chief Conductor, whoever he was, was bound to feel some distance between his work in front of the Orchestra and its results on the air.

Before 1952, 'Music' was part of the BBC's Entertainment Division (which included Features, Drama, Variety, Children's Hour, Gramophone Programmes, Outside Broadcasts and Recorded Programmes). 'Entertainment' was one of three 'supply divisions' responsible for giving the programme heads what they wanted. The reciprocity of the arrangement was expressed rather cautiously by Sir William Haley (24 July 1945): 'Supply Divisions will be encouraged to make suggestions for programmes to the Programme Heads. In fact, subject to the final right of veto resting with the Programme Heads, there must be an easy-running two-way traffic in ideas between the two sides.' In the competition which ensued between the three main Services, to carve out what each regarded as its share of the audience, the needs of those supplying the material were often overlooked.

The chief benefit of the new Third Programme (Programme C, as it was originally designated; 'C for Culture', as *The Times* dubbed it) was that it expanded the exploration of serious music in areas other than the nineteenth- and twentieth-century orchestral repertory for which the BBC Symphony Orchestra existed. Chamber music and pre-classical music formed perhaps the two areas of greatest expansion. New music, too, was prominent, especially on a smaller rather than a larger scale. The network acquired a distinct character, and a set of assumptions about its purpose and background was quick to enter the public's mind. 'No need to hurry back, darling,' says a professorial character down the phone as his young son sits bound and gagged on a nearby chair, 'Julian and I are thoroughly enjoying the Third Programme' (*Radio Times* cartoon, 8 November 1949). The critic Dyneley Hussey reported a comment overheard at a contemporary chamber music concert: 'It says here it was first performed in the Third Programme – oh dear, you know what that means!'

Idealistically, the BBC did not regard the Third Programme as a ghetto programme for the cultural élite, but as one rung in a ladder of educative entertainment in the Reith tradition. Haley declared (to the British Institute of Adult Education) that 'these three home programmes of the BBC will form part of a single co-ordinated whole and the whole will to the best of our ability be devoted to the enlightenment, entertainment and informing of the community and the slow but rewarding process of raising public taste'. In internal communications he was even more specific: classical music in the Light Programme should lead people on to the Home, where more substantial programmes were given, and thence to the Third. Waltzes from Strauss's *Der Rosenkavalier* on the Light, arias from the same opera on the Home, and a complete performance on the Third: what could express more fully the Reithian notion of broadcasting?

If the listening public did not turn out to have quite the flexibility of mind envisaged by the BBC Director-General, the plan nevertheless ensured one vital thing: that the output of each channel was not exclusive as to content. Serious music was to find a place on each network, especially on Home and Third. Which was just as well, for the habits of the listeners over the following years suggested on the whole a strong loyalty to one network. In the end, the notion of 'graded' networks was not Reithian. Reith's ideals were those of cultural unity; but now the divisions between each network's audience tended to cement the already existing class divisions of English society (in this case, the dividing line of upbringing rather than that of income). In the postwar period, the radical social changes brought about by the fact of war, by the inevitable levelling off in living circumstances which wartime economy brought about, by the social revolution which wartime legislation had created, and by the policies of the new Labour administration – these changes might have been expected to create a more evenly balanced society in Britain. The BBC, arguably out of touch or out of sympathy with these trends, reflected in its new programme structures a society which was already beginning to change.

So it was that the Third Programme did indeed become the channel of a cultural minority, and for the most part its listeners were not drawn across the wavebands to it from the other networks. But, as a network, it was none the worse for being conceived with the highest ideals and put into effect with great skill and integrity. For a relatively small audience (the figures presented by Asa Briggs seem to show that the network's listening public, after containing some open-minded experimenters, had by 1950 settled down to a hard core of 0.15% of the listening audience) the most lavish fare was provided.

With George Barnes as Controller and Etienne Amyot among the planners, and musicians such as Anthony Lewis and Denis Stevens among those responsible for major series, the products of the network were rich and varied. There could scarcely have been an apter expression of the spirit of the Third Programme than that it chose in 1950 to celebrate the bicentenary of Bach's death with three different performances of his *Art of Fugue*: uncompromising intellectualism could scarcely go any further.

So fruitful was the Third Programme in terms of all kinds of music until then rarely represented on the air that a new discussion began among the more thoughtful members of the broadcasting profession about the very availability of music. And this was a discussion with important consequences for the policy of the BBC Symphony Orchestra, for questions raised were: How much music should we hear? Do we hear great music too often? What is the place of unfamiliar music? What should the priorities in broadcasting music be?

Thinkers and theories

In the immediate postwar years, the answers to these questions had seemed clear. An exceptionally obvious, even naïve, set of answers was given by the short-lived Director of Music, Victor Hely-Hutchinson, who died in 1947. 'The ideal music policy for the BBC is not hard to define; it should be to give a representative picture of the musical activities of this country, together with a reflection of what is best among contemporary activities abroad.' Such a view would not perhaps have been supported by Adrian Boult, still less by Edward Clark, for both of whom it was the BBC's function to declare its own strong tastes and beliefs in what was musically worthwhile. Much of Boult's evidence to the Ullswater Committee in 1936 is concerned to rebut the notion that the BBC should simply 'reflect' musical activities in the country at large.

As for the Symphony Orchestra, Hely-Hutchinson expressed the view that 'experience has proved that no symphony orchestra can maintain its standard without the stimulus of reasonably frequent public performance; so, even if no other considerations were involved, it would be necessary from that point of view alone for the BBC to stage a certain number of public concerts'. Again, though those in charge of the Orchestra in the previous decade agreed that public concerts were necessary, to say that they existed purely for the Orchestra's good was a strange inversion of the situation: what about the exploration of the repertory neglected by other organisations? Hely-Hutchinson, writing after the bombing of Queen's Hall but before the building of the Royal Festival Hall, isolated as a major problem of music broadcasting a most curious fact:

the first stage in the planning of the BBC's music programmes must be the planning of public concerts; and at present, when there is no concert hall in central London, and only one hall suitable for the giving of really important public concerts . . . we are up against the staggering fact that the shape of the BBC's music programmes is ultimately conditioned by the availability or otherwise of the Albert Hall.

It was nice that there was little more to worry about than whether halls were available. Hely-Hutchinson's conclusion was that 'broadcasting music, unless it is to be an exotic growth, must be firmly planted in the musical activity of the country as a whole'.

Another essentially commonsense viewpoint was provided by Sir Steuart Wilson. Writing in the *BBC Quarterly* in 1950, ostensibly to commemorate 'Twenty Years of a Symphony Orchestra' (though not actually mentioning the name of the Orchestra's conductor, nor any of its concerts), Wilson said that 'the pattern of broadcasting of music does not – as a pattern – require fundamental re-setting: it requires constant watching lest the interests of one enthusiasm over-weigh the reasonable claims of another'. The problem was, then, one of balance. Or almost so: 'The evaluation of the known as against the potentialities of the unknown, the intelligent anticipations of what will soon be classified as "familiar" – all that is part of the duties of a Music Department with professional knowledge to explain to those whose business lies in interpreting such evaluations in terms of programmes.' Wilson also argued that an amateur appreciation of music 'up to any administrative level in the Corporation' hampered the professional's task. It was not a very hopeful view of broadcasting music which regarded the musician's role as merely that of anticipation, and enthusiasms of non-specialist musicians as a hindrance.

With his Arts Council experience, Wilson was on firmer ground in dealing with the radical changes in the musical profession brought about by wartime music-making and postwar economic expansion.

In 1930 there was no permanent orchestra of symphonic size – there are now four within the BBC and six outside the BBC who could be called contractually permanent, and three more whose personnel is predominantly, though not contractually, permanent. What will be the effect of these orchestras in the next twenty years of broadcasting? The Corporation has in the last few years made various moves towards the professional bodies – which in this case definitely exclude the trade unions – and it is possible that the picture in the next twenty years will change from the outside orchestras as the poor relations of broadcasting being given the occasional crumb from the planners' table, and become a working partner in a scheme of exchanging positions in a series of concerts both public and studio . . . the functions of the BBC are far more philanthropic than business-like . . .

Such an ambitious scheme was not to come to pass: it was not easy to tell outside orchestras what they ought to play, especially when economic conditions were insecure; they valued their independence above all else. But Wilson had pointed to the central fact that the BBC Symphony Orchestra no longer existed in an isolated world: it was one of many such bodies.

Perhaps the most significant contribution to the debate about broadcasting music around 1950 came from Herbert Murrill, who succeeded Wilson as Head of Music in 1950. A musician and composer, rather than primarily an administrator, Murrill was not afraid to declare in the title of another *BBC Quarterly* article what he saw as 'Broadcast Music: the Listener's Duty'. To him it was shocking that broadcast music enabled one to 'read a book, talk, knit, play cards and do a host of other things that will leave only a small part of your attention centred upon the loudspeaker. Some listeners quite habitually behave thus, and music for them becomes still further devalued . . .' Murrill's tone was moral in its insistence. He recalled working all day in an army hut with the radio on: the only reaction to the music was that when Stravinsky's *Duo Concertant* came on, someone wanted to turn the thing off. He recalled a friend who stepped into a taxi in Canada in the middle of the first movement of Beethoven's Fifth and left it in the middle of the slow movement. How to curb the appalling availability of great music?

As a broadcaster, Murrill saw no reason to give the answer 'broadcast less', for this would diminish the chances of this music making contact with an audience for the first time. It was vital to allow a new listener the chance to hear the Emperor Concerto – and different new listeners would listen at different times. No, Murrill placed the responsibility for controlling availability firmly in the hands of the listeners:

> The remedy, surely, must be for the listener to take his music with discrimination. It may be thought odd – it may be a matter for disapproval – that I advise careful listeners to turn off their sets. Yet what value can be ascribed to indiscriminate listening? It is a compliment neither to the BBC nor to the music broadcast, nor to the listener himself. Successful broadcasting depends upon a reciprocal act on the part of the broadcasting authorities and on the part of the listener himself. The originator's effort (however great) must be co-ordinated with the listener's effort (however small). The BBC's admitted duty to the music it broadcasts must, in my view, be matched by the listener's duty to the same music, less frequently admitted.

Murrill's view affected the provision of music by the BBC's central agent of large-scale music-making, the Symphony Orchestra, by clear implication. The balance between the familiar and unfamiliar in the Orchestra's output was a matter of central importance, and Murrill clearly leaned towards the view that the great masterpieces should not be over-available: that they gained their effect of greatness all the more from being set in context.

This view was taken up by Professor Gerald Abraham, who was in later years to become the BBC's Assistant Controller of Music. In a strong 'Plea for a wide Musical Policy' he remarked that 'it is much easier now to hear the Emperor Concerto or the Eroica Symphony than to see even *Hamlet*. The benefits of broadcasting music are obvious and numerous and must far outweigh the harm: nevertheless the potentiality of harm is there and it should be the concern of those responsible for musical broadcasting policy to see that the harm is reduced to the smallest possible proportion.' Abraham was sure that 'our trouble is a superabundance not merely of music but of the *best* music. The public demands the familiar masterpieces and the over-worked professional finds it much easier to give it the familiar masterpieces; both sides should be happy'. The remedy, he thought, was not 'a close season for the overworked masterpieces . . . the acknowledged masterpieces must go on being broadcast, if possible in model performances, to preserve our standards of greatness . . . The real remedy is a very great widening of the ordinary listener's field of musical experience.' This, he said, 'only a broadcasting authority can do as a long-term policy and in the teeth of well-meaning, fair and often highly intelligent criticism'. That was more like the fighting spirit of the 1930s. And, Abraham insisted, more out-of-the-way music should not be confined to the Third, for that would isolate it. It had to penetrate also on to the Home Service and Light Programme – a couple of unfamiliar Schubert songs instead of the hackneyed contents of the usual 'song recital'.

A new Music Division

In the field of orchestral music, *pace* Steuart Wilson's remarks about the use of outside orchestras, it was the BBC Symphony Orchestra which in 1950 was to be the instrument of these theoretical policies if they were to be put into practice. And among the planners of Music Department, later Music Division, the will to expand the orchestral repertory clearly existed. It was limited by two vital factors, however: the range of the planners' own tastes, and the position of Sir Malcolm Sargent at the head of Symphony Orchestra. Richard Howgill, who was Controller, Entertainment, became in February 1952 the first Controller, Music, when Music Division was established. He was a thoughtful administrator, a head of department who commanded admiration and respect. He was a strong advocate of the BBC's role in promoting the new music of established British composers: through him came the regular yearly commission of the Festival Hall season, from composers of the stature of Rubbra, Alwyn and Bliss, and the encouragement of the middle generation of composers – Tippett, Walton and Britten – if not of the youngest generation. He was surrounded by like-minded associates. Eric Warr, a planner of wide sympathies (who was later to be William Glock's right-hand man in running the Symphony Orchestra during the 1960s) had acted as Head of Music Programmes briefly following the creation of the Division. He then became Assistant Head to Maurice Johnstone, who had been Head of North Region music in Manchester. Johnstone was a composer, and had an encyclopaedic knowledge of the orchestral repertoire and the ability to create attractive programmes, which made him the central figure in the Department. As a friend and associate of Sargent's, he had been brought down to London as Head of Music Programmes partly on Sargent's recommendation and insistence. It was ironic that, as Sargent's man, he should be the first to become frustrated with the Chief Conductor's lack of rapport with Music Division, and the most eager campaigner for his replacement. There were other important members of the Department who worked under Howgill. Michael Whewell assumed responsibility for Symphony Orchestra programmes later in the decade. Leonard Isaacs and Peter Crossley-Holland held the posts of Music Organiser for the Third Programme and Home Service respectively, and then swapped jobs in 1954. (These programme music organiser posts lapsed in 1960; they were replaced with Chief Assistant posts, responsible for the planning of Choral and Orchestral Music, and of Chamber Music and Recitals. Still later, the responsibilities were spread around different producers in Music Division, and some were designated Chief Producers in various areas.) An important figure as Assistant Third Programme Music Organiser in the 1950s was Robert Simpson, a composer and administrator who was to become especially well known for his advocacy of the music of Havergal Brian. He later became a senior producer in Music Division, and resigned at the time of the Musicians' Union dispute in 1980 in protest against the changing values of the BBC. Simpson produced important concerts with the Symphony Orchestra when he was able to book their services; he was a strong critic of the system by which, after 1960, one man's judgement determined the programmes of the Proms and the Winter Season: this led him to withdraw a symphony from performance at the Proms after his resignation. Other distinguished figures in Music Division were Basil Lam, to whom fell much of the responsibility for the pre-classical repertory after the departure of Denis Stevens, and Harry Croft-Jackson, who undertook the administrative tasks of organising music programmes. By the end of the decade such figures as Peter Gould, Bernard Keefe, David Stone and John Manduell were members of Music Division.

Amongst all this expertise, what was missing at the top level of Music Division in the early 1950s was what the idiosyncratic Edward Clark had supplied in the 1930s: a finger on the pulse of European music. The music of certain unchallenged figures on the continent was supported, as will be clear from what follows. And in 1950 the neglect of a young generation of English composers and of a successful middle generation of composers on the continent was not as reprehensible as it became towards the end of the decade. A fossilisation of musical taste in the 1950s was not confined to the BBC: the Corporation reflected a national insularity which it was to be hard to conquer. But the fact remains that adventurous newcomers were scarcely recognised. The two outstanding figures of the postwar scene, Pierre Boulez and Karlheinz Stockhausen, were ignored: even their mentor, Olivier Messiaen, was scarcely given his due by the BBC. There was certainly no contact with the work of Henze, Nono and a host of other younger men on the continent. Backwaters were explored; risks were rarely taken. Such is a not unreasonable summary of the BBC's music policy as it affected the Symphony Orchestra in the 1950s.

Problems with Sargent

Sir Malcolm Sargent's relationship with the BBC was a difficult one from the beginning. Unlike Boult, Sargent never regarded himself as the servant of the Corporation; indeed it is difficult to think of any conductor who would have subordinated his own wishes to those of the BBC in the way that Boult had done during his twenty years. Nevertheless, Sargent's lack of desire to fit into the established working methods of the BBC Music Department was evident even in the discussions which preceded his appointment: it is neither to his credit nor to that of the BBC that these problems were not fully discussed and resolved before he took up his post.

The formal invitation to become Chief Conductor was issued to Sargent on 15 February 1950, and on 22 February Sargent replied in surprising terms. He proposed that he should also become Joint Head of Music Department with the new Head of Music who was to succeed Steuart Wilson, and also Conductor of the BBC Choir. Nicolls replied firmly that the post was to be that of Chief Conductor alone, but he added that 'Adrian is in a position to exercise considerable influence on the Music Department as an elder statesman, and you will be able to do so too'. Understandably, this was not what Sargent was looking for. He thought that official jurisdiction over matters in Music Department which concerned the Symphony Orchestra was indispensable to him. His demand having been turned down, he proposed to Nicolls on 23 February a 'gentleman's agreement', which would among other matters give him an option on at least half the Orchestra's public concert appearances; he said he was dissatisfied with Wilson's proposed allocation to him. Here, too, before his appointment, a possibility of conflict between Sargent and the BBC was made clear: his notions of conducting the Orchestra were centred around its public concert appearances; the studio performances were irrelevant to him. Boult had been exceptional in his willingness to conduct so much in the studio, but Sargent's view represented a potential sudden change of policy which was not foreseen.

The BBC presented Sargent with a detailed contract letter for him to sign, specifying all the details of his commitments to the Orchestra and outlining some of the working methods. Sargent, still hoping for a gentleman's agreement, asked to see the Director-General on the matter. He talked to Haley at the beginning of April, and immediately after the interview went to see the Head of Programme Contracts to say that, with the Director-General's agreement, a much freer form of contract was to be devised. Officials in Music Department felt, not for the last time, that they had been passed over. Richard Howgill wrote firmly to Nicolls (6 April):

> Sargent's tactics give one a growing feeling that a definition of duties is more necessary in his case than it might be in others, and that any laxity which strengthens his idea that he is God's gift to BBC music will make life intolerable not only to H[ead of] M[usic] and myself but to Programme Controllers and others . . .

Howgill reasserted what he saw as the accepted supremacy of the Music Department: 'I am not of course suggesting that his general musical views should not be welcomed, but I am most anxious that he should not think he can over-rule HM – or me – or appeal to some higher authority by virtue of his public prestige.'

Sargent had been told by Nicolls that as Chief Conductor he would have to use the existing machinery of Music Department, but as Howgill noted, 'he is obviously not satisfied and wants something different'. As an example of Sargent's expectation that the BBC would revolve around him rather than *vice versa*, Howgill cited his request to have the Symphony Orchestra made available for an afternoon choral concert. Sargent had wanted 'either the Third Programme opened up specially for it or the Home Service ordered to take it regardless of anything else they may think it advisable to do'. How-gill's firm line was generally supported. Sargent's modified suggestion to Haley that he should have a 'Musical Adviser' function outside the Music Department was turned down on 20 April. On 2 May formal terms of agree-ment were again presented to Sargent, and this time he concurred.

Sargent's arrangement with the BBC was exceptionally favourable: he was guaranteed a maximum of public exposure in his new post while being able to undertake outside engagements with freedom. The agreement stated that he would conduct 'as many rehearsals and performances as possible'; that he would normally conduct all public concerts outside London, and half of those in London; that all gramophone records made by the Orchestra would be conducted by him; and that outside engagements would be allowed. On the question of allocating his periods with the Orchestra, 'there shall be the fullest co-operation and exchange of information between the Corporation and yourself in deciding the occasions on which you will con-duct'. The important matter of programme planning was formulated thus: he would be responsible 'in co-operation with Head of Music and other appropriate members of the Corporation's staff for the programmes of the BBC Symphony Orchestra whether rehearsed and conducted by yourself, or, insofar as the Corporation may desire, by other conductors'. In other words, the BBC kept (as it always has) the artistic direction of the Orchestra firmly in its own hands: guest conductors and their programmes were only the concern of the Chief Conductor if the BBC wished to make them so. Sargent was provided with the usual accommodation and secretarial help in the BBC's offices, now housed in Yalding House, not far from Broadcasting House on the corner of Clipstone Street and Great Portland Street. His agreement was to run for an initial year from 16 July 1950 to 15 July 1951, and thereafter without limit, subject only to a year's notice. Thus Sargent was not subject to any fixed term: he might have been Chief Conductor for life. There was no age rule such as had been invoked in Boult's case.

Sir Adrian Boult's public farewell concert as Chief Conductor took place on 20 April 1950 at the Royal Albert Hall. The formalities of celebration were observed, but it was a muted occasion, tinged with regret that the whole period leading up to Boult's retirement had been so clumsily handled. (Sir William Haley, then Director-General, when reminiscing about the period nearly thirty years later, said that he hoped the BBC would not take the same course again.) In private, though, there were many expressions of good will and warm thanks from both the BBC and its Orchestra. Indeed, at a lunch given by Haley in Broadcasting House, Boult was so warmly praised that, as he recalls 'I began to wonder whether I had really been asked to go or had

Boult's farewell: Sir Adrian Boult's last concert as Chief Conductor on 20 April 1950. Above, with Paul Beard. Below, in the Royal Albert Hall

Sir Malcolm Sargent in his element: an ovation at the last night of the Proms, 1961

Smiles before the storm: rehearsals for Michael Tippett's Second Symphony in Maida Vale, a BBC commission which broke down briefly at its first performance. Above: Boult, Tippett and Paul Beard. Below: Boult, Tippett, Ralph and Ursula Vaughan Williams

'Let us make music together': Bruno Walter, a regular visitor to the Orchestra in the 1930s, rehearsing it again in Maida Vale in 1955

The magician: Sir Thomas Beecham, who played a leading role in the negotiations leading to the formation of the BBC Symphony Orchestra, returned to conduct it in a memorable performance of the Sibelius Second Symphony in the Festival Hall, 1954

Rudolf Schwarz, Chief Conductor of the BBC Symphony Orchestra from 1957 to 1962

Igor Stravinsky rehearses in Maida Vale Studio I for a late-night performance of his Oedipus Rex *at the Festival Hall, 1959*

'A quixotic outsider': William Glock, the BBC's new Controller, Music, in 1959

Leopold Stokowski, who in the 1963 Proms became the first foreign conductor ever to conduct a complete concert

Norman Del Mar, who gave the first performance of many of Glock's BBC commissions with the BBC Symphony Orchestra in the 1960s, and has continued to conduct the orchestra regularly

Planning a revolution: Hugh Maguire, who became leader of the Symphony Orchestra in 1963, with Antal Dorati, Chief Conductor 1963–6

To America: the BBC Symphony Orchestra's tour of the USA in 1965, when it performed a wide range of twentieth-century music. Left: off the plane William and Anne Glock, with Hugh Maguire behind them. Right: Dorati conducting in Carnegie Hall

Storm and stress: Antal Dorati, the vigorous new Chief Conductor of the BBC Symphony Orchestra, in 1963

insisted on going, to their great regret'. At a larger, more formal farewell dinner at the Connaught Rooms, Boult was presented with what Haley described as 'a Mozart of inkstands'. So Boult slipped quietly out of the picture, assuming almost immediately the conductorship of the London Philharmonic Orchestra, which was offered him by its manager Thomas Russell. But irritations continued to the last: Boult was peremptorily told to clear his office at the BBC (an ironic instruction, in view of the little use his successor ever made of it). It would be perhaps appropriate to close the account of Boult's staff career at the BBC not with the public concert on 20 April, but with the special Contemporary Music concert he gave at Maida Vale a week later, when – open-minded as ever – he introduced the cantata *Ulysses* by Matyas Seiber, the Piano Concerto by Christian Darnton, and gave the world première of a Symphony by Elizabeth Maconchy. Boult's service of a wide range of music has been his greatest achievement; for he is in so many ways an untypical example of a conductor. As Michael Kennedy wrote in the programme book for Boult's ninetieth birthday concert in 1979:

> Selfless is not the first word that comes to mind when one is considering conductors, but it can justly and accurately be applied to Boult. The other word that can be associated with him without fear of contradiction is integrity. The career of Adrian Boult is an epitome of the history of English music and of English music-making. . . . Three of the greatest figures in the so-called English musical renaissance – Elgar, Vaughan Williams and Holst – were his friends, and they gave him their friendship because of their gratitude to him for services to their music. Yet it is perhaps only in recent years, in his old age, that the general public, as opposed to musicians, has displayed affection as well as respect for Sir Adrian. He is not obviously a 'character'; he lacks Beecham's *braggadocio*, Barbirolli's endearing affectations, Sargent's dapper swagger. Far more anecdotes, apocryphal or not, are told about this trio than about Boult. In some ways, Boult's impatience with any kind of showmanship has done him a disservice. For many years, non-musicians – and even some unperceptive musicians – tended to think that such an unflamboyant personality and demeanour could only be correlated with unimaginative, even unexciting, performances. Added to this there was his appearance: tall, military in bearing and speech, suggesting a cartoonist's idea of the 'English Establishment' figure. As with Elgar and Bliss, this was deceptive and misleading. Boult is as emotionally committed to music as any of his more histrionic colleagues, but his passion is concentrated into interpretation of the score.

The first few months of Sargent's rule went swimmingly. The 1950

Proms were a success, and in one of the few unclouded letters which Sargent wrote to the BBC during his tenure of office, he declared to Haley on 18 September that 'my relationships with [the Orchestra] have been completely happy . . . the rest of your staff have been in every way helpful, there has not been one "awkward" moment with anyone'. He did add that 'there is still much to be done with the Orchestra', and during the following season he took the first steps towards what he hoped would be a radical revitalisation of their playing standard. His full plans for that problem were not to emerge for another eighteen months.

The 1950–51 season began to reveal some of the problems which the BBC's programme planners would face in Sargent's time. With the exception of Bartók's Concerto for Orchestra, all the works that Sargent conducted were from the standard repertory. Haydn, Mozart and Elgar on 29 November; Vaughan Williams and Brahms on 31 January; and Berlioz, Brahms and Bartók at the final concert of the season on 25 April 1951. In his studio concerts during that first season he showed more adventurousness. In November 1950 he conducted the Rawsthorne Piano Concerto, Moeran's Sinfonietta and Prokofiev's *Alexander Nevsky*. But it was left to hardier souls to do the bulk of the interesting work: in October Issay Dobrowen opened the Albert Hall series and conducted a selection of Russian music – Scriabin, Borodin and Liadov – in the studio; Vittorio Gui brought Italian novelties in October; and it was Boult not Sargent who gave the first performance of Alan Rawsthorne's Symphony for the Royal Philharmonic Society on 15 November (and repeated it in the studio on the next day). The one first British performance in the Symphony Concerts series – Poulenc's Piano Concerto – was conducted by Basil Cameron (with the composer as soloist). Of three large-scale works given at the Albert Hall, Mozart's C minor Mass was directed by Beecham, while two interesting revivals from prewar concerts, Debussy's *Le Martyre de Saint-Sébastien* and Purcell's *King Arthur*, were conducted respectively by Albert Wolff and Boult.

This was an inauspicious start. Both in the amount of conducting he was doing and in his repertoire Sargent came nowhere near the ideal required by the Symphony Orchestra. In the 1951 studio concerts the same story continued: the bulk of the work was done by such conductors as Walter Goehr (who on 25 January conducted the first in an ambitious Third Programme series surveying the work of Max Reger, devised by Donald Mitchell). Boult gave Schoenberg's *Pelleas und Melisande* on 19 February, Rubbra's Fourth Symphony on 10 February, Elsa Barraine's Second Symphony and Bartók's Viola Concerto with Primrose in March. In April Enesco came to do his own Symphony in E flat, Op. 13. Rafael Kubelik was a visitor in May (and included Martinů's and Roussel's Third Symphonies in his concerts).

The Royal Festival Hall opens

Sargent, however, was in charge of the major public event which followed the 1950–51 season: the series of concerts organised by the London County Council to open the new Royal Festival Hall on London's South Bank. It formed the main building (and, as it proved, the only permanent one) erected for the Festival of Britain. The Festival Hall, designed by Robert Matthew, caused a controversy which still rumbles. Beecham characteristically dismissed it as 'a monumental piece of imbecility and iniquity', but others welcomed its wide, cool foyers and its well-shaped auditorium, which gave a sense of intimacy to an audience of some 3000. About its acoustics there were more serious arguments, and subsequent modifications (including the installation of electronic reverberation techniques to enliven what was an exceptionally dry acoustic) have always roused argument. In 1951, the Festival Hall was a piece of 'new-wave' architecture: nearly thirty years later, it is still being cited as a fine example of postwar British building.

There were seven concerts in the opening celebrations: the first by a grand composite orchestra, one by the London Philharmonic, one by the London Symphony, and one by the London Mozart Players. The engagement of the BBC Symphony Orchestra to take the most prominent part in the Hall's opening celebrations was a token of its restored vigour at the end of the 1940s. The concerts were planned thus because it was hoped to engage Toscanini for the event. Owen Mase was to be Concerts Adviser to the new Hall, and his connections with the maestro and the BBC appeared to ensure the success of the partnership. Though the London Philharmonic, now subsidised by the LCC, might well have expected the prominent part in the series, Toscanini would agree to appear only with the BBC Symphony Orchestra. The details were concluded in August 1950 with Toscanini and programmes for his three concerts agreed: but because of an accident he had to cancel his visit. So the Festival Hall, having booked the BBC Symphony Orchestra, had to turn to Sargent to save the situation. He did so with typical aplomb, giving powerful and vivid performances of some of the favourite pieces from his repertory: Beethoven's Ninth (4 and 8 May, alongside the First Symphony and the Choral Fantasia), and an orchestral programme of Vaughan Williams' Sixth Symphony, Strauss's *Don Juan* and Debussy's *La Mer* (6 May). On 3 May he shared with Boult the conducting of the composite orchestra which played a sequence of British music at the opening ceremony of dedication by the Archbishop of Canterbury. It was the sort of occasion on which Sargent was at his best.

The BBC was slow to decide whether or not to transfer its regular series of Symphony Concerts to the Festival Hall. During preliminary discussions, the most worrying feature appeared to be the possible loss of the BBC's independence: might the LCC try to impose a programme policy on the new Hall? It was reported after an April 1950 meeting that

> there appeared to BBC members present to be an element of controlled planning in the LCC scheme which, together with the existence of their hall for some time without competition, might constitute a somewhat dangerous monopoly of aesthetic judgement. . . . We do not want our concert-giving activities submerged or fettered by those of the LCC.

Sargent disagreed; he would have preferred to take advantage of all the public attention focused on the new Hall and move there immediately. Caution, as usual in the BBC, prevailed. Both Steuart Wilson and W. W. Thompson, the Concerts Manager, argued strongly in favour of the Albert Hall for the 1951–2 season, and this was agreed. The move was made a season later, when the Festival Hall had aiready firmly established itself as a fine home for orchestral music.

Sargent was unhappy that, in the 1951–2 season, he was allocated only five out of the ten concerts in the Symphony Series, the last to be held at the Royal Albert Hall. But that represented exactly the proportion stated in his contract: his memory was sometimes selective as to the conditions he worked under. His programmes concentrated on classics and large choral works: the Verdi *Requiem* on 5 December; Berlioz's *Damnation of Faust* on 13 February (changed after the death of King George VI to *Messiah*); and, for the rest, Brahms, Elgar, Mozart and Strauss, Beethoven's Emperor and Holst's *Planets*. Interesting contributions were made by Basil Cameron (an all-Stravinsky programme on 26 March) and Clarence Raybould (a repeat of Hindemith's *Mathis der Maler*). There were also concerts by Barbirolli, Gui and Boult. The scheme lacked a coherent plan or sense of purpose; Sargent's concerts were not very successful in terms of audience.

Meanwhile, Sargent was making an increasing number of complaints in the highest quarters about his treatment by the Music Department. He lunched with Director-General Haley on 2 July 1951 and pointed out that he had only been given half the concerts in the forthcoming season; complained justifiably of the BBC's dilatoriness in moving to the Festival Hall; and then demanded to be consulted in special extra areas, especially the use of foreign conductors, in programme building, and in the selection of the choral repertoire, in which he had a special interest. More radical were his proposals to Haley for the staffing of the Orchestra. Instead of having staff posts with three-year contracts, he suggested that the whole Orchestra should be on yearly contracts, renewable at will but also able to be terminated without notice. This, Sargent felt, was the only way to maintain an orchestra which always played at the peak of its form and which had a commitment to fine performances.

Sargent was well known among orchestral musicians for his attitudes towards security in their profession. He had suggested in an interview back in 1935 that pensions for orchestral musicians were a mixed blessing, ensuring too comfortable a life: 'as soon as a man thinks he is in his orchestral job for life, with a pension waiting for him at the end of it, he tends to lose something of his supreme fire. He ought to give of his life blood with every bar he plays. Directly a man gets blasé or does not give of his very best, he ought to go. It sounds cruel, but it is for the good of the orchestra.' He later added that the feeling of instability about where next year's bread and butter was coming from had inspired many an artist to give of his best.

At the time, Sargent was very widely criticised for these remarks, though it is doubtful whether they were as crucially harmful to his reputation with orchestral musicians as his biographer Charles Reid suggests. What is clear from Sargent's requests to Haley in 1951 is that he did not change his mind even after fierce attacks on him. He was resolved to pursue the same course with the BBC Orchestra, and if possible to put his notion of 'creative insecurity' to the test. Of course, an assured wage and stable conditions of work underlay the whole conception of the BBC Symphony Orchestra from its foundation, and it was unlikely that even a Chief Conductor would be able to alter that. In fact, many long discussions had taken place in the BBC over the preceding few years in an effort to establish a workable pension scheme for orchestral members: it had only just come to fruition. There were plenty of opportunities in London for freelance orchestral musicians who preferred to do without that security: the BBC by the nature of its regular, often routine, work in the studio offered an alternative. But to Sargent, the BBC Symphony Orchestra had the capability to compete on equal terms in the London musical market-place with other orchestras whose lives were given over completely to public concert-giving.

Sargent's ambition to bring the BBC Symphony Orchestra a renewed measure of public acclaim was a worthy one. The BBC Music Department, however, saw this only as his desire to avoid work which was not glamorous. Nicolls briefed the Director-General about Sargent's demands, and wrote: 'Sticking out a mile in all Sargent's statements and arguments is his reluctance to conduct in the studio and a desire always to be conducting in public' (6 July 1951). Herbert Murrill, now Head of Music in succession to Wilson, replied to some more of Sargent's criticisms in a note to Nicolls (13 July). Sargent's concerts in the past Albert Hall season had not been box office successes, and other conductors deserved a chance. Sargent was always anxious to cut down on studio work. But Murrill admitted that the Music Department was perhaps at fault in not involving Sargent in their decision-making: 'I believe we have failed in some degree to keep Sir Malcolm informed of our proposals and to get his approval to names of visiting conductors. Sir Adrian was entirely co-operative in this respect.' One notes the fond recalling of Boult's era, which had now disappeared; it was perhaps idle to expect Sargent to behave in the same way. Besides, he was a busy man, without a full-time commitment to the BBC – and for that the BBC had only themselves to blame in appointing him. Sargent never used his office in Music Department, and rarely was seen in the building. Negotiations had to take place by phone or by visit to Sargent's flat next to the Albert Hall, which caused immense irritation.

Little over a year after he was appointed, Sargent complained to Nicolls (9 November) that 'the situation now seems exactly that which I was afraid of before joining your Corporation', though he assured his good will and signed himself 'Yours ever, Malcolm (who is anxious to stay happily in the BBC for years!)'. He wrote again on 17 November, this time more firmly. He complained that 'at present I have no position at all . . .' As to his using his office facilities: 'I must state frankly (as I am sure you have gathered) that I would not be happy for long in BBC office surroundings'. As far as his relationship with Music Department went, Sargent made it abundantly clear what he had expected: 'On joining I thought that the Music Department existed for the use of the Chief Conductor to assist him in his music-making, but in actual fact the Chief Conductor seems to exist solely for the use of the Music Department, if and when they want him.' The latter formulation was not far from the truth.

It was clear that there would have to be an effort to restore goodwill on all sides, and Nicolls proposed that he and Sargent should meet with Howgill and Murrill. Nicolls put down on paper with considerable frankness the problems which he felt Sargent should consider. The outstanding one was the amount of time Sargent spent with the Orchestra: it had been accepted that for the first two seasons Sargent's commitments were already firm when he was appointed, but 'it certainly was a surprise and a disappointment to me to find that, as far as one can judge, the rate of your outside engagements was not diminishing after two years. Quite frankly, I do not see (although this is only a layman's opinion) how you can be Conductor of the BBC Symphony Orchestra if other people of varying calibres conduct for about half the time.'

(In fact, this proportion was a diplomatic underestimate on Nicolls' part.) Nicolls referred to the 'vast change that has come about' through Sargent's absence from Yalding House, and wrote that 'it does not seem to me that as a general practice a collective business such as we are involved in can be conducted on the basis of the knowledge that you will normally be in town once a week and can be got on the phone at other times . . .' To balance this strong criticism, Nicolls added that he felt that there was (as Murrill admitted) cause to criticise the Music Department for its lack of liaison with Sargent over dates, programmes and conductors, and he reiterated 'that it is our firm wish that you should be the full-time conductor of our Orchestra and that your experience and musical knowledge and wisdom should be available in the field of broadcast music generally'.

The meeting was held at the end of November and no formal minutes were taken. Only three points were recorded: that Sargent would spend a regular half day a week in his Yalding office; that he would not as a rule attend orchestral auditions except in special cases, and that proposals for guest conductors must be submitted to him in each case (a suggestion that he approve a general list was not accepted). Nicolls added: 'It would be a mistake to record any other of the happenings as definite decisions.' The following year, when the Music Division was reorganised, Howgill reminded all members of staff of the necessity to consult Sargent on all matters pertaining to the Symphony Orchestra and also the Choral Society.

Reviving the Orchestra

There, for the moment, the matter rested. But meanwhile, another possible source of conflict was arising in Sargent's relationship with the Orchestra itself. It would be wrong to suggest that orchestral players wholly disliked Sargent. There were many for whom his arrival at the BBC was a breath of fresh air, a welcome change, and for a couple of seasons his dynamism, inexhaustible energy and lively style injected a spark into the Orchestra's playing which had previously been missing. The Orchestra became quickly used to his personal style, based as it was on an acute appreciation of the central role the conductor plays in the relationship with the audience at any symphony concert. It was perhaps unfortunate that, before he tried to improve the standard of the Orchestra's playing, Sargent's main concern in discussions with the players' Orchestral Committee was confined to the matter of whether the Orchestra should stand when he came on to the platform. Politely, but firmly, the Committee informed him that this was a gesture of spontaneous respect and affection which they reserved for distinguished guest conductors and foreigners, and that to make it an invariable rule would diminish its significance. Sargent accepted the prevailing view in that matter. Soon, though, there was bound to arise what both Music Department and Sargent knew was necessary, a substantial re-auditioning of orchestral players. In the string section in particular the accumulated members of many years had never been subjected to any strict control over their playing standard. In the postwar years the difficulty in obtaining new members of the required high standard had meant that players of lower ability had not been replaced. Re-auditioning had never been a regular part of the Orchestra's administration since its foundation, and it was bound to be a difficult business. Sargent, fortunately, had got nowhere with his scheme for a short-term contract orchestra, but in spite of his unwillingness to become involved with auditions, he had to supervise these crucial ones which would probably result in the sacking of some members.

The auditions took place in the spring of 1952, and they were thorough ones of their kind: set pieces, sight-reading, and performance of a choice of solo works were involved. There were complaints from orchestral members that these tests were suitable only for soloists, not orchestral players; but it was felt that each player should be equal to such a challenge. Nevertheless, when eight members were told that their contracts would not be renewed, a strong letter of protest was sent to Haley complaining about the nature of the auditions. But to no avail; everyone realised that, however painful, the maintenance of the Orchestra's standard was a prime concern.

Sargent paid little attention to the most important factor by which the standard could have been improved – for him to spend an increased amount of time with the Orchestra. Instead he contented himself with devising systems. The most famous, and notorious with the players, was the idea of rotating the positions of back-desk string players: instead of seating the strings in a standard order of seniority behind the leader and sub-leader, Sargent introduced a scheme whereby each pair of string players would take it in turns to play at the second, third, fourth (and so on) desks in their sections. Sargent thus hoped to ensure a more even quality of sound: instead of a general descent in quality towards the back, there would be a more solidly reliable quality of timbre throughout the sections. The section leaders, with whom Sargent discussed the matter over lunch, were not those to whom it applied, and so were not opposed to the idea. And there is no doubt that, when put into effect at the 1952 Proms, it helped to keep Orchestra members on their toes, swapping positions each concert. Ill-feeling, however, was the inevitable result, especially when old-established players were pushed back from their accustomed places – and also, less predictably, a certain loss of normal, confident ensemble. It was said that the younger players did not expect to sit in higher positions, and that the air of competitiveness that was introduced by the scheme was negative rather than positive. In time, though, the experiment seemed to work, and it remained in force (the practice is still used in many orchestras outside Britain). It also enabled Sargent to keep a close eye on all his personnel, not merely those who caught his eye (or ear) at the front of the ensemble. With typical rigour, Sargent insisted that the positions of the different desks be numbered on the floor of the Orchestra's Maida Vale studio, so that identification would be easy: but that was soon ignored in the day-to-day running of the scheme – playing in an orchestra, it was remarked, was not really like playing a game of hopscotch.

1952–3

Sargent continued to draw some fine results from the Orchestra, especially when he was directing prominent public concerts or when he was conducting a choral work. But his repertoire became hardly any broader. 1952 and 1953 brought no unexpected pieces in either public concerts or in the studio – with one notable exception. On 26 January 1952 the Orchestra was astonished to see that Sargent was down on their duty sheets to conduct the Five Orchestral Pieces, Op. 16, by Schoenberg. Had he agreed with the planners that he would try the work for the first time? All were aware of his oft-repeated attitude to most twentieth-century music from the continent; he was quite remote from the music of the Second Viennese School. Did this mark a change of heart? On the day of the studio recording he cancelled his appearance; Paul Beard directed the performance in his place. That was the end of Sargent's brief flirtation with Schoenberg; he never undertook another similar work.

In the studio during the first part of 1952, Sargent had only two substantial periods with the Orchestra. The first of these, in February, was disrupted by the death of King George VI: studio and public performances of Berlioz's *Damnation of Faust* were cancelled; *Messiah* replaced it in public, and a selection of sacred music extracts in the studio. Sargent's second period, in April, contained much more that was outside his normal repertoire. On 16 April Rudolf Firkusny came to give the British broadcast première of Martinů's Third Piano Concerto, and Sargent added to this the Fourth Symphony of Roussel. Later that week, Sargent gave a performance of the Mass by Julius Harrison, and on 19 April he included the Bloch Concerto Grosso for strings with obbligato piano. Glazunov's Sixth Symphony was performed on 26 and 27 April. Later isolated concerts by Sargent contained Balakirev's First Symphony, the *Concerto Gregoriano* by Respighi,

and the Second Piano Concerto by Rawsthorne (1 and 2 June) in which the
soloist was Clifford Curzon.

Major contributions to the season were again made by guest conductors.
Schoenberg's Op. 22 Songs were to have been given their first British per-
formance on 9 February under Raybould, but the King's death postponed
them until 3 May, when Walter Goehr conducted them alongside Elsa
Barraine's Second Symphony. Vittorio Gui again undertook a period with
the Orchestra in March, during which he gave Bloch's *Schelomo*, a British
première by Dallapiccola, and two symphonic poems by Roger-Ducasse.
Rudolf Schwarz directed Schoenberg's Violin Concerto on 20 March; Karl
Rankl included Scriabin's *Poem of Ecstasy* in his programme on 30 March;
Clarence Raybould conducted Bloch's Symphony in C sharp minor on 7 and
8 June; and Barbirolli arrived for a concert which included William Alwyn's
First Symphony and John Ireland's once-popular *Mai-Dun* Overture (now,
as the composer put it, 'hardly ever done') on 11 and 12 June. Another distinguished visitor was Leopold Stokowski who, perhaps surprisingly, included Rubbra's Fifth Symphony in his programme on 21 May, alongside
his own transcriptions of Bach and Purcell, Debussy's *Nocturnes* and Wagner's *Meistersinger* Overture.

One considerable disappointment for Sargent was that the smaller series
of Winter Proms, which he had conducted at the start of the year in 1951 and
1952, was abandoned. These concerts never caught on with the summer
Prom-going public and their programmes were miscellaneous, to say the
least. The scope of the concerts can be gathered from the titles the evenings
were given in 1952: 'Popular', 'British', 'Mendelssohn – Brahms', 'Berlioz –
Brahms', 'Popular', 'Popular', 'Berlioz – Strauss', 'Brahms – Haydn',
'Mozart – Brahms', 'Bach – Brahms – Beethoven', and 'Popular'. Basil
Cameron had shared the conducting with Sargent. Sargent proposed a
special Beethoven series to run in their place in 1953: his suggestion was not
taken up by the BBC.

The Orchestra made its first visits to the provinces under Sargent at the
end of 1951, with two concerts in Swansea and one in Cardiff, on 27–29
November. The adventurous programmes of previous provincial tours were
not maintained, though Britten's *Young Person's Guide to the Orchestra* was
played in both towns. In January 1953 Nottingham and Leicester were
visited, and again the *Young Person's Guide* was included.

1952–3: Coronation Year

In the 1952–3 season of public concerts Sargent undertook six of the ten
concerts, which gave him the pre-eminence he wanted. Vaughan Williams'

Sixth Symphony and *Sinfonia Antartica*, Beethoven, Strauss, Sibelius, Brahms, Elgar, two big choral works – the Verdi *Requiem* again and the Berlioz *Damnation of Faust* (cancelled the previous year). Two less usual works showed a distinct shift in the Sargent repertoire: Berg's Violin Concerto and the First Symphony by Rawsthorne (which Boult had premièred). Perhaps the influence of the BBC Music Department was beginning to show. In the same series Boult conducted Tippett's Concerto for Double String Orchestra and Mahler's Fourth Symphony; Gui, Barbirolli and Monteux all had concerts of interest.

In October 1952 a memorial concert was given at the Royal College of Music for Herbert Murrill, who had died tragically young after holding the post of Head of Music for less than two years. Cameron conducted the concert, which included Murrill's own Songs for Tenor and Orchestra, Stravinsky's *Apollo* and Fauré's *Pavane*. Studio concerts in the following season were again notable for the absence of Sargent, who conducted only a handful of programmes: these included choral works such as Holst's Choral Symphony and Stanford's *Requiem*, as well as repeats of Berlioz's *L'Enfance du Christ*, the Rawsthorne Symphony and the Berg Violin Concerto. He again conducted the Haydn oratorio, *The Return of Tobias*, but the bulk of the season's novelties and premières fell to the guests: Rudolf Schwarz in Bloch and Enesco (4 and 5 October) and later in Alwyn's Concerto Grosso No. 2; Cameron in John Gardner's First Symphony. Boult gave the British première of the Second Symphony by William Wordsworth and also of Frank Martin's Violin Concerto, while Raybould was entrusted with Hindemith's Symphony in E flat and the Viola Concerto by Quincey Porter, played by the Orchestra's principal viola, Harry Danks. Other important visitors included Georges Enesco, to direct his own unpublished Overture alongside Beethoven's Seventh Symphony; Paul Kletzki in Honegger's Fifth Symphony; and Hans-Schmidt Isserstedt, who took the Orchestra for a substantial period in November 1952, in the Third Symphony of Hartmann (previously broadcast in October 1951 from the ISCM Festival) and a British première of a Prelude by Jarnach. Walter Goehr, a constant supporter of new music throughout this period, directed Daniel Jones's Second Symphony. But Sargent did undertake two new works by Bloch on 11 April: his Concerto Grosso and *Sinfonia Breve*.

On 2 June 1953 Queen Elizabeth II was crowned in Westminster Abbey. To celebrate the occasion, a series of eight concerts was promoted at the Festival Hall by the Royal Philharmonic Society in association with the Arts Council, the BBC, and the London County Council. Beecham and the Royal Philharmonic Orchestra, Boult and the London Philharmonic Orchestra, Barbirolli and the London Symphony Orchestra all contributed concerts; the BBC Symphony Orchestra under Sargent appeared in two large choral concerts: on Wednesday 27 May, in Vaughan Williams' Sea Symphony, with the Walton Viola Concerto and Holst's *Perfect Fool*; and on 3 June, the day after the ceremony, in Britten's Spring Symphony and Elgar's First Symphony. On both occasions Sargent was in his element: directing choral works, and with the full glare of the public eye upon him on a royal occasion. In the studio, Sargent gave the first performances of two works commissioned by the BBC to mark the Coronation: Rubbra's Ode to the Queen, and Berkeley's Suite for Orchestra.

Sargent appears to have undertaken an increasing number of novelties – even if few of them could be called important works – in the seasons following 1952. He did not see it as his function to espouse untried works, and indeed in 1955 he was to declare as much when his Proms repertoire was criticised by Eric Blom of *The Observer*. He wrote to the newspaper defending his choice of the tried and tested. He explained with considerable candour that though he realised how many new works were heard at the Proms in the 1920s and 1930s, he thought it a pointless exercise: 'It would seem a waste of time that they were heard even on that occasion, when a better work would have given more pleasure and been of more importance to the audience.' This ingenuous statement brought an anguished plea from English composers, represented by Vaughan Williams and Peter Racine Fricker (ironically, since they were two living composers whose music Sargent had conducted), imploring the BBC not to abandon its policy of playing unconventional repertoire.

Sargent's obstructive attitude to even those works which the Music Department wished him to undertake, and his remoteness from all the decision-making in the BBC, led in 1953 to a growing feeling that his appointment had not developed as it should. A certain amount of flexibility was to have been expected in the first two years, as Sargent's commitments were already heavy when he took on the post and outside engagements were expected to take a fair proportion of his time. But, as Basil Nicolls had mentioned to him, this situation ought to have changed by the 1952–3 season. And Sargent's commitment to outside work had exceeded the BBC's expectations. In 1951, he had conducted so much for the Festival of Britain celebrations that the first rehearsal for the Proms had to be postponed so that he could take a rest; it had been insufficient and while conducting an extra concert for an outside body on 5 August during the Prom season, he had collapsed, and did not appear for the rest of August. Sargent was famed as the most energetic and inexhaustible of men, but the strain did sometimes tell, and the BBC felt that it was entitled to a higher share of priorities in its Chief Conductor's timetable.

Sargent criticised

1953 saw the first of a determined series of efforts by officials in Music Department to bring home to Management how bad was the relationship with Sargent, and to suggest that it should not continue. Herbert Murrill had expressed some of the main bones of contention before his death: 'The efficient training of the Symphony Orchestra demands the constant attention and presence of the Chief Conductor, at auditions as well as at concerts and rehearsals. This in Sir Malcolm's case we are not able to secure . . .' And, even more important, even if attendance was forthcoming, 'I have doubts of the results in terms of repertoire. The Third Programme concerts arranged by Sir Malcolm and Mr Isaacs contained few items of especial interest to the musical public served on that wavelength . . . There is a divergence of view here which is not easily bridged.' (The same applied, Murrill noted, to the choice of works to be recorded by the commercial record companies.) 'Sir Malcolm, as I understand, asks for authority not less than that of Head of Music in all matters affecting the Symphony Orchestra. In a special sense the Symphony Orchestra is *his* orchestra: but it is also the BBC's.'

To these criticisms the passage of time had added many more, mainly concerned with Sargent's methods of conducting business between himself and the BBC and about the musical results he was obtaining. A two-pronged attack was made at the beginning of June 1953; one official started a long dissertation on the problem with the statement that 'there should be a record of some of the many personal difficulties which beset our relationship with Sargent'. A typical example concerned Sargent's complaints that he was not consulted on the choice of guest conductors. When he was consulted, he invariably objected. When planning the group of concerts for May 1954, which would follow the Festival Hall season, the Music Department wished to invite Kubelik, but Sargent claimed that all the May concerts were his prerogative to conduct. Personal relationships became strained, in particular between Sargent and the man whom he had recommended should be brought from North Region to act as Head of Music Programmes, Maurice Johnstone. 'I am both amazed and dismayed to discover,' wrote Johnstone, 'to what an extent Sargent expects both staff and resources to be wholly at his disposal.'

Meanwhile, the musical standards of the Orchestra under Sargent's direction were being criticised. An internal report spoke of Sir Malcolm giving 'as shocking a performance of the Brahms First Symphony as I have ever heard in my life. Neither wind nor strings were able to phrase because of his heavy-handed 4-square beat.' Concerning Prom performances of Ravel and Sibelius, the report said: 'It was unfortunately obvious that not only is he out of sympathy with this music but that he did not know it.' Praising the Orchestra, the report continued: 'Sir Malcolm Sargent is fortunate to have so many principals whose innate musicianship determines that the Chief Conductor's chestnuts should be pulled out of the fire for him as often as possible.' The report concluded: 'May I recommend that Sir Malcolm Sargent's work . . . be restricted to popular programmes of inconsequential music . . . and routine works (plus the few choral works that he has made his own) . . .'

In these criticisms there was more than a hint of personal venom. Sargent's brilliant success with the public, especially at the Proms, the rapturous coverage given him by the Press, and his status as the most socially famous conductor in the country, roused the ire of those in the BBC who felt that his music-making was not of a quality to justify this image. In fact, Sargent's command of a small part of the repertory was unrivalled. He was idolised by choral singers, and his performances of big choral works were often supremely exciting. The BBC was mistaken in ever thinking that it could persuade Sargent to enlarge the area of his repertoire significantly; if the Corporation wanted a different kind of conductor, it could well be argued, it should not have appointed a glamorous one.

Sargent aggravated the situation, however, by his methods of dealing with complaints from the BBC. Letters of criticism which he wrote to Music Department officials were frequently read by him over the telephone to the immediate superior of the person concerned before they were delivered, ostensibly to obtain their approval. In September 1952, Director-General Haley retired from the BBC to become Editor of *The Times*, and Basil Nicolls also retired. (Nicolls was knighted at the time.) Sargent found that his close personal contacts with the higher management of the BBC had been reduced. But he was prepared to gild the lily of his agreements with them in an effort to appear the injured party. In August 1953, following the strong criticisms expressed of him, he wrote a handwritten pencil letter to Howgill: 'My dear Dick . . . In the Haley-Nicolls days it was clearly stated that they wished me to do as many public concerts as possible to build up the BBC Orchestra's prestige . . . It's a little hard if I do everything possible to make the Orchestra good for broadcasting and recording, and then am not certain of being allowed to show them off in public.' The clause starting 'if' is the significant one, for this was precisely what Sargent had not done.

Tempers flared, verbally and on paper. 'In my opinion Sargent is ingeniously incorrigible in his ambitious and deceitful manipulation of our machine – and I don't think there can be any respite until time is called by the management,' wrote Frank Wade, Howgill's assistant. The question of Kubelik's appearance in the 1954 May Festival was still unresolved at this time, and it was clear that Sargent meant to pursue the matter. The recently-appointed successor to Nicolls as Director of Home Sound Broadcasting, Lindsay Wellington (formerly the Head of the Home Service), felt it necessary to write to the new Director-General, Sir Ian Jacob, to explain that 'Howgill has been having a certain amount of trouble with Sargent for some time now', and Howgill himself explained to Jacob that

> there is only one reason for your being bothered with this matter. Sargent is likely to be waiting on your doorstep with the complaint that another conductor [Kubelik] has been pencilled for one of the four concerts that we give at the end of May 1954, and he will claim that this annual series is his to conduct in its entirety. This is not so . . .

Howgill, fairer than some of his staff who had borne the brunt of dealing with Sargent, spelled out to the Director-General that it was felt that Sargent was using the BBC appointment and its Orchestra for his own ends, and had a 'perpetual failure to see himself in the correct perspective as an instrument of BBC policy'. (Sargent, for his part, would never have dreamt of describing himself in such terms, and neither, one suspects, would the majority of the concert-going public.) But Howgill added: 'I must say that he and the Orchestra scored a success at Edinburgh. He thrives under festival conditions.' The crux of the matter as it concerned the Orchestra was that 'we are in dire need of a musician and orchestral trainer who could take full advantage of the opportunities we offer for a unique artistic enterprise . . .' That was the main objection to Sargent's tenure of his office, and it made personal considerations less important.

Sargent was told firmly that Kubelik would take part in the 1954 May Festival: it was to be a four-concert survey of Dvořák's work, to mark the fiftieth anniversary of his death; Sargent was to have the opening and closing concerts, plus the third, but Kubelik was to direct the concert performance of the opera *Rusalka* in the second concert. And there, for the moment, the matter rested officially, though the tussels with Music Department went on. During the 1953 Proms, the Orchestra travelled to Edinburgh for an important first performance, Michael Tippett's *Fantasia Concertante on a theme of Corelli*. But Sargent withdrew from conducting the première after seeing the score, and Tippett had to undertake both this first performance and the second performance at the Proms.

1953–4

In the Festival Hall, Sargent had six of the ten concerts, plus an extra concert at the Albert Hall which featured the Brahms *Requiem*. In the first concert (14 October) he directed a first performance, of Elizabeth Maconchy's Coronation Overture, *Proud Thames*; and in the 9 December concert there was a first London performance, of Peter Racine Fricker's Viola Concerto (played by William Primrose). He also included symphonies by Sibelius, Nielsen and Prokofiev, as well as Samuel Barber's First Symphony and Berlioz's *Harold in Italy*. The main bulk of Sargent's repertoire was concentrated on the choral works: on 11 November there was Walton's *Coronation Te Deum*, Holst's *Hymn of Jesus* and Honegger's *King David*, and in the last of the series on 31 March the Fauré *Requiem* and Walton's *Belshazzar's Feast*. The opening concert marked the farewell appearance of Kirsten Flagstad. The other conductors in the series were Beecham, who included Richard Arnell's *Symphonic Portrait: Lord Byron* on 25 November; Paul Kletzki, who was to have conducted Blacher's *Concertante*, though this was replaced by a Vivaldi Concerto Grosso; Barbirolli, who brought to London the William Alwyn Second Symphony which he had done with the Hallé; and Eugene Goossens with his famed reading of *The Rite of Spring*.

It was not an unattractive scheme; but strong evidence that it was not all that BBC programme planners might have wished of it was provided by the fact that in April, between the series and the Symphony Orchestra's May Festival, the Third Programme mounted its own series of five orchestral concerts in the Festival Hall. And the fare was very different from that provided by Sargent's Symphony Orchestra. Four of the concerts employed outside orchestras to give a selection of works which should surely have been featured in the BBC's main Symphony Concert series: on 12 April Walter Goehr conducted the first public performance in England of Messiaen's giant *Turangalîla Symphony*, with the London Symphony Orchestra; on 19 April Hans Rosbaud conducted the London Philharmonic Orchestra and Choir in Mátyás Seiber's cantata *Ulysses*; and then on 3 May Hermann Scherchen returned to conduct the first performance in England of Dallapiccola's opera *Il prigionero*. This series makes plain one of the ironies of the BBC's musical life in the 1950s: that while the Third Programme was at its most thorough in its exploration of neglected and significant twentieth-century pieces, the BBC's own Symphony Orchestra did not take a full part in that exploration.

Studio concerts in 1953–4 got off to a lively start with those two impulsive pieces of 1920s motor music, Ravel's *Bolero* and Honegger's *Pacific 231*, conducted in the same concert by Clarence Raybould. In October Walter

Goehr returned, ever adventurous, with *L'Ascension* by Messiaen and the *Greek Dances* by the Schoenberg pupil Nikos Skalkottas. At the time of Sargent's Festival Hall concert on 28 October, the Orchestra recorded a programme for television, *The Conductor Speaks*, in which Sargent introduced and conducted music by Strauss, Rimsky-Korsakov and Fauré. At the end of November and the start of December Sargent included an unusual number of non-mainstream works (at the time when he was also preparing the Barber Symphony and Fricker Viola Concerto): the *Sinfonia Concertante* by Szymanowski, with Irene Kohler; Berkeley's Flute Concerto, and Herbert Howells's *A Kent Yeoman's Wooing Song*. Hermann Scherchen returned for a concert, as did Heinz Unger; in December Boult conducted a concert to celebrate twenty-one years of Overseas Broadcasting with a daunting programme including music by six composers from Commonwealth countries: Douglas Lilburn (New Zealand), Arnold van Wyk (South Africa), C. J. A. Wadis (India), Healey Willan (Canada), John Antill and Arthur Benjamin (both Australia).

At the start of 1954 Sargent spent a substantial period with the Orchestra including a Festival Hall concert and visits to Birmingham and Hanley; works included the British première of the Concertino for trumpet, strings and piano by Jolivet, as well as Holbrooke's *Byron*. In March Stanford Robinson was entrusted with a new project by the Third Programme: a rehearsal and recording session of new works, which were not broadcast at once. This was an experimental venture which does not appear to have been often repeated. On this occasion the works were James Stevens's First Symphony, Leonard Scott's *Introduzione*, *Fugato*, *Andante*, and Kenneth Leighton's Overture, *Primavera Romana*.

During the first part of the year Sargent took the Orchestra to Bristol, Chester, Liverpool and Belfast. Two important visitors arrived in April and May: Pierre Monteux, who included the British première of Creston's Second Symphony and *Les Éolides* by Franck in his studio programmes; and Leopold Stokowski, who as usual conducted some English music – Vaughan Williams and Bax – as well as William Schuman's *Circus Overture* and (on 5 May) Glière's Concerto for coloratura soprano and orchestra, sung by Ilse Hollweg. Clarence Raybould conducted a studio performance of Frank Martin's *Golgotha*, of which Sargent was later to give the public British première on 16 April. Then came the much disputed May season of Dvořák concerts, and a visit to Southend, plus a group of English works in the studio – Bliss's *A Colour Symphony* and Gordon Jacob's *Laudate Dominum*, which Sargent conducted, and Lennox Berkeley's Concerto for two pianos, which Paul Beard had to direct in Sargent's absence.

The year saw a major change in the BBC's concert management office: W. W. Thompson, who had joined the BBC at the time it took over the Proms in 1927, retired after running every season of the BBC Symphony Orchestra's public concerts since its foundation. 'Tommy' Thompson had not only controlled the administrative side of public concert giving; he had taken a full part in advising on programme content, especially for the Prom seasons. With his retirement, a new scheme of organisation was introduced: George Willoughby, who had looked after the Orchestra's affairs since the war, was made Concerts and Orchestral Manager. (The administration of the Orchestra and of public concerts was thus united; they were to be separated again in 1964.) Under Willoughby, there were two assistants: Dorothy Wood, Thompson's experienced and invaluable No. 2, was now designated Assistant Concerts Manager; W. G. Paston, who had acted as Willoughby's assistant, had the title Assistant Orchestral Manager. R. G. Paterson, and later Freda Grove, were also assistants in the concerts department. Bill Edwards was orchestral porter (a post he was to retain almost until the Orchestra's fiftieth anniversary), and his senior, the remarkable Edgar Mays (an indispensable figure in Orchestra folklore, a gentle tyrant for conductors and players), was retained in the special post of Assistant (Orchestra and Artists).

To the Continent

In June 1954 Sargent took the Orchestra on its first tour of the Continent since he became Chief Conductor, and the first tour since June 1947. There were to be concerts in Düsseldorf, Hamburg, The Hague, Amsterdam, Maastricht and finally Brussels, with Clifford Curzon as solo pianist, all conducted by Sargent. Advance publicity emphasised Sargent's fame and popularity in England: 'The Conductor with the Carnation', was the headline in the *Düsseldorfer Nachrichten* for 10 June: 'His smile, his elegance and the carnation in his buttonhole are famous. He is no Bohemian and likes to relax at one of those magnificent social occasions that form the favourite topic of the illustrated papers. But as a musician he takes himself very seriously and relents neither for himself nor for his musicians . . .' The Orchestra arrived in Düsseldorf on 14 June, and immediately found itself the centre of a storm about whether the city's best grand piano should be transported to the Apollo Theatre from the Schumann Hall where it was housed. The city authorities refused to let it be moved, and it was only after negotiations between the British Council and the Mayor in person that the piano was moved. Nevertheless, the opening concert of the tour was a brilliant success. With Sargent at his most commanding, the programme of Beethoven's

Emperor, Britten's *Young Person's Guide* and Dvořák's Seventh Symphony proved an ideal mix. The papers wrote that 'even those who expected something out of the ordinary did not cease to be astonished. This English radio orchestra is of international standard and has developed a style of performance that lends it unmistakeable individuality . . . this is a perfect musical ensemble of confident artists . . .' 'The ensemble is technically above all praise . . . Sargent is a master of the art, which might be called a British characteristic, that of remaining detached and yet of giving what is actually in the score with fascinating definition and exactitude.' The Dvořák symphony, little known in Germany, was found especially interesting by the critics, while the Britten piece was thought a delightful way to introduce the Orchestra's virtuoso players to the audience.

Two days later the Orchestra moved to Hamburg, where it played for the first time in the famous Musikhalle. Wolfgang Vogler in *Die Welt* called the concert one

> that will long remain in our memories. . . . This orchestra has long been well known in Hamburg through the BBC transmissions. All the greater, then, is the pleasure derived from personal contact with the art of these British musicians. What were the special qualities? First of all the purity of sound, the rich and full string section, the sensitive woodwind and the brass, capable of both light and shade. Then there was the precision and effortless virtuosity of the ensemble, the clarity of sound even in the most powerful climax. . . . By no means the least important was the personal art of the youthfully slim, vital man on the rostrum with his energetic and vigorous gestures . . .

In this programme Curzon played the Rawsthorne Second Concerto, which was respected, and Sargent conducted the Vaughan Williams Fantasia on a theme of Thomas Tallis, which was loved. A critic in the *Hamburger Echo* expressed curiously the relevant sentiment that Sargent, 'a fiery and most active conductor who directs with such conviction', led one 'to forget that the gods have decreed that the creative inevitability of the artistic moment should be founded on the sweated labour of intensive rehearsal'.

From Germany the Orchestra travelled to Holland, which they had visited on their previous tour in 1947, and on 18 June played once again in Scheveningen. They were on this occasion the guests of the Holland Festival, and a large audience crowded the Kurzaal to hear Curzon in the Emperor, Haydn's Military Symphony (No. 100) and Vaughan Williams' Sixth Symphony. Impressions were mixed: few Dutch critics liked the Vaughan Williams, criticising it more for its length than for its idiom, but all praised

Sargent's vigorous conducting and the virtuosity of the ensemble. Many were surprised that no allowance had been made for the conventional Dutch habit of starting concerts late – but as the broadcast to England could not be kept waiting, Sargent was on the podium for both halves of the concert before many of the audience had taken their seats. 'Sit down, please,' he said, apparently rather sharply, as he was about to begin the second half.

And so to Amsterdam, where the concert on 19 June included Curzon in the Mozart A Major Concerto, K488, and the Walton Symphony which the Orchestra had played on its first Continental tour in 1936, and which the Amsterdam audience had had the chance of hearing played by their own orchestra, under Willem van Otterloo, just a few months previously. The Amsterdam audience was discriminating in its reaction to the concert: the critics said plainly that the Orchestra was too large and fierce for the Mozart Concerto (even though Sargent used a smaller group of strings to accompany the solo passages), and that Beethoven's Second Symphony did not show Sargent's technique at its best. With only a couple of exceptions, however, they praised the Walton Symphony as a most powerful work.

Then the Orchestra travelled to Maastricht and gave a concert which formed the climax of a week of events devoted to British culture (or at least one of the highlights – a local paper said that the other had been 'a cocktail' at the British Club on the previous evening). The Orchestra played in the old Dominican Church, which was nearly full. Britten, Holst and Delius all featured in the programme, plus the Dvořák Seventh Symphony and Berlioz's *Beatrice and Benedict* Overture. The critics' reactions were fascinating: Holst's *Perfect Fool* ballet music was thought to be 'rather empty' and even 'passé, uninteresting, noisy and unimportant', but the Delius works (*La Calinda* from Koanga and the *Irmelin* Prelude) were adjudged 'very beautiful' or at least 'very friendly'. The Britten *Young Person's Guide* was warmly welcomed: Britten 'shows himself to be an unparalleled master of instrumentation', and the performances were thought to be vivid and lively. At the end of the concert the Mayor of Maastricht presented Sargent with a huge laurel wreath with flowers and ribbons in the municipal colours.

So to the last journey and the last concert of the tour, which was in Brussels on 21 June. The series finished in great style with a concert at which Queen Elisabeth of the Belgians was present. It was a gala occasion, attended by the British Ambassador, Sir Christopher Warner, and many of the Embassy staff. Again the programme included the Vaughan Williams Sixth Symphony and Curzon in the Emperor, plus two of the short showpieces of the tour, the Berlioz and Brahms Overtures. The concert was a great success, if chiefly a social one: Sargent, always on the best of terms with royalty, got on extremely well with the musical Queen, and reported to delighted gossip columnists when he returned to London that she had invited him the following morning to accompany her in some Mozart violin sonatas.

A second attack on Sargent

The tour had proved that, in good conditions, the Orchestra could play excellently and was still responsive to the enlivening force of Sargent's direction. He was the ideal person to direct them on such occasions, making them play with precision and brilliance. If all the BBC's concerts had taken place in this atmosphere, Sargent might have been a more appropriate Chief Conductor; but it was impossible to avoid the routine aspects of the task. It would be wrong to say that Sargent had so alienated his musicians that they no longer played well for him: they continued to respect and enjoy his music-making, even though they had frequent disagreements with him. It was on the BBC side of the affairs that matters were becoming beyond redemption. In July 1954, just after this successful tour, Maurice Johnstone, the Head of Music Programmes, argued a case for taking the step of giving Sargent a year's notice as Chief Conductor, which would expire in July 1955, when he would have held the post for five years.

The case against Sargent from the BBC's point of view was overwhelming. He was an uneconomic proposition in that he devoted too little of his time to the Orchestra. The situation was likely to deteriorate, as he was still accepting large amounts of outside work for the 1954–5 season and was doing only about thirty per cent of the Orchestra's work with them. Artistically his results had been very mixed: 'Sargent is an immensely skilful conductor. His performances are always efficient and often vital but the heights and depths and poetry are beyond his vision . . . popular success in established music is his whole ambition.' It was thought that the Orchestra produced subtler results under guest conductors, and a press notice of such an occasion was quoted: 'The Orchestra played wonderfully: why doesn't it always?' As an administrative executive dealing with the BBC, Sargent had been a disaster, showing no appreciation of the nature of the BBC's work in planning and co-ordinating programmes for the various services; his absences were so frequent as to make regular consultation difficult. Johnstone wrote: 'The irony of the present regime lies in the bitter fact that the Orchestra is generally at its best when its chief conductor is absent. At such times relief is manifest . . .'

It was argued that Sargent was most successful as a guest conductor, on special occasions, when his gifts of vitality and drive could be put to best use. As a conductor of an orchestra which necessarily undertook routine studio engagements, and had to undertake unusual repertoire, he was not the right person. The case was sound. Johnstone wrote fiercely:

> Music is merely Sargent's shop window. He has no sense of public, artistic or functional responsibility. He is indifferent to the morale and welfare of the Orchestra.... His sense of loyalty to music staff is non-existent and his sense of co-operation is vestigial . . .

It has to be admitted in hindsight that the basic fault was not Sargent's, however. The leopard, particularly such a colourful one as Sargent, does not change its spots. The case that was made out against him was very substantially the one that could have been made out against appointing him in the first place. The BBC was idealistic in thinking that Sargent would adapt to its machine. It was also narrow in its view if it thought that, in the changed atmosphere of music-making after the war, any conductor would adopt the same attitude that Adrian Boult had maintained throughout his twenty years' service.

Unease about giving Sargent a year's notice – a far more positive step than simply deciding not to renew his contract, had it been for a fixed term – prevented Howgill from making a recommendation at that point. Besides, those less concerned with the day-to-day running of matters in Music Division felt that axes were being ground by the BBC musical bureaucrats which bore little relevance to artistic matters. Problems of administration were not grounds on which to dismiss a conductor, it was said. Sargent still had strong support among Orchestra members, from influential critics like Frank Howes, and from important members of the BBC hierarchy who did not begin to appreciate the points about musical standards or repertoire. For these people the prestige of Sargent's name linked to that of the Corporation in such vastly successful undertakings as the Proms or foreign tours was important, and well worth maintaining.

1954–5

So the matter rested. The 1954 Proms once again reasserted Sargent's prominence, for they were a Diamond Jubilee celebration of Wood's first Proms in 1895. Five orchestras shared the work (as in 1953) and Beecham appeared at the age of seventy-five for, unbelievably, only the second time – the first had been in 1915. But Sargent bore the 'major burden and stress of the arduous season', as Howgill put it in his introduction to the prospectus, and he of course conducted the actual Jubilee concert on 10 August, which included items from the first Henry Wood Prom. Sargent repeated from the studio the Jolivet Concertino, and revived Ireland's *These Things shall be* alongside his Piano Concerto for the composer's seventy-fifth birthday. Sargent's programmes included several novelties which had already been broadcast from the studio; he stepped down in favour of John Hollingsworth for Fricker's Piano Concerto and Denis Ap Ivor's *A Mirror for Witches*, and in favour of Malcolm Arnold for his Harmonica Concerto.

As if to reinforce the contrast between Sargent's regime and that of his predecessor, Sir Adrian Boult returned to the Orchestra for a long spell at the start of the 1954–5 season, including a typically wide-ranging selection of works: the large-scale choral work *Voices of Night* by Franz Reizenstein, the First Symphony of Robert Simpson, Tippett's Concerto for Double String Orchestra, Rubbra's Second Symphony, and Franck's Symphonic Poem *Les Djinns*. There were three performances of Frank Martin's Harpsichord Concerto with George Malcolm, and one of Pfitzner's Cello Concerto. This strong line-up culminated in the first Festival Hall concert of the season, which included Campoli in Moeran's Violin Concerto. The rehearsals of the Reizenstein are recalled as one of the few occasions when Boult lost his temper: the composer's eager and constant offers of advice finally became too much for the conductor. To Reizenstein's 'Could I just make one point, Sir Adrian?' Boult replied with a resounding 'No!' that echoed round the studio.

Equally welcome to the planners in the Music Division must have been the next long stint by a guest conductor, the Frenchman Jean Martinon. Through the second half of October he was able to explore a wide range of French music, paying special attention to the music of Roussel, whose four symphonies were all broadcast on the Third Programme in this period, along with his choral setting of Psalm 80. He did Prokofiev's ballet *Chout* and introduced his own *Sinfonietta*. Martin's *Petite Sinfonia Concertante* also appeared in the programmes. Martinon's Festival Hall concert featured Ravel's *L'Enfant et les Sortilèges*.

Not until November did Sargent come to the Orchestra for the first time that season, and the bulk of the work was in public. Two BBC concerts in the Festival Hall presented Shostakovich's Fifth Symphony and Rubinstein in Beethoven's Fourth Concerto (replacing the Emperor), and Delius's *A Mass of Life*. For the Royal Philharmonic Society, however, on 17 November Sargent and the BBC Orchestra gave one of the significant first performances in their collaboration: that of Rubbra's Sixth Symphony. More typical fare followed, when on 28 November Sargent took the Orchestra to the Albert Hall for a Beethoven concert in Holt's Celebrity Series; a Tchaikovsky programme was also given on 12 December. In December Beecham conducted a Festival Hall concert, which included a thrilling account of the Sibelius

Second Symphony, one of the highlights of the 1950s; the performance was later issued on record, complete with Beecham's grunts of encouragement. He also directed Mozart's C minor Mass in the studio. The Orchestra was permitted to pre-record its Christmas Day broadcast under Clarence Raybould on 21 December – a special exception was made to the rule of live broadcasts for this occasion. Stanford Robinson took the Orchestra through another rehearsal and record-session of new works: Daniel Jones's Concert Overture, Leonard Scott's Three Symphonic Studies and R. W. Mann's Music for Orchestra.

1955 opened with a tribute to Tippett on his fiftieth birthday, in the form of his own *Birthday Suite* (written for the birth of Prince Charles) conducted by Barbirolli. Sargent had a short period in the middle of the month in which he gave the London première of perhaps the longest-lived of the works he introduced: the cantata *Hodie* by Vaughan Williams. A Verdi *Requiem* at the Albert Hall and an HMV recording of Tchaikovsky's Fifth Symphony completed this visit. Sargent left for Philadelphia, and it was arranged that Eugene Ormandy should undertake an exchange visit to the BBC. He was in charge from 2 to 6 February, giving a Festival Hall concert including Barber's *Second Essay* for orchestra, and studio concerts featuring Persichetti's Fourth Symphony and *Epigraph* by the American composer Norman Dello Joio. Rudolf Schwarz also took the Orchestra in this period for a programme of curiosities: Peragallo's Violin Concerto (played by André Gertler), Hans Gál's Concertino, and Kenneth Leighton's Overture *Primavera Romana*, a work from Stanford Robinson's try-out sessions.

Sargent returned on 19 February, reviving Lambert's neglected choral work *Summer's Last Will and Testament* and then giving another popular concert for Harold Holt. He took the Orchestra to Norwich and Peterborough, did a Wood Birthday Concert at the Albert Hall, and then two Festival Hall concerts, each with points of interest: the first had Henry Holst playing the Frank Martin Violin Concerto; the second contained Bloch's *Sacred Service*. Sargent also gave the last of the Festival Hall concerts, with Tippett's *Ritual Dances*, but he did not work with the Orchestra in the studio during this period. The composer Hindemith returned to direct his Whitman *Requiem* setting. Other guests were William Steinberg, Walter Goehr (who conducted the *Cantata Secularis* by Seiber) and David Willcocks, who was entrusted with a repeat of Julius Harrison's Mass. Rudolf Schwarz returned for a distinguished series of three broadcast performances of Beethoven's *Missa Solemnis* on 15, 16 and 20 April, for which the soloists included Joan Sutherland and Peter Pears.

Then the Orchestra left for a provincial tour in the north of England under Sargent. Programmes were frankly popular, but audiences had the chance to hear Gina Bachauer in Rachmaninov's Third Piano Concerto (Blackburn and Leeds) or Ireland's Concerto (Bradford). Sheffield and Hull had purely orchestral concerts, dominated by the Berlioz *Symphonie fantastique*.

The now traditional May Festival of 1955 departed strikingly from the usual pattern: for once, Sargent did not conduct the majority of the concerts. The BBC had secured the return to the Symphony Orchestra of one of its best-loved conductors, Bruno Walter. This was one foreign guest conductor whose stature Sargent could scarcely dispute. However, Sargent himself entered into correspondence with Walter in an attempt to influence the programmes he chose, thus once again irritating the BBC administrators. The scheme as it finally emerged gave Sargent the prominence of the first and last concerts: the first included a première which was likely to attract wide attention, that of the Bliss Violin Concerto, while the last repeated Rubbra's Sixth Symphony and had Arrau as soloist – part of this was televised. At the centre of the Festival Sargent also directed Beethoven's Ninth, plus Kodály's *Missa Brevis*. Sibelius and Ravel, together with two Bach orchestrations, made up the scheme. This was surely the best group of programmes in Sargent's BBC life. Walter conducted Mahler's First, Bruckner's Ninth, Strauss's *Tod und Verklärung* and Mozart's *Requiem*. He was perhaps more passive, less inspiring to the Orchestra than on his visits in the 1930s, but he was nevertheless warmly welcomed and deeply revered by a new generation of audiences.

Just before the 1955 Proms, Aaron Copland visited the Orchestra to conduct his own *Appalachian Spring* in a programme otherwise directed by Vilem Tausky, who on 11 June gave the British première of Martinů's Sixth Symphony. And Boult produced the Orchestra's contribution to an ambitious Liszt series for the Third Programme with four works, Psalm 13, the *Cantico del Sole*, *Hymne de l'enfant*, and two episodes from Lenau's *Faust*.

The 1955 Prom season brought out of the studio the Panufnik *Sinfonia rustica*; Sargent repeated his performances of the Rubbra Sixth Symphony and the Bliss Violin Concerto. He included a sequence from Walton's opera *Troilus and Cressida*, which he had premièred at Covent Garden. But John Hollingsworth again undertook many of the novelties, and the one major new work, Gordon Jacob's Cello Concerto, was performed by the Bournemouth Orchestra under Charles Groves. The Orchestra appeared again at the Edinburgh Festival at the end of August, though with less interesting programmes than previously; Shostakovich's fine Tenth Symphony was broadcast for the first time in this country.

A third offensive

Meanwhile Sargent's position was still unresolved. It had been discussed endlessly during the year within the BBC, and some outside opinions had been sought. Caution had so far prevailed, but as the anniversary of Sargent's engagement came round, Maurice Johnstone once more pleaded for the ending of his contract:

> Views against replacement have been based on factors neither essential nor relevant to the two basic issues which are 1. the terms of Sargent's contract [which are] completely contrary to normal practice, i.e. a symphony orchestra should have a permanent conductor in the fullest sense of the word . . . 2. the failure of Sargent as a musical leader, administrator and employee in an organisation with very great musical responsibilities . . . Sargent's methods, and his attitude towards music staff, have antagonised most of your colleagues . . . I think you are well aware that a happy and successful professional relationship is . . . impossible.

Johnstone asked again for 'a totally different type of permanent conductor'.

The feeling that the attacks on Sargent were partly personally motivated prevented action being taken. But during the following season matters finally came to a head. Sargent's appearances with the Orchestra were prominent in public (six out of the ten symphony concerts) but very sparse in the studio. He began the Festival Hall season with Vaughan Williams' *Job* and inaugurated a Sibelius symphony series on the Third Programme for the composer's ninetieth birthday. Then he returned for the first public performance in this country of Frank Martin's *Golgotha* on 9 November (a work which had been prepared by Raybould for studio performance) and a studio concert including Holst's *Beni Mora* oriental suite. A popular Tchaikovsky concert for Holt in the Albert Hall and a television concert completed this week. At the end of November he gave a Beethoven concert, and accompanied two unusual violin concertos, by Lars Erik Larsson and Benjamin Frankel. A longer period in January and February included several celebrations of Mozart's bicentenary (including the C minor Mass at the Festival Hall) and also Rubbra's Improvisation for violin and orchestra. Television recorded the Berlioz *Symphonie fantastique* and there was a performance of Honegger's Fourth Symphony in the studio; and that was about all. On 21 March the Festival Hall series ended with the first performance of Rubbra's specially commissioned Piano Concerto, played by Denis Matthews, alongside Verdi's *Te Deum* and Vaughan Williams' *Dona nobis pacem*.

Once again the repertoire for which the BBC was chiefly known had to be conducted by others. The season's chief guests were Sir Eugene Goossens, who included the gimmicky Concerto for Jazz Band by Rolf Liebermann in his Festival Hall concert, and did weightier matters in the studio, including Fricker's Second Symphony (4 November) and Enesco's *Sinfonia Concertante* for cello and orchestra. On 28 and 29 October he directed his own large-scale oratorio *The Apocalypse*. Walter Goehr gave the British première of the Second Piano Concerto by the young American Lukas Foss, and Stanford Robinson directed a 'new works recording session' of Graham Whettam's Second Symphony for soprano, chorus and orchestra. The Orchestra also contributed to an important studio opera production of Bartók's *Bluebeard's Castle* under Stanford Robinson in the Camden Theatre on 12 November 1954. In December and January Alfred Wallenstein spent long periods with the Orchestra with a wide-ranging repertoire including American music by Dello Joio and Walter Piston (Fourth Symphony), Berlioz's *Romeo and Juliet* and a curiosity by Charles Loeffler, *The Dream of Tintagiles*, with Harry Danks as viola soloist. Ernest Toch's Second Symphony was heard on 13 and 14 January. A distinguished visitor at the end of 1955 was Otto Klemperer: he gave a Festival Hall concert of Debussy, Mozart and Brahms, and in the studio conducted the Bruckner Seventh Symphony and Brahms's *German Requiem*.

February 1956 should have been dominated by the visit of Hans Schmidt-Isserstedt, but that month the Musicians' Union called a strike of all BBC orchestral musicians, the only such strike to have affected the Symphony Orchestra before the more serious dispute in its fiftieth year. Ironically, the problems were not ones which especially concerned the BBC's staff orchestras, for what was being argued were the rates of pay for casually employed musicians, and the terms of their contracts which allowed for the televising of broadcasts. The Musicians' Union also wanted the BBC to agree not to use its house orchestras on television, a request which an Industrial Court had already turned down in 1953. Staff orchestras became involved in the dispute because it coincided with negotiations about an increase in minimum salaries for staff musicians. In particular, the BBC was about to increase the extra payments for television work, and the scales were being discussed with the Union. But lack of agreement about the casual rates caused these negotiations to be suspended. A statement by Sir Ian Jacob, the Director-General, said that 'the BBC places a high value on the services of all those musicians who contribute to the broadcasting service . . . although it must continue to resist any proposed terms and conditions which it feels to be unreasonable and not in the interests of the broadcasting service and its listeners and viewers . . .' The strike went on for a fortnight, and broadcasting suffered remarkably little: one Festival Hall concert was cancelled, and foreign tapes of performances conducted by Schmidt-Isserstedt had to be substituted for studio concerts. By 24 February, though, the Orchestra was back in action, giving the first broadcast performance of Fortner's *Capriccio and Finale*, while on 26 February it played the Blacher *Concertante* which should have featured in the Festival Hall concert.

With the Orchestra back, Sargent again took it on a tour which went as far as Ireland. Londonderry and Belfast were on the schedule, and there were also visits during the season to Huddersfield, Swansea, Bristol and Salisbury Cathedral. For reasons which are not entirely clear, the May Festival in 1956 appeared only in a very truncated form: two concerts, both conducted by Pierre Monteux, each including a French work: the Bizet *L'Arlésienne* Suite on 9 May and Chausson's Symphony in B flat on 11 May. Sargent, as so often, was busy with other things.

Scandinavia by air

In June 1956 Sargent took the Orchestra on another major continental tour, this time to Scandinavia. It was the first occasion on which the Orchestra had flown on tour; for some it was their first experience of aircraft. It was made the more memorable by the importance of the concerts that were to be given: two contributions in Helsinki to the Sibelius Festival honouring the 91-year-old composer; and concerts in Stockholm which were to be attended not only by the Swedish Royal Family, but by Queen Elizabeth and Prince Philip (who were in Scandinavia for the opening of the Olympic Equestrian Games). Sargent was in his element. The opening concerts took the Orchestra to the famous Tivoli Gardens in Copenhagen. King Frederick attended the concerts and followed the scores, for he was an enthusiastic amateur conductor. (Sargent even offered him one of the rehearsals, but the King treated the offer as a gesture of politeness, no more.) The Copenhagen programmes mixed display pieces with serious works in a manner calculated to win both respect and enthusiasm: Vaughan Williams' London Symphony in the first, plus Dvořák's *Carnaval*, Brahms's Academic Festival Overture and Rimsky's *Capriccio Espagnol*. In the second, the Tchaikovsky *Pathétique*, and Sargent's favourite display piece for his Orchestra, the Britten *Young Person's Guide*. This was topped up with Grieg's Lyric Suite and two overtures, Sullivan's *Di Ballo* and Berlioz's *Beatrice and Benedict*. Scarcely programmes to challenge serious listeners, but they had the desired effect and the popular enthusiasm was enormous.

Orchestra members enjoyed themselves greatly, with Sargent as keen a participant in the post-concert parties as anyone (though he was under considerable physical strain, and after these two concerts was reported to be in need of sustained rest). Then to Norway, where the third, now well-established, Bergen Festival was host to the Orchestra for two concerts. These were the fourth and fifth in a series exploring many byways of Scandinavian music, and it was appropriate that the BBC should play some native works. Sargent included in the first programme two short pieces, one *Siljuslatten* by Harald Saeverud, born in 1897, and in the other *Carnival in Paris* by Johan Svendsen (1840–1911). After those concerts on 5 and 7 June, there was another journey to a third Scandinavian nation, Finland, for the Sibelius Festival in Helsinki. Two concerts were given on Sunday 10 and Monday 11 June, both all-Sibelius programmes. *Finlandia, En Saga*, and the *Three Historical Scenes*, Op. 25 were followed by the First Symphony in the opening concert; and then *Tapiola*, the Third and Seventh Symphonies in the second concert. Sargent was grateful for the acclaim which he received from experts in Sibelius's music for his readings, for he had often been criticised by English critics for his departure from the supposedly authentic readings of Kajanus. The day following the second concert, the aged Sibelius himself played host to Sargent and some members of the Orchestra at his home in Järvenpää. They brought with them a book of signatures from the whole Orchestra and staff, which they presented to him. Sargent was photographed with the composer, and brought back in return a signed photograph of Sibelius, inscribed 'with gratitude and admiration'.

And so to Sweden, to Stockholm, where one of the most glamorous occasions in the Orchestra's career took place in the Konserthuset on 12 June. In the presence of the Queens of Sweden and England with Prince Philip, Princess Margaret and members of the Swedish Royal family, Sargent conducted Sidelius's First Symphony, Britten's *Young Person's Guide*, Haydn's London Symphony and an overture by the Swedish composer Hilding Rosenberg. The concert was a triumph – one of the landmarks of Sargent's career. Indeed, according to his biographer Charles Reid this was the concert which was recalled for Sargent on his deathbed by Lord Mountbatten. 'You have been one of our great ambassadors throughout the Commonwealth and all over the world. I shall never forget your concert in Stockholm . . . At the end the whole audience stood up. All over the place you put Britain's name sky-high.' Sargent would have wished no more than to have brought about such an event. He was honoured by the King of Sweden the next day with the award of Commander of the Order of the North Star; and that night concluded the Orchestra's tour with an Elgar, Beethoven and Brahms programme in the Konserthuset. It was a great climax to Sargent's career with the Orchestra.

Sargent removed

Ironically, it was just after this triumph that Sargent's position was finally reconsidered. His attitude to contemporary music had been the subject of more complaints. One concerned his broadcast of the Frankel Violin Concerto, where he instructed the announcer to introduce it with the sentence: 'Although it is contemporary music, it is a work of appealing intensity.' The Salisbury Cathedral concert also brought complaints from those who felt that Sargent made himself too much the centre of attention on the occasion. In response to a request from Leonard Isaacs that he conduct a modern work, Sargent replied, after looking at the score: 'I cannot understand how any composer could allow himself to write a work so completely lacking in melodic interest . . . It is just another of those compositions which consist really of a succession of modern harmonies. I don't know what modern composers are coming to . . .'

Perhaps the most powerful move, however, came in a considered report on the Orchestra's playing standard from a member of the BBC staff who did not deal regularly with Sargent nor have any personal axe to grind against him. Robert Simpson, the Assistant Third Programme Music Organiser, submitted a frank discussion of the playing of every section of the Orchestra, and concluded:

> The above strictures may seem harsh, and I would like to qualify them by saying that with very few changes of personnel, the Orchestra could still be one of the best in Europe. For this the right conductor is needed. The present holder of that office is, in my opinion, unsuitable. . . . In order to make this Orchestra what it ought to be, one of the major ones of the world, it is necessary to have a conductor who has the following qualities:
> a) Devotion to music and willingness to become a genuine member of the BBC.
> b) A powerfully authoritative and utterly professional technique coupled with a striking and unequivocal artistic personality, both sensitive and dynamic.
> c) Breadth of musical sympathies and readiness to be the selfless vehicle of new and unfamiliar music as well as that in the repertory.

It was clear that Sargent fulfilled only part of the first and of the second of these demands. The pressure for change within the BBC was now overwhelming, and, following a further insistent series of demands from Maurice Johnstone at the beginning of April, Howgill realised that action had to be taken. He had probably acted wisely in delaying as long as possible, for he wished to be sure that the matter would be beyond dispute when it was finally raised with the BBC management. He gathered together the most recent reports on the Orchestra, some detailed accounts of the Department's workings with Sargent (or rather, lack of them), and sent them to Lindsay Wellington, the Director of Home Broadcasting. With a somewhat weary reluctance, he added this note:

> There is little in the attached documents with which I can disagree and most of the strictures on Sargent have been discussed at various times between you and me over the past few years. If I have been over-tolerant I have not lacked patience but we have got nowhere with it all and it is impossible for me to go on regarding the present state of affairs as satisfactory. I am not referring to day-to-day difficulties but to artistic results. Sargent started as Chief Conductor of the BBC Symphony Orchestra with the 1950 Promenade Concerts and now, after nearly six years, none of us can say with conviction that the Orchestra is the aesthetic body of the highest class that we feel it could and should be. The simple fact is that it is just not a trained orchestra in the full artistic meaning of the term. . . . Sargent has enjoyed the title of Chief Conductor but has remained in essence a guest who conducts it more often than do other conductors. He has had, in effect, the best of both worlds. What is really required is a conductor who will concentrate on the orchestra and its programmes in close collaboration with ourselves for approximately six weeks in every eight from October to June inclusive and who will not during the period compete with us in any way. I do not think that such an arrangement would be acceptable to Sargent at this stage of his career or that having regard to his limitations any noticeable improvement would result.
>
> I propose, therefore, that Sargent be given notice of the termination of his contract to take effect at the end of June, 1957, with no reason given other than that we shall wish to make a change after seven years. I propose also that at the same time we offer him a contract to continue with the Promenade Concerts on the same numerical basis and, of course, tell him that we will hope to continue to engage him from time to time as a guest conductor.

It was a moderate, wise summary of a situation which had roused many passions; and it was effective. Howgill and Wellington between them ensured that the decision was carried through. Sargent was informed, and sought an interview with Director-General Sir Ian Jacob. As a result of Sargent's representations, Jacob came back to Howgill with an astonishing suggestion which was clearly Sargent's: that there should be two associate Chief Conductors of the Symphony Orchestra. One would be responsible for the Orchestra and carry the major part of the work from October to May, including the training of the Orchestra; the other would be Chief Conductor of the Prom season from July to September, and would participate in the winter work to the extent required by the Music Division. The role of conductor for foreign and provincial tours would be divided, a decision on each occasion being taken by the Music Division according to circumstances. Jacob concluded that this 'is not of course a final specification, but it sets out the kind of arrangement which might give us what we want while being fair to Sargent'. Howgill's reaction is not reported, except that the word 'fair' on Jacob's note has been quizzically underlined. The suggestion was clearly absurd, simply because the work of the second conductor, which Sargent envisaged for himself, did not amount to anything like that demanded of a Chief Conductor. But it was clearly necessary that the break between the BBC and Sargent be seen to be as minor as possible. The BBC would obviously wish to retain Sargent's services in connection with the Proms, for which he had built up a following which helped to ensure the success of the series. So a compromise was suggested: there would be a new Chief Conductor, but Sargent would have the title of Conductor-in-Chief of the Promenade Concerts. Sargent would also be the Chief Guest Conductor of the Orchestra, doing a minimum of six weeks between each September and June, with two concerts in the Royal Restival Hall symphony series included. Foreign tours which had been already agreed and the May Festival in 1959 would be Sargent's responsibility.

These terms were agreed by all concerned on 29 August. A statement which was as positive as possible was issued on 11 September 1956:

> In order to give Sir Malcolm Sargent greater freedom for his many engagements it has been mutually agreed by him and the BBC that from the autumn of 1957 he will relinquish his post as Chief Conductor of the BBC Symphony Orchestra. He will be Conductor-in-Chief of the Promenade Concerts, and chief Guest Conductor of the BBC Symphony Orchestra in sound and television at other times of the year.

The Sargent era was effectively over, even though there was a year's more music-making to come. Sargent, as might have been expected, communicated the news to his Orchestra in the most dramatic way possible. Not a word had been heard of the decision, though its possibility had been frequently discussed. The evening the announcement was due to be made was the Tuesday in the last week of the Proms season. The BBC Orchestra was not playing that night, and so Sargent, with the lavish generosity to individual musicians which had marked all his dealings with them, took Orchestra members out to dinner at one of his favourite haunts, the restaurant at

London Zoo. Players recalled the quite exceptionally relaxed atmosphere at the party, as the Proms neared their close, with Sargent at his most witty and charming. Then, just before ten, Sargent insisted that the radio was put on. As Orchestra members sat listening, baffled, to the Home Service news, they heard the brief formal announcement which was being issued to the press that evening. Immediately the atmosphere of the evening changed. Taken quite unawares, the musicians did not know how to react; in a stunned atmosphere the party broke up. Sargent, at his most emotional, burst into tears. He stood at the door and grasped each member by the hand as they left, the tears pouring down his face. He thanked each player individually for their work. To many of them it was a disconcerting, unbearable experience.

1956–7

The 1956–7 season was something of a limbo, during which Sargent played out his notice. In fact, during that Festival Hall series he conducted more concerts than ever before, mainly because Igor Stravinsky, who was to have conducted a concert of his own music, became ill and was unable to do more than attend the concert on 5 December at which his Symphony in C, Symphony of Psalms, and complete *Pulcinella* were performed. Sargent's other concerts included Haydn's *Seasons*, Shostakovich's Ninth Symphony with Bax's Violin Concerto, Elgar's *The Dream of Gerontius* (as a Henry Wood birthday concert), Vaughan Williams' Eighth, Orff's *Carmina Burana* with the *bonne bouche* of the first London performance of Walton's Johannesburg Festival Overture. Sargent chose to play himself out as Chief Conductor with Schubert's Ninth Symphony, the Nocturne *Paris* by Delius, and Strauss's Four Last Songs sung by Lisa Della Casa.

Several other of the season's concerts were marked by last-minute changes. The first performance of Alwyn's Third Symphony, commissioned by the BBC to open the season on 10 October, was given by Beecham instead of Barbirolli. The first appearance in the series of Rudolf Kempe had to be cancelled through illness, and Hermann Scherchen returned with the inconsiderable novelty of Villa-Lobos's Harp Concerto, in its British première (21 November). The only other performance of note was in the 24 October concert conducted by Pedro de Freitas Branco when, alongside Turina and Ravel, Rawsthorne's Second Violin Concerto was premièred by Endré Wolf.

A further disappointing aspect of this season was that the May concerts of 1957 had to be cancelled altogether. The four concerts were all to be conducted by Bruno Walter, and were to feature some of the works he had performed in the studio during the previous season. But he fell ill, and in

March it became clear that he would be unable to come. As the programmes
were never published, their intended contents should be recorded:

Sunday 12 May	*Haydn*........................	Symphony No. 102
	Mahler...........................	Symphony No. 4
Wednesday 15 May	*Mozart*............	Overture: The Magic Flute
		Symphony No. 36
		Eine kleine Nachtmusik
		Masonic Funeral Music
		Symphony No. 41 in C
Sunday 19 May	*Schubert*...........................	Symphony No. 5
	Brahms........................	A German Requiem
Wednesday 22 May	*Bruckner*........................	Symphony No. 9
		Te Deum

One other extra set of concerts did take place as planned, however: performances of Elgar's two oratorios *The Kingdom* (on 29 May) and *The
Apostles* (on 12 June), a BBC Home Service promotion to mark the centenary
of Elgar's birth. Boult conducted the first, Sargent the second.

For the Royal Philharmonic Society in February 1957, Sargent conducted
the British première of Walton's Cello Concerto, with Piatigorsky as soloist;
and he once more became involved in a squabble in the Press. Among the
chorus of praise for Walton's piece, Peter Heyworth in *The Observer* struck a
dissenting note: 'There is something rather alarming about the stagnant
quality of Walton's recent music.' Sargent wrote to say that Heyworth's
statement had 'no justification whatsoever' and that Walton was merely
'discarding the superfluous and growing in sincerity. I wish the same could
be said of more of our modern composers.' Sargent then challenged Heyworth's notions of composers' development by asking that he place Beethoven's symphonies in chronological order: No. 4 and No. 8 would surely
come before No. 3, and so on. Heyworth replied testily: 'Beethoven is hardly
a happy example of a composer who did not in each work extend his idiom . . .
I never suggested that a composer has to develop systematically in a straight
line . . . Walton's recent music seems to me to show no vital development at
all.'

Celebrating – and curtailing – the Third Programme

The season which ended the Sargent era coincided with one of the BBC's
most lavish celebrations. The tenth anniversary of the Third Programme
was celebrated in the week beginning 30 September 1956, and it was decided
to invite a number of composers to write works specially for the occasion.
The list of chosen composers is a good indication of Third Programme taste

in the period: chamber music works were requested from Peter Racine Fricker, Alun Hoddinott, Anthony Milner, Kenneth Leighton and Phyllis Tate. For orchestral works the planners went abroad, and approached Ibert, Blacher, Holmboe, Petrassi and Martinů. All except the last accepted: Martinů offered his recently completed *Frescoes of Piero della Francesca* which had been written for Kubelik, but when it became clear that the première in Salzburg would be in August 1956, this was regretfully declined. Frank Martin was then approached; he was unable to write a work, so the commission passed to Andrzej Panufnik. The one Englishman in this group was Michael Tippett, who was preparing to write his Second Symphony. Tippett was insistent, however, that there should be no time deadline.

The plan was to broadcast the orchestral works from the studio in the course of the few months after the anniversary: the Petrassi to be conducted by Robinson in October, the Ibert by Monteux and the Blacher by Sargent in November, and the Tippett in December. But Tippett's work was certainly not going to be ready, and Petrassi asked that his be delayed until the end of the year. Then on 15 January 1957 he wrote to Howgill saying that it was still not ready. 'We can control many things just as we desire, but the creative imagination submits to secret laws which are impossible to rationalise.' The première was delayed until June, with a Prom performance planned for September. The Holmboe was substituted in December, and Panufnik was asked to conduct his own work in January. Ibert and Blacher both produced their works on time.

It is worth recalling here that the BBC's commissioning policy during the late fifties was quite straightforward: one major work was requested for each winter season of concerts, and the BBC also commissioned a smaller work for the Cheltenham Festival. The products of this policy were chamber works by Benjamin Frankel, John Addison, Grace Williams, Kenneth Leighton and Mátyás Seiber, and the following orchestral works:

William Alwyn...Symphony No. 3
Iain Hamilton...The Bermudas
Daniel Jones...Symphony No. 5
Roberto Gerhard...Symphony No. 2

Only a few commissions in this period did not materialise: a notable one was that to Benjamin Britten. He was offered the symphony concerts commission for 1957–8 as 'the obvious choice, but he is still unable to undertake the commission owing to outstanding commitments though he wished to do so at some later date'. So the offer was renewed for 1960, and Britten accepted to write a piece for the Mahler centenary of that year. Unfortunately it was never completed: Britten was ill, and it was also rumoured that he was unsympathetic to performances by the Symphony Orchestra.

It was ironic that less than a year after the Third Programme's tenth anniversary, its activities should have been drastically curtailed by BBC economies. As a result of these economies announced in April 1957, the Third Programme's output was reduced to three hours every night; this involved the loss of the Symphony Orchestra's Thursday concert. A new 'Network Three' was to be introduced to carry spoken word programmes. The Controller of the Third Programme ruled that the scope of the programme was to be drastically curtailed: there was no longer to be any catering for 'extremely specialised' interests. There would be fewer series, no renaissance or medieval music, no oriental music, and so on: the best possible performances of the central parts of the repertory were suggested as a worthy aim in place of the previously wide coverage. There was widespread outrage. Public opinion was roused, and a Third Programme Defence Society (later renamed the Sound Broadcasting Society) came into existence with the support of many distinguished names in Britain and such important figures from abroad as Albert Camus, Jean Cocteau, André Malraux, Jacques Maritain and François Mauriac. A deputation to Broadcasting House in July consisted of T. S. Eliot, Laurence Olivier, Michael Tippett, Vaughan Williams, and four officers of the Society. But the Society could do little to prevent the BBC's plans taking effect, and it remained unsatisfied. The broadcasts of the Wednesday concerts on the Home Service also suffered, but in all the effect was not as great as some of the critics feared: the BBC was certainly taken by surprise at the wide range of the outcry against its changes.

At the beginning of 1958, the changes were surveyed by a member of the Third Programme staff, who noted the losses sustained: among the most serious, he felt, were

> the repeat of the Symphony Concerts, with the advantages this gave for the second hearing of a new or difficult work . . . the regional orchestral concerts, which every week included some new work. This has given rise to a bottleneck of new works which . . . command attention and hearing. . . . Big series are now impossible without crowding out other things . . . the tendency to make demands on the rehearsal time of the BBC Symphony Orchestra from other quarters makes it impossible to envisage, as hitherto, including a complete series of symphonies of a particular composer (whether contemporary or not) in a given quarter or even six months.

Though the BBC had claimed that 'more music' would be heard on the Home and Light, though less on the Third, it could not disguise the fact that the non-music Network Three (from around 6 pm to 7.45 pm each night) restricted the Third's range of music, thus curtailing much of its adventurousness.

Music policy

During the Sargent era, the relationship of the Symphony Orchestra and its repertoire to the broadcast output had been raised only infrequently. During these years discussion of policy at the Music Direction meetings held in Music Department tended to centre round details of programming and conductors. But general matters did occasionally occur, and in 1955 there was a consideration of the problem of equating the Orchestra's quality of work with its quantity of output. It was resolved to make the main Wednesday and Sunday programmes run more smoothly together, with a repertory piece instead of a novelty on the Sunday; Richard Howgill felt that seven concerts a fortnight (with Home and Third Programmes forgoing one of their appointed four in alternation) was the maximum load possible on the Orchestra. In 1956 a plan was mooted to regularise the use of guest conductors and ease the strain on the Orchestra. Two assistant conductors were to be appointed to look after studio dates which Sargent did not want to do, and which it would be inappropriate to ask guest conductors to undertake. Stanford Robinson and Norman Del Mar were given this perhaps unenviable task for a trial six months between 1956 and 1957.

It was still felt important for the Orchestra's broadcasts to be live: a suggestion in 1957 from the Third Programme that it should record the usual Friday concert to be used at any time convenient to the network during the following week was strongly resisted by the Music Division. The Department also had to hold out against requests to modify its public concert programmes by the Controller of the Home Service, who felt that there was too much choral music and new music in the Wednesday Symphony Concert series.

When the first of many working parties was appointed to enquire into the orchestral policy of the BBC in August 1957, it reported back with a strong defence of the *status quo*.

> The working party was agreed that the Symphony Orchestra is a unique instrument in our national musical life, performing a wide and varied repertoire at a high level of accomplishment. It did not consider that its disbandment could be seriously contemplated, and had no recommendations for change in its size and construction.

And when Howgill raised with BBC management the fact that Symphony

Orchestra pay was low compared with that of the freelance orchestras (a situation which was to become more marked in the 1960s), he was put firmly in his place by Lindsay Wellington: 'I think we all know very well what the position is. Our orchestra is the highest paid salaried orchestra. Freelance orchestras exist and by being freelance they avoid PAYE [Pay As You Earn taxation]. They also run the risks of being freelances – no pensions, no holiday pay, etc.' It was to be some years before this fundamental complacency over the Symphony Orchestra's position could be disturbed.

Contemporary music was discussed very rarely, and usually with a note of worry. When it was suggested in August 1956 that the music of Henze, Boulez and others was not receiving sufficient attention on the air, there was a discussion as to how it was possible to establish whether their music was of sufficiently high quality to be broadcast. 'On balance it was felt that to broadcast a few of their better works would not blunt our reputation for acute critical assessment.' This sentence might stand as a memorial to the BBC's insular musical policy in the 1950s.

This discussion may be seen as a background to a concert which was broadcast on 3 March 1957 at 8 pm on the Third Programme. It was a recording of an event at the Institute of Contemporary Arts, whose concerts were at that time directed by William Glock. There was absolutely no publicity given to the programme; not a word about the works in *Radio Times*. It consisted of:

Nono..Canti per 13
Boulez...Le Marteau sans maître
Stockhausen .... Zeitmasze
Webern...Concerto Op. 24

Few could have suspected that this eccentric intrusion into the BBC's 1950s' music policy would become almost the standard fare of the 1960s.

When music policy was formulated during the 1950s, there was a note of self-congratulation which now reads unhappily. In 1958, Howgill reported:

> The senior music critic in this country has said that the BBC is giving us in abundance music adapted to all tastes and all mental ages. We can assume that, in saying this, Mr Ernest Newman is judging the BBC from its total music output, which is what the BBC would like all its critics to do rather than pick on certain sections of it . . . it is hard to conceive that the music-lover cannot obtain reasonable gratification of his tastes.
>
> There is consciousness of the following omissions, or at least inadequacy of representation: Music for string orchestra . . . Cantatas, oratorios and Masses . . . Madrigals . . . Cathedral Music . . . Modern British songs . . .

Lieder . . . Organ music. There should be room for more contemporary music, particularly the twentieth-century masters and British music, avant-garde experiments, medieval, renaissance and oriental music and occasional special projects . . .

Modifications on the lines set out above, though perhaps necessitating a little more time for music, should leave little for the critics to say of this branch of the BBC's output.

A successor to Sargent

The BBC Symphony Orchestra still had the capacity to return to its form as one of the world's great orchestras, and it occasionally played at that top form. But who was the musician who could give it the devotion, commitment and inspiration that it needed? In 1956 there were various suggestions to replace Sargent: Jascha Horenstein, it was thought, might well contemplate an offer; foreign conductors of the stature of van Beinum or Kletzki would certainly have been interested. There was much to say for returning to Kubelik with a new offer. Walter Susskind's name was often mentioned in the BBC. Those who most keenly wished to finish with Sargent, however, had a candidate whom they felt to be ideal. In Birmingham, Rudolf Schwarz had been achieving very fine results in a wide repertoire. He was now a British subject, and had an open-minded attitude to the music he conducted. He had already done much work with the BBC Symphony Orchestra in a wide range of music. Between 1952 and 1957 he had directed works by nearly fifty composers, of the stature of Schoenberg, Stravinsky, Bartók, Bax, Bliss, Kodály, Strauss and Vaughan Williams. He had been enthusiastic about new and neglected works, and had fallen in well with the requests of the Music Division. Moreover, his personal qualities were in marked contrast to those which had recently dominated the scene: with his selfless service to the music, putting it always before his personal gain, and his gentle integrity in all dealings with people, he had a strong claim to be an ideal candidate for the post.

Schwarz was one of the many European musicians who had suffered at the hands of the Nazis – and he suffered much more directly than many who escaped early in the regime's life. Born in 1905, he had become a junior conductor at the Düsseldorf Opera House at the age of eighteen, and had soon joined Josef Krips as conductor at the Karlsruhe State Theatre. This and a growing number of other conducting engagements were brought to an end by the Nazis. Schwarz was arrested and taken during the war to Belsen, where he was subjected to torture which has marked him all his life, as well as restricting his physical movements. He was rescued from Belsen by the

allied forces in 1945 and went to Sweden, where he began to resume his
activities as a conductor. He then came to England, where he became musical
director and conductor of the Bournemouth Municipal Orchestra; and in
1951 he moved to Birmingham, where he developed the playing of the City
of Birmingham Symphony Orchestra immeasurably over the following five
years, broadening their repertoire and creating consistent standards.

The administrators of the BBC's Music Division felt they could work
with Schwarz, and their confidence was a large factor in determining Howgill
to approach him. It was not a complicated matter to resolve. Schwarz was
delighted to be asked to undertake the task and willing to fall in with all the
BBC's contractual conditions. He saw Howgill in August 1956 and the
matter was sealed in a quite simple letter of invitation.

> Further to discussion between us, I am now writing to confirm our earnest
> wish that you should undertake the task of Chief Conductor of the BBC
> Symphony Orchestra from immediately after the termination of the
> Promenade Concert season which ends on 14 September 1957. On the
> understanding that you will be able to accept this invitation, the contractual
> terms can be finally settled on the lines already known to you after my return
> from leave on 24 September.

The letter was sent on 5 September, so that Schwarz would be able to confirm that he had been approached as soon as Sargent's change of position had
been announced. In Birmingham, Alderman Lloyd of the Orchestra's committee 'accepted the resignation and congratulated the BBC on acquiring the
services of a sensible musician and an admirable man'. Nothing could have
been smoother. Howgill drew up a revised statement of policy with regard to
the Chief Conductor and repertoire of the Symphony Orchestra. It differed
little from that conceived as an answer to Sargent in 1953. The proportion of
the year's Festival Hall concerts to be taken by the Chief Conductor was set
at half (five out of ten), and tours were now 'normally' to be undertaken by
the Chief Conductor. The vexed question of allocating responsibility between the BBC and the conductor for programming and guest conductors
was newly formulated:

> The choice of both works and artists for the BBC Symphony Orchestra's
> programme rests in the first place with the Head of Music Programmes and
> his staff working with the Chief Conductor in respect of the content of his
> own programmes. The over-all responsibility for programme content must,
> however, rest with the Controller of Music.
>   The Chief Conductor will be responsible for the artistic standard of the

personnel of the BBC Symphony Orchestra and will make such reports as are required. Any action involving personnel consequent on this will be initiated by the Orchestral Manager in consultation with the Chief Conductor, referring where necessary to the Controller of Music.

The Chief Conductor will be provided with an office and a secretary to enable him to maintain the required close contact with the Music Division Staff concerned with programmes and concert and orchestral management and to deal with outside correspondence.

These statements consolidated the BBC's control over the choice of guest artists, and re-established the Music Division's priority in choosing works for programmes not conducted by the Chief Conductor.

The term of Schwarz's contract was set for a fixed five years. Initial periods with the Orchestra during the 1956–7 season went very well, and on 2 May Howgill wrote to Schwarz: 'I feel that there is every reason to congratulate you on your recent extensive periods with the Orchestra for which you are to be artistically responsible. Paul Beard . . . could not have been more enthusiastic about the prospects for the future.' Schwarz for his part was delighted. He wrote to Howgill (5 May): 'I have never before felt such waves of goodwill, such a congenial atmosphere, and such complete co-operation.' The scene looked set for a most successful collaboration.

Schwarz's first season

Rudolf Schwarz took up his duties with the Symphony Orchestra at the start of the 1957–8 season; the season's programmes, planned with his collaboration, at once displayed a renewed sense of purpose and openness. Almost every programme contained a British work: his first concert began with Walton's *Portsmouth Point*, and his last included Rubbra's Seventh Symphony. Gordon Jacob's Third Suite, Seiber's cantata *Ulysses*, and Britten's fine *Sinfonia da Requiem* all featured in Schwarz's concerts. There were two BBC commissions: Iain Hamilton's *The Bermudas*, a choral work (30 October), conducted by Schwarz; and the Second Symphony of Michael Tippett (5 February). It was hoped that Hans Schmidt-Isserstedt, a keen advocate of Tippett's music, would be able to conduct this concert, a notorious one in the Orchestra's annals, but just before the season's plans appeared Sir Adrian Boult was approached to take over the première. Other last-minute changes included the replacement of Szymanowski's *Sinfonia concertante* in the 27 November concert. Rubinstein asked to be released from the work; he played Saint-Saëns and Schumann instead. Sargent was given his agreed two concerts in the season: the first was to have included

Sibelius's Fourth Symphony, but was replaced by the British première of Shostakovich's Eleventh; the second consisted of the Berlioz *Damnation of Faust*. The final guest was Jascha Horenstein, who had been suggested for the Chief Conductorship: he brought with him Aaron Copland's Third Symphony (13 November). Commenting on the plans, Lindsay Wellington wrote: 'This looks to me to be a pretty well mixed bag – familiar and un-familiar works, concentration on our own new conductor, Malcolm doing works which suit him, and some first class artists for the concertos.' (Besides Rubinstein, Myra Hess, Cherkassky, Tortelier and Andor Foldes were all featured.) On 12 February 1958 the Orchestra also contributed to the Royal Philharmonic Society series, giving the first performance of Roberto Gerhard's Violin Concerto.

In the event, the success of the season was varied. However much the Orchestra respected Schwarz's integrity and undemonstrativeness in re-hearsal, the critics were slow to respond to his approach. On the platform Schwarz was reserved and inactive compared with Sargent, and to some this evidently meant that the end result was less exciting. It soon became clear that, as far as success with the public was concerned, Schwarz would have an uphill struggle. Iain Hamilton's ambitious piece found little popular success either. This cantata for baritone solo, chorus and orchestra was in five sections, the first written in Hamilton's own individual twelve-note tech-nique, the later choral sections in 'free tonality'. The text, compiled by Hamilton himself, drew together descriptions of the Bermudas from accounts of the island's discovery by Silvestre Jourdain in 1610, culminating with Andrew Marvell's poem 'Where the remote Bermudas ride'.

Also mixed were the reactions to Shostakovich's new Eleventh Sym-phony under Sargent. This work had been planned for performance as part of the Third Programme Tenth Anniversary celebrations, and was based on the events of the Russian uprising of 1905. Enjoyably, some first-hand reactions to this piece were preserved by the BBC's Audience Research Department: some twenty per cent of the Third Programme panel tuned in, and the most complimentary remark about the work was that it was 'inter-mittently interesting'. Another listener felt that it did not put Shostakovich among the immortals, while a third was annoyed because 'Shostakovich has nothing to say and says it very loudly'. One reported: 'The opening bars sounded like Vaughan Williams. As the performance went on (and how it went on!) I began to wish it *were* Vaughan Williams . . .' So much for the BBC's enterprise in mounting the work.

Tippett's symphony

The première of the Tippett Second Symphony was a major occasion. This too had been a Third Programme anniversary commission, but Tippett had accepted it only on condition that there was to be no time factor involved. He kept in close touch with Howgill during the composition, sending him regular reports about its progress.

> The (short) symphony that I have been pondering for the last three years and for which I have now cleared the decks, is a work which has to be of the very best I have and therefore cannot be driven. This is so serious to me that I'd have to forgo, reluctantly, the commission if we had to set an absolute time limit.

Tippett wrote again in July 1956 apologising for the delay, but adding that 'the real pleasure to me is that it *still* looks like being one of the best works I have ever done. I feel that I have not yet put a note wrong.' It was later agreed not to attempt to put it in the anniversary year's programme, but to delay it until 1957–8. Tippett to Howgill: 'You can be perfectly assured as to the date you have chosen . . . the very beginning of an important piece takes a long time . . . but the time is over and it flows.' It was not until 14 November 1957 that Tippett was able to write: 'I have just this moment finished copying with ink the full score of the (your) Symphony. It has ended in a blaze of sound and it still seems to me one of the best things I have done . . . I don't know quite why I have been so excited by it.'

When Schmidt-Isserstedt was unavailable, other continental figures experienced in the performance of new music were considered for the première, in particular Paul Sacher; he was considered to be little known in London, and Rudolf Kempe was preferred. In case a foreign guest could not be found, the Music Direction Meeting approved either Norman Del Mar or Stanford Robinson as possible British conductors. But in the end it was realised that the première was too important, and Sir Adrian Boult was engaged for the date – only in the July before the season started. Tippett acknowledged that the Symphony was his most difficult work from the point of view of orchestral technique: a challenge both to players and conductor. It begins with a complex flurry of string writing. At the première, which was broadcast live, this passage broke down. Boult immediately stopped the Orchestra, turned to the audience and said words to the effect of 'I'm sorry. Entirely my fault, we'll begin again.' He thus acknowledged that the responsibility for the breakdown was his, and tried to exonerate the Orchestra. But some of the critics were less sure, and in their reviews explicitly or implicitly blamed the quality of the string playing for the collapse of the opening bars. Tippett kept silent on the subject for some time; the Orchestra concluded that he blamed them. A fortnight later, he wrote to both Schwarz and Paul Beard, thanking the Orchestra for all their work in connection with the Symphony, praising them highly, and removing any blame for the mishap. Beard read this letter to the Orchestra at rehearsal: it was received with applause and cheers. Schwarz explained to Tippett: 'The Orchestra were (if not upset) rather disappointed that you refrained from letting them know . . . of your appreciation, so they had to conclude that you had been little satisfied with their efforts.' Schwarz defended the Orchestra, and Howgill concurred. He wrote to Schwarz: 'I am most impressed with your letter. I intend to support the line you have taken . . . it is a marvel to me what the BBC Symphony Orchestra achieved.' In all this, the position of Boult was ignored, as it had to be if the Orchestra's face was to be saved. Boult, by once again accepting the most difficult of tasks at the BBC's wish (at the last minute, and not as their first choice), was a poor choice for scapegoat. As one of the listeners who contributed to the controversy after the première noted, he could easily have ploughed on in the hope that the Orchestra would pull itself back together again and the mistake would not be noticed. Nevertheless, the incident did a great deal to damage the Orchestra's prestige at a time when it badly needed support. Three days after the première, Boult and the Orchestra gave an impeccable rendering of the Symphony in a studio broadcast on the Third Programme.

During the season Schwarz took the Orchestra to Ireland and the provinces: a larger number of visits than usual included Brighton, Southampton, Wells, Exeter and Truro Cathedrals; Plymouth and Huddersfield. Cork, Limerick and Londonderry were visited in Ireland, Belfast had three concerts and Dublin one. The practice of having a British work in every programme was restored: Ireland, Bax and Walton were featured. The Belfast concerts were well attended by enthusiastic audiences, and the final Dublin concert brought 2000 people. 'The tremendous enthusiasm shown for the conductor and Orchestra after Sibelius No. 5 and Schubert's C major gave a tremendous uplift to all concerned,' reported George Willoughby, the Concerts Manager. 'The tour was an excellent thing for conductor and Orchestra, and one noticed a feeling of growing rapport between them.'

1958 also saw the Orchestra's previously-planned visit to the Brussels Exposition. Sargent had been engaged to conduct before the change in his contract arrangements. The brief visit was enlivened by such arrangements as that in Ostend, where the concert was billed to start at 9 pm, whereas the Home Service was expecting a relay from 8 to 9. At the first concert of the

Brussels Exposition, the King of the Belgians and the Duke of Edinburgh were to be present. Their arrival delayed the start of the concert by twenty minutes: England was to broadcast the second part of the concert (*Belshazzar's Feast*) which had to finish punctually because another live broadcast followed. The Concerts Manager was expected to organise a specially shortened ten-minute interval for a stage full of 350 people and an audience full of dignitaries. He despaired, and risked London's wrath by simply postponing the start of the relay by fifteen minutes. The following live broadcast was cut.

In Ostend administration was not all that it might have been. Marjorie Thomas, one of the soloists in *The Dream of Gerontius*, was dismayed to see that Elsie Morison's name was on the posters; Denis Matthews was rather more amused when a man was observed painting out 'Concertino [sic] in A, K488' and substituting 'Concerto en ré mineur K466' on the afternoon of the concert. 'Don't worry,' he said, 'whatever Malcolm starts I'll tag along.'

Working with Schwarz

Meanwhile Schwarz continued to deepen his understanding and collaboration with the Orchestra. His rehearsals were detailed: each matter of balance, phrasing, rhythm and shape was settled and talked out, so that there was complete confidence at the time of performance as to what was needed, without being worried by details. He never asked for anything to be done in a particular way without explaining why: frustrating to some who hated talk, but to the musicians in the Orchestra invaluable. He was always intent that the players should listen to each other, not merely watch him. He never lost his temper: hardly ever – there was one occasion when the unmusical singing of a soprano drove him to distraction.

Schwarz was a perfectionist. And he was a musician's conductor. These two qualities help to explain why he sometimes failed as well as why he succeeded. In a talk broadcast some years later, one of his fervent admirers among the Orchestra, the distinguished principal oboist Janet Craxton, had this to say about his methods:

> He is one of my ideals as a conductor in that he is always trying to reach the truth of the music and his interpretation is always based on that rather than a feeling of adding his personality to the music. To help him he has the gift of a very acute ear and an unfailing sense of tempo. . . . His choice of tempi never appears hurried and they always seem to come from the music in a natural way . . .
>
> At the performance [he] gives the impression of such total immersion in

the music (almost as if he withdraws into the work) that one might have the impression that he was unaware of the orchestra or audience, but this is naturally very far from true; he is concentrating his whole attention on the work and its overall shape. This is, I find, a very great help to one's own total concentration on the music. In effect, you are very much aware of his heart and spirit in control and never troubled by niggly details.

In retrospect the musical highlights of our five years with him were probably for most of his insight into and love and affection for Schumann, his moving but unsentimental and unexaggerated performances of Mahler, fine performances of Bruckner, Dvořák and Strauss, his musically sane performances of all the classical repertoire including beautiful performances of Schubert symphonies, particularly the Ninth, and, for me, a most memorable Beethoven Ninth. He showed a genuine love and understanding of the French music that we played with him and he was always a great champion of British composers, showing a different but very positive approach to the works of Elgar in particular. He never got bogged down by any traditional approach, and the resulting distortion that so often goes with it. We performed most of the Elgar symphonic works with him and I for one welcomed the sweeping off of some of the old cobwebs! . . .

Rudolf Schwarz was always interested in new but what he would call legitimate musical works, and I remember his enthusiasm for the Britten *Nocturne*, of which we gave the first performance. Also the care and effort that he put into the preparation of Roberto Gerhard's symphonies. He was and still is a champion of those composers who write what he feels is musical sense, and he will take endless pains to rehearse their works thoroughly and to do them justice at performance. . . .

He was the first to praise performances that he admired and to congratulate a player or players in the orchestra if he felt that they had distinguished themselves. It is very easy for any orchestra to become cut off from their management and in an establishment as large as the BBC, this is even easier, so that this contact and interest in the playing of his Orchestra was of enormous value to the players.

He never took his position as principal conductor lightly and never ceased to interest himself in the welfare and well-being of his players. He has been criticised for being too kind and lacking the ruthless streak that some feel necessary in a conductor in order that he may part with a player who is perhaps past his best and replace him with new blood. Personally, I feel that loyalty and justice are enormously important in an orchestra and although you may well gain in one way by making these changes, you can often lose something else.

1958–9

For the 1958–9 season there was a new look to the BBC's publicity material. Streaked yellow and grey covers for the prospectus and programmes, with white music stands standing out against an infinitely receding background. A lively little essay by Noël Goodwin enticed listeners into the list of forthcoming concerts. In all, there was a feeling of confidence that the new season had much to offer. Schwarz conducted half the concerts, and the range of the series was broadened by the inclusion of a new-found classic of the early baroque repertory: the *1610 Vespers* by Monteverdi. There was new music, too: a commission, the Fifth Symphony by Daniel Jones, and the British première of the Piano Concerto by Petrassi. Ingenious programme planning juxtaposed Rachmaninov's Rhapsody and Blacher's Variations, both on the famous theme of Paganini; two important works from the English repertory: Walton's Violin Concerto and Vaughan Williams' Fourth Symphony; Bartók's First Piano Concerto and Berg's Violin Concerto; Kodály's *Psalmus Hungaricus*; and classic symphonies including Brahms's Second and Fourth, Mahler's Fifth and Beethoven's Third. Guest conductors were distinguished: Schmidt-Isserstedt, Rudolf Kempe and Barbirolli; a new visitor, Nino Sanzogno; and towering above them all, Igor Stravinsky, who came at vast expense (£900, at least three times as much as any other conductor in the season) to direct an evening of his own music on 10 December. The most recent work included was *Agon*, which had been premièred in the USA only the previous year. There was also the Symphony in Three Movements, *Apollo*, and dances from *The Firebird*. Schwarz ended the season with Mahler's Fifth Symphony.

Among the highlights of the broadcasting year were the first performance of Britten's *Nocturne* from the Leeds Festival, sung by Peter Pears, a work for which Schwarz had special enthusiasm (16 October). Schwarz and Herbert Bardgett conducted another Leeds centenary concert the next day, with the Kenneth Leighton Cello Concerto and Charpentier's soon-to-be-famous *Te Deum*. Under Stanford Robinson, the BBC Men's Chorus with the Symphony Orchestra performed Martinů's *Mass for the Field of Battle* (9 November), and Rudolf Kempe conducted a series of studio concerts including Bloch's *Baal Shem Suite* (16 November). On Saturday 6 December, a pair of exchange concerts broadcast Danish music from London (in which Schwarz conducted the Orchestra) and British music from Copenhagen (by the Danish State Radio Symphony Orchestra, conductor Thomas Jensen). 1959 began with studio concerts under Schwarz (Rubbra's Viola Concerto) and Schmidt-Isserstedt (Three Pieces for Cello and Orchestra by Seiber, with Amaryllis Fleming); the first performances of Berkeley's

Concerto for Piano and Double String Orchestra were given by Colin Horsley at the Royal Philharmonic Society and again in the studio (11, 14 February). Daniel Jones repeated his commissioned Fifth Symphony in a concert which also included the *Six Monologues for Everyman* by Frank Martin; and Nino Sanzogno's studio concerts around his Festival Hall appearance included the British première of Dallapiccola's *Canti di Liberazione*, Hartmann's Sixth Symphony, and Pizzetti's *Canti della stagione alta*. In March, too, Sargent included the *Symphonic Variations* by Bentzon in a studio concert (14 March).

The season's visits included Southend, Hull, a visit to the Hallé's home in Manchester (with Tippett's Piano Concerto), Bradford, Bournemouth, Peterborough and Norwich, Ipswich and Portsmouth (where the Orchestra reopened the Guildhall). The Orchestra was invited to the Cheltenham Festival, where it gave the first performance of the Piano Concerto by Malcolm Lipkin, born in Liverpool in 1932 (with Lamar Crowson as soloist), and in the second concert the first public performance in Britain of Iain Hamilton's Violin Concerto, Op. 15, completed in 1952 and first broadcast in 1956. The first public performance had been given in Vienna with Wolfgang Schneiderhan; Manoug Parikian played it on this occasion.

So the decade came towards its close with a feeling of solid achievement: Schwarz and the Symphony Orchestra were working well together, and the limited ambitions of the BBC's Music Department were at last being realised in the programmes of the Winter Season and studio concerts. But the year 1959 saw a change in the BBC's Music Division which was to upset this calm equilibrium completely. Though it could scarcely have been foreseen at the time, a revolution was on the horizon.

7
Winds of Change
1959-71

Tilting at windmills

The appointment of William Glock as the BBC's Controller, Music (in succession to Richard Howgill) came as a shock to the musical world both inside and outside the BBC. In 1959 Glock was not part of the British musical establishment, from whose ranks the post was expected to be filled. He was (as Peter Heyworth of *The Observer* described him) a 'quixotic outsider', who had spent much of his life arguing causes which conventional wisdom thought eccentric and irrelevant. Glock had been organ scholar of Caius College, Cambridge, and then studied the piano with Schnabel in Berlin; he appeared at the Proms in 1940. He worked first as a music critic for the *Daily Telegraph* and then from 1934 for *The Observer*, where it was said that he earned the displeasure of his last editor, Ivor Brown, by neglecting the standard repertoire and conventional concerts in favour of a wide range of music from Byrd to Britten. He was finally dismissed in September 1945 for ignoring the week's concerts yet again to write an appreciation of Bartók (who had died during the month) in which Glock wrote that Bartók had 'the genius of the greatest' and – to Ivor Brown's annoyance – remarked that 'no great composer has ever cared how "pleasant" his music sounds'.

Glock's two major ventures of the postwar period were the Summer School of Music which he established, first at Bryanston School and later at Dartington Hall in Devon, and his magazine *The Score*. The aims of the two were similar: to bring into British musical life an awareness of the most adventurous musical developments on the Continent. At Bryanston and then at Dartington the leading continental composers – Hindemith, Gerhard, Stravinsky, Sessions, and later Nono, Berio (his classes translated by a young Englishman, Peter Maxwell Davies), Lutoslawski and Elliott Carter – came to teach a new generation of young English composers; in *The Score* they wrote about their work, and a lively young group of writers tackled the problems of postwar musical developments with a seriousness which was missing from the passing, usually dismissive references for which the national press found room.

Glock was one of the outside experts called upon during the 1950s to advise the BBC through its Central Music Advisory Committee. He was Chairman of the Music Section at the Institute of Contemporary Arts in London, and had proposed a series of collaborative concerts with the BBC in the late 1950s; the programmes had proved too strong for the taste of most of the BBC Music Department at the time, though isolated events were broadcast.

By 1959, however, there was a realisation that the work of Boulez and Stockhausen, Nono and Berio, though still unintelligible to many, was forming a coherent mainstream tradition of postwar music on the Continent. Glock was one of a tiny number of people in this country who was informed about these developments; he believed in them, and had shown that he had the administrative and creative skill to bring them to a wider public at Dartington. He was one of the few radical and lively minds in English music. Richard Howgill, the retiring Controller of Music, argued strongly for Glock's appointment. He had struck up a friendship with him in the 1950s, when they both served on the Committee of the International Musicians' Association. He respected Glock's views and admired his energy and enthusiasm. Whether he realised just how radical Glock might be as Controller is open to question. But Howgill often showed shrewd judgement: though essentially a cautious man, regarded by his staff as an inactive Controller, he made the right decision when the moment came – as he had when terminating Sargent's contract as Chief Conductor. But Glock's educational work at Dartington had also attracted the attention of those in charge of the Guildhall School of Music, and at the same time as the possibility of the BBC post arose, he was pressed to become a candidate for the post of Principal at the Guildhall. There was a promise of a new college in the Barbican in the near future (though it was in fact to be nearly twenty years before it came to pass), and the opportunity to form a new generation of young English musicians in a broad-minded tradition. It was an important chance. Fortunately for the concert life of this country, Glock took the advice of Michael Tippett and of his own outspoken younger sister, and just as he was on the point of appearing for a final interview at the Guildhall decided instead to join the BBC. He became Controller, Music in the autumn of 1959.

It was not without some distress that Symphony Orchestra members learned of Howgill's retirement, which was announced in February 1959. On their behalf, Sidonie Goossens wrote to him on 14 February:

It was with great regret that we read the news of your coming retirement. We had not realised it would be so soon, in fact we had hoped it would never be realised. We feel that we shall lose a very good friend of the Orchestra; one who has helped to fight and win our battles. We do appreciate all that you have done for us.

Howgill replied with his thanks, and with the declaration that 'it is essential to my mind that the BBC Symphony Orchestra should be one of the major preoccupations of whoever is responsible for BBC music and I shall impress this important point on my successor'. William Glock was not slow to take up the challenge; the Symphony Orchestra and its work immediately became one of his most important priorities.

Starting a revolution

A wide-ranging revolution such as Glock wished to achieve in BBC music was not going to be easy to begin. It involved the revitalisation of music programmes, of the public concerts given by the BBC, and of the Symphony Orchestra itself. Glock began in two ways: first, by broadening the base by which contemporary music was selected for performance on the air; and second, by arguing the case for a livelier and fuller public concert season. Both these tasks he was able to initiate in his first few months in the job, before the end of 1959. To ensure that a wider selection of new music was passed for performance, he arranged for the co-option onto the BBC's reading panel of some musicians conversant with this repertoire, including Iain Hamilton, Humphrey Searle and David Drew, who would listen to playbacks and look at scores of new works.

For a larger public concert season, Glock put up a general case to Lindsay Wellington, Director of Sound Broadcasting. On the sympathetic and open-minded response of men like Wellington, and his successor Frank Gillard, depended a great deal of the success or failure of Glock's intended revolution. In December 1959 Glock proposed that the number of Festival Hall concerts should be increased from ten to twelve a season, for three reasons:

1. It is tremendously important for the players to get out of the studio as often as possible. Public concerts strengthen the morale, improve the standards, and enhance the prestige of the Orchestra.
2. It would enable the BBC to make a greater impact on London's musical life, to present a larger and more varied repertory and to introduce one additional conductor of international standing. Apart from our own concerts, very few enterprising orchestral programmes are given at the Royal Festival Hall – not more than a dozen or so in a season.

3. It would mean two extra relays from a public hall and these are almost always far more exciting for the radio listener than transmissions from the studio.

The virtues of the case were not obvious. For several seasons the BBC concerts at the Festival Hall had been drawing distressingly small audiences. As Glock wrote, the 1959–60 season had started with a 52% house for Ansermet (who included the London première of Honegger's *Christmas Cantata*), a 45% house for Schwarz (giving the première of Gerhard's Second Symphony), and then a 29% audience for the second Schwarz concert (Stravinsky, Britten and Schubert's Ninth). Massimo Freccia, giving a miscellaneous programme on 25 November, had drawn only a 34% attendance. It was scarcely surprising that Wellington asked in reply 'whether it helps or harms us to put on concerts which draw audiences as small as the one which recently came to hear Massimo Freccia?' Glock had the chance to dissociate himself from some of the programme planning that had preceded him, and point to the future. 'The BBC's job,' he replied on 1 January 1960, 'is to put on programmes that others can't, not that others wouldn't if you paid them . . . the Freccia evening seems to me an example of all that we should avoid.' He said that, given good guest conductors and better programmes, 'I'm ready to guarantee an audience of at least twice the size; that will follow quite naturally from all the rest. The musical world is only too ready to acclaim a lively and enterprising policy. Allies are swarming round, just waiting for something worthwhile to support. . . .' It was a necessarily over-confident declaration.

Matters regarding the Festival Hall series could hardly get worse; the manager of the Hall, Ernest Bean, only added fuel to Glock's fire when he wrote in February 1960 to complain about the BBC's poor performance there. He felt that 'there is an inherited aura of mediocrity about BBC concerts which keeps people away. This is distressing to me because the programmes you are putting on ought to put your concerts well ahead of many of the others in the minds of discerning concert-goers. . . .' The BBC's concerts averaged an attendance over the previous two seasons of 54% – by far the lowest of the organisations which regularly promoted concerts at the hall. Schwarz had drawn good audiences only when bringing famous soloists with him in popular works: a 92% house for Rubinstein; Stravinsky had drawn a full house, as had Sargent with Moisewitsch. But there was little else that looked hopeful in Bean's analysis of the situation.

This all made Glock's plea to change the programming and strike out afresh the more cogent. He was already achieving considerable public interest with the chamber concerts given live at the Maida Vale Studios; the Thursday Invitation Concerts, juxtaposing new and old music in the most imaginative manner, had an immediate public impact. This series had begun on 7 January 1960 with a programme that brought together Mozart string quintets and *Le Marteau sans maître* by Boulez. The concerts explored a remarkably wide range of music, all set in unusual contexts. They represented Glock's first major declaration of intent for BBC radio music; in the field of chamber music, they paralleled much he was later to attempt with the Symphony Orchestra in the field of orchestral music. Characteristic programmes in the first season included a symmetrical scheme of Britten choral music, Bach harpsichord music and (at the centre) Purcell's Ode, *Welcome to all the pleasures* – the Britten and Purcell directed by, and the Bach played by, George Malcolm. Henze's Chamber Music of 1958 followed Dowland songs with lute and Beethoven's Serenade Op. 25. Stravinsky's Concerto for two pianos and Bartók's Sonata for two pianos and percussion were separated by Bach's Fifth Cello Suite (Bach is always, as Glock later remarked in a Prom prospectus, a good mixer). A lighter programme presented the piano quintets of Beethoven and Mozart, with the *Hommage à Haydn* pieces of Debussy, Dukas, Hahn, d'Indy, Ravel and Widor, plus the second series of Debussy's *Images*. Glock's instinct for juxtaposing the very old with the very new also found a place in the series. One programme presented a sequence of the Victoria Requiem, the Stravinsky Cantata, and a Bach motet. Another had as its centrepiece Machaut's *Messe de Notre Dame*. Before and after that came two performances of Boulez's *Improvisation No. 2 (Mallarmé)*, later to be incorporated in *Pli selon pli*. And to open and close the programme, music from a period almost equidistant between Machaut and Boulez – motets by William Byrd. In these concerts and many others, Glock showed how conventional notions of programme planning could be altered, even overturned, and could give way to schemes which provided a revealing setting for the music played. As in all the best concerts, in a good Glock Invitation Concert the whole was greater than the sum of its parts.

Into these concerts, and into the programmes of the Promenade Concerts, went Glock's major creative effort in his first year. Having set the tone of his planning for radio music, he brought into the BBC's Music Division, initially on short-term contracts, musicians of like mind – Alexander Goehr, David Drew, Stephen Plaistow, Leo Black, Hans Keller – whose imagination and skill developed the programmes in the succeeding few years. Goehr and Drew soon moved on, but Plaistow, Black and Keller became full-time members of the Music Division. The changes which Glock wrought in the content and spirit of the Promenade Concerts are discussed in more de-

tail in David Cox's *The Henry Wood Proms*. We should note here that his first
season introduced to the Proms the Schoenberg Op. 31 Variations and the
Webern Six Orchestral Pieces, Op. 6 (entrusted to the Royal Liverpool
Philharmonic Orchestra under John Pritchard). The BBC Symphony
Orchestra contributed the first public performance of Eugene Goossens'
Phantasy Concerto, the first London performance of Iain Hamilton's
Scottish Dances, and the première of a newly-commissioned Overture,
Derby Day, by William Alwyn. But other orchestras contributed the other
important premières, by Musgrave, Ives and Berg. It was clear from this
first Prom season that Glock was wary about entrusting difficult works to the
BBC Orchestra, for it was overworked during the Proms and had become
unused, during the last ten years of its existence, to playing the most
adventurous twentieth-century repertory.

Early plans

One of Glock's earliest triumphs was to persuade Stravinsky to conduct, and
the Festival Hall to house, a performance of *Oedipus Rex* for the Third
Programme on 9 November 1959. This took place at the extraordinary hour
of 11pm on a Monday night, following the Festival Hall's normal concert,
and was broadcast live – a bold piece of planning which Glock never
attempted to equal in his late-night Prom concerts of the early 1970s. The
speaker in *Oedipus Rex* was Jean Cocteau, and the performance was repeated
by the same forces (for the benefit of listeners unable to stay awake until
midnight) at 8.55pm on the Saturday of the same week, from Maida Vale
Studios. Apart from this event, the 1959–60 Symphony Concerts season
(planned before Glock arrived at the BBC) had concluded without any
sensations: Rubbra's Violin Concerto had been premièred on 17 February by
Endré Wolf under Schwarz; Oivin Fjeldstad brought Fartein Valen's Third
Symphony to his concert on 9 March; and Schwarz juxtaposed Beethoven's
Ninth Symphony with Bliss's choral work *Pastoral*. The now traditional
May Festival followed the main concert season. This was directed by the
Italian conductor Nino Sanzogno, who had first appeared with the Orches-
tra in the previous year. He was a regular conductor at La Scala, Milan, and
one of the prime movers in the Venice Biennale, the contemporary music
festival which attracted wide international attention. (He had brought
Walton's opera *Troilus and Cressida*, which the BBC had commissioned, to
La Scala, and was known as an advocate of new British music.) Glock's hand
was active in the balance of his four programmes: two conventional (a Verdi
Requiem and a Russian programme) and two unusual. The first of these
included the British première of Dallapiccola's *Sacra Rappresentazione: Job*,

and the second brought to England for the first time the *Musique Funèbre* in memory of Bartók by the Polish composer Witold Lutoslawski, as well as Malipiero's Third Symphony. The Lutoslawski was juxtaposed with Bartók's Sonata for two pianos and percussion, Mozart's Concerto for two pianos and Debussy's *Jeux*. It was a distinctive mixture, of which much more in similar vein was to be heard in the future.

Meanwhile Glock had planned a new winter season for the Symphony Orchestra. With twelve concerts, he was able to extend the range of activity – and it was notable that he did so mainly in concerts with guest conductors. Prominent among these was Bruno Maderna, who had two concerts, and Hans Rosbaud, who had one. On 19 October Maderna gave, almost unbelievably, the first public performance in Britain of the Schoenberg Op. 22 Songs, alongside the symphonic extracts from Berg's *Lulu* and Stravinsky's *Les Noces*. Then on 16 November he conducted part of Stravinsky's *Perséphone* and Ravel's *L'Heure Espagnole*. To Rosbaud fell one of Glock's typically ingenious schemes: a symmetrical programme enclosing two performances of Stravinsky's *Movements* for piano and orchestra (British première), framed by Blacher's *Orchester-Ornament* Op. 44 and Schoenberg's Violin Concerto, with Webern's Op. 6 pieces and Hindemith's Op. 38 Concerto at the centre. Then there was a series of large choral works: Schwarz began the season with Mozart's *Requiem*, and ended it with Beethoven's *Der glorreiche Augenblick* (the text rewritten by Hermann Scherchen, to make it a twentieth-century hymn to peace); on 30 November the outstanding young conductor, Lorin Maazel, made his first appearance in England with Mahler's Second Symphony; Sargent contributed Berlioz's *L'Enfance du Christ* on 25 January; and Jascha Horenstein returned for Beethoven's *Missa Solemnis* on 22 February. Schwarz's other concerts included some premières and some earlier music than was usual: on 2 November the season's commission, Malcolm Arnold's Fourth Symphony, was premièred alongside Bach's Cantata No. 21. On 14 December the great forty-part motet by Tallis, *Spem in alium nunquam habui*, was included, and the 8 February concert saw Schwarz giving the first performance of Gerhard's *Collages*. It was a cautious season; but the weight of significance had already begun to shift from the Honegger–Frank Martin–Rubbra–Walton axis which had dominated the fifties in the BBC to a concentrated attention on the Schoenberg–Webern–Stravinsky–Gerhard line of development. Glock's tastes were beginning to be evident.

Stink bombs in Venice

The visit of the Symphony Orchestra to the Venice Biennale in 1961 proved to be a sensation in many ways. The whole enterprise was organised at the last minute: plans were still being approved in January and February for the event, which was to take place in April. The main purpose of the visit was that the Orchestra should give the first performance of Nono's opera *Intolleranza 1960*, conducted by Bruno Maderna. In addition there was to be a symphony concert of British works. Arrangements for the tour, which had been slipped into the Orchestra's schedule between a visit to Ipswich and an Irish tour starting at Belfast, were continually disrupted. Plane failure meant that the whole of the first day's rehearsal in Venice was lost; the symphony concert was only a moderate success, since Vaughan Williams' Fourth Symphony was regarded as relentlessly old-fashioned by the festival audience (a couple of whom booed at the end) and only Britten's *Nocturne* really made a mark. Nono's work was an ambitious left-wing story based on an idea by Angelo Maria Ripellino; it dealt with an emigrant miner, oppressed and exploited, who finds through a series of traumas the way back to a fruitful life; Nono called it 'a story of our times; it shows the awakening of man's conscience when, rebelling against the pressures of circumstances, he looks for a reason, a human basis of life.' The opera's sentiments were unlikely to appeal to any fascist sympathiser in Italy, and indeed, unknown to the Orchestra, neo-fascist movements were planning their own right-wing demonstrations against the piece: rumours appeared in the press on the day of the première.

The Nono opera was originally to have been performed on 11, 13 and 15 April, though the first performance was subsequently postponed until the 13th. It was relayed direct to England. Almost as soon as it began there were noisy interruptions from a well-organised group of protesters, who obviously gathered some support from other members of the audience whose dislikes in the piece were purely musical. Maderna carried on against the barracking, but then a new element entered the protest: stink bombs began to descend from the upper regions of the theatre. Most of the bombs hit the orchestra pit, and so the players bore the brunt of the attack. George Willoughby, the Concerts and Orchestral Manager, thought the circumstances justified ringing down the curtain: 'Conditions in the orchestra pit were appalling . . . the players were anxious for the security of their instruments. I would have understood it if any of the players . . . had refused to come back after the interval. . . .' But Maderna insisted on carrying on, and eventually won a moderate victory against the protesters. The whole incident received great publicity in a gleeful British press: for once events were so amazing that it was difficult to exaggerate them. For the second performance of the opera on Saturday night, 15 April, everything went off much more smoothly, though a repeat demonstration was feared. The police were present in large number: rumour had it that the reason they had not appeared on the first night was that the opera itself contained not a few slighting references to the role of the police in society.

1961–2

In the 1961–2 season, which was to be Schwarz's last as Chief Conductor, Glock used his quota of twelve concerts to present a few thematic ideas, to explore the twentieth-century repertory in some breadth, and also to push the limits of the programmes back in time. Schwarz conducted Masses by Mozart (opening concert, 4 October), Haydn (13 December) and Beethoven (21 March), and devoted an evening to Bach's *St John Passion* (21 February). His other concert on 1 November included Part III of Schumann's *Faust*; this was nicely balanced by Liszt's *Faust* Symphony which completed the season on 4 April under Izler Solomon. There was another visit by Stravinsky, this time to direct his *Perséphone* complete (a concert for which the Festival Hall, with unusual flexibility, agreed to a starting time of 5 pm on Sunday 29 October). The other visitors were Pierre Monteux, who added to the Stravinsky theme with the *Symphony of Psalms*; Erich Leinsdorf, who directed Bruckner's Ninth; Sargent in the Berlioz *Te Deum*; and Jean Martinon in Debussy's *Le Martyre de Saint-Sebastien*. Michael Tippett made a brief appearance on 1 November, conducting his own *Divertimento on Sellinger's Round*. The two concerts which bore the closest imprint of Glock's attention, however, were those of 29 November and 24 January. The first was designated a Schoenberg Tenth Anniversary Concert: Bruno Maderna conducted a formidable programme of the Orchestral Variations, the orchestral version of the First Chamber Symphony and *Verklärte Nacht*. In addition there were two British premières: *Prelude to Genesis*, Op. 44, and *A Survivor from Warsaw*, Op. 46. The second concert was conducted by Michael Gielen: it included two performances of Webern's Five Pieces, Op. 10, Stravinsky's *Agon*, music by Mozart and – almost scandalously – the British première of a work by Messiaen, *Reveil des oiseaux*, which had been written over ten years previously in 1953. That such works still remained to be heard in England in 1964 was an indictment of the country's narrow musical culture. The season made a bold impression: an unusual selection of classics was juxtaposed with a wide selection of twentieth-century music. Like all the best Glock programmes, each had a strong profile.

One feature was notably absent from the winter season: new commissions. Glock had decided to shift the focus of attention for commissioned works to the Proms, where they might have a better chance of public success. It was clearly important that the range of these commissions be increased from the one major work per year which had become standard in the fifties. Glock's first move was to propose that, supposedly to safeguard against composers' difficulties in producing works to deadlines, the BBC should have 'a reserve of compositions . . . I could plan about three years ahead . . .' He suggested to Wellington a substantial list of composers he would like to approach immediately: for 1961, Elisabeth Lutyens, Alexander Goehr, Malcolm Williamson and Anthony Milner; for 1962 Peter Maxwell Davies, Alan Rawsthorne, Nicholas Maw and Thea Musgrave; for 1963 Iain Hamilton, Peter Racine Fricker and possibly Tippett; and for 1964 Hugh Wood, Priaulx Rainier . . . It was a fine list, and it achieved its end. Instead of being allowed a set amount of money for individual commissions, Glock first obtained from the BBC a cumulative amount over a three-year period; this amount was then increased; finally there was an agreement that the whole commissioning fund was inadequate. A study comparing BBC commissioning fees with those abroad pointed clearly to the paltry nature of the sums of money involved. By August 1961 the money available had been increased sevenfold, enabling Glock to plan as he wished; and he decided that on the whole greater public attention would be gained, and a readier audience found, if commissions were heard at the Proms – and not necessarily played by the BBC Symphony Orchestra. In the 1961 Proms, two of the promised commissions – Elisabeth Lutyens's work, *Symphonies* for solo piano, wind, harps and percussion (28 July) and Alexander Goehr's *Hecuba's Lament* (24 August) – were played by the BBC Symphony Orchestra, both conducted by John Carewe. But a considerable amount of other adventurous repertory went elsewhere, including Malcolm Williamson's Organ Concerto and Anthony Milner's Divertimento for string orchestra. Because Sargent was associated with the BBC Symphony Orchestra, its programmes inevitably contained the high proportion of classics which he contributed to the seasons.

Towards a new conductor

Glock was already beginning to concern himself with the future of the Symphony Orchestra. It was difficult to dispute the fact that its work had stagnated; that it had the reputation of being a boring orchestra which sometimes played well. The Orchestra needed enlivening. The remedies were, in part, what they had always been: better players and more public concerts. But there was also another serious problem, that of the Orchestra's conductor. Rudolf Schwarz's musicality had been appreciated by the Orchestra more than it had by the Festival Hall public, and in general the qualities of his performances had not communicated themselves to a very wide audience. The critics were particularly aggressive, and in the first months of Glock's controllership there had been something of a crisis, brought on by Schwarz's performance of Mahler's Ninth Symphony on 9 December at the Festival Hall. Both *The Times* and the *Daily Telegraph* attacked the performance as a 'travesty'. *The Times* wrote:

> We seldom hear so blatant a misrepresentation of any work as Mr Rudolf Schwarz offered. . . . It is not as if the work admitted of various interpretations. . . . The absurdity of his conception would be manifest to all if the symphony had been by Beethoven or Brahms . . . he tore the nobility, the anguish, the sarcasm, the very vitals, from a grand symphony, and flung it over his shoulder at us, limp and featureless.

These extremely strong words were echoed in Donald Mitchell's report in the *Daily Telegraph*:

> Mr Schwarz's performance began badly . . . went from bad to worse . . . the unhappy climax of this travesty of an interpretation was reserved for the very slow last movement, through which the conductor swept at a brisk and unfeeling pace.

Even Neville Cardus, who was more polite, called it a 'misleading translation of Mahler'. Schwarz was so hurt by the violence of these criticisms that he at once offered his resignation to the BBC. It was naturally refused; as Glock wrote to him two days after the concert: 'We cannot accept the possibility of any extreme action such as your typically sensitive and public-spirited gesture seems to invite. There is no question, in other words, of the BBC submitting to an outbreak of unfavourable, let alone vicious, press notices. Do please therefore continue your work.' Schwarz complied, and carried on. But the criticism did not abate, and in 1960 one of the planners in Music Division responsible for orchestral programmes, Leonard Isaacs, declared that he thought there was 'a concerted and premeditated effort by the gentlemen of the press to belittle [Schwarz] on every possible occasion'.

Many of the Orchestra continued to enjoy their work with Schwarz, but it was clear that he could not provide the spearhead of a revolution such as Glock intended, nor that he would have the general acclaim in public concerts which was so necessary if the BBC's concert season was to become more successful. Glock might have liked to approach Bruno Maderna, whose musical sympathies were close to his own; but Maderna was unwell, and the first consideration had to be that of orchestral training. Glock began to work towards the notion of inviting a group of guest conductors to undertake the bulk of the year's work, in an effort both to revitalise the spirit of the Orchestra and to find a trainer who could bring about the changes which he intended over a longer period.

It was important that there should be maximum confidence in all quarters in this scheme of guest conductors, and that included Schwarz himself who would play an important part in the plan. Glock waited until they were in Venice together in April 1961, during the Nono performances, and met him to explain the problems which confronted the BBC, the changes he wanted to bring about in the Orchestra, and the different role he saw for Schwarz in these plans. Schwarz was delighted with the scheme – it would enable him to concentrate on the repertoire he loved, and work in the relative calm of the studio more than in the competitive atmosphere of the London concert hall where he had been uneasy ever since moving from the provinces. With typical foresight and lack of personal self-interest, Schwarz had the interests of the Orchestra at heart. It was agreed that he would step down as Chief Conductor as from August 1962, in order to make way for a new team among whom he would be a prominent figure. Glock went out of his way to emphasise that the aim was to implement a policy, not merely respond to criticism. He later wrote: 'Our future plans have been evolved in an attempt to find a positive solution to the many problems that face a radio orchestra, with its formidable repertory, and not in response to press criticisms, which I for one have often found unjust, unbalanced and mechanical.' The change of policy was agreed by the beginning of 1962, and in April the announcement was made to the press that a group of conductors, including Colin Davis, Malcolm Sargent, Dean Dixon, Antal Dorati, Rudolf Kempe and Rudolf Schwarz, would lead the team for the next season. Also involved would be Michael Gielen, Jan Krenz, Lorin Maazel, Norman Del Mar, Igor Markevitch and Jean Martinon.

Press reaction to this announcement was understandably baffled and hostile. *The Times* proclaimed: 'Not the Way to Make the BBC Orchestra First-rate,' and wrote:

> Orchestral players are apt to say that there are no bad orchestras, only bad conductors. But almost all of us would agree that a conductor is necessary to the musical health of a permanent symphony orchestra, and the recent announcement that the BBC Symphony Orchestra is to work without a permanent conductor, after the imminent expiry of Mr Rudolf Schwarz's present contract, is disquieting indeed. . . . This policy of divided rule is at the moment an unwise one for the BBC Symphony Orchestra, because the orchestra lacks, and has for many years lacked, exactly that sure-founded

virtuosity and strong musical character without which versatile development is attempted in vain. The material is admirable enough, and it can, under a Stravinsky, a Rosbaud, a Maazel, an Izler Solomon, be welded together into the semblance of a splendid orchestra. When a less dynamic conductor comes along, the orchestra's achievement is seen to have been founded upon sand, for the playing reflects more of the conductor's shortcomings than of his worthwhile musical qualities. It begins to sound like a second-rate orchestra, and not a first-rate one on an off-night. And this is precisely what the symphony orchestra of the British Broadcasting Corporation – as near to a state-owned orchestra as we have – cannot afford to do.

An injection of energy

In fact, Glock had already settled on the man whom he thought would be best able to invigorate his Orchestra. It was clear from the plans for the Festival Hall season in 1962–3 who was in effect, if not in fact, Chief Conductor of the BBC Symphony Orchestra. Antal Dorati had come to England with a brilliant reputation as a rebuilder of orchestras. First with the Dallas, Texas, Symphony Orchestra, then with the Minneapolis Symphony Orchestra, and since arriving in Britain with the London Symphony Orchestra, Dorati was a conductor who all agreed had an electric effect on performers and audiences alike. He had a fine administrative mind, a deep interest in the *minutiae* of individual players' performances, and a clear vision of what a great orchestra should be. The composer Roberto Gerhard was the link between Dorati and Glock. Gerhard had first met Dorati when he was living in Barcelona in the early 1930s and Dorati had visited the town with the Monte Carlo Ballet. Gerhard left Spain at the time of the Civil War and settled in Cambridge, where he came to know Glock well. He spent some time at the end of the 1950s as visiting professor of music at Ann Arbor, Michigan, and it was there that he made contact again with Dorati, who was conducting the Minneapolis Symphony Orchestra. Gerhard told Dorati of Glock's musical vision, and told Glock of Dorati's lively work. When Glock was looking for a new orchestral trainer, Dorati was an obvious choice. He was thus able to reply to press criticism in October 1962:

> There has recently been a good deal of controversy over the BBC's decision not to appoint a chief conductor for its Symphony Orchestra, at least for the next two years ... The question is: who at the present moment is the right man for such a task, and how long is 'long enough'? Well, we have asked Antal Dorati, and he will conduct the Orchestra for rather less than five months over the next two seasons. His own view is that this gives him

sufficient scope; and having heard two or three of his rehearsals since he arrived about ten days ago, and seen him and the players conspiring their utmost to do well, I think you are going to get some splendid concerts . . .

By 1962 Glock was beginning to explore radical ways in which the functioning of the Orchestra could be improved. Since the post-war explosion of freelance orchestral work, at which time many players had left the Orchestra, conditions in London had continued to favour the freelance employment of musicians. There was no longer the same attraction in the musical profession for the steady employment which an organisation such as the BBC could provide for the seasoned professional. There was now a new generation of young, first-rate orchestral players: to them, a lifetime's performance in one orchestra was not sufficient for musical fulfilment. These intelligent, highly talented players wanted the stimulus and satisfaction of playing in chamber music as a regular alternative to orchestral work; they wanted to appear as soloists in concertos; they wanted to earn good money from extra recording or film work. A varied, diverse life along those lines was readily available in London during the early 1960s. Survival in this freelance world was not easy, but for the best players it provided the most profitable and most enjoyable means of existence.

It was realised that the only way to attract the finest players to the BBC Symphony Orchestra would be to ensure that they could be offered a generous amount of free time for other activities. And life in the Orchestra had to be purposeful enough to satisfy the best talent available. How could this be achieved? The only method would be to release important players, especially principals, from the binding 33-hour weekly contract which gave them so little freedom. This meant in its turn that the work of section principals would have to be shared between two players on a rota basis. A co-principal scheme, such as worked in continental orchestras but had not been tried here, might be the answer. Glock wanted a flexible arrangement: in the woodwind section, a half-and-half agreement which the leading players would work out among themselves; in the strings, a scheme of sharing the principal's work so that more important players would have time off.

To enliven the regular life of the Orchestra, Glock argued strongly for bringing it out of the studio more often. Writing in March 1962, when the plans were first forming in his mind, he said he had been 'profoundly impressed by the different level and impact of our own performances at the Royal Festival Hall from those of the LSO and Philharmonia, who are constantly having to project the music to an audience . . .' At first he wanted to increase by a large amount the number of public concerts in the provinces, so that for every two studio dates there would be one public appearance. (This would have meant increasing the number of out-of-town concerts to around twenty.) He subsequently revised his estimate of what was necessary: as long as the Orchestra played outside the studio once a fortnight, he felt that would be a sufficient improvement on the prevailing situation.

A plan of action

By the spring of 1962, just under three years after he took over, Glock was in a position to spell out his conclusions about the Symphony Orchestra's needs to the BBC management. He devoted a substantial part of his report to the Board of Governors in 1962 to this problem, and identified four basic requirements for rebuilding the Orchestra, which he later expanded in more detail to Lindsay Wellington: 'I think we are all agreed that the top priority in BBC music at present (apart from trying to maintain programmes that make the *Radio Times* exciting to read every Thursday) is an attempt to rejuvenate and reconstruct the Symphony Orchestra.' His four requirements were:

1. The choice of a new leader, and of a team of conductors who will insist on a high standard of orchestral technique and discipline.

The first part had already been accomplished, for Paul Beard had retired at the end of the 1962 Proms after serving the Orchestra with great distinction since 1936. Hugh Maguire had been appointed in his place. The second part could begin to be put into effect with the emergence of Glock's temporary plan for guest conductors.

2. A planning of programmes and of rehearsal schedules so that conductors and players are allowed more adequate preparation than now – and this means reducing the total number of concerts given by the Symphony Orchestra.

Glock thought that the Symphony Orchestra should reduce its output from around 102 concerts a year (apart from the Proms) to around ninety, the shortfall to be provided by the BBC regional orchestras. This would make possible adequate rehearsal for each event; Glock stressed that 'there should not be too many difficult works to learn . . . there should be more repeats than is usually now the case'. (The number of repeat performances had dropped considerably with the curtailment of the Third Programme.)

3. The next, and I think crucial, point is the need to strengthen the Symphony Orchestra by bringing in a number of outstandingly good players.

This, Glock admitted, would be expensive; to employ all the co-principals envisaged in his scheme would cost about £17,000 a year. But a start could be made where most needed, in the string sections, while exploring other possibilities; this would reduce the cost considerably. Five new rank-and-file strings were also badly needed, and an extra horn was also desirable.

    4. A planned policy of taking the Symphony Orchestra out of the
       studio rather more than at present.

This final point had already been discussed, and Glock drew the conclusion that for a preliminary outlay of around £8000 per annum a radical change could be achieved in the standards of the Symphony Orchestra.

In essence, Glock's plan was agreed by BBC management; it was made clear that a solid improvement in attendances at public concerts was to be expected as a result, and that a close control should be kept over the regional orchestras' expanded contribution to the radio network concerts each year. Though Glock would have liked to bring in new co-principal woodwind players immediately, he contented himself with these improvements for the time being.

'Creative unbalance'

Glock's plans for the Orchestra should be seen in the context of his policy for BBC music as it developed during the first years of his appointment as Controller. In 1963 he made an important declaration of intent in a lecture delivered in the BBC Concert Hall on 'The BBC's Music Policy'. Referring to the catalogue of music broadcast on the radio (a document drawn up annually by the BBC), he tried to dissipate fears that there had been an undue amount of new music on the air since he had taken over:

> The catalogue shows not only what a vast range of music the BBC does broadcast, but also the prominence that is given to the great masters. It is worth saying this because we have acquired a reputation during the last three years for giving contemporary music a great run for its money. The fact is that we have not given even a minute more to contemporary music than before. What we have tried to do, both with the music of the past and with that of the present day, is to make a strong impact, to choose a high percentage of important works, and to limit the number of those secondary and incidental pieces which belong rather to the Spa repertory, and which are apt to make faint reading in the *Radio Times* and dull or inanimate listening.
>
> So far as contemporary music is concerned – contemporary music of challenging difficulty – the catalogue shows that during 1961 the BBC broadcast, for example, three pieces by Pierre Boulez, two by Luigi Nono, one by Stockhausen, one by Maxwell Davies; and that the total time devoted to Anton Webern during the whole year was about two hours.

Sidonie Goossens, one of the earliest members of BBC ensembles at Savoy Hill, and principal harpist of the BBC Symphony Orchestra for all its first fifty years, in 1926 (above), and with Igor Stravinsky, Maida Vale, December 1958

Colin Davis rehearses for his first concert as Chief Conductor of the BBC Symphony Orchestra in October 1967, with the pianist Victoria Postnikova

An ebullient Colin Davis, around 1961

Mastermind: Pierre Boulez, on one of his first visits to the BBC Symphony Orchestra in 1965. He became Chief Conductor in 1971

Percussion battery: Pierre Boulez as a rehearsal is set up in Maida Vale Studio I for his Pli selon pli, *which was given its first complete London performance on 7 May 1969 in the Festival Hall*

Electronic complications: Diego Masson (left) and Pierre Boulez (centre) working with BBC engineers on Boulez's . . . explosante-fixe *. . . at the Proms, 1973*

Composers and conflicts: two leading musicians whom Glock invited to direct the BBC Symphony Orchestra; both had difficulties with the Orchestra. Left: Karlheinz Stockhausen, who initiated the Orchestra into his world of 'total improvisation' in 1970. Right: Peter Maxwell Davies, who conducted the unsuccessful Prom première of his Worldes Blis *in 1969; the piece was convincingly revived by the Orchestra in 1973*

Fewer problems: two British composers working with the Orchestra in 1969. Left: Malcolm Arnold. Right: Sir Lennox Berkeley

From railway shed to concert hall: The Round House, Camden Town, where the BBC Symphony Orchestra gave concerts of new music from 1971. Above: an engraving of the railway engine house. Below: Pierre Boulez in the Round House during rehearsals for a BBC concert, March 1974

Prom quadrophony: Stockhausen's Carré, *for four orchestral groups, played twice at a late-night Promenade Concert in September 1972*

BBC Controller, Music: William Glock, who retired in 1972 (left), and Robert Ponsonby, introducing his first season of Proms in 1974

A short-lived partnership: Rudolf Kempe, Chief Conductor of the BBC Symphony from 1975 until his death in May 1976. One of the handful of concerts he conducted with the Orchestra was a brilliant Prom on 29 August 1975. Above: rehearsing for the concert. Below Dvořák's New World *Symphony*

Why then the reputation? It may have been partly the placing of some of these works in prominent contexts, such as the Thursday Invitation Concerts or the Proms, partly the fact that we included them at all – for no one will pretend that it is easy for the ordinary intelligent music-lover to come to terms with Stockhausen and other avant-garde composers, or with Webern either for that matter. Yet the BBC has always been prepared to exhibit new works of any consequence, however difficult; to act, if you like, as a kind of information bureau. And the works in question constitute, in any case, a minute ingredient of the total music output.

Of course, the controversy over the BBC's choice of contemporary music involves much more than an almost invisible dose of Boulez and Stockhausen. It involves Schoenberg as well, whose works have been treated as a rightful part of the repertory only during the last few years. Above all, though, it involves the very principle of choice; for there is no doubt that judgement is more difficult to exercise with confidence in this field than in any other. Nevertheless, if you are prepared to put a foot anywhere, then you must be prepared to put it wrong. In the end, contemporary music as a whole will surely gain from an attempt to uphold standards, to look for whatever seems vital even if it is often forbidding.

Glock established the principle that was to dominate his period as Controller: 'that if you are to maintain an interesting repertory, a repertory that will be relevant and stimulating, then you should not only broadcast every imaginable kind of good music but also try to sense the things that at any given moment need perhaps a little more than their natural share of programme time'. How was this vital choice of emphasis to be made? Glock went on:

This may sometimes happen in reaction against previous neglect, and then one must judge the moment when the 'campaign' should be halted and the music be left to take care of itself (e.g. with Schoenberg just about now); or it may be the result of something that is in the air, that comes from divining to some extent what people would want to hear (I wonder if this is not the case with the BBC's important series of Mahler symphonies, two or three years ago?) Such things are difficult to define, and difficult to grasp in practice. But one thing seems certain. Nothing truly alive and worthwhile could ever be achieved by working to a system of quotas. And who, after all, is to decide what those should be? The right principle seems to be that of a creative unbalance, as I have just tried to describe; and behind this, again and always, the exercise of every ounce of judgement one may possess.

The principle of 'creative unbalance' was one which linked Glock's work with that of the Music Department of the 1930s. Instead of a faithfulness which merely reflected public taste, Glock – like Sir John Reith, Sir Adrian Boult and Edward Clark before him – determined to lead public taste and to anticipate its enthusiasms.

In his lecture, Glock made it clear that the Symphony Orchestra formed a central part of his undertaking. In a phrase he might later have reconsidered, he said that 'it is the state of the Symphony Orchestra, perhaps more than anything else, which gives evidence of our aspirations and our critical standards, and which affects, for good or ill, the general attitude towards all our musical activities.' He acknowledged that

> too often in the past we have asked the Symphony Orchestra to perform almost impossible feats of preparation, have relied on their adaptability and remarkable skill in sightreading to pull us through programmes for which others would have demanded at least twice as much rehearsal. Perhaps this is the natural tendency in broadcasting, an inevitable result of trying to open up frontiers that would otherwise remain closed, of presenting the listener with the fullest possible range of musical experience. But we are now engaged on a policy of compromise.

On the planning of orchestral programmes he expressed the possible conflicts of high standards and wide repertory:

> Thus there is a never-ending struggle between one vital ingredient of broadcasting and another. One must be continually prepared to make adjustments, and yet never yield too far in the matter of repertory. It is better to include a small chamber of horrors than to cry halt and treat contemporary music of any vitality as a disaster from which the listener must be carefully shielded. For the planning of broadcast programmes is not a question of taste, but rather of judgment and of receptiveness; and those with the most responsibility and the most influence must be more liberal than the others, more receptive to every kind of music from Boulez to Mozart to Pérotin. Of course they will not feel themselves deeply involved in this entire territory of music; no one could. But neither will they try to suppress works of generally accepted importance, even though they might not wish to hear these works themselves.

Glock's critics would argue that he did just this: he did not programme works that he did not wish to hear himself, works by a whole generation of English composers whose only fault was that they were conservative. But was their music of 'generally accepted importance'? Glock judged not, and turned his attention elsewhere.

To the acute problems of programming the BBC Symphony Orchestra's public concert season Glock devoted a special section of his lecture:

> Whereas the Proms encompass a whole world of orchestral music, with contrasts and proportions that can be carefully chosen, the concerts at the Festival Hall are isolated events, and perhaps too few in number to express much else than an adventurous determination to provide what others probably will not. The problem as to what to include in these prestige programmes is by no means easy to solve. We tend to aim as often as we can at a concert consisting of only one work – an opera or a Passion or some gargantuan symphony; and failing that, two works; and failing that, three. In other words, we turn away from the conventional patterns and try to plan a series of 'events', to find works that will make a fresh and exciting and grandiose impact. But although it may seem that the available repertory is so large that one is conscious above all of a giddy freedom of choice, in practice this is by no means the case. The recent performance of *Benvenuto Cellini* was a worthwhile 'event', or so we thought. But what about a double operatic bill consisting of Schoenberg's *Von Heute auf Morgen* and Ravel's *L'Enfant et les sortilèges*? What kind of audience would that attract? We decided: none at all; and so we began to look for a strong and attractive piece that would go well with the Schoenberg to make one programme, and the same with the Ravel, to make another. This is a perfectly reputable method of programme building, and really better both for those listening at home and for the actual audience in the hall. We have sometimes made the mistake in recent years of piling enterprise on enterprise until neither orchestra nor audience could quite assimilate all that was put before them. Now we have changed our tactics, and partly because of this, and partly perhaps because of the Symphony Orchestra's new and growing reputation, the Festival Hall audiences have gone up by 60 per cent since last season. That is an encouraging figure, because I do not think the choice of works has ever fallen below the level of interest that the BBC ought to provide. And that others share this view is shown by the scheme that is now being developed, to persuade some of the leading London orchestras to share in a series of adventurous programmes at the Festival Hall 'in the weeks when there are no BBC concerts'.

These remarks point to the fact that Glock found it much easier to make his special impact on musical taste *via* the Proms rather than the Winter Season of concerts: this was something that was to remain true until Boulez and Glock together reorganised and expanded that series in the early 1970s. But Glock did not let the difficulties stand in the way of his planning, and he finished his lecture with a declaration which he would stand by for ten years: 'Whatever else may happen, there is one thing we intend to maintain; and that is liveliness.'

A radical reorientation of the BBC's music policy was laid out in this lecture. Glock minimised its differences from the policy of the 1950s, but in fact they could hardly have been greater. He reinterpreted the spirit of the 1930s, and resolved to draw the BBC and the musical public belatedly into the postwar era.

1962–3 season

In the 1962–3 Festival Hall season the first stage of Glock's plans for the Orchestra was put into action. In effect, though not in title, Antal Dorati was the Orchestra's Chief Conductor: he had the opening concert (3 October), with Beethoven's Ninth, and three others including Britten's Spring Symphony (6 February) and Berlioz's *Benvenuto Cellini* complete on 23 January. His other concert (14 November) brought together four major twentieth-century figures: Bartók (*Cantata profana*); Schoenberg (*Dance round the Golden Calf* from *Moses und Aron* for the first time on a London concert platform), Tippett (a new *Preludium* for brass, bells and percussion), and Stravinsky (*The Rite of Spring*). Other conductors in the season had one concert each: Michael Gielen gave the British première of Schoenberg's drama *Die Glückliche Hand*; Norman Del Mar conducted Mahler's Sixth Symphony; Boult conducted the British première of Shostakovich's Twelfth Symphony; Colin Davis directed Stravinsky's *Apollo* and Mozart's *Requiem*; Lorin Maazel conducted Bach's B minor Mass; while Dixon, Sargent and Martinon had more conventional programmes.

In this 1962–3 season the first of the new players were introduced into the string sections at the front desks. Hugh Maguire was leader with Norman Nelson as deputy leader (Arthur Leavins had a short period as 'Répétiteur', but left for the sunnier climate of the BBC Concert Orchestra). In the second violins Trevor Connah joined Jeffrey Wakefield as co-principal, with Belle Davidson as sub-principal; in the violas John Coulling joined Harry Danks, with Joan Wolstencroft as sub-principal. The cello section was distinguished by the addition of Kenneth Heath to the front desk, with Alexander Kok; Frank Ford was sub-principal; in the double basses Gerald Drucker and Gerald Brinnen became the co-principals.

New manager, new orchestral schemes

Thus the first stage of Glock's plans had succeeded; there was a new and vital quality in the Orchestra's string leadership. The second stage was to apply the same process to the wind section, and to improve the quality of the rank-and-file strings. Glock now had the collaboration of Dorati in his plans. And in the middle of 1963 the devoted and long-serving George Willoughby retired as Orchestral Manager (though he remained with the BBC for a while as Concerts Manager). It was thus possible to find a new manager for the Orchestra who was especially sympathetic to the Glock–Dorati approach. Glock invited Paul Huband, Head of Music in Manchester, to fill the post. He was to be in command of the Orchestra, working closely with them not from Yalding House but in the Maida Vale Studios. (The public concert arrangements were to remain in Yalding House, with Music Division.) Huband's influence on the next ten years of the Orchestra's existence was a vital one. Through all the challenges of reorganisation he maintained the morale of players and did all the detailed work which helped to realise the ambitions of Glock. He became the important diplomatic link between the BBC's administration – especially the Programme Contracts and managerial departments – and the day-to-day running of the Orchestra.

The next stage of the operation was full of problems. It was clear that if a workable co-principal scheme was to be introduced for the woodwind section, then delicate negotiations would have to take place. Most of these negotiations were undertaken personally by Glock before Huband's arrival. The woodwind principals in the 1962–3 season were the flautist Douglas Whittaker, the oboist Janet Craxton, the recently-appointed clarinettist Colin Bradbury (who had succeeded Ralph Clarke after the 1960 Proms), and the bassoonist Geoffrey Gambold. Glock proposed that they themselves should suggest partners with whom they could happily co-operate. These could be found among the lower-ranked players in each section, or from outside 'star' names. The original plan was to ask each principal to play both first and second in the section on different occasions. But none of the players wanted to do all the work of the section principal, and all of them objected to playing second to their co-principals. It was therefore resolved that the work should be split between the two players on a half-and-half basis; each player would play only half-time.

The situation worked out differently in each section. In the flutes the number two, David Butt, joined Douglas Whittaker as co-principal. In the oboes Janet Craxton, who had been a strong admirer of Rudolf Schwarz and was less enthusiastic about the new regime, left to concentrate on solo and chamber music; two new co-principal oboists, Terence McDonagh and Sidney Sutcliffe, were appointed. In the clarinets Jack Brymer was approached to share the work with Colin Bradbury, which he agreed to do. And in the bassoon section William Waterhouse joined Geoffrey Gambold as co-principal. Douglas Moore and Neill Sanders became co-principal horns. Most of these players had joined by the start of the 1963–4 season; William Waterhouse joined in January 1964, and the co-principal wind scheme formally took effect from that date.

With the rank-and-file string sections of the Orchestra, the difficulties were more marked. An intensive advertising campaign to recruit new members had met with little success: there were sixty-eight applicants, forty-five of whom were given auditions. Not one was of the standard required. The reason was that the rates offered to players were not competitive. On the open market, players could earn twice as much as in the BBC's rank-and-file, and have the additional benefit of being taxed as self-employed persons. Huband argued against accepting poor players:

> If we take the easy course of recruiting the inadequate players who can be engaged, the way to the Orchestra's further progress will be barred and we shall gradually lose our liveliest and most talented principals who are with us because they are ambitious for the Orchestra. If, on the other hand we are given the means to meet and defeat an unfavourable 'player's market' by offering the right salaries and conditions of work, we shall then be able to attain the high standard which will rival that of first-class orchestras in other countries.

More money was needed. But it would be impossible to increase all salaries. So Huband's suggested compromise was to create an order of seniority among the rank-and-file positions. There would then be a sequence of seven players, all on special salaries, before the basic rank-and-file was reached, thus lessening the effect of the low salary.

Glock took up all these points, in a note of 27 April 1964, in an effort to persuade the BBC management to spend more money on the renewal of the Orchestra.

> The first criterion in judging an orchestra is its string playing. If this is thin, acid and lustreless then the noblest brass in the world and the most poetic and accomplished woodwind are the enhancement and decoration of a non-existent structure . . . we have made great progress, partly through bringing in a number of excellent leaders and partly because the strings as a whole have begun to play with the greater sweep and ambition that comes from the consciousness of an upward curve in the fortunes of the orchestra . . . the present moment is a critical turning-point . . . if we recruit indifferent players because those are the best we can get then we shall be a serious rival to the provincial orchestras but to no-one else. But if we plunge for a bolder

solution, and make it possible to enlist some of the first-class players we know to be interested in joining the Orchestra, then we can do honour to the BBC both at home and abroad.

There was one other essential difficulty to be overcome in making employment in the Symphony Orchestra attractive to those in the freelance world. That was the income tax position. As salaried employees of the BBC, Orchestra members were taxed at source on Schedule E; freelance musicians were self-employed, paying tax on Schedule D. The former had the benefits of a pension scheme; the latter had the benefits of extensive tax-deductible expenses. It would be wrong to suggest that all preferred the latter: there was a new breed of orchestral player – young professionals with families – to whom considerations of security and permanence were important. The problem was that they were as yet an emerging generation; the most distinguished players had other priorities, and it would be difficult for the BBC to retain their services without changing the status of their employment.

A radical proposal

The immense and largely unexpected problems that the reorganisation of the Orchestra had thrown up demanded radical solutions. In the middle of 1964 Paul Huband and the Head of Programme Contracts (who was responsible for all the detailed arrangements of orchestral members' contracts) drew up a comprehensive seventeen-point document for discussion. It first outlined the problem. The BBC had declared its intentions for the Orchestra: in the words of Frank Gillard, 'to make what is already a very fine orchestra into the country's best'; and in those of William Glock, 'to restore the Symphony Orchestra to the pre-eminent position it held before the war'. The paper stressed that restoring the Symphony Orchestra to such a pre-eminent position could only be achieved at high financial cost.

The problem with regard to string players was that 'there are only a limited number of string players of really high quality and they are insufficient to meet the present demand. This means that in what is very decidedly a seller's market their value now stands at an unprecedentedly high level.' To combat this, the paper proposed a large-scale regrading of string players (such as Huband had outlined earlier).

The paper then turned to the taxation problem, and explained that the tightening of the tax laws now meant that it was impossible for the BBC to offer contracts which would enable musicians to remain self-employed, while at the same time contributing to the BBC pension fund.

It had been hoped that this extension of BBC paternalism [the pension fund]

would have the effect of making musicians feel that their position was closer
to that of staff and making them less likely to leave the BBC's service in order
to improve their immediate financial position by working as a freelance or
joining an orchestra which paid higher rates but had no pension scheme.
This hope has not been fulfilled. It is no doubt in the nature of musicians that
they prefer more cash now to long-term provisions for retirement. . . .

Only those few principals who had joined the new co-principal scheme in the
preceding year had been exempted from the requirement to join the pension
scheme. But now Huband and his colleague proposed that all members
should have the option of withdrawing from the scheme, and that no new
members should be forced to join.

While we are reluctant to do anything to reduce the extent of BBC paternalism or to encourage the natural improvidence of musicians, we are convinced
that the only hope of achieving the BBC's aims for the Symphony Orchestra
is to give all members the option of withdrawing from the scheme and to
make it voluntary for anyone joining the Orchestra. This is a cornerstone of
the present scheme.

The next proposal was, for the BBC, equally radical. Aware of the fact that
members of all non-salaried orchestras had ample opportunities for chamber
music, session work, or simply leisure, the paper proposed that every member of the BBC Symphony Orchestra should have the automatic right to opt
out of a proportion of the work undertaken by the Orchestra in any year.
'The absences would not necessarily be used for outside work or even for
practising: their primary aim would be to ensure that what has been called
the "new look" orchestral musician enjoys reasonable leisure and the physical absence from the studios which are essential to prevent staleness.'

Finally, the paper came to the matter of the cost, which would be high:
around an extra £23,000 a year. In conclusion, the paper argued:

It is appreciated that the changes proposed . . . may appear somewhat
sweeping. It must be emphasised, however, that while the BBC never
formally relinquished its ambition to possess the finest symphony orchestra
in the country, the measures previously taken have never been sufficiently
bold or far-reaching. We are convinced that the time has come to face the
problem squarely and to do our utmost to ensure that players of the requisite
calibre are available in all positions in all sections. In the present state of the
market, we cannot guarantee that the measures proposed here will achieve
their aim, but they appear to us to be the absolute minimum that offers any
serious prospect of success.

This excellent but revolutionary set of proposals, amounting to a plan for a total restructuring of the Orchestra, came at a bad time in the BBC's affairs. Money was short, the Corporation was committed to large programme expansions in the radio field (including the start of the Music Programme), and there was less than total belief in the need to maintain the very large number of musicians employed by BBC house orchestras throughout the country. The reaction to the plan from BBC management was definite (10 August): the Director of Sound Broadcasting was

> unwilling to contemplate any proposition which involves current expenditure of this order.... If we were to spend anything like the [amount] proposed for the Symphony Orchestra we would virtually remove the prospect of developments in other directions for a long time ahead and we should be steering too high a proportion of our available funds to finance this orchestra.

The Director of Administration suggested that 'you must therefore finally reconcile yourselves to the fact that our present difficulties with the Orchestra must somehow be remedied at very much lower cost . . . I think you had better consult together and if you can see a way of making progress draw me in again.'

With this, the possibility of making the BBC Symphony Orchestra unquestionably the pre-eminent orchestra in England disappeared for the time being. Only a week after the full scheme was turned down some modified schemes which would not involve major expense were discussed. The main points agreed were that the pension fund should be made optional as suggested. Members should be offered a choice between a salaried post and a 'first-call' contract (that is, one in which they were given the option to do all the work undertaken by the Orchestra, but could choose what they wished to undertake). Second, a modest system of free time could be introduced in the string sections of the Orchestra. Even these proposals did not survive the attention of BBC management, however. The free-time scheme was allowed, but the optional use of the pension scheme by all players was vetoed. Instead, a 'Retainer Contract' was introduced, which was applicable only to twelve players – those vacancies which needed most urgently to be filled. This was a much smaller step forward than Huband had envisaged. Moreover, there were delays and administrative complications, and as a result most of the new recruits were not available to the Orchestra until well into 1965.

There is a certain irony in the schemes that were presented for the Orchestra's renewal in 1964. They all involved to a greater or lesser extent the dismantling of the whole edifice of a permanent, contracted orchestra which

was, essentially, the structure which had been built in 1930. Then the Orchestra had been in a unique position in the country, and able to attract
the best players as a result; by 1964 that same position had become a
barrier in the way of attracting the best players. So it gradually gave way.
The extent it gave way was, roughly, the extent to which the Orchestra
became a finer group of players. But the financial restrictions imposed by
BBC Management and reluctance of the administrative department radically
to change the basis of the Orchestra's contracts effectively ensured that the
structure of a permanent orchestra remained, and that the BBC did not
compete with the other London orchestras on equal terms in the free market.
The result was, typically, a compromise; it pleased few people. And so the
matter remained open in the succeeding years; the Orchestra improved,
more gradually than Dorati, Huband and Glock had wished, and proposals
to increase its prestige continued to surface.

Dorati's work

As these negotiations dragged on, Antal Dorati was making great strides
forward with the Orchestra. He had been employed as the 'conductor chiefly
responsible for training the Symphony Orchestra' for two years from the
autumn of 1962. At the start of the 1963–4 season he was given the formal
title of Chief Conductor; but before then he had made the case strongly to
Glock that two years was too short a time in which to achieve a revolution,
and that the length of his appointment should be extended. At that point,
when good progress was being made, Glock was eager to agree. He had a
couple of younger men in mind for an appointment later in the decade, but
neither would be ready as soon as 1964. So he wrote to Frank Gillard (14
January 1963): 'I would like to suggest that we ask Antal Dorati to continue
for two more years . . . that is to say, from September 1964 until June 1966.'
The Board of Management gave their support, with the provision that they
would eventually like to see an English conductor in the post.

By the time Dorati formally took over as Chief Conductor, he was established with a brief running to the middle of 1966 which would involve him in
four or five visits a year with a minimum of twelve weeks' work a year. His
agreement included a restatement of the relationship between the BBC's
Chief Conductor and the Music Division. Dorati asked to be consulted on
'soloists, repertoire, and the administration of the orchestra', as well as on
guest conductors. Glock insisted to Dorati's agent that 'where guest conductors and their programmes are concerned, the BBC must have freedom
of choice, but agree to keep Mr Dorati fully informed of their plans'.

Paul Huband had joined the Orchestra's administrative staff at the start of the 1963–4 season. He was soon writing enthusiastically to Glock of the effect that Dorati's vital and purposeful approach was having on the players. Sparks flew, often, and tempers were lost, but on the whole the results were productive. Dorati himself reported the progress of the first months to Glock at the end of 1963:

> The Orchestra started in low morale and played rather weakly. This soon improved, and by the end of November the picture – and sound – was entirely changed. Fine performances were given of the following works: – Beethoven: Symphony No. 7; Brahms: Symphony No. 2; Dvořák: Symphonies 6 and 7; Britten: Bridge Variations and Simple Symphony; Mahler: Symphony No. 4; Verdi: Requiem; Bach: Cantata No. 21; Skalkottas: Violin Concerto; Partos: Sinfonia Concertante for viola and orchestra.
>
> The concerts at the Festival Hall posed a special problem because of the immense difference in acoustics from Studio I, and because of a feeling of inhibition especially of the string players at these concerts. It cannot be stressed often enough that it would be of immeasurable help to the BBC SO to play more and more public concerts and also to get out of Studio I for an increasing number of broadcast concerts. I repeat here the idea which I proposed earlier to give some of these concerts at the town halls of various suburbs of London such as Walthamstow, Watford and Wembley, and to make out of these broadcast concerts some special event for the local community in question by issuing invitations mostly to people of that suburb.

Dorati concerned himself in great detail with the reports on individual orchestral members, and on the relationship between himself, Glock and Huband which would ensure the smooth running of the machinery. He saw this trinity as the centre of the enterprise. In his report to Glock he drew a diagram, depicting himself as the one responsible for playing standards, Huband for all organisation and the relationship with other BBC bodies (he should, thought Dorati, absorb the Concerts Management department), and Glock, the artistic director of the enterprise, whom Dorati asked to meet regularly to be kept informed of guest conductors, and so on. Dorati declared his belief that 'great orchestras grow only in an atmosphere of "selfish isolation" . . . that they are always made by "romantic" leaders, energetic dreamers'. And it was just such an energetic dreamer that Dorati tried to be over the following seasons. For some considerable time the results were excellent. Like every other conductor of the time, Dorati found programme planning with Glock one of the most stimulating experiences of his job. Glock would usually visit Dorati in his Rome house, and spend a few days during which ideas were thrown forwards and backwards between them. Glock never liked programme planning in isolation as much as he did when confronted by a conductor of similar tastes, who would reject suggestions and bring forward his own. For those who were able to witness some of these planning sessions as third parties, they were electrifying experiences. And the programmes that resulted from the fray grew in impressiveness. The job of translating them into practical terms, however, was a daunting and detailed one. Glock relied heavily on the support of two men. Eric Warr was Assistant Head of Music Programmes, and after Maurice Johnstone's departure in 1960 he absorbed those duties of Head of Music Programmes which Glock did not undertake himself (the post itself was suspended during this period). Warr dealt with all the Symphony Orchestra's concerts, helping with planning and administration until his retirement in 1967. Later, Christopher Samuelson, whom Glock brought into Concerts Management to help him with the planning process for the public concerts, both winter season and Proms, became an indispensable assistant. On their meticulous labour in the 1960s depended the success of many of Glock's inspirations.

In the 1963–4 season Dorati conducted five of the twelve concerts, and they included three major premières. In the first concert on 2 October, Stravinsky's *The Flood* was performed here for the first time, alongside *Oedipus Rex* and the *Firebird* suite; on 13 November the British première of Schoenberg's *Von Heute auf Morgen* was given (with Mahler's Fourth Symphony); and in the last concert of the season (1 April 1964) there was Roberto Gerhard's new BBC commission *The Plague*, for speaker, chorus and orchestra (with Mahler's Ninth Symphony). English music was not neglected, however: Alan Rawsthorne's choral work *Carmen Vitale* was given its first performance on 16 October under Norman Del Mar. Dorati also conducted two large choral works, the Verdi *Requiem* and the Beethoven Ninth Symphony; the Verdi was performed just after John F. Kennedy's assassination, and was dedicated to his memory. The other conductors in the season were the veteran Ernest Ansermet (in Ravel's *L'Enfant et les sortilèges*) and Sargent in Holst's Choral Symphony. Dean Dixon conducted Mahler's Seventh, and the young Colin Davis, then music director at Sadler's Wells, conducted Berlioz's *Romeo and Juliet*.

An important newcomer

The most influential pair of concerts in the season were barely noticed at the time. One was in the Festival Hall, and one took place a week earlier in the unlikely venue of the Assembly Hall, Worthing. They presented the first appearances with the BBC Symphony Orchestra of the French composer and conductor, Pierre Boulez. The Worthing programme was not well suited to his talents: Mozart (*Magic Flute* Overture), Chopin (Piano Concerto No. 2, with Vladimir Ashkenazy), Schubert's Fifth Symphony, and Debussy's *La Mer*. Of the Chopin Boulez said later: 'It was terrible, I felt like a waiter who keeps dropping the plates.' An internal report mentioned that he conducted the Mozart 'in the manner of an ignorant military bandmaster.' With pouring rain on the journey, cold tea in the rehearsal break, and a less than confident performance, this was an inauspicious début. In his Festival Hall concert, however, Boulez was given a chance to explore his specialities, and the resulting programme was a mixture which was to recur many times in the Orchestra's history. Boulez gave the British première of his own work, *Le Soleil des eaux*, then the Stravinsky Symphonies of wind instruments, Webern's Op. 6 Pieces, the Bach–Webern *Ricercare*, Mozart's C minor Adagio and Fugue, and Debussy's *Images*. His rapport with the Orchestra was such that Glock invited him to join them on the American tour he was planning for 1965. For that tour and, in the succeeding years, for the Festival Hall seasons and the Proms Glock and Boulez were to put together programmes that would contradict every accepted notion of programme-building, and would illuminate the twentieth-century repertory as never before.

The 1964–5 season, because of the refurbishment of the Festival Hall, was split between there and the Albert Hall. The first six concerts, between October and February, all featured works including chorus, such as would be suitable to the larger hall's acoustics. Dorati conducted Beethoven's *Missa Solemnis*; Franz-Paul Decker conducted Mozart's Vespers and Bruckner's F minor Mass; and then David Willcocks did a programme of Purcell's *King Arthur* preceded by Britten's *Sinfonia da Requiem*. After Christmas, Sargent revived Constant Lambert's *Summer's Last Will and Testament* alongside Holst's *The Planets*; Dorati returned for the Berlioz *Damnation of Faust*; and Lorin Maazel was the guest conductor for Haydn's *The Creation*. Back in the Festival Hall, four quite conservative programmes in March and April presented only one new work, though that was a demanding one: Hans Werner Henze's Cantata, *Novae de infinito laudes*, which the composer conducted on 17 March. For the rest, Haitink in Brahms, Stravinsky and Bruckner, Dorati in Berlioz, Bartók and Mahler, or Haydn, Berg and Stravinsky were on offer. These were programmes which saw the Orchestra through the difficult period of reorganisation, and which prepared the way for the adventure of 1965.

The Proms flourish

Through the years from Glock's first Promenade Concert season of 1960 to his fifth in 1964, the scope and range of the programmes had been expanded in an unprecedented manner. Complete concert performances of opera from Glyndebourne were presented in 1961 (*Don Giovanni*) and 1962 (*Così fan tutte*) and twice in 1963 (*Le Nozze di Figaro* and Monteverdi's *L'Incoronazione di Poppea*). Foreign conductors and guest orchestras played an increasingly important role – in 1963 Leopold Stokowski and Carlo Maria Giulini both directed concerts, and Georg Solti and his Covent Garden forces gave a Wagner evening. Solti and Covent Garden returned the following season (as did Stokowski) to celebrate the seventieth anniversary of the Proms with a concert performance of Verdi's *Otello*. Perhaps the most striking new element was the vast number of important, classic works which Glock introduced to the Proms for the first time – there were fifty-six works in 1961 that had never been heard before, including Haydn symphonies and the Mozart *Requiem*. Audiences lapped up the new experiences that were on offer: a remarkable aspect of Glock's success in planning the Proms was that he found his audiences were not deterred by one unfamiliar work in an otherwise popular programme. The more conservative audiences on London's South Bank could be relied on to empty the hall if there was an 'advanced' work in the programme: many of Glock's most interesting Festival Hall concerts were poorly attended. But at the Proms, Glock found that he could follow a Beethoven first half, conducted by Sargent, with Schoenberg's Violin Concerto, and still draw the largest audience of the season.

Glock made the most of his Prom audiences' open-mindedness. Increasingly, the BBC Symphony Orchestra – which, as has been noted, started the 1960s at the Proms playing the standard repertoire under Sargent – branched out into more adventurous fields. As Sargent became more willing to relinquish the platform for half-concerts (he was always a great supporter of Glock's plans, which he realised were enlivening the concerts he loved so much), the Orchestra's programmes became a mixture of standard fare and exotic innovation. The Orchestra also began to undertake more of Glock's continuing commissions. 1962 was an outstanding season in this respect, with two works – Nicholas Maw's *Scenes and Arias* and Peter Maxwell Davies' *Fantasia on an 'In Nomine' of John Taverner* – which have established themselves as significant British works. There were new works by Rawsthorne and Berkeley. By 1964, Glock felt confident enough to entrust all five BBC commissions in the season to the Symphony Orchestra; these were by Bernard Naylor, Reginald Smith Brindle, William Alwyn, Priaulx Rainier and Richard Rodney Bennett – the last an *Aubade* in memory of the assistant Prom conductor who did so much of the new repertory in the fifties, John Hollingsworth. New works were now conducted either by the composer – a long-standing tradition which Glock appears to have wisely, and gently, phased out – or by younger conductors whom Glock did much to support and promote during this period, especially Norman Del Mar and John Carewe. It was during these Prom seasons that the strong personality of Glock's regime made itself most clearly evident. And for all those who objected to Glock's strong declaration of his own taste in broadcast programmes or the Thursday Invitation Concerts, there were found few among them to criticise the wealth and range – and, most important, the popularity – of his Prom programmes. Through these years the BBC Symphony Orchestra, from being at first something of an outsider in this activity, came to assume a central role in the development.

A new Music Programme

One other innovation characterised these early Glock years. 1963 saw the largest expansion of the BBC's radio networks since the postwar reorganisation into Light, Home and Third. There had always been an anomaly in the use of the available airtime, in that the Third Programme and Network Three were heard only in the evenings, leaving their frequency unused during the daytime. Towards the end of the 1950s, a committee set up under the Assistant Director of Sound Broadcasting to consider local broadcasting began to examine the problem of wavelengths, and its terms of reference were widened to include the whole of sound broadcasting. It reported in September 1959, and some of its recommendations were included in the BBC's submissions to the Pilkington Committee, which met soon after. Pilkington endorsed the suggestion of the BBC that the spare airtime on the Third Network should be used for a popular, day-long music programme. The notion of a music programme had the beauty of simplicity; it was something that many continental stations already possessed. But it must be stressed that the idea originally arose from broadcasting policy, not from needs expressed by Music Division. Seventy more hours of music broadcasting a week represented a huge and somewhat frightening addition to the BBC's responsibilities. The problem would be to give it shape and purpose, to avoid the possibility of its becoming mere aural background.

The BBC's detailed planning for the music programme was initiated in April 1960, shortly after William Glock's arrival as Controller. Though Glock took a keen interest in the new programme, his main energies were, as noted above, directed elsewhere; the work of planning the Music Programme was undertaken by John Manduell, later to be Director of the Royal Northern

College of Music, and Chairman of the Arts Council's Music Advisory Panel. The Controller of the new programme was not, as might have been expected, the Controller of the Third Programme. The Music Programme was brought instead under the aegis of the Home Service; Ronald Lewin and then Gerard Mansell guided its fortunes until the reorganisation of those networks into Radios 3 and 4 in 1970. This system of control was, perhaps, a declaration that the new programme was to be firmly popular, not esoteric; a policy which the Assistant Director of Sound Broadcasting spelled out to the Board of Governors:

> . . . we shall have to keep in mind that the majority of the potential audience for it are music lovers with fairly simple and conservative tastes, and that our first task is to attract and build up an audience for this new programme venture.

This policy was reaffirmed by Frank Gillard to Glock: 'If we fail to find an audience of reasonable size for the Programme, we shall before long become embarrassed by it. In general, therefore, the Music Programme should not be regarded as a channel for new, difficult and advanced music.'

John Manduell's plans for the Music Programme followed this policy. There was still opportunity, in the evenings, for especially challenging listening; during the day, as Manduell wrote, 'Our chief desire is to give listeners the opportunity to enjoy the mainstream of good music whenever they want it'. And the notion that the BBC should simply provide music for its listeners was supported by another planner of the Programme, Hans Keller:

> Who are we musicians-by-birth – constitutional foreground listeners there-fore – to tell people what to do with the music we put at their disposal? Our duty boils down to – to make good music available to all who can be dis-covered to want it.

This was not a view which would find favour with Keller and other musicians when the BBC attempted to push to its logical limits the concept of 'streamed' broadcasting in *Broadcasting in the Seventies*, published in 1969. But for the time being it provided an adequate basis for the Music Programme. Under Manduell's direction, the portmanteau titles – Studio Portrait, Further Hearing, Music Making, Overture, Morning Concert, Intermezzo – all became established; some have remained to the present.

The implications of this vast expansion of music broadcasting for the provision of orchestral music were considerable. The first stage of the Music Programme was a Sunday service, from 8 am to 5 pm, introduced on 30

August 1963. This immediately began the transfer of orchestral programmes (the Sunday Symphony Concert was the first example) away from the Home Service. As the second stage came into operation on 12 December, with the inauguration of a weekday morning service, it was clear that the Home Service would lose most of its music programmes to the new service. Streamed broadcasting was being accomplished before the term had been invented. From 20 March 1964, the full service was introduced, running to 6.30 pm on weekdays; midday orchestral concerts, particularly on Wednesdays, presented concerts by regional symphony orchestras, both BBC and non-BBC.

The BBC Symphony Orchestra's pattern of work was not radically altered by the Music Programme. The burden of the expansion was carried by the provincial orchestras and – most significant – by a large increase in 'needle time', the broadcasting of commercial gramophone records. (The Musicians' Union agreed to this increase only because a commensurate increase in the employment of live musicians was to be given with the foundation of a BBC Training Orchestra based in Bristol.) But the Symphony Orchestra found, from this time on, that the wide dissemination of its work was narrowed. Its studio concerts were increasingly fitted into the schedules of the new programme and the evening Third Network wherever they suited the planners. The attention given to its studio work on the air was reduced – a problem which was to continue after the reorganisation into Radios 3 and 4.

The Music Programme was an undoubted success. Although doubts were raised in the BBC about its gradual introduction (Glock made a strong plea in November 1962 that the whole Programme should 'begin with a bang' on 1 January 1964), the wisdom of Manduell's plan became evident. The introduction of major series – Haydn symphonies and Bach keyboard music in stage one; Schubert piano music and Haydn quartets in stage two; organ recitals and Bach cantatas in stage three – all helped to accumulate interest in the new broadcasts. Musical organisations throughout the country were happy with the extra employment it gave to orchestras and to recitalists: many concerts were recorded live in regional centres. And there was an increased opportunity to hear recordings of outstanding foreign concerts. Against these benefits, however, must be set the loss to the Orchestra of a general public which encountered its broadcasts, perhaps by accident, on a mixed broadcast service.

Abroad again

The Orchestra's touring commitments had become more extensive during the Sargent years, for he was a popular figure abroad; but Schwarz had

found much less international success, and these activities had become reduced. One of Dorati's aims for the Orchestra was to give it several major
international tours which would act as a focus and encouragement for its
work. As Dorati wrote to Glock in May 1963:

> The position of the BBC Symphony Orchestra is, just because of its secure
> entrenchment within the BBC, a very peculiar one – and when I knew (after
> my first experience with it) that it can go far, I deliberately thought to arrange
> 'outside activities' such as tours – as the only way of survival of this orchestra
> as a first class body. These tours are not a luxury.

The logical start for such a project was a tour of America. Dorati had many
contacts there because of his work with American orchestras. Through the
impresario Sol Hurok, Glock was able to obtain a unique invitation from the
composer William Schuman, the President of the recently-opened Lincoln
Center in New York, for the orchestra to give a series of six concerts there in
April and May 1965 (though eventually the concerts had to be given in
Carnegie Hall). Other concerts would be arranged around this central
feature: the tour would last three weeks, and Hurok suggested a total of
fifteen concerts including the six in New York. Glock thought that with a
contribution from BBC management the tour might cover its costs, and in
requesting permission for the venture he argued strongly for the effect it
would have on the Orchestra: 'I need hardly say what a great experience
such a tour would be for the Orchestra, and what prestige (one hopes) it
would bring to the BBC.' The tour was agreed in 1963.

By late 1964, with the tour looming in the coming May, and with far less
achieved in the way of the reorganisation of the Orchestra than had been
hoped for, there was considerable worry among those responsible as to
whether it was fair to expose an orchestra in the middle of a revolution to the
pressures and demands of such a tour. Glock had arranged a challenging set
of programmes with a high proportion of twentieth-century music in them;
and he had taken the bold step of inviting Pierre Boulez to share the tour
with Dorati. Boulez was still an unknown quantity in the orchestral world,
but George Szell had shown confidence in him by inviting him to the Cleveland Orchestra, and Glock thought that the risk involved – bearing in mind
the programmes it enabled him to plan for the Orchestra – was well worth
while. Boulez had been planned to appear in New York two seasons previously, to construct the world première of the revised version of his *Doubles*;
so it was prescient of Glock to invite him to include this work in his BBC
programmes and to make his delayed New York début with it.

The problem of the Orchestra's string players was still, however, acute.

Delays in introducing the special Retainer Contract meant that new players, though accepted for the Orchestra, would not be free until after the tour. In response to strong concern expressed, Glock attempted to postpone the tour; but it was far too late for such action, for plans were well advanced in the States. It was decided to go ahead, and make the very best possible of a difficult situation. In the event, the members of the Orchestra rose brilliantly to the occasion and showed the resourcefulness which the situation demanded. Because of the tour's prestige, and because it fell at the end of the London concert season, it was possible to recruit a small, high-quality group of special players for the Orchestra, who took leave of absence from their own ensembles for the five-week period of rehearsal and tour. 'The result was immediate,' as Huband later reported, 'and the tour produced some very fine playing carried out with pride, good humour and exemplary behaviour in varying conditions.'

American triumph

The tour was very demanding. The Orchestra left on 24 April 1965 and returned on 16 May. Dorati and Boulez shared the conducting. Jacqueline du Pré made her first appearances in America; the other soloists were the pianist John Ogdon and the soprano Heather Harper. Concerts were given as follows:

25 April	Boston	7 May	New York
26 April	Stamford	8 May	New York
28 April	New London	9 May	Washington
29 April	Hartford	11 May	Syracuse
30 April	New York	12 May	Corning
1 May	New York	14 May	New York
4 May	Durham	15 May	New York
6 May	Philadelphia		

And the repertoire list was daunting:

Stravinsky	Symphonic Poem: Le Chant du Rossignol
	Symphonies of Wind Instruments
	Four Studies
	The Rite of Spring
Bartók	Ballet Suite: The Miraculous Mandarin
	Piano Concerto No. 1
Schoenberg	Five Orchestral Pieces, Op. 16
Webern	Six Pieces for Orchestra, Op. 6
	Variations for Orchestra, Op. 30

Berg	Three Fragments from Wozzeck
Shostakovich	Symphony No. 10
Blacher	Concertante Music for Orchestra, Op. 10
Schuller	Dramatic Overture
Gerhard	Concerto for Orchestra
Copland	Music for a Great City
Britten	Our Hunting Fathers
Tippett	Piano Concerto
Boulez	Doubles
Mahler	Symphony No. 4
Elgar	Cello Concerto in E Minor
Vaughan Williams...........	Symphony No. 4 in F Minor
Debussy	Ballet: Jeux
	Images
Beethoven	Piano Concerto No. 5 in E flat Major
	(Emperor)

Glock's lively report on the tour to the Board of Management may be quoted directly:

The Symphony Orchestra's visit to the United States was, on the whole, a great success. It brought out the best in the players, and developed them noticeably as a team; and it earned good marks for the BBC by offering a repertory such as no other orchestra on tour had ever dared to present – a repertory which suited their style of performance, as well as contributing a new flavour to the American season. There is no doubt, in fact, that a series of programmes consisting entirely of twentieth-century music was exactly the right choice for New York; and it was welcomed nearly everywhere else as well. If we had taken Brahms and Beethoven we should have invited comparison with the Boston and Cleveland orchestras – and especially with their illustrious string-playing. As it was, the concerts made an exciting impact. Composers were heartened by our celebration of contemporary music. Conductors and instrumentalists I met were full of enthusiasm for the delicacy of the Orchestra's playing, for the relaxed style of the strings, and for the naturalness of tone-production which they contrasted with the relentless onslaught of some of the American orchestras. The critics, too, gave generous recognition as the following excerpts will show:

'Choice of repertory and the standards of performance served as a welcome reminder of what conductors, orchestras and concerts are for.'
                                                                    (*Boston Globe*)

'The BBC Symphony Orchestra is one of Europe's finest . . .'
                                                    (*New York Times*)
'Boulez . . . led a surpassingly beautiful performance (of Debussy's
Jeux). The orchestra responded with the best kind of playing, in
which all the instrumental textures had a light, sensuous sound.'
                                                    (*New York Times*)
'A superlative programme – superlatively played – of Webern's Six
Pieces, Op 6, the Three Fragments from Berg's *Wozzeck*, Debussy's
Images, and Boulez's *Doubles*.'   (*New York Herald Tribune*)
'Of the numerous orchestras that have visited Carnegie Hall this year,
the one that I would most welcome as a resident ensemble was the last.
Unfortunately, it already enjoys a position of honor as the No. 1 pride
of the British Broadcasting Corporation, but that was only the more
reason, after its series of six concerts spread over successive Fridays
and Saturdays, to envy the audience that hears it regularly. Under the
alternating guidance of Antal Dorati and Pierre Boulez, the BBC
Symphony impressed me as being every bit as resourceful in a variety
of styles as the New York Philharmonic, and more than a little better-
sounding.'   (*The Saturday Review*)
'Come back soon, gentlemen. You are England's finest.'
                                              (*New York World Telegram*)

Together with these encouraging notices, there was a steadily growing sentiment in New York that our concerts were the most significant musical event
during those three weeks – a triumph for twentieth-century music and for
the BBC.

So much for the artistic side, though I would like to add a word about the
splendid halls (and audiences) both in Boston and Philadelphia, and about
Pierre Boulez, who gave some magnificent concerts and is undoubtedly the
finest conductor we have had for years. Luckily he has three favourite
orchestras – the Cleveland, the Concertgebouw and ourselves. Under his
direction the BBC Symphony Orchestra surpasses itself, and every concert
of his has a quality of excitement which makes it very difficult to settle down
for hours afterwards.

The tour was a gruelling but enjoyable experience for the Orchestra:
apart from a few heart-stopping moments during *The Rite of Spring* under
Dorati in New York, the performances went better than anyone could have
hoped. Parties were given by the British cultural representatives in New
York, and in Washington Sir Patrick Dean provided a champagne supper for

the entire Orchestra and staff, which proved to be a special highlight of the tour.

The article by Benjamin Boretz of *The Nation*, which appeared in *The Sunday Times* in London on 16 May, summed up the reaction of American opinion to the Orchestra's achievement:

The decision to send the BBC Symphony Orchestra to the United States with programmes of twentieth-century music was as remarkable for its intelligent assessment of the qualities of the American musical environment as the concerts themselves were for their revelation of the executive and interpretative capacities of the Orchestra, its two conductors and the participating soloists. But this was perhaps the less to be wondered at in view of our long-standing ties with the British musical community, and particularly with the present musical director of the BBC, which are certainly stronger than to any other transatlantic milieu. Thus our admiration for William Glock goes back to the days when *Score* magazine, of which he was founder and editor, was for us an essential lifeline for non-historical musical communication.

Of the two conductors, moreover, Pierre Boulez's activities as lecturer at Darmstadt, and his presence recently at Harvard and other American universities, have brought him closer to American musical life than any other major Continental musician, while Antal Dorati was of course a familiar part of the American musical scene for many years as resident conductor in Dallas and later Minneapolis. Yet up to this visit by the BBC Orchestra Boulez had never conducted in New York (having twice been unable to fulfil announced engagements with the New York Philharmonic) and given his extraordinary European reputation as a conductor of the 'classic' twentieth-century literature, his position as successor to Hans Rosbaud (a deeply revered figure here) at the Baden-Baden Sudwestfunk, as well as the predominance on his programmes of important twentieth-century masterworks, this resulted in a particular degree of interest in the two programmes under his direction . . .

. . . the ensemble's discipline seemed first-rate and the flexibility it revealed in producing radically different sonorities under Boulez and Dorati was quite spectacular.

But perhaps the most striking aspect of these concerts was that for once an obviously 'good idea' had been carried out with real intelligence and responsibility; as if the directors of the BBC had understood that the announcement of a project is not quite equivalent to its fulfilment, and had therefore enabled the expenditure of as much care in the preparation of the performances, and in the assembling of programmes of genuine musical significance and interest, that might be capable of making a real contribution to the musical experience of American listeners, as in the preparation of appropriately elaborate brochures. As a result we have had a sense of experiencing at first hand the life of another musical culture, and it is an experience we shall not only cherish but would like to repeat often and very soon again.

Unpleasing to the BBC, however, was the financial result of the tour, which was less satisfactory than expected. Audiences outside New York and Washington were good, but in those major centres the unfamiliar programmes and a lack of publicity ensured small paying audiences. The BBC stood to lose far more than Sol Hurok did by a small box-office return, and indeed the tour was so costly that Frank Gillard declared that 'had we known when the project was first launched that it would require such a large subsidy, the idea would certainly have been abandoned. Our salvation was the special non-recurrent grant made by the Board to Sound Broadcasting in 1964-5, out of which we were able to meet practically the full cost.'

Dorati would dearly have loved to take the Orchestra on other major tours. A Commonwealth tour, taking in a long journey across Canada, was planned for the end of 1965, but did not materialise. And other ambitious projects were viewed with more caution after the financial results of the American visit became known. A tour of Africa, which Dorati proposed, was out of the question because it would have involved some concerts to segregated audiences in South Africa. But the major project which did go ahead was the notion of a tour to Eastern Europe; that was to come to fruition in 1967.

Planning the future

Back in England, the Orchestra came down to earth with a bump. The summer of 1965 was a difficult period, for the enthusiasm which all members had put into the challenge of the American tour was dissipated when it was realised that the plans for reorganising the Orchestra, for better conditions of work and for more contractual freedom had all been delayed by managerial caution within the BBC. Four important players left, and the level of vacancies returned to that of the previous year; morale became low during the Prom season, where the Orchestra's heavy burden of work was dominated by often routine concerts under the direction of Sargent.

Moreover, Dorati's fire and dedication had been somewhat dulled in the face of the slow progress towards the changes he wanted to see. So Glock began to make plans for the future. He had already written to Dorati's agent earlier in the year, reminding them that Dorati's engagement would end in June 1966:

> As you know we asked Mr Dorati to come in the first instance for two years, and then prolonged this to four years which we regarded as a fruitful arrangement both from our point of view and his. But we also thought of four years as a maximum period.

Dorati, writing to Glock in the autumn of 1965, agreed:

> I have to tell you at this time that I shall not be in the position to renew our agreement which will end in June 1966. The past years in the BBC Symphony Orchestra were interesting and exciting . . . I shall relinquish the post of Chief Conductor with regret as I have become very fond of that Orchestra. However, if I would not regret to leave, it would not have been worthwhile to come!

The arrangement was to lapse by mutual agreement. Glock could now turn towards the other possible choices he had considered earlier in the decade for the post of Chief Conductor. Of them Colin Davis had made the most striking impression. A last-minute substitution for Otto Klemperer in a performance of *Don Giovanni* at the Festival Hall in 1959, a growing reputation with performances conducting the English Chamber Orchestra and the Chelsea Opera Group as well as his regular work with Sadler's Wells Opera since 1961, Davis was clearly at that time the brightest young English conductor on the scene. Glock had known and admired him for many years: as long ago as 1948 at the Bryanston Summer School of Music, Davis had conducted a performance of a Mozart Piano Concerto with Glock as soloist. So Glock did not waste time. He combined a trip to Amsterdam to book the Concertgebouw Orchestra for the 1967 Proms with a visit to Colin Davis, who was making guest appearances there. He spent an evening with him, persuaded him to accept the job from September 1967 onwards, and reported back to Frank Gillard, 'I need hardly say that I am delighted to have brought this off, though naturally nervous – perhaps because of the very speed of our negotiations!' It was hoped to have the appointment approved and an announcement made as soon as possible.

In fact there were many details to be negotiated about the nature of Davis's contract. Glock wanted him to make his services available as continuously as possible: there was a special stipulation that he would not be absent from the Orchestra for more than two months in any year. A press conference announced for early November had to be postponed while the terms of the contract were finalised. The public learned of the appointment on 14 December 1965: Davis would take up his post on 21 September 1967, just four days before his fortieth birthday.

Meanwhile, there remained the problem of the 1966–7 season. Davis, who had just made his Covent Garden debut, was heavily booked for operatic appearances in London and New York over the following year, and there was no question of his taking over early. The tour of Eastern Europe, which was now a fully-fledged exchange with the Moscow Radio Symphony Orchestra (which would visit the 1967 Proms) had to take place in January 1967, while the Orchestra was without a principal conductor. The solution which had covered the 1962–3 season was again brought into effect: the Orchestra would be under the care of a distinguished group of guest conductors, this time including Bernard Haitink, Mario Rossi, Sir John Barbirolli, Rudolf Kempe and Pierre Boulez. Barbirolli and Boulez would lead the Orchestra on the Russian tour. Thus Glock aimed to bridge the gap from Dorati to Davis.

1965–7

Dorati's last season as Chief Conductor was an impressive one in which the music of Beethoven and Mahler figured large. In the Festival Hall he conducted Mahler's Second Symphony (6 October) and Sixth Symphony (2 February), Beethoven's *Missa Solemnis* (16 February), and Berlioz's *Te Deum*. Gerhard's Concerto for Orchestra (which had been premièred on the American tour and then given at the Cheltenham Festival) was included on 2 February, and there was an orchestral concert of Britten, Prokofiev and Beethoven, with Daniel Barenboim in the Emperor Concerto, on 1 December. There were guest appearances by Sargent, Rudolf Kempe, Norman Del Mar, Christoph von Dohnanyi (who conducted Henze's Fifth Symphony on 3 November), Erich Schmid and Walter Susskind (who did Mahler's Tenth Symphony in Deryck Cooke's complete performing version, first heard in Britain at the 1964 Proms). At the centre of the season came the first performance of a BBC commission from Michael Tippett, which the composer conducted: *The Vision of St Augustine*, a highly complex work juxtaposing two texts in Latin drawn from St Augustine's confessions, set for baritone, chorus and orchestra. Glock continued his advocacy of the work of Pierre Boulez by inviting him to contribute two important programmes to the season: for the last concert, Stravinsky's *The Rite of Spring* was juxtaposed with Debussy's Three *Nocturnes* and Webern's Opp. 29, 30, and 31. On 16 March there was to have been a complete performance of Boulez's *Pli selon pli*, alongside the Mallarmé settings of Ravel and Debussy.

This would have brought the work to London for the first time, in the season following its performance in Edinburgh by Hamburg Radio forces. Unfortunately, after an unprecedentedly long set of rehearsals – nine in all – it became clear that to perform the whole work would be impossible. The day before the concert it was decided to perform only the first three sections, and the programme was extended with Stravinsky's *Song of the Nightingale*, Webern's Symphony, and his Five Orchestral Pieces, Op. 10. The concert had been preceded by provincial dates in Leicester and Nottingham, so the substitute works were already well rehearsed.

Dorati's final season also included a special concert of his own works – the *Madrigal Suite* and Symphony – which was recorded in the studio on 8 April, the day before his sixtieth birthday. Ironically, it was the occasion for his last outburst of temper at the Orchestra, when a percussion instrument that fell over in the closing pages of the Symphony did so a second time during a retake. But afterwards all was smiles. This concert preceded the formal farewells, which took place after a group of studio recordings, in which Dorati demonstrated all the great strengths of his repertoire – there was Berlioz and Bartók, Stravinsky, and finally Beethoven's *Missa Solemnis*. He also gave the British première of Messiaen's *Et exspecto resurrectionem mortuorum*, which he would introduce in public at the 1966 Proms. After the last concert on 9 June there was a farewell ceremony at which Hugh Maguire spoke, and Dorati replied, saying that he was happy at all he had done, and sorry that not more had been achieved. He later recalled, 'I still feel the same way, and am constantly watching from a distance to see if one of my successors succeeds in what I failed to accomplish – that is, in liberating the BBC Symphony from its "slavery to the microphone".' Dorati's achievement had in fact been very great; he had been the prime mover in a renewal of the Orchestra and had given it a new self-confidence. Some of the outstanding results are preserved on record – Gerhard's First Symphony, Bartók's *Miraculous Mandarin*, Messiaen's *Chronochromie*; others, like the American tour, remain strong in the memories of those who took part. Dorati had not, though, maintained the impetus of his first two years with the Orchestra: it was time for a change. His broader ambitions – to make the Orchestra more independent from the BBC – had much to commend them. His notion that the Orchestra must be 'an island', distinct from the sea around it, was one with which many of those concerned with the Orchestra agreed. But his grandiose schemes often conflicted with the less glamorous day-to-day work of making the Orchestra play better.

In 1966–7 Glock had to programme his season without the binding force of a Chief Conductor. As Chief Conductor designate, Colin Davis was present to open the series with Haydn's *Creation* on 12 October, and in the second concert Erich Schmid conducted Schoenberg's *Erwartung* with Annamaria Bessel. On 30 October the Third Programme presented a performance of the massive *Gothic Symphony* by Havergal Brian – the result of the constant efforts on behalf of this composer by Robert Simpson, now a senior producer in Music Division. Mario Rossi conducted Stravinsky's *Symphony of Psalms* on 9 November, while Bernard Haitink (continuing the Mahler boom with a performance of the Second Symphony) drew warm praise for his 'grasp of the huge structure . . . the BBC Symphony Orchestra realised Mahler's harsh tonal palette to perfection'. Bruckner's Sixth under Christoph von Dohnanyi (7 December) and Berlioz's *Romeo and Juliet* under the Israeli conductor Gary Bertini (1 February) followed and then Shostakovich's Fourth Symphony, in which an ailing Sir Malcolm Sargent was replaced by Charles Groves (15 February). Rudolf Kempe's Beethoven Ninth Symphony on 1 March coincided with the Queen's opening of the new concert halls next door to the Festival Hall – the Queen Elizabeth Hall and the Purcell Room. Members of the BBC Orchestra contributed to the opening celebrations of the Elizabeth Hall two days later with the first performance of Elisabeth Lutyens's *And suddenly it's evening*, for tenor and eleven instruments.

Then Pierre Boulez returned for an outstanding and important series of concerts. He began with a programme of Webern, Schoenberg and Bartók (8 March), as *The Financial Times* reported: 'The BBC with the invaluable aid of Pierre Boulez continues the excellent work of helping us to understand the music of the present day by giving repeated performances of the music of yesterday.' The unique achievement of Boulez's concerts was also stressed in *The Sunday Times*, where David Cairns was straightforward about his Webern performances: 'He is the first person to have made an English orchestra play the music as if it meant something, and that is that.' Reports were more mixed of Boulez's all-Stravinsky evening in the Festival Hall on 15 March; and the all-Berg concert of 20 March proved strong meat for some, though Andrew Porter in *The Financial Times* thought the concert had 'a revelatory quality. Boulez conducting seems to think with the mind of the composer himself. He does not "interpret"; he shows.' In the *Daily Telegraph* Peter Stadlen, who should know, declared that 'everything was just right'. On 29 March, Boulez's exploration of early twentieth-century masters should have taken a leap into the present with the first British performance of the newly revised version of his own *Éclat*, in a concert for the Royal Philharmonic Society. But the work was not yet ready, and so another one-composer concert took its place – this time all Debussy, with *Le Martyre de*

Saint-Sébastien, the *Prélude à l'après-midi d'un faune*, and the *Nocturnes*. *Éclat* first appeared on 7 May, in a studio recording.

The adventures of the season were not over, for the 12 April concert under Norman Del Mar brought a revival of Hugh Wood's *Scenes from Comus* (a 1966 Proms commission); Hans Schmidt-Isserstedt conducted Mahler's Ninth on 10 May; and on 24 May came one of the boldest importations of the whole Glock period – the British première of the *St Luke Passion* by Penderecki, a then little-known 33-year-old Polish composer. The conductor, invited for the occasion, was Henryk Czyz; the performance was to be repeated at the Proms. Many agreed on the deep impressiveness of the work: a large audience cheered at the end, and critics wrote admiringly of its brilliant range of technical accomplishments. Some thought it 'the nearest the avant-garde has come to producing a universal masterpiece' (John Warrack, *Sunday Telegraph*), while William Mann, now no longer anonymous as Music Critic of *The Times*, attacked its 'powerful aroma of speciousness'. Peter Heyworth in *The Observer* concluded unhappily that the work did not bridge the gap between the avant-garde and the concert-going public, because 'its foundations remain as insecure as the defiantly eclectic ground on which they are raised'. The opportunity was also taken to include other Penderecki works in a broadcast: his *Threnody for the victims of Hiroshima* and the first performances of *De natura sonoris No. 1*.

Eastern challenge

The highlight of the season, however, was the January visit to Eastern Europe. This tour was an extraordinary challenge to the Orchestra: it was playing music which was unfamiliar, in countries where the reaction would be unpredictable; it was encountering new circumstances of concert-giving, new kinds of audiences, and, of course, new political pressures. The tour schedule was gruelling; far more than in any previous tour, the detailed arrangements were subject to frequent change and cancellation. Relatively untroubled concerts in Czechoslovakia and Poland provided a gentle preparation for the administrative confusion which greeted the Orchestra in Russia. Rehearsal halls were rarely available when promised; the concerts in Leningrad, for example, were timed to start at 7 pm, but this turned out to be a most unusual hour for that city, and so they were deferred until 8 pm. Extensive negotiations had to take place with the Russians on the subject of sound and television recording, which were not satisfactorily concluded. In spite of all these behind-the-scenes troubles, however, the concerts were successfully beyond anyone's hopes. Boulez and Barbirolli between them led the Orchestra to new heights: the players were encouraged by the lively response of the audience – in Russia, music by Webern and Boulez was greeted with standing ovations and had to be encored: every twentieth-century piece was greeted with enthusiasm. Jacqueline du Pré, who had been such a success on the American tour, was again outstanding in performances of the Elgar Cello Concerto with Barbirolli. The tour ended in considerable disorder, since the tour's promoters had not made arrangements for the flight home on the date agreed and many musicians were delayed in Russia an extra day, causing ill feeling and broken engagements in London. Nevertheless, the result of the tour was one of immense satisfaction at the musical results – and, says William Glock, it was the time he first thought keenly that Pierre Boulez would be an ideal Chief Conductor for the Orchestra.

Davis takes over

Colin Davis was due to assume his leading role with the Orchestra in September 1967. But before this a cloud was cast over the 1967 Prom season by the illness of Sir Malcolm Sargent, and Davis came into prominence when he took over several of Sargent's concerts. It was a memorable season for the Orchestra in several ways: the Penderecki *St Luke Passion* was repeated, Gerhard's Symphony No. 3 (with electronics) was included, and there were commissions from Humphrey Searle and Thomas Wilson. In one spectacular evening, Glock had the Orchestra split around the Albert Hall arena for Stockhausen's *Gruppen*. Then there was the highly charged emotion of the last night, which Colin Davis conducted: Sargent insisted, against his doctor's advice, on making the short journey across the road from Albert Hall Mansions to the stage of the Hall, to reassure his devoted promenaders that he would be with them next year. The audience's enthusiasm was unbounded, and the scene was transmitted live to millions on television. But less than a month later, Sargent died. An era in the Proms, and an era in British music, was suddenly over. As the dominating personality of the Proms, Sargent would prove as hard to replace as Henry Wood had been before him; but in Glock's time, and after, a single personality became less important – the music, in all its range and variety, took centre stage.

Colin Davis formally took over as Chief Conductor of the Orchestra at the start of the 1967–8 season. He had described the appointment as 'the greatest challenge of my life, and the completion of my professional education'. Talking to *The Times*, he had this to say about the post:

I have never held such a position with a symphony orchestra before. The opportunities are immense: the orchestra has the widest repertory of any, both because of its function as a broadcasting orchestra and because sufficient funds are available to make its existence independent of public attendance. Besides, the position of chief conductor with the BBC Symphony Orchestra is the nearest thing we have in London to the American musical director, and therefore carries with it far more personal responsibility for the standard of the Orchestra.

The BBC Symphony under Boult was, before the war, the best orchestra in the country. Dorati, Boulez, and others have shown that the Orchestra can play with its old brilliance; perhaps I may be able to get, in some way, the flame of their achievement to burn more steadily. I have the greatest respect for William Glock. More than anyone he has changed the musical scene here over the past five years, and I support his interest in new music wholeheartedly, but I hope he will join me in trying to persuade composers to write for the Symphony Orchestra. There is life in it yet, even though it is avoided by most of the avant-garde who, I suspect, consider it an old-fashioned invention like Stephenson's Rocket.

After all, composers in contributing new works to the repertory are helping to keep alive a communal activity which poses most of the problems of the world at large. I think we need to work for something bigger than ourselves, even though we fight so hard to assert our individuality.

The Times music critic commended the BBC for choosing a British conductor and thought that 'the breadth of Mr Davis's musical sympathies will surely be an asset in his new post. The BBC Symphony Orchestra has by the nature of its broadcasting function to cover a huge, indeed comprehensive repertory of music . . .' A note of caution was sounded that Davis's periods with the Orchestra might be too short for 'conductor and orchestra to work together to best advantage . . .' And it was already rumoured that Davis was tipped to succeed Georg Solti 'in due course' as Music Director at Covent Garden, though he had only just made his début at the Opera House.

Davis did indeed have broad musical sympathies, but he did not have a very wide repertoire when he joined the Orchestra. Though he had considerable orchestral experience, having spent two years with the BBC Scottish Symphony Orchestra, during which he must have conducted around 300 concerts, his previous permanent post had been with the Sadler's Wells Opera Company. In February 1967 he wrote to John Douglas Todd, the producer in Music Division at that time responsible for the Orchestra: 'Please remember that I am only familiar with a tiny corner of the repertory. Initiate me gently and with kindness or I shall finish up in an asylum! William [Glock] must try to build a repertoire between myself and the Orchestra . . .'

Davis was perhaps unduly modest. The wide range of works he was able to conduct during his first season demonstrated the range of his repertoire. He began with two major Festival appearances: a Bartók and Stravinsky programme at Edinburgh; Tippett and Gerhard at the Berlin Festival. Then he began the Festival Hall season with Gerhard's Concerto for Orchestra alongside Beethoven's Eroica Symphony. Large works in the rest of the season included Mozart's C minor Mass, Berlioz's *Romeo and Juliet* (replacing the planned *Damnation of Faust*), Stravinsky's *The Rite of Spring*, and Mozart's *Idomeneo*, which was given a concert performance to end the season. Davis also did Tippett's Second Symphony and the newly revised version of Nicholas Maw's *Scenes and Arias* – a piece which *The Times*, under the heading 'Maw's inflammatory erotics', described as 'a wonderfully tender and exhilarating document of modern romantic feeling'. Davis's busy first season for the Orchestra also included the melancholy duty of directing a memorial concert for Sir Malcolm Sargent on 27 October; Elgar's *Nimrod* prefaced the first Festival Hall concert for the same reason. This concert, with Victoria Postnikova as the soloist in the Schumann Piano Concerto, drew much public attention: the *Daily Telegraph* noted that 'throughout, the Orchestra responded in a manner that promises a brilliant partnership with its new conductor'. And Beethoven's Eroica had 'a splendidly energetic, vital performance'.

The Berlin Festival appearances in September were notable for one dramatic incident – which occurred not in Davis's programmes but in that conducted by Pierre Boulez on 30 September. It was a time of student protest and unrest in Germany; unknown to the authorities, a number of protesters had bought seats and smuggled leaflets into the hall. In the middle of Webern's very short and quiet Op. 6 pieces, people started making their way down from the gallery to the platform – no one was quite aware what was happening until it became clear they were not simply leaving the hall. They mounted the platform and began to scatter leaflets through the Orchestra and the auditorium. Boulez, momentarily surprised but cool as ever, stopped conducting and moved to one side. Then the real purpose of the demonstration became clear – the protesters moved to the microphones which were transmitting the concert all over Europe and proceeded to shout out their protests in German. They had skilfully chosen to make the maximum impact on the listening audience. Then the hall staff and Orchestra platform staff had to close in to remove them, and for the first and last time in his life Bill Edwards, the indefatigably good-humoured BBC orchestral porter, had to bundle people off a concert platform by force. The incident was short, and not especially violent – not as disrupting to the Orchestra as the stink bombs in Venice in 1961. But it made clear the alarming possibilities of broadcasts for advertising and transmitting such incidents, and security had to become a larger consideration in the future on continental tours.

Recording and touring

Colin Davis took the Orchestra into the field of television and commercial recordings with more success than any of his predecessors. Already in this first season television recorded two Beethoven symphonies from the Fairfield Halls, Croydon; and later two Haydn symphonies from Portsmouth and Elgar's Second Symphony from Watford. Davis took part in a Hungarian exchange concert, conducting the Elgar *Introduction and Allegro* and Bartók's Second Piano Concerto for broadcast to Hungary, while the Hungarian Radio Symphony Orchestra broadcast Kodály's *Summer Evening* and Vaughan Williams' Fourth Symphony. Later in the season, television recorded a workshop on the music of Walton in which Davis and the Orchestra took part. Davis conducted at three major English music festivals in July: a Berlioz concert for the English Bach Festival in Oxford; a repeat of the Gerhard Concerto for Orchestra at Aldeburgh; and Haydn's *The Seasons* for the City of London Festival in St Paul's Cathedral. The Orchestra also visited the Cheltenham Festival, where under Norman Del Mar they gave the British première of Gerhard's *Epithalamion*.

The biggest undertaking of Davis's first season, however, was the German tour which took place in January 1968; he shared the conducting with John Pritchard. Davis's programmes included the Gerhard Concerto for Orchestra, Tippett's Second Symphony and Britten's *Les Illuminations*, as well as standard classics. The Orchestra visited Frankfurt, Düsseldorf, Essen, Munich, Nuremberg, Tübingen, Freiburg, Heilbronn, Höchst, Hanover, Kiel and Hamburg: a busy schedule which was to be the first of several such regular annual tours, as the Orchestra's reputation for twentieth-century music grew in Europe.

1967-8 saw important changes of personnel at the top of the Orchestra. Hugh Maguire had resigned as leader in 1967 in order to resume his active career in chamber music and solo work; Trevor Williams led the Orchestra for some months until Hugh Bean took over. Eli Goren joined him as co-leader in 1968, and when Bean left a year later Goren was joined by Bela Dekany, and a long-standing and successful collaboration was inaugurated.

Economics and problems

Through this exhausting and demanding period, Davis became preoccupied with and often depressed by the unresolved problems facing the Orchestra.

Since the major advances of the Dorati period, the many difficulties created by the efforts to improve the Orchestra's standard had not begun to be resolved. It was generally agreed during 1966 that the success of all the improvement schemes depended on a solid upgrading of the whole Orchestra's pay. If this was not put into effect, then the BBC would simply be uncompetitive and could resign itself to losing all the best players to the freelance London orchestras. This principle made sense; but it was the time of a pay freeze and of severe economic constraints. This was the year of the seamen's strike and the devaluation of the pound – a low point for the British economy in the 1960s. The BBC was under pressure to conform. There was some support from higher management for the notion that the BBC should simply defy the freeze, as the Arts Council had done. In November 1967, shortly after Davis took over the Orchestra, there was an informal dinner for Glock, Davis and the BBC's administrative heads at which the difficulties were considered: it was reluctantly concluded that a bonus scheme might be the best way of temporarily solving the crisis, rather than the more radical step of scrapping all the present contracts and devising a new basis for employment.

The urgency of the question seemed to be accepted by BBC management, but there were countless complications. In December, the Head of Administration noted that 'Colin Davis rang a few days ago in desperation, obviously not realising the sort of difficulties we are in over these matters'. Davis himself had been trying to take the Orchestra's side, for he was very anxious that an improvement in their conditions of employment should take place quickly: if possible before the German tour. But by Christmas it became clear that little could be finalised. In December, cautious negotiations on the subject of a salary rise took place with outside bodies; it was suggested that the Orchestra's situation should be compared to that of the salaried orchestras of the opera houses at Covent Garden and Sadler's Wells; but, as the BBC management rightly pointed out, 'the role and character of the Covent Garden and Sadler's Wells orchestras makes them radically different from our own, with which the chief comparison is the main London symphony orchestras which are not salaried, and whose rank-and-file earnings have risen so much in the last few months as to precipitate our present crisis'. The internal discussions reached a climax: it was agreed within the BBC to increase all orchestral members' pay from January 1968: the argument was to be based on 'recognising the élite role of the Symphony Orchestra'. The increase was thought scarcely sufficient to solve the problem of rank-and-file recruitment, but it was an important start. However, the very next day, the Legal Adviser of the BBC ruled that (although a London weighting increase could be agreed at once) any general salary increase had to be referred to the Post Office, the Government department responsible for broadcasting. Glock and Davis had to depart for the German tour in January with nothing settled.

At this point the whole of the BBC Management came into the picture. The Post Office referred the proposed salary scheme to the Department of Economic Affairs, which turned it down. The Department said it was not possible to give an across-the-board increase: all that was feasible within the terms of the Government's White Paper would be an incentive scheme. While some Corporation officials believed that an incentive scheme could be devised which would meet the Government's formulation, it was realised by the musicians taking part in the negotiations that such a notion would be scarcely plausible. What was an 'extra return' in terms of orchestral performance? The Board of Management finally decided to ask the Post Office to approve a bonus scheme for the rank-and-file strings; it was also prepared to institute the scheme proposed back in 1964 which would grade positions in the string sections, so that there would be very few purely rank-and-file places left in the Orchestra. In the end, a modified scheme involving a compromise around all these possibilities was agreed: with London weighting, a 'ladder' scheme and selected bonuses, the Orchestra's pay was increased by small amounts. But there was still no radical solution such as Glock and Davis had hoped. They anxiously sent cables from Germany asking what the conclusion of the negotiations had been. Administration officials assured Glock that all that could be done was being done: 'All the forces of the BBC have been involved over the past fortnight, from DG and the Board of Management downwards.' There was a stalemate.

Through all these negotiations, the climax of Glock's efforts on behalf of the Orchestra since he became Controller, there was a feeling of inevitable failure in the air. The fact was that the Orchestra could not take an undisputed high priority in the BBC's financial affairs such as it had in the 1930s. With the rise of television and the expansion of the BBC's operations in so many diverse fields, the only argument for supporting the Symphony Orchestra had now to be that it really cost very *little* compared with a network of television programmes. Inevitably, too, the argument about its prestige cut little ice in the BBC: though its events were public and were important, they reached far smaller audiences than the BBC commanded in other media. The Symphony Orchestra had to reconcile itself to accepting a lower place in the BBC's scheme of activity than it had previously enjoyed. Nevertheless, in this 1967-8 crisis, some members of the BBC management made a supreme effort to argue on its behalf. It was unfortunate that the crisis was partly brought about by, and coincided with, economic conditions which could scarcely have been less propitious. Management could argue, quite justifiably, that in the end it was the Government and not the BBC which at this moment had forced the Symphony Orchestra to make do with second best.

But evidence that orchestral pay was not high in BBC management's priorities was not slow to appear. Later that year the BBC inaugurated its Policy Study Group, following up the process of internal investigation by the American management consultants McKinsey and Co., which led to the publication of the controversial discussion document 'Broadcasting in the Seventies' in July 1969. That plan suggested that the BBC needed only five orchestras (including the Symphony Orchestra), which employed 279 musicians. Three orchestras (including the Scottish Symphony) and the BBC Chorus were to be disbanded if alternative funding was not found; and the future of three more (the Concert, Welsh and Northern Ireland) was put in doubt. There was a fierce outcry from the musical world and the press to the proposals, and even the Government (in the person of John Stonehouse, Postmaster-General) urged the BBC to reconsider. In August 1969 Lord Hill and Charles Curran visited the Prime Minister, and in return for a rise in the licence fee and the acceptance of its plans for local radio, the BBC withdrew its plans to disband any orchestra.

The debate over 'Broadcasting in the Seventies' was only just beginning; the outcry showed that the BBC was still under some public pressure to maintain its traditionally large number of salaried musicians. The BBC Symphony Orchestra's existence was not at this time threatened, but it became ever more unlikely that it would receive the substantial financial input which would have made it competitive with the best in the country. Not until Pierre Boulez took over the Orchestra, nearly four years later, was there to be a salary increase which gave it stability and an assured standard. Colin Davis's efforts bore fruit only after his departure.

From Amy to Weill

In spite of all its problems, the Orchestra continued to give an astonishingly wide range of programmes, in the studio as well as in the concert hall. There was little competition from commercial concert-giving bodies in London. As the *Annual Register* remarked, 'The Festival Hall clings to its audience partly by virtue of the unenterprising character of its own concerts'. Standards of performance at the Queen Elizabeth Hall during its first year of operation were variable. The one bright spot on a gloomy scene was the founding of the London Sinfonietta, which under David Atherton began a consistent, creative support of new music that paralleled in the chamber orchestral field what Glock had achieved with the BBC Symphony Orchestra at the Festival Hall and the Proms.

The BBC's workload was exceptionally varied in this period: there was Gary Bertini conducting and recording the two little-known symphonies by Kurt Weill, and giving the British première of Penderecki's Music from the Psalms of David; Carlo Franci directing Dallapiccola's *Tre Laudi*; Gilbert Amy in the British première of his own *Triade*; John Carewe in a Stravinsky programme including *Le Rossignol*; John Pritchard in Gunther Schuller's *Seven Studies on themes of Paul Klee*; Henze's *Five Neapolitan Songs*, conducted by Erich Schmid. All these examples, from a few months in 1967–8, show how widely Glock interpreted his task of bringing little-known music from outside England to this country.

The Symphony Orchestra also contributed to other music programmes, both in radio and television. At the start of Glock's period as Controller, Lionel Salter, as head of television music, had managed to include several programmes by the Orchestra in his TV series *Concert Hall*, but this work had declined, and later in the decade, when Humphrey Burton and John Culshaw were in charge of music on television, the Symphony Orchestra was more often seen either in direct concert relays, usually from the Proms, or in specially prepared documentaries, such as those by Pierre Boulez on the Second Viennese School or by John Warrack on Walton. One fine example was recorded in the autumn of 1968: Boulez's exposition of 'The New Rhythm of Music', based on performances by the Symphony Orchestra of Stravinsky's *The Rite of Spring* and Bartók's Music for Strings, Percussion and Celesta. The Orchestra continued to broaden its outlook by giving major performances of opera on radio, especially when Lionel Salter returned to radio as Head of Opera. In 1966, under Walter Susskind, it played in Hindemith's *Cardillac*, giving the original version of a major work which the Orchestra had introduced complete to this country in the Thirties under Clarence Raybould. In 1967 Mozart's *La Clemenza di Tito* and Tchaikovsky's *The Empress's Shoes* were also performed, under Gary Bertini and Norman Del Mar. The most ambitious operatic undertaking of the period was Wagner's *Tristan und Isolde*, given in German with a largely British cast under Colin Davis – a recording which was fraught with problems and which was only broadcast more than a year later, to appreciative notices from the critics.

'Rain on a parched land'

Overshadowing all these events was the series of public concerts and studio recordings undertaken by Pierre Boulez. As *The Observer* put it, 'Pierre Boulez descends on the Festival Hall like rain on a parched land'. During the Davis years, Glock invited Boulez to undertake a major proportion of the Orchestra's work in each season. When he returned to the BBC Orchestra at the end of its German tour, his schedule was crowded and varied. Three very different Festival Hall concerts were what the public saw; but these were preceded by studio concerts: one of Berg, Wagner and Varèse; one of Ravel and Berlioz; and an all-Schoenberg programme that consisted of the *Music for a cinema scene*, the Piano Concerto, the Op. 16 Pieces and the Op. 31 Variations. Only then did the strongly planned sequence of Festival Hall concerts take place. First came Mahler's Fifth Symphony (with the Berg Violin Concerto). As William Mann noted, 'Boulez approaches Mahler from this end of musical history, from Berg rather than Wagner'. In *The Financial Times* Ronald Crichton found it 'an enthralling experience'; some critics felt he rushed the last movement (which, it was later learned, he did not actually like).

The next concert was a Royal Philharmonic Society event; three contrasted works by twentieth-century masters were included. *Chronochromie* by Messiaen and *Arcana* by Varèse used the full orchestra, and then a chamber group gave Boulez's own *Le Marteau sans maître*; scarcely standard Philharmonic Society fare. In *The Observer*, Peter Heyworth was held enthralled by *Le Marteau*'s 'cool lyricism and steely yet infinitely delicate counterpoint' – yet he admitted to having been baffled by the piece when it first appeared. The performances by the Orchestra were universally praised: the work of Boulez the educator and stimulator of public taste was beginning to have an effect. The climax of his visit was a repeat performance of Stockhausen's three-orchestra piece *Gruppen*, which had been given at the Proms with great success the previous season. Michel Tabachnik and Edward Downes joined Boulez in the direction. In the Festival Hall the three orchestras were placed on stage and in the two side annexes. This meant that for the audience in the stalls the sound had a better wrap-around effect than in the Albert Hall, where only promenaders in the arena caught the full spatial effect. The quality of sound was also much clearer. On many listeners it made a great effect: the hall was crowded with young people. The performance was praised as 'magnificently assured and sonorous' in the *Daily Telegraph*; 'admirable because it was so clear and precise,' wrote William Mann in *The Times*. Mann was the work's chief supporter: 'The effect is fantastically exhilarating not just in weight of separated sound, but in dynamic and rhythmic variety and contrast.' He thought the Festival Hall's clarity preferable to the Albert Hall's space: 'It must have been in anticipation of music so detailed, so fascinating for the ear to analyse and distinguish that the Festival Hall was built.' It was one of the high points of the Glock era at the BBC.

This brilliant series of Boulez explorations would not have been possible without the less glamorous work of Colin Davis as the Orchestra's Chief Conductor. For, at the same time that Boulez was taking the Orchestra into untried paths of the newest music, Davis was trying to consolidate the Orchestra's expertise in the field of the great classics. He did not neglect new works; nor was he unsympathetic to them. In a revealing letter to Glock, Davis recalled a conversation with Boulez in which the latter had praised Stockhausen's music. Davis suggested to Glock that Stockhausen himself be invited to direct a concert with the Orchestra (a plan that Glock undoubtedly had in mind, which was to come to a kind of fruition in 1970). But Davis said that he felt it his role to concentrate on those things which Boulez did not do: recent British orchestral music, and performances of Beethoven, Mozart and others. Davis's priority was to make the Orchestra a better musical instrument.

Davis expressed his essential philosophy in a letter to Hans Keller of the BBC's Music Division. He wrote that his problem was one of

> building up a repertoire which we can actually play in public. I know that playing in public is not the reason for the existence of the BBC Symphony Orchestra, but while it does appear in public, it has got to be as good as it can be and the only way an orchestra can be good is to have a repertoire which it knows so well that it produces the required standard. Please don't think I am not willing [to try a number of new works] . . . I am just as perplexed as you are.

Keller rightly isolated one problem in the Orchestra's scheduling:

> If you were able not to use studio recordings as rehearsals for public concerts, or at least slightly to reduce this practice, one would, of course, be able to cope with this problem of content a little more easily.

Nevertheless, studio concerts continued to be arranged around public concerts, simply because rehearsal time for public events was so limited and because they were planned around conductors' availabilities. The possibility of the Orchestra's contributing unrelated work in response to requests from producers in the BBC's Music Division was something that became less likely in this period; the situation eventually drew strong complaints from individual producers.

So Davis's main achievements were in mainstream repertoire. Dating from this period with the Orchestra are his recordings with them of some of Beethoven's symphonies and piano concertos with Stephen Bishop, and of Haydn's *The Seasons*. Later there were to be the Mozart operas: *Idomeneo*, *Le Nozze di Figaro*, as well as the Mozart *Requiem*, Berlioz's *Benvenuto Cellini*, and less likely things – a Tchaikovsky record, and one of popular operatic overtures. These recordings helped to increase the Orchestra's proficiency and maintain its standard in conventional music to an extent that (some would argue) was absent later, when Boulez took over as Chief Conductor.

A fruitful autumn

At the start of the 1968–9 season, Davis was scarcely inactive in the field of recent music: in his first Festival Hall concert he repeated an important Prom commission from the summer, Harrison Birtwistle's *Nomos*. Later that autumn he returned to the music of Roberto Gerhard, giving the first public performance of his Fourth Symphony. The Symphony Orchestra's autumn was otherwise very varied; probably too varied for the good of the Orchestra, which did not benefit from the stability of working with only a few outstanding conductors. The Orchestra played under Rudolf Schwarz, David Atherton, Moshe Atzmon (in a new Piano Concerto by William Mathias), Eliahu Inbal (in a successful Festival Hall concert including the Schoenberg Violin Concerto), John Pritchard, Boult, Norman Del Mar, Szymon Goldberg, and others. There were strongly contrasted contemporary music events: a fiftieth-anniversary concert of music by Lili Boulanger, conducted by the aged Nadia Boulanger; a concert of French music by Barraqué, Masson and Gilbert Amy, conducted by Amy; then, only a couple of days later, a first broadcast performance under Norman Del Mar of Part Three of Granville Bantock's oratorio *Omar Khayyám*; and a concert of music by Arthur Bliss, under the composer's direction. It would be wrong to accuse the Orchestra of being narrow in its selection of twentieth-century music in this period.

Colin Davis restored the Orchestra's equilibrium during a substantial period in January and February 1969 during which it visited Holland. It played mainly Berlioz to celebrate his centenary: it was a happy coincidence that the Berlioz centenary fell in Davis's years with the BBC Orchestra, for he was a foremost interpreter of the composer. Later that season he did *The Damnation of Faust* at the Festival Hall and in Bath. The expansion of his repertory into big romantic works, planned during the previous year, began at this time: Bruckner's Seventh Symphony and Liszt's huge *Dante* Symphony were both recorded in the studio. The latter performance was later praised as a model of its kind by the Liszt scholar and composer Humphrey Searle; Davis went on to do more large-scale Liszt, though never the oratorio *Christus*. The next project of his continuing Mozart series followed: *La Clemenza di Tito* in a concert performance at the Festival Hall. He ended this period with two premières of British works: the Royal Philharmonic Society concert on 5 February brought Walton's *Capriccio burlesca* (like the Gerhard Fourth Symphony, an import from the New York Philharmonic's 125th anniversary celebrations), and Thea Musgrave's Clarinet Concerto. Gervase de Peyer was the soloist in this work, which William Mann thought 'ranks among the most powerful and original of her works'. The Concerto was enjoyed, and it added to the significant tally of new British pieces which Colin Davis introduced with the Orchestra.

The next part of 1969 saw the Orchestra featuring Bruckner's Symphonies: it played the Eighth with Reginald Goodall, the Fourth with Franz-Paul Decker, and the Sixth at the Festival Hall with Christoph von Dohnanyi. A guest appearance was to have been made by Haitink, but he was indisposed on the day of the concert; John Pritchard hurried across from Covent Garden to rehearse and conduct the Beethoven Choral Symphony and Stravinsky's *Symphony of Psalms*. The most auspicious guest appearance of the period, however, was that of the Russian conductor, Gennadi Rozhdestvensky, who in a studio concert, a visit to Leicester and a Festival Hall concert invigorated the Orchestra's playing and gave brilliant accounts of two Shostakovich symphonies, the Eighth and Ninth, with Tchaikovsky's *Manfred* and a Piano Concerto by Schedrin previously unheard in this country. Rozhdestvensky was to be in constant demand by the Orchestra in this period, but his appearances were all too often cancelled. Later, though, the relationship was to bear fruit. Other major events were the long-delayed inclusion of Messiaen's *Turangalîla* Symphony in the Orchestra's repertory: Charles Groves, who had given a successful performance in Liverpool with his own orchestra, conducted.

A new conductor-elect

During the season it became known that Davis had, as expected, been approached by Covent Garden to succeed Georg Solti as Music Director. Glock feared that Davis might be encouraged to leave his BBC post early, but in discussions with Sir David Webster of the Royal Opera House managed to agree on a formula whereby Davis could remain as Chief Conductor at the BBC until the end of the 1970–1 season, while doing slightly less work; and then take over at Covent Garden in the autumn while retaining a close connection with the BBC as Chief Guest Conductor. And Glock was able to announce that Davis's successor would be Pierre Boulez: a bold choice, but one that was in tune with the development of Glock's plans.

So when Boulez appeared in the Festival Hall on 7 May to conduct his own *Pli selon pli* alongside music by Varèse, it was for the first time as Chief Conductor-elect of the BBC Symphony Orchestra. The occasion could not have been more auspicious. Here, for the first time complete in London, was Boulez's orchestral masterwork, which he had given with the Hamburg Radio Orchestra in Edinburgh, and which he had been revising on and off for some twelve years, now as finished as it was ever likely to be. Whatever the reactions to this work might be, the performance and the concert were a clear declaration of intent for the Orchestra's future. Some thought it a central experience of twentieth-century music: 'If you were not there last night, you should have been listening to the radio; and if you were not, nothing I write can tell you very much about its essence, and that is sad' (Dominic Gill in *The Financial Times*). Others tried to be more explicit:

> Each detail is immaculately finished. There are no rough edges or blurred outlines. An astonishingly elaborate web of sound is realised with such precision and lucidity that in what seemed an almost miraculously polished performance by the BBC Symphony Orchestra, it gleamed and fluttered like a vast, elaborate and wonderfully mysterious piece of jewelry (Peter Heyworth, *The Observer*).

It was a brilliant ending to a season which had re-established the Orchestra's prowess in many fields: Beethoven symphonies, Mozart operas, big romantic masterpieces, and now the most demanding of post-war scores.

Davis Proms

The Promenade concerts of the Colin Davis years enlarged the scope and adventurousness of the BBC Symphony Orchestra's programmes. There were large-scale, one-work programmes, such as Schoenberg's *Jacob's Ladder* in 1968; Davis gave two Berlioz works in 1969 – the *Grande Messe des Morts* to open the season, and *Beatrice and Benedict*, performed with spoken dialogue by actors from the Royal Shakespeare Company. In 1970 he conducted *Messiah* on one evening, and Act III of Wagner's *Tristan und Isolde* on another. (He also conducted the first British performance of Kurt Weill's cantata *The Lindbergh Flight*, which he later revived in the Festival Hall.) Maazel conducted the Verdi *Requiem* in 1969, and the 1970 season opened with a massive undertaking: the British première of Messiaen's latest work, *La Transfiguration de Notre Seigneur Jésus-Christ*, under Serge Baudo. Often, the Symphony Orchestra shared its programmes with other groups; it regularly appeared alongside the Accademia Monteverdiana of Denis Stevens, complementing that group's baroque music with Beethoven's Eroica under Davis, or Elgar's First Symphony under Boult. In 1969 it appeared in the same concert as Musica Reservata. Colin Davis shared other concerts, too: he provided a Mozart second half in 1968 for Frederic Prausnitz's taxing first half of Busoni, Wolpe and Dallapiccola. The next year, Ives and Gerhard were complemented by Beethoven's Violin Concerto.

The Albert Hall acoustics were improved in 1968 by the addition of mushroom-like reflectors which crowded into the dome and reduced the reverberation time: no longer could it be said (in the words attributed to Beecham) that the Albert Hall was the only place where a young composer could hear his new work played twice.

Through these Prom seasons ran the continuing strand of Pierre Boulez's brilliant, individualistic programmes with the BBC Symphony Orchestra. Typical was this 1968 combination of solo, chamber and orchestral music:

Messiaen .... Chronochromie
Boulez..Le Marteau sans maître
Stockhausen...Piano Piece No. 10
Berg..Three Orchestral Pieces Op. 6

and this, from the same year:

Varèse .... Arcana
                                                                   Ionisation
Stravinsky...Le Roi des Etoiles
                                                             Requiem Canticles

In 1969 he repeated his own *Pli selon pli*, performed complete during the previous Winter Season. And in 1970 his three programmes were as follows:

Stravinsky...Suite: The Firebird
Bartók...Piano Concerto No. 2
Ravel...Ballet: Daphnis et Chloé

Schoenberg...Pierrot Lunaire
Mahler...Symphony No. 5

Debussy .... Nocturnes
Messiaen......................Et exspecto resurrectionem mortuorum
Stravinsky...The Rite of Spring

Some players and listeners still feel that Boulez's work with the Orchestra was at its freshest and most inspired during the Proms of these years –

certainly the results of the collaboration remain in the memories of many who were present.

As a final strand to the Symphony Orchestra's contribution to the Prom programmes of the Davis period, there were the new works. Some of these Glock made an effort to present in an original way. In 1968, John Tavener's *In alium* and Don Banks's Violin Concerto, both new commissions, were played under Norman Del Mar and followed by Thea Musgrave's Concerto for Orchestra. Then, during the interval, the audience was invited to take part in a ballot to select which work should be played again in the second half, before Stockhausen's *Kontakte*. Tavener's piece won, though it was not clear whether this proved anything. The 1969 premières were presented less sensationally: Alan Bush's Scherzo for wind and percussion and Malcolm Arnold's Concerto for two pianos made little impact; Peter Maxwell Davies's *Worldes Blis* was a disaster – the composer conducted, the Orchestra was uncommitted, the piece lasted much longer than advertised, and some of the audience walked out – and it was several years until the work's reputation was salvaged by means of a powerful revival by Colin Davis and the Symphony Orchestra. Berio's *Sinfonia* with its pop elements and parts for the Swingle Singers, was the most striking of the year's importations, while of the new works Hugh Wood's Cello Concerto made the most lasting impression.

In 1970 Glock again tried something different with a commissioned work. The Orchestra found itself in the middle of an extraordinary concert late on the evening of 13 August. It was spread around the Albert Hall arena to play Tim Souster's *Triple Music II*, its three sections directed by David Atherton, Justin Connolly and Elgar Howarth. The performance was preceded by a piece by Terry Riley, and followed by forty minutes of improvisation from The Soft Machine. This three-part concert followed one earlier in the evening, in which the Academy of St Martin-in-the-Fields played Bach; both concerts were televised, and it was possible to spend some four hours in the company of the BBC and of a mind-boggling variety of music. This was the boldest of Glock's Prom experiments, and nothing quite like it was ever attempted again.

Another experiment in which the Symphony Orchestra found itself involved was the effort to change the pattern of the traditional Last Night. Efforts to remove some favourite elements, for example the Elgar *Pomp and Circumstance March No. 1* with its added audience participation, were howled down by the press and public: in 1969 *Land of Hope and Glory* was first dropped and then reinstated. So in 1970 Glock commissioned a new work for the Last Night from Malcolm Arnold, in which some traditional elements were reworked. The most striking ingredient in the piece was the Sailor's Hornpipe, a much-loved element in all Wood and Sargent Last Nights, but rewritten in 5/8 time – demanding an exceptional rhythmic facility in the stamping from the audience. The piece was not revived. New experiments were tried; and eventually the format of the concert returned to something nearer its traditional form. As with all Glock's more outlandish schemes, opinion was split between those who thought it brought a necessary breath of fresh air into a stale atmosphere, and those who thought it interfered unnecessarily with time-honoured tradition. In the end, for all the attention it received, the Last Night was peripheral to the main business of expanding the Prom repertory and providing ever more imaginative programmes – and this was something that Glock did with unequalled skill.

Towards Boulez

The 1969–70 and 1970–1 seasons looked more and more like a preview of a Boulez era with the Orchestra. It could be argued that the balance during this period between the twin influences of Davis and Boulez created an ideal working environment which was not surpassed later. The mixture can be seen to its best effect in the foreign tours of those years, which Boulez and Davis shared – to Bratislava, Vienna and Budapest in 1970; to Germany and Switzerland in 1971. The Orchestra took post-war pieces such as Stockhausen's *Punkte* mixed with twentieth-century classics like Debussy's *Jeux* and Stravinsky's *The Rite of Spring*. In Germany Davis conducted Harrison Birtwistle's *Verses for Ensembles* and Tippett's *Fantasia concertante on a theme of Corelli*, as well as Bruckner's Seventh Symphony.

Davis continued to include premières in his concerts with the Orchestra: in October 1969 there was Shostakovich's Second Symphony, with its factory siren and rousing choruses, which was surprisingly receiving its British première. In a concert at the Sheldonian Theatre in Oxford, he introduced the Second Violin Concerto of Gordon Crosse, with Manoug Parikian as soloist. Desmond Shawe-Taylor wrote that it showed 'marked progress by one of the real hopes of English music'. Stephen Walsh thought it 'a substantial achievement' and noted that its 'clarity was emphasised by Colin Davis's beautifully gauged reading with the BBC Symphony Orchestra'. On the whole, however, Davis's repertory in the Festival Hall season concentrated on the large-scale masterpieces: Handel's *Messiah*, Berlioz's *Harold in Italy*, Stravinsky's *Oedipus Rex*, Holst's *The Planets*. For the Royal Philharmonic Society he conducted Elgar's *Falstaff*, Lalo, and Purcell's *Come ye sons of art away*. The adventurous weight of this well-planned season was borne by guest conductors: John Pritchard gave the first performance of

Iain Hamilton's *Circus*, a BBC commission, 'a shapely, communicative work' (*The Times*). Erich Leinsdorf directed the British première of Elliott Carter's Piano Concerto with Jacob Lateiner. This complex work had taken five years to cross the Atlantic. Some were puzzled, but Stephen Walsh wrote in *The Times*, 'I found the performance, as I find the work, both absorbing and enthralling'; while in *The Financial Times* Ronald Crichton admitted that

> the concerto is not easy listening. It has a nasty habit of becoming elusive, baffling or downright prickly just when one thinks one has been following the composer's drift, even when the ear is still seduced by fascinating sounds, delicate, incredibly sensitive, often on their rarefied level, witty and entertaining.

Michael Gielen conducted a major concert of first hearings in England of music by Donatoni, Berio and Nono. This was, as *The Observer* put it,

> one of the few big orchestral events of the winter season that has done much to extend our knowledge of the outside world. . . . Berio's . . . *Epifanie* (1959–61), which was splendidly played by the BBC Symphony Orchestra under the manifestly expert direction of Michael Gielen, is a score of dazzling virtuosity. Apart from Stockhausen's *Gruppen* and Boulez's *Pli selon pli*, I can think of no post-war work that expands the range of the symphony orchestra with so impressive a combination of imaginative daring and technical surefootedness.

Weber's *Oberon* was revived for a complete concert performance under John Pritchard. Then there were two Boulez concerts to end the season; the second should have included the first performance of a new version of his *Éclat*, but that was postponed. Instead, Stravinsky and Messiaen's *Oiseaux exotiques* complemented the complete Ravel *Daphnis and Chloe* – which was 'as overwhelming as I have ever known' (Edward Greenfield, *The Guardian*).

Improvising with Stockhausen

In fact, this Festival Hall season was in several ways less exciting than Glock had originally envisaged. In particular, the 19 November concert had been planned to follow up the success of Stockhausen's *Gruppen* with a complete evening of his music including *Telemusik*, *Setz die Segel*, *Zyklus* and *Punkte*. There were enormous complications over this programme, particularly because of its use of electronics and of improvisation. Stockhausen's requests for equipment, though reasonable enough, were unlike any which the Festival Hall or the BBC's engineers had been faced with before. The head of Radio Broadcasting Operations expressed the opinion that 'we have neither the apparatus nor the effort available for the work *Setz die Segel* . . .' Tim Souster, who was assisting Stockhausen in the preparation of the project, objected strongly that the equipment was not out of the ordinary and that if the BBC could not provide the effort, no one could; but the project was postponed. It was agreed to stage the concert as a special extra event in the Albert Hall during January 1970, where it was hoped there would be more flexibility. However, this too became problematical, and finally it was thought wisest to make the concert a studio event in Maida Vale on 14 January. Meanwhile, Stockhausen was becoming ever more demanding of rehearsal time and facilities. He wanted to see the solo percussionist for *Zyklus* for two and a half hours every day he was in London. He wanted the whole Orchestra made available to play *Setz die Segel*: previously four solo players were to be brought from Germany to participate in this piece, which was entirely based on improvisation. John Pritchard had been engaged to conduct the one conventional work in the programme, *Punkte*, but there was a confusion about the version of the score that was being used. Stockhausen wrote: 'It would be wise that Mr Pritchard prepares himself for this 1966 version, otherwise, he will have a hell of a time.' The concert score was rushed to Naples, where Pritchard was conducting, but it became bogged down in the Italian customs and never surfaced. Stockhausen received his contract for the concert only on 12 December, and did not agree to the conditions in it.

In all these circumstances, it was a near-miracle that the event took place. But it did, and for the first time the BBC Symphony Orchestra was initiated into the mysteries of 'total improvisation'. Stockhausen himself declared the event 'historic': it was, he suggested, the first time a Western symphony orchestra would play together, without a conductor, notes that were not determined by another man. The highlight of the concert was undoubtedly *Setz die Segel zur Sonne*, which was played in a darkened Maida Vale I. The entire score for the piece consisted of the following English translation of a text by Stockhausen:

Play one note long enough
for you to hear its individual vibrations

Sustain it
and listen to the notes of the others
– to all of them simultaneously, not to individual ones –
and move your note slowly
until you reach perfect harmony

and the total sound turns into gold
to pure, calmly radiating fire

The Orchestra was split into four groups around the studio. In the middle, Stockhausen and four assistants controlled potentiometers which directed the sound into loudspeakers around the room. Many thought the results unsatisfactory. There was much uncertainty among the players about what they should be doing, and open hilarity in some quarters. In *The Financial Times*, Dominic Gill reported that

> ... the success of the piece was going to depend more than anything on the willing spirit and sympathy of the players: and not all of the BBC SO seemed willing. A number of their sounds, indeed, seemed specially remote from the spirit of the text: some brass cat-calls and raspberries, flung challengingly from end to end of the hall; one or two suppressed giggles; an oddly abrupt section of tapping and blowing that began from nothing and ended nowhere. Not, one felt, a very successful account – even though there were some few scattered moments of genuine pleasure and tension. ... the lights went up to reveal a marvellous tableau of studio doormen in one corner, bunched together in stunned disbelief.

It was clear that Stockhausen's intentions required a different kind of player from those schooled in conventional techniques. Even the BBC Symphony Orchestra, experienced as it was in the newest of new music, could scarcely cope with this. (In future years, Stockhausen was to find specialist collaborators for this kind of work in the London Sinfonietta.) The experiment was not quickly repeated. There was, however, another abortive project to mount a major Stockhausen work in the Festival Hall: his work continued to be played by the Orchestra under other conductors; and a full-scale performance of his *Momente* was later imported from abroad into the Symphony Concerts season.

Less outlandish but no less lively events also took place in the studio during the 1969–70 season. Lawrence Foster conducted Charles Ives' rambling, sprawling Fourth Symphony; Heribert Esser directed Peter Racine Fricker's Toccata for piano and orchestra with Margaret Kitchin; Boulez returned for a TV programme on Varèse and Ives. The ageing Darius Milhaud conducted a programme of music by himself and Satie, including, for the first time in Britain, his Tenth Symphony; while Boult contributed a fine unfashionable programme of English music: Finzi's *Dies Natalis*, Parry's Symphonic Variations, Holst's *Hymn of Jesus*. With Goehr's *Little Symphony*, Messiaen's *Couleurs de la Cité Céleste*, Deryck Cooke's completion of Mahler's Tenth Symphony, plus a return visit from Rozhdestvensky (though not to the Festival Hall), Tadeusz Baird's *Espressioni varianti* and Malcolm Arnold's Sixth Symphony, the Orchestra's advocacy of recent works could not have been more wide-ranging.

It was the same story in the following year. At the start of the 1970–71 season, two important composers conducted their own music: there were studio concerts by Aaron Copland (including his First Symphony and *Statements*) and by Ernst Křenek (*Perspectives*, Three fragments from *Karl V*, and *Four plus three makes seven*). Then in the Festival Hall on 21 October Boulez returned with a new version, still not complete, of his *Éclat*, now re-titled *Éclat-multiples*, which was played in the same programme as Bartók's *Duke Bluebeard's Castle* and Stravinsky's Symphonies of Wind Instruments; later in the month *Éclat-multiples* was taken to Paris. The ten minutes of *Éclat* had been doubled in length, and the scoring had been expanded from a chamber group to a small symphony orchestra (still featuring the solo instruments of the original). *Éclat-multiples* remains an open-ended work, to which more sections will be added. Some small revisions and explanations were made even before the Paris performance, and that lasted 24 minutes.

Eliahu Inbal was to have visited the Orchestra in November, but he fell ill. This gave the chance for one of the most famous replacements in the Orchestra's history to make an impression on London audiences: the 26-year-old Andrew Davis, who had only just taken up his post as assistant conductor of the BBC Scottish Symphony Orchestra (after success in a conducting competition in Liverpool). The main work on Inbal's Festival Hall programme was Janáček's *Glagolithic Mass*. Davis scored a personal triumph at the performance, which ensured him continued attention from the Symphony Orchestra in the years that followed; indeed his international career, which took off with remarkable speed during the 1970s, may be dated from that concert. Later that season he again replaced a conductor in the Festival Hall series, this time Gennadi Rozhdestvensky in an RPS concert. Besides Andrew Davis other conductors who would soon be well known worked with the Orchestra in these months: Edo de Waart, Raymond Leppard (soon to be principal conductor of the BBC Northern Symphony Orchestra) and Bernhard Klee.

One disappointing loss during this season was the British première of Messiaen's *Poèmes pour Mi* in its orchestral version, which John Pritchard was to have conducted on 17 March; it was delayed until the Prom season. But there were two significant premières which remained. *Quadrivium* by Bruno Maderna was conducted by the composer. Dominic Gill described it as 'a large piece, around half an hour long, full of exuberant, romantic, well-

wined music, expertly constructed, beautifully scored. I liked it a lot . . .'
Maderna also conducted Mahler's Ninth Symphony, which Gill found 'both
convincing and moving. In human, dramatic terms often very impressive . . .
the final pages were absolutely right . . .' Two new works were given in a
special concert held during the ISCM Festival: *An Imaginary Landscape* by
Harrison Birtwistle, and *Siebengesang* by the oboist-composer Heinz
Holliger. Peter Stadlen of the *Daily Telegraph*, who had been to more ISCM
Festivals than any English critic, wrote that '*Siebengesang* . . . is one of the
most important compositions ever to have been presented in a Festival of the
International Society for Contemporary Music . . . I cannot readily imagine
an oboist who will not be pining to play what is surely the finest and, for that
matter, the most demanding concerto written for his instrument.'

Davis moves on

Colin Davis's share of the work, during this, his last season as Chief Conductor, was necessarily smaller than previously because of his growing commitments to Covent Garden. But he took up one important British work, the
Cello Concerto by Hugh Wood; and one revival, *The Lindbergh Flight*, by
Kurt Weill. He also directed several major works: Beethoven's *Cantata on
the Death of the Emperor Joseph II*, and the Choral Symphony; Stravinsky's
Perséphone, and Mahler's *Das Lied von der Erde*. He covered a typical range
of works with the Orchestra in his last major period in the studio during
January 1971: Tippett's *Fantasia concertante*, Verdi's Four Sacred Pieces,
an all-Dvořák programme, Sibelius, some Wagner, some Berlioz, and Elgar's
Second Symphony. He then left for Italy on an exchange visit with Mario
Rossi of the Italian radio orchestra; Rossi visited the BBC and gave the
Verdi *Requiem* at the Festival Hall. For Davis, the gruelling German tour
followed, and then nothing more until he returned as a guest conductor in
the next season.

Colin Davis's short period with the BBC Orchestra never quite worked
out as intended. Prevented at the start from restoring the Orchestra to the
supreme quality he desired for it, he was soon engaged in the next chapter of
his career, and the Orchestra was soon engaged in its: Covent Garden loomed
large for Davis, while Boulez came to dominate the Orchestra's activities. So
Davis was able to achieve only a part of what he had wanted. He did a great
deal for the solid base of the Orchestra's repertoire, and he took it into the
recording studio with a greater regularity, and with more central works, than
had been done for a long time. His performances of recent British music had
cogency and persuasiveness; the works by Wood, Birtwistle, Crosse, Maw
and Musgrave which he performed have all stood the test of time. It is true

that Davis's repertory with the Orchestra could at times have been mistaken for Malcolm Sargent's. But he did this repertory not for reasons of self-advancement, but because he believed that it was the right repertory for the Orchestra. This judgement was fundamentally sound, especially with Boulez so active in the years that Davis was Chief Conductor. That Pierre Boulez was able subsequently to make the BBC Symphony Orchestra into an unrivalled instrument for twentieth-century music is due in no little measure to Colin Davis's work in the period up to 1971.

The BBC and London

The BBC Symphony Orchestra continued to stand out from the other London orchestras by virtue of its programme planning and because of the extensive rehearsal it could give to new works. Pierre Boulez's dynamism did not go unnoticed by the London orchestras; in May and June 1969 he gave an important series with the London Symphony Orchestra called 'Cross-roads of Twentieth-Century Music' which proved highly popular as well as significant. But for the rest of the year, as the *Annual Register* recorded, 'the orchestral fare served up evening after evening in the Royal Festival Hall went only to show that the concert-going public at large was not much interested in music as a stimulant so long as it could have it as an anodyne, not concerned with adventure, but with reassurance, aesthetic security.' In 1971, the same publication complained that the Festival Hall's spring concerts were 'woefully routine [with programmes] designed along ruthlessly unimaginative lines'.

In the world of London's orchestral concert-giving, the BBC provided a contribution that was all too often isolated. The competition between the four public orchestras at the Festival Hall had results which were unfortunate for both programmes and performances. Neither did it benefit the economic condition of the public orchestras. Yet there seemed to be just enough, or not quite enough, work to go round. In the five years since the London Orchestral Concerts Board had been set up in the wake of the Goodman Report, a measure of co-ordination and financial stability had been achieved among London's orchestras. But were more radical measures needed? The Peacock Report on Orchestral Resources in Great Britain, which appeared in 1970, thought they were. It suggested that London's public orchestras should be reduced from four to two – an idealistic rather than a practical proposal. The Arts Council, in the person of its Chairman Lord Goodman, went so far as to dissociate itself from this recommendation in its foreword to the published report, thus ensuring the proposal little chance of a serious discussion. For ten more years, the problem of London's over-lavish and duplicatory orchestral resources was put on ice.

New priorities inside the BBC

In the twenty years since 1950, the BBC's stance towards its Symphony Orchestra and to all its orchestral resources had undergone a significant change. No longer was the case for their support unquestionable; it had constantly to be argued. For better or for worse, 'Broadcasting in the Seventies' had changed the face of the BBC radically before the Seventies had even begun. The hard-headed economic considerations of that document, its deathless, dangerous declaration that 'ends must be tailored to means', caused open conflict with the public and with members of the BBC's own staff in the national press, which made the country aware that the BBC was a divided organisation, vulnerable to economic pressures, and that its priorities were changing. In January 1971 the Controller of BBC 1 television, Paul Fox, set the severely practical tone of the BBC management's discussion of their problems, when he wrote in *The Listener* about the problems of television support for more programmes of high cultural content.

> It doesn't require particularly sharp intelligence to spot that the BBC's costs would go up considerably and that the audiences would go down considerably. What happens then on the cost factor alone? . . . the very existence of the licence fee would be imperilled, loyalty to the BBC's professional standards would disappear, and the end would be in sight for public service broadcasting.

Thus, with its sights set firmly on inexpensive programmes which attracted large audiences, BBC television advanced into the 1970s. And such views were not confined to television executives: a few months later (in July 1971) Mark White, Head of Radio 1, wrote to *The Listener* to say that his network could not attempt experimental programmes: 'We must attempt to cater for the kind of audience that is available to us at the times we are broadcasting. During the hours it is on the air Radio 1 attracts some 45% of the total radio audience. So it must be clear, therefore, that during that time we cannot cater for any minorities.' Serious music was not exempt from these attitudes: in a compelling address to the Royal Musical Association in 1972, Brian Trowell (for a while the BBC's Head of Opera) quoted these and other documents to show the radical change in tone that the BBC's provision of music had undergone since the days of Sir John Reith. Trowell was to broadcast the central points of his address in a Radio 3 programme; but his attack was so violent, and the BBC-organised discussion that followed was so incoherent, that the recording was never broadcast.

The question of provision for minority taste was crucial. The BBC was clearly over-provided with orchestral resources, much of which served, on Radio 3, a rather small minority. In *Broadcasting in the Seventies* the BBC had flown the kite of large-scale orchestral disbandment, and had been firmly put in its place by the public and by Parliament. Charles Curran's summary of the situation (in another *Listener* article, 11 June 1970) was a fair one:

> The Government asked us to reconsider our proposal. In effect they said to the BBC – and in this they were reflecting a feeling expressed very generally in Parliament: 'You may have too many orchestras but we want you to continue to employ them because somebody has to. They are needed nationally.' By implication, of course, the Government was also accepting that the cost of maintaining the orchestras was a fair charge on the licence revenue, and – presumably – that the licence fee would have to be calculated to take account of this cost. Faced with this request, and in the light of public discussion, the BBC agreed to maintain its employment of musicians at broadly the present level. In other words, we agreed to the Government's request that we should continue to bear a large share of the national musical patronage. . . . I understand the reasons for the Government's action. If the number of orchestras in the country were to fall below a certain level, it would mean either a more limited national musical repertoire, or a wide repertoire with a lower standard of execution. A really high standard of performance must rest on the broad base of public performance in quantity, because only this quantity can give opportunity for perfection. From that base the top orchestras can draw on a ready supply of skilled musicians. The higher the skill, the less the demand for rehearsals, the more ambitious the works that can be performed. It is a wholly logical argument. The present situation, as I have said, implies, first, an acceptance by Government that the BBC must continue to extend musical patronage beyond the strict needs of broadcasting and, secondly, its continued agreement to the use of licence revenue for this purpose – and that, in an era when the BBC needs every penny of the licence revenue to meet the specific requirements of broadcasting.

Curran's points about performance standards are perhaps arguable. A large amount of music-making does not necessarily stimulate great music-making; it would be difficult to maintain the case that the performances of the BBC's regional orchestras significantly affected those of the BBC Symphony Orchestra, except by the occasional transfer of players. The BBC needed its orchestras because they performed a repertoire that outside ensembles rarely touched: this was a point that BBC management was slow to grasp. The BBC's employment of orchestral musicians was not only a market force, an economic factor in the profession, but an artistic force, a matter of the highest importance to the balance of the repertory. Also most significant were the regional orchestras' services to their local communities – and this was a field in which the BBC fairly believed that it should share its burden with outside bodies such as the Arts Council in England, Scotland and Wales. This subsequently came about in Wales, but not in Scotland. Nor was the BBC's licence fee raised to a level commensurate with a continued support for all its orchestral resources. But it was to be another decade before this situation came to a head.

Meanwhile, the BBC Symphony Orchestra entered the 1970s with a degree of muted confidence. It could no longer enjoy an undisputedly high priority in the BBC's financial planning; but it had a certain status, it had a special role, and, with the approach of Pierre Boulez as Chief Conductor, it had the opportunity to become again, as it had been in the 1930s, a leader in the field of contemporary music. The balance of justified pride and economic concern with which top BBC management now regarded the BBC's musical patronage was aptly summed up by Charles Curran in his 1970 article:

> The BBC commitment remains, as Reith described it in 1924, 'music for all'. But now the audience is vastly bigger; it is more sophisticated and more demanding. It knows what it wants: a wide range of music of the highest quality . . . Each year the audience asks more of its music-makers. They are never disappointed.
>
> The BBC is proud of its part in . . . the musical life of the nation as a whole. It may perhaps be forgiven if at times it wonders a little ruefully whether its dedication to the tasks which it shouldered nearly fifty years ago is not too readily taken for granted.

8

A French Revolution?
1971-75

A declaration of war

The appointment of Pierre Boulez as Chief Conductor of the BBC Symphony Orchestra was not just a confirmation of his growing importance as an international conductor, or a consolidation of his already important part in each of the Orchestra's recent seasons. It was, on his part and that of William Glock, a declaration of war on the prevailing pattern of London concert life. Boulez's intention was to create a new model of what musical life could be like in a big city; Glock, while less didactic in spirit, aimed to show that just as the Proms had been revivified and broadened in scope during the 1960s, so in the 1970s the BBC Symphony Orchestra could similarly contradict some preconceptions about its role and function. Together, they set out to prove that a traditional symphony orchestra could provide the basis for a new approach to concert-giving.

By now, Boulez and Glock were old friends; they knew each other's thinking in great detail – the points at which they converged and where they differed. They agreed on the most important ingredients of the scheme: diversification and experiment. They disagreed over some of the means to be used: Boulez thought planning should be firmly thematic, while Glock never liked to have his ideas constrained by a straitjacket. Boulez wanted a strong profile over each season; Glock knew that, with the complexities of the BBC's organisation, all that could be hoped for would be some outstanding events which would stick in the memory. Together, they hoped to be able to achieve at least a couple of seasons of music-making which demonstrated that concerts in which the music of our time formed a major part of the programmes could be a lively success in London.

The appointment of Boulez had a long history behind it. When Glock first invited him to the BBC in 1964, they had already been acquainted for many years. They had corresponded since the early 1950s; Boulez regularly sent Glock advance programmes of his Domaine Musical concerts in Paris.

His allegiance was firmly to the music of Webern rather than to that of Schoenberg; when Schoenberg died on 13 July 1951, Boulez wrote an article at Glock's invitation for his magazine *The Score*. 'Schoenberg is dead!', it proclaimed in a famous sentence. 'I do not hesitate to write, not out of any desire to provoke a stupid scandal, but equally without hypocrisy and point-less melancholy, SCHOENBERG IS DEAD.' The article was typical of Boulez for its strongly-emphasised stance, its flavour of polemic. But it had a very wide influence as a declaration that the development of musical language in the 1950s was to draw its inspiration not from Schoenberg, but from Webern. Boulez's *Structures* for two pianos, which dates from the same period, made this intention palpable: its Section Ia was as rigorously organ-ised a serial passage as had been written up to that time, determining not only pitches by serial methods but also duration, timbre and volume. (Messiaen had shown a path towards this development in his *Mode de valeurs et d'intensités* of 1949.) Boulez's music made a great impact among the avant-garde. Glock kept in close touch with him and heard the première of his *Le Marteau sans maître* at the ISCM Festival of 1955 in Baden-Baden. He then invited Boulez and his Domaine Musical Ensemble to London in 1957 for a concert under the auspices of the Institute of Contemporary Arts, featuring *Le Marteau* and music by Stockhausen, Webern and Nono. (It was reluct-antly broadcast by the BBC: see Chapter 6.)

By this time Boulez was conducting twentieth-century music regularly. He did so, he says, because performances of the Second Viennese School repertory were generally so bad. He recalls only Hermann Scherchen and Hans Rosbaud as reliable conductors of Schoenberg and Webern: such men as René Leibowitz, who directed Webern's Symphony Op. 21 in Paris after the war, made the music unintelligible, he says. Boulez began to expand from directing his own chamber concerts at the end of the 1950s, when he con-ducted at the Donaueschingen Festival of contemporary music in Germany, replacing Hans Rosbaud who was ill. He had an arrangement with the South-West German Radio Orchestra to work as composer-in-residence and to conduct some smaller concerts; and from 1963 he conducted the other orchestra that Rosbaud has been associated with, the Concertgebouw of Amsterdam. He was soon to be approached by George Szell to make guest appearances with the Cleveland Orchestra. William Glock stepped in first, and invited him to give concerts in 1964 and 1965 in London, at the Proms and in the Winter season.

Boulez's repertoire was then extremely small. Fifteen or twenty works were all that the two men could agree on: Berg, Schoenberg, Webern, Stravinsky, Debussy, with a little of Berlioz, Haydn and Schubert. Yet within a couple of years that number had grown, and Boulez was already established as a world-class conductor of his own repertoire through the BBC Symphony Orchestra's American tour and some deeply impressive performances at the Proms. Glock later recalled:

> He conducted Debussy's *Images* at his very first appearance at the Proms – I shall never forget the heart-rending beauty of *Les Parfums de la nuit* and the transition from that to the next piece, *Le Matin d'un jour de fête* with its distant march rhythm. . . . Boulez realises the music from within and with a naturalness and intensity that can't be imitated.

The relationship Boulez formed then with the BBC Orchestra soon became a close one. His note to them after that 1965 Prom still survives: 'To the BBC Symphony Orchestra. Before leaving London I'd like to express to you my deep gratitude for last night's concert. I enjoyed not only the way you performed but also and not least, the effort you made to rehearse in such a short time a programme which was not really easy. Thank you for the music and the friendship. PB.'

Plans for Paris

The growth of that relationship in the extraordinary concerts of the Festival Hall seasons in 1967 and after, in the East European tour of 1967, and in the partnership with Colin Davis before 1971, has already been touched on. It was with the successes of that Russian tour fresh in his mind that Glock turned towards the idea of Boulez as Chief Conductor. However, there was at that time no possibility that this could be realised. Boulez was engaged in far more complex negotiations which were supposed to lead to a post which he regarded as central to his life's work. He was to become Musical Director of the Paris Opéra, a fact often ignored in discussions of Boulez's career. The chief conductorships of the two orchestras in London and New York which he was eventually to undertake in the seventies were, as late as 1967, no more than a dream. Boulez had violently criticised French music-making on several occasions. In her biography of him, Joan Peyser records in detail the struggle which Boulez had after 1964 with André Malraux, the French Minister of Cultural Affairs, who instituted a commission to enquire into French musical life. Boulez's advice was rejected by the commission, and he vowed to have nothing more to do with Parisian music-making. But the break was not as radical as his biographer implies, for there were still those in official positions in Paris who realised that his was one of the few brilliant minds in French music. One of these was Jean Vilar, who was in charge of the department under which the Paris Opéra and Opéra Comique are controlled – a department separate from that of Malraux's ministry. Vilar invited Boulez and Maurice Béjart to prepare a report on the state of the Opéra's workings, concentrating on its artistic policy. Boulez was to have a completely free hand in devising new schemes of work for the house, but more important, if the report was accepted, he was to become director of the newly-reorganised Opéra. It was a prospect few creative men would have turned down.

The Paris Opéra inquiry enabled Boulez to develop in his own mind for the first time the possibilities of changing a big city's orientation towards music through administrative means. Most radical thinkers would have thought it inappropriate or impossible to bring about change through such bastions of the establishment as opera houses (a stance which Boulez later adopted himself). But in 1967 the chance was there to reconstruct one city's musical life around a revivified opera house, with theatre, dance, music, workshops, a new building which would be appropriate for contemporary work, and a traditional but discriminating repertory of opera. Boulez and Béjart prepared their report, and submitted it to Vilar, who was enthusiastic. Boulez recalled that the name Opéra was to be dropped; instead it would become known as the 'Centre for Music and Theatre'. However, May 1968 saw the student uprising in Paris and the fierce backlash of the De Gaulle government. Boulez was disgusted with the reactionary political situation, as was Vilar, on whom there was pressure to fall in with the counter-revolutionary line. Vilar refused, and quickly resigned. The Paris Opéra plan was dead.

A walk at Scheveningen

Only now was Boulez free to accept the possibility of the BBC post. In June 1968 Glock travelled to visit him in Holland, where he was conducting concerts with the Hague Orchestra. They met on the sea-front at Scheveningen, near the Kurzaal where the BBC Symphony Orchestra had appeared in the past. They walked on the beach for several miles and discussed plans endlessly: plans which would translate some of Boulez's hopes for musical life in a capital city into reality in London. Glock was excited to have found a conductor who responded so immediately to his ideas, who understood questions of administration and saw music in its organisational framework. Glock recalls:

> We walked for six or seven miles along the beach. . . . In asking him to become the next Chief Conductor of the BBC Symphony Orchestra I was influenced not only by the marvellous performances he had often given, but also by my long association with him . . . and by my admiration for him as a

composer, as a man of brilliance and imagination, and as a human being.
Someone wrote of him that he is a clairvoyant observer of everything around
him, and his judgements can certainly be violent at times. But there is
nothing small in his behaviour, any more than in his conducting.

Boulez, for his part, knew that success or failure in London would depend
on Glock's obtaining support for their radical plans within the BBC. There
was one problem. Glock had already been Controller of Music at the BBC
for nine years, and was due to retire in 1970 when he would be two years
beyond the official BBC retiring age of sixty. Boulez could not take over until
1971. So he insisted on one condition if he were to come to the BBC – that
Glock should stay on long enough to be able to collaborate with him. This
meant that Glock had to request an extension of another two years beyond
his already generous retiring age of sixty-two. It was agreed: Glock's
appointment as Controller was prolonged for another two years; Boulez's
contract was for three seasons. Though Glock would leave during Boulez's
second season, they would be able to outline plans for the third. Boulez was
immensely excited by the possibilities of the post. When he drove into
Amsterdam to collect his agent Howard Hartog, following his discussions
with Glock, he became so animated that with rare confusion he became
completely lost in the suburbs of Amsterdam.

How much time would Boulez spend with the Orchestra? This question
was crucial to the influence which a Chief Conductor could acquire over his
players. Colin Davis had in the later years of his contract underfulfilled it by
several concerts each season. But Boulez was at first prepared to make a
substantial commitment. Discussing the details with Howard Hartog,
Glock agreed on a five-month period annually with the Orchestra for three
years from September 1971, with a minimum of forty concerts a year. Two
further renewals of the contract for a year were possible. With forty concerts
(including studio appearances) a very strong set of programmes could be
obtained. Agreement on that basis was reached in January 1969.

But then complications ensued. An extraordinary offer of another chief
conductorship was made to Boulez on 1 April by the New York Philharmonic Orchestra – and it was no April Fool's joke. Boulez saw an opportunity
to change the profile of musical life in two major cities instead of just one.
Any other man might have regarded it as impossible to combine both jobs,
but Boulez, with his inexhaustible energy and self-discipline, considered
that he might be able to combine the two. Without committing himself in
New York, he returned to England to discuss the new problem with Glock.
Glock frankly tried to talk him out of the American offer. He felt (a justified

feeling in the event) that Boulez had a better chance of success in London; that the BBC provided a much firmer base for doing a large proportion of twentieth-century music than did the New York Philharmonic, and that he would have to fight fewer battles in London. Glock thought he had succeeded, and left for a holiday. However Boulez returned to New York to carry on negotiations. He was careful not to imperil the BBC scheme, and the management of the New York Philharmonic agreed that he would appear for a very short period in the 1971–2 season, so that the BBC schedule need be altered very little. With these provisos, Boulez decided to accept the New York post. In May he returned to England, and on 30 May, just two days before the New York appointment was announced, Glock had to submit a revised scheme for Boulez's post to the BBC's management. Thanks to Boulez's acceptance of a workload that would have killed other men, the scheme remained almost intact: Boulez would now conduct the BBC Symphony Orchestra for four months of the year instead of five; there would be thirty-two concerts instead of forty. Only seven weeks would be spent in New York for 1971–72 and four months a year thereafter, and the New York management would work closely with Glock to ensure that the schedules dovetailed. In the years when he spent eight months in his two permanent posts, Boulez agreed that he would undertake no further conducting. Glock appended a typically dry note to his document: 'Much will depend on Boulez's stamina, but as most conductors live as long as Titian perhaps all will be well.'

Plans and policies

In the two years between his appointment and his taking up the post in September 1971, Boulez developed rapidly his ideas of what he hoped to achieve in London. As Glock recalled, 'His convictions grew that reforms were needed, and as time went on letters would arrive from Boston, Provence, Baden-Baden – wherever he happened to be working at the moment – with a call to arms'. In an interview with Peter Heyworth of *The Observer*, published when he began his first season, Boulez explained some of his aims in detail:

HEYWORTH: *Can you outline your policy as chief conductor of the BBC Symphony Orchestra?*
BOULEZ: I am coming at the instigation of William Glock, the BBC's head of music, because we have many ideas in common about what we feel needs to be done. We don't want to give a series of concerts like so many menus, so that all you remember at the end of the season are a few isolated events – a

good work, a good performance and so on. We want to give each season a profile, so that it isn't easily forgotten, so that one can say ah yes, that was the year of so and so.

Can you put that in more concrete terms?

The idea is to operate on three levels. Three, because, although I want to have a plan, I don't like the idea of putting the season into a strait-jacket. The first level is what I call *retrospective*, and that runs on two parallel lines. The first is to take a composer of the seventeenth to the nineteenth century, who is famous but insufficiently performed, or who wrote a lot of works that are very rarely performed. For the coming season we've chosen Haydn, and we're going to perform him mainly in St John's, Smith Square, because that's the size of building he wrote for.

And the other retrospective?

One of the classical composers of the twentieth century, and for that we're starting with Stravinsky. Not just as an act of homage, but to try to get a general view of his music and see what he really means in the music of our time. We're also going to put on short pre-concerts. These will consist of chamber music works that orchestral concert audiences might not otherwise hear. We also have plans for post-concerts at St John's in 1972–3.

The second level?

The idea here is to draw attention, not to individual composers, but to forms. This coming season, unfortunately, we haven't been able to realise this approach. But what I want to do is to take a form like, for instance, the cantata and trace its evolution from, let's say, Schütz to Stockhausen's *Momente*. And then the third level is what I call *prospective*. These concerts are going to take place in the Round House, and in their programmes I have put the accent on discovery – discovery of new works, new media, new composers, new ways of expression. . . .

You haven't necessarily chosen works that you think are masterpieces?

If you present twenty new or recent works, you can't have twenty masterpieces. That never was the case, and it never will be. We have to try to get rid of the idea that when we listen to new music we are searching for the masterpieces of the future. The aim is to explore what is going on today, and if something valid or valuable turns up, then we can be pleased. Some of the works may be more important for indicating a direction than for themselves.

I'm keen to get the audience to participate in this exploration, to react to what is played. My plan is to give a very brief introduction to each piece. Very brief, because I don't want to burden people with details of a work they haven't yet heard. Then, afterwards, I want to have a discussion and, if there's time, to perform again at least part of the work. And I hope the musicians will also join in the discussion.

But I want a real discussion, so that the differences of opinion are ventilated.

Why aren't you going to give these concerts in the Festival Hall?

First of all, it's too big. And then, I think it's too formal. You see, I think we must get the right kind of atmosphere. I don't want these concerts to be events you go to just to admire the performances. The musicians and myself will be dressed like the audience, so that we are all visibly part of it. I want to create a feeling that we are all, audience, players, and myself, taking part in an act of exploration . . .

There is a need for a new approach to concert life that will bring it into touch with what composers are doing today. Look at Wagner: he didn't only compose, he built a model opera house and created the conditions in which his own music could be performed.

What I want to do is to create models of concert life in two cities – London and New York. After that, anyone can do it. But if I don't, I fear nobody will – that's what's so distressing. And that's why I've been invited by the New York Philharmonic and the BBC. It's not just because of my ability as a conductor. There are plenty of conductors as good as me and some who are much better in parts of the repertory. But it's the ideas I want to put into practice that count . . .

I want to create conditions in which the music of our own time is once again an integral part of concert life. That's a creative task and that's why I accepted it.

These comments may fruitfully be compared with what actually happened during Boulez's period as Chief Conductor. Boulez was to be attacked later for planning a revolution that failed; but his declaration then and now was that he did no more than set out to create a 'model' of concert life which others might or might not follow. However, Boulez's detailed outline of his intentions here reveals much that did *not* occur during his Chief Conductorship – thematic programming, planned retrospectives, pre-concerts and post-concerts, extensive audience participation.

A new concert profile

The Boulez era was inaugurated in September 1971. The plan of the 1971–2 public concert season was radically different from anything which had gone before. In parallel to the expansion of the Proms from the Albert Hall to other venues, the Symphony Concerts series was now not confined to the Royal Festival Hall. 'A conventional hall attracts conventional audiences to conventional programmes,' Boulez said. So there were two extra series: one, of new music, in the Round House at Chalk Farm (where Proms had already been presented in the summer of 1971); and one, of classical and pre-classical music, in the Church of St John's Smith Square in Westminster (which already housed the BBC's very successful series of lunchtime concerts). These two buildings became hallmarks of the Boulez period. The Round House, a bare, gaunt railway shed designed by Stephenson in 1847, in which engines were once housed and turntabled (hence its shape and name), was in those days very flexible in its programming and in its seating arrangements; it was ideal for the kind of informal encounter with new music which Boulez hoped would bring a whole new young audience to BBC concerts. The atmosphere was informal (some said chaotic); the railway lines to Euston were still uncomfortably close for comfort during some of the quietest modern music. The place was not as spruce as the Festival Hall, but then the idea was not to use a hall which was regimented or over-organised: it was well known as a location for pop concerts and adventurous theatre.

St John's Smith Square, magnificently restored after wartime bombing, was used both as a concert hall and a recording studio (though still consecrated as a church). A splendid four-square baroque building, by Thomas Archer, it was designed under the Fifty New Churches Act of 1711. Nikolaus Pevsner and others had argued that it was one of the few truly baroque pieces of architecture in London and perhaps the finest – certainly few other ecclesiastical buildings showed the spirit of continental baroque architects, of Borromini and Bernini, so clearly as this church with its unconventional plan and its massive elaborate decoration. The internal spaces, unencumbered by large aisles, were ideal for seating a quite large orchestra on the floor of the church; only the absence of raised seating made life difficult for the audience. Dressing-room facilities were limited here, but the management was flexible, and there was already a production box installed with broadcasting equipment.

Into these two strongly contrasted buildings Glock and Boulez put the most adventurous ideas of their first joint season. The outlines followed Boulez's plan. All the works presented in the Round House were to be first British performances; these concerts were to be introduced by Boulez himself and were to be followed by discussions. In St John's programmes were to be based, as Boulez intimated, on the music of Haydn. There was an element of a theme in the Festival Hall season: Stravinsky was to be featured with two concerts devoted to his music. Boulez also had ambitious ideas for informal pre- and post-concerts. In St John's these were to take the form of informal chamber music recitals (linked to the evening's music) which would take place downstairs in the crypt of the church, where drinks and meals could be served. In the Festival Hall they were to be short, informal programmes to whet the appetite for the evening's main events, planned for the thirty minutes between 7.15 and 7.45, leaving a short interval before the full concert at 8. They would happen perhaps in the foyer or in the auditorium, and might be devoted to small-scale works relevant to the evening's concert. In the event none of this scheme was realised exactly as Boulez had intended. At St John's plans for post-concerts were abandoned even before programmes had been discussed. At the Festival Hall there was the recurrent problem of the regular Wednesday evening organ recital in the hall to consider. The BBC Symphony Orchestra traditionally gave its concerts on Wednesdays (other nights being allocated to the four public orchestras supported by the London Orchestral Concerts Board); organ recitals, too, invariably occurred on that night from 5.55 to 6.55. The only possibility for holding pre-concerts on Wednesdays, therefore, was to choose nights outside the organ recital season. So it was that in the first season it was possible to organise two particular 'pre-concerts' – chamber music by Stravinsky preceding both the concerts including his music. But even these two events did not quite materialise with the spirit Boulez intended: they simply became incorporated into extra-long concerts which started at 7.30, with the chamber music section lasting until just after eight; then there was an interval, and parts two and three of the evening, the concert proper, followed. The 'pre-concerts' were equally formal in style, and tickets were required for admission. In future seasons it proved impossible to present these pre-concerts with point and purpose, and it was also impossible to circumvent the Festival Hall's inflexible planning. So they too disappeared.

New orchestral planning

Major changes in orchestral planning were brought about by Boulez's programme plans. In a return to the Symphony Orchestra's earliest practice (so as to make fuller use of the groups of orchestral players needed for the Round House and Smith Square concerts), the Orchestra was to be split into two, as it had been during the 1930s. While one group rehearsed and played the small-scale public concerts, another was to rehearse and record a studio concert. This scheme was administered by Paul Huband, the Orchestra's General Manager, who had been joined in 1970 by William Relton (a former colleague in the BBC's Manchester Music Department) as Orchestral Manager. The plan ensured an increased broadcast output from the Orchestra, which in its turn was used as justification for a necessary salary rise which made the Orchestra more competitive with outside bodies. The opportunity was also taken, when Boulez took over, to change other features of the Orchestra's life. The co-principal scheme in the woodwind was modified: instead of a half-and-half arrangement a clear seniority was established – one principal did 70% of the work, the other 30%. Only in the horn section was a half-and-half scheme retained, since it was preferred by Alan Civil, who had brought such distinction to the Orchestra since he joined in 1966. At this time, too, during Boulez's first season, another distinguished brass player joined: John Wilbraham became principal trumpet. Praise of Civil's and Wilbraham's playing became constant features of press notices in the Boulez period.

Indeed, in all sections the Orchestra was now stronger than it had been for some years. In 1969 Bela Dekany had joined Eli Goren as co-leader – a highly successful partnership which was to survive until Goren retired in 1977. Colin Bradbury was now principal clarinet; the outstanding young oboist David Theodore joined during the 1972 Proms; and following the retirement of Douglas Whittaker in 1970 (having served the Orchestra for nearly twenty years), David Butt became principal flute. The full orchestral strength now stood at 101, the highest establishment since 1939. Morale was very high. Boulez took a close interest in every individual player in the Orchestra and was meticulous about attending auditions. Standards improved through the period and the Orchestra's work was full of challenges.

The splitting of the Orchestra provided much variety: while John Eliot Gardiner was preparing the first of the St John's series, with Mozart's Vespers and Haydn's *Harmoniemesse*, Gilbert Amy was in the Maida Vale studios directing *Wildtrack* by Bernard Rands. While Colin Davis was rehearsing Stravinsky and Haydn for St John's in November, George Malcolm was taking the rest of the Orchestra through a delightful Saint-Saëns anniversary concert. The St John's programmes were launched first, and they proved an attractive scheme: John Eliot Gardiner, John Pritchard, Colin Davis, Raymond Leppard, Andrew Davis, Charles Mackerras and Boulez conducted. All the programmes included the music of Haydn or Stravinsky. Two of the concerts, including, improbably, Boulez's, were all-Haydn. One of the series, on 14 February 1972, was cancelled because of power cuts: the programme had to be pre-recorded in the studio.

A contemporary partnership

The Boulez–BBC partnership was inaugurated with a Festival Hall concert of Varèse, Stravinsky and Bartók, and then, six days later, with a concert to open the festival 'Musikprotokoll 1971' at Graz. This programme proved, if proof were needed, that the BBC Symphony Orchestra had returned to its

'*From the heart to the heart*': *Colin Davis rehearses Beethoven's* Missa Solemnis *for the first night of the 1976 Proms, in place of Rudolf Kempe*

Andrew Davis, who had his first major success in London with the BBC Symphony Orchestra, standing in at the last moment for Eliahu Inbal

John Pritchard, Chief Guest Conductor of the BBC Symphony Orchestra from 1978

Rozhdestvensky at work: in rehearsal at Maida Vale, with Rodney Friend, co-leader, 1980

Sir Charles Mackerras, Chief Guest Conductor 1976–8

'I find this one of the best orchestras in the world': Gennadi Rozhdestvensky, with his wife Victoria Postnikova, at the press conference in September 1977 to announce his appointment as Chief Conductor

The BBC Symphony Orchestra, 1980. Violins: Rodney Friend, co-leader

Horns: Alan Civil, co-principal (right)

Cellos: Ross Pople, principal

Brass: Jim Gourlay, tuba principal

Rodney Friend, co-leader

Colin Bradbury, principal clarinet
Geoffrey Gambold, principal bassoon

Sidonie Goossens, principal harp

John Wilbraham, principal trumpet until 1980

Above: Summer home; The Royal Albert Hall, South Kensington, with Prom queue. Below: Winter Home; The Royal Festival Hall, the South Bank; the Orchestra with Bela Dekany, co-leader

'*I send you all my profound good wishes and every hope for the half-century to come*' : *Sir Adrian Boult greets the BBC Symphony Orchestra on its fiftieth anniversary, 22 October 1980*

status of the 1930s, as one of the world's leading advocates of contemporary music. The works played were:

Elliott Carter...............Concerto for Orchestra (European première)
Harrison Birtwistle...............................An imaginary landscape
Boulez .... Éclat-multiples
Stravinsky.............................Symphonies of wind instruments

– a programme which could stand as a typical but outstanding example of the Orchestra's unique achievement.

The Orchestra went to Vienna, where it repeated the Carter and Boulez works, and played Schoenberg's Orchestral Variations (which it had introduced in public there in 1936), alongside music by Debussy, Bartók, Mahler and Haydn. These concerts were a brilliant success; there seemed to be nothing Boulez and the Orchestra could do wrong for continental audiences and critics.

Back in London, the Festival Hall concerts provided strikingly varied fare. The series was not as unified in its programmes as Boulez might have wished, and was rather in line with Glock's desire to go 'one step at a time'. But each concert was memorable. Michael Gielen conducted Ligeti's *Requiem* (which was to become famous for providing background music to the film *2001*); Andrew Davis returned in Bach's *St John Passion*; Charles Groves introduced a new Gordon Crosse work *Memories of morning: night*; John Pritchard launched into Ives' Fourth Symphony; Louis Frémaux took over a programme (which had first been Rozhdestvensky's and then Sergiu Commissiona's) which formed part of the Stravinsky theme. On 5 April, Colin Davis contributed *Threni* to the Stravinsky celebration, and then on 19 April Boulez returned for one of his most challenging programmes. This was to include a 'pre-concert' of Stravinsky, and was to juxtapose Schoenberg's *Jacob's Ladder* (itself a major undertaking for one concert) with Stravinsky's *A sermon, a narrative and a prayer*, and was also to include the British première of Boulez's own work *e.e. cummings ist der dichter*. (The title, Boulez assures us, is due to a mistake on the telephone, when his secretary said to an orchestral manager in German, 'The title is not decided yet, but I can tell you this: e.e. cummings is the poet.' Somehow the middle part of the sentence was not heard, and the title duly appeared on his next schedule. So he kept it.) It is a measure of the demands which Boulez made on the BBC that this concert had no fewer than sixteen rehearsals of various kinds: a prospect which would have made it quite impracticable for any commercial body. In the Boulez work, the Schola Cantorum of Stuttgart took part; echoing Boulez's wish for informal dress, they wrote to the BBC, 'We have our own individual clothes, not dinner-jackets; we have no uniforms because we are no soldiers'. *The Sunday Times* reported that the new Boulez work 'attempts to mirror in musical terms the poet's tricky, trickling typographical lay-out; whether or not it achieved that aim, it charmed the ear by its delicate flutterings, both vocal and instrumental, did not outstay its welcome, and sounded still better on repetition'.

At the end of the winter season, the Orchestra left for a tour of France and Switzerland in which Boulez conducted every concert – on nine consecutive days, from 3–12 May. *Éclat* was included in both short and long versions, Hugh Wood's Cello Concerto was taken as a representative British work, and Berio's *Epifanie* was revived in Paris.

Round House risks

The series of concerts in the Round House did not begin until the winter of 1972. It had been hoped to have six concerts, but this proved impracticable: instead, there were two pairs of two concerts, in January and May; Boulez conducted three, while the other was directed by Michael Gielen. (A fifth concert, similar in type, was given in studio on 6 May 1972 under Diego Masson.) Programmes were risky. Boulez saw no need to programme master-pieces: his intention was to stimulate discussion and provoke ideas. At the first event, he introduced it as 'more a meeting than a concert', but he did include a strong Stockhausen work, *Mixtur*, in the programme as well as a piece by Bruno Maderna which he admired. The third work was a BBC commission: Justin Connolly's *Tetramorph*. The complications which these concerts involved for BBC staff were extensive. Only the Maderna was for 'conventional' orchestra. Connolly's piece used pre-recorded tape; the synchronisation between tape and strings had to be managed by a machine on stage which flashed a red light every five seconds. Stockhausen's *Mixtur* required live sounds to be electronically modified; the sound was mixed in the auditorium by Hugh Davies, who had frequently collaborated with Stockhausen in English performances of his works. Stockhausen was to have come to England himself but in the end he withdrew. He wrote detailed instructions to Boulez: 'It is important that the BBC starts collecting a fair number of plastic boxes (soap containers etc) of varying sizes. These are needed for scraping the surface of the tam-tam.' There were two days of sectional rehearsals for the five groups of instruments; Catherine Comet from Paris was engaged alongside Boulez to direct the rehearsals.

On the night, Boulez wished his introductions and the post-concert dis-cussion to be as spontaneous as possible. The result was that his introduc-tions rambled slightly and the discussion was less than cohesive. Some

questions were written down and submitted during the interval: Did Boulez
enjoy conducting the Maderna? Was there any scope for interpretation in
this music? Does aleatoric freedom turn the conductor from an interpreter
into a creator? Others were taken live, and were difficult to hear. Justin
Connolly cast some doubt on the value of his own commission by describing
the inflexible conditions he had been given, including limits as to the available players and to length. The introductions were included in the broadcast, but the question time was only recorded for possible future use. There
was a large and enthusiastic audience for this first concert: nearly 600 seats
were sold.

William Mann described the feeling of the concert well in *The Times*
(19 January).

> The atmosphere of the Round House is informal. The performers are as
> casually dressed as the audience who can buy seats or (for half price) lounge
> promenade fashion in vacant spaces. Concerts start at 9 pm and are con-
> ducted in the manner of *Musica Viva* with spoken programme notes, live
> musical illustrations, a performance of each work, and finally question-time
> due to end by 11.45 pm. The hours may deter some willing patrons – the
> auditorium was jam packed until the interval but emptied steadily after 11
> o'clock – though they encourage a receptive atmosphere if you don't have to
> worry about getting home.
>
> The question-time period was not ideally helpful, especially when
> Boulez called for spoken questions (inaudible) from the audience. His
> introductions, very illuminating, could have been less discursive. The aptest
> proportions for such an event are never found at once. But for best effect the
> most worthwhile and difficult works should be performed twice in the same
> concert, or repeated in subsequent concerts, so that their qualities may
> shine more brightly in numerous, differently concocted performances.

Dominic Gill in *The Financial Times* broadly agreed:

> A simple, excellent idea – but one which we may be tempted to take too much
> for granted: how little time ago it was after all that a taste even of Webern or
> Schoenberg in a BBC/Boulez programme raised eyebrows, provoked public
> alarm!
>
> The real disappointment was the discussion: too short (racing an early
> deadline), too one-sided (why not a panel of speakers, not the conductor
> alone?). The BBC should give more thought to this end of their evening;
> properly developed, it could prove to be the most vital and illuminating part.

The same pattern continued at the second concert, though here Boulez had trouble with his radio microphone and some of his introductions were inaudible in the hall. The critics were once again enthusiastic.

> Let's have three cheers for Pierre Boulez's BBC concerts in the Round House, a welcome alternative to the conventional symphony concert. After the second one on Monday we know now that we aren't asked to expect masterpieces but to make acquaintance, more closely perhaps than formal concerts allow, with fairly recent progressive works that do not immediately explain themselves to everyone who might enjoy them (William Mann, *The Times*).

The concert was as lively and as complicated as the first: here the difficulties centred not only round electronics, but around staging. The concert was to have included a piece by David Bedford called *With 100 Kazoos*, which was going to include audience participation on toy kazoos that would be distributed during the concert. But Boulez and Glock drew the line at this piece – perhaps on grounds of quality, as was reported of Boulez; perhaps on grounds of practicality, as was reported of Glock. The prospect of rivalry between 100 'official' kazoo players and members of the audience was not discounted; nor was the potential effect on members of the Orchestra. Did the Musicians' Union intervene on the grounds of amateur participation in a professional concert? At any rate, the piece was replaced by *Foxes and Hedgehogs* by the American Eric Salzman, which was given its first British performance. This was a music-theatre work involving movement, visual effects, costume, and sections of the piece which had to be recorded and played back during the performance. (The Musicians' Union would not allow the extracts to be taped during rehearsal, so a tape using a different performance had to be used in its place.) As described by Meirion Bowen in the *Guardian*, the piece included 'members of separate instrumental groups arriving casually as though for a rehearsal, ear-splitting amplification systems, the soloist entering from the back, chattering away in baby talk, symbolic coloured spots, and speeded-up movie projections'. He found the whole thing pretentious and Andrew Porter wrote that 'frankly, it all seemed rather a mess', but others enjoyed it. The programme also included a string piece, *Ramifications*, by Ligeti, which was given two hearings, and the first performance of a BBC commission, *Mésalliance*, by Bernard Rands, 'which proved to be a piano concerto in which the orchestra proposed semi-ordered chaos and was gradually tamed by the soloist who ended the work by himself as violently and as anarchically as they' (William Mann, *The Times*). 'Roger Woodward played his scatty piano part with bright-eyed abandon' (*Guardian*).

This concert raised the question of quality in Boulez's experimental ventures: put bluntly, did it matter if some of the pieces turned out to be
rubbish? Boulez himself, in the post-concert discussion, refused to be drawn
into judgements of quality. He saw the function of the series as that of simply
presenting works and talking about them. Critics also began to be irritated
by Boulez's offhand manner during question-time. The conductor laughed
at an objection to his performance of the Ligeti *Ramifications* (that he had not
observed the silent bars which the score indicates that the conductor should
beat at the end of the piece), saying that there was no point beating when
there were not notes – a curious attitude to rests in music. Questioners who
had submitted their written questions were sometimes asked to come to the
front of the hall and reword their query: a disconcerting experience which
inhibited rather than enlivened the proceedings. Slowly, it was discovered
that 'informal concerts' were more difficult to run than formal ones.

The third concert of the series, directed by Michael Gielen but introduced by Boulez, also had a change of programme: there was to have been
another BBC commission, from Hugh Wood, but he said just after the
season had begun that he would not be able to finish his new piece. Fortunately Glock was able to substitute a new work from a senior English composer, Elisabeth Lutyens. She had just completed *Counting your steps*, for
voice, flute and percussion. Gielen included a work of his own, and there
was music by Busotti and Betsy Jolas. In *The Financial Times* Gillian Widdicombe summed up the result: 'One hit, one hard, one plain, one cold'. She
thought the Lutyens a success, the Busotti lacking in warmth, the Jolas
rather too ordinary, and the Gielen difficult to grasp; other listeners disagreed and had less trouble enjoying the pieces. Boulez's introductions
continued to attract criticism. The BBC had encouraged him to make them
shorter, and even on this occasion scripted (which Boulez thoroughly
disliked), but they were not always clear, and Widdicombe declared that 'as
broadcaster and introducer, he could still profit in lessons in communication
. . .' Though Boulez was present to speak, there was a smaller audience than
for the concerts he conducted.

The last concert of the series was, like the first two, a popular success. The
main attraction was another staged work, commissioned from Peter Maxwell
Davies. *Blind Man's Buff* was based on a scene from a Büchner play; it
involved a king and a jester, with a mime and a dancer, costumed instrumentalists on stage, and an off-stage string band. The production, staged by
William Fitzwater, made use of various effects: 'Bright heraldic banners,
coloured lights, a sulphurous flash from the gates of hell, bags of toys, innumerable masks, a death's head.' The music was generally found less

interesting than these extravagant accessories. Included in the rest of the concert should have been Maurizio Kagel's *Hallelujah II*, but that was cancelled and a work by the Canadian Murray Schafer substituted: *Requiem for a party girl*, which provided a virtuoso vehicle for the soprano Jane Manning. Globokar's *Discours II* for solo trombone (played by the composer, with other trombonists from the Orchestra) opened the concert. Questions in the discussion verged on the flippant: Was putting down the trombone mutes on the floor during the Globokar part of the piece? Or, more relevantly, how could Davies' theatre piece be appreciated over the radio?

Towards a second season

This question raised one of the fundamental problems about the Round House series which time did not quite solve. As conceived by Boulez, the evenings were loosely constructed, broken up by talk, punctuated by pauses and generally relaxed. For a broadcast audience, however, that sort of experience was unsatisfactory: not being part of the atmosphere, they could easily feel that the evening was disorganised, slow and not very coherent. Boulez's informality had to be restrained for the listening audience: in the end, all spontaneity dropped out of the presentation. There was also the problem of establishing an audience in the hall. There had been considerable enthusiasm in this first season, but only for the Boulez concerts. When the second season was billed to open with Bruno Maderna conducting a concert, with a mostly American programme of music by Morton Feldman and Jacob Druckman, the audience seemed to disappear. To avoid undue embarrassment in the hall, the concert was transferred to Maida Vale, and members of the public were invited to turn up on the night without payment. Maderna's *Amanda* was given two performances, alongside Feldman's *The Viola in my Life No. 4* and Druckman's *Incenters*.

When Boulez himself returned, however, audiences picked up. He gave concerts in November 1972 and February 1973, each including fine works by well-known figures: Messiaen in the first (*Couleurs de la Cité Céleste*) and Stockhausen in the second (*Kreuzspiel*). The first also featured the music of a notorious figure, Iannis Xenakis, known to English audiences through the work of Lina Lalandi's English Bach Festival, and the second that of a well-known English composer, Roger Smalley. The mixture was much better, and it worked. The quality of the major works was unarguable, and Smalley's Sonata for Strings was praised as serious and substantial.

None of these concerts turned out as planned. Boulez should have included his *e.e. cummings* piece on 19 February, but it was not ready; and Luciano Berio should have directed a complete programme of his music on

26 March, but a programme could not be agreed. Hugh Wood's new work was again programmed in this concert, and then postponed to the next season. Instead, this last concert featured music by Alsina and Berio. It was extremely popular, for it featured Cathy Berberian as well as the music of Berio. Diego Masson directed the first public performance of Alsina's *Schichten* (which he had done in the studio), and Berio's *Chemins IIC*. In the second half Berberian performed Berio's astonishing virtuoso theatre-piece *Recital*. This was altogether the best concert of the series, and drew the largest audience in spite of Boulez's absence. Dominic Gill said it was 'the last, and possibly also the most successful of the present series of informal programmes at the Round House introduced by the composer or conductor', and found *Recital* 'a moving, often deeply beautiful, revelation'. *Chemins IIC* was found 'exciting', and *Schichten* 'just as exciting, but essentially more lightweight and humorous'. Meirion Bowen wrote that 'Berberian left one spellbound', and in *The Times* Stephen Walsh said that '*Recital* is beyond question one of Berio's most moving works . . . I loved it'. This programme had all the best features of the series – a reliably excellent work by a well-known composer, an interesting, already-tried work by a lesser-known composer, and one star performer.

A new experiment in presenting the concerts was tried in that season. On 19 February Michael Hall, a BBC music producer, 'interviewed' Boulez on the works; John Amis talked to Berio during the following concert. The experiment, even if it was thought successful, was not repeated in the following season.

A new format

It was clear that the Round House concerts needed a firmer format, something which would give a shape and purpose to the good intentions of the series. There had been constant complaints, for example, about the intelligibility of Boulez's own English. For the next season (all the concerts fell in the first three months of 1974) there was a new musical shape to the programme, and a new idea for the talk. Robert Ponsonby had now taken over as Controller, Music, from Glock (see Chapter 9), and he devised the new plan with Boulez. Each of the four concerts had the same outline: one première, one revival of a recent work, and one twentieth-century masterpiece. Only the masterpiece was introduced, by someone chosen for their speaking ability rather than just for their eminence. All four speakers were composers: in the first concert there was Hugh Wood on Schoenberg's *Pierrot Lunaire*; in the second Gordon Crosse on the Bartók Sonata for two pianos and percussion; in the third Bernard Rands on Berio's *Circles*; and in the last Alexander

Goehr on Berg's Chamber Concerto. The talks were scripted, and were produced for radio with great care by Veronica Slater of Music Division. The new works were by Jean-Claude Eloy, Hugh Wood (his new song cycle), Tim Souster and Bernard Rands. The revived works were by Ligeti (*Ramifications*), Birtwistle, Varèse and Stockhausen. The scheme was most successful, and the audiences were consistently high, except for the concert which Boulez did not conduct.

Dominic Gill in *The Financial Times* described the series as a revamp,

> perhaps the most successful and workable so far, of the BBC's Round House concerts scheme that began in 1971.
>
> The BBC Symphony is still the orchestra for the series; and Pierre Boulez is still the conductor – though he has dropped, on good advice, the lengthy preambles with music examples that he used to give for each work before it was played. The idea otherwise remains essentially the same: to provide in an inexpensive and informal setting polished and professional performances, also broadcast live, of worthwhile modern pieces that particularly deserve first hearing or repetition; and afterwards to give the audience the chance to participate in a discussion (informal and non-broadcast) with the composers and performers concerned.

All the concerts were well received, though Eloy's new work was not found especially interesting. Wood's Song cycle on Poems of Neruda was given an unsatisfactory performance, and Tim Souster's *Song of an average city*, with electronic taped sound, was thought by some to be merely trendy.

The same scheme was followed in 1974–5, but Boulez could direct only two of the concerts. Once again, four different composers introduced the masterworks in the series: Bernard Rands on Boulez's *Le Marteau sans maître*; Thea Musgrave on the orchestral arrangement of movements from Berg's Lyric Suite; Hugh Wood on Schoenberg's *Ode to Napoleon Bonaparte*; and Malcolm Williamson on Messiaen's *Seven Haikai*. New works were Barry Guy's *D*, Naresh Sohal's *Dhayan I*, a BBC commission; Edward Cowie's *Leighton Moss: December Notebook*; and Tona Scherchen's *Khouang*. The revivals were of Maderna's *Amanda*; Gerhard's *Pandora*; Robin Holloway's *Evening with angels*; and Bernard Rands' *Mésalliance*. Boulez conducted the first and last concerts, David Atherton directed the second and Elgar Howarth the third. The Howarth programme drew an acceptable audience, as did the Boulez *Marteau*, but the other two had disappointingly small houses.

The Round House concerts had not exactly failed: while Boulez was there to inspire them they had made a considerable impact, drawn an audience, and developed. But they proved, like much else in this period, that what would work for Boulez could not necessarily be adapted to other conductors. And Boulez was not constantly in charge of the proceedings for long enough, in a way that would have built up an audience prepared to trust his tastes. Had the concerts formed only one series among many such series in London, all providing stimulating fare, there would have been few worries about ensuring that every work heard was a masterpiece. But instead they were the only such concerts: a highly-publicised set of four isolated events in the concert season, promoted by the BBC and broadcast to a potentially wide audience. In retrospect, it is possible to argue that emphasis on quality should have been paramount, even at the expense of programming so many new, untried works. Only then would the concerts have gained wide respect and become an indispensable part of any open-minded concert-goer's schedule. Instead, they became largely hit-or-miss events, sometimes fascinating, sometimes dull. Boulez, certainly, had wished for no more; on his terms, the concerts had worked. But such informal public encounters with recent music deserved a more permanent place in London's concert life. Like much of the Boulez revolution their effect was temporary. There were to be only one and a half more Round House seasons after Boulez gave up the Chief Conductorship; the format and content of the series was modified, and continued to flourish in the very different surroundings of the London colleges of music.

Series at St John's

The first season in Smith Square had been attractive: Haydn and Stravinsky had made a good pairing, and the concerts were well planned. But there were not many good composers who could form the basis of such a plan – at least among those whom Boulez and Glock felt the need to give special exposure. The choice for 1972–3 fell on Webern; an excellent choice, but one which changed the complexion of these concerts from ones of classic music, contrasted with the Round House programmes, to ones which complemented and illuminated the Round House and Festival Hall series. There was some doubt as to whether the St John's concerts should start at a normal evening concert time, or earlier. The Smith Square management wanted a short concert which would catch people on their way home from Westminster. It was decided that the concerts should start at 6.15 pm; but they were of normal length. A revised notion of informal post-concerts in the crypt was abandoned. The programmes, however, were scarcely light listening for evening commuters. They were fine examples of Glock's planning but were, perhaps, in the wrong context.

Boulez's opening and closing concerts would not have been out of place in the Round House: the first was a symmetrical scheme of Schoenberg (with the tiny *Herzgewächse* twice) surrounded by Webern, starting with Schubert choruses and ending with Nono choral works. The last used Mozart's C minor Serenade to introduce a counterpoint of Webern (Opp. 13, 14 and 17) with Stockhausen (*Kreuzspiel* and *Kontrapunkte*). There was more Webern in programmes from Erich Leinsdorf and Erich Schmid. Both Hans Zender and John Pritchard included Haydn symphonies and modern pieces: the first, Morton Feldman's *The Rothko Chapel*, and Zimmermann's *Stille und Umkehr*; the latter, Birtwistle's *The Fields of Sorrow*, a seven-minute choral work written for the Dartington Summer School of Music, and praised as 'powerful, delicate music'.

The choral involvement in this series was expanded in the following season, Robert Ponsonby's first, when all the concerts had a vocal emphasis and involved the BBC Singers. There were now five concerts (as against six the previous year and seven in the first season): Boulez had two, Andrew Davis, Barenboim and Pritchard one each. Schubert was featured: his A flat Mass and the Second and Third Symphonies were heard. Other sacred choral works were Bruckner's E minor Mass, Haydn's *Harmoniemesse* and Schubert's *Lazarus*. Schoenberg, Stravinsky, Tippett, Bartók, Hindemith and Boulez (a repeat of *e.e. cummings ist der dichter*) completed the programmes. Once again, the scheme produced some individually attractive concerts but failed to fix itself in the public's mind.

The inclusion of choral works was popular, however, so in Boulez's final season as Chief Conductor, Ponsonby and he made a wider selection. Boulez had thought of choral music by Liszt and Weber as a theme, but this could not be realised: 1974–5 began with John Eliot Gardiner conducting a notably successful Fauré *Requiem* which filled the hall; Raymond Leppard directed his own edition of Cavalli's *Missa Concertata*; Colin Davis included the Stravinsky Mass and Schubert's Mass in G; and Boulez conducted Schumann's rare *Der Rose Pilgerfahrt* (a work praised by George Bernard Shaw). There was a good sprinkling of twentieth-century music through the series: Maw's Sonata for two horns and strings, Schoenberg pieces, Berg's Chamber Concerto, Gerhard's Harpsichord Concerto, plus a little Brahms including some chamber music (the Horn Trio). Nevertheless, this fine selection of works failed to find consistent audiences; the St John's concerts remained as broadcasts in search of a public. (They now started at 6.30 pm, with the broadcast relay delayed until 8.00 pm). Boulez had originally intended that they should explore music suitable for the building: but Haydn was initially the only eighteenth-century composer for whom Boulez showed any affinity, and baroque music could scarcely have used the Orchestra to best advantage. Instead, any small-scale music was thought suitable, and there was little coherence to the various schemes. The St John's concerts foundered temporarily for lack of an idea to build them on; it was to be a couple of years before one emerged.

Festival fare

If the more distinctive impression of Boulez's seasons was given by the concerts outside the Festival Hall, he nevertheless managed to bring a great deal that was new into that home of repetitive programme-planning. In 1972–3 he gave concerts of twentieth-century classics, for example, Stravinsky's *Symphony of Psalms*, Berg's Violin Concerto and Ravel's *Daphnis and Chloe* (8 November). He expanded his own repertory by exploring the music of Schumann (Scenes from *Faust* on 7 March, the *Overture, Scherzo and Finale* on 25 October) and by performing Mahler's Sixth Symphony. Then he gave two varied and purposeful concerts: in the first Berlioz's *Harold in Italy* (Peter Schidlof) and Messiaen's *Poèmes pour Mi* (Felicity Palmer) were preceded by Webern and Webern arrangements of Bach and Schubert; in the second, which ended the season, Webern's three last works, Opp. 29, 30, 31, came together with Bartók's Concerto for Orchestra and the European première of Berio's Concerto for Two Pianos (which had been commissioned for and performed by the New York Philharmonic). This work was greeted with surprise and relief by the critics: Jeremy Noble in the *Sunday Telegraph* summed up reaction when he wrote that 'beneath an immediately attractive surface it gives the impression of a rich inventiveness and above all, of the coherence one has missed in Berio's recent music'. Martin Cooper called it 'easily approachable', and Stanley Sadie in *The Times* wrote that 'it is not, of course, merely agreeable or seductive. It is a complex and finely sculpted work, using limited means and reaching a high degree of intensity . . . The performance was assured enough to reach beyond the notes of this complex score to the intensity and richness of the expression behind it.'

Boulez's own concerts were not the only highlight of the season. For the first and last time in its fifty-year history, the BBC series played host to visiting musicians. Both Glock and Boulez were anxious to present one of Stockhausen's most important recent works, the cantata *Momente*, which he wrote in 1961–2, revised in 1965, and had just reordered. But after the problems of the composer's 1970 visit and the acute difficulties of the score, it was agreed that as a special exception the BBC Symphony Orchestra would not undertake the performance: a ready-made performance could be imported. This would also ensure Stockhausen's own participation. So members of the Musique Vivante Ensemble of Paris were invited, along with the Choir of the

Westdeutscher Rundfunk and the soprano Gloria Davy; Stockhausen directed. It was a remarkable concert. As for *Gruppen*, the hall was well filled by an enthusiastic young audience: the work puzzled many, but delighted too. The evening lasted two and a quarter hours, with interval. William Mann wrote:

> *Momente*, in its present version, is a fascinating piece, greatly inventive in musical and paramusical activity. The singers have the best of it, especially the soloist – Miss Davy's vocal assurance and personal charm must have won all hearts. Radio listeners missed the procession of chorus and brass from terrace level down to the platform – and perhaps their percussion contributions, delightful to behold. Though long, it is an entertaining piece, as well as conducive to inward meditation. It sounds well, and like nothing else; probably that is its chief claim on an audience's interest and future loyalty.

This concert, to avoid the interruption of the Festival Hall's organ recital between rehearsal and concert, with all the resetting of electronic equipment, took place on a Monday. Two days later, the BBC Symphony Orchestra was back in the hall for a première of a very different kind: Anthony Milner's Symphony, which had been promised a performance in the previous Prom season but (much to the composer's annoyance, which was publicised in *The Times*) had been postponed to this later date. Glock argued, in a letter to *The Times*, that this placing in the winter season gave the long work a better chance of full rehearsal in sympathetic conditions. John Pritchard directed it with evident sympathy, and it was enjoyed in the hall, although it proved too unadventurous for the taste of most critics. Elsewhere in the programmes Glock's hand was evident in the planning. It had originally been hoped that Rafael Kubelik would open the season with Beethoven's Ninth, preceded by Honegger's Second Symphony, but he withdrew. In his place Lorin Maazel was engaged: but he did not wish to do the Honegger. In a characteristically bold move, Glock engaged the Martindale Sidwell Singers to provide a complete contrast: the five-part Mass of William Byrd, which made a sublime and serene prelude to the Beethoven; this was surely a first performance in the Festival Hall. Guests during the season included Bruno Maderna (who conducted Mahler and Webern), Hans Schmidt-Isserstedt, Erich Leinsdorf and John Eliot Gardiner. Settings of the Mass formed one theme of the series: Bach's B minor and Mozart's C minor were heard as well as Byrd's. Colin Davis contributed to three important concerts: a performance of Tippett's Third Symphony which he had premièred with the London Symphony Orchestra; and then a performance of Gerhard's Fourth Symphony which formed part of a European Broadcasting Union concert in the

Festival Hall which was shared between the BBC Orchestra and the London Sinfonietta. (A loud cry of 'Rubbish' was heard over the air at the end of the concert; through the agency of the EBU, this was no doubt one of the most widely disseminated such cries in musical history.) Finally, for the Royal Philharmonic Society season, Colin Davis brought out of the studio the First Symphony by the 74-year-old Alexander Tcherepnin, a work whose all-percussion Scherzo had caused it to belong to the noble tradition of works which caused a riot in Paris. (Shouts of 'Barbare!' and 'Renvoyez-vous à Moscou!' had interrupted the movement.) Both work and performance were praised enthusiastically on this occasion: *The Times* even wanted to hear more symphonies by Tcherepnin, but has not, so far, had the chance.

A short season

In 1973–4 only ten dates were made available to the BBC by the Festival Hall; fewer than usual were available and the Hall had to favour the four public orchestras. So Robert Ponsonby, in the first Winter Season for which he was responsible, had to plan economically. Boulez had four concerts, Davis two, Pritchard, Kempe, Maderna and Barenboim one each. (There were also two concerts for the Royal Philharmonic Society.) Many of the season's plans were altered by unforeseen events: Maderna's concert was to have included the British première of his *Biogramma*, but the Hallé Orchestra programmed that first, so the Third Oboe Concerto was included in its place. Then Maderna fell seriously ill shortly before the concert. John Carewe, who had conducted so many new scores for the BBC, was asked to take over the première, and Raymond Leppard directed the Berlioz *Te Deum* which followed. Boulez included Maderna's *Aura* of 1972 in his programme on 20 March, in place of his own new work which was unfinished. In November Maderna died: Boulez's new work was to draw its inspiration from his death. Boulez's exploration of Mahler was to have continued with the Second Symphony to open the season, but this was replaced by the Fourth (with Felicity Palmer), which made room for the British première of *Photoptosis* by Zimmermann, one of the few pieces Boulez imported from his New York programmes, and Bartók's Music for Strings, Percussion and Celesta. Boulez had hoped to bring to London some of his discoveries among the music of Liszt. For 20 March he wanted to arrange a pre-concert of the strange choral work *Via Crucis* (which had been one of the successes in his Liszt series in New York). This failed to materialise. So did other ambitious plans, including a complete concert performance of Weber's *Euryanthe*, which Colin Davis was to have conducted in his 7 November concert. (Vaughan Williams' Sixth Symphony was heard instead.) Davis's other major project came off, however: a performance with a linked recording of Tippett's oratorio *A Child of our Time*, in which the BBC Singers and the BBC Choral Society took part. The other guest conductors had strongly contrasted programmes: Pritchard did a Boult-like concert of Britten, Walton (Violin Concerto) and Holst's *Hymn of Jesus*; while Barenboim, who was to have included the Schoenberg Piano Concerto, directed Schubert and Bruckner (Dietrich Fischer-Dieskau was ill; his place in orchestrations of Schubert and Wolf songs was taken by Benjamin Luxon). Rudolf Kempe was unable to conduct the last concert of the season as planned; it was taken over by Charles Groves.

A final flourish

Boulez's far more successful final season as Chief Conductor was also planned with Robert Ponsonby, and saw one of his most ambitious projects: a performance (and recording) of Schoenberg's incomplete opera *Moses und Aron*. This was a popular triumph, a performance which argued the work's attractiveness to a large audience which was unfamiliar with it. But it drew strong criticism from Schoenberg specialists. It was the most outstanding of three important one-work programmes, which also included Berlioz's *Romeo and Juliet* (13 November) and Mahler's Third Symphony (20 November). Boulez's two final concerts as Chief Conductor offered varied fare. On 2 April his new work was given its première: it was at first called *Memoriales*, but Boulez later changed the title to *Rituel: in memoriam Maderna*. *Rituel* came as a surprise to most commentators on Boulez's music. Its hieratic grandeur, severity of sound and feeling of harmonic stasis was in marked contrast to his earlier works: as Paul Griffiths writes in his book on Boulez's music, 'He imposes extraordinary restrictions not only on register but also on formal shape and harmonic variety ... It is possible that *Rituel* will come to be seen ... as an extreme and untypically austere instance of the later Boulez's derivation of whole works from a few basic harmonic ideas'. The Orchestra was divided up into eight groups – which rehearsed separately under the composer. The music is a sequence of verses and refrains; the latter are made up of massive, sonorous chords. (For a 1977 Prom performance, Boulez revised these refrains, delaying the entries of some of the instrumental groups, making the chords less overwhelming.) Bartók's *Cantata profana* and *Miraculous Mandarin* Suite complemented *Rituel*, and the concert also included a revival of *Aum* by Bernard Rands. In his last concert there were two quasi-operatic fairy tales: Stravinsky's *Le Rossignol* and Ravel's *L'Enfant et les sortilèges*.

The season was short of wholly new works: the only other première, of

Arnold Cooke's Fourth Symphony, came in a Royal Philharmonic Society concert under John Pritchard. But there were important revivals, none more effective than that of Peter Maxwell Davies' *Worldes Blis*. This had been a failure at its first Prom performance under the composer's direction: Davies withdrew the piece. But he had come to the conclusion that the work's importance could be seen in better perspective against his more recent music, and so allowed it to be performed again. After many difficulties and worries about the complexities of the work in rehearsal, which nearly led to the cancellation of the performance, it was given under Colin Davis – with a forceful effect that no one who was there will forget. Davis also included Vaughan Williams' Fourth Symphony a fortnight later (19 March). Andrew Davis brought to London for the first time the Fourth Symphony of Robert Simpson, a symphony based on the model of Beethoven (whose Second Leonora Overture and Third Piano Concerto completed the programme). Charles Groves once again stepped into the breach to open the season, in the absence of Josef Krips, with Bruckner's Sixth; and Bernhard Klee was a newcomer to the series, including Goehr's *Pastorals* and Schoenberg's Piano Concerto with Charles Rosen in his two concerts.

The Proms: commuting and expanding

The Promenade Concert seasons when Boulez was Chief Conductor – to which may be prefixed the outstanding 1971 season, since it began the trend they all exhibited – carried still further the diversification which had marked Glock's seasons in the 1960s. The music, it seemed, could hardly become more varied, so an attempt was made to provide venues more suitable for the varied wealth of music by taking concerts out of the Royal Albert Hall to other venues in London. So the Proms visited Covent Garden (with stalls removed) for a staged performance of *Boris Godunov* with Boris Christoff. The BBC Symphony Orchestra appeared in the other two unfamiliar places: Westminster Cathedral, for Beethoven's *Missa Solemnis* under Colin Davis, and the Round House, for a twentieth-century programme under Pierre Boulez. As Glock wrote:

> These three occasions express rather more than the natural tendency of a festival to spread its wings; their purpose is really to offer in each case a more immediate or authentic experience than would otherwise be possible . . . With the Round House . . . the aim is partly to achieve a kind of informality that would be difficult in the Albert Hall.

But the Albert Hall was not abandoned, nor was its number of concerts reduced. The BBC Symphony Orchestra, within the first week of the 1971 season, played Mahler's Eighth Symphony under Colin Davis; C. P. E. Bach under Roger Norrington; a Mozart–Mendelssohn–Mahler programme; and a juxtaposition of Beethoven's Eroica with Berlioz's *Te Deum*, both under Colin Davis. The second week brought two Boulez programmes; the third, two predominantly English programmes under Boult and Del Mar, and the Viennese night under John Pritchard. Pritchard also gave the British première of the orchestral version of Messiaen's *Poèmes pour Mi*; Jascha Horenstein conducted Bruckner's Fifth Symphony. The Orchestra kept less strange company this season than it had in the late 1960s, though it did perform Mozart's *Requiem* after Bach's *Goldberg Variations*, and Schubert's Ninth Symphony after Beethoven's *Archduke* Trio (in which the conductor, Daniel Barenboim, had played the piano).

In 1972, Boulez chose what Glock called 'a formidable range of programmes', from the *Missa Solemnis* to Messiaen and Elliott Carter, from Mahler's Sixth Symphony to a two-evening presentation of Wagner's *Parsifal*. Colin Davis repeated Mahler's Eighth Symphony, and Norman Del Mar conducted the Seventh. (A visiting orchestra, the Munich Philharmonic, added to the Mahler theme with the Second Symphony.) The Symphony Orchestra's adventures in the season included a Round House concert at 10 pm, devoted to Boulez, Holliger and Maxwell Davies. In another late-night concert, this one at the Albert Hall, Stockhausen's four-orchestral piece *Carré* was played twice. Both in 1971 and 1972 there were new works for the Last Night: the first, Malcolm Williamson's *The Stone Wall*, an opera with audience participation, and the second, Gordon Crosse's more subdued *Celebration*. The major première in 1972 was Elliott Carter's Concerto for Orchestra, for the first time in Britain; it was supported by a group of American works, including George Crumb's *Echoes of Time and the River*, also new to this country.

The expeditions of the 1971 season were modified in 1972. Covent Garden had been able to promote its own series of Prom performances for several days at a time, under the sponsorship of the Midland Bank – the BBC's solitary venture there had shown the way forward to a most flourishing series. Westminster Cathedral's acoustic was more carefully considered than it had been in 1971 and Monteverdi's *1610 Vespers* chosen – a performance under John Eliot Gardiner which could have become a Prom tradition in subsequent years. The Round House, now a firm part of the BBC's Winter Season, was retained. As the *Annual Register* put it, the 1972 Prom season was 'outstanding both for the variety of what it offered and for the sheer depth of momentous events'.

The turn of the year from 1972 to 1973 saw Glock's bold revival of a popular pre-war idea, the Winter Proms. This short season of Albert Hall concerts had been held on and off in the 1930s; Henry Wood was furious when it was casually cancelled by the BBC. It had been revived briefly after the war and was again cancelled after the 1952 season, this time to Sargent's annoyance. Glock thought he might be able to achieve in the winter what he had already achieved in the summer – a gathering of all London's most youthful, most open-minded audiences in the Albert Hall. But the season failed to catch on. The Symphony Orchestra contributed four programmes to the week's events: two under Boulez, one with Boult and one with Lorin Maazel. The only really successful concert, however, was that by the Berlin Philharmonic Orchestra under Herbert von Karajan, which gave two Beethoven symphonies; the concert was part of the 'Fanfare for Europe' which somewhat unconvincingly heralded Britain's entry into the European Economic Community. Given a few more years, this new Winter Prom season might have established itself; but the auguries were not good, and the BBC was in no mood to spend extensively on a new season whose purpose was not altogether clear.

In 1973, the last Prom season that Glock planned, the same outside venues were used, with one addition, that of the Brompton Oratory. But all the Symphony Orchestra's concerts were in the Albert Hall: they included Berlioz's *L'Enfance du Christ* under Colin Davis, Schoenberg's *Gurrelieder* under Pierre Boulez (which the Orchestra recorded), and Mahler's Third Symphony, also with Boulez. There was an all-Stravinsky concert with Boulez, an all-Haydn concert with Raymond Leppard, a Bartók and Haydn concert with Antal Dorati. Boulez's other concerts included his . . . *explosante-fixe* . . ., and there were premières by Nicola Lefanu and Elisabeth Lutyens. Norman Del Mar took over the Last Night; it was scarcely up Boulez's street. These were only the highlights of the BBC Symphony Orchestra's appearances: giving over twenty concerts, it dominated the season.

Robert Ponsonby's first season of Proms showed itself better at programming than at mathematics. Ponsonby noted that Henry Wood's first Prom took place on 10 August 1895, and declared the BBC Symphony Orchestra's concert on 10 August 1974 to be celebrating 'the 80th anniversary of the Proms'. It was the eighteenth *season*, but, therefore, the seventy-ninth anniversary, a fact which was noted with glee by the BBC's critics. But there was much else to be enthusiastic about in the Symphony Orchestra's programmes: Boult returning in two half-concerts, Schubert's Ninth Symphony and Holst's *The Planets*; Boulez repeating *Gurreleider* and Stockhausen's *Gruppen*; premières by Malcolm Williamson, Martin Dalby and

Robin Holloway; Tippett's *A Child of Our Time* under Davis; a significant appearance by Rudolf Kempe; and a new conductor for the Last Night, Sir Charles Groves. Intriguing juxtapositions included Mahler's Second Symphony following Mozart's E flat Piano Quartet (which Ponsonby included as a tribute to a neglected facet of his predecessor's skills: Glock, who had appeared at the Proms back in 1940, returned to play the piano; he was joined by members of the Lindsay Quartet). On another occasion there were orchestral, organ and piano works by Liszt in one half-concert, before Dvořák's New World Symphony.

The Orchestra gave twenty-three concerts that season, and twenty-two in the following one, which marked the end of Pierre Boulez's term as Chief Conductor. He chose to bid farewell early in the season with three massive concerts: Mahler's Eighth Symphony, Schoenberg's *Moses und Aron*, and his own *Pli selon pli*. The Orchestra continued under a wide range of conductors, including Colin Davis, Rudolf Kempe, John Pritchard, Norman Del Mar (who took on the Last Night again) and – in an all-American programme – Aaron Copland. The Orchestra visited Westminster Cathedral for John Tavener's large and impressive work *Ultimos Ritos*, and it gave premières by Edward Cowie, David Bedford and Arnold Cooke. The demands of the season were very great; the standard of performance that was maintained was astonishingly high – such was the verdict, repeated year after year through the Boulez era, on the Symphony Orchestra's work at the Proms.

Studio labours; public triumphs

So energetic was Boulez in his work with the Symphony Orchestra, and so widely did he expand its public engagements (both in London and on tour), that the studio work of the Orchestra during his years seemed an unbelievable extra burden on its schedule. But it should be recorded, to show that the breadth of interest in the Orchestra's programmes did not decline. In the first season there was Boult, returning to celebrate the thirtieth anniversary of the Orchestra's wartime move to Bedford, with a Parry/Vaughan Williams/Elgar programme; Erich Schmid directing a newly completed version of Prokofiev's Cello Concertino; Baird's Four Essays and Sessions' Piano Concerto under Bernhard Klee; Schoenberg's arrangement of Brahms's G minor Piano Quartet under Brian Priestman. There were British premières of four American works under Harold Faberman; Weill's Violin Concerto under Elgar Howarth followed by Busoni's Violin Concerto under Daniel Barenboim; music by Dallapiccola and Nono conducted by Piero Bellugi. From earlier ages there was Handel's *L'Allegro ed il Penseroso*

(Charles Mackerras), extracts from Rameau's *Dardanus* (Raymond Leppard), and Carissimi's *Balthazar* (Peter Gellhorn).

In November 1972 the BBC celebrated its fiftieth anniversary. Ambitious
plans were proposed for orchestral music to take its full part in the celebrations: one suggestion was that a week-long festival should be held at the
Albert Hall featuring not only the Symphony Orchestra but all the BBC
regional symphony orchestras. New works were to be commissioned from
two international figures, Boulez and Messiaen, and from four British composers. In the event the celebration was reduced in size; it was modest and
effective. A televised concert was given by the Symphony Orchestra in the
Albert Hall, at which Boult and Boulez shared the conducting. The two men
established a warm relationship: Boulez spoke warmly of Boult's contribution to contemporary music in Britain, and admitted that he had learned
much from Boult's direction of great classical works such as Schubert's
Ninth Symphony. Brian Large directed the successful television relay.

In the studio in January 1973 Andrew Davis conducted Ives; Hans
Zender presented Messiaen; Carlos Chavez directed a programme of his
own music. Boulez tried out a large range of works: Birtwistle's *Nenia on the
Death of Orpheus*, Messiaen's *Poèmes pour Mi*, Ravel's *L'Heure espagnole* and
L'Enfant et les Sortilèges, and scenes from Schumann's *Faust*. At the end of
the season, Boulez took the Orchestra on an Italian tour – another strenuous
schedule, with the most demanding programmes: eleven consecutive performances – followed by three concerts at the Vienna Festival. Not everything was well known to the Orchestra: in Rome Boulez's tribute to
Stravinsky, . . . *explosante-fixe* . . . was given its first European performance
in the revised version (the work has been revised again since then).

In a break from the 1973 Proms, Boulez took the Orchestra to Edinburgh,
including in one notable programme his own *e.e. cummings ist der dichter*,
Holliger's *Siebengesang* and Berg's Three Orchestral Pieces, Op. 6 (26
August). Scarcely surprising that in this period the Orchestra was in constant
demand abroad, receiving far more invitations than it could fulfil.

The 1973–4 season also presented some surprising contrasts: a contribution to the Radio 3 series *Orpheus Britannicus*, in which Norman Del Mar
conducted the première of Denis ApIvor's *Neumes*, with Bax's First Symphony, Walton's Partita and Delius's *Life's Dance*. Later in the season he
gave Rawsthorne's First Piano Concerto. Thea Musgrave's *Memento Vitae*
was conducted by James Loughran; music by Hugh Wood and Tippett
under Andrew Davis; Paul Patterson's Trumpet Concerto with Elgar
Howarth – even if Boulez neglected British music, the BBC's Orchestra did
not do so.

The May 1974 tour took the Orchestra around Germany, Austria and Switzerland – again with Boulez conducting every concert. One disruption marked the tour: in Innsbruck the soloist, Clifford Curzon, objected to performing his concerto on the piano which was also to be used for Bartók's Music for Strings, Percussion and Celesta; when no agreement could be reached with the BBC he returned home. Christoph Eschenbach replaced him. Boulez's repertoire on this tour was hair-raising – fourteen different works, in the German part of the tour, in five concerts on successive nights. First came Hanover, Nuremberg, Linz, Vienna, Innsbruck, Munich, Zürich, Bern, Basel. Then the highlight of the visit: a concert in Baden-Baden, the town Boulez made his home after his arguments in France. Here the European Broadcasting Union presented a concert celebrating the era of the 1950s in Baden-Baden with works begun in that period: Berio's *Allelujah II*, Haubenstock-Ramati's *Petite musique de nuit*, Stockhausen's *Kontrapunkte*, and Boulez's own *Figures/Doubles/Prismes*. It was an exhausting concert, given in cramped and difficult conditions, but Orchestra members were royally entertained afterwards at Boulez's own expense. Then they went on to Stuttgart, Düsseldorf, Berlin, and finally Hamburg, with Mahler's Sixth Symphony. The repertoire also included Bernard Rands's *Wildtrack I*, and Alexander Goehr's Three pieces for wind band, from *Arden Must Die*. The tour, like so many in the 1970s, was difficult, demanding, not altogether enjoyable, but highly successful.

Studio concerts in 1974–5 saw the start of an important new series, conceived by Robert Ponsonby, called 'The Composer Conducts', in which composers attempted to do just that, with mixed success. Hans Werner Henze launched the series well with two programmes that included his *Der Vorwurf*, Three Symphonic Studies, *Ariosi* for soprano, violin and orchestra, Symphony No. 5, Concertino, *Los Caprichos*, *Antifone*, and *Nachtstücke und Arien*. In January Thea Musgrave conducted her *Obliques*, Viola Concerto, and *The Five Ages of Man*; the following season another expert composer-conductor, the Polish Witold Lutoslawski, directed his First Symphony, Cello Concerto, Funeral Music, and *Trois Poèmes d'Henri Michaux*. But two of this series of concerts ran into severe trouble. Peter Maxwell Davies cancelled his appearance because of what he felt was an uncooperative attitude on the part of certain players in the Orchestra. And the Polish composer Krzyzstof Penderecki, in a well-publicised incident, left the rehearsals for his concert because of disruption by isolated players; this recording was taken over by Brian Wright and Kerry Woodward, who both worked with the BBC Singers. These problems could be put down to sheer intransigence on the part of some musicians towards music they disliked; but they had played plenty of such music under Boulez. There is probably a more fundamental reason: that the Orchestra had become so used to the absolute precision and accuracy of Boulez's own methods that they rapidly became impatient and unprofessionally disruptive when faced with anyone who did not match up, as a conductor, to Boulez's unusual standards of efficiency. This was a special problem of discipline which the Orchestra's management had to face. Fortunately, the incidents did not recur.

Other important concerts included Charles Groves conducting Goehr, Hugh Wood and Roberto Gerhard (Gerhard's Symphony No. 2, entitled *Metamorphoses*, was given in its unfinished version, including the first performance of the last movement in its unrevised form: a newly-complex genre of première), and Diego Masson in Berio's *Bewegung*. Bernhard Klee returned for a substantial period, and included the huge, late-romantic Lyric Symphony by Schoenberg's son-in-law Alexander Zemlinsky, which was later recorded by the Orchestra. Vernon Handley gave the first performance of Anthony Milner's *Midway*, a cantata for soprano and chamber orchestra, alongside works by Lennox Berkeley and Arthur Bliss.

But the biggest adventure of Boulez's last season was the tour to Japan: thirteen concerts between 7 and 25 May 1975 conducted by Boulez and Charles Groves, in a splendidly varied repertoire including Mahler's Fourth Symphony, Boulez's *Rituel*, Maxwell Davies's *Stone Litany*, and Birtwistle's *Nenia*; Tippett's *Concertante Fantasia*, Walton's *Partita* and Britten's Piano Concerto. Soloists were Jan de Gaetani (in the Mahler, Davies and Birtwistle) and Michael Roll (in Britten and Mozart). This most ambitious of all the Orchestra's tours was given a special attraction because it coincided with, and was part of the celebrations for, the visit to Japan of the Queen. The Royal Ballet was also touring, and there was an exhibition of drawings from the Royal Collection. There was a flurry of enthusiasm for all things English. The tour was managed by the Nippon Cultural Centre, in association with the Hochhauser agency. There was British Council support and local industrial sponsorship. Some of the concerts were broadcast – the last, live by satellite. In spite of doubts at the Japanese end, Ponsonby and Boulez determined to programme boldly, and were well rewarded by enthusiastic, often young audiences for all the modern works. The administrative arrangements went smoothly (Orchestra members were astonished to find their hotel rooms correctly booked on arrival in Tokyo), and the Orchestra was royally entertained by the Japanese. There were concerts in Tokyo, Koriyama, Nagoya, Kobe, Osaka, Kyoto, Gifu and Yokohama. In *The Listener*, Robert Ponsonby set down some diary notes on the early part of the tour:

Tokyo 7 May

The BBC Symphony Orchestra, a party of 120 or so, boarded its JAL jumbo yesterday, embarking upon a Japanese tour of thirteen concerts which was to culminate in a live transmission to Britain eighteen days later. . . . At the capital (larger than London) we were met by the Nippon Cultural Centre, promoting the tour, the British Council, guaranteeing it, and by CBS/SONY, for whom Pierre Boulez records. Bouquets were presented and a Womble played God Save the Queen – Her Majesty had arrived a few hours before us – improbably on the violin. There was much photography.

Tokyo 8 May

Reconnaissance of the 4000-seat NHK hall during a concert by the NHK Symphony Orchestra suggests a somewhat unflattering acoustic favouring the higher frequencies: cellos and basses sound thin. But at our own first rehearsal the sound is perceptibly warmer. The concert, tele-recorded with great expertise and admirable discretion by NHK, attracts an audience which grows and grows: a public transport strike means that many have walked to it. Berlioz's *Romeo and Juliet* music seems less accessible to the Japanese than either Maxwell Davies's *Stone Litany* or the Bartók Concerto for Orchestra, of which Boulez gives a characteristically brilliant performance. (His stamina is astonishing. Almost throughout the flight he was reading, with unwavering concentration.)

Tokyo 11 May

We travel by bus to Koriyama, a town of 250,000 in the north. Its civic pride is immense; its reputation transformed by seven enlightened 'samurai' who have made possible periodic concerts by orchestra of world class. A boys' choir greets us, huge bouquets are distributed, short speeches are made. But the platform will not contain Boulez's *Rituel* and a rapt young audience listens wide-eared to the second *Daphnis* Suite instead, with Debussy's *Jeux* and the complete *Firebird*. After the concert the entire party is 'clapped' into the Town Hall for an unforgettable buffet banquet.

Osaka 14 May

Arriving at Osaka we find Britten's Simple Symphony being piped, in our honour, through the hotel's muzak channel – a well-meant tribute. In nearby Kobe Boulez conducts the complete *Daphnis* ballet, the performance marvellously paced, rhythms and tempi cogently related, sensuous and brilliant. The Orchestra respond splendidly; I don't expect to hear it better done.

Osaka 16 May

Jan de Gaetani sings the *Wozzeck* fragments in Osaka's Festival Hall. . . .
With Schoenberg's Five Pieces, to start, and Mahler 4, to end, they complete
an exceptionally successful programme. Much credit is due to the Nippon
Cultural Centre for accepting the BBC's wish and need to perform such
programmes. Many of the works we are carrying must be receiving their first
public performances here. Audiences are admirably receptive: Birtwistle's
Nenia, Maxwell Davies's *Stone Litany*, Boulez's *Rituel* are absorbed with
relative ease – the last most readily of all.

Los Angeles 17 May

The Orchestra move on to Kyoto, Japan's ancient capital, I to Los Angeles,
bound for New York. (I arrive, surprisingly, after twelve hours in the air,
somewhat earlier the same day.)

Looking back on Japan, I find the dominant impression is of a combined
energy and discipline unequalled even in Germany. Its people are by contrast exceedingly well-mannered and considerate. . . . Over the high wall of
the garden of the Heian shrine in Kyoto come not the frail sounds of the
koto or samisen but those of a western conservatoire hard at work – a
soprano exercising, a Chopin study, a violinist practising the double-stop-
ping in the slow movement of the Mendelssohn Concerto . . .

London 24 May

The climax, and conclusion, of the Symphony Orchestra's tour is a concert
in the NHK hall transmitted live by satellite at 1900 hours in Tokyo,
received here at 1100 hours, in actual fact one half-second later. The music
comes over with miraculous, crystal clarity, close but finely balanced. Better
still, the vitality of the occasion, the resilience of the Orchestra, Boulez's
mastery in Debussy, Stravinsky and his own *Rituel*, the spontaneous involvement of the audience, are excitingly conveyed. The combined technical
achievement of NHK and BBC, at the service of music, is breath-taking.
And the Orchestra make fine ambassadors.

Many besides Ponsonby agreed that the Japanese tour marked a high
point in the Orchestra's life. Paul Huband, who had seen the Orchestra
through the previous twelve years – the Glock regime, the Dorati and Davis
years, the attempts at reorganisation – felt that on this tour the Orchestra
played under Boulez at a level they never surpassed.

Looking back at Boulez

For the members of the Orchestra, working with Boulez as Chief Conductor was a challenging, stimulating, but (some thought) a narrowing experience. Boulez is a perfectionist, and any orchestra responds to that. He is a conductor who knows precisely what he is doing – and who can hear exactly what the orchestra is doing. These qualities might be thought necessary in every conductor; but any orchestral player will say that the number of conductors who possess them can be quickly counted up. You were never playing in the dark with Boulez, they say; if you did something wrong it was noticed – and that keeps you on your toes. Boulez would take great care with the balance of small sections, of tiny combinations of instruments, to make sure that phrases which should match did not become muddied in the texture, and that tuning was precise, not approximate. He could take infinite pains over these matters. Also important to orchestral players was the fact that he did not interfere with matters he regarded as the players' prerogative – the production of the notes, breathing, bowing, tone and timbre. He treated the players with respect as masters of their instruments and got the same in return. If something went wrong his tone was usually puzzled: 'Is there a problem there?' He saw the role of conductor as that of a master balancer, a co-ordinator. The music did not become part of him, still less was it transformed by his personality into something other than the composer intended. It simply spoke through his agency. In this respect, Orchestra members with long memories compare him to another great conductor from their history – Toscanini. Although the two conductors' ways of making music and their temperaments were very different, many of the things for which they strove were similar. Both had a miraculous ability to clarify a score: to balance it correctly, to let its essential parts be heard. What Alex Nifosi once said of Toscanini could well apply to Boulez: 'Time and again we were fascinated by the way he brought out some detail not usually heard in a complex welter of sound – some strand of instrumental colour never before brought to the surface – not brought out at the expense of real musical interest but in addition to it . . .' William Glock added some further points about Boulez's methods.

> One thing I don't ever remember him mentioning at a rehearsal is string sound. Intonation, yes; and that affects the carrying power of the strings. You could say that he aims at eloquence, but never at sumptuousness. Another thing is that in trying to achieve a vital balance between all the various details of a score, he very rarely seems to suppress anything. He's much more likely to say, for example, can we please hear the flute or the clarinet more clearly there? It's what he believes the composer wanted to be heard, and the process of trying to reach that is positive not negative. . . .

As you know, he conducts without a baton. It's just possible that this arose from the fact that most of his early concerts were with small ensembles. But I doubt it. I know that he himself considers that a stick prevents him from expressing himself. One of his most noticeable styles in conducting is the use of an undulating or wave-like gesture which makes orchestral musicians instinctively play in long lines without accents. When Boulez wants an accent, but without changing the general character of the music at that point, he brings his body into it, making a forward body movement. That reminds me of a conversation we had during one of the BBC Orchestra's foreign tours, in which Boulez talked very interestingly about the difference between German and French rubato; one with the whole body, as it were; the other, a swift movement of the arm. There's no doubt that he thinks intensely about all these things.

On the rare occasions when the tempi in a Boulez concert are different from anything that has happened during rehearsal, then the players say they are invariably faster. Boulez, sometimes accused of being ice-cold, admits that he gets excited, but that he's not obliged to show it. Outward excitement, he says, uses up inner excitement.

Boulez is supremely efficient. And he works extraordinarily hard. The second quality may be one associated with conductors, but the first is not always as true. No one has put on more complicated programmes with the BBC Orchestra than Boulez, but his rehearsal requirements have always been absolutely precise. He knows exactly what can be done and what cannot, and he is not likely to change his mind at a later date. He knows how to organise a rehearsal without fuss, even when there are countless platform changes, switches of personnel, electronics and staging to consider. For orchestral administrators, concert managers, orchestral porters, he is the easiest, kindest and best organised of conductors. Relations between conductor and players, conductor and planners, were both exceptionally trouble-free during his regime. Moreover, his energy and enthusiasm are immense. Some, like Joan Peyser in her book, have found this difficult to understand, and have searched (in vain) for emotional weak links in his life, and for other preoccupations besides music. As anyone who plays under him or works with him comes to realise, music is his motivating force, and he pursues it (or it pursues him) with single-minded obsessiveness. Boulez did more work with the BBC Orchestra than any Chief Conductor since Boult. In the later seasons he consistently over-fulfilled his contract, giving ten or twelve extra concerts each season. Hence his powerful effect on the Orchestra, and his transformation of it into one of the outstanding vehicles for contemporary music. How does he manage to do so much? As he once put it to William Glock, 'I sleep fast'.

Against all this must be put the long-term effects on the Orchestra of its becoming a specialist body. Even those who disliked much of the repertoire that Boulez introduced (and it is always a minority of orchestral players who feel anything like the same commitment to new music that the planners and conductors do) are united in saying that he did it well. But at what loss? There can be no doubt that during Boulez's period, certainly after Colin Davis ceased to do so much work with them, the Orchestra's ease in the classical repertoire diminished. Boulez never felt it necessary to concentrate on depth of string sound, richness of wind chording, warmth of phrasing and other matters to which the conductors of big romantic music devote so much attention. The whole thrust of his activity was to show how orchestral music – Debussy, Ravel, even Mahler and Brahms – could sound without those qualities.

Some deduced from the lack of these qualities that Boulez was not a real musician at all, but merely a technician. Or else that he was a limited musician who lacked certain crucial qualities. This view was put strongly by Hans Keller – a close associate of Glock during his early days at the BBC, and before his retirement in 1979 the BBC's Chief Assistant, New Music – in his book *1975 (1984 minus 9)*:

> Boulez cannot phrase – it is as simple as that. So far as all available evidence goes, of which there is plenty, he does not know what a phrase is. In that respect, his conducting of Bach, Beethoven or Wagner is absolutely identical: with all the precision and translucence he achieves, with all his so-called rhythm which is really metre, he does not bring about a single well-shaped phrase – the reason being that he ignores the harmonic implications of any structure he is dealing with, to the extent of utterly disregarding harmonic rhythm and hence all characteristic rhythm in tonal music. . . .
>
> What the habitual non-phraser does . . . is to replace phrasing by pace (everything too fast), and rhythm by 'beat', by motoric pseudo-excitement. The result is that while you can hear things which you shouldn't, you can't hear things which you should, especially in a rich texture, partly or wholly contrapuntal: they're past before you can say blast you.

How successful was Boulez? Musically, he achieved more in his London post than he did in New York. There were immense pressures in New York for him to conduct music to which he was not especially suited, because he was providing the only full subscription series by a professional symphony orchestra in the city. After his first two seasons, he weakened his resolve to keep a high proportion of twentieth-century works in the programmes, and directed many standard classics. In London, there were four other excellent orchestras to take care of the standard classics: Boulez could concentrate without any problems on the repertory that he did best.

Organisationally, his plans met with less success. Boulez now admits that little in London was changed by his period as Chief Conductor. 'Persistence is the first quality I did not have,' he says. 'If I had been completely a conductor I would have stayed for ten or fifteen years. Then I would have done something.' Nevertheless, he argued, one can look back 'and see a period that stands out as very special, with a profile and a personality'. The compromises that took place were simply because 'some ideas are not palatable to an audience . . . you cannot do it all for empty houses . . . the actuality must coincide at some point with what people want'.

In the end, it was Glock's plan that succeeded rather than Boulez's. There was no real thematic planning of the Festival Hall season, no pre-concerts or post-concerts, no radical alteration of London concert-going habits. Boulez would have liked much more contact with television; Glock was not especially interested. But a whole series of memorable individual events took place, in which the central twentieth-century orchestral repertoire was newly illuminated. Boulez grew in stature: from the original list of twenty works drawn up with Glock in 1964, he expanded his repertoire to 184 works by the time he relinquished the Chief Conductorship. And if his most ambitious schemes did not succeed – well, the privilege of experiment is to fail. The diversification of the Orchestra's activities has in fact continued to the present, and will expand, for example, when the Barbican Concert Hall opens.

The Boulez era (which is still not over, for he maintains close links with the Orchestra in his work at IRCAM) may well be seen as one of the landmarks of Britain's musical life in this century. It pointed some possible directions for renewal; it had little effect on the conservative pattern of concert life. It was that strange phenomenon, a revolution that changed nothing.

9

From Kempe to Rozhdestvensky
1973-80

A change of control

The creative partnership between Pierre Boulez and Sir William Glock (as he became in the 1970 Honours List) had lasted some nine years, but Boulez's time as Chief Conductor only just overlapped with Glock's time as Controller, Music. Glock had obtained a two-year extension of his appointment; he had to retire in December 1972, when Boulez's second season had just begun – though he was able to plan the 1972–3 season and the 1973 Proms. The question of his successor was of crucial importance to the Orchestra. Would the new Controller support the direction in which Boulez was taking the Orchestra, or would he reverse those trends? The field of possible successors sympathetic to Glock's views was not wide: like Boulez, Glock was an isolated figure; he had derived his initial success from the fact that very few people agreed with his musical sense of direction. Through the 1960s Glock had confounded his critics with the success of his broader Proms policy; he had brought new music into a central place in all the BBC's musical activities – not just in the Symphony Orchestra programmes, but in the famous Invitation Concerts, in some chamber concerts and studio broadcasts, and to a lesser extent in regional programmes. The foresight of Glock's actions was, of course, recognised by 1972; but elsewhere, too much of the musical world was as fossilised as it had been twelve years before, when Glock's efforts at the BBC began.

There was considerable public speculation as to his successor, though it proved to be poorly informed. When the name was announced the only surprise, as the *Guardian* reported, was that it had been so rarely mentioned during all the speculation following the announcement of Glock's retirement. Robert Ponsonby, at the age of forty-five, was an experienced figure in the world of musical administration. He had been appointed Director of the Edinburgh Festival at only twenty-nine and he had resigned from that post in 1960, because of the acute shortage of money available to run a leading

396

international festival. He had subsequently worked in America, and then back in England for the Independent Television Authority. In 1964 he had returned to Scotland as Administrator of the Scottish National Orchestra. In collaboration with Alexander Gibson, he had been very closely involved in modern music there: a trail-blazing series of new-music performances and workshops called 'Musica Nova' brought figures like Henze and Berio to Scotland, and the Orchestra gradually grew in international fame and strength. With a background both in broadcasting and in orchestral administration, and with wide musical interests, Ponsonby looked in retrospect to be ideally suited to the BBC post. His only serious rival had an operatic background – though the same festival background – and was less experienced in orchestral administration.

There were fears, however, because Ponsonby's views on new music were not widely known. He recalls, very soon after his appointment was announced early in 1972, introducing himself to a Press reporter on the phone and being told: 'Oh, you're the man who's going to change all William Glock's work at the BBC!' In fact, it had not taken him very long to become completely won over by the talent, purposefulness and charm of Pierre Boulez. Ponsonby visited the Orchestra on its 1972 tour, and was profoundly affected by what he saw and heard: the enthusiasm for Boulez which audiences showed; the commitment to Boulez's methods with the Orchestra, and the high quality of the resulting music-making. At the Swiss town of La Chaux-des-Fonds, which has a population of only 40,000, Ponsonby saw 3500 people crowd into a cold and uncomfortable ice-rink to hear and applaud a programme of music by Varèse, Stravinsky, Hugh Wood and Boulez himself. That evening, he says, made a deep impression on him and showed him the remarkable spell that Boulez casts on audiences – especially those without prejudices and preconceptions about modern music. Boulez, for his part, was also won over. He had been deeply reluctant to work with anyone except Glock, with whom he had a close understanding; he knew little of Ponsonby's work. His first letter to Ponsonby sounded an apologetic warning note: 'You must understand that I am not prejudiced . . .' Ponsonby recalls: 'I think he imagined me as a hopelessly conservative English type, and I had visions of him as dynamic, destructive and violent – we both couldn't have been more wrong.' Ponsonby's open-minded enthusiasm for Boulez's work quickly smoothed over any possible differences.

Ponsonby's first major task as Controller was to plan for the Symphony Orchestra's future. Boulez's three-year contract was to end in 1974; Ponsonby immediately asked him to stay for another year. In spite of his pressing commitments, and the imminent establishment of the new centre of acoustical and musical research in Paris which he was to head, Boulez agreed. Ponsonby then had to establish a successor from the 1975–6 season. He was well aware that no conductor could follow directly in line; besides, with Boulez as a guest conductor in future seasons, it would be possible to carry on his kind of work while restoring to the Orchestra some of its necessarily lost ease in the romantic and classical repertoire. Ponsonby decided to approach the most distinguished available figures. It was no secret that he at first hoped to attract Sir Georg Solti: discussions took place over a period of almost a year, from the moment Ponsonby's appointment was announced. A special Promenade Concert was arranged for 23 July 1973, at which Solti appeared with the Orchestra for the first time, and as Alan Blyth reported in *The Times*, the auguries looked fair:

> Solti had a double first at the Albert Hall last night. He was making his debut with the BBC Symphony Orchestra and conducting his first symphonic, as distinct from operatic, Prom. The affair with the Orchestra seemed such a happy one that rumours of a future marriage are to be encouraged. The evening's major work was Bruckner's Seventh Symphony, and it is a long time since I have heard the Orchestra's strings play with so much warmth and glowing tenderness, or the brass with so much refulgence. All obviously responded to Solti's impulsive, very committed direction.

Like Ponsonby, Solti wished to make the Orchestra the best in London, to extend the Boulez revolution that had ensured its prominence in contemporary music into other fields. He was extremely interested in individual players and in raising salary levels to attract the very best talent. Following his experience at the Prom concert, he was more than willing to continue discussions. So at the start of September 1973, after a series of visits to Solti, Ponsonby with his BBC associates 'flew to Paris on the hottest day of the year and sweltered with Solti for three protracted and very friendly hours'. But Solti finally decided to refuse the post. He felt that he would not have time to do the BBC job properly, that he had no guarantee that the BBC could raise salaries enough to attract the players he wanted, and that the offer of the Principal Guest Conductorship with the London Philharmonic Orchestra (under exceptionally favourable conditions, in which he could plan and conduct his own season-within-a-season) was more attractive. He could continue to conduct opera and to maintain his extensive American commitments; and he would have more free time. In retrospect, the marriage might not have worked: Solti could well have been unhappy with BBC bureaucracy. As his subsequent association with the LPO as Chief Conductor proved, Solti was greatly concerned with hiring and firing players; the BBC jealously guarded its independence in this regard.

So with Solti withdrawn from the scene, Ponsonby had to start again. By the middle of September, he was already flying to Munich to open discussions with Rudolf Kempe. It appeared that Kempe, the Artistic Director and Principal Conductor of the Royal Philharmonic, was not wedded to them for ever, and that he might welcome the prospect of a change. Agreement was reached with comparative ease, and the appointment was announced at the beginning of December. The *Daily Telegraph* reported that 'the BBC have pulled off a remarkable coup . . . Kempe is one of the most widely respected conductors on the international circuit . . .' The *Guardian* noted that he is 'regarded as a musician's musician . . . Mr Kempe has been appointed as the best man for the job, irrespective of nationality . . .'

A short collaboration

Rudolf Kempe was indeed one of the most outstanding of international conductors. Born in 1910 near Dresden, he had begun his career as an oboist and pianist, and had then moved swiftly to prominence as an opera conductor in Leipzig. In the forties he worked in Chemnitz, and in 1949 he moved to Dresden; in 1952 he was appointed musical director of the Bavarian State Opera in Munich, the company with which he appeared for the first time at Covent Garden in 1953. He scored a great success at Covent Garden, and returned there often, giving ten memorable *Ring* cycles between 1955 and 1961 and several Strauss operas. As conductor of the Royal Philharmonic, he had broadened its scope and brought it from a somewhat unstable reputation among London's commercial orchestras to be equal in standard with its rivals. He was also conductor of the Munich Philharmonic, since 1967, and would retain his connection with them. He was unsurpassed in the late romantic repertoire, especially Bruckner and Strauss, and it was hoped that he would have precisely the deepening effect on the BBC Symphony Orchestra's playing that Ponsonby had hoped for from a new conductor. Kempe had had an intermittent relationship with the Symphony Orchestra over many years; long-standing members of the Orchestra had already come to know him well and respect his music-making deeply. In the past, his concerts had often provoked the critics to surprise that the Orchestra could play so well. In November 1958 he did a Festival Hall concert, and even *The Times*, which was then attacking the Orchestra regularly for its standards, said:

Faced with a conductor whose beat is unambiguous and whose interpretative intentions are forthright and full of character, the BBC Symphony Orchestra sat up at their third concert of this season and began to play in the polished manner expected of them. Mr Kempe showed how efficient are their principal players . . .

And again six years later, after Kempe had had a bout of serious illness:

Rudolf Kempe made a triumphant return to this country with the BBC Symphony Orchestra at the Fairfield Hall. His performances of symphonies by Brahms and Beethoven showed if anything, that the spell he casts over an orchestra is even more potent than formerly.

Orchestra members recalled rousing performances of *Ein Heldenleben* and of Tchaikovsky's Fifth Symphony in the Albert Hall where, as Harry Danks said, 'I really thought the roof of the Albert Hall must collapse on us all'.

There were a few dissenting voices in the chorus of praise. Some thought Kempe a retrograde step to take after Boulez, that a conductor more in sympathy with contemporary music should have been chosen – but where was one, available and of international standing? And the usual letters to the Press complained that Kempe was not English, that the BBC Symphony Orchestra had a duty to encourage British talent. (Speculation as to the possible British candidates had centred around John Pritchard, Alexander Gibson, who was linked with Ponsonby through the Scottish National Orchestra, and Andrew Davis.) But Ponsonby was clear that he wanted a fine orchestral trainer with a good central repertoire as Chief Conductor: special tastes could be catered for by guest conductors, especially as Boulez would still be active. Kempe's association with the Orchestra was to begin as soon as possible. He was to make guest appearances with them in the 1973–4 Winter season, the 1974 and 1975 Proms, and then to begin his full-time post with the 1975–6 season. During that first year, because of his advance en-gagements, he would not be able to devote the full proportion of his time to the Orchestra, but it would increase to a maximum in 1976–7. The plan never came to fruition. He did appear briefly during the Proms of 1974, and gave a handful of concerts with the Orchestra at the start of his season as Chief Conductor. (There was one other important change at the start of Kempe's first season: Paul Huband, the Orchestra's General Manager since 1963, retired, and William Relton succeeded him. Huband had come to the Orchestra at one of its low points, and left it at one of its highest moments – his contribution had been vital to that achievement.)

From the few concerts which Kempe gave with the Orchestra, it was possible to see what he might have achieved. The glorious accounts of Janáček's Sinfonietta during the 1974 Proms and Dvořák's New World

Symphony in 1975 made the Orchestra sound richer and stronger than it had for some time. At the start of his tenure as Chief Conductor, he conducted Hindemith's *Symphonia Serena* and Haydn's London Symphony in the studio on 4 October 1975, and then coupled the Haydn with Mahler's *Das Lied von der Erde* in the Festival Hall on 8 October. Then, on 12 October, there was a televised concert from Croydon: Britten's Four Sea Interludes from *Peter Grimes*, Prokofiev's First Piano Concerto with Michel Béroff, and Janáček's Sinfonietta again. Notable in all these performances was the breadth of tone and rhythmic strength which Kempe managed to draw from the Symphony Orchestra.

There was to be only one more concert: on 18 February 1976 at the Festival Hall, Kempe conducted Tippett's Concerto for double string orchestra, the Berg Violin Concerto, and the Brahms Fourth Symphony. *The Financial Times* wrote, 'Rudolf Kempe is doing great things for the BBC Symphony Orchestra. Closing one's eyes . . . this might have been any of London's orchestras on a good night. Opening them, the reason is clear: Kempe has taken the Boulez-induced precision of recent years and has added to it a rhythmic unity . . . the orchestra is with him all the way.' That, alas, was the sum of Kempe's achievement with the Orchestra. By the time of his next concerts with them, in March 1976, he was already a sick man: though how sick, few realised. It was hoped that he would recover; there were concerts in April, and he had a full programme planned for the 1976 Proms, including a *Missa Solemnis* on the opening night. But in May, Kempe died suddenly. He was sixty-five; scarcely very old, in a world of conductors which then included an active Böhm at eighty-one, Boult at eighty-seven and Stokowski at ninety-four.

Players were quick to acknowledge Kempe's achievement with the Orchestra. Eli Goren, the co-leader, recalled that

> from the first to the last rehearsal, he would progressively inform the orchestra how he saw a particular work, and how he was going to portray it. Most of this was done by the unusual clarity of his beat and gesture. His comparatively few verbal comments were spoken quietly and almost leisurely, giving the orchestra time to consider the point. The result was that, in the performance, everybody was able to give his best.

Harry Danks, the principal viola in the Orchestra for many years, gave a detailed account of Kempe's working method in a broadcast talk which was heard, ironically, just before Kempe's death.

> His approach and manner are usually very quiet but firm, tinged with a dry

sense of humour. This is terribly important to an orchestral musician for a conductor without a sense of humour usually turns out to be an uninteresting director. . . .

Kempe seems to have the knack of conveying the correct amount of information in the minimum number of words. He never appears to find it necessary to ask for the music to go quicker or slower, louder or softer; this is all conveyed through his personality and power to grip the orchestra. . . .

Kempe is considerate and experienced with his type of rehearsing; he knows exactly what he wants and what is terribly important, how to obtain it. In my experience he never makes an orchestra over-play at rehearsal and when he has worked with a group of players over a period and understands them, and they, him, he appears to leave well alone and it all becomes a very enjoyable experience in making music and earning a living: for me, a delightful combination. . . .

Ponsonby himself paid tribute to Kempe's 'inner dedication to music' which 'revealed itself when he came on the rostrum. There his genius for communication emerged . . . he achieved with his orchestras a deep and immediate rapport.' Ponsonby pointed to the fact that Kempe's range of repertoire in his first concerts had been wide, and that his future programmes would have included music by Schumann, Mahler, Shostakovich, Stravinsky, Roussel, and Francis Burt. 'He would also have conducted some Richard Strauss, though, on the whole, the less familiar works. On the horizon was a concert performance of *Daphne* . . .' Nevertheless, it must be admitted that Kempe's limited range of sympathies might well have made life difficult for the BBC orchestral planners in the future, had he lived to serve his full contract: there might not have been the flexibility of programming which they had become accustomed to enjoy. His health was known to be poor; it was unlikely that he would have stayed beyond the three years of his agreement.

Looking for a new direction

With the illness and death of Kempe, Ponsonby was faced with unenviable short-term and long-term problems. In the short term, there were Festival Hall concerts and an important group of Proms for which replacements had to be found. In the long term, the question of the Chief Conductorship was now reopened. In the Festival Hall Kempe's programmes were a Debussy, Bloch and Beethoven concert for the Royal Philharmonic Society, and a performance of Haydn's *The Creation*. In between, there was a concert in Brighton of Tippett, Strauss and Brahms. Raymond Leppard undertook the first, Alun Francis directed *The Creation*, while John Pritchard did the

Brighton concert. The next group of concerts in April and May passed to
Loughran, Erede, Boettcher and Bernhard Klee: Erede conducted the Verdi
Requiem; Klee, Mahler's First Symphony. Colin Davis conducted the
opening night of the Proms, with a notably successful *Missa Solemnis*; John
Eliot Gardiner took over for the repeat performance of *The Creation*; Rafael
Frühbeck de Burgos and Andrew Davis took over concerts, and Raymond
Leppard conducted what was to have been Kempe's Beethoven Ninth
Symphony.

For the remainder of the season, and for the season to follow, Ponsonby
could either rush into a new appointment of Chief Conductor (almost certainly having to approach someone of less than world rank) or he could rely
on the services of distinguished guest conductors. He had, however, conceived a definite idea for a new appointment, and it was an idea which could
not be rushed. So through the 1975–7 period, the Orchestra worked under a
vast number of different conductors, relying on special guests and distinguished visitors who each brought their particular expertise to bear on the
situation. The period was not a happy one for the Orchestra: morale flagged
in the absence of positive leadership. Some conductors aroused enthusiasm;
others did not. Boulez was not in a position to give the Orchestra more of his
time; his return visits, however, were highlights of the period, Colin Davis,
increasingly busy not only at the Royal Opera but in Boston, and with a wide
range of recordings and tours, relinquished his Chief Guest Conductorship;
it was taken up by Charles Mackerras, who in the midst of busy schedules
was able to conduct a substantial number of events. Boulez, too, gave up his
guest conductorship in 1977 when he started full-time work at IRCAM.
His place was taken by Michael Gielen, one of the few conductors who had
shown an aptitude and enthusiasm for a repertoire similar to that of Boulez:
indeed, many who were suspicious of Boulez's popularity preferred Gielen's
reserved, thoughtful manner with new music.

1975–7

The 1975–6 season began with an outstanding period of work. The Orchestra visited *Europalia* in Brussels and then Grenoble with Boulez, in a
programme of Maderna, Birtwistle, Globokar and Boulez. There were
sessions under Colin Davis. And there was Kempe as well: Kempe, Davis,
Boulez in one month – the situation looked ideal. Rudolf Schwarz also returned; Boulez directed the British première of Messiaen's huge *Des canyons
aux étoiles* for the Royal Philharmonic Society. At this important concert,
Boulez presented Messiaen with the gold medal of the Royal Philharmonic
Society. As Peter Heyworth noted in *The Observer*, '. . . few would question

that it was appropriate so to honour Olivier Messiaen. On a stage that each year seems more disconcertingly bare, he remains one of a handful of senior composers of indisputable stature and originality.' But there were many reservations about the new work itself, its length and repetitiveness. In the studio, Frederick Prausnitz gave an eightieth birthday concert for Roger Sessions including his Eighth Symphony, and Norman Del Mar directed Nicola Lefanu's *The Hidden Landscape* with Rawsthorne's Third Symphony.

Boulez was back in the Festival Hall in the new year, for a Hungarian programme including the British premières of Ligeti's *San Francisco Polyphony* and Sandor Balassa's *Iris*; Bartók's *Duke Bluebeard's Castle* completed the programme: this concert was widely praised. There was some disappointment over the Ligeti piece; as Paul Griffiths wrote in *The Times*, '. . . the polyphonic weave made for the San Francisco Symphony Orchestra is to a large extent a tangle. The glistening surfaces which have abounded in his recent works are muggy here, the polyphonic layers barely distinguishable, the ideas undistinguished.' Balassa's *Iris* was liked by Dominic Gill: '. . . a good score . . . and a hundred times more honest and invigorating than most of the patronising piffle presented to us lately by London orchestras in the guise of "something new".' But, as he noted,

> . . . it was the performance of Bartók's *Duke Bluebeard's Castle* which entirely dominated the evening: a magical, memorable performance which I would not have missed for the world.
>
> It is difficult to remember hearing the BBC Symphony Orchestra ever play so well. Their performance had a quickness and a finesse, as well as a continuity and breadth, which they can probably achieve under no other conductor: every gesture a marvellous unanimity, every line precisely placed, each colour exactly mixed . . .

Harold Farberman contributed more American music: Macdowell, Sessions, Grant Still, Barber and Crumb; Raymond Leppard conducted a Weber anniversary concert at St John's Smith Square. John Pritchard gave three one-composer programmes in the studio, of music by Bartók, Schubert and Walton, and then a Festival Hall concert with Henze's Second Piano Concerto (with Paul Crossley). Paul Griffiths reported that 'the BBC Symphony Orchestra seemed set last night to show themselves a body of relentless virtuosos, and with John Pritchard to conduct they made a fair impression of brilliance'. An important première of the season was Jonathan Harvey's *Inner Light* (*III*), a BBC commission, composed for orchestra and electronic tape. Four speakers surrounded listeners in the Festival Hall with quadraphonic sound, controlled by the composer from the auditorium; the counterpoint of orchestral sound was directed by Michael Gielen. The piece lasted over thirty minutes; most listeners found some difficulty in following its shape, but enjoyed the sound of the piece. Back in the studio, Malcolm Arnold and Michael Tippett both directed programmes in the series 'The Composer Conducts', Elgar Howarth an interesting English programme of Britten, Maconchy, Lefanu and Constant Lambert. Andrew Davis juxtaposed Lutoslawski's Funeral Music with Beethoven's Eroica Symphony.

Two major public appearances ended the pre-Prom season: under Colin Davis, the Orchestra contributed to the Festival Hall's twenty-fifth anniversary series with a new work commissioned by the BBC, Peter Racine Fricker's Symphony No. 5 for organ and orchestra. Davis revived Tippett's *The Vision of St Augustine* in the same concert. At Cheltenham, Lawrence Foster presented an American programme including the British première of Roger Sessions' Concerto for violin, cello and orchestra.

In 1976–7 the season was inaugurated by Boulez in the studio, with one all-Berlioz and one all-Schoenberg programme. Then the Orchestra was involved in the semi-finals and finals of the Rupert Foundation Conductors Competition, which the BBC now helped to present, providing the Orchestra on which the conductors aimed to prove their ability. Charles Groves conducted half the final concert; the winner was Ivan Fischer who later that month replaced Erich Schmid in a studio concert. (Fischer, and some later winners, have had the chance to work with several BBC orchestras; the competitive nature of the event has recently been changed, however, and it is now known as the Rupert Foundation Conductors Awards.) Rarities followed under Bryden Thomson, Balakirev's Second Piano Concerto, with Hamish Milne; while for the Radio 3 programme 'The Innocent Ear' (in which the music is identified only after it has been performed), the Orchestra recorded Busoni's Violin Concerto, a Symphony in B flat by Van Maldere, and Rubbra's First Symphony. Other conductors in the period included Raymond Leppard, Mark Elder, Brian Wright, Samuel Friedemann (in Shostakovich's Fourth and Fifth Symphonies), Gunter Herbig and Hans Vonk. One major project occupied four days at the start of 1977: the recording of Iain Hamilton's new opera for radio, *The Death of Tamburlaine*, which the BBC had commissioned. On 10 January Norman Del Mar conducted the slow movement of Mahler's Fourth Symphony in a memorial celebration for the Mahler and Wagner scholar Deryck Cooke, who had been in charge of the BBC's Music Information Unit. At the end of the season there were appearances at festivals in St Albans (with Peter Dickinson's Organ Concerto replacing Justin Connolly's, which was unfinished), and Swansea (where Erede repeated the Verdi *Requiem*).

The Festival Hall series in 1976–7 included concerts under Yuri Arano-vich, John Pritchard, Erich Schmid, Andrew Davis, Michael Gielen, Colin Davis, John Eliot Gardiner and Charles Mackerras; the main interest was in the revival of Schoenberg's *Die glückliche Hand* by Gielen and in the Walton birthday concert given by Colin Davis. There was also a concert under Boulez for the Royal Philharmonic Society. The continental tour by the Orchestra in 1977 took it to Germany: an exhausting thirteen-concert trip on which the conducting was shared between Mackerras (who was unable to come to the first concerts, and was replaced by Norman Del Mar), James Loughran and Charles Groves. Modern works on the programmes included the Britten Violin Concerto, Maxwell Davies' *St Thomas Wake* and Goehr's *Pastorals*. The tour ended, untypically, with an all-Beethoven concert which Mackerras added in Rotterdam. In June, Sir Adrian Boult made one of his last public appearances, conducting the Orchestra in a concert to open the Royal Albert Hall's jubilee week, in Schubert's Ninth Symphony.

Inaugurating IRCAM

The 1977–8 season was to be the last without a chief conductor. It was especially notable for two Festival Hall concerts under Boulez; in between them he took the Orchestra to Paris to complete the inauguration of his new Institute de Récherche et Coordination Acoustique/Musique in the Georges Pompidou Centre. For the opening of IRCAM, Boulez had devised a comprehensive series of concerts called 'The Passage of the Twentieth Century'. The BBC Symphony Orchestra contributed the two final con-certs. Boulez was not content to repeat pieces which he had already per-formed with the Orchestra, though he had covered nearly all the great twentieth-century orchestral works in his concerts with them. Two of the major pieces in the concerts had not been performed by Boulez in England: the Fourth Symphony of Charles Ives (30 November) and the new *Hago-romo*, a BBC commission from David Lumsdaine (1 December), which should have been heard in the previous year's Proms. Around these pieces were classic Boulez fare: in the first concert Debussy's *Jeux*, Berg's *Altenberg-Lieder* and Schoenberg's Orchestral Variations; in the second, Boulez's own *Le Soleil des eaux* (revised version), Ligeti's *San Francisco Poly-phony* and Nono's *Il canto sospeso*. In the *Guardian* Christopher Ford reported that the Orchestra played 'with much polish and subtlety . . . the visit was an artistic success of a considerable order'. Boulez's Festival Hall concerts did not duplicate this material, except for a performance of *Le Soleil des eaux*. There was Stravinsky's *Firebird*, and an ambitious pro-gramme of Wagner (*Das Liebesmahl der Apostel*) and Schoenberg (*Die*

Jakobsleiter). Boulez was also able to share the conducting on the season's continental tour in the following May: he took pieces by Webern, Birtwistle, Bartók, Berg, Stravinsky and himself to Vienna, Zagreb, Zürich, Lausanne and Paris; Charles Mackerras conducted concerts in Bratislava, Budapest, Maribor and Paris, which included Iain Hamilton's *Aurora*.

Outstanding events in the Festival Hall season during 1977-8 included a Vaughan Williams centenary concert and a seventieth birthday concert for Olivier Messiaen, under Serge Baudo, which included the early *Hymne au Saint-Sacrement*, as well as *Oiseaux exotiques* and *Et exspecto resurrectionem mortuorum*. Kurt Sanderling, Walter Susskind and Charles Mackerras contributed to the series. Outside engagements included a programme of new Canadian music for the *Musicanada* festival, a visit to Brighton with Mackerras, a recording of Zemlinsky's Lyric Symphony under Franco Ferra, and an appearance at the Cheltenham Festival under David Atherton, when Iain Hamilton's new *Scena: Cleopatra* (a festival commission) was premièred. In the studio interesting concerts were conducted by Zoltan Pesko (the Szymanowski *Sinfonia concertante*, Cherubini *Requiem* and works by Petrassi); by Mackerras (an all-Janáček programme); and Brian Wright (Rubbra's Fourth Symphony and Holst's Choral Symphony). The Orchestra's programmes ranged as widely as before, but without the binding force of a Chief Conductor they sometimes seemed miscellaneous.

In and out of Smith Square

During the years since Boulez had ceased to be Chief Conductor, the question of the concert series which he had inaugurated – at St John's Smith Square, and at the Round House – was a constant preoccupation for the BBC. Each had had its moments of success under the direction of Boulez, and the diversification they provided was welcome. Could they be carried on in some different form? Before the 1975-6 season, the first since Boulez had left, the answer looked depressingly like a straight 'No'. The year 1975 was one of economies throughout the BBC, and the prospect of saving money by cancelling either or both of these series was attractive to some. Ponsonby insisted that the Round House series, which had acquired a strong reputation for presenting new music and commissioned works, should be retained. The Smith Square series, less popular with the public, was reluctantly transferred to the Concert Hall of Broadcasting House, where the programmes were given before an invited audience (very much as at the Maida Vale Studios, though with rather more of a sense of occasion). A considerable sum of money was to be saved by the transfer, yet the Orchestra's output was maintained.

It was initially agreed that the transfer should take place for at least two seasons. The 1975–6 season featured Edward Downes, Mackerras, Pritchard and Leppard, with at least one twentieth-century work in each programme. The following season, an attractive scheme of concerts was planned, based on Haydn symphonies and Mozart violin concertos. They were prominent in almost all the programmes, which were conducted by Erich Schmid, John Pritchard, John Poole, Hans Vonk, Walter Susskind and Colin Davis. It was decided to go back to St John's at once, after a gap of only a year. This series re-established the popularity of the concerts, and confirmed the decision to base their programmes on classic works. In 1977–8 Haydn's choral works were featured; Ivan Fischer, Ferdinand Leitner and Kurt Masur conducted concerts there. In 1978–9, a broader set of programmes featured music by Hindemith, and presented the new Chief Conductor (see below) in Webern and Schubert, then in Weill and Hindemith, and in Berlioz's *L'Enfance du Christ*. Charles Mackerras conducted Beethoven's *Cantata on the Death of the Emperor Joseph II*, alongside Frank Martin's *Petite Symphonie Concertante* and the *Trauermusik* by Hindemith (which he had written for a BBC Symphony studio concert to mourn the death of King George V, see p. 117). Later in the season Prokofiev's incidental music to *Hamlet* was given a first hearing in England.

The growing emphasis of the series on choral music, and the success of concerts involving the BBC Singers led to a decision to make the 1979–80 season a joint one by Orchestra and Singers. The BBC Singers had already promoted its own thematically-planned seasons at St John's in 1978–9, featuring early music; for the new joint season the title 'Sacred and Profane' was chosen, and the programmes were based around British choral and orchestral music, both sacred and secular. Several pieces which had been in the repertory of the Orchestra during the 1930s were revived, including Bliss's Music for Strings and Frank Bridge's tone-poem *Summer*. Each concert included a piece by Britten. Guest conductors included Paul Sacher and John Pritchard.

From Round House to Royal College

While the Smith Square series disappeared and then reappeared, the BBC's connection with the Round House was gradually changed. In the first post-Boulez season, 1975–6, there were again four concerts, only the first conducted by Boulez. Elgar Howarth, David Atherton and Michael Gielen completed the series. Though the programmes were felt to have achieved a good, stable format, audiences were disappointingly small, and the third concert (like Maderna's in the second season) was transferred to the studio because of 'unforeseeable technical difficulties'. Boulez's programme included a BBC commission from Sven David Sandström, *Utmost*; Howarth's, the London première of *Le Terrazze* by John Buller; in Atherton's concert, there was the first performance of sections of Stephen Reeve's . . . *aux régions éthérées* . . ., for three instrumental ensembles, another BBC commission; in Gielen's, there was the newly-revised version of Nicholas Maw's *Life Studies*, with No. 2 heard for the first time. Music by Nono, Schoenberg, Webern, Hugh Wood, Dallapiccola, Birtwistle and Boulez made up the programmes.

Press comment on the Sandström commission was mixed:

> The BBC had thought it would be (in the words of Robert Ponsonby, Controller of Music) 'rather pleasant, as a kind of thank you, if we commissioned a young Swede to write for the Round House' – in response to the special attention given by Swedish Radio to British music.

Thus reported Dominic Gill in *The Financial Times*, but then said that 'Pleasant gesture it may have been: but pleasant the work was not'. Buller's piece, which dates from 1967–8, was strongly disliked by some critics, but Edward Greenfield in the *Guardian* thought it 'remarkable for its strikingly simple but imaginative use of electronic tape . . . a cogent and eventful score'. In the Maida Vale concert, Stephen Reeve's piece made 'a scrappy, disjointed impression' on *The Financial Times*, while *The Times* said that the 'desultoriness of the music tells heavily against it' – but it was scarcely possible to judge the work, as its two final sections were omitted (without any clear explanation) in the performance. Though the premières in this season received a poor press, the standards of performance of the classic twentieth-century works were consistently praised.

In 1976–7 four concerts were again planned. Two featured Boulez: in the first there was a new Michael Finnissy work; the second included the British première of a major American work, Elliott Carter's *A mirror on which to dwell* (sung by Jane Manning). The third concert was to be directed by Stockhausen. This last, on 7 February 1977, would have been the culmination of a long project which was also to include a performance in the same month of *Hymnen* at the Festival Hall. The programme was at an advanced stage: *Formal* and *Spiel* were originally planned for the Round House, and later the *Drei lieder*, *Spiel* and the recent *Harlequin*. But the problems of mounting *Hymnen* were immense, particularly with the inflexibility of the Festival Hall's planning machinery. As with *Momente*, it was eventually decided that the concert would have to be moved from a day when rehearsal and performance would be interrupted by an organ recital; it was replanned on Monday 14 February. Eventually, with accumulated problems, it had to be dropped altogether. The Round House programme, adapted by the addition of choral works, was then proposed for the Festival Hall. But the BBC thought it unsuitable, as all the music was small-scale. So the plans fizzled out.

The BBC was then left with a Round House concert which might well not draw a large audience in the absence of Stockhausen. So the decision was taken to alter the two final concerts of the season, which were now to be conducted by Elgar Howarth and Diego Masson. Instead of merely transferring them to Maida Vale studios, William Relton, now General Manager of the Symphony Orchestra, suggested that they be turned into Invitation Concerts. Two of the London colleges of music were asked if they would like to play host for the occasions, and both Sir David Willcocks at the Royal College of Music and Sir Anthony Lewis at the Royal Academy of Music readily agreed. So in February, at the Royal College, Howarth conducted John Casken's *Kagura*, and Hugh Wood introduced Webern's Op. 21; Ligeti's display pieces *Aventures* and *Nouvelles Aventures* were revived with great success. On 21 February at the Royal Academy, Masson conducted his own choice of work, *Il gigante Golia* by the French-resident composer George Aperghis; part of Alexander Goehr's triptych of music-theatre pieces, *Naboth's Vineyard*, was revived, with Stravinsky's *Renard*.

The success of these two concerts led to the decision to share the 1977–8 season between the Round House and the London colleges of music instead. By this season the new buildings of the Guildhall School of Music and Drama were open in the Barbican (though the long-awaited large concert hall in that complex was not yet ready for use). Two concerts were given there, one at the Royal College and one at the Royal Academy. The programmes, as in the previous season, were devised in close collaboration with two of BBC Music Division's specialists in new music, Stephen Plaistow and Veronica Slater. At the College on 18 October, Peter Maxwell Davies conducted his own *Leopardi Fragments*, Simon Bainbridge gave *World* by Michael Finnissy for the first time in this country, and Stockhausen's *Kontakte* was revived by pianist Jan Latham-Koenig and percussionist James Holland. At the Guildhall on 14 November, Hans Zender conducted British premières of two of his recent works, and Henze's *Being Beauteous* was given alongside music by Webern. At the Academy on 9 March, Lionel Friend conducted Nicholas Maw's *Sinfonia*, Durko's *Turner Illustrations*, and Messiaen's *Couleurs de la cité céleste*. At the Guildhall on 23 March, Gary Bertini conducted music by Gerhard, Schnittke and Dallapiccola. The Round House concerts formed a small festival in February: Elgar Howarth premièred a new John Buller work, and Lionel Friend introduced a Robert Saxton piece to this country.

In 1978–9 the Round House was not used for the series. Alterations to its stage and auditorium, making it more suitable for stage shows, had made it far less easy to accommodate a large orchestra. The BBC continues to use the venue, especially during the Promenade Concert season, but only for chamber-sized ensembles. And in the new 'College Concerts' an important precedent was established: another ensemble, the London Sinfonietta, was invited to share in the series of concerts. This enabled programmes to be broader, for both chamber and orchestral forces could be included. The BBC Symphony Orchestra undertook three concerts: Mark Elder in Stravinsky and Birtwistle at the Guildhall; Lionel Friend in Goehr, Nigel Osborne, Denisov and Stravinsky at the College; and Michael Gielen in Stravinsky, Zimmermann, Goehr and Webern, again at the Guildhall. In the 1979–80 season, the significance of the series was increased: it was enlarged to six concerts, shared equally between the Symphony Orchestra and the Sinfonietta. Stephen Plaistow, now the BBC's Chief Producer, Contemporary Music, devised the programmes and produced them. There was an extra new venue, in the Logan Hall of London University. The Orchestra's contribution included the première of Nigel Osborne's Cello Concerto and the British première of Zimmermann's Concerto for two pianos, while the Sinfonietta gave the first performances of BBC commissions from Douglas Young and Stephen Reeve, as well as British premières by Henri Pousseur. Late Stravinsky provided the connecting thread to the series: *A Sermon, a narrative and a prayer*, *Requiem Canticles*, and *Threni* were all played by the Orchestra. It would be hard to think of an orchestral concert series in this country which more closely matches the achievements of Edward Clark's contemporary music series in the 1930s – also given before invited audiences, also juxtaposing recent classics with new works from Britain and Europe. The continuity of the BBC's work for contemporary orchestral music has been one of the main themes of this book, and in the College Concerts it finds a lively expression today.

A Russian surprise

Robert Ponsonby's search for a new Chief Conductor had begun immediately after the death of Rudolf Kempe. For once the newspapers were right – or at least, one of them. In the *Guardian*, during May 1976, Christopher Ford surveyed the available field, including John Pritchard (about to give up his directorship at Glyndebourne Opera, but in fact contracted to the Cologne Opera), Bernard Haitink (who could scarcely have combined his new responsibilities at Glyndebourne with the BBC), and Andrew Davis (who was dismissed as too young, though he was in fact by no means excluded from the running). From Symphony Orchestra members, there was immediate reaction to the possibility of a British conductor, and a strong plea to Ponsonby to preserve the international flavour of the Boulez and Kempe appointments; names mentioned included Wolfgang Sawallisch, Kurt Sanderling and Kurt Masur. But Ford's article went on:

> The one name whose very mention causes excitement among BBC musicians (as among most others) is that of the great Soviet conductor Gennadi Rozhdestvensky, now 46. After difficulties in the past, which caused him to cancel so many British appearances that orchestras became chary of booking him, he seems to be relieved of pressure. He is halfway 'out', as chief conductor of the Stockholm Philharmonic, a post arranged at Prime Ministerial level between Palme and Brezhnev.
>
> Rozhdestvensky's contract at Stockholm ends early next year, after which he will become 'permanent guest conductor' of the Cleveland Orchestra. He has no contract post in the Soviet Union, and there is no reason why Cleveland and the BBC could not be combined (Boulez ran the New York Philharmonic and the BBC SO at the same time while living in Baden-Baden). His London agent is known to be interested in the possibility.
>
> His home is still in Russia and, politically, Rozhdestvensky must remain a potential pawn – a knight, anyway – but musically he would be a marvellous answer.

Ponsonby had met Rozhdestvensky at the Edinburgh Festival back in 1960, when he had given some supremely exciting concerts with the Leningrad Philharmonic. On the last morning of the 1960 Festival (Ponsonby's last as director) Rozhdestvensky shared the triangle with Rostropovich in a performance of the Toy Symphony which Ponsonby conducted: Ian Wallace, Leonid Massine, Alexander Gibson and Lord Harewood were among the other participants. Rozhdestvensky had the reputation of being an orchestral magician, one of the rare conductors to whom players responded instantly and enthusiastically; certainly, each of his collaborations with the BBC Symphony Orchestra in the past had been an outstanding success. But what was the possibility that Russia would release him? And were other orchestras also interested in approaching him when his contract in Stockholm ran out? Ponsonby decided at least to try and approach Rozhdestvensky. He knew his agent, the London firm of Victor Hochhauser, very well, and they had been in close touch with Russia.

One problem lay in the BBC's status with the Russian authorities. It might well be easier to make approaches to Russia through the formal channels of a well-known body like the BBC, and in this sense it was an advantage. But the BBC's political independence, which it jealously guarded, and the activities of its External Services in broadcasting to Russia, might well have made it an organisation with which the Russians would not wish to have close links. In this sense it was a disadvantage. Ponsonby, working very largely in the dark, determined to make the requests through the official channels. And though, as he recalls, he had no favourable answers for some time, neither did he receive any firm refusals. So he persevered.

In September 1976 Ponsonby and William Relton travelled to Berlin, where Rozhdestvensky was conducting Shostakovich's *The Nose* at the Festival. They talked with him over supper after the performance, and asked him if he would be interested in the appointment. He was enthusiastic at the prospect, but warned that the Stockholm post had been arranged at the highest level. In November 1976 negotiations were opened with the Russian Embassy in London through its cultural attaché, and with Vladimir Popov of the Ministry of Culture in Moscow. In February 1977 the Embassy said that a decision would have to be delayed; but there was no unfavourable reaction. Ponsonby was able to enlist the help of the BBC's Director-General, at the time Sir Charles Curran, in the negotiations; they both lunched with the Russian Ambassador at the Café Royal, though it was discovered that he had more pressing matters to discuss with Curran than mere music. Still, no firm barriers were put in the way, and it was hoped that an answer would be forthcoming by April. But then the Russians again postponed a decision, this time until 'the second half of 1977', which was leaving matters rather late. Ponsonby flew to Stockholm in May to meet Rozhdestvensky, who expressed very strong enthusiasm and assured him that everything possible was being done to hasten matters. He assured Ponsonby of his co-operation in the project, and thought that with the BBC's help the appointment could be obtained. (There had been no objections to his accepting a guest post with the Cleveland Orchestra.) Meanwhile, the matter rested with the Ministry of Culture in Moscow. In June a decision was promised by July; in July, one by August. The uncertainty became tantalising. Rumours drifted back from Moscow of cocktail parties at which cultural officials had said Rozhdestvensky was welcome to work with any London orchestra 'except the BBC's'. Communications with Moscow consisted almost entirely of messages from London, left unanswered.

In the middle of this period of waiting, the matter became public knowledge. Rumours of an appointment were persistent, and when he announced the 1977 Proms programmes at the usual Press conference Ponsonby knew that he would be questioned on the subject. He agreed an announcement with Moscow:

> The Ministry of Culture and Gennadi Rozhdestvensky are doing their best to enable him to find time amongst his other engagements to accept the Chief Conductorship of the BBC Symphony Orchestra.

He added: 'I fervently hope this appointment will be achieved very soon. No one can say any more at the moment.'

Ponsonby travelled to the Salzburg Festival in August, and while he was there telephoned Moscow. Rozhdestvensky's mother told him that the appointment had been agreed – and a telegram just after from Rozhdestvensky suggested the same – but there was no official confirmation, and it was not until the end of October that Ponsonby and Relton were able to visit Moscow to conclude the arrangements. They met with the officials of GOSKontserts, the official Russian artists' agency, on 24, 25 and 26 October. The first question Ponsonby had to ask the Russians was: 'Is the appointment really confirmed?' to which he received the reply: 'I assure you, you would not be sitting here if that were not the case'. The BBC were eager to contract Rozhdestvensky for five years; the Russians offered less, and a compromise of three years was finally agreed. On the last day of negotiations two contracts were signed, one in English, one in Russian. Ponsonby described the discussions as 'strenuous but friendly'.

Rozhdestvensky travelled to London in November 1977, when the announcement of his appointment was made. Replying to questions, he said, 'I find this one of the best symphony orchestras in the world'. He was to take over the Orchestra in the 1978–9 season, and would appear with them in the 1978 Proms. He was to undertake between twenty and thirty concerts a year: a small number compared to those that Boulez conducted, but perhaps the maximum that any other international figure was likely to accept. Many chief conductors, some at the head of two orchestras a continent apart, spent much less time with their ensembles. The Orchestra would still have to wait nearly a year before Rozhdestvensky joined them; it was a long wait, but worth while.

Gennadi Rozhdestvensky is not among that small group of international conductors whose names are well known to the public through countless recordings and well-promoted concerts. In spite of the acclaim which has greeted his concerts in England, he has never previously been among the conductors whom the public orchestras rushed to engage each season – perhaps because his availability has been limited, and because of the unpredictability of his cancellations in the past. His background is unfamiliar.

He was born in 1931 into a family of Russian musicians. His father Nicolai was a conductor, his mother a singer. The father conducted at the Moscow Conservatoire, while Gennadi heard his mother singing around the house. He recalls Russian composers of the time coming to the house to rehearse; his first musical memory is of Mozart's *Marriage of Figaro* in a concert performance, which he heard when he was five. Two years later he began to study the piano, but the war intervened. The family was evacuated to Gorky (Nizhny Novgorod) on the Volga, but Gennadi returned to Moscow in 1943 to continue with his piano studies. Only when he was fourteen did his mind turn to conducting. His teachers in the Moscow Conservatoire included Lev Oborin and Professor Anosov, but he left before the end of his course there because he was offered the post of assistant conductor at the Bolshoi Theatre. Soon after, he became a full-time conductor there, specialising in ballet. It was in this guise that he was first seen in England, during the Bolshoi's historic visit in 1956 to Covent Garden, at which the famous ballerina Ulanova appeared, and Rozhdestvensky conducted. Later he was to return often to England, appearing at the Edinburgh Festival (where Ponsonby first met him) and at the Proms; he appeared most frequently in London with the London Symphony Orchestra. In 1966 he was appointed Musicial Director of the Bolshoi, where he had married one of the company's ballerinas, Nina Timofeyeva. He moved into the field of opera, raising the standards of the company and putting on important revivals of Russian operas. But he did not stay long in charge, though he still conducts there, becoming instead head of a small, homespun group, the Moscow Chamber Opera. He also teaches at the Conservatoire. He has preferred to travel as widely as possible, and the Soviet authorities have put few restrictions in his way: he has appeared in more than thirty different countries. He retained for many years the artistic directorship of the Moscow Radio and Television Orchestra, but gave that up in 1974, before taking on the Stockholm Philharmonic.

Rozhdestvensky has not been entirely free of criticism from official Soviet sources. Shortly before he took up the BBC post, in March 1978, an adventurous new staging of Tchaikovsky's *The Queen of Spades* in Paris, which he was to conduct, was violently attacked in the Soviet newspaper *Pravda*. The attack came from a former colleague at the Bolshoi, Zhuraitis, who said that the version of the opera prepared by composer Alfred Schnittke and producer Yuri Lyubimov was 'a calculated act of destruction of a Russian cultural monument', 'a monstrous enterprise' produced by 'lovers of sensations'. But no official action was taken against the distinguished Russians involved. Rozhdestvensky has remained a Russian citizen and intends to do so. No political action has been involved in his appointment and the BBC and Russian authorities try to keep political considerations to a minimum. Rozhdestvensky has served Russian music and music-making loyally in the course of his career: his freedom to travel is the gift of the Russian government, and at present it is freely given.

Rozhdestvensky is now married to the Russian pianist Victoria Postnikova, well known here for her controversial second prize in the Leeds Piano Competition of 1966 (one of the jurors, Hans Keller of the BBC, made public the fierce disagreements in the jury, arguing that she deserved first prize). She appeared with him at his début as Chief Conductor, in the 1978 Proms.

Rozhdestvensky arrives

Rozhdestvensky arrived for that first Albert Hall concert with the Orchestra in August 1978. There was an exceptional flurry of press activity: Rozhdestvensky was uneasy about giving interviews, declaring that his job was to conduct, not to talk, but the papers found much to write about his appointment and his conducting style, and were uniformly enthusiastic. Gillian Widdicombe in *The Observer* exclaimed:

> *A miracle?* Yes, the BBC has achieved a miracle in capturing Rozhdestvensky . . . as Chief Conductor of the BBC Symphony. By far the finest Russian conductor of our time, he will work for up to three months a year in Britain; and he will remain a Soviet citizen. . . .

The Sunday Times reported the comment of one violinist: 'He conducts with his face . . . He might not have a strong beat, but you know exactly what he wants just by the twitch of an eyebrow.' A programme on Radio 3, introduced by John Warrack, told listeners of 'The Art of Gennadi Rozhdestvensky', using Russian recordings. Warrack played some of Stravinsky's *The Soldier's Tale* and said that

> like Stravinsky, Gennadi Rozhdestvensky is an international musician with deep Russian roots; unlike him, he is not becoming an exile in leaving Russia. There is no fear that, as in *The Soldier's Tale* which he was conducting there, frontiers are closed or any risks are involved in crossing the wrong ones. He is the first Soviet conductor of whom it can truly be said that he is, musically, also a citizen of the world.

And in the same programme, Yehudi Menuhin said:

> I am delighted that we have this intermingling of musical cultures. I have always felt that the English have so much to give in the way of style and

initiative which other orchestras simply don't have, to that extent. Orchestras that are *drilled*, like those that Rozhdestvensky has had, are certainly
superb instruments and wonderful machines: but he will find in London, as
he has already found, a quality which is nowhere else. . . .

The Russian tradition of music-making . . . has been influenced by German conductors, with a tremendous discipline and seriousness. They are
still, in that respect, refreshingly old-fashioned. They have a very strong
Germanic element which is always fighting with their passionate Russian
one. Their interpretations will vary from the most classical Tchaikovsky to
the most romantic: at their very best, like Rozhdestvensky, they will fuse the
two. They will create a synthesis which clears the music of all false senti-
mentality but gives it an incredible power. It is a very important quality –
that combination of the Slav and the Teutonic.

The omens were good, and by the day of the Prom concert, there was
much celebration of the new marriage. At the morning rehearsal expectations ran high, and Rozhdestvensky had already established a strong rapport
with the Orchestra. He was able to stand back from the performance, not
bothering to conduct while he listened to a point of balance, and then he
discussed it with leader Bela Dekany as the music went on. He gauged the
acoustics of the hall, shouted crisp directions across the Orchestra without
ever disturbing the performance. Not a moment of time was wasted; only the
crucial bits of the symphony were rehearsed, to give time for his wife to try
the piano. There were plenty of light moments in the rehearsal; but nothing
became out of hand. The players were visibly alert, and afterwards enthusiastic. Rozhdestvensky does not keep the Orchestra a minute longer than
necessary before dismissing them – on the night the result is a fresh, alert,
supremely responsive performance. He gave Mozart's Symphony No. 32,
Britten's *Diversions* for piano left hand (with his wife at the piano), and
Shostakovich's Fourth Symphony. The *Daily Telegraph* praised the
'stimulating, unhackneyed programme that augurs well for their future
collaboration'. The programme was televised, and Rozhdestvensky talked in
the interval to Michael Berkeley. Unusually, the concert drew not only
notices from the critics, but a delightful leader column in the *Guardian*
which conveyed some first impressions of the man:

In repose, Gennadi Rozhdestvensky looks a mild-mannered, unexceptional
man, roughly half way in appearance along a line drawn between Mr
Arthur Lowe of the Army Game* and Mr Gerald Kaufman of the Depart-

---

Recte: Dad's Army. *The Grauniad* triumphs again.

ment of Industry. In action, as thousands of television viewers will have discovered to their immense joy and pleasure when he conducted the BBC Symphony Orchestra for the first time at the Proms on Saturday, he is an altogether different kettle of caviare. For sheer elastic mobility, Mr Rozhdestvensky's face is in the Marcel Marceau class. But it isn't his face alone which he employs to communicate the emotions in the music to his happily-enslaved orchestra: there is the lift of an eyebrow here, the explosive flick of a finger there, the moment of total immobility, as the music flows on about him; even at one stage, as Shostakovich (whose Fourth Symphony he was conducting) interrupted a sentimental tune of his own with a sudden derisive snort in the brass, a schoolboy sticking-out of his tongue. And then there is the baton: to outward appearance, a conventional stick of wood, such as any conductor might carry – but transformed in Rozhdestvensky's hands now into a rapier, now into a whip, and next into a strange oscillating object hovering above his head, such as in country districts might send the timorous onlooker rushing to the constabulary, raving of Unidentified Objects . . . he promises to be a most exciting, even a magical, adornment to the British concert scene.

When Rozhdestvensky came to the Festival Hall for the first of his concerts in the 1978–9 Winter Season, he brought a challenging programme which displayed his current specialities: Russian music (two rare works by Prokofiev) and English music (Elgar's Second Symphony). The critics were unanimous in their praise. David Cairns wrote in *The Sunday Times*:

> It has taken the BBC more than two years to replace Rudolf Kempe . . . to judge by the playing of the Orchestra under Gennadi Rozhdestvensky . . . the time has been well spent and the patient search for a successor handsomely rewarded . . . I shall be surprised if Rozhdestvensky's advent does not herald a splendid epoch in the orchestra's fortunes.

Max Loppert in *The Financial Times* agreed:

> Gennadi Rozhdestvensky's first Festival Hall concert as chief conductor of the BBC Symphony Orchestra on Wednesday was a brilliant affair. The Orchestra's response to his masterly communicative powers is already appreciable; it has sloughed off the tired, lacklustre form of recent months, and is already – on the evidence of the two roof-raising Prokofiev works in the programme, and of the Elgar Second Symphony, which closed it – on the way to becoming a virtuoso ensemble of the best and most musical kind.
>   . . . Rozhdestvensky possesses, at the end of those simian arms, two of the wittiest, most precise, most expressive hands of any conductor before the

public; . . . his installation at the BBC is the very best thing to have happened to the London orchestral scene in a long time.

And Stephen Walsh in *The Observer* commented that

there's reason to hope that Gennadi Rozhdestvensky's tenure as chief conductor of the BBC Symphony Orchestra, which started last month and bore its first Festival Hall fruits on Wednesday, will bring a new and much needed sparkle to concert life on the South Bank.

Rozhdestvensky is not only in the front rank as conductor and musician. He has also managed to reach the age of 47 without being touched by the dead hand of media images or plated in the instant chromium of the A and R do-it-yourself pocket conductor factory, suppliers to the trade for too many years.

It is . . . an excellent appointment, and a notable feather in the BBC's already well-plumed cap.

Before the Festival Hall concert, Rozhdestvensky had travelled with the Orchestra to the Flanders Festival and Brussels at the end of September, giving Elgar's *Enigma Variations*, Tchaikovsky's Fifth Symphony, Bruckner's F minor Mass with the BBC Singers and the BBC Symphony Chorus. Two days after his first Festival Hall concert, he was in the Maida Vale Studios, conducting Brahms's First Serenade and then, on 18 October, he gave his first concert at St John's Smith Square. There was a large audience, even though Webern was on the programme. Once again Rozhdestvensky's neat, unflappable technique was in evidence; the precision and control seemed natural even when things went not quite right at the end of Webern's Op. 21 pieces. Some Schubert songs in Webern's arrangements, not previously heard here, were sung by Jill Gomez, and he ended with Schubert's First Symphony.

A few days later, I watched Rozhdestvensky at work in the Maida Vale Studios on his next Festival Hall concert. This was the first rehearsal of an unfamiliar work by an unfamiliar composer: Franz Schreker's *The Birthday of the Infanta*, based on Oscar Wilde's little story. The Orchestra was massive, its arrangement complicated, but through all the difficulties Rozhdestvensky preserved a perfect calm; when the moment came to begin, his huge, Henry Wood-like baton swept over the Orchestra, and that same feeling of absolute confidence which one had noticed at the Prom rehearsal swept through the hall. There were numerous innaccuracies to tidy up, puzzlement for the mandolines as to where their entry was, but Rozhdestvensky rehearsed with efficiency and restraint. There were few of the jovial pleasantries that had marked previous rehearsals: this was hard, solid work. But the atmosphere was one of concentration: the Orchestra was once more in the hands of a master craftsman, who knew exactly what he wanted.

To a surprising extent, there was little said in these early rehearsals about tone and interpretation. Rozhdestvensky seemed to assume that he would communicate what he wanted by simpler means – and indeed he did. The sound which the Orchestra immediately made in rehearsal for Stravinsky's *Petrushka* was quite unlike that it would have made in the same piece under Boulez: for Boulez the excitement would have derived from a lean, hard sound, whereas here it was a broad, full sound, controlled with a solid rhythmic edge which prevented the ensemble ever becoming uncertain. This Schreker/Stravinsky/Scriabin concert drew as good notices as the first. Desmond Shawe-Taylor noted in *The Sunday Times* that 'everything, so far, conspires to suggest that Mr Ponsonby has made a happy choice' of new conductor; reflecting on the season's programmes, he said that they 'have a distinctly fresh look; without being eccentric, they explore avenues long neglected by other conductors'.

Rozhdestvensky returned in December for another Festival Hall concert, in which his advocacy of English and Russian music was again evident. The Russian part of the programme, Arvo Pärt's *Cantus to the memory of Benjamin Britten*, unfortunately did not materialise, as the corrected orchestral parts failed to arrive from Russia. Hugh Wood's *Scenes from Comus* was a notable revival of a piece which was generally acknowledged to be among the finest of Glock's commissions for the Proms. Then to Brighton, a town Rozhdestvensky loves, where he was able to spend a free day in between two concerts. In the first programme was Prokofiev's Fifth Symphony and Tchaikovsky's Fourth; in the second, an adventurous selection of small-scale pieces which he repeated in St John's Smith Square the following night – Kurt Weill's Violin Concerto (with wind instruments), played by Erich Gruenberg; Hindemith's Sinfonietta in E; and Grieg's Holberg Suite. Of the Smith Square concert, the *Daily Telegraph* wrote:

> Rozhdestvensky is proving a stimulus to the BBC Symphony Orchestra in more than one way. The improvement in standards of playing is already a matter of common knowledge, and so is the opening to the East he has brought about in his choice of programmes . . . an exuberant, virtuoso performance . . .

In the studio he recorded Rachmaninov's First Symphony, and then travelled to Bedford for a Prokofiev–Glazunov–Rachmaninov programme with Iona Brown. In St John's just before Christmas, he conducted Berlioz's

L'Enfance du Christ, a concert which failed to be broadcast on Radio 3 because it unluckily coincided with a very shortlived strike, over a pay settlement, by BBC employees. The performance was revived in the 1980 Proms, this time in Westminster Cathedral.

Rozhdestvensky's next period with the Orchestra, in March and April 1979, was devoted to a further exploration of Prokofiev and Shostakovich, including British premières of works by both composers. Elgar's First Symphony was added to a growing list of major twentieth-century British works which he conducted; later in that visit was to come Walton's Symphony. These performances raised controversy, in much the same way that Toscanini's readings of Elgar caused controversy in the thirties: criticised by those well acquainted with the works' performing tradition in this country, they were heard as powerful and freshly-conceived interpretations by other listeners. Shostakovich provided the whole programme for Rozhdestvensky's Festival Hall concert in this period: the dour, late *Suite on verses of Michelangelo* in its orchestral version, the Second Violin Concerto and the Overture *Columbus*.

Around these successes the BBC's Festival Hall series seemed to gather strength and character in 1978–9. There was a half-Lutoslawski concert with the composer conducting his Concerto for Orchestra; Charles Mackerras in an Eastern European programme of Dvořák, Janáček, Bartók and Kodály, and in an English programme of Musgrave, Walton and Holst. Foreign guests included Kurt Sanderling and Hans Vonk. In a major concert of the season, David Atherton gave the first European performance of Elliott Carter's Symphony of Three Orchestras, an American bicentennial commission which should have reached England earlier. This masterly 15-minute score was recorded by the Orchestra two days before in the studio, and then repeated at the Proms. It was complemented by a revival of Tippett's *The Vision of St Augustine*. The season's success was sealed by the welcome return of Boulez, reviving Debussy's *Le Martyre de Saint-Sébastien* (which seems to appear regularly in the Symphony Orchestra's programmes every ten or twenty years) alongside Berlioz's extraordinary *Tristia* and Debussy's *Le jet d'eau*.

1979–80

Rozhdestvensky returned to the Orchestra at the start of the 1979–80 season. The season was delayed – by thirty-five minutes, to be precise. Rozhdestvensky's complete performance of Tchaikovsky's ballet *The Sleeping Beauty* was held up pending the arrival of a trombonist (who had been caught in a traffic jam). The concert was just about to be cancelled when he arrived, and one of the most notable performances of the collaboration so far took place (it had been recorded the previous week, and the recording was released to mark the Orchestra's fiftieth anniversary). *The Financial Times* wrote that 'since Boulez's departure from the BBC Symphony Orchestra, it has needed a conductor no less radical, but warmer-hearted, less narrowly tuned, to re-establish Tchaikovsky without snide condescension in the Orchestra's repertory. And who better than Gennadi Rozhdestvensky?' And the *Guardian* reported that 'there was . . . a feeling in the air that the players welcomed this holiday from the normal symphonic round. For the music-lover who has become inured to hearing the great ballet scores chopped about, distorted in speeds, under-rehearsed and conducted by mediocrities, it was an evening of unmixed pleasure.'

Rozhdestvensky's advocacy of English music led him to revive Vaughan Williams' *Sancta Civitas* on 21 November: a work rarely heard in London. 'Mr Rozhdestvensky controlled it quite beautifully,' wrote *The Times*. As Edward Greenfield reported in the *Guardian*, 'What a welcome contrast he presents to Pierre Boulez on this particular point, a conductor of the BBC Symphony Orchestra who actually has something to tell us about our own music.' He included Bridge's *Summer* and Britten's *Phaedra* with Sarah Walker at St John's. In *The Times* William Mann praised the performances: the Frank Bridge was 'exquisitely played, moulded with scrupulous finesse by the conductor, but sounded quite overwhelming'; the Britten was 'given a performance of riveting intensity'.

Rozhdestvensky contributed three more concerts to the BBC's Festival Hall season (plus an extra concert with the Orchestra for the Royal Philharmonic Society), including a 75th-birthday year account of Tippett's Second Symphony, and a new BBC commission from Rozhdestvensky's compatriot and friend Alfred Schnittke, the Symphony *St Florian*, which William Mann thought might be a suitable work for the Three Choirs Festival – it was not entirely clear whether this was a compliment.

The remainder of the Festival Hall winter season brought the two Chief Guest Conductors of the Orchestra into prominence. Michael Gielen was drawing increasingly appreciative notices from the Press. In *The Financial Times* Andrew Clements wrote:

Michael Gielen's contribution to the BBC Symphony Orchestra's concert profile is underplayed and underrated. As one of the Orchestra's chief guest conductors his capabilities in contemporary music and evident fondness for the dustier corners of the nineteenth-century German orchestral repertory give a valuable thrust to the BBC's middle-aged approach to its South Bank concerts. It's tempting to regard Gielen as a latter-day surrogate for the sadly missed Boulez; the parallel is not exact, though – Gielen lacks Boulez's moments of revelation and substitutes instead a reliability in the symphonic mainstream.

He gave three Festival Hall concerts (and another for the Royal Philharmonic 1980 Proms, a period disrupted by a Musicians' Union strike over proposed premièring a commission from Alexander Goehr as well as his own *Penta-phonie* and a new work for organ and orchestra by Peter Racine Fricker. Fricker's work was found disappointing, lacking in identity. But Goehr's choral work *Babylon the Great is Fallen*, written for the fiftieth anniversary celebration of the BBC Symphony Chorus, roused more respect, if not enthusiasm. In *The Times* Paul Griffiths said he thought the piece 'sounds to have enough monumental earnestness to establish for itself some sort of niche. It was perhaps intended to become a staple item for the big amateur choruses.' But he and other critics noted an academic flavour in the music which removed some of its immediacy.

John Pritchard was newly installed as a Chief Guest Conductor at the start of the 1979–80 season. A popular and respected figure on the international conducting scene, he had held no permanent post in England since he left Glyndebourne to take charge of the Cologne Opera. He has a wide range of musical sympathies and was willing to undertake challenging programmes: in the past he had premièred Tippett's opera *A Midsummer Marriage*, and as conductor of the Royal Liverpool Philharmonic had introduced a wide range of new music. He had premièred the work he now revived in the BBC's series: Peter Maxwell Davies' *Second Fantasia on an 'In nomine' of John Taverner*, which was performed alongside the Mozart *Requiem*. He also gave a Walton and Mahler programme in the Festival Hall as well as two programmes of English music in St John's Smith Square. Boulez had one concert in the series with his own *Éclat-multiples* (which was then taken to the Graz Festival). It had been planned to present the première of a further expanded version of the piece, but this was not ready: the nine-year-old version was heard again. Mark Elder revived a notable Prom success, John Buller's *Proença*, which was also recorded.

There was one other major change at the start of 1980. Rodney Friend, who had been leader of the London Philharmonic Orchestra and then concertmaster of the New York Philharmonic, returned to London as leader of the BBC Orchestra, sharing the work with Bela Dekany. Eli Goren, the much-valued co-leader, had left two years before to concentrate on solo work, teaching and chamber music. So the Orchestra moved towards the

1980 Proms, a period disrupted by a Musicians' Union strike over proposed BBC orchestral economies (see p. 432).

The fiftieth anniversary season of the BBC Symphony Orchestra opened in public, after a tour of Spain, a week before the anniversary date; it was planned to include concerts in public and in the studio by all the surviving Chief Conductors of the Orchestra (see Appendix E). There was a sole exception: Sir Adrian Boult, who had slipped away from the conductor's podium as unobtrusively as he had always mounted it, quietly declaring his intention not to be seen to decline in public.

At work in 1980

The pattern of the BBC Symphony Orchestra's work is now rather different from that which was inaugurated in 1930. The splitting of the Orchestra into different ensembles (a practice which was current throughout the 1930s and was revived in the Boulez period) has almost disappeared. There is no extensive light music content such as the first players had to tolerate. And the Orchestra is generally far less bound to the studio – there are more public concerts, more provincial visits and, especially, more foreign tours such as were unknown in the first five years of the Orchestra's existence. But the principles behind all that work are the same: to provide the widest possible range of orchestral music played to the highest standard, for broadcast audiences, and to give first-rate public concerts which explore a repertory that commercial bodies find it difficult to undertake.

The present-day administrative structure of the Orchestra may be characterised as byzantine, labyrinthine, bureaucratic or simply clumsy. But it works. It is the inevitable result of the BBC's expansion that the task that occupied a small handful of people in one BBC building in 1930 now occupies a huge number of people scattered throughout the BBC's empire. The organisational task is today far more complex than it was fifty years ago. There are two important centres of activity: the Orchestra's own premises at the BBC's Maida Vale Studios, and the BBC Music Division offices at Yalding House in Great Portland Street, near Broadcasting House. At Maida Vale, all the Orchestral Management staff have their offices. The General Manager of the Symphony Orchestra – at present William Relton, a former brass player and BBC producer in Manchester, still active as a conductor and adjudicator of brass bands – heads the department and guides the artistic policy of the Orchestra under Controller, Music. The Orchestral Manager, Lawrie Lea, deals with all matters of personnel and is responsible for the general administration of the orchestral players. Complex details of orchestral rehearsals, the requirements for players, extras and deputies, are dealt with by the orchestral assistant, Elizabeth Williams, and two staff responsible for players' bookings and contracts. Central to this operation is a huge card index showing the scoring of most of the works the Symphony Orchestra has played in its lifetime. This historic index dates back to the time when Henry Wood's Concert Manager, W. W. Thompson, first joined the BBC, when the Corporation took over the Proms and before the Symphony Orchestra was even founded. It includes many details of conductors' special preferences, of decisions made in the past because of stage-space, halls, and so on. Does Boulez use off-stage brass in Stravinsky's *Firebird*? Did Wood double the wind in Beethoven 8? Did Boult use a second trumpet here, or a third trombone there? Such *minutiae* can often be established from this index. Charts of orchestral players' work dominate the walls in this office; records of past performances line the shelves and disappear back into a musty cupboard. (The older records have recently been transferred to BBC Written Archives.) Constant contact with individual players, the issuing of work schedules and the careful planning of rehearsals are the basis of this work – making sure that the orchestral machine functions efficiently and humanely.

Maida Vale also houses the Symphony Orchestra librarians and the orchestral porters, on whom the entire responsibility of the Orchestra's stage-setting and instrument transport depends. Central to this operation until his recent retirement was Bill Edwards, who joined the BBC at Savoy Hill when he was fifteen and was with them, except for the war years, all his working life. His memory goes back through every Chief Conductor and most players in the Orchestra; everyone, from Pierre Boulez down, has praised him as the man who kept the Orchestra functioning on tour, who made sure that players are there to begin rehearsals and on stage in time for concerts – and who always did it with a smile. He is, with Sidonie Goossens and Sir Adrian Boult, one of the central surviving personalities of the Orchestra's history.

In Yalding House, the public concerts and the broadcasting arrangements for studio concerts are co-ordinated. Concerts Management department works under Controller, Music, and is answerable to the General Manager of the Symphony Orchestra as part of his Symphony Orchestra unit. This department is headed jointly by Concerts Organiser (until recently Freda Grove), who is responsible for all matters of contact with outside bodies, booking halls, arranging concert details of tours and provincial visits; and by Concerts Manager, Christopher Samuelson, who works closely with the Controller on all details of programmes and artists for the Symphony Orchestra's winter season and Promenade Concerts. Staff in this department also includes an assistant who plans rehearsal schedules for public concerts in collaboration with Orchestral Management, and is a point of contact for outside soloists and conductors. A finance assistant works under Concerts Organiser and keeps records of all the financial transactions, the budgeting and accounting of each public concert or series. She deals also with the issue of concert tickets to artists, the press and BBC officials.

Formerly under the Symphony Orchestra, but now part of Music Information Unit, the printed programmes and publicity for all BBC public concerts including the Proms are prepared – now using an IBM computer typesetter with an extensive memory bank. The BBC's collection of programme notes is authoritative and probably unrivalled. The task of commissioning, editing and updating them has traditionally fallen to the Controller of Music's chief assistant: first Gerald Abraham, then Lionel Salter, and Stephen Plaistow; now Guy Protheroe, Music Presentation Editor, has that task. Prom and winter season programmes are kept, in bound volumes, in Concerts Management; they are meticulously corrected with last-minute changes, and form an invaluable reference tool both for information on pieces of music and for details of the BBC's performances.

There are many other necessary collaborations: between the Controller of Music, the General Manager of the Symphony Orchestra and the Controller of Radio 3, on whose network the vast majority of the BBC Symphony Orchestra's output is broadcast; between departmental heads under the Deputy Managing Director, Radio, to ensure that the output is balanced; between the orchestral planners in the BBC's regional centres, to prevent excessive duplication of material; between orchestral management and Programme Contracts; between instrument hirers, studio bookings clerks, librarians, and countless indispensable secretaries.

In the studio

Most of the Orchestra's rehearsals and studio performances still take place in the BBC's Maida Vale Studios, the converted ice rink in Delaware Road, near Warwick Avenue that the Orchestra first occupied in 1934. Its largest studio, Maida Vale I, is still not ideal, though its lighting, ventilation and seating have been improved. (The most recent replacement, in 1980, was the roof of the building, which was leaking heavily into some of the offices and studios. At a cost of £120,000 it was completely replaced by a steel roof.) But it is a regular, happily-tolerated home for the Orchestra, with its own canteen; other orchestras in London do not operate under such conditions of stability. Studio recordings take place under the experienced control of the BBC's senior music studio managers. They are responsible for the balancing, taping and all technical aspects of the session, and their comments on the end result may influence the time and day when the programme is broadcast. The atmosphere of a public performance is always maintained: often an audience is present; but even when there is no audience in the studio, works are played through complete. Musicians' Union regulations at present insist that the 'recording' part of a session is carefully distinguished from the 'rehearsal' section. Retakes are sometimes necessary, but are generally discouraged. There is no extensive doctoring and editing of BBC Symphony Orchestra studio performances such as a record company would expect to undertake: the flavour of a continuous performance is thought most important. When an audience is in the studio, an announcer from Radio 3 or 4's Presentation Department will introduce the programme; at other times, the music alone is recorded and is provided with introductory material when it is broadcast.

In recent years, the live broadcasting of the Orchestra has been entirely restricted to its public concerts. (Even some of these, with starting times inconvenient to the radio networks, have been given 'delayed broadcasts' later on the same evening: the early evening series at St John's Smith Square was treated in this way.) Gone are the fixed points of the week when the radio audience could reliably expect to hear a BBC Symphony Orchestra studio concert. Programmes are now slotted in where they suit the radio schedules and the taste of the planners; some studio recordings wait many months before they are scheduled to be broadcast. This, it can be argued, is a necessary result of the crowded, diverse programmes on Radio 3, but it has unfortunate results for the Orchestra: the attention of the public is not focused on a major part of its work (some in the BBC would say the fundamental part of its work) and its adventurous, wide-ranging programmes in the studio are barely noticed. This increases the feeling of routine that some of the players feel in this section of their work; they may never notice when or whether a particular studio concert reaches the public. If Orchestral and Radio 3 schedules would permit one regular live broadcast from the studio, and the firm placing of other programmes within a month of recording, at a fixed time of the week, much might be done to give the Symphony Orchestra more of the prominence it deserves in the BBC's output.

In public

Public concerts are the most visible aspect of the Orchestra's work, yet there is much here which is scarcely obvious to the public eye. The broadcast is supervised by one member of the Concerts Management department; on complex occasions, one of Music Division's producers may take this responsibility (as happened frequently during the Round House series, and at non-Albert Hall Prom concerts). He must co-ordinate the announcer with the artists, warn the studio of unexpectedly short or long timings which will cause the programme to over-run or under-run, and ensure that conductors enter at the right moment. He has to take the difficult decisions: should we go on with the concert even though the second clarinet is not here? How long can we let the interval over-run? Do we cancel the concert or can we change the programme? What happens when a soloist collapses?

To the announcer falls the central task of keeping the listener linked to the public concert audience. He has, it is hoped, all the relevant information on performers and music; he has to draw it together into a coherent introduction; he must fill in if the artists are late appearing, or rapidly adjust his material if they arrive early. He must give something of a sense of the atmosphere of the occasion to bring it alive to the listener. Radio 3's announcers, headed by Presentation Editor Cormac Rigby, have forged close links with the public and are well-known, respected figures: their distinctive style gives a special character to the Symphony Orchestra's broadcast output.

Problems ahead

What are some of the tasks facing the BBC Symphony Orchestra as it enters its second half-century? Essentially they are those that have preoccupied it since the end of the war: to provide both a special identity for its public concerts, and a varied and satisfying life for its players in the face of growing pressures. These pressures come both from the framework of concert life in London, and from the BBC's economic problems. In its central concert season, that given in the Festival Hall, the Orchestra must still compete on unequal terms with the four public symphony orchestras whose motivation is, primarily, that of survival. Because the BBC opts out of the battle to programme all the popular orchestral works with star artists on the South Bank, it inevitably loses audiences. Ideally, it should establish its series so that it does not appear to be in competition with the London Symphony, London Philharmonic, Philharmonia and Royal Philharmonic concerts. But a move to any other less conventional London venue, such as the Royal Albert Hall or the Coliseum, would risk reducing the audience still further. More hopeful is the opening of the Barbican Concert Hall, where the BBC Orchestra will make some appearances in the Hall's inaugural season; this may help to relieve pressure on the South Bank and change the balance of orchestral concert-giving. But it remains to be seen how long it will take for the hall to build up a new audience.

The depressing effect that the Royal Festival Hall's policy – or rather, non-policy, since its only aim has been to avoid too frequent repetition of popular works – has had on London's orchestral programmes has been often criticised. With too many orchestras competing for the same audience, the results are inevitably unsatisfactory. But every effort to alter this situation has met with justified opposition from the four public orchestras, which feel that they have just enough work to survive, and that they ought to be funded on the more generous level of their continental counterparts. As mentioned above (p. 354), in 1970 the Peacock Report suggested that two rather than four London orchestras should receive special funding; but this radical proposal was rejected by the Arts Council when it published the report. At the end of the decade, a renewed approach from the public orchestras to the Arts Council for a higher level of funding gave rise to an even more radical proposal, which originated from the Council's Music Advisory Panel: that one of the four orchestras be established on a full-time contract basis (while the other three were maintained at their present level of subsidy) enabling it to develop a more permanent membership, rehearse contemporary music, and generally to programme adventurous, not necessarily commercial, works. None of the orchestras was happy with the loss of self-governing status and control over artistic policy that the move would have necessitated; in the event, a cutback in the Arts Council grant removed any hope that the Treasury would provide the extra money – estimated at well over £1 million – to establish such a contract orchestra.

The irony of this proposal was that the BBC Symphony Orchestra, in 1930, had been just such a 'million-pound orchestra' – it had emerged from an unsatisfactory freelance orchestral world in London offering contracts with good salaries, a solid year-long basis of work, and challenging programmes. And it had attracted the best players. But the apparatus of that contracted orchestra had to be to some extent dismantled in the 1960s in order to compete with the flourishing freelance scene and to attract again the liveliest young players into the Orchestra. Now, in 1980, it was clear that it would take a massive injection of funds to establish a contract orchestra in London which was clearly superior to its competitors: the BBC had the framework for such a development, but not the funds.

Money problems

Funds, income and output became a pressing problem for the BBC. Throughout the 1970s, the emphasis within BBC management was on the production of the BBC Symphony Orchestra, not on its special repertoire or its standard. As in the bleak days after the Second World War, output was

considered before excellence of performance. As a result of McKinsey &
Co's analysis of music output during its investigation into the BBC, an
agreed breakdown of Radio 3 output was drawn up in 1969. This categorised
precisely the various departmental contributions to the network – drama,
talks, chamber music, orchestral music, and so on – and quantified them in
broadcast hours. This quota was controlled by Director of Programmes,
Radio; Gerard Mansell, who had chaired the BBC Policy Study Group, was
the first holder of this post in 1970. The quota system still exists, and is controlled by the Deputy Managing Director, Radio. It is regularly modified in
collaboration with department heads, to meet the changing needs and the
changing availability of broadcast hours.

The Symphony Orchestra's contribution to Radio 3 has remained fairly
stable: it was estimated in 1970 as seventy-four concerts annually, totalling
some 111 hours of broadcast time. This estimate specifically allowed for such
major events as performances of Boulez's *Pli selon pli*, Wagner's *Tristan und
Isolde* and Berlioz's *Requiem* (these three projects in the season before the
quota was drawn up had absorbed some thirty-five rehearsal sessions, the
equivalent of several broadcast concerts). But when finalised in 1972, the
quota expected seventy-nine concerts a year, around 115 hours. This
excluded the Symphony Orchestra's major contribution to the Prom season
(usually around twenty-five concerts) and its non-broadcast concerts on
tour. As early as the 1972–3 season, the Orchestra fell behind its quota by
some ten hours, because of extra rehearsals demanded by Boulez's concerts.
This provoked complaints from Radio management – 'I am very concerned
at this large shortfall in broadcasting return from our most costly orchestra' –
in spite of the fact that the events thus prepared had a prestige importance
out of all proportion to the time they absorbed. It was hoped that the
splitting of the Orchestra for the Round House and St John's concerts when
Boulez took over in 1971–2 would lead to increased output, but this proved
to be exaggerated. Not even Boulez, it was noted, could hope to predict the
amount of rehearsal an as-yet-unwritten new work would demand.

Through the decade, the BBC Symphony Orchestra has in fact usually
maintained and sometimes surpassed its contribution to the Radio 3 quota:
121 hours in 1973–4; 117 hours in 1974–5; 103 hours in 1975–6; 129 hours
in 1976–7; and so on. And the radio planners have not always broadcast all
the available material in a given year, so that the Orchestra's representation
on the air has been less than its status would suggest that it ought to be. But
the fundamental conflict between quantity and quality of output has remained a central issue: it would be an easy task for the Symphony Orchestra
to satisfy the planners and accountants of the BBC by producing more pro-

grammes that contained uninteresting material and had been inadequately rehearsed. That, however, would run counter to the whole purpose of its fifty-year existence; a purpose which the musical administrators now have to maintain.

The concern of BBC management for the Corporation's orchestral economics is understandable, for the pressures here have been intense. Since the BBC had bowed to government and public pressure and had backed down on the proposals of *Broadcasting in the Seventies* to abolish a large number of orchestral jobs, it had to look for other ways of sharing the burden. In January 1976, Howard Newby, just appointed Managing Director, Radio, gave a BBC lecture in which he floated the possibility of outside collaboration in the costs of the orchestras. Mentioning that the BBC's twelve orchestras employed some 589 musicians, he said:

> It is a commitment greater than is required for the needs of broadcasting, and you may wonder whether that is entirely right. A different system could be imagined in which the BBC had fewer orchestras, or no orchestra at all, and spent the money (it would be about £2·8 million in the current financial year) on the four London symphony orchestras and the other orchestras outside London.

The position of the BBC Symphony Orchestra was never seriously threatened by these proposals, but in this sentence Newby had actually raised the possibility of its ceasing to exist. Later in the lecture, however, he declared:

> The BBC Symphony Orchestra in particular is free from the tyranny of the box office, and can in its studio and public concerts enlarge the understanding and appreciation of music. The appointment of Pierre Boulez as the principal conductor in 1971 was – in the words of Sir William Glock – as important for orchestral playing in this country as the engagement of Toscanini had been in the 1930s, and more important, of course, for the understanding of twentieth-century music. This is to honour musical tradition in a way no other organisation could – no other organisation is big enough, can plan ahead with as much confidence and, as a result, hold an enlightened balance between popular taste and the demands made by the art of music itself.

The central point of his talk, however, was this:

> There is no blinking the fact that the cost of the house orchestras is a significant proportion of the radio budget. It is, as I see it, too high. I should welcome any opportunity to share the financial responsibility in some way

consistent with the Charter and justify the sharing on the grounds that the orchestras represent a national as well as a broadcasting interest.

But little progress was made: the collaboration between the BBC and the Welsh Arts Council in support of the BBC Welsh Symphony Orchestra proved difficult to duplicate elsewhere. So the BBC reached the end of the 1970s, and the beginning of a new financial crisis, without the problem of its orchestral resources being alleviated in any way.

The result was obvious and painful. Drastic cuts were suddenly proposed as part of a large package of economies which planned to save £130 million: in February 1980 the winding-up of five orchestras was proposed – including the BBC Scottish Symphony Orchestra. This would save £500,000 a year, and represented an eight per cent cut in the BBC's expenditure on music. The Musicians' Union reacted fiercely to the loss of any jobs; even those who acknowledged that some orchestral jobs had to go were dismayed that the Scottish Broadcasting Council had chosen to axe its own orchestra. And so, on 16 May 1980, the Musicians' Union voted 5–1 to strike against the BBC, and on 1 June the members of the BBC Symphony Orchestra, in common with all musicians employed by the BBC, stopped work. The stage was set for bitter negotiations and a hard battle.

The issues raised by the dispute were wider than the immediate dismissals, though those were inhumane enough to shock many. Was the BBC now moving towards the abandonment of all orchestral employment, preferring to rely instead on whatever outside bodies and freelance groups could offer? The BBC claimed that the last licence fee increase set by the Government had been inadequate to cover the costs of the orchestras. Would a further inadequate increase in the future mean the end of more orchestras?

The 1980 Proms at once became a principal issue in the dispute. Radio's Managing Director, Aubrey Singer, maintained that the concerts were of 'less consequence than the music policy of the orchestras for the future', and made it clear that they would not take place if the dispute were not settled – and that no one else would be permitted to stage them. On 23 June, Sir Adrian Boult wrote to *The Times* to propose that the Proms should be heard in the Albert Hall, and recorded for broadcast after the dispute was settled. BBC management welcomed the suggestion, but the Musicians' Union rejected it.

Negotiations took place through the agency of ACAS, the Government's conciliation and arbitration service, but neither side was prepared to back down. Positions hardened, and a settlement seemed far away. There were lunchtime performances by striking musicians outside Broadcasting House

– I chanced on a fine account of Mozart's C minor Serenade by wind players from the Symphony Orchestra. The much-photographed picket lines included visits of support from Charles Groves, Lennox Berkeley, Geraint Evans, Norman Del Mar, Lady Barbirolli and Sidonie Goossens. Meanwhile extensive public interest in the dispute and the possibility of the cancellation of the Proms led to a debate in the House of Commons on Friday 27 June. Though MPs strongly voiced their feelings against the abolition of the BBC Scottish Symphony Orchestra in particular, too many of the suggested remedies – the abolition of Radio 1, BBC local radio, or the thinning of BBC administrative posts – were unlikely to be seriously contemplated by the BBC. And the Government held out no hope of a special licence fee increase to cover the situation: it merely emphasised the BBC's point that live music on the air would scarcely be reduced by the proposals.

On Friday 11 July the situation seemed beyond redemption. The BBC submitted a new set of proposals to the Musicians' Union, which included the setting-up of a Scottish Sinfonia of fifty-four players in place of the Scottish Symphony Orchestra. The Union rejected the alterations, saying they were merely 'cosmetic'. That evening, the Orchestra of the Royal Opera House Covent Garden gave a concert under the BBC Symphony Orchestra's former Chief Conductor Sir Colin Davis, in aid of the Union's hardship fund. The BBC cancelled the First Night of the Proms, and warned that more cancellations would have to follow. On 18 July 1980, for the first time in the history of the Proms, the First Night failed to take place. The BBC broadcast a gramophone recording of the programmed work, Elgar's *The Apostles*, while members of the BBC Symphony Orchestra staged at the Wembley Conference Centre a popular prom concert of Tchaikovsky and Berlioz. Sir Colin Davis conducted. Sir Adrian Boult sent a message of support. There was a small but enthusiastic audience of about 1000. But the twin substitutes for the first night of the Proms 1980 offered proof, if proof were needed, of how much the BBC and live musicians needed each other: apart, they could achieve little.

While the Musicians' Union proceeded with its plans for more Wembley Proms – engaging at least one conductor, Pierre Boulez, who had not been able to appear in the BBC's own season – negotiations were restarted at the House of Commons. A select committee set up as a result of the Commons debate reported with exceptional speed, and suggested that Lord Goodman be asked to mediate in the dispute. The BBC's Director-General, Sir Ian Trethowan, accepted the suggestion cautiously, adding that the negotiations should continue to be under the aegis of ACAS. When negotiations restarted, it was thought that they might arrive only at a compromise solution for the staging of the Proms: suggestions from the Arts Council and the Association for Business Sponsorship of the Arts were already being considered. But in fact Lord Goodman was able to take both sides back to the principles at stake behind the dispute. Within days, by the early hours of 24 July, the two sides had reached a solution to the whole issue. It was announced that the BBC would, as the Union had demanded, withdraw all the notices of dismissal to the orchestra members. The Northern and Midland Radio Orchestras would be retained until spring 1981, and then their members would be assured of a period of freelance employment; the BBC Scottish Symphony Orchestra would be saved, though the Scottish Radio Orchestra would go in its place. (The complications caused by this arrangement have yet to be resolved.)

The BBC Symphony Orchestra, which was not threatened by the dispute but was closely affected by it, ironically came out of the final agreement with a benefit: it was proposed that, subject to the next Government licence fee increase, its personnel would be increased to 110 players, bringing it close to its original strength in 1930. The Proms were quickly restored; only twenty concerts were lost; and the Symphony Orchestra began the delayed season on 7 August with a programme of Ravel, Messiaen and Mahler's Fourth Symphony, under its Chief Guest Conductor John Pritchard.

All this was scarcely a happy lead-in to the BBC's fiftieth anniversary season, for it raised the question: did the BBC still value its finest orchestra? Fortunately, the anniversary concert itself, held on 22 October, fifty years to the day since the inaugural concert, suggested that it did. The concert was televised and broadcast to a wide audience; it was attended by Prince and Princess Michael of Kent. George Howard had recently succeeded Sir Michael (now Lord) Swann as Chairman of the Board of Governors (an appointment greeted with delight in BBC musical circles, since his support of and interest in the Symphony Orchestra when a Governor of the BBC had always been considerable). At the concert he spoke appreciatively of the Orchestra's contribution to musical life, and looked forward to its next fifty years.

The concert's programme aptly summed up the Orchestra's commitment to twentieth-century music, both British and foreign, and highlighted the tastes of Chief Conductor Gennadi Rozhdestvensky: there was music by Vaughan Williams, Prokofiev and Stravinsky. During the concert, Sidonie Goossens, the one founder member who is still playing with the Orchestra, was fêted and presented with a gift from her colleagues (she was awarded the OBE in the 1981 New Year's Honours List). And during the next few days the critics in the national press added to the refrain of praise for the Orchestra's achievement: a fitting parallel to the acclaim the Orchestra received after its first concert in 1930.

> ... on Wednesday a great occasion was worthily celebrated. The Festival Hall was packed; the programme was appropriate; the performances glowed and glittered ... Such skill and enthusiasm, applied to countless new scores as well as to what are now standard classics, seemed to guarantee another fifty years of fruitful life to our indispensable BBC SO (Desmond Shawe-Taylor, *Sunday Times*).

> It was a time to enjoy and ponder the standard the orchestra has achieved under its present chief conductor, Gennadi Rozhdestvensky, and to reflect on the glories of the past half-century ... no orchestra has done so much for native music ... a reminder of the inestimable job the orchestra has done in bringing us new music from abroad ... proving their unrivalled experience in twentieth-century music (Paul Griffiths, *The Times*).

> ... an occasion of major importance ... with memories of the BBC's summer of discontent still green, the unique significance of the Orchestra in our musical life, as a living musical organism among so many musical fossils, has this year been so firmly underlined ... it was a splendid evening of music-making, a vivid demonstration of the Orchestra's current state of robust health ... concern with live and living music has always been the Orchestra's most valuable preoccupation (Max Loppert, *The Financial Times*).

The first fifty years were over; the next fifty have already begun.

Bibliography

A select list of books consulted

Bartók, Béla: *Letters*, edited and annotated by Janos Demeny (Faber, 1971)
Beecham, Sir Thomas: *A Mingled Chime* (Hutchinson, 1944)
Bliss, Sir Arthur: *As I Remember* (Faber, 1970)
Blom, Eric: *Music in England* (Penguin, 1942)
Blyth, Alan: *Colin Davis* (Ian Allan, 1972)
Boulez, Pierre: *Conversations with Célestin Deliège* (Eulenburg, 1976)
Boult, Sir Adrian: *My Own Trumpet* (Hamish Hamilton, 1973)
Briggs, Asa: *The History of Broadcasting in the United Kingdom*
    Vol. 1: *The Birth of Broadcasting* (OUP, 1961)
    Vol. 2: *The Golden Age of Wireless* (OUP, 1965)
    Vol. 3: *The War of Words* (OUP, 1970)
    Vol. 4: *Sound and Vision* (OUP, 1979)
Brook, Donald: *Conductors' Gallery* (Rockliffe, 1945)
Brymer, Jack: *From Where I Sit* (Cassell, 1979)
Burrows, A. R.: *The Story of Broadcasting* (Cassell, 1924)
Carner, Mosco: *Alban Berg* (Duckworth, 1975)
Chamier, J. Daniel: *Percy Pitt, of Covent Garden and the BBC* (Edward
    Arnold, 1938)
Chesterman, Robert (ed.): *Conversations with Conductors* (Robson, 1976)
Clark, Ronald: *Royal Albert Hall* (Hamish Hamilton, 1958)
Colles, H. C.: *Walford Davies* (OUP, 1942)
Cox, David: *The Henry Wood Proms* (BBC Publications, 1980)
Curran, Sir Charles: *A Seamless Robe: Broadcasting – Philosophy and
    Practice* (Collins, 1979)
Dorati, Antal: *Notes of Seven Decades* (Hodder & Stoughton, 1979)
Eckersley, Roger: *The BBC And All That* (Low, Marston, 1946)

Elkin, Robert: *Queen's Hall, 1893–1941* (Rider, 1944)
  Royal Philharmonic (Rider, 1947)
Foreman, Lewis (ed.): *British Music Now* (Paul Elek, 1975)
  Havergal Brian and the Performance of his Orchestral Music (Thames Publishing, 1976)
Foss, Hubert and Goodwin, Noël: *London Symphony* (Naldrett, 1954)
Griffiths, Paul: *Boulez* (OUP, 1978)
Hibberd, Stuart: '*This – is London . . .*' (Macdonald & Evans, 1950)
Howes, Frank: *Full Orchestra* (Secker & Warburg, 1942)
Jackson, Gerald: *First Flute* (Dent, 1968)
Jacobson, Bernard: *Conductors on Conducting* (Macdonald & Jane's, 1979)
Jefferson, Alan: *Sir Thomas Beecham: a Centenary Tribute* (Macdonald & Jane's, 1979)
Keller, Hans: *1975 (1984 minus 9)* (Dobson, 1977)
Kennedy, Michael: *The Hallé Tradition* (Manchester University Press. 1960)
  Barbirolli (Hart-Davis, 1971)
  Portrait of Elgar (OUP, 1968)
  The Works of Ralph Vaughan Williams (OUP, 1964)
Lutyens, Elisabeth: *A Goldfish Bowl* (Cassell, 1972)
Moore, Jerrold Northrop (ed.): *Music and Friends: Letters to Sir Adrian Boult* (Hamish Hamilton, 1979)
Pearton, Maurice: *The London Symphony Orchestra at 70* (Gollancz, 1974)
Pettitt, Stephen: *Dennis Brain: a Biography* (Hale, 1976)
Peyser, Joan: *Boulez: Composer, Conductor, Enigma* (Cassell, 1977)
Pirie, Peter J.: *The English Musical Renaissance* (Gollancz, 1979)
Pound, Reginald: *Sir Henry Wood* (Cassell, 1969)
Previn, André (ed.): *Orchestra* (Macdonald & Jane's, 1979)
Reich, Willi: *Schoenberg: A Critical Biography* (Longman, 1971)
Reid, Charles: *John Barbirolli* (Hamish Hamilton, 1971)
  Thomas Beecham: An Independent Biography (Gollancz, 1961)
  Malcolm Sargent: (Hamish Hamilton, 9th ed. 1973)
Reith, J. C. W.: *Into the Wind* (Hodder & Stoughton, 1949)
Ronald, Sir Landon: *Myself and Others* (Low, Marston, 1931)
Russell, Thomas: *Philharmonic Decade* (Hutchinson, 1945)
  Philharmonic Project (Hutchinson, 1952)
Salter, Lionel: 'BBC', in Oscar Thompson, *International Cyclopedia of Music and Musicians*, (Dent, 10th ed. 1975)
Scholes, Percy: *Everybody's Guide to Broadcast Music* (OUP/Hodder, 1925)
Scott-Sutherland, Colin: *Arnold Bax* (Dent, 1973)

Seaman, L. C. B.: *Post-Victorian Britain, 1902–51* (Methuen, 1966)

Shead, Richard: *Constant Lambert: His Life, his Music and his Friends* (Simon Publications, 1973)

Shore, Bernard: *The Orchestra Speaks* (Longmans, Green, 1938)

Skelton, Geoffrey: *Paul Hindemith* (Gollancz, 1975)

Stuart, Charles (ed.): *The Reith Diaries* (Collins, 1975)

Vaughan Williams, Ursula: *Ralph Vaughan Williams: A Biography* (OUP, 1964)

Walter, Bruno: *Of Music and Music-making* (Faber, 1961)

Wood, Sir Henry J.: *My Life of Music* (Gollancz, 1938)

Young, Percy: *A History of British Music* (Benn, 1967)

Letters to Edward Clark are preserved in the British Library's Department of Manuscripts, Add. 52256 and 52257.

There are fuller bibliographies of material concerning broadcasting in the volumes of Asa Briggs's *History of Broadcasting in the United Kingdom*.

APPENDIX A
Personalia

This outline list of relevant BBC personnel is intended as a guide to the changing posts of those mentioned in the text. It is neither complete, nor precisely faithful to the many redesignations or job titles and responsibilities which frequently occur in the BBC. For full details, reference should be made to the bi-annual staff lists of the BBC.

(a) BBC Administration

Director-General

Sir John Reith	1927–38
F. W. Ogilvie	1938–42
R. W. Foot	1942–4
Sir Cecil Graves	1942–3
W. J. Haley	1944–52
Sir Ian Jacob	1952–9
Sir Hugh Greene	1960–9
Sir Charles Curran	1969–77
Sir Ian Trethowan	1977–

Controller (Programmes)

Roger Eckersley	1924–34
Cecil Graves	1934–8
Basil Nicolls	1938–44
Lindsay Wellington	1944–5

Senior Controller

Basil Nicolls	1944–8

Director of Sound Broadcasting

Basil Nicolls	1948–52
Lindsay Wellington	1952–63
Frank Gillard	1963–8

Managing Director, Radio

Frank Gillard	1969–70
Ian Trethowan	1970–5
Howard Newby	1976–8
Aubrey Singer	1978–

Assistant Controller, Programmes

Roger Eckersley	1935–6
Lindsay Wellington	1936–42
Richard Howgill	1942–5

Director of Programmes, Radio
(Deputy Managing Director, Radio)

Richard Marriott	1959–70
Gerard Mansell	1970–1
Howard Newby	1971–5
Douglas Muggeridge	1975–80
Charles McLelland	1980–

Controller, Entertainment

Roger Eckersley	1934–5
Richard Howgill	1945–52
Michael Standing	1952–9

Controller, Home Service
(Radio 4 from 1970)

Lindsay Wellington	1945–52
Andrew Stewart	1953–7
Ronald Lewin*	1960–5
Gerard Mansell*	1965–9
Anthony Whitby	1969–75
Clare Lawson Dick	1975–6
Ian McIntyre	1976–8
Monica Sims	1978–

Controller, Third Programme
(Radio 3 from 1970)

George Barnes	1946–8
Harman Grisewood	1948–52
John Morris	1953–8
Howard Newby	1958–71
Stephen Hearst*	1972–8
Ian McIntyre	1978–

---

* *Also responsible for the*
Music Programme, 1963–9

440

THE BBC SYMPHONY ORCHESTRA

(b) Music Department
(from 1952, Music Division)

Director of Music
Percy Pitt	1924–30
Adrian Boult	1930–42
Arthur Bliss	1942–4
Victor Hely-Hutchinson	1944–6
Kenneth Wright (Acting)	1946–8

Head of Music
Sir Steuart Wilson	1948–50
Herbert Murrill	1950–2

Controller, Music
Richard Howgill	1952–9
William Glock	1959–72
Robert Ponsonby	1972–

Assistant Director of Music
Owen Mase	1931–3
Aylmer Buesst	1933–5
Kenneth Wright	1935–7

Deputy Director of Music
Dr Reginald Thatcher	1937–43

Assistant Director (Head) of Music
Herbert Murrill	1946–50

Assistant Controller, Music
Frank Wade	1953–5
Gerald Abraham	1962–7
Lionel Salter	1967–74

Chief Assistant to Controller, Music
Stephen Plaistow	1974–79
Peter Dodd	1979–

Programme planners
Edward Clark	1927–36
Julian Herbage	1927–46

Music Department members
Owen Mase	1930s
Kenneth Wright	1930s

Music assistants between 1946 and 1952
Eric Warr	Basil Lam
Anthony Lewis	Basil Douglas
Denis Stevens	Desmond Osland
John Lowe	Edward Lockspeiser
Lennox Berkeley	Robert Collet

Head of Music Programmes, Radio
Maurice Johnstone	1952–60
Eric Warr (*Assistant Head*)	1960–6
Peter Gould	1971–5

Eleanor Warren	1975–7
Ernest Warburton	1977–

Third Programme Music Organiser
Leonard Isaacs	1950–4
Peter Crossley-Holland	1954–60

Home Service Music Organiser
Peter Crossley-Holland	1950–4
Leonard Isaacs	1954–60

Music Programmes Organiser
Herbert Murrill	1942–6
Leonard Isaacs	1946–50
Frank Wade	1951–3
Desmond Osland	1953–4
Harry Croft-Jackson	1955–6

Producer, BBC Symphony Orchestra programmes
Michael Whewell	1953–60
John Douglas Todd	1960–70

Chief Assistant, Orchestral & Choral
Leonard Isaacs	1960–4
Hans Keller	1964–72

Chief Assistant, Chamber Music & Recitals
Hans Keller	1960–4
Peter Gould	1964–71

Chief Producers, Music Division
Leo Black	1971–
Eleanor Warren	1971–6
Paul Hamburger	1978–

Chief Assistant, New Music
Hans Keller	1972–9

Chief Producer, Contemporary Music
Stephen Plaistow	1979–

(c) BBC Symphony Orchestra

Chief Conductor
(no appointment)	1930–1
Sir Adrian Boult	1931–50
Sir Malcolm Sargent	1950–7
Rudolf Schwarz	1957–62
(vacant)	1962–3
Antal Dorati	1963–6
(vacant)	1966–7
Colin Davis	1967–71
Pierre Boulez	1971–5
Rudolf Kempe	1975–6

(vacant)	1976–8	Dorothy Wood	1930–63
Gennadi Rozhdestvensky	1978–	Freda Grove	1955–63
Assistant Conductor		*Assistant Orchestral Manager*	
Clarence Raybould	1936–45	W. G. Paston	1950–63
Stanford Robinson	1946–8	*General Manager, Symphony Orchestra*	
Chief Guest Conductor		Paul Huband	1963–75
Colin Davis	1971–6	William Relton	1975–
Pierre Boulez	1975–7	*Orchestral Manager*	
Charles Mackerras	1976–8	W. G. Paston	1963–70
Michael Gielen	1977–	William Relton	1970–5
John Pritchard	1978–	Lawrie Lea	1975–
Leader(s)		*Concerts Organiser*	
Arthur Catterall	1930–6	Freda Grove	1964–80
Paul Beard	1936–62	Daphne Smith	1980–
Hugh Maguire	1962–7	*Concerts Manager*	
Trevor Williams	1967	Christopher Samuelson	1966–
Hugh Bean	1967–9	*Assistant (Artists and Orchestral)*	
Eli Goren	1968–77	Edgar Mays	1934–70
Bela Dekany	1969–	William Edwards	1970–9
Rodney Friend	1980–	*Chief Orchestral Porter*	
Concerts Manager		William Fussell	1930s–51
W. W. Thompson	1927–54	William Edwards	1951–70
Orchestral Manager		*Orchestral Supervisor*	
Richard Pratt	1930–46	Myra Thomas	1978
George Willoughby	1946–54	Jamie Pearson	1979–
Concerts and Orchestral Manager		*Orchestral Assistant*	
George Willoughby	1954–63	Elizabeth Walker	1966–74
Assistant Concerts Manager		Elizabeth Williams	1974–
R. G. Paterson	1940–61		

Members of the BBC Symphony Orchestra to 22 October 1980

This includes all players listed in BBC records as contracted to the Orchestra during its first fifty years; it excludes all temporary players and players seconded from the other BBC orchestras during World War II. Corrections and further information are welcome. The BBC contracts of some original members began before 1930; the earlier dates are shown. Contracts for the full-time BBC Symphony Orchestra began before the 1930 Promenade Concerts season, in July 1930, when the Orchestra first met to rehearse. The complete Orchestra did not appear in public until 22 October 1930.

ALEXANDRA, J. P. *Horn*	1933–7	BAILEY, Irene *Violin*	18.8.46–26.4.47
ALKER, John *Bassoon*	20.9.64–5.7.65	BAKER, Julian *Horn*	11.1.70–8.1.77
ALLEN, Eric *Percussion*	20.12.59–21.9.63	BARLOW, Frances *Violin*	15.10.67–
ALMGILL, Frank *Flute*	1923–25.9.45	BARLOW, Harry *Tuba*	27.7.30–1932
ANDERSON, Angus *Violin*	5.1.69–19.11.72	BARNES, Arthur *Horn*	21.8.30–19.3.43
ANDERSON, James *Tuba*	27.2.72–17.10.78	BARNES, Michael *Tuba*	16.3.69–10.10.71
ANDERSON, John *Oboe*	22.8.76–	BARR, Herbert *Trumpet*	27.7.30–15.7.50
ANDREWS, Bernard *Violin*	20.7.38–28.7.64	BATES, Doris *Violin*	29.3.28–16.7.49
ARNOLD, Malcolm *Trumpet*	23.9.45–16.1.46	BEAN, Hugh *Leader*	12.11.67–11.11.69
ASHCROFT, Anne *Violin*	31.12.74–	BEARD, John *Viola*	28.12.47–2.2.63
BAILEY, Enid *Violin*	20.7.30–18.12.47	BEARD, Paul *Leader*	4.10.36–15.9.62

BEATTIE, Cecil *Cello*   20.7.30–15.6.63
BEERS, Bernard *Cello*   1930–1938
BENDER, Charles *Timpani*   1930–1937
BENTLEY, Lionel *Violin*   4.8.35–3.5.46
BERCOVITCH, Jack *Violin*   26.7.36–6.4.63
BESZNAK, L. R. *Violin*   1935–1940
BIRD, Mary *Violin*   1.7.79–
BIRKS, Heather *Viola*   1.7.79–
BLACKFORD, G. *Cello*   1930–1935
BLECH, Harry *Violin*   1930–1936
BLUNDELL, William *Flute*   21.10.46–5.1.52
BODDINGTON, Robert *Flute*   5.10.32–21.9.35
                                          & 20.7.37–28.3.53
BOR, Samuel *Violin*   20.7.30–21.9.46
BOYCE, John *Cello*   19.4.66–6.8.77
BRADBURY, Colin *Clarinet*   18.9.60–
BRADLEY, Francis *Horn*   1934–1937
BRADSHAW, Graham *Cello*   2.7.78–
BRADSHAW, Howard *Timpani*
                                          14.12.68–1.5.71
BRADY, Patricia *Timpani & Percussion*
                                          14.6.64–1.7.67
BRAHAM, Editha *Violin*   20.7.30–1933
BRAIN, Aubrey *Horn*   7.10.28–11.12.45
                                          & 21.1.51–1.8.51
BRAY, Eric *Viola*   20.7.30–31.10.46
BRETT, Audrey *Violin*   29.3.70–
BRETT, Maurice *Violin*   29.3.70–
BREWER, Charles *Tuba*   10.4.38–8.7.64
BRIGGS, Roger *Cello*   20.7.30–7.9.46
                                          & 29.1.61–14.11.70
BRINNEN, Gerald *Double Bass* 20.5.56–
BRODIE, Janice *Cello*   6.4.80–
BROWN, Jack *Violin*   14.8.49–15.6.63
BROWN, Norah *Viola*   18.8.46–26.4.47
BROWNE, Geoffrey *Oboe*   3.10.67–3.7.71
BROWNE, L. *Violin*   20.7.30–1945
BRYANT, Raymond *Horn*   31.12.50–16.5.53
BRYMER, Jack *Clarinet*   15.9.63–14.3.72
BUNBURY, Zingra *Viola*   13.4.52–26.6.62
BURGESS, Norman *Trumpet*   30.3.74–
BURNESS, John *Bassoon*   17.10.65–
BURROWS, V. *Horn*   27.7.30–1932
BURTON, Daniel *Double Bass* 20.7.30–26.7.47
BUTLER, Alfred *Contra-Bassoon*
                                          20.7.31–19.9.64
BUTT, David *Flute*   17.7.60–
BUTTERWORTH, John *Horn*   11.12.77–
BUXTON, Paul *Violin*   22.10.67–28.10.79
CAMDEN, Archie *Bassoon*   20.7.33–30.4.46
CAPRARA, Ennio *Violin*   20.7.30–28.12.47
CARRELL, Norman *Viola*   20.7.30–4.2.48

CASS, William *Violin*   20.7.30–17.9.60
CASTALDINI, Joseph *Bassoon*   9.8.36–19.9.53
CATTERALL, Arthur *Leader*   20.7.30–19.7.36
CAWS, Jennifer *Oboe*   13.7.80–
CHAPMAN, Robin *Flute*   16.9.62–1.4.70
CHESTERMAN, Edmund *Double-Bass*
                                          20.7.30–12.1.46
CHEVREAU, Jeanne *Harp*   20.7.30–31.1.53
CHIMES, John *Timpani*   6.7.75–
CHISHOLM, Allan Sedman *Cello*
                                          20.9.70–1.6.74
CIVIL, Alan *Horn*   21.9.66–
CLARK, Raymond *Cello*   20.7.30–3.2.45
CLARKE, Ralph *Clarinet*   4.11.28–1.12.60
CLEVELAND, Anthony *Violin*   6.8.67–
CLOUGH, Thomas *Trombone*   30.6.74–21.4.76
COCKERILL, Albert *Double-Bass*
                                          20.7.30–3.1.41
COLEMAN, William *Bass Trombone*
                                          17.7.43–19.9.59
COLYER, Ronald *Violin*   31.12.74–6.1.80
CONDRON, Marie *Violin*   16.8.53–18.6.66
CONHOFF, Cornelius *Double Bass*
                                          20.7.30–2.8.47
CONNAH, Trevor *Violin*   11.2.63–
COOKSON, Michael *Viola*   16.7.67–16.5.70
COPPERWHEAT, Winifred *Viola*
                                          20.7.30–1938
CORDELL, Joyce *Cello*   14.11.48–4.7.59
COTTRELL, Josephine *Viola*   20.7.52–15.7.67
COULLING, John *Viola*   18.11.62–
CRAWFORD, John *Violin*   29.8.76–
CRAXTON, Janet *Oboe*   19.9.54–14.9.63
CROWLEY, Regan *Violin*   18.4.76–
CRUFT, Adrian *Double Bass*   25.1.48–30.7.49
CRUFT, Eugene *Double Bass*   1926–16.7.49
CUNINGHAM, Juliet *Double Bass*
                                          16.7.50–
CURSUE, Alfred *Horn*   12.10.30–1.6.47
DALWOOD, E. *Clarinet*   10.10.48–15.3.53
DALZIEL, Alan *Cello*   6.3.66–3.11.75
DANIELS, Muriel *Cello*   6.4.75–15.2.78
DANKS, Harry *Viola*   20.7.37–16.9.78
DANKS, Ysobel *Violin*   5.11.61–31.7.65
DAVIDSON, Belle *Violin*   20.7.31–9.10.76
DAVIS, Caroline *Violin*   1.3.75–22.7.78
DAVIS, Russell *Cello*   20.9.70–1.6.74
DAWSON, Russell *Violin*   17.10.76–
DEKANY, Bela *Leader*   1.1.69–
DE MONT, William *Cello*   19.5.35–27.1.45
DENBIN, Sidney *Cello*   18.1.48–
DENISON, John *Horn*   1934–1935

DICKASON, H. *Violin* 1930–1931
DICKIE, Thomas *Bassoon* 1931–1933
DIXON, Vivien *Violin* 6.7.58–
DODD, Edwin *Violin* 7.8.66–
DOMMETT, Leonard *Violin* 17.7.49–5.8.50
DRUCKER, Gerald *Double Bass* 16.8.53–18.4.64
DUFFIELD, Michael *Viola* 3.6.65–
DUNK, Roderick *Double Bass* 4.7.79–
DUNN, F. V. *Violin* 20.7.30–1932
DURIE, Winifred *Viola* 3.6.56–4.6.60
EAST, Denis *Violin* 30.3.47–17.5.48
EAST, Ruth *Cello*
EASTOP, Susan *Bassoon* 16.7.79–
EASTWOOD, Harry *Percussion* 1.8.37–31.5.47
EDWARDS, Gwynne *Viola* 20.7.31–19.8.47
ELLINGFORD, Constance *Violin*
20.7.30–1.7.72
ELLIFF, Jillian *Violin* 14.7.63–2.6.79
ELLIS, Ruth *Violin* 5.1.75–
ELMITT, Martin *Cello* 6.4.80–
ELMS, Frederick *Violin* 21.3.48–16.2.56
EMERY, Terence *Percussion* 5.7.64–
ENGLAND, Richard *Violin* 21.12.47–30.8.77
ENGLISH, Cyril *Violin* 18.10.42–18.1.47
6.8.50–22.8.53
& 21.1.61–23.9.67
ESSWOOD, Peter *Cello* 15.11.77–
EVANS, David *Trombone* 26.11.76–14.10.78
EVANS, Michael *Cello* 20.7.58–29.11.59
FAIRLESS, Margaret *Violin* 20.7.30–1932
FALKNER, A. *Trombone* 1929–1937
FALLOWS, Roger *Clarinet* 23.7.72–
FAWCETT, Norman *Bassoon* 2.10.32–19.7.40
FENTON, Desmond *Violin* 29.9.63–6.3.65
FIELD, John *Oboe* 1923–20.7.47
FISKE, Andrew *Horn* 13.10.46–10.11.62
FLACK, Lambert *Flute* 20.7.33–15.3.52
FLASZYNSKI, Alfred *Trombone* 1.10.64–
FLETCHER, Elisabeth *Harp* 23.4.72–
FLETCHER, John *Tuba* 6.7.64–14.9.68
FLOYD, Denzil *Horn* 16.9.62–30.12.78
FOOTTIT, Jane *Violin* 17.10.76–
FORD, A. *Cello* 20.7.30–1940
FORD, Elsie *Double Bass* 4.9.46–26.6.51
FRANCIS, John *Cello* 18.12.38–4.11.46
FRANKLIN, Roland *Timpani & Percussion*
1927–8.10.50
FRANKS, Arthur *Violin* 9.4.50–27.7.75
FREYHAN, Peter *Cello* 4.12.77–
FRIEND, Rodney *Leader* 1.1.80–
GALE, Jocelyn *Cello* 5.3.78–4.3.79
GALWAY, James *Flute* 27.8.66–17.9.66

GAMBOLD, Geoffrey *Bassoon* 20.9.59–
GARVIN, Alfred *Trombone* 1.8.37–15.6.47
GARVIN, Sidney *Trombone* 3.8.30–11.6.46
GASKELL, Helen *Oboe* 2.10.32–31.12.66
GAUNTLETT, Ambrose *Cello* 1925–27.9.47
GEORGIADIS, John *Violin* 25.11.62–24.2.63
GILBERT, Geoffrey *Flute* 18.7.48–20.9.52
GILLEGIN, Ernest *Timpani & Percussion*
20.7.30–24.2.52
GLADDEN, Mary *Viola* 20.7.30–1937
GLOSSOP, Keith *Cello* 2.2.75–19.6.76
GLYNN, William *Tuba* 1933–1937
GMITRUK, Hanna *Violin* 2.9.79–
GOOD, Ronald *Violin* 20.7.31–9.4.42
GOOSSENS, Sidonie *Harp* 6.11.27–
GOREN, Eli *Leader* 15.9.68–31.12.77
GORING, Lionel *Bassoon* 5.10.47–16.3.71
GOURLAY, James *Tuba* 1.4.79–
GOROWSKI, John *Violin* 14.3.65–9.10.76
GRAHAM, Breta *Violin* 4.9.55–
GRANT, W. *Horn* 2.1.38–4.10.60
GRAY, John *Double Bass* 17.7.55–30.7.58
GRAY, Thomas *Viola* 21.5.65–5.12.66
GRAY, V. *Horn* 1936–1937
GRAYDON, M. *Horn* 1931–1935
GREEN, Horace *Cor anglais* 10.10.37–20.4.46
GREENHALGH, Jack *Double Bass*
1952–22.12.63
GRIFFITHS, D. *Oboe* 1929–1930
GURRY, Keith *Violin* 10.9.78–
HAINTON, J. *Violin* 1928–1930
HALLAM, George *Violin* 10.2.80–
HALL, Ernest *Trumpet* 1929–19.9.53
HAMILTON, Harold *Horn* 1943–24.8.50
HAMILTON, Horace *Trumpet* 20.7.30–14.6.47
HAMILTON, John *Violin* 20.7.30–15.9.62
HANDY, James *Horn* 7.7.78–
HARDING, Kenneth *Viola* 8.4.28–10.3.63
HARMS, Molly *Violin* 12.8.56–2.10.73
HARRIS, Ronald *Horn* 15.1.61–30.11.63
HARRISON, John *Viola* 3.1.54–26.12.59
HART, Muriel *Viola* 20.7.30–25.7.52
HARVEY, Peter *Bass Trombone*
20.5.66–29.5.70
HAYES, John *Violin* 30.3.47–23.12.50
HEALY, Michael *Violin* 19.3.72–7.6.73
HEATH, Desmond *Violin* 1.2.48–25.10.58
HEATH, Kenneth *Cello* 16.9.62–31.10.65
HEPTON, Albert *Violin* 20.7.30–8.4.50
HEPTON, Joseph *Violin* 18.8.46–30.6.73
HERMAN, Godfrey *Double Bass*
22.1.78–

HESTER, Norman *Double Bass*
14.10.34–21.1.56
HIGHAM, Gwendolen *Violin*   30.3.47–30.7.52
HILL, F. W. *Violin*   1930–1935
HILL, Nicholas *Horn*   1.3.70–31.10.77
HILL, Gwendoline *Violin*   18.9.76–
HINCHLIFF, Ernest *Bassoon*   20.7.30–15.7.50
HINCHLIFFE, Jessie *Violin*   20.7.30–20.7.46
HOBDAY, Claude *Double Bass*   20.7.30–19.10.40
HODGES, Peter *Double Bass*   4.5.80–
HODKINSON, Frederick *Cello*   4.10.36–4.6.41
& 28.3.43–2.3.46
HOLLAND, James *Percussion*   2.1.72–
HOPKINSON, James *Flute*   1.1.36–19.4.48
HOUGHTON, Doris *Violin*   20.7.31–18.8.40
HOUSTON, Dudley *Violin*   21.5.65–30.11.73
HOWARTH, Herbert *Double Bass*
2.12.34–19.7.52
HUMFRESS, Gordon *Viola*   6.10.46–28.1.63
HURSEY, John *Cello*   17.4.77–3.9.77
HYLAND, Jane *Cello*   31.7.77–15.12.79
IVES, Paul *Cello*   30.10.68–25.2.74
IVESON, John *Trombone*   19.3.65–3.12.69
JACKSON, Gerald *Flute*   31.7.38–23.2.46
JACKSON, Harry *Horn*   27.7.30–26.7.31
& 5.10.41–2.3.46
JENNINGS, Anthony *Clarinet*   17.7.55–
JEZARD, Mary *Violin*   31.3.35–14.9.46
JOHNSON, D. *Percussion*   2.4.72–
JONES, David *Double Bass*   11.4.65–8.8.70
JONES, John *Trombone*   20.7.38–14.3.46
JONES, Hilary *Cello*   23.1.77–
JONES, Justin *Violin*   31.12.74–23.6.79
JONES, Philip *Trumpet*   3.10.67–18.9.71
JONES, William *Viola*   3.10.52–16.7.66
JUDD, Anthony *Bassoon*   8.11.53–16.4.54
KAHN, Charles *Viola*   1936–42
18.8.46–26.12.53
KANTROVITCH, Ula *Cello*   1.11.46–15.6.63
KARA, Jasmine *Viola*   29.4.51–
KENNEDY, Lauri *Cello*   20.7.30–6.10.35
KENNING, H. *Violin*   20.7.30–1938
KENT, Norman *Viola*   10.3.63–
KESZEI, Janos *Timpani*   23.4.72–26.8.78
KETTEL, Gary *Timpani & Percussion*
3.10.71–30.11.74
KHAMBATTA, Tessa *Violin*   3.2.80–
KILLEN, Clifford *Double Bass*   5.9.71–
KING, Russell *Flute*   6.4.52–13.11.54
& 17.7.55–29.11.59
KING, Kenneth *Violin*   1.5.66–31.12.69
KIRBY, James *Horn*   20.7.37–27.7.46

KITCHEN, John *Violin*   20.9.59–26.2.66
KNEALE KELLEY, S. *Violin*   20.7.30–1932
KNOWLES, J. G. *Viola*   1932–1937
KNUSSEN, Albert *Cello*   1.10.34–10.9.39
& 18.1.42–1.7.43
KNUSSEN, Stuart *Double Bass*   1.12.53–21.11.57
KOK, Alexander *Cello*   10.7.60–31.3.65
KOK, Felix *Violin*   27.12.63–26.5.65
KOOS, Joseph *Cello*   10.1.66–12.8.68
KRAUS, George *Double Bass*   14.7.63–
LAMBERT, Betty *Violin*   17.7.49–11.7.59
LANGSTON, Sidney *Trombone*   21.8.30–22.8.47
LANNIGAN, Patrick *Double Bass*
13.4.80–
LARKIN, Christopher *Horn*   8.7.79–
LEAR, Walter *Bass Clarinet*   21.8.27–25.4.55
LEAVINS, Arthur *Violin*   17.2.57–30.11.62
LEE, Philip *Violin*   14.12.65–
LEES, John (senior) *Timpani & Percussion*
1926–5.2.55
LEES, John (junior) *Timpani & Percussion*
22.7.51–15.7.69
LEWIS, Carl *Violin*   30.3.47–2.9.72
LEWIS, Nina *Violin*   22.10.50–15.6.63
LEWIS, Peter *Viola*   18.9.66–
LINDON, Geoffrey *Bass Trombone*
2.3.58–23.5.66
LIPMAN, H. *Violin*   1945–
LOCK, Rosemary *Violin*   31.1.75–6.2.80
LONES, Gwen *Violin*   1930–1948
LOVEDAY, Martin *Violin*   9.7.78–
LOVELL, Pat *Violin*   20.4.47–3.9.68
LUCAS, Patience *Viola*   20.7.30–17.8.46
LUDLOW, John *Violin*   9.7.61–7.10.61
& 23.9.62–17.11.63
MACDONAGH, Terence *Oboe*   20.7.30–7.6.47
& 15.9.63–2.5.72
MACKAY, G. S. *Violin*   1929–1930
MCGEE, Andrew *Violin*   16.9.62–20.10.62
MACKINTOSH, Ian *Trumpet*   20.7.52–16.5.79
MACKINTOSH, Jack *Trumpet*   20.7.30–19.7.52
MACLENNAN, Avril *Violin*   20.12.69–
MCTIER, Duncan *Double Bass*   6.7.75–20.8.77
MAGUIRE, Hugh *Leader*   16.9.62–31.3.67
MAGUIRE, Francis *Double Bass*
22.10.67–21.9.74
MALCOLM, Spence *Violin*   20.7.30–23.8.42
MANNING, Gerald *Viola*   31.12.68–
MARCUS, Marshall *Violin*   9.10.77–8.3.79
MARINARI, G. Paul *Cello*   1.12.35–25.8.60
MARJORAM, Keith *Double Bass*
24.1.60–2.3.63

MARTIN, Charles *Cello*　27.3.77–
MASON, Berkeley *Organ & Celesta*
　　　　　　　　　　　1931–1935
MASON, Denis *Horn*　21.11.65–30.6.69
MASON, Lena *Violin*　5.10.30–2.2.41
MASON, Timothy *Cello*　23.3.75–29.12.76
MAYER, John *Violin*　21.5.65–1.11.67
MEACHEM, John *Violin*　2.1.26–5.11.44
MEASHAM, David *Violin*　2.10.60–9.3.63
MELLIARD, David *Viola*　10.4.66–
MERRETT, James *Double Bass*　16.1.66–3.9.74
MESSITER, Christine *Flute*　23.4.72–
MEYER, Robert *Double Bass*　18.1.59–13.10.59
MILLER, Robin *Oboe*　3.10.71–3.3.76
MILLER, Rose *Cello*　9.8.59–4.12.62
MILNE, Helen *Viola*　20.7.30–1931
MONT-CLAR, Yvonne *Violin*　21.7.40–30.7.52
MOORE, Douglas *Horn*　20.7.37–5.4.69
MOORE, K. *Violin*　1935–1939
MORONEY, Maurice *Flute*　30.1.55–14.7.56
MORRIS, Patricia *Flute*　28.6.76–
MOSS, Geoffrey *Double Bass*　17.3.58–23.2.63
MURCHIE, Robert *Flute*　20.7.30–1938
MURRAY, G. T. *Double Bass*　20.7.30–1939
MUSCANT, Peter *Cello*　20.7.30–10.7.60
NEAL, Maurice *Double Bass*　28.1.51–20.1.67
NELSON, Norman *Violin*　16.9.62–26.9.65
NEW, Herbert *Clarinet*　1.10.36–23.9.72
NEWTON, Richard *Bassoon*　20.7.30–19.9.59
NIFOSI, Alex *Cello*　20.7.30–17.8.72
NOLAN, Francis *Flute*　19.7.70–1.11.75
NORRIS, Robert *Double Bass*　1.10.34–14.4.67
NUTTY, Kevin *Percussion*　2.1.72–
O'DONNELL, Manus *Violin*　20.7.30–29.12.45
　　　　　　　　　　　& 26.7.53–10.7.60
ORFORD, John *Bassoon*　19.12.71–3.2.79
OTTWAY, Harry *Horn*　29.7.51–26.9.69
OVENS, Raymond *Violin*　15.9.63–29.9.65
OVERTON, William *Trumpet*　23.4.35–7.3.74
OWEN, J. W. *Violin*　20.7.30–1932
PANTLING, Jess *Oboe*　4.11.28–19.3.55
PARRY, Martin *Flute*　14.8.66–14.4.74
PARSONS, Anthony *Trombone*　25.1.70–
PARTRIDGE, Bernard *Violin*　5.10.68–5.9.69
PATEMAN, Diana *Violin*　18.8.46–17.11.46
PEATFIELD, Thomas *Violin*　20.7.31–20.9.58
PENNEY, Mary *Violin*　18.8.46–12.4.73
PENNY, Barbara *Violin*　17.9.61–13.2.64
PETERS, William *Violin*　25.1.48–25.7.52
PETTS, Frederick *Viola*　19.10.36–30.7.52
PINCHES, Jack *Trombone*　4.1.48–15.9.73
PIRANI, Lelia *Violin*　1932–1935

POOL, Robert *Violin*　23.9.79–
POOLE, Peter *Violin*　3.12.65–31.12.77
POPLE, Ross *Cello*　1.11.76–
POPPLEWELL, Kenneth *Violin*　2.4.50–22.12.62
POWELL, Frederick *Double Bass*
　　　　　　　　　　　20.7.30–16.2.46
POWRIE, Douglas *Cello*　4.9.55–5.1.66
PRITCHARD, E. *Trumpet*　27.7.30–15.9.45
PRITCHARD, Eric *Timpani*　4.5.52–13.7.63
　　　　　　　　　　　3.11.63–2.11.71
PROBYN, Frank *Horn*　27.7.30–1932
PULLEN, Julia *Violin*　13.11.77–6.1.79
PUSEY, Violet *Violin*　1.11.31–19.6.47
REVELL, Henry *Cello*　20.7.30–15.11.58
RICHARDS, Leslie *Violin*　18.8.46–8.7.61
RISDON, Joseph *Trombone*　20.7.30–14.6.47
RITCHIE, Ian *Viola*　14.10.34–20.7.46
ROBAY, Ealasaid *Violin*　18.8.46–28.2.47
ROBERTSON, George *Viola*　18.12.60–21.12.63
ROBINSON, Ronald *Double Bass*
　　　　　　　　　　　27.7.30–20.8.49
ROSS, Angus *Violin*　7.11.33–11.5.46
ROSTALL, J. *Violin*　20.7.30–1931
RUTLEDGE, Ernest *Violin*　1923–31.8.50
SAINTON, Philip *Viola*　20.7.30–2.2.44
SAMUEL, Mary *Viola*　21.5.65–6.5.58
SANDERS, Neill *Horn*　23.9.62–14.5.66
SANSOM, Carolyn *Cello*　3.12.61–14.2.63
SARGON, Eric *Viola*　20.7.52–
SCANNELL, William *Tuba*　22.10.40–1.12.45
SCHEFFEL-STEIN, Renata *Harp*
　　　　　　　　　　　21.8.49–7.12.53
SCOTT, Brian *Double Bass*　4.8.63–22.3.67
SCOTT, Graeme *Viola*　30.3.80–
SELWYN, Edward *Oboe*　14.4.35–18.9.54
SENTER, John *Cello*　30.3.75–23.1.77
SEVILLE, Clifford *Flute*　15.9.63–20.8.66
SHACKLETON, A. *Trombone*　30.8.31–1938
SHEEN, Celia *Violin*　25.8.63–11.2.65
SHERMAN, Alec *Violin*　20.7.30–1938
SHINEBOURNE, Jack *Cello*　20.7.30–2.1.43
SHORE, Bernard *Viola*　20.7.30–14.9.45
SIMPSON, Claire *Violin*　31.12.74–
SIMPSON, Richard *Oboe*　4.2.73–3.2.74
SLATER, Joseph *Flute*　2.12.34–23.9.48
SMITH, H. R. *Tuba*　27.7.30–1932
SMITH, I. *Viola*　31.7.38–1940
SMITH, Peter *Horn*　4.4.71–23.8.79
SOLOMON, Andrew *Flute*　4.11.56–11.6.60
SOUTHWORTH, Linda *Viola*　3.8.30–9.11.45
SPENCER, Sheila *Viola*　16.7.50–10.1.79
SQUIRE, Barry *Violin*　17.7.29–26.6.43

STAGG, Richard *Flute*   6.7.75–
STAINER, Charles *Flute*   1930–1933
STAMP, Jesse *Trombone*   1930–1932
STEELE, Elise *Violin*   28.12.47–13.8.49
STEIN, J. *Violin*   1930–1931
STIRLING, David *Timpani & Percussion*
                                  1.7.79–
STONE, Leonard *Violin*   20.7.30–19.5.31
                                  & 29.6.42–22.12.45
STRATFORD, Ernest *Violin*   20.7.30–19.7.39
                                  & 17.12.44–28.7.45
STURTIVANT, Donald *Violin*   20.7.52–31.3.58
SUGDEN, Margaret *Viola*   19.5.46–30.7.52
SUTCLIFFE, Sidney *Oboe*   15.9.63–14.3.71
SUTHERLEY, Susan *Cello*   6.7.75–29.12.76
SUTTIE, Alan *Timpani*   6.10.63–16.4.66
SUTTON, Allan *Violin*   30.4.47–25.7.52
SUTTON, Stanley *Double Bass*
                                  13.10.29–21.1.50
SWAINSON, James *Viola*   26.7.70–23.12.78
TAIT, Enid *Violin*   26.7.36–30.3.46
                                  & 30.3.47–21.12.60
TAYLOR, Derek *Horn*   17.1.64–
TAYLOR, Frank *Trombone*   1923–10.5.43
TESKEY, W. J. *Trombone*   9.8.36–8.7.64
THEODORE, David *Oboe*   6.8.72–6.1.79
THOMAS, David *Oboe*   6.3.80–
THONGER, Aubrey *Horn*   9.10.32–25.2.50
THORNTON, Evelyn *Violin*   20.7.30–26.7.41
THORNTON, H. F. *Horn*   1930–1937
THURSTON, Frederick *Clarinet*   1923–27.6.46
TOMALIN, Michael *Violin*   1963–1964
TOOKEY, William *Violin*   20.7.31–22.8.43
TOWNSEND, Barrie *Viola*   30.12.62–
TOWNSHEND, Jacqueline *Viola*
                                  31.3.35–4.6.51
TSCHAIKOV, Anissim *Clarinet*   21.8.27–18.6.47
TSCHAIKOWSKY, Urik *Violin*   24.4.49–4.8.50
TURNER, Laurance *Violin*   20.7.30–30.9.39
TYACK, Richard *Bass Trombone*
                                  1.11.70–
UNGERSON, Julius *Violin*   20.7.30–20.7.46
VAN KAMPEN, Anthony *Double Bass*
                                  27.2.72–29.3.78
VELLA, Oliver *Cello*   1.2.48–14.8.48
VERRALL, Colin *Violin*   19.3.65–24.8.68

VIGAY, Denis *Cello*   30.4.64–30.9.72
VOCADLO, Bernard *Cello*   11.12.66–1.6.74
WAKEFIELD, Jeffrey *Violin*   16.9.62–
WAKS, Nathan *Cello*   26.10.69–30.5.70
WALKER, Edward *Piccolo*   20.7.30–19.10.37
WALKER, George *Violin*   13.4.47–23.8.47
WALTON, John *Double Bass*   17.7.49–19.9.53
WALTON, Richard *Trumpet*   24.2.63–
WARBURTON, Harold *Cello*   6.6.43–5.4.58
WARREN, Brian *Flute*   4.12.60–29.5.63
WASHBOURNE, Kathleen *Violin*
                                  20.7.30–4.7.64
WATERHOUSE, William *Bassoon* 1.1.64–
WATSON, Donald *Clarinet*   13.2.73–
WATSON, Henry *Horn*   20.7.34–20.11.62
WEBB, Robert *Viola*   13.8.47–7.6.50
WEBSTER, Gilbert *Percussion*   10.8.36–30.11.71
WELCH, Timothy *Viola*   3.6.79–
WHEELHOUSE, F. H. *Percussion*   1930–1937
WHELAN, Patrick *Clarinet*   10.8.30–31.7.48
WHITE, Ian *Viola*   22.2.63–12.1.64
WHITING, Joan *Oboe*   12.1.75–30.6.79
WHITTAKER, Alec *Oboe*   1930–1937
WHITTAKER, Douglas *Flute*   3.2.52–29.9.70
WHITTAKER, Stephen *Timpani & Percussion*
                                  1.8.37–15.7.50
WHONE, George *Violin*   20.7.52–16.7.55
WILBRAHAM, John *Trumpet*   23.4.72–
WILLIAMS, Trevor *Violin*   8.8.63–29.2.68
WILLS, Anne *Violin*   18.12.66–
WILSON, Albert *Bassoon*   20.7.30–23.3.46
WILSON, Iaan *Trumpet*   3.12.72–
WILSON, John *Double Bass*   20.10.46–21.7.54
WILSON, Marie *Violin*   20.7.30–30.9.44
WINFIELD, Roger *Oboe*   10.11.62–10.3.63
WINTHORPE, Thomas *Trombone* 1.4.79–
WOLFE, Anne *Viola*   20.7.30–15.12.45
WOLFE, John *Cor Anglais*   16.11.47–
WOLSTENSCROFT, Joan *Viola*   2.10.50–4.7.64
WOODAGE, Wesley *Trumpet*   16.7.50–15.3.71
WOODHOUSE, Charles *Violin*   1929–1931
WOOTTON, Stanley *Cello*   14.1.45–15.8.53
WYAND, Hugh *Viola*   20.7.30–19.7.40
WYATT, E. *Violin*   20.7.30–19.7.31
YOUNG, Joseph *Violin*   20.7.30–28.6.47
ZABLUDOW, Michael *Violin*   14.7.63–9.10.76

First performances by the BBC Symphony Orchestra 22 October 1930-22 October 1980

1. Dates given are those on which the works were performed by the Orchestra. Until the 1950s, broadcasts were almost invariably live. After that time, studio broadcasts were recorded for future transmission; performance dates do not necessarily coincide with those on which the works were broadcast.
2. A query after the performance description indicates that either (a) a claim is made in the BBC's records which is open to doubt but has not been disproven; or (b) that no claim was made at the time by the BBC but no other previous performance in that category has so far been traced. Further information and corrections are welcome.
3. In the 1930–31 season, the smaller sections of the Orchestra were not identified in *Radio Times* (except for the Chamber Orchestra which played for the ISCM Festival in Oxford, July 1931, and on a few other occasions). Between 1931 and 1939, sectional performances were listed, and are recorded here. For an explanation of the sections, see pp. 35–6. All public concerts were given by the full Orchestra (Section A).

Abbreviations
Place:
S – BBC Studio
QH – Queen's Hall
FH – Royal Festival Hall
AH – Royal Albert Hall
PP – People's Palace
SJSS – St John's Smith Square
RH – The Round House
A name of a British town indicates a provincial visit by the Orchestra, or a wartime public concert in Bristol or Bedford.
A name of a foreign town indicates a tour abroad by the Orchestra.

Abbreviations
Performance:
fp – First performance (world première)
fep – First European performance
fup – First United Kingdom performance (British première)
fbp – First broadcast performance
fubp – First broadcast in United Kingdom
flp – First London performance
(public) – First public performance in this category (ie previously broadcast from studio)
(c) – BBC commission

Date	Composer	Work	Conductor	Place (See Key)	Perf	Section of Orch
18 Nov 30	Debussy	Pelléas et Mélisande	Pitt	S	fubp?	
10 Dec 30	Schoenberg	Pelleas und Melisande	Scherchen	QH	fup	
9 Jan 31	Schoenberg	Erwartung	Schoenberg	S	fup	
9 Jan 31	Bach, arr. Schoenberg	Prelude and Fugue in E flat, 'St Anne'	Schoenberg	S	fup	
12 Jan 31	Sidney Jones	Daddy Longlegs	Lewis	S	fp	
21 Jan 31	Poulenc	Concert champêtre	Ansermet	QH	fup	
28 Jan 31	Stravinsky	Four Studies	Ansermet	QH	fup	
28 Jan 31	Stravinsky	Overture: Mavra	Ansermet	S	fup	
1 Feb 31	Stravinsky	Eight Easy Pieces (Suites Nos. 1 & 2)	Stravinsky	S	fubp	
15 Feb 31	Mossolov	Factory – The Music of Machines	Boult	QH	fup	
27 Feb 31	D'Erlanger	Requiem Mass	Robinson	S	fp	
27 Feb 31	Quilter	I arise from dreams of thee	Quilter	S	fp	
6 Mar 31	Hindemith	Konzertmusik, Op. 49	Bridge	S	fup	
7 Mar 31	Coates	Suite: From Meadow to Mayfair	Lewis	S	fbp	
7 Mar 31	Frazer-Simson	Ballet: A Venetian Wedding	Lewis	S	fbp	
25 Mar 31	Bliss	Morning Heroes	Bliss	QH	flp	
27 Mar 31	Richard Strauss	Kampf und Sieg	Boult	S	fup	
29 Mar 31	Kodály	Dances of Marosszek	Wood	S	fup	
24 Apr 31	Scott	Passacaglia No. 1	Morales	S	fbp	
24 Apr 31	Guridi	Una Aventura de Don Quijote	Morales	S	flp	
24 Apr 31	Falla	Ballet: The Three-Cornered Hat	Morales	S	fbp	
8 May 31	Webern	Five Movements for String Orchestra, Op. 5	Webern	S	fup	
8 May 31	Schoenberg	Music to accompany a Cinema Scene, Op. 34	Webern	S	fup	
20 May 31	Mayerl	Selection: The Millionaire Kid	Lewis	S	fbp	
20 May 31	Lehár	Selection: The Land of Smiles	Lewis	S	fbp	
3 Jun 31	German	A Princess of Kensington (selection)	Lewis	S	fbp	
24 Jun 31	Falla	Master Peter's Puppet Show	Falla	S	fubp (complete)	
24 Jun 31	Falla	Harpsichord Concerto	Wood	S	fubp?	

Date	Composer	Work	Conductor	Place	Perf (See Key)	Section of Orch
23 Jul 31	Leff Knipper	Suite Lyrique, Op. 18	Scherchen	(ISCM)	fups	(Chamber Orchestra of 51 players)
23 Jul 31	E. Halffter	Sinfonietta	Halffter	Oxford		
23 Jul 31	Maklakiewicz	Four Japanese Songs for Voice and Orchestra	Fitelberg	at 3 pm S at 8.55 pm	fbps	
27 Jul 31	Webern	Symphony, Op. 21	Scherchen		fup (not b'cast)	
27 Jul 31	Palester	Symphonic Music	Fitelberg		fup (not b'cast)	
27 Jul 31	Mortari	Rhapsody for Orchestra	Casella		fup (not b'cast)	
27 Jul 31	Dukelsky	Symphony No. 2	Fitelberg		fup	
28 Jul 31	Juan Castro	Three Symphonic Pieces	Casella	QH	fup (not b'cast)	
28 Jul 31	Quinet	Three Symphonic Movements	Quinet	(ISCM)	fup (not b'cast)	
28 Jul 31	Vaughan Williams	Benedicite	Boult		fbp	
28 Jul 31	Vogel	Two Studies for Orchestra	Scherchen		fup	
28 Jul 31	Roussel	Psalm 80	Boult		fup	
20 Aug 31	Fogg	Bassoon Concerto	Fogg	QH	fp	
20 Aug 31	Elgar	Nursery Suite	Elgar	QH	fp (public)	
22 Aug 31	Webern	Passacaglia	Wood	QH	fup	
5 Sep 31	Poulenc	Aubade for Piano and 18 Instruments	Wood	QH	fup?	
10 Sep 31	Bradford	Variations on a Popular Theme	Wood	QH	fp	
17 Sep 31	Delius	A Song of Summer	Wood	QH	fp	
19 Sep 31	Berners	Luna Park	Wood	QH	fp (public)	
19 Oct 31	Richard Strauss	Macbeth	Strauss	S	fubp?	
21 Oct 31	Richard Strauss	Three Hymns of Hölderlin	Strauss	QH	fup	
25 Oct 31	Sibelius	Night Ride and Sunrise	Cameron	S	fup?	
13 Nov 31	Schoenberg	Variations for Orchestra, Op. 31	Boult	S	fup	(Studio Orch)
25 Nov 31	Holst	Hammersmith (Prelude and Scherzo)	Boult	QH	fp (c)	
25 Nov 31	Walton	Belshazzar's Feast	Boult	QH	flp	
18 Dec 31	Lambert	Concerto for Piano and Small Orchestra	Lambert	S	fp	(Chamber Orch)

Date	Composer	Work	Conductor	Place (See Key)	Perf	Section of Orch
22 Jan 32	Busoni	Violin Concerto	Boult	S	fubp?	
24 Jan 32	Honegger	Symphony (No. 1)	Ansermet	S	fup	
1 Feb 32	Leifs	Three Icelandic Folk Dances	Hely-Hutchinson	S	fbp	
3 Feb 32	Prokofiev	Violin Concerto No. 1	Malko	QH	fup?	
5 Feb 32	Mossolov	Piano Concerto	Malko	S	fup	
5 Feb 32	Shostakovich	Symphony No. 1	Malko	S	fup	
10 Feb 32	Bax	Sinfonia Concertante (Winter Legends)	Boult	QH	fup	
12 Feb 32	Krein	Cello Concerto, Op. 25	Lewis	S	fup	
12 Feb 32	Coates	Concert Waltz: Dancing Nights	Coates	S	fbp	E
17 Feb 32	Hindemith	Konzertmusik, Op. 50	Wood	QH	fup	E
11 Mar 32	Haydn Wood	Scherzo in the Olden Style	Lewis	S	fp	
27 Apr 32	Bliss	A Colour Symphony (revised version)	Boult	QH	fp	B
1 May 32	Heward	Quodlibet	Heward	S	fp	B
1 May 32	Sibelius	Oceanides	Heward	S	fup?	
20 May 32	Delius	A Village Romeo and Juliet	Beecham	S	fbp	
25 May 32	Coates	Ballet: The Jester at the Wedding	Lewis	S	fbp	E
13 Jul 32	Leigh	Interlude for Theatre Orchestra	Lambert	S	fbp	C
13 Jul 32	Roseingrave, arr. Lambert	Overture in F	Lambert	S	fp	C
13 Jul 32	Satie	Ballet: Mercure	Lambert	S	fup	C
11 Aug 32	Bainton	Epithalamion	Bainton	QH	fp (public)	
16 Aug 32	Ravel	Piano Concerto for the Left Hand	Wood	QH	fup	
17 Sep 32	Delius	A Song of Summer	Wood	QH	fp	
23 Oct 32	Roussel	Concert, Op. 34	Pitt	S	fup	
30 Oct 32	Gibbs	Symphony in E	Boult	S	fp	D
20 Nov 32	Wood	Suite: Moods	Lewis	S	fp	C
2 Jan 33	Hindemith	Philharmonic Concerto	Wood	QH	fup	
10 Jan 33	Coates	Suite: London Every Day	Lewis	S	fp	C
16 Jan 33	D'Erlanger	Prelude Lyrique	Lewis	S	fp	D
20 Jan 33	Roussel	Symphony No. 3	Boult	S	fup	D
29 Jan 33	Benjamin	Violin Concerto	Benjamin	S	fp	B

Date	Composer	Work	Conductor	Place	Perf (See Key)	Section of Orch
1 Feb 33	Vaughan Williams	Piano Concerto	Boult	QH	fp	
5 Feb 33	Monn, arr. Schoenberg	Cello Concerto in G minor	Clark	S	f(u)p?	
8 Feb 33	Schoenberg	Variations for Orchestra, Op. 31	Schoenberg	QH	fup (public)	
14 Feb 33	Haydn Wood	Manx Tone Poem, Manin Veg Veen	Lewis	S	fp	E
1 Mar 33	Haydn Wood	Violin Concerto	Lewis	S	fp	D
4 Mar 33	Quilter	Pastoral Dance	Woodgate	S	fp	C
8 Mar 33	Berg	Three Fragments from Wozzeck	Wood	QH	fup (public)	
19 Mar 33	Hindemith	Konzertmusik, Op. 48	Wood	S	fup	
22 Mar 33	Hindemith	Das Unaufhörliche (The Perpetual)	Wood	QH	fup	
24 Mar 33	Hindemith	Das Lehrstück	Boult	S	fup	D
10 Apr 33	Pizzetti	Rondo Veneziano	Pizzetti	S	fup	D
14 Apr 33	Berg	Three Pieces from the Lyric Suite	Webern	S	fup	D
21 Apr 33	Berg	Chamber Concerto	Webern	S	fubp	D
21 Apr 33	Krenek	Durch die Nacht	Webern	S	fup	D
21 Apr 33	Moeran	Farrago (Suite)	Clifford	S	fp	C
26 May 33	Kodály	Skékely Fonó (The Spinning-Room)	Kodály	S	fup	D
30 May 33	Wolf-Ferrari	Idillio Concertante for Oboe and Orchestra	Clark	S	fup	
30 May 33	Hindemith	Kammermusik, Op. 24 No. 1	Clark	S	fubp	
30 May 33	Respighi	Antiche Danze ed Arie	Clark	S	fup	
11 Sep 33	Besly	Mary's Blue Eyes	Woodgate	S	fp	C
16 Sep 33	Honegger	Symphonic Movement No. 3	Wood	QH	fup	
3 Oct 33	Delius	Idyll	Wood	QH	fp	
8 Nov 33	Bartók	Piano Concerto No. 2	Boult	QH	fup	
25 Nov 33	Haydn Wood	Suite: A Day in Fairyland	Lewis	S	fp	C
29 Nov 33	Bruckner	Symphony No. 9 (original version)	Boult	QH	fup	
22 Dec 33	Honegger	Cris du Monde	Boult	S	fup	D
1 Jan 34	R. O. Morris	Symphony in D	Boult	QH	fp	
8 Jan 34	Toch	Bunte Suite	Braithwaite	S	fup	C
10 Jan 34	Bridge	Rhapsody for Piano and Orchestra, Phantasm	Bridge	QH	fp	
12 Jan 34	Delius	Fantastic Dance	Boult	QH	fp	

Date	Composer	Work	Conductor	Place (See Key)	Perf	Section of Orch
12 Jan 34	Ireland	Legend for Piano and Orchestra	Boult	QH	fp	
26 Jan 34	Shostakovich	The Nose (excerpts)	Malko	S	fup	D
26 Jan 34	Miaskovsky	Symphony No. 7	Malko	S	fup	D
26 Jan 34	Prokofiev	Symphonic Suite: Four Portraits	Malko	S	fup	D
26 Jan 34	Prokofiev	Portraits	Malko	S	fup	
31 Jan 34	Prokofiev	Piano Concerto No. 5	Walter	QH	fup	
7 Feb 34	Mahler	Symphony No. 9	Boult	QH	flp	
21 Feb 34	Busoni	Piano Concerto	Boult	S	fubp	
10 Mar 34	Berg	Der Wein	Scherchen	S	fup	
14 Mar 34	Berg	Wozzeck	Boult	QH	fup	
18 Mar 34	Holst	Lyric Movement for Violin and Orchestra	Boult	S	fp	B
26 Mar 34	Weigl	Piano Concerto in F minor	Braithwaite	S	fup	E
3 Apr 34	Satie	Jack-in-the-box, Suite No. 1	Foster Clark	S	fup	
27 Apr 34	Stravinsky	Mavra	Ansermet	S	fup?	D
25 May 34	Bartók	Cantata profana	Buesst	S	fup	D
1 Jun 34	Wood	Market Day	Wood	S	fp	E
9 Jun 34	Cowen	Orchestral Ballad: The Magic Goblet	Cowen	S	fp	D
30 Aug 34	Tapp	Metropolis	Wood	QH	fp	
30 Aug 34	Cooke	Concert Overture No. 1	Wood	QH	flp	
22 Sep 34	Kodály	Dances from Galanta	Wood	QH	fup	
29 Sep 34	Bach, arr. Respighi	Prelude and Fugue in D	Wood	QH	fp	
19 Oct 34	Prokofiev	Symphony No. 3	Prokofiev	S	fup	D
19 Oct 34	Prokofiev	Suite de Ballet: Chout	Prokofiev	S	fbp	D
6 Nov 34	Richard Strauss	Salome	Coates	S	fubp (complete)	
23 Nov 34	Milhaud	Suite: Maximilian	Lambert	QH	fup?	D
28 Nov 34	Stravinsky	Perséphone	Stravinsky	S	fup	
21 Dec 34	Hindemith	Symphonie: Mathis der Maler	Hindemith	S	fup	
6 Jan 35	Farjeon	Phantasie Concerto	Raybould	S	flp	C
16 Jan 35	Grace Williams	Overture	Woodhouse	S	fp	D
18 Jan 35	Sessions	Suite from The Black Maskers	Raybould	S	fup?	D

Date	Composer	Work	Conductor	Place	Perf (See Key)	Section of Orch
18 Jan 35	Gershwin	Second Rhapsody	Raybould	S	fup?	D
18 Jan 35	Bliss	Mélée Fantasque	Bliss	S	fbp	D
18 Jan 35	Copland	Dance Symphony	Raybould	S	fup?	D
23 Jan 35	Shaporin	Symphony in C minor	Coates	QH	fup	
6 Feb 35	Holst	Scherzo	Boult	QH	fp	
3 Mar 35	Delius, trans. Tertis	Double Concerto for Violin, Viola and Orchestra	Boult	S	fp	B
20 Mar 35	Frescobaldi, arr. Malipiero	Toccate	Boult	QH	fup	
20 Mar 35	Malipiero	Sinfonia (No. 1)	Boult	QH	fup	
20 Mar 35	Berg	Symphonic Excerpts from Lulu	Boult	QH	fup	
21 Mar 35	Erdmann	Serenade	Clifford	S	fup	E
27 Mar 35	Schubert, arr. Weingartner	Symphony in E (No. 7)	Weingartner	QH	fup	
10 Apr 35	Vaughan Williams	Symphony No. 4 in F minor	Boult	QH	fp	
12 Apr 35	Mossolov	Turkmenian Music	Clark	S	fp	D
20 Apr 35	Conen	Miniature Variations (Humoresque)	Lewis	S	fp	E
25 Apr 35	Bach, arr. Webern	Ricercare from The Musical Offering	Webern	S	fup	
28 Apr 35	Haydn Wood	Overture: Apollo	Raybould	S	fp	E
7 May 35	Coates	Song of Loyalty	Coates	S	fp	E
21 Jun 35	Debussy, orch. Goossens	Dance: En Blanc et Noir	Goossens	S	fup	B
21 Jun 35	Wagner, trans. Goossens	Chorus of Gibichungs	Goossens	S	fup	B
28 Jun 35	Janáček	Glagolithic Mass	Wood	S	fubp	B
4 Jul 35	Prokofiev	The Love for Three Oranges	Coates	S	fup	B
6 Jul 35	Mozart	Rondo in A, K.386	Raybould	S	fp	C
29 Jul 35	Honegger	Cello Concerto	Clifford	S	fubp	
20 Aug 35	Demuth	Nachtmusik	Demuth	S	fup	C
2 Sep 35	Herman, orch. Wood	Suite: High Street	Lewis	S	fp	C
12 Sep 35	Bliss	Suite from the Film Music: 1935	Bliss	QH	fp (in concert form)	
19 Sep 35	Shostakovich	Symphony No. 1	Wood	QH	ftp (public)	
19 Sep 35	Mossolov	Three Songs with Orchestra	Wood	QH	fup	
26 Sep 35	Bartók	Hungarian Peasant Songs (orchestral version)	Wood	QH	fup	

Date	Composer	Work	Conductor	Place (See Key)	Perf	Section of Orch
5 Oct 35	Larsson	Concerto for Saxophone and Strings	Wood	QH	fup (public)	C
8 Oct 35	Handel, arr. Herbage & Greaves	Perseus and Andromeda from Jupiter in Argos	Raybould	S	fp	C
9 Oct 35	Dunhill	Suite from Ballet: Dick Whittington	Dunhill	S	fp	C
14 Oct 35	Gibbs	Dance Suite: Fancy Dress	Lewis	S	fp	E
23 Oct 35	Berg	Three Pieces from the Lyric Suite	Boult	QH	fup (public)	C
27 Oct 35	Grayson, orch. Jacob	In Linden Time	Lewis	S	fbp	
6 Nov 35	Walton	Symphony No. 1	Harty	QH	fp (in complete form)	C
29 Nov 35	van Dieren	Overture	Braithwaite	S	fup	D
29 Nov 35	Darnton	Piano Concerto	Braithwaite	S	fup	D
29 Nov 35	Lloyd	Symphony in F	Lloyd	S	fp	D
30 Nov 35	Toomey	Celtic Tunes for String Orchestra	Woodgate	S	fp	C
8 Dec 35	Alwyn	English Overture: The Innumerable Dance	Buesst	S	fp	C
16 Dec 35	Busoni	Indian Fantasy	Lambert	S	fubp	
20 Dec 35	Markievitch	Le Paradis perdu	Markievitch	S	fp	D
25 Dec 35	Bizet	Symphony No. 1	Harty	S	fbp	E
3 Jan 36	Hyde	Piano Concerto No. 1	Buesst	S	fbp	C
5 Jan 36	Haydn Wood	Suite: Frescoes	Lewis	S	fp	C
17 Jan 36	Beck	Innominata	Boult	S	fbp	D
17 Jan 36	Copland	Music for the Theatre	Boult	S	fbp	D
17 Jan 36	Bridge	Oration for Cello and Orchestra	Kabasta	S	fp	D
19 Jan 36	Richard Strauss	Overture: Die schweigsame Frau	Bridge	S	fubp	
22 Jan 36	Hindemith	Trauermusik for Viola and Orchestra	Boult	S	fp	D
29 Jan 36	Lambert	Summer's Last Will and Testament	Lambert	QH	fp	
9 Feb 36	Roussel	Symphony No. 4	Boult	S	fup	B
21 Feb 36	Malipiero	Three Preludes to comedies by Goldoni	Clark	S	fup	D
21 Feb 36	Malipiero	Filomela e l'Infatuato	Clark	S	fup	D
23 Feb 36	Shostakovich	Symphony No. 3	Malko	S	fup	B
27 Feb 36	Greenwood	Salute to Gustav Holst	Greenwood	S	fp	D

Date	Composer	Work	Conductor	Place (See Key)	Perf	Section of Orch
8 Mar 36	Bantock	A Pagan Symphony	Boult	S	fp	B
18 Mar 36	Shostakovich	Lady Macbeth of Mtsensk	Coates	QH	fup	
20 Mar 36	Maconchy	Concerto for Piano and Chamber Orchestra	Boult	S	fbp	C
25 Mar 36	Bartók	Cantata profana	Boult	QH	fup (public)	
3 Apr 36	Sorozabal	Basque Sketch: Mendian	Morales	S	fup	D
6 Apr 36	Kodály	Theatre Overture	Sargent	S	fubp	D
9 Apr 36	van Dieren	Symphony, Op. 6	Lambert	S	fbp?	C
11 Apr 36	Phillips	Surrey Suite	Lewis	S	fp	C
13 Apr 36	Grétry, arr. Meyrowitz	Suite: La Rosière Républicaine	Lewis	S	fbp	C
15 Apr 36	Darnton	Concerto for Viola and String Orchestra	Lemare	S	fbp	E
15 Apr 36	Maconchy	Great Agrippa	Lemare	S	fbp	E
15 Apr 36	Thorpe Davie	Dirge for Cuthullin	Heward	S	fp	D
30 Apr 36	Britten	Our Hunting Fathers	Boult	S	fbp/fup	
1 May 36	Berg	Violin Concerto	Webern	S	fup	D
2 May 36	Warner	Suite: Camera Snaps	Lewis	S	fp	C
16 May 36	Murrill	Cello Concerto	Murrill	S	fp	D
19 May 36	Creith	Violin Concerto	Lambert	S	fp	E
23 May 36	Godfrey	Hornpipe	Lewis	S	fbp	E
23 May 36	Russell Williams	Symphonic Fantasia	Buesst	S	fp	D
24 May 36	D'Erlanger	Ballet: Les Cent Baisers	Boult	S	fbp	B
29 May 36	Mase	Lights Out	Boult	S	fp	E
5 Jun 36	Mary Callander	Suite	Boult	S	fp	D
5 Jun 36	Vogel	Ritmica Ostinata	Boult	S	fup	D
6 Jun 36	Woodgate	Marginale	Woodgate	S	fp	E
17 Jun 36	Still	Afro-American Symphony	Harty	S	fup	B
19 Jun 36	Berkeley	Jonah	Raybould	S	fp	
16 Jul 36	Anson	Concerto for Two Pianos and Strings	Barbirolli	S	fp	C
20 Jul 36	Del Campo	El Scherzo del Borriquillo	Morales	S	fp	C
20 Jul 36	Françaix	Concertino	Morales	S	fup	C
27 Jul 36	Rudolph Dolmetsch	Spring Tidings	Dolmetsch	S	fp	D

Date	Composer	Work	Conductor	Place (See Key)	Perf	Section of Orch
31 Jul 36	Kabalevsky	Symphony No. 2	Coates	S	fup	D
31 Jul 36	Coates	Concerto in C	Coates	S	fp	D
21 Aug 36	Speer	Fantasy: Impressions	Harrison	S	fbp	C
1 Sep 36	Boyce	Overture: The Power of Music	Lambert	S	fp (modern)	
10 Sep 36	Sibelius	The Ferryman's Brides	Wood	QH	fup	
25 Sep 36	Fritz Hart	Fantasy: Cold blows the Wind	Hart	S	fup	C
2 Oct 36	Richard Strauss	Violin Concerto	Clifford	S	fubp?	
3 Oct 36	Bach, arr. Casella	Chaconne for Full Orchestra	Wood	QH	fup	
17 Oct 36	Stoll	Ballet Suite: The Blonde Persian	Lewis	S	fp	C
30 Oct 36	Rathaus	Serenade	Raybould	S	fup	D
30 Oct 36	White	A Revel	Raybould	S	fp	D
30 Oct 36	Rootham	Symphony in C minor	Rootham	S	fbp	D
13 Nov 36	Kodály	Te Deum	Boult	S	fp	D
13 Nov 36	Vaughan Williams	Dona Nobis Pacem	Vaughan Williams	S	fbp	D
16 Nov 36	Pakeman	Day that I have loved	Raybould	S	fp	E
19 Nov 36	Godfrey	Overture: Torland	Lewis	S	fbp	E
9 Dec 36	Berg	Violin Concerto	Wood	QH	fup (public)	
16 Dec 36	Jacob	Fiddle Concerto	Jacob	S	fp	B
17 Dec 36	Phillips	Overture: Charles II	Phillips	S	fup	E
17 Dec 36	Phillips	A Moorland Idyll	Phillips	S	fp	E
18 Dec 36	Hindemith	Cardillac	Raybould	S	fup	D
20 Dec 36	Prokofiev	Violin Concerto No. 2	Wood	S	fup	B
22 Dec 36	Haydn Wood	A Manx Overture: The Isle of Mountains and Glens	Wood	S	fp	E
7 Jan 37	Hindemith	Violin Concerto (Kammermusik No. 4)	Braithwaite	S	fp	C
15 Jan 37	Colin M. Campbell	Thais and Talmaae	Campbell	S	fup	C
16 Jan 37	Lovelock	Second Suite for Orchestra	Lovelock	S	fbp	C
16 Jan 37	Britten	Soirée Musicale	Lewis	S	fbp	C
16 Jan 37	Coates	Saxo-Rhapsody	Lewis	S	fbp	C
16 Jan 37	Milhaud	Christophe Colomb	Milhaud	S	fup	B

Date	Composer	Work	Conductor	Place (See Key)	Perf	Section of Orch
27 Jan 37	Vaughan Williams	Five Tudor Portraits	Boult	QH	flp	C
31 Jan 37	Kridel	Cantata No. 4	Bernard	S	fp	E
1 Feb 37	Anthony Collins	Pastoral: Topley Pike	Collins	S	fp	
10 Feb 37	Rachmaninov	The Bells	Wood	QH	flp	E
22 Feb 37	Harrison	Autumn Landscapes for Strings	Harrison	S	fp	D
26 Feb 37	Wilson	Double Concerto	Wilson	S	fp	E
1 Mar 37	Ferrers	Songs of a Roman Legion	Ferrers	S	fbr	
7 Mar 37	Handel, arr. Schoenberg	Concerto for String Quartet and Orchestra	Boult	S	fubp	E
12 Mar 37	Mompou, orch. Isaacs	Four Catalan Songs and Dances	Raybould	S	fbp	E
12 Mar 37	Wallace	Symphonic Poem: Sister Helen	Raybould	S	fbp	E
17 Mar 37	Busoni	Doktor Faust	Boult	QH	fup	
19 Mar 37	Bowen	Piano Concerto No. 4	Boult	S	fp	E
8 Apr 37	Bright	Theme and Variations	Raybould	S	fup	
28 Apr 37	Roussel	Petite Suite Op. 39	Lambert	S	fubp	D
30 Apr 37	Rubbra	Symphony No. 1	Boult	S	fp	
30 Apr 37	Lucas	Sinfonia Brevis	Boult	S	fp	
4 May 37	Bax	London Pageantry	Coates	S	fp	B
6 May 37	Bantock	King Solomon	Bantock	S	fp	D
9 May 37	Walton	A Coronation March: Crown Imperial	Boult	S	fp(c)	B
13 May 37	Ireland	These things shall be	Boult	S	fp(c)	B
13 May 37	Coates	Suite: Springtime	Coates	S	fp	C
28 May 37	Tommasini	Il Carnevale di Venezia	Toscanini	QH	fup	
11 Jun 37	Felix White	Nocturne	Lewis	S	fp	E
18 Jun 37	Jacob	Variations on an Original Theme	Harrison	S	fbp	D
11 Aug 37	Stoll	Suite: Princess Margaret Rose	Lewis	S	fp	C
18 Aug 37	Satie	Relâche: Suite	Lambert	S	fubp	
24 Aug 37	Kodály	Ballet Music	Wood	QH	fup	
7 Sep 37	Bowen	Rhapsody	Boult	S	fbp	C
8 Oct 37	Szymanowski	Overture Op. 12	Boult	S	fup	D
8 Oct 37	Szymanowski	Violin Concerto No. 2	Boult	S	fup	D

Date	Composer	Work	Conductor	Place	Perf (See Key)	Section of Orch
8 Oct 37	Szymanowski	Ballet: Harnasie	Boult	S	fup	D
9 Oct 37	Wood	Suite: Cities of Romance	Lewis	S	fp	E
18 Oct 37	Curzon	Suite: Robin Hood	Lewis	S	fp	C
21 Oct 37	Geehl	A Comedy Overture	Lewis	S	fp	C
22 Oct 37	Bloch	Three Poems of the Sea	Raybould	S	fup	B
27 Oct 37	Gerhard	Albada: Interludi i Dansa	Raybould	S	fup	B
29 Oct 37	Roussel	Concertino, Op. 57	Raybould	S	fup	
5 Nov 37	Franckenstein	Praeludium	Franckenstein	S	fup	D
9 Nov 37	Roussel	Padmâvâti (excerpts)	Boulanger	S	fup	
18 Nov 37	D'Erlanger	Incidental Music: Sappho	Lewis	S	fbp	E
28 Nov 37	Robert Cox	Overture: The Golden Fleece	Lewis	S	fbp	E
3 Dec 37	Rawsthorne	Clarinet Concerto	Lemare	S	fbp	E
5 Dec 37	Hindemith	Symphonic Dances	Hindemith	S	fp	B
14 Dec 37	Roussel	Piano Concerto in G	Wood	S	fup?	
15 Dec 37	Bantock	Five Ghazals of Hafiz	Raybould	S	fp	E
17 Dec 37	Beck	Serenade for Flute, Clarinet and Strings	Munch	S	fup?	D
17 Dec 37	Rieti	Piano Concerto No. 2	Munch	S	fup?	D
17 Dec 37	Haba	Overture: Nova Zeme	Munch	S	fup?	D
18 Dec 37	Pattman	Cinderella	Lewis	S	fbp	C
22 Dec 37	Milhaud	Suite Provençale	Milhaud	S	fup	D
31 Dec 37	Phillips	Overture: Revelry	Phillips	S	fp	E
7 Jan 38	Bartók	Music for Strings, Percussion and Celesta	Scherchen	S	fup?	E
7 Jan 38	Dallapiccola	Tre Laudi	Scherchen	S	fup	E
8 Jan 38	Jones	Overture: Elsinore	Lewis	S	fbp	C
8 Jan 38	Britten and Berkeley	Suite: Mont Juic	Lewis	S	fp	C
9 Jan 38	Miaskovsky	Symphony No. 14	Malko	S	fup	B
10 Jan 38	Hindemith	Symphonic Dances	Boult	Newcastle	fup (public)	
12 Jan 38	Hindemith	Symphonic Dances	Boult	QH	ffp	
24 Jan 38	Greenwood	Symphonic Movement	Lambert	S	fp	E
26 Jan 38	Prokofiev	Violin Concerto No. 2	Prokofiev	QH	fup (public)	

Date	Composer	Work	Conductor	Place (See Key)	Perf	Section of Orch
26 Jan 38	Prokofiev	Symphonic Suite No. 2: Romeo and Juliet	Boult	QH	fup	E
29 Jan 38	Milford	Violin Concerto	Raybould	S	fp	E
30 Jan 38	Thiman	Ballade: Barbara Allen	Lewis	S	fp	
4 Feb 38	Maconchy	Viola Concerto	Lambert	S	fbp	E
10 Feb 38	Haydn Wood	Overture: Love and Life	Lewis	S	fp	
16 Feb 38	Schumann	Violin Concerto in D minor	Boult	QH	fup	D
18 Feb 38	Schmidt	Symphony No. 4	Kabasta	S	fup	
22 Feb 38	Malipiero	Symphony No. 2	Boult	QH	fup	D
25 Feb 38	Woodgate	A Song of Joys	Woodgate	S	fbp	E
17 Mar 38	Haydn Wood	Rhapsody: King Orry	Wood	S	fp	E
1 Apr 38	Richard Strauss	Symphony in F minor (No. 2)	Raybould	S	fbp	D
8 Apr 38	Rivier	Symphony No. 2	Boult	S	fup	D
8 Apr 38	Křenek	Piano Concerto	Boult	S	fp	D
8 Apr 38	Berg	Three Orchestral Pieces, Op. 6	Boult	S	fup	D
11 Apr 38	Victor Buesst	Concerto for Three Pianos and Orchestra	Buesst	S	fp	C
23 Apr 38	Handel	La Resurrezione	Herbage	S	fup (modern)	C
2 May 38	Arthur Wood	Ballade: Strolling Players	Arthur Wood	S	fp	D
11 May 38	Demuth	Portraits (1935)	Raybould	S	fp	
13 May 38	White	Sinfonietta in C	Hervard	S	fp	
13 May 38	Rathaus	Suite: The Lion in Love	Raybould	S	fp	B
24 May 38	Bax	Paean	Wood	QH	fp (Royal concert)	
25 May 38	Fuleihan	Concerto	Fogg	S	fbp	
17 Jun 38	Berkeley	Domini est Terra	Fulton	QH (ISCM)	fbp	B
24 Jun 38	Webern	Das Augenlicht	Scherchen	QH (ISCM)	fup	
2 Aug 38	Brookes	Three Midsummer Dances	Lewis	S	fp	C
8 Aug 38	Lambert	Suite from the Ballet: Horoscope	Lambert	QH	fp	
18 Aug 38	Britten	Piano Concerto	Wood	QH	fp	

Date	Composer	Work	Conductor	Place (See Key)	Perf (See Key)	Section of Orch
19 Aug 38	Henman, orch. Wood	Olde Wayes	Lewis	S	fp	C
19 Aug 38	Campbell	Five Dances for Orchestra	Lewis	S	fp	C
25 Aug 38	Rowley	Piano Concerto in D	Braithwaite	S	fp	C
3 Sep 38	Bliss	Film Music: Conquest of the Air	Bliss	QH	fp (in concert form)	
10 Sep 38	Walton	Façade (Second Suite)	Wood	QH	fp	
30 Sep 38	Carse	A Romantic Legend	Raybould	S	fp	
5 Oct 38	Vaughan Williams	Serenade to Music	Wood	AH	fp (with players from other orchestras)	C
31 Oct 38	Benjamin	Jamaican Song & Jamaican Rumba	Lewis	S	fp	E
31 Oct 38	Grieg, trans. de Mont	Four Lyric Pieces	Lewis	S	fbp	E
3 Nov 38	Coates	The Enchanted Garden	Coates	S	fp	D
4 Nov 38	Stravinsky	Dumbarton Oaks	Boulanger	S	fup	E
4 Nov 38	Préger	Il viendra vers toi	Boulanger	S	fp	E
4 Nov 38	Françaix	Le Diable boîteux	Boulanger	S	fup	E
9 Nov 38	Goossens	Two Nature Poems	Goossens	QH	ffp	
17 Nov 38	Eberl	Piano Concerto	Raybould	S	fup	C
2 Dec 38	Burkhard	The Vision of Isaiah	Raybould	S	fup (complete)	D
16 Dec 38	Howells	Concerto for String Orchestra	Boult	S	fp	B
16 Dec 38	Rubbra	Symphony No. 2	Boult	S	fp	B
23 Dec 38	Tapp	Overture: Beachy Head	Collins	S	fp	C
24 Dec 38	Jacob	Galop	Lambert	S	fp	E
2 Jan 39	Boyce, arr. Lambert	Overture: The Cambridge Ode	Lambert	S	fp (modern)	E
3 Jan 39	Thomas Wood	Daniel and the Lions	Woodgate	S	fp	E
6 Jan 39	William Busch	Piano Concerto	Raybould	S	fp	D
6 Jan 39	Rawsthorne	Three French Nursery Songs (Orchestral version)	Raybould	S	fp	D
6 Jan 39	Chisholm	Symphony No. 1	Raybould	S	fp	D
9 Jan 39	Casella	Concerto Romano	Raybould	S	fup	D
3 Feb 39	Benjamin	Suite: Cotillon	Raybould	S	fp	C

Date	Composer	Work	Conductor	Place (See Key)	Perf	Section of Orch
9 Feb 39	Haydn Wood	Suite: East of Suez	Haydn Wood	S	fp	C
10 Feb 39	Hindemith	Nobilissima Visione	Ansermet	S	fup	E
27 Feb 39	Martinů	Cello Concerto	Clifford	QH	fbp	E
1 Mar 39	Harty	Poem: The Children of Lir	Harty	S	fp	
13 Mar 39	Rota	Serenata	Braithwaite	S	fup	
15 Mar 39	Hindemith	Mathis der Maler	Raybould	QH	fup (complete)	D
17 Mar 39	Rootham	Symphony No. 2	Boult	S	fp	
3 Apr 39	Janáček	The Fiddler's Child	Raybould	S	fubp	
10 May 39	Gerber	Prelude: Stonehenge	Lewis	S	fp	E
3 Jun 39	Harty (arr.)	John Field Suite	Harty	S	fup	B
13 Jun 39	D. Moule Evans	Poem for Orchestra: Cliff Castle	Cameron	S	fp	D
24 Jun 39	Filz	Bohemian Symphony in A	Coates	S	fbp	B
20 Jul 39	Veress	Divertimento	Lambert	S	fbp	C
17 Aug 39	Britten	Two Songs from Les Illuminations	Wood	QH	flp	
17 Aug 39	Bliss	Piano Concerto	Wood	QH	fup	
22 Aug 39	Pizzetti	Concerto in C	Raybould	S	fup	C
24 Aug 39	Barber	Essay for Orchestra (No. 1)	Wood	QH	fup	
24 Oct 39	Grace Williams	Symphonic Legend: Rhiannon	Idris Lewis	S	fp	
1 Nov 39	Vaughan Williams	Five Variants of Dives and Lazarus	Boult	Bristol	fup	
8 Nov 39	Schubert, orch. Gal	Divertissement	Guy Warrack	S	fp	
8 Dec 39	Roussel	Sinfonietta for Strings	Bernard	S	fbp	C
21 Dec 39	Haydn Wood	Theme and Variations for Cello and Orchestra	Haydn Wood	S	fp	
12 Apr 40	Britten	Les Illuminations	Boult	Bristol	fbp (complete)	
6 Jun 40	Britten	A Canadian Kermesse	Raybould	S	fp	B
11 Jun 40	Carr	Overture: Sir Walter Raleigh	Lewis	S	fp	B
11 Jun 40	Rawsthorne	Cantata: Kubla Khan	Redman	S	fp	C
21 Jun 40	Bax	Symphony No. 7	Boult	Bristol	fup	
9 Dec 40	Thiman	Variations on a Theme of Elgar	Raybould	S	fp	B
12 Mar 41	Bridge	Overture: Rebus	Wood	S	fbp	
7 Apr 41	Holland	Billingham Marshes	Raybould	S	fbp	

Date	Composer	Work	Conductor	Place (See Key)	Perf
28 Apr 41	Britten	Violin Concerto	Raybould	Bristol	fbp
29 Apr 41	Arne, arr. G. Bush	A Little Concerto for Piano and String Orchestra	Harvey	Bristol	fbp
17 May 41	Clifford	Five English Nursery Tunes	Boult	S	fbp
24 May 41	Dyson	Unison Song: Motherland	Dyson	S	fp
4 Jul 41	Alden Carpenter	A Song of Faith	Woodgate	Bristol	fup
10 Jul 41	Quilter	A Song of Freedom	Woodgate	S	fp
7 Aug 41	Haydn Wood	Overture: Minerva	Raybould	S	fbp
14 Sep 41	Carpenter	Violin Concerto	Raybould	S	fbp
3 Nov 41	Alwyn	Pastoral Fantasia for Viola and String Orchestra	Boult	S	fp
3 Nov 41	Walton	Overture: Scapino	Walton	S	fup
20 Nov 41	Bartók	Divertimento for Strings	Greenbaum	S	fbp?
8 Dec 41	Prokofiev	Alexander Nevsky (music for the film)	Boult	S	fup
18 Jan 42	Milhaud	Fantasie Pastorale	Boult	S	fbp
11 Feb 42	Gerhard	Suite from the ballet: Don Quixote	Lambert	Cambridge	fp
12 Feb 42	Gerhard	Suite from the ballet: Don Quixote	Raybould	S	fbp
16 Feb 42	Dyson	Violin Concerto	Boult	S	fp
23 Mar 42	Dunhill	Divertimento	Harrison	S	fbp
6 Apr 42	Rowley	Suite in A (from music by Dibdin)	Boult	S	fbp
28 May 42	Harris	Symphony No. 3	Boult	AH	fup
1 Aug 42	Copland	Billy the Kid	Wood	AH	fup
4 Aug 42	Harris	Heroic Prelude	Harris	AH	fp
6 Aug 42	Benjamin	Rondo: Prelude to Holiday	Wood	AH	fup
7 Aug 42	Rowley	Three Idylls for Piano and Orchestra	Boult	AH	fp
8 Aug 42	Demuth	Valses graves et gaies	Demuth	AH	fp
13 Aug 42	Lucas	Suite Française	Lucas	AH	fp
14 Aug 42	Rubbra	Symphony No. 4	Rubbra	AH	fp
19 Aug 42	Dunhill	Triptych for Viola and Orchestra	Boult	AH	fp
22 Aug 42	Gipps	Symphonic Poem: Knight in Armour	Wood	AH	fp
22 Aug 42	Gibbs	Dance Suite	Boult	AH	fp
15 Oct 42	Braithwaite	Suite of 18th-Century Country Dances	Raybould	S	fbp

Date	Composer	Work	Conductor	Place (See Key)	Perf
19 Oct 42	Holbrooke	Double Concerto (Tannerlane)	Raybould	S	fbp
22 Oct 42	May	Suite of Irish Airs	Boult	S	fbp
16 Nov 42	Mozart	Symphony in B flat K.45	Carner	S	fbp
21 Dec 42	Khachaturian	Ode to Stalin	Boult	S	fup
22 Dec 42	Gibbs	Concertino for piano	Boult	S	fbp
7 Jan 43	Grace Williams	Sinfonia Concertante	Raybould	S	fp
20 Mar 43	Jacob	Sinfonietta	Raybould	S	fp
9 Jul 43	Braithwaite	Crab Apple Fair	Raybould	S	fbp
10 Jul 43	Walthew	Mosaic in ten pieces for Viola and Orchestra	Raybould	S	fbp
19 Jul 43	Shebalin	Overture Op. 25	Boult	AH	fup
20 Jul 43	Chavez	Sinfonia India	Boult	AH	fup
29 Jul 43	Weisgall	American Comedy 1943	Weisgall	AH	fp
29 Jul 43	Copland	A Lincoln Portrait	Boult	AH	fup
29 Jul 43	William Schuman	Symphony No. 3	Boult	AH	fup
31 Jul 43	Khachaturian	Lezginka	Boult	AH	fup
3 Aug 43	Dunhill	Waltz Suite	Dunhill	AH	fp
6 Aug 43	Dale	The Flowing Tide	Boult	AH	fp
10 Aug 43	Rubbra	Sinfonia Concertante	Boult	AH	fp
13 Aug 43	Busch	Cello Concerto	Boult	AH	fp
14 Aug 43	Van Wyk	Saudade for Violin and Orchestra	Boult	AH	fup
17 Aug 43	Kabalevsky	Suite from Colas Breugnon	Boult	AH	fup
18 Aug 43	Moeran	Rhapsody No. 3 for Piano and Orchestra	Boult	AH	fp
6 Sep 43	Phillips	Sinfonietta	Phillips	S	fp
21 Sep 43	Murrill	Country Dances	Boult	S	fbp
1 Oct 43	Berkeley	Divertimento for Strings, Op. 18	Boult	S	fp (c)
7 Oct 43	Milford	Sinfonietta for Small Orchestra	Milford	S	fp
22 Oct 43	Tippett	Fantasia on a theme of Handel	Boult	S	fbp
26 Oct 43	Dyson	Overture: The Canterbury Pilgrims	Dyson	S	fbp
11 Nov 43	Cooke	Piano Concerto	Raybould	S	fp
17 Nov 43	Stravinsky	Symphony in C	Boult	Bedford	fup

Date	Composer	Work	Conductor	Place (See Key)	Perf
18 Nov 43	Alwyn	Concerto Grosso (No. 1)	Raybould	S	fp
19 Nov 43	Evans	Overture: The Spirit of London	Raybould	S	fbp
22 Nov 43	Bax	Violin Concerto	Wood	S	fp
13 Dec 43	Tate	Elegiac March	Boult	S	fp
17 Jan 44	Rubbra	Sinfonia Concertante for Piano and Orchestra	Boult	S	fbp
1 Feb 44	Bush	Overture: Resolution	Raybould	S	fp
20 Feb 44	Hindemith	Symphony in E flat	Raybould	S	fup
20 Mar 44	Berkeley	Symphony (No. 1)	Raybould	S	fbp
3 May 44	Goossens	Symphony No. 1	Cameron	S	fbp
13 Jul 44	Shostakovich	Symphony No. 8	Wood	S	fup
5 Aug 44	Maconchy	Suite: Puck Fair	Boult	S	fp
13 Sep 44	Scott	Fantasia for Strings	Raybould	S	fbp
20 Sep 44	Bartók	Violin Concerto No. 2	Boult	S	fup
30 Sep 44	Bizet, arr. Douglas	Suite No. 2: Jeux d'enfants	Raybould	S	fbp
10 Oct 44	Glière	Overture on Slavonic Tunes	Raybould	S	fup
1 Nov 44	Goossens	Phantasy Concerto for Piano and Orchestra	Boult	Bedford	fup
2 Nov 44	Heming	Threnody for a Soldier killed in Action	Raybould	S	fbp
13 Nov 44	Baker	Aubade	Raybould	S	fp
17 Nov 44	Sowande	Africania	Sowande	S	fp
17 Nov 44	Moeran	My Country	Raybould	S	fp
18 Dec 44	Busch	Cello Concerto	Raybould	S	fbp
21 Dec 44	Prokofiev	A Toast to Stalin	Boult	S	fup
24 Dec 44	Coates	Suite: The Three Elizabeths	Coates	S	fp
4 Jan 45	Bax	Polish Christmas Carols	Woodgate	S	fp
6 Jan 45	Martinů	Lidiče Memorial	Raybould	S	fup
22 Jan 45	Haydn Wood	Phantasy for Strings	Haydn Wood	S	fbp
26 Jan 45	Evans	Vienna Rhapsody	Raybould	S	fbp
1 Feb 45	Seiber	Four Greek Songs for Soprano and Strings	Harrison	S	fbp
15 Feb 45	Lutyens	Salute for Orchestra	Raybould	S	fp
22 Feb 45	Frumerie	Variations and Fugue for Piano and Orchestra	Raybould	S	fup

Date	Composer	Work	Conductor	Place (See Key)	Perf
4 Mar 45	Walton	Memorial Fanfare	Boult	AH	fp
7 Mar 45	Moeran	Sinfonietta	Barbirolli	S	fp
25 Jun 45	Demuth	Fantasia and Fugue	Raybould	S	fp
25 Aug 45	D. Moule Evans	Poem for Orchestra: September Dusk	Evans	AH	fp
25 Aug 45	William Schuman	A Free Song for Chorus and Orchestra	Boult	AH	fup
29 Aug 45	Britten	Four Sea Interludes and Passacaglia (Peter Grimes)	Boult	AH	flp (public)
29 Aug 45	Whyte	Festival March	Whyte	AH	fp
3 Sep 45	Veprik	Song of Jubilation	Cameron	AH	fup
7 Sep 45	Schoenberg	Piano Concerto	Cameron	AH	fup
10 Sep 45	Dunhill	Overture: May-time	Boult	AH	fp
14 Sep 45	Vaughan Williams	Thanksgiving for Victory	Boult	AH	fp (public)
14 Sep 45	Walton	Suite from Henry V	Walton	AH	fp (public)
4 Oct 45	Darnton	Symphony No. 3	Raybould	S	fbp
24 Oct 45	Rawsthorne	Cortèges	Cameron	PP	fbp
28 Nov 45	Bartók	Violin Concerto No. 2	Boult	AH	flp
9 Dec 45	Martinů	Symphony No. 2	Boult	S	fup
16 Jan 46	Knipper	Suite	Raybould	PP	fup
16 Jan 46	Copland	Appalachian Spring	Raybould	PP	fup
27 Feb 46	Kodály	Variations for Orchestra	Ansermet	PP	fup
6 Mar 46	Bartók	Concerto for Orchestra	Boult	AH	flp
8 Mar 46	Bliss	Theme and Cadenza for Violin and Orchestra	Salter	PP	fbp
10 Apr 46	Moeran	Cello Concerto	Boult	PP	fp
22 Apr 46	Stevens	Violin Concerto	Fistoulari	PP	fp
1 May 46	Jacob	Symphony No. 2	Boult	PP	fp
14 May 46	Searle	Piano Concerto in D minor	Boult	PP	fp
22 May 46	Maklakiewicz	Symphonic Poem: Grünwald	Lambert	PP	fup

Date	Composer	Work	Conductor	Place (See Key)	Perf (See Key)
7 Jul 46	Mohaupt	Town-Piper Music	Fitelberg		fup
7 Jul 46	Lutyens	Three Symphonic Preludes	Clark	Covent Garden (ISCM)	fp
7 Jul 46	De Roos	Piano Concerto	Van Lier		fup
7 Jul 46	Barraine	Symphony No. 2	Rosenthal		fup
7 Jul 46	Prokofiev	Ode to the End of the War	Boult		fup
14 Jul 46	Loucheur	Nocturne	Rosenthal		fup
14 Jul 46	Palester	Violin Concerto	Fitelberg		fup
24 Aug 46	Creston	Poem for Harp and Orchestra	Boult	AH	fup
28 Aug 46	Berkeley	Nocturne for Orchestra	Boult	AH	fp
3 Sep 46	Hindemith	Symphonic metamorphoses on themes of Weber	Lambert	AH	fup
11 Sep 46	Ireland	Overture: Satyricon	Cameron	AH	fp
16 Sep 46	Bliss	Suite: Adam Zero	Lambert	AH	fp (public)
17 Sep 46	Strauss	Oboe Concerto	Boult	AH	fup
21 Sep 46	Milhaud	Deux Marches	Lambert	AH	fup
29 Sep 46	Britten	Festival (Occasional) Overture, Op. 38	Boult	S	fp (c)
5 Oct 46	Kodály	Concerto for Orchestra	Kodály	PP	fup
30 Oct 46	Creston	Threnody	Goossens	AH	fup
2 Nov 46	Goossens	Symphony No. 2	Goossens	PP	fup
6 Nov 46	Diamond	Rounds for Strings	Herrmann	S	fup
6 Nov 46	Ives	Prelude & Fugue from Symphony No. 4	Herrmann	S	fup
6 Nov 46	Herrmann	The Devil and Daniel Webster	Herrmann	S	fup
16 Nov 46	Martinů	Symphony No. 4	Kubelík	PP	fup
27 Nov 46	Bartók	Piano Concerto No. 3	Boult	AH	fup
4 Dec 46	Nabokoff	Biblical Symphony	Munch	S	fup
7 Dec 46	Honegger	Symphony No. 3 (Liturgique)	Munch	S	fup
11 Jan 47	Ivanov-Radkevich	Russian Overture	Cameron	AH	fup
17 Jan 47	Hadley	The Hills	Boult	AH	fp
15 Feb 47	Bridgewater	Piano Concerto	Boult	S	fbp
16 Apr 47	Honegger	Joan of Arc at the Stake	Cameron	S	fup

Date	Composer	Work	Conductor	Place (See Key)	Perf
21 Jul 47	Rawsthorne	Oboe Concerto	Rawsthorne	AH	flp
23 Jul 47	Haydn	Organ Concerto in C	Boult	AH	fup
25 Jul 47	Hely-Hutchinson	Symphony for Small Orchestra	Boult	AH	flp
8 Aug 47	Duruflé	Trois Danses	Robinson	AH	fup
20 Aug 47	Jacob	Concerto for Bassoon, Strings and Percussion	Boult	AH	fp
22 Aug 47	Piston	Symphony No. 2	Boult	AH	fup
26 Aug 47	Lutyens	Petite Suite	Boult	AH	fp (public)
5 Sep 47	Novák	Triptych on a chorale theme of St Wenceslas	Boult	AH	fup
21 Sep 47	Lucas	Litany	Raybould	S	fp
22 Nov 47	Finzi	Ode for St Cecilia's Day	Boult	AH	fp
4 Feb 48	Honegger	Joan of Arc at the Stake	Cameron	AH	fup (public)
7 Feb 48	Villa-Lobos	Chôros No. 6	Villa-Lobos	S	fup
26 Feb 48	Cooke	Processional Ode	Boult	Cambridge	fp
21 Apr 48	Vaughan Williams	Symphony No. 6	Boult	AH	fp
29 Jul 48	Vaughan Williams	Partita for double string orchestra	Vaughan Williams	AH	fp (public)
13 Aug 48	Stevens	Fugal Overture	Sargent	AH	fp
23 Aug 48	Kabalevsky	Piano Concerto No. 2	Sargent	AH	fup
25 Aug 48	Rawsthorne	Violin Concerto	Sargent	AH	flp
28 Aug 48	Auric	Overture	Auric	AH	fup
13 Sep 48	Scott	Oboe Concerto	Robinson	AH	fp
16 Sep 48	Milhaud	Suite Française	Sargent	AH	fup
15 Nov 48	Tippett	Birthday Suite	?Boult	S	fp
20 Nov 48	Dallapiccola	Suite: Marsia	Scherchen	S	fp
29 Dec 48	Honegger	La Danse des Morts	Boult	S	fup
22 Jan 49	Tippett	Birthday Suite	Sargent	AH	fp (public)
22 Jan 49	Howells	Corydon's Dance: Scherzo in Arden	Sargent	AH	fp (public)
22 Jan 49	Jacob	Festival March	Sargent	AH	fp (public)
26 Jan 49	Rubbra	Symphony No. 5	Boult	AH	fp
5 Feb 49	Lajtha	In Memoriam	Boult	S	fup

Date	Composer	Work	Conductor	Place (See Key)	Perf
16 Feb 49	Stravinsky	Ballet Suite: Orpheus	Ansermet	AH	fup
19 Feb 49	Stravinsky	Mass	Ansermet	S	fup
26 Feb 49	Cooke	Symphony (No. 1)	Boult	S	fp
5 Mar 49	Cluzeau Mortet	Llanuvas	Raybould	S	fup
5 Mar 49	Chavez	Sinfonia de Antigona	Raybould	S	fup
5 Mar 49	Gnattali	Braziliana	Raybould	S	fup
5 Mar 49	Allende	Tonada No. 11	Raybould	S	fup
5 Mar 49	Villa-Lobos	Chôros No. 10	Raybould	S	fup
26 Mar 49	Bax	The Bard of the Dimbovitza (revised version)	Boult	S	fp
26 Mar 49	Villa-Lobos	Symphony No. 7	Villa-Lobos	S	fp
4 Jun 49	Copland	Symphony No. 3	Boult	S	fbp
10 Jun 49	Caplet	Epiphanie for Cello and Orchestra	Boult	S	fup
10 Jun 49	Roussel	Bacchus et Ariane, Suite No. 1	Boult	S	fup
5 Aug 49	Searle	Overture to a drama	Sargent	AH	fp
15 Aug 49	Goossens	Fantasy for Piano and Orchestra	Goossens	AH	flp
15 Aug 49	Goossens	Sinfonietta	Goossens	AH	flp
16 Aug 49	Jacob	Fantasia on the Alleluia Hymn	Sargent	AH	flp
29 Aug 49	Leighton Lucas	Chaconne in C sharp minor	Lucas	AH	fp (public)
24 Sep 49	Ladmirault	Prélude: Tristan et Iseult	Boult	S	fup
1 Oct 49	Mahler	Symphony No. 2	Walter	AH	Second up
12 Nov 49	Rawsthorne	Concerto for String Orchestra	Del Mar	S	fbp
19 Nov 49	Barraud	Piano Concerto	Boult	Cambridge	fup
3 Dec 49	Nystroem	Sinfonia Espressiva	Boult	S	fbp
17 Dec 49	Daniel Jones	Tone Poem: Cystuddiau Branwen	Daniel Jones	S	fbp
4 Mar 50	Sauguet	Sinfonie Expiatoire	Désormière	S	fubp
1 Apr 50	Hindemith	Piano Concerto	Boult	S	fup
27 Apr 50	Maconchy	Symphony	Boult	S	fp
27 Apr 50	Seiber	Ulysses, for Tenor, Chorus and Orchestra	Boult	S	fbp
6 May 50	Pizzetti	Symphony in A	Boult	S	fup
27 May 50	Milhaud	Kentuckiana	Milhaud	S	fup

Date	Composer	Work	Conductor	Place (See Key)	Perf
27 May 50	Milhaud	Le Bal Martiniquais	Milhaud	S	fup
27 May 50	Milhaud	Symphony No. 3 (Te Deum)	Milhaud	S	fup
9 Jun 50	Thomson	Symphony No. 3	Boult	S	fup
25 Jul 50	Bax	Concerto for Orchestra and Piano (left hand)	Sargent	AH	flp
26 Jul 50	Douglas	Warra-Wirrawaal	Post	AH	fup
21 Aug 50	Jacob	Symphonic Suite (Suite No. 2)	Sargent	AH	flp
23 Aug 50	Sowerby	Organ Concerto in C	Sargent	AH	fup
8 Sep 50	Lutyens	Viola Concerto	Hollingsworth	AH	fp
15 Sep 50	Vaughan Williams	Fantasia on the Old 104th Psalm Tune	Sargent	AH	flp
25 Oct 50	Ghedini	Concerto dell'Albatro	Gui	S	fubp
8 Nov 50	Poulenc	Piano Concerto	Cameron	AH	fup
11 Nov 50	Sibelius	Four Legends for Orchestra (revised version)	Cameron	S	fp (of complete cycle)
15 Nov 50	Rawsthorne	Symphony (No. 1)	Boult	AH	fp
24 Feb 51	Sessions	Symphony No. 2	Boult	S	fup
3 Mar 51	Murrill	Cello Concerto No. 2	Cameron	AH	fp
31 Mar 51	Ravel	Une barque sur l'océan	Boult	S	fup
18 Apr 51	Howells	Hymnus Paradisi	Sargent	AH	fbp/flp
14 Jun 51	Malipiero	Symphony No. 5	Sargent	S	fup
31 Jul 51	Castelnuovo-Tedesco	Concerto da Camera for Oboe and Strings	Sargent	AH	fp
6 Aug 31	Johnstone	A Cumbrian Rhapsody: Tarn Hows	Johnstone	AH	flp (public)
22 Aug 51	Sainton	Serenade Fantastique for Oboe and Strings	Sainton	AH	flp (public)
31 Aug 51	Daniel Jones	Five Pieces for Orchestra	Jones	AH	fp
7 Sep 51	Bush	Symphonic Suite: Piers Plowman's Day	Bush	AH	fup
14 Sep 51	Fricker	Symphony No. 1	Sargent	AH	flp (public)
13 Nov 51	Matthews	Queen of Ithaca	Raybould	S	fbp
13 Nov 51	Busoni	Fantasia Contrappuntistica (orch. version)	Raybould	S	fbp
5 Mar 52	Dallapiccola	Symphonic Fragments from the Ballet Marsia	Gui	S	fup
20 Mar 52	Schoenberg	Violin Concerto	Schwarz	S	fubp
16 Apr 52	Martinů	Piano Concerto No. 3	Sargent	S	fubp

Date	Composer	Work	Conductor	Place (See Key)	Perf
3 May 52	Schoenberg	Songs with Orchestra, Op. 22	Goehr	S	fup
6 Nov 52	Wordsworth	Symphony No. 2	Boult	S	fbp
15 Nov 52	Jarnach	Prelude for Orchestra	Schmidt-Isserstedt	S	fup
6 Dec 52	Porter	Viola Concerto	Raybould	S	fubp
10 Jan 53	Martin	Violin Concerto	Boult	S	fubp
17 Jan 53	Ibert	Symphonie Concertante	Sargent	S	fup
7 Feb 53	Ben–Haim	Symphony No. 1	Van Beinum	S	fup
18 Mar 53	Rankl	Symphony No. 1	Rankl	S	fubp
21 Mar 53	Fulton	Sinfonia Pastorale	Boult	S	fbp
8 Apr 53	Bell	The Strain Upraise	Raybould	S	fp
9 Apr 53	Honegger	Monopartita	Sacher	S	fubp
11 Apr 53	Bloch	Concerto Grosso No. 2	Sargent	S	fp
11 Apr 53	Bloch	Sinfonia Breve	Sargent	S	fp
15 Apr 53	Rubbra	Viola Concerto	Sargent	FH	fp
6 Jun 53	Rubbra	Ode to the Queen	Sargent	S	fp (c)
6 Jun 53	Berkeley	Suite for Orchestra	Sargent	S	fp (c)
25 Jul 53	Walton	Coronation Te Deum	Sargent	AH	flp (public)
29 Jul 53	Berkeley	Flute Concerto	Sargent	AH	fp
19 Aug 53	Jongen	Symphonic Concertante for Organ and Orchestra	Sargent	AH	fp
29 Aug 53	Tippett	Fantasia Concertante on a theme of Corelli	Tippett	Edinburgh	fp
3 Sep 53	Tippett	Fantasia Concertante on a theme of Corelli	Tippett	AH	flp
10 Sep 53	Howells	A Kent Yeoman's Wooing Song	Tippett	AH	fp
3 Oct 53	Skalkottas	Five Greek Dances	Goehr	S	fup
8 Oct 53	Absil	Le Zodiaque	Fjelstad	S	fup
8 Oct 53	Valen	Le Cimetière Marin	Fjelstad	S	fup
14 Oct 53	Maconchy	Coronation Overture: Proud Thames	Sargent	FH	fp
9 Dec 53	Fricker	Viola Concerto	Sargent	FH	flp
17 Dec 53	Malipiero	El Mondo Novo	Scherchen	S	fup
8 Jan 54	Tansman	Sinfonia Piccola	Kletzki	S	fup
3 Feb 54	Alwyn	Symphony No. 2	Barbirolli	FH	flp

Date	Composer	Work	Conductor	Place (See Key)	Perf
12 Feb 54	Vermeulen	Passacaglia and Cortège	Van Beinum	S	fup
19 Feb 54	Gerhard	Pedrelliana	Castro	S	fp
20 Feb 54	Jolivet	Concertino for Trumpet, Strings and Piano	Sargent	S	fup
12 Mar 54	Hamilton	Clarinet Concerto	Goossens	S	fubp
14 Apr 54	Creston	Symphony No. 2	Monteux	S	fup
4 Jun 54	Jacob	Laudate Dominum	Sargent	S	fbp
24 Jul 54	Alwyn	Harp Concerto	Sargent	AH	fp
29 Jul 54	Bliss	A Song of Welcome	Sargent	AH	fp (public)
30 Jul 54	Maconchy	Concertino for Bassoon and Strings	Sargent	AH	fp
6 Aug 54	Benjamin	Symphony	Benjamin	AH	flp
7 Aug 54	Jolivet	Concertino for Trumpet, Strings and Piano	Sargent	AH	fup (public)
14 Aug 54	Burkhard	Overture: The Hunting Parson	Sargent	AH	fup (public)
14 Aug 54	Arnold	Harmonica Concerto	Arnold	AH	fp
14 Aug 54	Rachmaninov	Symphonic Dances	Sargent	AH	fup (public)
20 Aug 54	Cannon	Symphonic Study: Spring	Sargent	AH	fp (public)
31 Aug 54	Leighton	Violin Concerto	Sargent	AH	fp (public)
13 Sep 54	Aplvor	Symphonic Suite: A mirror for witches	Hollingsworth	AH	fp
24 Sep 54	Simpson	Symphony No. 1	Boult	S	fup
29 Sep 54	Martin	Harpsichord Concerto	Boult	S	fup
5 Nov 54	Martinon	Sinfonietta	Martinon	S	fup
17 Nov 54	Rubbra	Symphony No. 6	Sargent	FH	fp
14 Jan 55	Rankl	Symphony No. 4	Rankl	S	fbp
19 Jan 55	Vaughan Williams	A Christmas Cantata, 'Hodie'	Sargent	FH	flp
21 Jan 55	Peragallo	Violin Concerto	Schwarz	S	fup
26 Jan 55	Harold Noble	Mass	Schwarz	S	fp
28 Jan 55	Jacob	Sinfonietta No. 3	Schwarz	S	fbp
30 Jan 55	Leighton	Overture: Primavera Romana	Schwarz	S	fbp
4 Feb 55	Persichetti	Symphony No. 4	Ormandy	S	fup
29 Apr 55	Creston	Symphony No. 3	Wallenstein	S	fup
29 Apr 55	De Lamarter	Overture from the Suite, The Betrothal	Wallenstein	S	fup

Date	Composer	Work	Conductor	Place (See Key)	Perf
11 May 55	Bliss	Violin Concerto	Sargent	FH	fp (c)
11 Jun 55	Martinů	Symphony No. 6 (Fantaisies symphoniques)	Tausky	S	fup
27 Jul 55	Panufnik	Sinfonia Rustica	Panufnik	AH	fp (public)
2 Aug 55	Walton	Duet, Act II, Troilus and Cressida	Sargent	AH	fp (concert)
19 Aug 55	John Veale	Panorama	Hollingsworth	AH	fp (public)
30 Aug 55	Shostakovich	Symphony No. 10	Sargent	Edinburgh	fubp
7 Sep 55	Menotti	Overture: Amelia goes to the Ball	Hollingsworth	AH	fup (public)
12 Sep 55	A. Brott	Overture: Royal Tribute	Brott	AH	fup
17 Sep 55	Weber	Symphony No. 1 in C	Cameron	AH	fup (public)
21 Oct 55	Beck	Symphony No. 4	Goossens	S	fup
26 Oct 55	Liebermann	Concerto for Jazz Band and Symphony Orchestra	Goossens	FH	fup
28 Oct 55	Goossens	The Apocalypse	Goossens	S	fup
9 Nov 55	Martin	Golgotha	Sargent	FH	fup (public)
18 Nov 55	Foss	Piano Concerto	Goehr	S	fup
16 Dec 55	Loeffler	Death of Tintagiles for Viola d'amore and Orchestra	Wallenstein	S	fubp
28 Dec 55	Piston	Symphony No. 4	Wallenstein	S	fup
4 Jan 56	Dello Joio	Variations, Chaconne and Finale	Wallenstein	S	fup
13 Jan 56	Toch	Symphony No. 2	Wallenstein	S	fup
18 Jan 56	Rubbra	Improvisation for Violin and Orchestra	Sargent	FH	fup
24 Feb 56	Fortner	Capriccio and Finale	Schmidt-Isserstedt	S	fubp (public)
7 Mar 56	Hartmann	Symphony No. 3	Jochum	FH	fp
21 Mar 56	Rubbra	Piano Concerto in G	Sargent	FH	fup
4 Apr 56	Robert Hughes	Essay for Orchestra	Susskind	S	fup
21 Jul 56	Milhaud	Harp Concerto	Sargent	AH	fup
23 Jul 56	Kodály	Variations on a Hungarian Folk-Song, The Peacock	Sargent	AH	flp (public)
24 Jul 56	Surinach	Sinfonietta Flamenca	Sargent	AH	fup

Date	Composer	Work	Conductor	Place (See Key)	Perf
11 Aug 56	J. Addison	Suite from the Ballet: Carte Blanche	Addison	AH	fp (public)
14 Aug 56	Searle	Piano Concerto No. 2	Hollingsworth	AH	ffp (public)
17 Aug 56	Saeverud	Siljuslatten	Sargent	AH	fup (public)
5 Sep 56	Hoddinott	Concerto for Clarinet and Strings	Sargent	AH	flp (public)
7 Sep 56	Bush	Concerto Suite for Cello and Orchestra	Bush	AH	ffp (public)
13 Sep 56	Hamilton	Symphonic Variations	Sargent	AH	flp
14 Sep 56	Greenwood	Viola Concerto	Hollingsworth	AH	fp
10 Oct 56	Alwyn	Symphony No. 3	Beecham	FH	fp (c)
12 Oct 56	Blacher	Fantasy for Orchestra	Robinson	S	fp (c)
19 Oct 56	De Seixas	Suite Ancienne	Freitas-Branco	S	fup
19 Oct 56	Barraud	Offrande à une ombre	Freitas-Branco	S	fubp
24 Oct 56	Rawsthorne	Violin Concerto No. 2	Freitas-Branco	FH	fp
2 Nov 56	Berger	Rondo Ostinado	Goossens	S	fup
2 Nov 56	Ibert	Bacchanale	Goossens	S	fp (c)
21 Nov 56	Villa–Lobos	Harp Concerto	Scherchen	FH	fup
28 Dec 56	Holmboe	Symphonic Metamorphosis: Epitaph	Robinson	S	fp (c)
11 Jan 57	Panufnik	Rhapsody	Panufnik	S	fp (c)
23 Jan 57	Walton	Johannesburg Festival Overture	Sargent	FH	flp (public)
25 Jan 57	Tansman	Violin Concerto	Sargent	S	fup
1 Feb 57	Blomdahl	In the Hall of Mirrors	Del Mar	S	fup
8 Feb 57	Lutoslawski	Concerto for Orchestra	Sargent	S	fubp
13 Feb 57	Walton	Cello Concerto	Sargent	FH	fup
12 Apr 57	Tansman	The Prophet Isaiah	Schwarz	S	fup
19 Apr 57	Blacher	Study in Pianissimo	Schwarz	S	fup
25 May 57	Bacewicz	Overture for Orchestra	Del Mar	S	fup
31 May 57	Gerhard	Symphony (No. 1)	Boult	S	fup
22 Jul 57	Martin	Overture: Athalie	Sargent	AH	ftp (public)
24 Jul 57	Fricker	Litany for double string orchestra	Fricker	AH	fp (public)
17 Aug 57	Ibert	Bacchanale	Sargent	AH	fup
23 Aug 57	Henze	Ode to the West Wind for Cello and Orchestra	Hollingsworth	AH	fup

Date	Composer	Work	Conductor	Place (See Key)	Perf
30 Aug 57	S. Bate	Piano Concerto No. 3	Hollingsworth	AH	fp
30 Aug 57	Reizenstein	Overture: Cyrano de Bergerac	Hollingsworth	AH	flp (public)
31 Aug 57	Rawsthorne	Dance Suite: Madame Chrysanthème	Rawsthorne	AH	fp
5 Sep 57	Martinů	Piano Concerto No. 4 (Incantations)	Sargent	AH	flp
12 Sep 57	Leighton	Cello Concerto	Leighton	AH	flp
26 Oct 57	Milhaud	Symphony No. 6	Milhaud	S	fup
30 Oct 57	Hamilton	The Bermudas	Schwarz	FH	fp (c)
10 Nov 57	Guarnieri	Piano Concerto	Horenstein	S	fup
25 Jan 58	Bloch	Proclamation for Trumpet and Orchestra	Sargent	S	fubp
5 Feb 58	Tippett	Symphony No. 2	Boult	FH	fp (c)
8 Feb 58	Williamson	Overture: Santiago de Espada	Boult	S	fbp
12 Feb 58	Gerhard	Violin Concerto	Schwarz	FH	fp
22 Mar 58	Havergal Brian	Symphony No. 9	Del Mar	S	fbp
31 May 58	Haydn	The Storm (1792)	Boult	S	fbp
31 May 58	Haydn	Litany (1730)	Boult	S	fp (modern)
17 Jul 58	Susskind	Nine Slovak Sketches	Susskind	S	fubp
20 Jul 58	Bowen	Festal Overture	Susskind	S	fbp
23 Aug 58	Hoddinott	Harp Concerto	Sargent	AH	flp
5 Sep 58	Shostakovich	Piano Concerto, Op. 101	Sargent	AH	fup
10 Sep 58	Martin	Etudes for string orchestra	Miles	AH	fup
12 Sep 58	G. Bush	Symphony No. 1	Miles	AH	flp (public)
16 Oct 58	Britten	Nocturne for Tenor and Small Orchestra	Schwarz	Leeds	fp
17 Oct 58	Charpentier	Te Deum	Bardgett	Leeds	fup (modern)
25 Oct 58	Henkemans	Harp Concerto	Schwarz	S	fup
19 Nov 58	Crossley-Holland	Chansonnier des puys d'amore	Schwarz	S	fbp
6 Dec 58	S. V. Tarp	Comedy Overture No. 2	Schwarz	S	fbp
6 Dec 58	Hermann Kappel	Concertino for Strings	Schwarz	S	fubp
6 Dec 58	P. R. Olsen	Symphonic Variations	Schwarz	S	fbp
6 Dec 58	Fricker	Symphony No. 2	Jensen	S	fubp

Date	Composer	Work	Conductor	Place (See Key)	Perf
31 Dec 58	Shostakovich	Piano Concerto No. 2	Sargent	S	fubp
29 Jan 59	Seiber	Three Pieces for Cello and Orchestra	Schmidt-Isserstedt	S	fubp
8 Feb 59	John Veale	Kubla Khan	Schwarz	S	fp
11 Feb 59	Berkeley	Concerto for Piano and Double Orchestra	Berkeley	FH	fp
14 Feb 59	Berkeley	Concerto for Piano and Double Orchestra	Berkeley	S	fbp
15 Feb 59	Serge Lancen	Piano Concerto	Schwarz	S	fup
18 Feb 59	Daniel Jones	Symphony No. 5	Jones	FH	fp (c)
28 Feb 59	Dallapiccola	Canti di Liberazione	Sanzogno	S	fup
4 Mar 59	Petrassi	Piano Concerto	Sanzogno	FH	fup
13 Mar 59	Bentzon	Symphonic Variations	Sargent	S	fup
8 Apr 59	Lajtha	Symphony No. 7	Goossens	S	fup
11 Apr 59	Goossens	Violin Concerto	Goossens	S	fp
12 Apr 59	Rota	Variations on a Gay Tune	Goossens	S	fup
16 Apr 59	Fried	Concerto for Two Pianos & Orchestra	Sargent	S	fup
18 Apr 59	Martinů	The Epic of Gilgamesh	Sargent	S	fup
8 May 59	von Einem	Symphonic Scenes	Freccia	S	fp
23 May 59	Leighton	Passacaglia, Chorale and Fugue	Leighton	S	fubp
23 May 59	Schoeck	Summer Night	Schwarz	S	fup
5 Jun 59	Fortner	Fantasy on BACH	Schwarz	S	fup
12 Jun 59	Martinů	Fantasia Concertante for Piano and Orchestra	Schwarz	S	fp
16 Jul 59	Lipkin	Piano Concerto	Schwarz	Cheltenham	fup (public)
17 Jul 59	Hamilton	Violin Concertino	Schwarz	Cheltenham	flp
25 Jul 59	Whettam	Dance Concertante	Sargent	AH	fp (public)
6 Aug 59	Ibert	Symphonie Concertante for Oboe and Strings	Hollingsworth	AH	flp (public)
15 Aug 59	Milhaud	Concerto for Percussion and Small Orchestra	Sargent	AH	flp
19 Aug 59	Williamson	Piano Concerto	Hollingsworth	AH	flp
3 Sep 59	Leighton	Burlesque	Leighton	AH	fp (public)
9 Sep 59	Berkeley	Symphony No. 2	Berkeley	AH	flp

Date	Composer	Work	Conductor	Place (See Key)	Perf
7 Oct 59	Honegger	Une Cantate de Noël	Ansermet	S	flp
28 Oct 59	Gerhard	Symphony No. 2	Schwarz	FH	fp (c)
25 Nov 59	Ghedini	Pezzo Concertante	Freccia	FH	flp
28 Nov 59	Malipiero	La Cena	Freccia	S	fubp
19 Dec 59	Milner	Variations for Orchestra	Schwarz	S	fbp
30 Dec 59	Lopatnikoff	Concerto for Two Pianos and Orchestra	Schwarz	S	fup
10 Feb 60	Badings	Concerto for Two Violins and Orchestra	Schwarz	FH	fup
12 Feb 60	Suchon	Metamorfozy	Schwarz	S	fup
17 Feb 60	Rubbra	Violin Concerto	Schwarz	FH	fp
5 Mar 60	S.-E. Bäck	Violin Concerto	Fjeldstad	S	fup
9 Mar 60	Valen	Symphony No. 3	Fjeldstad	FH	fup
12 Mar 60	Valen	Symphony No. 3	Fjeldstad	S	fubp
23 Apr 60	Copland	Quiet City	Copland	S	fup
23 Apr 60	Copland	Suite: The Tender Land	Copland	S	fup
27 Apr 60	William Schuman	Violin Concerto	Schwarz	S	fup
7 May 60	Jolivet	Concerto for Flute and Strings	Jolivet	S	fubp
7 May 60	Constant	24 Preludes	Schwarz	S	fup
14 May 60	Jacob	Passacaglia Stereophonica	Schwarz	S	fp
20 May 60	Strauss	Japanische Festmusik	Groves	S	fup
29 May 60	Lutoslawski	Musique Funèbre for String Orchestra	Sanzogno	FH	fup
13 Jul 60	Maw	Nocturne	Schwarz	Cheltenham	flp (public)
14 Jul 60	Smith Brindle	Cosmos for Orchestra	Gibson	Cheltenham	fp (public)
15 Jul 60	Frankel	Symphony, Op. 33	Frankel	Cheltenham	fup
6 Aug 60	Hamilton	Scottish Dances	Robinson	AH	flp (public)
7 Sep 60	Goossens	Phantasy Concerto for Violin and Orchestra	Goossens	AH	fp (public)
8 Sep 60	Alwyn	Overture: Derby Day	Sargent	AH	fp (c)
14 Oct 60	Dallapiccola	Variazioni	Schwarz	S	fubp
19 Oct 60	Schoenberg	Songs with Orchestra, Op. 22	Maderna	FH	fup (public)
31 Oct 60	Maw	Nocturne	Schwarz	FH	fbp
31 Oct 60	Frankel	Symphony Op. 33	Frankel	S	fbp

Date	Composer	Work	Conductor	Place (See Key)	Perf
2 Nov 60	Arnold	Symphony No. 4	Arnold	FH	fp (c)
4 Dec 60	Gal	Idyllikon	Schwarz	S	fup
31 Dec 60	Bergman	Aubade	Schwarz	S	fup
4 Feb 61	Seiber	Renaissance Suite	Schwarz	S	fbp
8 Feb 61	Gerhard	Symphony No. 3, Collages	Schwarz	FH	fp
10 Mar 61	Stravinsky	Monumentum in memoriam Gesualdo	Rosbaud	S	fup
22 Mar 61	Stravinsky	Movements for Piano and Orchestra	Rosbaud	FH	fup
13 Apr 61	Nono	Intolleranza, 1960	Maderna	Venice	fp
6 May 61	S.-E. Bäck	Sinfonia da Camera	Schwarz	S	fup
24 May 61	Bacewicz	Music for Five Trumpets, Percussion and Strings	Schwarz	S	fup
27 May 61	Berkeley	Suite: A Winter's Tale	Berkeley	Norwich	fp
1 Jun 61	Lutyens	Music for Orchestra	Maderna	S	fp
1 Jun 61	Messiaen	Oiseaux Exotiques	Maderna	S	fup
1 Jun 61	Nono	Composizione 1	Maderna	S	fup
4 Jun 61	Zafred	Viola Concerto	Schwarz	S	fup
7 Jun 61	Reizenstein	Piano Concerto No. 2	Schwarz	S	fp
10 Jun 61	Bush	Dorian Passacaglia and Fugue	Schwarz	S	fp
12 Jul 61	Hamilton	Five Love Songs for Tenor and Orchestra	Schwarz	Cheltenham	fp
13 Jul 61	R. R. Bennett	Journal for Orchestra	Del Mar	Cheltenham	fp
14 Jul 61	Bush	Dorian Passacaglia and Fugue	Schwarz	Cheltenham	fp (public)
28 Jul 61	Lutyens	Symphonies for solo piano, wind, harp and percussion	Carewe	AH	fp (c)
11 Aug 61	Ravel, arr. Goossens	Le Gibet	Goossens	AH	flp
24 Aug 61	Goehr	Hecuba's Lament	Goehr	AH	fp (c)
16 Sep 61	Gerhard	Two songs from The Duenna	Cameron	AH	fp (public)
21 Nov 61	ApIvor	Yerma	Goossens	Camden	fp
29 Nov 61	Schoenberg	Prelude to Genesis, Op. 44	Maderna	FH	fup
2 Dec 61	Frankel	Serenata Concertate, Op. 37	Frankel	S	fp
7 Jan 62	Spisak	Concerto Giocoso	Skrowaczewski	S	fup

Date	Composer	Work	Conductor	Place (See Key)	Perf (See Key)
20 Jan 62	Gielen	Variations for Forty Instruments	Gielen	S	fup
24 Jan 62	Messiaen	Reveil des Oiseaux	Gielen	FH	fup
24 Feb 62	Smith Brindle	Homage to H. G. Wells	Smith-Brindle	S	fp
10 Mar 62	John Vincent	Symphony in D	Boult	S	fup
27 Mar 62	Delius	Fennimore and Gerda	Robinson	Camden	fup
14 Apr 62	Elliott Carter	A Holiday Overture	Solomon	S	fup
5 May 62	Mendelssohn	Concerto for Two Pianos	Schwarz	S	fup
31 May 62	Veerhoff	Mirages for Orchestra	Rosbaud	FH	fp
31 May 62	Stravinsky	A Sermon, a Narrative and a Prayer	Rosbaud	FH	fup
31 May 62	Henze	Antifone	Rosbaud	FH	fup
31 May 62	Klaus Huber	Cujus Legibus Rotantur Poli	Rosbaud	FH (ISCM)	fup
4 Jun 62	Camillo Togni	Helian Di Trakl, Op. 39	Rosbaud	S	fup
4 Jun 62	Maurice Jarré	Mobiles	Rosbaud	S	fup
4 Jun 62	Baird	Erotics for Soprano and Orchestra	Rosbaud	S	fup
11 Jul 62	Hoddinott	Symphony No. 2	Schwarz	Cheltenham	fp
12 Jul 62	Lutyens	Quincunx, Op. 44	Del Mar	Cheltenham	fp
13 Jul 62	Frankel	Symphony No. 2	Schwarz	Cheltenham	fp
31 Jul 62	Berkeley	Five Pieces for Violin and Orchestra	Berkeley	AH	fp
15 Aug 62	Rawsthorne	Medieval Diptych for Baritone and Orchestra	Del Mar	AH	fp (c)
31 Aug 62	Maw	Scenes and Arias	Del Mar	AH	fp (c)
13 Sep 62	Maxwell Davies	Fantasia on an 'In Nomine' of John Taverner	Maxwell Davies	AH	fp (c)
10 Oct 62	Messiaen	Chronochromie	Gielen	S	fup
13 Oct 62	Penderecki	Tren, for 52 Instruments	Gielen	S	fubp
17 Oct 62	Schoenberg	Die glückliche Hand	Gielen	FH	fup
14 Nov 62	Tippett	Praeludium for Brass, Bells and Percussion	Dorati	FH	fp
6 Dec 62	Britten	A War Requiem	Britten/Meredith/Davies	Westminster Abbey	flp
1 Jun 63	Bartók	The Miraculous Mandarin	Dorati	S	fp (complete)
9 Aug 63	Berkeley	Four Ronsard Sonnets for Tenor and Orchestra	Berkeley	AH	fp (c)

Date	Composer	Work	Conductor	Place (See Key)	Perf
11 Sep 63	Fricker	O longs désirs: song cycle for Soprano and Orchestra	Fricker	AH	fp (c)
28 Sep 63	Skalkottas	Violin Concerto	Dorati	S	fup
2 Oct 63	Stravinsky	The Flood	Dorati	FH	fup
16 Oct 63	Rawsthorne	Carmen Vitale	Del Mar	FH	fp
13 Nov 63	Schoenberg	Von Heute auf Morgen	Dorati	FH	fup
24 Nov 63	Partos	Viola Concerto	Dorati	S	fup
14 Dec 63	Silvestri	Three Pieces for String Orchestra	Silvestri	S	fbp
4 Mar 64	Boulez	Le Soleil des eaux	Boulez	FH	fup
1 Apr 64	Gerhard	The Plague	Dorati	FH	fp (c)
2 May 64	R. Hall	Symphony No. 4	Gielen	S	fp
17 Jul 64	Lutyens	Music for Orchestra III	Dorati	Cheltenham	fp (c)
29 Jul 64	Naylor	Cantata: Sing O my love	Halsey	AH	fp (c)
5 Aug 64	Smith Brindle	Creation Epic	Brindle	AH	fp (c)
19 Aug 64	Alwyn	Concerto Grosso No. 3	Alwyn	AH	fp (c)
3 Sep 64	Rainer	Cello Concerto	Del Mar	AH	fp (c)
11 Sep 64	Bennett	Aubade	Carewe	AH	fp (c)
10 Oct 64	Koechlin	Les Bandar-Log	Dorati	S	fup
25 Apr 65	Gerhard	Concerto for Orchestra	Dorati	Boston	fp
25 Apr 65	Britten	Our Hunting Fathers	Dorati	Boston	fp in USA
29 Apr 65	Boulez	Doubles	Boulez	Hartford	fp
6 May 65	Tippett	Piano Concerto	Dorati	Philadelphia	fp in USA
9 Jul 65	Gerhard	Concerto for Orchestra	Del Mar	Cheltenham	fup
2 Aug 65	Wood	Scenes from Comus	Del Mar	AH	fp (c)
4 Aug 65	Hamilton	Cantos for Orchestra	Del Mar	AH	fp (c)
3 Oct 65	Castiglioni	Apreludes	Dorati	S	fup
11 Oct 65	Tharichen	Timpani Concerto	Kempe	S	fup
17 Oct 65	Blacher	Clementi Variations	Kempe	S	fup
30 Oct 65	Ruggles	Portals for String Orchestra	Copland	S	fubp
7 Jan 66	Sessions	Piano Concerto	Schmid	S	fup
19 Jan 66	Tippett	The Vision of St Augustine	Tippett	FH	fp (c)

Date	Composer	Work	Conductor	Place (See Key)	Perf (See Key)
31 Jan 66	Skalkottas	Suite No. 2	Dorati	S	fp
31 Jan 66	Skalkottas	Piano Concerto No. 2	Dorati	S	fup
7 Feb 66	Dallapiccola	Requiescant	Dorati	S	fubp
21 Mar 66	Hindemith	Cardillac	Susskind	Camden	fup (revised version)
8 Apr 66	Dorati	Madrigal Suite	Dorati	S	fp
8 Apr 66	Dorati	Symphony	Dorati	S	fup
7 May 66	Boulez	Éclat	Boulez	S	fup
6 Jun 66	Messiaen	Et exspecto resurrectionem mortuorum	Dorati	S	fp
28 Jul 66	Varèse	Ecuatorial	Prausnitz	AH	fup
4 Aug 66	Crosse	Ceremony for Cello and Orchestra	Del Mar	AH	fp (c)
2 Sep 66	Boulez	Éclat	Boulez	AH	fup (public)
13 Sep 66	Schuller	Sequences from Movements for Flute and Strings	Schuller	AH	fup
13 Sep 66	Ives	Symphony No. 4	Schuller	AH	fup (public)
5 Oct 66	Shostakovich	Cello Concerto No. 2	Davis	FH	fep
3 Mar 67	Lutyens	'And suddenly it's evening' for tenor and eleven instruments		QEH	fp (c)
15 May 67	Penderecki	De Natura Sonoris (No. 1)	Czyz	S	fup
24 May 67	Penderecki	St Luke Passion	Czyz	FH	fup
18 Jul 67	Rainier	Aequora Lunae	Del Mar	Cheltenham	fp (c)
2 Sep 67	Stravinsky	Requiem Canticles (15–18)	Boulez	Edinburgh	fep
6 Nov 67	Penderecki	From the Psalms of David	Bertini	S	fup
20 Nov 67	Amy	Triade	Amy	S	fup
8 Apr 68	Malipiero	Symphony No. 1	Rossi	S	fubp
12 Jul 68	Gerhard	Epithalamion	Del Mar	Cheltenham	fup
12 Aug 68	Tavener	In alium	Atherton	AH	fp (c) (twice)
12 Aug 68	Banks	Violin Concerto	Del Mar	AH	fp (c)
23 Aug 68	Birtwistle	Nomos	Davis	AH	fp (c)
15 Oct 68	Mathias	Piano Concerto No. 3	Atzmon	Swansea	fp
30 Oct 68	Boulanger	Psalm : Du fond de l'abîme	Boulanger	Croydon	fubp
20 Nov 68	Barraqué	Clarinet Concerto for Six Instrumental Groups	Amy	FH	fp

Date	Composer	Work	Conductor	Place (See Key)	Perf
20 Nov 68	Amy...	Trajectoires	Amy	FH	fup
27 Nov 68	Bantock	Omar Khayyám (Part Three)	Del Mar	S	fbp
4 Dec 68	Gerhard	Symphony No. 4	Davis	FH	fp (public)
16 Dec 68	Bliss...	Ballet Music: The Lady of Shalott	Bliss	S	fup
23 Jan 69	Bellini	Mass in A Minor	Gellhorn	S	fbp
23 Jan 69	Rubbra	In Die et Nocte Canticum	Gellhorn	S	fbp
5 Feb 69	Walton	Capriccio burlesca	Davis	FH	fup
5 Feb 69	Musgrave	Clarinet Concerto	Davis	FH	fp
17 Mar 69	Schedrin	Piano Concerto	Rozhdestvensky	S	fup
7 May 69	Boulez	Pli selon pli	Boulez	AH	flp (complete)
16 May 69	Tcherepnin	Piano Concerto No. 2	Tcherepnin	S	fup
16 May 69	Tcherepnin	Symphony No. 1	Tcherepnin	S	fup
22 Jul 69	Berio	Sinfonia	Berio	AH	fup
29 Jul 69	A. Bush	Scherzo for Wind Orchestra with Percussion	Bush	AH	fp (c)
16 Aug 69	Arnold	Concerto for Two Pianos and Orchestra	Arnold	AH	fp (c)
26 Aug 69	Wood	Cello Concerto	Davis	AH	fp (c)
28 Aug 69	Maxwell Davies	Worldes Blis	Maxwell Davies	AH	fp (c)
24 Sep 69	Milhaud	Musique pour l'Indiana	Milhaud	S	fup
24 Sep 69	Milhaud	Symphony No. 10	Milhaud	S	fup
16 Oct 69	Rosenthal...	Musique de Table	Rosenthal	S	fup
22 Oct 69	Shostakovich	Symphony No. 2	Davis	FH	fup
14 Jan 70	Stockhausen	Setz die Segel zur Sonne	Stockhausen	S	fup
14 Jan 70	Stockhausen	Punkte	Pritchard	S	fup
21 Jan 70	Hamilton	Circus	Pritchard	FH	fp (c)
29 Jan 70	Crosse	Violin Concerto No. 2	Davis	Oxford	fp
9 Mar 70	Baird	Espressioni Varianti	Gielen	S	fup
18 Mar 70	Donatoni	Etwas rühiger im Ausdrück	Gielen	FH	fup
18 Mar 70	Berio	Epifanie	Gielen	FH	fup
18 Mar 70	Nono	Il Canto Sospeso	Gielen	FH	fup (public)
25 Mar 70	Elliott Carter	Piano Concerto	Leinsdorf	FH	fup

Date	Composer	Work	Conductor	Place (See Key)	Perf
17 Jul 70	Messiaen	La Transfiguration de notre Seigneur Jésus-Christ	Baudo	AH	fup
23 Jul 70	Ives	Tone Roads Nos 1 and 3	Foster	AH	fup (public)
23 Jul 70	Ives	The Pond	Foster	AH	fup
25 Jul 70	Weill	The Lindbergh Flight	Davis	AH	fup
13 Aug 70	Souster	Triple Music II	Atherton/Connolly/Howarth	AH	fp (c)
8 Sep 70	Lutyens	Essence of our Happinesses	Del Mar	AH	fp (c)
12 Sep 70	Arnold	Fantasy for Audience and Orchestra	Davis	AH	fp (c)
25 Sep 70	Chavez	Sinfonia de Antigona	Copland	S	fup
25 Sep 70	Fine	Serious Song for String Orchestra	Copland	S	fup
21 Oct 70	Boulez	Éclat-multiples (incomplete version)	Boulez	FH	fp
23 Nov 70	Hamilton	Piano Concerto (revised version)	Downes	S	fp
30 Nov 70	Amy	Cette étoile enseigne à s'incliner	Amy	S	fup
31 Mar 71	Maderna	Quadrivium	Maderna	FH	fup
2 Jun 71	Birtwistle	An imaginary landscape	Boulez	FH	fp (c)
2 Jun 71	Holliger	Siebengesang	Boulez	FH	fup
7 Jun 71	Smith Brindle	Apocalypses	Segerstam	Cheltenham	fp
7 Jun 71	Blomdahl	Chamber Concerto	Segerstam	Cheltenham	fup (public)
6 Sep 71	Newson	Arena	Boulez	RH	fp (c)
7 Sep 71	Messiaen	Poèmes pour Mi (orchestral version)	Pritchard	AH	fup
18 Sep 71	Williamson	The Stone Wall: opera for Audience and Orchestra	Davis	AH	fp (c)
18 Oct 71	Carter	Concerto for Orchestra	Boulez	Graz	fep
8 Nov 71	Ligeti	Requiem	Gielen	S	fup
10 Nov 71	Ligeti	Requiem	Gielen	FH	fup (public)
27 Nov 71	Prokofiev (completed Kabalevsky and Rostropovich)	Cello Concertino	Schmid	S	fubp
8 Dec 71	Crosse	Memories of morning: night	Groves	FH	fp (c)
17 Jan 72	Maderna	Juilliard Serenade	Boulez	RH	fup
17 Jan 72	Connolly	Tetramorph	Boulez	RH	fp (c)
17 Jan 72	Stockhausen	Mixtur (version for small orchestra)	Boulez	RH	fup
31 Jan 72	Ligeti	Ramifications	Boulez	RH	fup

Date	Composer	Work	Conductor	Place (See Key)	Perf
31 Jan 72	*Rands*	Mésalliance	*Boulez*	RH	fp (c)
31 Jan 72	*Salzman*	Foxes and Hedgehogs	*Boulez*	RH	fup
27 Feb 72	*Crumb*	Echoes of time and the river	*Farberman*	S	fup
27 Feb 72	*Sessions*	Symphony No. 5	*Farberman*	S	fup
27 Feb 72	*Farberman*	Ballet: The Losers	*Farberman*	S	fup
27 Feb 72	*Feldman*	The viola in my life (version 4)	*Farberman*	S	fup
6 Mar 72	*Globokar*	Fluide	*Masson*	S	fup
6 Mar 72	*Xenakis*	Avrova	*Masson*	S	fup
6 Mar 72	*Alsina*	Funktionen	*Masson*	S	fup
6 Mar 72	*Berio*	Chemin IIb	*Masson*	S	fup
10 Apr 72	*Folas*	Quatre plages	*Amy*	S	fup
19 Apr 72	*Boulez*	e.e. cummings ist der dichter	*Boulez*	FH	fup (twice)
22 May 72	*Bussotti*	Three madrigals	*Gielen*	RH	fup
22 May 72	*Lutyens*	Counting your steps	*Gielen*	RH	fup
22 May 72	*Folas*	Points d'aube	*Gielen*	RH	fup
22 May 72	*Gielen*	Four poems of Stephan George	*Gielen*	RH	fup
29 May 72	*Globokar*	Discours II	*Boulez*	RH	fup
29 May 72	*Schafer*	Requiem for a party girl	*Boulez*	RH	fp (c)
29 May 72	*Maxwell Davies*	Blind Man's Buff	*Boulez*	RH	fup
10 Aug 72	*Carter*	Concerto for Orchestra	*Boulez*	AH	fup
14 Aug 72	*Zimmermann*	Canto di Speranza	*Del Mar*	AH	fup
21 Aug 72	*Lambert*	Formations and Transformations	*Davis*	AH	fp (c)
4 Sep 72	*Crumb*	Echoes of time and the river	*Farberman*	AH	fup
7 Sep 72	*Stockhausen*	Carré	*Amy/Tabachnik/Dufallo/Vis*	AH	fup (twice)
16 Sep 72	*Crosse*	Celebration	*Davis*	AH	fp (c)
1 Oct 72	*Hartmann*	Concerto funèbre	*Schmid*	S	fubp
5 Oct 72	*Nono*	España nel corazón	*Bellugi*	S	fubp
14 Oct 72	*Druckman*	Incenters	*Gielen*	S	fup
14 Oct 72	*Maderna*	Amanda	*Gielen*	S	fup (twice)
27 Nov 72	*Alsina*	Funktionen	*Boulez*	RH	fup (public)

Date	Composer	Work	Conductor	Place (See Key)	Perf
13 Dec 72	Feldman	The Rothko Chapel	Zender	SJSS	fup
13 Dec 72	Zimmermann	Stille und Umkehr.	Zender	SJSS	fup
10 Jan 73	Eloy	Equivalences	Masson	S	fup
10 Jan 73	Birtwistle	The Fields of Sorrow	Pritchard	SJSS	fbp
17 Jan 73	Milner	Symphony	Pritchard	FH	fp (c)
7 Feb 73	Alsina	Schichten	Masson	S	fup
19 Feb 73	Smalley	Sonata for strings	Boulez	RH	fp
17 Mar 73	Christopher Shaw	Peter and the lame man	C. Davis	S	fp
26 Mar 73	Alsina	Schichten	Masson	RH	fup (public)
26 Mar 73	Berio	Recital I	Boulez	RH	fup
11 Apr 73	Berio	Concerto for two pianos	Boulez	FH	fep
13 May 73	Boulez	. . . explosante-fixe . . . (revised version)	Boulez	Rome	fep
6 Jul 73	Rands	Wildtrack II	Pritchard	Cheltenham	fp
7 Aug 73	Lefanu	The Hidden Landscape	Del Mar	AH	fp (c)
17 Aug 73	Boulez	. . . explosante-fixe . . .	Boulez	AH	fup
7 Sep 73	Lutyens	De Amore	Lovett	AH	fp
10 Oct 73	Zimmermann	Photoptosis	Boulez	FH	fup
24 Oct 73	Maderna	Oboe Concerto No. 3	Carewe	FH	fup
17 Nov 73	Aptvor	Neumes	Del Mar	S	fp
21 Jan 74	Eloy	Faisceaux-diffractions	Boulez	RH	fup (public)
18 Feb 74	Wood	Song-cycle to poems by Neruda	Howarth	RH	fp (c)
11 Mar 74	Souster	Song of an average city	Boulez	RH	fp (c)
18 Mar 74	Rands	Aum	Boulez	RH	fp (c)
18 Mar 74	Maderna	Aura	Boulez	RH	fup
10 Jul 74	Apostel	Passacaglia, Op. 50	Atherton	S	fp
30 Jul 74	Williamson	Hammarskjöld Portrait	Pritchard	AH	fp (c)
8 Aug 74	Holloway	Domination of Black	Groves	AH	fp (c)
6 Sep 74	Dalby	Viola Concerto	Del Mar	AH	fp (c)
28 Sep 74	Gerhard	Metamorphoses (Symphony No. 2)	Groves	S	fp of unrevised last mvt.

Date	Composer	Work	Conductor	Place (See Key)	Perf
3 Nov 74	Goehr	Chaconne for wind instruments	Boulez	Leeds	fp
25 Nov 74	Guy	D	Boulez	RH	fp
9 Dec 74	Henze	Der Vorwurf	Henze	S	fup
11 Dec 74	Henze	Los Caprichos	Henze	S	fup
11 Dec 74	Henze	Antifone	Henze	S	fup
2 Jan 75	Beck	Clarinet Concerto	Schmid	S	fup
15 Jan 75	Cooke	Symphony No. 4	Pritchard	FH	fp
27 Jan 75	Sohal	Dhayan I	Atherton	RH	fp
10 Feb 75	Copie	Leighton Moss: December Notebook	Howarth	RH	fp
2 Apr 75	Boulez	Rituel	Boulez	FH	fp (c)
4 Jun 75	Milner	Cantata: Midway	Handley	S	fp
6 Aug 75	Cooke	Cello Concerto	Groves	AH	fp (c)
8 Aug 75	Bedford	Twelve Hours of Sunset	Poole	AH	fp (c)
2 Sep 75	Copie	Leviathan	A. Davis	AH	fp (c)
10 Nov 75	Sandström	Utmost	Boulez	RH	fp (c)
12 Nov 75	Messiaen	Des canyons aux étoiles	Boulez	FH	fup
24 Nov 75	Buller	Le Terrazze	Howarth	RH	ffp
18 Jan 76	Lefanu	The Hidden Landscape	Del Mar	S	?fubp
6 Feb 76	Balassa	Iris	Boulez	FH	fup
6 Feb 76	Ligeti	San Francisco Polyphony	Boulez	FH	fup
23 Feb 76	Reeve	... aux régions éthérées	Atherton	S	fp (c)
27 Feb 76	Crumb	Variations for Orchestra	Farberman	S	?fubp
3 Mar 76	Harvey	Inner Light (III)	Gielen	FH	fp (c)
8 Mar 76	Maw	Life Studies	Gielen	RH	fp of No. 2
27 Mar 76	Patterson	Wildfire	Seaman	FH	fp (c)
5 May 76	Fricker	Symphony No. 5 for Organ and Orchestra	C. Davis	FH	fp (c)
4 Jul 76	Sessions	Concerto for Violin and Cello	Foster	Cheltenham	fup
19 Aug 76	Blake	Violin Concerto	Groves	AH	fp (c)
15 Nov 76	Finnissy	Pathway of sun and stars	Boulez	RH	fp (c)

Date	Composer	Work	Conductor	Place (See Key)	Perf (See Key)
29 Nov 76	Sinopoli	Drei Stücke aus 'Souvenirs à la mémoire'	Boulez	RH	fup
29 Nov 76	Carter	A mirror on which to dwell	Boulez	RH	fup
3/7 Jan 77	Hamilton	The death of Tamburlaine	Atherton	S	fp (c)
21 Feb 77	Aperghis	Il gigante Golia	Masson	RAM	fup
9 Jun 77	Dallapiccola	Three questions with two answers	Pesko	S	fep
8 Jul 77	Dickinson	Organ Concerto	Atherton	St Albans	fbp
11 Jul 77	Buller	Proença	Elder	S	fp (c)
28 Jul 77	Henze	The Raft of the Medusa	Atherton	AH	fup
6 Aug 77	Buller	Proença	Elder	AH	fp (public)
12 Aug 77	Bennett	Actaeon	Susskind	AH	fp
18 Oct 77	Finnissy	World	Bainbridge	RCM	fup
2 Nov 77	Lokshin	Symphony No. 5	Barshai	S	fup
4 Nov 77	Freedman	Tapestry	Bernardi	SJSS	fup
4 Nov 77	Beecroft	Improvisation No. 2	Bernardi	SJSS	fup
4 Nov 77	Schafer	Son of Heldenleben	Bernardi	SJSS	fup (Musicanada)
4 Nov 77	Aitken	Spiral	Bernardi	SJSS	fup
4 Nov 77	Hétu	Piano Concerto	Bernardi	SJSS	fup
9 Nov 77	Zender	Zeitstrome	Zender	S	fubp
14 Nov 77	Zender	Muji No Kyo	Zender	Guildhall	fup
1 Dec 77	Lumsdaine	Hagoromo	Boulez	Paris	fp (c)
6 Feb 78	Buller	The mime of Mick, Nick and the Maggies	Howarth	RH	fp (complete)
5/6 Feb 78	Weill	The Protagonist	Atherton	S	fup
10 Feb 78	Sinopoli	Tombeau d'armor II	Boulez	RH	fup
19/20 Feb 78	Weill	The Tsar has his photograph taken	Atherton	S	fup
20 Feb 78	Saxton	Reflections of Narziss and Goldmund	Friend	RH	fup
18 Mar 78	Paynter	Galaxies for Orchestra and Audience	Keefe	FH	fp (c)
16 May 78	Hamilton	Scena: Cleopatra	Atherton	Cheltenham	fp
16 May 78	Schubert, ed. Newbould	Symphony No. 7	Atherton	Cheltenham	fbp
5 Aug 78	Hamilton	Scena: Cleopatra	Atherton	AH	flp
11 Oct 78	Prokofiev	Ode to the End of War	Rozhdestvensky	FH	fup (public)

Date	Composer	Work	Conductor	Place (See Key)	Perf
24 Oct 78	Schreker	Suite: The Birthday of the Infanta	Rozhdestvensky	FH	fbp
14 Nov 78	Denisov	Flute Concerto	Friend	RCM	fup
3 Dec 78	Webern	Siegfrieds Schwert	Atherton	FH	fp
3 Dec 78	Webern	Three Orchestral Studies on a Ground	Atherton	FH	fp
5/6 Jan 79	Bantock	Omar Khayyám	Del Mar	S	fbp (complete)
17 Feb 79	Williamson	Fiesta	Friend	Milton	fup
17 Feb 79	Williamson	Les Olympiques	Friend	Keynes	fup
19 Feb 79	Carter	Symphony of Three Orchestras	Atherton	S	fup
21 Feb 79	Carter	Symphony of Three Orchestras	Atherton	FH	fup (public)
28 Feb 79	Prokofiev	Incidental music to Hamlet	Rozhdestvensky	SJSS	fup
4 Apr 79	Shostakovich	Overture: Columbus	Rozhdestvensky	FH	fup
27 Jul 79	Crumb	Star-Child	Howarth/Hicks/Friend/Snell	AH	fup
30 Jul 79	Lutoslawski	Les espaces du sommeil	Lutoslawski	AH	fup
10 Aug 79	Wooldridge	Five Italian Songs	Gielen	AH	fp
31 Aug 79	Pärt	Cantus to the memory of Benjamin Britten	Rozhdestvensky	AH	fup
6 Sep 79	Knussen	Symphony No. 3	Tilson Thomas	AH	fp (c)
9 Oct 79	Denisov/Pärt/Schnittke/ Rozhdestvensky	Pas de quatre	Rozhdestvensky	S	fup
16 Oct 79	Osborne	Cello Concerto	Friend	Logan Hall	fp
19 Nov 79	Lokshin	Symphony No. 3	Rozhdestvensky	S	fup
5 Dec 79	Fricker	Laudi Concertati	Gielen	FH	fp
12 Dec 79	Goehr	Babylon the great is fallen	Gielen	FH	fp (c)
20 Feb 80	Gielen	Pentaphonie	Gielen	FH	fup
24 Feb 80	Zimmermann	Dialogue: Concerto for Two Pianos and Orchestra	Gielen	RCM	fup
4 Mar 80	Knaifel	The Canterville Ghost	Rozhdestvensky	RCM	fup
23 Apr 80	Schnittke	Symphony No. 2 (St Florian)	Rozhdestvensky	FH	fp (c)
25 Aug 80	George Benjamin	Ringed by the flat horizon	Elder	AH	flp
15 Oct 80	Prokofiev, ed. Rozhdestvensky	The White Swan	Rozhdestvensky	FH	fup

The concerts of contemporary music complete programmes 1931-39

These concerts were given before invited audiences in the Studio. Concerts omitted did include the BBC Symphony Orchestra; they were devoted to chamber music. Titles have not been standardised: they are printed as in *Radio Times*.

———————————— **Fifth Season, 1931** ————————————

I.   Friday 9 January 1931

ARNOLD SCHOENBERG

Margot Hinnenberg-Lefebre (soprano) The BBC Orchestra Leader, Arthur Catterall
Conducted by Arnold Schoenberg

Prelude and Fugue in E flat, for organ ....*Bach, trans. Schoenberg*
(Transcribed for full Orchestra)
Erwartung ....*Schoenberg*

II.   Friday 13 February 1931

HOLST and VAUGHAN WILLIAMS

Megan Thomas (soprano) Steuart Wilson (tenor) Clive Carey (bass)
The BBC Orchestra Conductors, Adrian Boult and R. Vaughan Williams

Savitri (An episode from the Mahabbarata) ....*Holst*
Job (A Masque for Dancing) ....*Vaughan Williams*

III.   Friday 6 March 1931

John Armstrong (tenor) Emma Lübbecke-Job (piano) Robert Murchie (flute)
Terence MacDonagh (cor anglais) The International String Quartet
The BBC Orchestra Conducted by Frank Bridge

Fifth Quartet (first performance) ....*Bernard van Dieren*
The Curlew (Four poems by W. B. Yeats) ....*Peter Warlock*
Concert music 1930, for piano, brass and harps................................*Paul Hindemith*

IV.   Tuesday 31 March 1931

The Brosa String Quartet The BBC Orchestra Conducted by Frank Bridge

Enter Spring ....*Frank Bridge*
Concerto for String Quartet and Orchestra (1929).........................*Conrad Beck*

There is a Willow grows aslant a Brook ....*Frank Bridge*
(Impression for small Orchestra, 1927)
Concerto grosso for Orchestra (1930) ....*Igor Markievitch*

V.   Friday 8 May 1931

Enid Cruickshank (contralto) The BBC Orchestra Conducted by Anton Webern

Five Movements for String Orchestra..*Webern*
(Transcription from String Quartet, Op. 5)
Song of the Wood Dove (Gurrelieder) ....*Schoenberg*
(Transcription for Chamber Orchestra by the composer)
Music to accompany a Cinema Scene (Op. 34) ....*Schoenberg*

VI.   Wednesday 24 June 1931

MANUEL DE FALLA

Manuel de Falla (harpsichord) Mary Hamlin (soprano) Frank Titterton (tenor)
Roy Henderson (baritone)
The BBC Orchestra Leader, Arthur Catterall Conducted by Sir Henry Wood
and Manuel de Falla

Suite, El Amor Brujo.. ....*Manuel de Falla*
Concerto for harpsichord, flute, oboe, clarinet, violin
   and violoncello ....*Manuel de Falla*
Master Peter's Puppet Show ....*Manuel de Falla*
(conducted by the composer)

VII.   Thursday 23 July 1931

Drawn from programmes of ISCM Festival Oxford and London, July, 1931

Eva Bandrowska-Turska The Wireless Singers
The BBC Chamber Orchestra Conducted by Hermann Scherchen

Lyric Suite for small orchestra, Op. 18 (1928) ....*Leff Knipper*
Quatre chansons japonaises, 1930 ....*Jan Maklakievicz*
(conducted by Gregor Fitelberg)
Ame en peine (Soul in Torment) (Unaccompanied) (1925) ....*Jean Hure*
(conducted by Stanford Robinson)
Three a capella Choruses, Op. 43 (1930)...*Egon Wellesz*
(conducted by Stanford Robinson)
Sinfonietta in D (1923–27) ....*Ernesto Halffter*
(conducted by the composer)

——————————— Sixth Season, 1931-2 ———————————

I.   Friday 13 November 1931

ARNOLD SCHOENBERG

The BBC Studio Symphony Orchestra Leader, Arthur Catterall Conductor, Adrian Boult

Verklärte Nacht (Op. 4) for string orchestra ....*Schoenberg*
Variations for Orchestra (Op. 31)..*Schoenberg*

II.   Friday 18 December 1931

Odette de Foras (soprano) Arthur Benjamin (piano)
The BBC Chamber Orchestra Conducted by Constant Lambert

Suite from the Ballet Romeo and Juliet ....*Constant Lambert*
Ephemera (W. B. Yeats), for soprano and small orchestra ....*Patrick Hadley*
Concerto for piano and small orchestra ....*Constant Lambert*
(first performance)
Seven Poems by Li-Po (trans. by Shigeyoshi Obata) for
   soprano and small orchestra ....*Constant Lambert*
Rout...*Arthur Bliss*

III.   Friday 22 January 1932
                                       FERRUCCIO BUSONI

Joseph Szigeti (violin) The BBC Orchestra (Section D) Leader, Arthur Catterall
Conductor, Adrian Boult

A Comedy Overture, Op. 38 (1897–1904) ....*Busoni*
Concerto in D for violin and orchestra, Op. 35a (1899)..................................*Busoni*
Turandot – Orchestral Suite from the Music to Gozzi's
   Drama, Op. 41 (1913) ....*Busoni*

IV.   Friday 5 February 1932

Solomon (piano) The BBC Orchestra (Section D) Conducted by Nikolai Malko

Symphony (No. 1) ....*Shostakovich*
Concerto for piano and orchestra...*Mossolov*
Two Studies for Orchestra ....*Vogel*

V.   Friday 4 March 1932
                                       BÉLA BARTÓK

Béla Bartók (piano) The BBC Orchestra (Section D) Leader, Arthur Catterall
Conducted by Sir Henry Wood

First Suite for Orchestra (Op. 3) ....*Bartók*
Rhapsody for piano and orchestra (Op. 1) ....*Bartók*
The Amazing Mandarin – Music from the Mimodrama (Op. 19) ....*Bartók*

VII.   Friday 13 May 1932

May Blyth (soprano) The BBC Orchestra (Section D) Led by Laurance Turner
Conducted by Sir Henry Wood

Theme and Thirteen Variations (Op. 69) ....*Ernst Křenek*
Three Fragments from Wozzeck ....*Alban Berg*
Passacaglia (Op. 1)..*Anton Webern*

———————————————Seventh Season, 1933———————————————

III.   Friday 20 January 1933

Victor Hely-Hutchinson (piano) Ernest Lush (piano)
The BBC Orchestra (Section D) Led by Laurance Turner Conductor, Adrian Boult

Escales (1922)... ....*Jacques Ibert*
Concerto for two pianos ....*Arthur Bliss*
Symphony in G minor, Op. 42..*Albert Roussel*
(first performance in this country)

V   Friday 24 March 1933

Tudor Davies Arthur Cranmer Harry Tate Harry Tate Jnr
The Wireless Chorus (Section C) Chorus Master, Cyril Dalmaine Wireless Military Band
The BBC Orchestra (Section C) Led by Marie Wilson Conductor, Adrian Boult

Lehrstück (The Lesson) ....*Hindemith*

VI.   Friday 21 April 1933

Hedda Kux (soprano) Rudolf Kolisch (violin) Eduard Steuermann (piano)
The BBC Orchestra (Section D) Led by Laurance Turner Conducted by Anton Webern

Three Movements from the Lyric Suite..................................... ....*Alban Berg*
(Transcribed for string orchestra by the composer)
Durch die Nacht, for soprano and chamber orchestra (1930–1) ....*Ernst Křenek*
Kammerkonzert for piano and violin with thirteen wind
  instruments (1924)..*Alban Berg*

Friday 26 May 1933

Enid Cruickshank ....Housewife
Harold Williams ....Suitor
Parry Jones ....A Youth
Ina Souez..............................The Girl
Roy Henderson ....A Masker, dressed as a flea

The BBC Chorus (Section B) Chorus Master, Cyril Dalmaine
The BBC Orchestra (Section D) Led by Laurance Turner Conducted by Zoltán Kodály

Skékély Fono (The Spinning-room) ....*Kodály*

——————————————— Eighth Season, 1933–4 ———————————————

II.   Friday 22 December 1933

Kate Winter (soprano) Betty Bannerman (contralto) Harold Williams (baritone)
The Wireless Chorus (Section B) The BBC Orchestra (Section D)
Led by Laurance Turner Conducted by Adrian Boult

Cris du Monde ....*Arthur Honegger*

III.   Friday 26 January 1934

Parry Jones (tenor) The BBC Orchestra (Section D) Led by Laurance Turner
Conducted by Nicolai Malko

Four Portraits and a Dénouement (Op. 49);
  Symphonic Suite from the Opera, The Gambler ....*Prokofiev*
Symphony No. 7 ....*Miaskovsky*
Suite from the opera, The Nose ....*Shostakovich*

VI.   Friday 27 April 1934
STRAVINSKY

Oda Slobodskaya (soprano) Kate Winter (soprano) Betty Bannerman (contralto)
Mary Jarred (contralto) Tudor Davies (tenor) Roy Henderson (baritone)
Victor Hely-Hutchinson, Berkeley Mason, Ernest Lush, Edwin Benbow (pianos)
The Wireless Chorus (Section B) Chorus Master, Leslie Woodgate
The BBC Symphony Orchestra (Section D) Led by Laurance Turner
Conducted by Ernest Ansermet

Mavra, a comic opera in one act ....*Stravinsky*
Les Noces, a ballet for solo voices, chorus, percussion
  and four pianos ....*Stravinsky*

VII.   Friday 25 May 1934
BÉLA BARTÓK

Trefor Jones (tenor) Frank Phillips (baritone) Bela Bartók (piano)
The Wireless Chorus (Section A) Chorus Master, Leslie Woodgate
The BBC Symphony Orchestra (Section D) Led by Laurance Turner
Conducted by Aylmer Buesst

Two Portraits ....*Bartók*
Piano Concerto No. 2 ....*Bartók*
Cantata Profana ....*Bartók*

────────────────── Ninth Season, 1934–5 ──────────────────

I.   Friday 19 October 1934
SERGE PROKOFIEV

The BBC Symphony Orchestra (Section D) Led by Marie Wilson
Conducted by Serge Prokofiev

Symphony No. 3 (Op. 44)..*Prokofiev*
Chout, Suite de Ballet (Op. 21) ....*Prokofiev*

II.   Friday 23 November 1934

Marcelle Meyer (piano)
The BBC Symphony Orchestra (Section D) Led by Marie Wilson
Conducted by Constant Lambert

Five Studies for piano and small orchestra .... *de Roos*
Overture for chamber orchestra .... *Erik Chisholm*
Partita for piano and small orchestra .... *Markievitch*
Suite, Maximilian .... *Milhaud*

III.   Friday 21 December 1934

HINDEMITH

Irene Kohler (piano)
The BBC Orchestra (Section D) Led by Laurance Turner Conducted by Paul Hindemith

Concert Music (for piano, brass and harps) .... *Hindemith*
Symphonie, Mathis der Maler .... *Hindemith*

IV.   Friday 18 January 1935

Solomon (piano)
The BBC Orchestra (Section D) Led by Laurance Turner
Conducted by Arthus Bliss and Edward Clark

Suite from the Black Maskers .... *Roger Sessions*
Mêlée fantasque (conducted by the composer) .... *Arthur Bliss*
Second Rhapsody .... *George Gershwin*
Dance Symphony .... *Aaron Copland*

V.   Friday 8 February 1935

BBC Symphony Orchestra Conducted by Edward Clark

The Tuppenny-ha'penny Opera .... *Weill*

VIII.   Friday 28 June 1935

Laelia Finneberg (soprano) Doris Owens (contralto) Walter Widdop (tenor)
Stanley Riley (bass)
The BBC Chorus (Section A) Chorus Master, Leslie Woodgate
The BBC Orchestra (Section B) Leader, Arthur Catterall Conducted by Sir Henry Wood

Msa Glagolskaya (Slavonic Festival Mass) .... *Janáček*

————————————Tenth Season, 1935–6————————————

II.   Friday 29 November 1935

Music by British Composers

Adolph Hallis (piano)
The BBC Orchestra (Section D) Led by Laurance Turner
Conducted by Warwick Braithwaite and George Lloyd

Overture (first performance in England)... *Van Dieren*
Concerto for Pianoforte and orchestra... *Darnton*
(first performance in England)
Symphony in F (first performance) .... *George Lloyd*

III.   Friday 20 December 1935

Oda Slobodskaya (soprano) Betty Bannerman (mezzo-soprano) Parry Jones (tenor)
The BBC Chorus (Section A) Chorus Master, Leslie Woodgate
The BBC Orchestra (Section D) Led by Laurance Turner Conducted by Igor Markievitch

'Le Paradis perdu' (Paradise Lost) (first performance) ....*Igor Markievitch*

IV.   Friday 17 January 1936

Florence Hooton (violoncello)
The BBC Orchestra (Section D) Led by Marie Wilson
Conducted by Frank Bridge and Adrian Boult

Innominata ....*Conrad Beck*
Oration (Concerto elegiaco) for violoncello and orchestra...............................*Bridge*
(first performance) (conducted by the composer)
Music for the Theatre ....*Aaron Copland*

V.   Friday 21 February 1936

MALIPIERO

Ina Souez (soprano) Heddle Nash (tenor) Bradbridge White (tenor)
Stanley Pope (baritone)
The BBC Men's Chorus Chorus Master, Leslie Woodgate
The BBC Orchestra (Section D) Led by Laurance Turner Conducted by Edward Clark

Preludes to Three Comedies of Goldoni..*Malipiero*
   1. La bottega de Caffe 2. Sior Todero Brontolon
   3. Le barruffe Chiozzotte
Filomela e l'infatuato, Musical Drama in Three Parts ....*Malipiero*

VII.   Friday 1 May 1936

ALBAN BERG MEMORIAL CONCERT

Louis Krasner (violin)
The BBC Orchestra (Section D) Led by Laurance Turner Conducted by Anton Webern

Introductory Announcement
Two Pieces for String Orchestra (from Lyric Suite) ....*Berg*
Violin Concerto (First Performance in England) ....*Berg*

VIII.   Friday 19 June 1936

Joan Cross (soprano) Jan van der Gucht (tenor) William Parsons (baritone)
The BBC Chorus (Section A) Chorus Master, Leslie Woodgate
The BBC Orchestra (Section F) Led by Laurance Turner
Conducted by Clarence Raybould

Jonah (first performance) ....*Lennox Berkeley*

———————————— **Eleventh Season, 1936–7** ————————————

I.   Friday 13 November 1936

Renée Flynn (soprano) Roy Henderson (baritone)
The BBC Chorus (Section A) Chorus Master, Leslie Woodgate
The BBC Orchestra (Section D) Conducted by Ralph Vaughan Williams and Adrian Boult

Te Deum (first performance) ....*Kodály*
Dona Nobis Pacem, A Cantata for soprano and baritone soli,
    chorus and orchestra (first broadcast performance) ....*Vaughan Williams*

II.   Friday 18 December 1936

Cardillac – the Goldsmith ....Arthur Fear
The Daughter ....Noel Eadie
The Officer ....Frank Mullings
The Goldmerchant............................Norman Walker
The Cavalier ....John McKenna
The Lady...Miriam Licette
The Captain ....Dennis Noble

The BBC Chorus (Section A) Chorus Master, Leslie Woodgate
The BBC Orchestra (Section D) Leader, Paul Beard
Conducted by Clarence Raybould Assistant, Arnold Perry

Cardillac ....*Paul Hindemith*
(First performance in England)

III.   Saturday 16 January 1937

A Concert Performance of 'Christophe Colomb'
An Opera in Two Parts by Darius Milhaud
(First performance in England)

The Story Teller...........................Stuart Robertson
The Speakers ....Robert Chignell
                                         Christian Darnton
                                         Martin Boddey
Isabella......................................May Busby
Christopher Columbus ....Endreze
Christopher Columbus II ....William Parsons
The Messenger ....
The Majordomo ....
The Beadle ....Parry Jones
The Cook....................................
The King of Spain ....
The Commandant ....Samuel Worthington
Huichtlipochtli ....
and Margaret Godley, Doris Owens, Bradbridge White, Martin Boddey, Stanley Riley,
            Victor Harding, Victor Utting, Samuel Dyson
The BBC Choral Society Chorus Master, Leslie Woodgate
The BBC Orchestra (Section B) Leader, Paul Beard
Conducted by Darius Milhaud Assistant, Arnold Perry

VI.   Friday 9 April 1937
                    VAN DIEREN MEMORIAL CONCERT

Margaret Godley (soprano) Betty Bannerman (contralto) Bradbridge White (tenor)
              Henry Cummings (baritone) Stanley Riley (bass)
         The BBC Chorus (Section A) Chorus Master, Leslie Woodgate
 The BBC Orchestra (Section D) Leader, Paul Beard Conducted by Constant Lambert

Comedy Overture, Anjou ....*van Dieren*
Symphony, Op. 6 ....*van Dieren*

VII.   Friday 30 April 1937
                            BRITISH MUSIC

               Sophie Wyss (soprano) Aubrey Brain (horn)
    The BBC Orchestra (Section D) Leader, Paul Beard Conductor, Sir Adrian Boult

Our Hunting Fathers, A symphonic cycle for soprano and
    orchestra ....*Benjamin Britten*
Sinfonia Brevis for horn and orchestra ....*Leighton Lucas*
Symphony (No. 1) ....*Edmund Rubbra*

———————————— **Twelfth Season 1937–8** ————————————

I.   Friday 8 October 1937
                    SZYMANOWSKI MEMORIAL CONCERT

                        Antonio Brosa (violin)
    The BBC Orchestra (Section D) Leader, Paul Beard Conductor, Sir Adrian Boult

Concert Overture in E, Op. 12...*Szymanowski*
Violin Concerto No. 2, Op. 61 ....*Syzmanowski*
Movements from the Ballet, Harnasie, Op. 55 ....*Syzmanowski*

III.   Friday 17 December 1937

  Robert Murchie (flute) Frederick Thurston (clarinet) Marcelle Meyer (piano)
                       The Brosa String Quartet
    The BBC Orchestra (Section D) Leader, Paul Beard Conducted by Charles Munch

Serenade for flute, clarinet and strings ....*Conrad Beck*
Concerto for string quartet and orchestra ....*Valls*
Second Concerto for piano and orchestra ....*Rieti*
Overture, Nova Zeme (New Earth) ....*Alois Haba*

IV.   Friday 7 January 1938

                        Noel Eadie (soprano)
           The BBC Orchestra (Section E) Led by Laurance Turner
                    Conducted by Hermann Scherchen

Fuga from the *Musikalisches Opfer* of J. S. Bach ....*orch. Anton Webern*
Tre Laudi ....*Luigi Dallapiccola*
Music for Strings, Percussion and Celesta ....*Béla Bartók*

V.   Friday 4 February 1938

May Blyth (soprano) Bernard Shore (viola)
The BBC Orchestra (Section D) Leader, Marie Wilson Conducted by Constant Lambert

Suite, L'Envoi d'Icare ....*Markievitch*
Concerto for viola and orchestra ....*Maconchy*
Swan Song, Five Poems for soprano and orchestra ....*Darnton*
Tripartita ....*Vogel*

VI.   Friday 4 March 1938

Dennis Noble (baritone) Alan Bush (pianoforte) The BBC Men's Chorus
The BBC Orchestra (Section E) Led by Laurance Turner Conductor, Sir Adrian Boult

Concerto for pianoforte and orchestra, with baritone solo
   and male voice chorus in the last movement ....*Alan Bush*
   Text by Randall Swingler

VII.   Friday 8 April 1938

Ernst Křenek (pianoforte)
The BBC Orchestra (Section D) Led by Marie Wilson Conductor, Sir Adrian Boult

Symphony No. 2 in C, for string orchestra.......................................*Jean Rivier*
(First performance in England)
Concerto for pianoforte and orchestra..*Ernst Křenek*
(First performance)
Three Orchestral Pieces ....*Alban Berg*
(First performance in England)

──────────────── **Thirteenth Season, 1938–9** ────────────────

II.   Friday 4 November 1938

Hugues Cuénod (tenor) Dora Conrad (bass) Stanley Bate (piano)
The BBC Orchestra (Section E) Led by Marie Wilson Conducted by Nadia Boulanger

Overture...*Antoni Szalowski*
Concertino for piano and orchestra...*Stanley Bate*
L'oiseau blessé
La grenouille qui veut se faire aussi gros que le boeuf..................*Marcelle de Manziarly*
Dumbarton Oaks Concerto..*Igor Stravinsky*
(British première)
Chanson épique...*Ravel*
Il viendra vers toi..*Leo Préger*
(First performance)
Le diable boîteux)..*Jean Françaix*
(British première)

III.   Friday 2 December 1938

May Blyth (soprano) Parry Jones (tenor) Ronald Stear (bass)
The BBC Chorus (Section A)
The BBC Orchestra (Section D) Leader Paul Beard Conducted by Clarence Raybould

The Vision of Isaiah, an oratorio for soloists, chorus
    and orchestra ....*Willy Burkhard*
English translation by D. Miller Craig

IV.   Friday 6 January 1939

William Busch (pianoforte) Sophie Wyss (soprano)
The BBC Orchestra (Section D) Leader, Paul Beard Conducted by Clarence Raybould

Concerto for pianoforte and orchestra..*William Busch*
(First performance)
Three French Nursery Songs ....*Alan Rawsthorne*
(First performance of orchestral version)
Symphony No. 1 ....*Erik Chisholm*
(First performance)

V.   Friday 10 February 1939

May Blyth (soprano)
The BBC Orchestra (Section B) Leader, Paul Beard Conducted by Ernest Ansermet

Ostinato ....*Conrad Beck*
Symphonic Fragments from Lulu ....*Alban Berg*
Suite, Nobilissima Visione ....*Hindemith*

APPENDIX D

The BBC Symphony Orchestra: a discography

Recordings are listed under the name of the conductor, in alphabetical order of composer. This is not a list of currently available recordings, for which reference should be made to the most recent number of the Gramophone Classical Catalogue. An asterisk denotes the recording was reissued on BBC ARTIUM 4001 (4 record set) to mark the 50th anniversary of the BBC Symphony Orchestra.

SIR JOHN BARBIROLLI
arr. Barbirolli ....Elizabethan Suite ....HMV ASD 2496
Beethoven ....Symphony No. 3 ....HMV ASD 2348
                                                HMV SXLP 30209

SIR THOMAS BEECHAM
Sibelius ....Karelia Suite: Intermezzo & Alla
                        marcia ....HMV DB 6248
Sibelius ....Symphony No. 2 ....WORLD RECORD ST 1085
                                                WORLD RECORD SH 1007

LUCIANO BERIO
Berio ....Epifanie (Cathy Berberian) ....RCA LSC 3189
                                                RCA SB 6850
Berio ....Allelujah (with Pierre Boulez,
                        conductor) ....RCA RL 11674

GARY BERTINI
Weill ....Symphonies Nos. 1 and 2 ....HMV ASD 2390
                                                ARGO ZRG 755

PIERRE BOULEZ
Bartók ....Duke Bluebeard's Castle ....CBS 76518
Bartók ....Music for strings, percussion and
                        celesta ....CBS SBRG 72652
Bartók ....Two Rhapsodies for violin and orch
                        (Menhuin) ....HMV ASD 2449
Berg ....Chamber Concerto (Barenboim) ....CBS SBRG 72614
Berg ....Violin Concerto (Menuhin) ....HMV ASD 2449
Berg ....Five Songs Op. 4 (Lukomska) ....CBS SBRG 72614
Berg ....Seven Early Songs (Harper)..............COLUMBIA M 32162
Berg ....Three Pieces Op. 6 ....CBS SBRG 72614
Berlioz ....Les Nuits d'été (Minton, Burrows) ......CBS 76576

Berlioz..................La Mort de Cléopatre (Minton) ....CBS 76576
                                                                  61891
Birtwistle...............The Triumph of Time.....................ARGO ZRG 790
Boulez..................Le Soleil des eaux (Nendick,
                             McDaniel, Devos).......................HMV ALP 2092
                                                                  HMV ASD 639
                                                                  ARGO ZRG 756
Boulez..................Pli selon pli (Lukomska).................CBS 72770
Messiaen...............Poèmes pour Mi (Palmer)...............ARGO ZRG 703
Schoenberg............Gurrelieder....................................CBS 76377-8
Schoenberg............Moses und Aron...........................CBS 79201
Schoenberg............Five Pieces Op. 16...........................CBS 76577
Schoenberg............Accompaniment to a film scene Op. 34...CBS 76577
Schoenberg............A Survivor from Warsaw (Reich)......CBS 76577
Schoenberg............Variations for Orchestra Op. 31.........CBS 76577
Stravinsky............The Firebird, Suite No. 1..............CBS SBRG 72652
                          Reach out for Boulez
Berg.....................Seven Early Songs: Die Nachtigall....⎫
Stravinsky............The Firebird: Infernal Dance..........⎭ CBS 73333

SIR ADRIAN BOULT
Auber..................Overture: Masaniello.....................HMV DB 2364
Bach.....................Suite No. 3....................................HMV DB 1963-5
Bach arr. Pick-
   Mangiagalli.........Violin Sonata No. 6: Prelude............HMV DB 1965
Beethoven............Symphony No. 8 in F.....................HMV DB 1764-6
                                                                  HMV DB 7172-4
Beethoven............Piano Concerto No. 3 in C minor
                             (Solomon)...............................HMV DB 6196-9
Beethoven............Overture: Coriolan........................HMV DB 2101
Beethoven............Overture: Egmont...........................HMV DB 1925
Berlioz..................Overture: Le Carnaval Romain........HMV DB 2078
Berlioz..................Overture: Les Francs Juges..............HMV DB 3131-2
*Berlioz...............Overture: King Lear........................HMV DB 3093-4
*Bliss..................Music for Strings...........................HMV DB 3257-9
Borodin...............Prince Igor: Polovtsi March.............HMV DB 3094
Brahms...............Piano Concerto No. 1 in D minor
                             (Backhaus)...............................HMV DB 1839-43
Brahms...............Piano Concerto No. 2 in B flat
                             (Schnabel)...............................HMV DB 2696-701
                                                                  WORLD RECORD H 109
Brahms...............Hungarian Dances Nos. 19, 20, 21......HMV DB 3814
Brahms...............Hungarian Dances Nos. 19, 21.........HMV DB 1804
Brahms...............Tragic Overture............................HMV DB 1803-4
Chopin, orch. Elgar...Piano Sonata in B flat minor:
                             Funeral March..........................HMV DB 1722
Elgar..................Cello Concerto (Casals)....................HMV DB 6338-41
                                                                  J. 153-50 141
                                                                  WORLD RECORD H 121
                                                                  HMV HLM 7110
Elgar..................The Dream of Gerontius: Prelude......HMV DB 2194
Elgar..................Enigma Variations..........................HMV DB 2800-2

Elgar	Imperial March	HMV DB 3163
Elgar	Introduction and Allegro for strings	HMV DB 3198–9
Elgar	Sospiri	HMV DB 3199
Elgar	Symphony No. 2	HMV DB 6190–5
Gluck	Overture: Alceste	HMV DB 3129
Holst	The Hymn of Jesus (BBC Chorus)	DECCA SXL 6006
		DECCA JB 49
Holst	The Planets	HMV DB 6227–33
Holst	The Planets: Jupiter	HMV 7P 204
Holst	The Planets: Mars	HMV 7P 203
Humperdinck	Overture: Hansel und Gretel	HMV DB 1758
Mendelssohn	Overture: The Hebrides	HMV DB 2100
Mendelssohn	Overture: Ruy Blas	HMV DB 2365
Mendelssohn	Overture: A Midsummer Night's Dream	HMV DB 6242–3
Mendelssohn	A Midsummer Night's Dream: Nocturne	HMV DA 1318
Mendelssohn	A Midsummer Night's Dream: Wedding March	HMV DB 6243
Meyerbeer	Le Prophète: Coronation March	HMV DB 3163
Mozart	Symphony No. 32 in G	HMV DB 6172
Mozart	Symphony No. 41 in C (Jupiter)	HMV DB 1966–9
Mozart	Overture: Così fan tutte	HMV DB 2190
		HMV DB 3814
Mozart	Overture: Der Schauspieldirektor	HMV DB 1969
Mozart	Horn Concerto No. 3 in E flat (A. Brain)	HMV DB 3973–4
Nicolai	Overture: The Merry Wives of Windsor	HMV DB 2195
Saint-Saëns	Samson et Delilah: Bacchanale	HMV DB 2077
Schubert	Symphony in C major	HMV DB 2415–20
Schumann	Overture: Manfred	HMV DB 2189–90
*Sibelius	Night Ride and Sunrise, Op. 55	HMV DB 2795–6
Sibelius	Oceanides, Op. 73	HMV DB 2797
		WORLD RECORD SH 237
Sibelius	Romance in C, Op. 42	HMV DB 3972
Tchaikovsky	Capriccio Italien	HMV DB 3956–7
Tchaikovsky	Eugene Onegin: Polonaise	HMV DB 3132
Tchaikovsky	Marche Slave	HMV DB 3971
Tchaikovsky	Serenade for strings in C	HMV DB 3303–5
*Vaughan Williams	Fantasia on a theme of Thomas Tallis	HMV DB 3958–9
Vaughan Williams	Job	HMV DB 6289–93
		HMV DB 9024–8
Wagner	Parsifal: Good Friday Music	HMV DB 1677
Wagner	Tristan und Isolde: Prelude	HMV DB 1757
Wagner	Overture: Die Meistersinger	HMV DB 1924
Walton	Overture: Portsmouth Point	HMV DA 1540
Walton	March: Crown Imperial	HMV DB 3164
Weber	Overture: Euryanthe	HMV DB 3130
Weber	Overture: Der Freischütz	HMV DB 1678
Anon.	God save the King	⎫
	The British Grenadiers	⎬ HMV DB B9420
Arne	Rule Britannia	⎭

Various ....National Anthems of the Allies ....HMV C 3232

FRITZ BUSCH
*Mozart ....Symphony No. 36 in C (Linz) ....HMV DB 2187–8
Strauss..................Till Eulenspiegel ....HMV DB 2191–3

JOHN CAREWE
David Bedford.........Music for Albion Moonlight
                  (Manning) ....ARGO ZRG 638

SIR COLIN DAVIS
Bartók ....Piano Concerto No. 2 (Bishop-
                  Kovacevich) ....PHILIPS 6542 206
                                              PHILIPS SAL 3779
                                                PHILIPS 839 761 LY
Beethoven ....Symphony No. 2 in D ....PHILIPS 9500 160
Beethoven ....Symphony No. 3 in E flat (Eroica) ......PHILIPS 6500 141
Beethoven ....Symphony No. 4 in B flat.................PHILIPS 9500 032
Beethoven ....Symphony No. 5 in C minor ....PHILIPS 6500 462
Beethoven ....Symphony No. 6 in F (Pastoral) ....PHILIPS 6500 463
Beethoven ....Symphony No. 8 in F ....PHILIPS 6500 462
Beethoven ....Piano Concerto No. 1 in C
                  (Bishop-Kovacevich).....................PHILIPS 6599 594
                                              PHILIPS 6500 179
Beethoven ....Piano Concerto No. 2 in B flat...........PHILIPS 6599 595
Beethoven ....Piano Concerto No. 3 in C minor ......PHILIPS 6500 3155
                                                PHILIPS 6599 596
Beethoven ....Piano Concerto No. 4 in G ....PHILIPS 6599 975
Beethoven ....Overture: Coriolan ....PHILIPS 6500 141
                                                PHILIPS 6580 048
Beethoven ....Overture: Egmont...........................PHILIPS 9500 032
Beethoven ....Overture: Leonora No. 1 ....PHILIPS 6580 064
Beethoven ....Overture: Leonora No. 3 ....PHILIPS 9500 160
Berlioz..................Benvenuto Cellini ....PHILIPS 6500 494–7
Berlioz..................Benvenuto Cellini (selections) ....PHILIPS 6833 249
Gerhard ....Symphony No. 4 ....ARGO ZRG 701
Gerhard ....Violin Concerto (Neaman) ....ARGO ZRG 701
Grieg ....Piano Concerto (Bishop-Kovacevich) ...PHILIPS 6500 166
Handel, arr. Sargent .Saul: Dead March..........................BBC RE 10
Haydn ....The Seasons ....PHILIPS SAL 3698–700
                                                PHILIPS 839 719–21
Haydn ....The Seasons (selections) ....PHILIPS 6580 019
Mendelssohn ....Overture: The Hebrides ....PHILIPS 6580 048
                                                PHILIPS 6833 109
Mozart ....Idomeneo ....PHILIPS SAL 3749–9
                  (Shirley, Davies, Rinaldi, Tinsley,   PHILIPS 839 758–60
                  Tear, Pilley, Dean, BBC Chorus)   PHILIPS 6598 710–2
Mozart ....Le Nozze di Figaro ....PHILIPS 6500 272–5
                  (Wixwell, Ganzarolli, Grant, Tear,   PHILIPS 6598 698 701fi
                  Hudson, Norman, Freni, Minton,
                  Casula, Watson)
Mozart ....Le Nozze di Figaro (highlights) ....PHILIPS 6500 434

Mozart	Requiem (Donath, Minton, Davies, Nienstedt)	PHILIPS SAL 3649
		PHILIPS 802 862 LY
		PHILIPS 6598 694
Mozart	Overture: Le Nozze di Figaro	PHILIPS 6833 133
Mozart	Overture: Die Zauberflöte	PHILIPS 6596 026
		PHILIPS 6580 048
Nicolai	Overture: The Merry Wives of Windsor	PHILIPS 6580 048
Schumann	Piano Concerto (Bishop-Kovacevich)	PHILIPS 6500 166
Stravinsky	Concerto for piano and wind (Bishop-Kovacevich)	PHILIPS SAL 377
		PHILIPS 839 761 LY
Tchaikovsky	Violin Concerto (Accardo)	PHILIPS 9500 146
Tchaikovsky	Sérénade Mélancolique, Op. 26	PHILIPS 9500 146
Tchaikovsky	Valse Scherzo, Op. 34	PHILIPS 9500 146
Tippett	A Child of Our Time (Norman, Baker Cassilly, Shirley-Quirk, BBC Chorus BBC Choral Society)	PHILIPS 6500 985
Tippett	A Child of Our Time: Steal away	PHILIPS 6598 950
Wagner	Overture: Die Meistersinger	PHILIPS 6580 048

The Last Night of the Proms (1969, 1970, 1971)
Arne, arr. Sargent ...Rule Britannia (Bainbridge)
Berlioz The Trojans: Hail, all hail to the Queen
Elgar Pomp and Circumstance March No. 1
Mendelssohn Octet in E flat: Scherzo
Parry, orch. Elgar ...Jerusalem PHILIPS 6588 011
Wagner Wesendonck Lieder (Norman): Träume; Schmerzen
Walton A Song for the Lord Mayor's Table; The Contrast; Rhyme (Bainbridge)
Williamson The Stone Wall

NORMAN DEL MAR

Gerhard	Concerto for Orchestra	ARGO ZRG 553
Lutyens	Quincunx (Nendick, Shirley-Quirk)	ARGO ZRG 622
Maw	Scenes and Arias (Manning, Howells, Procter)	ARGO ZRG 622
Rawsthorne	Symphony No. 3	ARGO ZRG 553

ANTAL DORATI

Bartók	Divertimento for Strings	MERCURY MG 50416
		MERCURY SR 90416
		PHILIPS SAL 3569
Bartók	The Miraculous Mandarin (complete)	MERCURY MG 50416
		MERCURY SR 90416
		PHILIPS SAL 3569
		PHILIPS 6543 003
Bartók	The Miraculous Mandarin (Suite)	PHILIPS 6582 011
Gerhard	Symphony No. 1	ARGO ZRG 752
		HMV ASD 613

Gerhard ....Suite: Don Quixote ....ARGO ZRG 752
                                                                   HMV ASD 613
Koechlin ....Les Bandar-Log, Op. 126.................HMV ASD 639
                                                                   HMV ALP 2092
                                                                   ARGO ZRG 756
Messiaen ....Chronochromie ....HMV ASD 639
                                                                   HMV ALP 2092
                                                                   ARGO ZRG 756

MARK ELDER
Buller ....Proença (Walker) ....UNICORN

SIR EDWARD ELGAR
Elgar ....The Kingdom: Prelude ....HMV DB 1934
                                                                   HMV BOX 70802
                                                                   WORLD RECORD H 139
*Elgar ....Overture: Cockaigne.......................HMV DB 1935-6
                                                                   HMV ALP 1464
                                                                   HMV HLM 7061
Elgar ....Pomp and Circumstance Marches
                        Nos. 1, 2, 4.............................HMV HLM 7005
                                                                   HMV HLM 7061
Elgar ....Pomp and Circumstance Marches
                        Nos. 1 & 2 ....HMV DB 1801
Elgar ....Pomp and Circumstance March No. 4...HMV DB 1936
                                                                   HMV HLM 7093

FRANCO FERRA
Zemlinsky ....Lyric Symphony (Dorow, Nimsgern)...ITALIA ITL 70048

SIR CHARLES GROVES
The Last Night of the Proms 1974 ......BBC REH 290
Elgar ....Pomp and Circumstance March No. 1...BBC RESL 48

HERBERT HANDT (and eleven members of the BBC SO)
Lutyens ....And suddenly it's evening ....ARGO ZRG 638

SERGE KOUSSEVITSKY
Sibelius ....Symphony No. 7 in C ....HMV DB 1948-6
                                                                   HMV DB 7388-93
                                                                   WORLD RECORD H 174

ZOLTAN PESKO
Dallapiccola............Three Questions with Two Answers ...ITALIA ITL 70044
Maderna ....Aura ....ITALIA ITL 70044
Petrassi ....Concerto No. 1; Concerto No. 8 ....ITALIA ITL 70009
Petrassi ....Concerto No. 2; Concerto No. 7 ....ITALIA ITL 70005

FREDERICK PRAUSNITZ
Gerhard ....Symphony No. 3, Collages ....HMV ASD 2427

GENNADI ROZHDESTVENSKY

Tchaikovsky ....Ballet: The Sleeping Beauty
(complete) .... BBC ARTIUM 3001

SIR MALCOLM SARGENT

Brahms ....Four Serious Songs, Op. 121
(Ferrier) (live, 12 Jan 49) ....DECCA LXT 6934
Britten ....A Young Person's Guide to the
Orchestra (Variations and Fugue on a
theme of Purcell) ....HMV BLP 1101/BSD 754
HMV SXLP 30114
Elgar ....Cello Concerto (Tortelier) ....HMV BLP 1043
Elgar ....Wand of Youth: Suite No. 2 ....HMV BLP 1019
Handel..................Suite: The Water Music ....HMV BLP 1059
Handel..................Suite: Royal Fireworks Music...........HMV BLP 1059
Holst ....Oriental Suite: Beni Mora, Op. 29
No. 1 ....HMV BLP 1101/BSD 754
HMV SXLP 30126
Holst ....The Planets ....HMV ALP 1600
HMV ASD 269
WORLD RECORD ST 1096
CFP 175
FANFARE SIT 60025
Holst ....The Planets: Mercury ....HMV HQM 1115
Holst ....The Planets: Mars and Jupiter ....HMV 7ER 5112
HMV RES 4254
Holst ....The Planets: Uranus and Neptune .....HMV 7ER 5123/RES 4260
Humperdinck ....Overture: Hansel und Gretel ....HMV 7ER 5029/DB 21591
Mendelssohn ....A Midsummer Night's Dream
(complete) ....HMV ALP 1261–4
Mendelssohn ....Ruy Blas: Overture ....HMV DB 21601
Rachmaninov ....Symphony No. 3 ....HMV ALP 1118
MFP 2078
Rawsthorne ....Piano Concerto No. 2 (Matthews) ......HMV HQM 1025
HMV BOX 508003
HMV CLP 1164
Rubbra..................Piano Concerto in G, Op. 85
(Matthews)..............................HMV HQM 1103
HMV BOX 508003
HMV CLP 1164
Sibelius ....Symphony No. 1 in E minor ....HMV ALP 1542
HMV ASD 260
MFP 2018
CFP 132
Sibelius ....Symphony No. 2 in D ....HMV ALP 1639
HMV MFP 2052
Sibelius ....Symphony No. 5 in E flat.................HMV ALP 1732
HMV CFP 114
Sibelius ....Finlandia, Op. 26 ....HMV 7ER 5029/7P 319
Sibelius ....Pohjola's Daughter, Op. 49 ....HMV ALP 1732
CFP 114
Tchaikovsky ....Symphony No. 5 ....HMV ALP 1236
Tchaikovsky ....Marche Slave, Op. 31 ....HMV DB 21569

Tchaikovsky ....Symphony No. 5: Waltz ....HMV 7ER 5067
Vaughan Williams ...Fantasia on a theme by Thomas Tallis...HMV BLP 1019
                        Collection
Chabrier ....Le Roi malgré lui: Fête polonaise ......⎫
Dvořák.................Slavonic Dance in E minor, Op. 72
                        No. 2 ....
Elgar ....Pomp and Circumstance March No. 1...⎪ HMV ALP 1658
Litolff ....Concerto Symphonique No. 4:   HMV ASD 536
                        Scherzo (Cherkassky) ....⎰ WORLD RECORDS T 602
Sullivan ....Overture: Di Ballo .... CFP 154
Tchaikovsky ....Eugene Onegin: Letter Scene
                        (Hammond) ....
Tchaikovsky ....Quartet No. 1: Andante cantabile ......⎭
                        Last Night of the Proms 1966
Arne.....................Rule Britannia   ⎫
Elgar ....Symphony No. 1 (extract)
Delius ....Brigg Fair (extract)   ⎬ BBC RE 10
Parry ....Jerusalem
Wood ....Fantasia on British Sea Songs
Walton.................Belshazzar's Feast (extract)   ⎭

                        GERARD SCHURMANN
Schurmann ....Six Studies of Francis Bacon ....CHANDOS ABR 1011
Schurmann ....Variants for small orchestra ....CHANDOS ABR 1011

                        RUDOLF SCHWARZ
Dvořák.................Serenade for strings in E ....HMV ALP 1821
Dvořák.................Slavonic Dances, Op. 46 and 72
                        (complete) ....HMV ALP 1820–1
Dvořák.................Slavonic Dances No. 3 in A flat,
                        No. 8 in G minor ....HMV 7P 351

                        ARTURO TOSCANINI
Beethoven ....Symphony No. 1 in C ....HMV DB 3537–40
                                                              VICTOR LCT 1023
                                                              WORLD RECORD H 134
Beethoven ....Symphony No. 1: Minuet and Trio ...HMV DB 3350
Beethoven ....Symphony No. 4 in B flat................
                                                              HMV ALP 1598
                                                              WORLD RECORD H 134
*Beethoven ....Symphony No. 6 in F (Pastoral) ....HMV DB 3333–7
                                                              HMV ALP 1664
                                                              VICTOR LCT 1042

Beethoven ....Overture: Leonora No. 1 ....HMV DB 3896–9
                                                              HMV ALP 1598
Brahms ....Tragic Overture...........................HMV DB 3349–50
                                                              HMV XLP 30079
Mozart ....Overture: Die Zauberflöte ....HMV DB 3550
                                                              HMV XLP 30079

Rossini	Overture: La scala di seta	HMV DB 3541
		HMV ALP 1664z
		HMV XLP 30079
		WORLD RECORD H 112
Weber	Invitation to the Dance	HMV DB 3542
		HMV XLP 30079

Unofficial recordings

Brahms	Symphony No. 4 in E minor	ARTURO TOSCANINI SOCIETY
Wagner	A Faust Overture	ATS 1008
Verdi	Requiem Mass (Milanov, Thorborg, Roswaenge, Moscona, BBC Chorus)	OLYMPIC ATS 1108–9

Unissued recordings (held by EMI) Recorded in 1935 except where stated

Beethoven	Symphony No. 7 in A
Brahms	Symphony No. 2 in D (recorded 1938)
Brahms	Symphony No. 4 in E minor
Cherubini	Overture: Anacreon
Debussy	La Mer
Elgar	Enigma Variations
Geminiani	Concerto Grosso Op. 3 No. 2
Mendelssohn	A Midsummer Night's Dream: Nocturne and Scherzo
Mozart	Symphony No. 35 (Haffner)
Rossini	Overture: Semiramide
Sibelius	Symphony No. 2 in D (recorded 1938)
Wagner	A Faust Overture
Wagner	Parsifal: Prelude and Good Friday Music
Wagner	Siegfried's Funeral March

BRUNO WALTER

Beethoven	Overture: Fidelio	HMV DB 2261
*Brahms	Symphony No. 4 in E minor	HMV DB 2253–7
Mozart	Symphony No. 39 in E flat	HMV DB 2258–60
		DA CAPO IC 147–50 178

RALPH VAUGHAN WILLIAMS

Vaughan Williams	Symphony No. 4 in F minor	HMV C3367–70
		WORLD RECORD H 128

SIR HENRY WOOD

Vaughan Williams	Serenade to Music	COLUMBIA LX 757–8
		COLUMBIA SED 5553

Coarse-groove shellac discs at 78 rpm

Prefixes:
HMV	DB, C	(12")
	DA, B	(10")
COLUMBIA:	LX	(12")

Microgroove Mono LPs at 33⅓ rpm

Prefixes:
DA CAPO		(12")
DECCA:	LXT	(12")
HMV:	ALP	(12")
	BLP	(10")
	CLP	(12")
	HLM	(12")
	HQM	(12")
	J	(12")
MUSIC FOR		
PLEASURE	MFP	(12")
MERCURY		
WORLD	MG	(12")
RECORDS	H	(12")
	SH 237	(12")
BBC	BOX 70802	(12")
	4001	(12")
TOSCANINI	RE	(12")
SOC.		(12")
OLYMPIC		(12")

Microgroove Stereo LPs at 33⅓ rpm

Prefixes:
ARGO	ZRG	(12")
CLASSICS		
FOR PLEASURE	CFP	(12")

CBS	A11	(12")
COLUMBIA	M	(12")
HMV	ASD	(12")
	BOX 508003	(12")
	SXLP	(12")
DECCA	SXL	(12")
	JB	(12")
ITALIA	ITL	(12")
FANFARE	SIT	(12")
WORLD		
RECORDS	SH 1007	(12")
	ST	(12")
PHILIPS	A11	(12")
RCA	LSC	(12")
	RL	(12")
	SB	(12")
MERCURY	SR	(12")
BBC	3001	(12")
	REH	(12")
	RESL	(12")

Microgroove Mono discs at 45 rpm

Prefixes:
HMV	7ER	(7")
	7P	(7")
COLUMBIA	SED	(7")

Microgroove Stereo discs at 45 rpm

Prefixes:
	RES	(7")

The fiftieth anniversary season 1980-81

Concerts in the Royal Festival Hall unless specified.

Wednesday 15 October 1980

Gennadi Rozhdestvensky (conductor) Victoria Postnikova (piano)
Jill Gomez (soprano) Sarah Walker (mezzo-soprano)
Kenneth Woollam (tenor) John Shirley-Quirk (baritone) BBC Symphony Chorus

Dreams .... *Prokofiev*
The White Swan..*Prokofiev, ed. Rozhdestvensky*
Piano Concerto No. 2 in G minor..*Prokofiev*
A Child of Our Time..*Tippett*

Wednesday 22 October 1980 (Fiftieth anniversary of first public concert)

Gennadi Rozhdestvensky (conductor) Itzhak Perlman (violin)

Symphony No. 5 in D major ....*Vaughan Williams*
Violin Concerto No. 1 in D major ....*Prokofiev*
The Rite of Spring..*Stravinsky*

Wednesday 5 November 1980

David Atherton (conductor) BBC Singers (women's voices)

Fireworks .... *Stravinsky*
Symphony No. 1..*Gerhard*
The Planets..*Holst*

Wednesday 19 November 1980

Michael Gielen and Witold Lutoslawski (conductors)
Heinz Holliger (oboe) Ursula Holliger (harp)

Concerto for oboe and harp (British première) ....*Lutoslawski*
Symphony No. 9 in D minor ....*Bruckner*

Sunday 30 November 1980 Royal Albert Hall

Colin Davis (conductor)
Julia Varady, Yvonne Kenny, Alison Hargan, Elizabeth Connell,
Sarah Walker, Peter Lindroos, Donald McIntyre, Norman Bailey
BBC Symphony Chorus London Symphony Chorus
Philharmonia Chorus Southend Boys Choir

Symphony No. 8 ....*Mahler*

Wednesday 3 December 1980

Gennadi Rozhdestvensky (conductor) Walter Klien (piano)

Waltz, München (second version)..*Strauss*
*Symphony No. 1...*Tippett*
Piano Concerto (1945)...*Hindemith*
Waltz, Les Patineurs...*Waldtenfel*

*A new work had been commissioned from Hugh Wood but was not ready.

Wednesday 10 December 1980 (Royal Philharmonic Society concert)

Gennadi Rozhdestvensky (conductor)
Ida Haendel (violin) BBC Singers BBC Symphony Chorus

Song of the high hills...*Delius*
Violin Concerto ....*Delius*
Symphony No. 6 ....*Shostakovich*

Monday 19 January 1981 (European Broadcasting Union concert)

James Loughran (conductor)
Edith Vogel (piano) Felicity Lott (soprano) Stafford Dean (bass) BBC Singers

Fantasia in C minor for piano, chorus and orchestra................................*Beethoven*
Three Orchestral Pieces, Op. 6 ....*Berg*
Cantata on the death of Emperor Joseph II ....*Beethoven*

Wednesday 11 February 1981

Antal Dorati (conductor)
Michael Rippon (speaker) Sheila Armstrong (soprano) Sarah Walker (mezzo-soprano)
Anthony Rolfe Johnson (tenor)
BBC Singers BBC Symphony Chorus Southend Boys Choir

The Plague ....*Gerhard*
Spring Symphony ....*Britten*

Wednesday 18 February 1981 (Royal Philharmonic Society concert)

Michael Gielen (conductor) Elizabeth Söderström (soprano) Thomas Allen (baritone)

Lyric Symphony ....*Zemlinsky*
Symphony No. 7 in A ....*Beethoven*

Wednesday 25 February 1981

Michael Gielen (conductor) Margaret Price (soprano) Alfreda Hodgson (mezzo-soprano)
Kenneth Riegel (tenor) Roland Hermann (speaker and baritone)
BBC Singers (men's voices) BBC Symphony Chorus

A Survivor from Warsaw ....*Schoenberg*
Symphony No. 9 in D minor (Choral) ....*Beethoven*

Wednesday 11 March 1981

Pierre Boulez (conductor) Daniel Barenboim (piano) Siegmund Nimsgern (baritone)

Four Orchestral Pieces Op. 12 ....*Bartók*
Piano Concerto No. 1 ....*Bartók*
Die glückliche Hand ....*Schoenberg*
Amériques ....*Varèse*

Wednesday 25 March 1981 (Bartók anniversary concert)

Gennadi Rozhdestvensky (conductor) Sylvia Sass (soprano) John Mitchinson (tenor)
Brian Rayner Cook (baritone) BBC Singers BBC Symphony Chorus

Cantata profana ....*Bartók*
orch. Kodály: Five Songs ....*Bartók*
Ballet, The Wooden Prince ....*Bartók*

Wednesday 1 April 1981 Royal Albert Hall

Gennadi Rozhdestvensky (conductor) Sarah Walker (mezzo-soprano) Robert Tear (tenor)
Jules Bastin (bass) BBC Singers BBC Symphony Chorus

Romeo et Juliette ....*Berlioz*

Wednesday 8 April 1981

Elgar Howarth (conductor) and soloists BBC Singers

Symphony No. 99 in E flat..*Haydn*
Variations on a Hungarian folk song, The Peacock.........................*Kodály*
Concert suite from Le Grand Macabre...*Ligeti*

Sunday 12 April 1981 Royal Albert Hall (Berlioz Festival)

Brian Wright (conductor) Stuart Burrows (tenor)
BBC Symphony Chorus Goldsmiths Choral Union

Grande messe des morts ....*Berlioz*

Wednesday 15 April 1981 Royal Albert Hall (Berlioz Festival)

John Pritchard (conductor) Elizabeth Söderström (soprano) Peter Schidlof (viola)

Overture, King Lear ....*Berlioz*
Les nuits d'été ....*Berlioz*
Harold in Italy ....*Berlioz*

Wednesday 29 April 1981

Gennadi Rozhdestvensky (conductor) Sheila Armstrong (soprano) Kenneth Collins (tenor)
John Shirley-Quirk (baritone) BBC Symphony Chorus

Music for strings, percussion and celeste ....*Bartók*
Scènes de ballet ....*Stravinsky*
The Bells ....*Rachmaninov*

Saturday 2 May 1981

Gennadi Rozhdestvensky (conductor)
Colin Carr (cello)

Concerto for Double String Orchestra ....*Tippett*
Cello Concerto in E minor ....*Elgar*
St Thomas Wake: Foxtrot for Orchestra ....*Maxwell Davies*
The Young Person's Guide to the Orchestra ....*Britten*

The Orchestra's work in its fiftieth anniversary season also includes:

COLLEGE CONCERTS 12 November (Nicholas Cleobury), 28 January (Lionel Friend), 4
March (Michael Gielen). New works by Robert Saxton, Jonathan Lloyd; British premières
by Roger Smalley, Luciano Berio, Arvo Pärt, Zsolt Durko, Wolfgang Rihm.

ST JOHN'S SMITH SQUARE 29 October (Paul Sacher), 17 December (Rudolf Schwarz). Haydn
Symphonies and Masses.

PROVINCIAL VISITS Leeds 18 October, Huddersfield 19 October, Bedford 12 December (all
Gennadi Rozhdestvensky), Bedford 21 January (Gerard Akoka), Peterborough 29 March
(Rozhdestvensky) Fairfield Hall, Croydon, 16 January (Vladir Ponkin), 5 February (Israel
Edelson)

COMMERCIAL RECORDINGS Prokofiev Violin Concertos: Itzhak Perlman (Gennadi Rozhdestvensky). Schoenberg: Die Glückliche Hand (Pierre Boulez).

STUDIO RECORDINGS Music by Schnittke, Denisov, Sofia Gubaidullina, Delius, Shostakovich
(Rozhdestvensky); Schreker, Busoni, Zemlinsky, Webern, Schoenberg, Jonathan Harvey
(Michael Gielen); Strauss: *Guntram*, original version (John Pritchard); Strauss: *Ariadne
auf Naxos* Gerhard (David Atherton); Gerhard, Britten (Antal Dorati); Schoenberg,
Bartók (Pierre Boulez); Brahms (Rudolf Schwarz); Ligeti (Elgar Howarth); Antheil,
Hindemith, Henze, Křenek (Nicholas Cleobury); Graham Whettam (Sir Charles Macker-
ras); Philip Cannon, Bliss (Brian Wright); 'The Composer Conducts': Oliver Knussen.

FOREIGN TOURS Antwerp, Paris, Barcelona, 26 September – 2 October (Gennadi Rozhdest-
vensky): Britten, Elgar, Shostakovich, Strauss, Stravinsky. Geneva, Basle, Zürich, Lau-
sanne, Berne, 8–12 January (Gennadi Rozhdestvensky and Brian Wright): Britten, Elgar,
Maxwell Davies, Mozart, Schoeck, Shostakovich, Tchaikovsky. Peking, Shanghai, Tokyo,
Mito, Yokohama, Seoul, Fukuoka, Kagoshima, Kurashiki, Osaka, Kyoto, 14 May–2 June
(Gennadi Rozhdestvensky, Norman Del Mar): Britten, Elgar, Holst, Nicholas Maw,
Maxwell Davies, Bartók, Tippett, Stravinsky, Strauss.

APPENDIX F

The BBC Symphony Chorus
1928-80

Queen's Hall, 23 November 1928. The first performance of Granville Bantock's oratorio *The Pilgrim's Progress*, commissioned by the BBC to mark the tercentenary of the birth of John Bunyan; and the first appearance of the BBC's new National Chorus. It was an appropriate beginning, for the BBC's choir (renamed the BBC Chorus in 1932, the BBC Choral Society in 1935, and as from October 1977 the BBC Symphony Chorus) has always had the most adventurous repertory of any large choral group in the country; it has sung the great choral classics, but throughout its fifty years of existence has taken part in a remarkably wide variety of British premières and first performances, singing rare and neglected works.

It was on 12 June 1928 that the Control Board of the BBC approved the formation of an amateur chorus of 250 voices. Opinion outside the BBC was firmly against the new corporation rivalling existing musical organisations and so membership of the new chorus was invited only from those who sang – and would continue to sing – with existing bodies. The venture was to be co-operative, and there was to be no poaching of talent. Nevertheless, in response to broadcast announcements, some 2000 applications were received. On receiving details of the duties involved, a considerable number withdrew, but almost 1500 singers were auditioned. Stanford Robinson, already on the BBC's staff, was appointed Conductor. Ernest Wood, Secretary of the Civil Service Choir, became Honorary Secretary. Robinson later wrote: 'How gaily Ernest Wood and I started on the task of auditioning the hundreds of applicants . . . and how tired but how proud we were when we assembled for the first rehearsal on the evening of 28 September 1928.'

That first rehearsal began with the National Anthem, and then plunged into *The Pilgrim's Progress*, which had to be learnt in just two months. The Chorus' work was rewarded: Bantock, who conducted the concert, said it was one of the most memorable occasions of his life, and *The Times* commented: 'The singing of the National Chorus, which was heard for the first time on this occasion, proved that a fine choir has been collected and well trained by Mr Stanford Robinson.' But this was only the beginning. The next February the Chorus gave the first London performance of Eric Fogg's *The Hillside* – and, in 1930, participated in one of the most important events in London's musical life: the British première of Mahler's Eighth Symphony; Sir Henry Wood conducted the performance on 15 April 1930. In December of that year the Chorus appeared for the first time with the new BBC Symphony Orchestra, in Beethoven's *Missa Solemnis* under Hermann Scherchen.

Outstanding events in the following years included the première of *Morning Heroes* by Bliss, on 25 March 1931; the London première of *Belshazzar's Feast* by Walton (now a staple diet of every choral society) under Boult on 25 November 1931; Stravinsky's Symphony of

Psalms with the composer present, on 27 January 1932; and perhaps the greatest challenge of those early years, the British première of Hindemith's massive oratorio *Das Unaufhörliche*, which Wood conducted on 22 March 1933.

In 1932, Stanford Robinson was, to the great regret of members, transferred to the Theatre Orchestra, which he conducted for many years. He was succeeded briefly by the colourful figure of Cyril Dalmaine, who took over in July. In his autobiography, written under the pseudonym Jonah Barrington, Dalmaine said his appointment 'typifies one of the early weaknesses in BBC administration – the allocating of jobs to the lowest bidder'. His salary was raised slightly from what it had been as Robinson's assistant, but he was not given a new assistant. 'What is a Chorus Master? A stupid title, anyway – bearing an analogy to a harbour-master or a ring-master . . . in plain English, a chorus master is one who does the donkey work for others . . .' It was plain that Dalmaine was not ideally suited to the job, and indeed within two years he left the BBC, a victim (as he put it) of 'the BBC's absorbed and all-pervading interest in man's relations with woman' which was 'at that time proverbial'.

After that interlude, the Choral Society (as it became from its 1935 season) was fortunate enough to find a chorus master who was wholly dedicated to the work of preparing the Society for the many arduous engagements it undertook. Leslie Woodgate held the post from 1934 until he died in 1961, and he raised the choir from the position of being, as Sir Henry Coward told Woodgate in 1936, 'nearly as good as my Yorkshire choir' to being comparable with any in the country. Important performances of new works continued: on 11 April 1934 there was Holst's Choral Symphony; on 28 November in the same year the British première of Stravinsky's *Perséphone*. In January 1935 Albert Coates conducted one of the 1930s' curiosities: the Symphony in C minor by Yuri Alexandrovich Shaporin, whose *On the Field of Kullikorvo* was another of the Russian works undertaken by the chorus in this period. Bartók's *Cantata profana* on 25 March 1936 under Boult; the London première of Vaughan Williams' much-loved *Five Tudor Portraits* on 27 January 1937; and, perhaps most remarkable of all, the British première of Busoni's *Doktor Faust*, which took place on 17 March 1937, also conducted by Boult.

Under Leslie Woodgate, the Choral Society achieved maturity; and all accounts of the period agree that the occasions which marked that maturity were the concerts given at the end of the 1930s under the direction of Arturo Toscanini. When Toscanini was first persuaded to come to England, he would not consider working with an amateur chorus. But eventually he accepted the challenge of a performance of Beethoven's Ninth Symphony with the BBC Choral Society. The young Charles Groves prepared the chorus and that night in October 1937 is still remembered as a highlight of the Society's existence. The Brahms *Requiem*, the Verdi *Requiem* and Beethoven's *Missa Solemnis* were all performed under Toscanini's direction in the following two years, in a series of concerts in the BBC's London Music Festival which were the highlights of the capital's musical life in the prewar years.

The Second World War interrupted the activities of the Choral Society as it did many other artistic ventures. In August 1942, in wartime London, a chance meeting took place near the Albert Hall between Leslie Woodgate and the Society's Secretary, at which it was agreed that the chorus should not remain inactive, and that conditions permitted the resumption of activities. On the first Friday of January 1943, about 100 members assembled for wartime rehearsals, which continued until flying bombs interrupted them for about six weeks (during which period four members lost their lives).

After the war, activities began again in earnest. The Society worked towards its coming-of-age, its 21st birthday in 1949, and to mark that anniversary several special events took place, among them the first performance in London of a work by Leslie Woodgate, his oratorio *Simon Peter*. The BBC commissioned a choral work from Lennox Berkeley to mark the occasion: *Colonus' Praise* was premièred at the Proms on 13 September 1949. In 1949 there were thirty-five members remaining from the original chorus of 1928: some remained for many years to come. The year after the Society's birthday, a momentous change took place in the direction of the BBC's music: Adrian Boult, who had conducted many of the performances in the 1930s and 1940s as the BBC's Director of Music and Chief Conductor, passed retiring age and was not asked to remain with the Corporation. In 1950 the post of Chief Conductor of the BBC Symphony Orchestra was given to Malcolm Sargent, and there began an era in which the performance of the great choral works became a particular feature of BBC concerts.

Sargent was especially devoted to choral music, and choirs were exceptionally dedicated to him. His special skills with singers were well described by Bernard Shore (the former principal viola of the Symphony Orchestra) in his book *The Orchestra Speaks*: 'He is able to instil into the singers a life and efficiency they never dreamed of. You have only to see the eyes of a choral society screwing into him like hundreds of gimlets, to understand what he means to them. He is hypnotic with the choir – he plays upon the imagination and minds of the singers like a mesmerist.' Under Sargent the emphasis in the Society's repertoire shifted from adventurous new continental works to the twentieth-century compositions of British composers: Howells's *Hymnus Paradisi*, Vaughan Williams' *Sea Symphony*, Delius's *Sea Drift*, Ireland's *These things shall be*; such works, along with the classics of the choral repertory, Haydn's *The Creation*, Beethoven's Ninth and the *Missa Solemnis*, Handel's *Messiah* – these were the backbone of the Sargent era. Premières there were, too, though fewer than before: significant works included *Golgotha* by Frank Martin, *Hodie* by Vaughan Williams; other important events included the ceremonial opening of the new Royal Festival Hall in 1951 and a memorial concert for King George VI.

While Leslie Woodgate continued to be Chorus Master of the Society, Sargent was succeeded as Chief Conductor of the Symphony Orchestra by Rudolf Schwarz. This took place in 1957; Sargent continued to conduct the Society on many occasions (particularly at the Proms), but a change in direction was immediately apparent with the inclusion in programmes of such new works as *The Bermudas* by Iain Hamilton (on 30 October 1957) and such (then) rare works at Monteverdi's *1610 Vespers* (on 20 October 1958). Schwarz also conducted *Ulysses* by Mátyás Seiber for two concerts in December 1957. In 1958 the Choral Society made one of its all-too-rare visits abroad. They travelled to Aachen, where they gave an *a cappella* concert under Leslie Woodgate including Britten's *Hymn to St Cecilia*, and then went on to the Herkulesaal in Munich, where Handel's *Messiah* was performed. Only in 1978, twenty years later, did they travel abroad again, and this is an aspect of the Society's work which it is hoped may be developed in the future.

The arrival of William Glock at the BBC as Controller, Music, in 1959, had the same revolutionary effect on the Choral Society as on every other department concerned with music. In addition, the Society suffered a sudden loss in 1961 with the death of Leslie Woodgate, who had guided it through twenty-seven years of its existence. On 15 June 1961, a memorial concert was held, directed by Keith Falkner (who had been a soloist in the first concert in 1928) and by George Thalben-Ball. Peter Gellhorn took over the post of Chorus Master, which he held for some eleven years until 1972. Under the Glock régime modern works began to reassume a vital part in the Society's repertoire. On 1 August 1963 the London première of Britten's *War Requiem* (first performed the preceding year at Coventry

Cathedral) was given, with Britten and Meredith Davies conducting. Later that year Raws-thorne's *Carmen Vitale* was a choral commission; and at the beginning of 1963 the Society faced one of its greatest challenges, a new work by Hans Werner Henze called *Novae de Infinito Laudes*. This was given two performances under the composer's direction: on 17 March 1965, and again at the Proms on 27 August. Distinguished visitors in this period included Ernest Ansermet (conducting Honegger's *King David*) and Leopold Stokowski (in Mahler's Second Symphony).

In what he described as 'an act of faith', Glock promoted in 1967 the first performance in England of the *St Luke Passion* by the Polish composer Krzysztof Penderecki – a modern reworking of the traditional large-scale Passion setting which made exceptional demands on the choir. The work was repeated in the Proms on 2 August of that year. A typical example of the extraordinary demands made on the chorus during the Proms each year was the succession of works performed during that season: in addition to the Penderecki, they sang Mahler's Second Symphony, Walton's *Belshazzar's Feast*, Liszt's *Faust* Symphony, Berlioz's *Grande Messe des Morts*, Delius's *Appalachia*, Vaughan Williams' *Serenade to Music*, Schubert's E flat Mass and the obligatory Beethoven Ninth!

Under Antal Dorati, Chief Conductor of the Symphony Orchestra from 1963 to 1967, the Choral Society had sung Mahler, a great deal of Stravinsky, some Britten, and much Beethoven. When Colin Davis took over in 1967, a new group of composers came to the fore: Berlioz, Liszt (the *Dante* as well as the *Faust* Symphonies), and Michael Tippett. This last connection brought the Choral Society its opportunity to make its first recording for a commercial company in its recent life (though Mendelssohn's *Elijah* had been recorded as long ago as 1930): Tippett's oratorio *A Child of Our Time* was recorded under Davis's direction for Philips.

There was also a succession of major contemporary works in those years: *Voices of Night* by Reizenstein in 1969; *La Transfiguration de Notre Seigneur Jésus-Christ* by Messiaen at the first night of the Proms in 1970; and the *Requiem* by György Ligeti in 1971. By the following season, Colin Davis had departed to take up the post of Music Director at Covent Garden, and he had been succeeded by the composer and conductor Pierre Boulez. There was also a change of chorus master: in 1972 Peter Gellhorn was succeeded by John Poole, who directed several of the concerts in this period, including Dvořák's *Te Deum* and Bruckner's F minor Mass.

The Boulez repertoire, as with the Orchestra, was immediately distinctive: Schoenberg's *Gurrelieder* was given performances, and became a commercial recording for CBS Records. Stravinsky, Ravel, Debussy and Mahler were prominently featured, while of the romantics Berlioz, Schumann (the *Faust* Scenes) and Brahms (the *Requiem*) all appeared more than once. During this period the Society sang under many guest conductors: the young Andrew Davis made his unexpected London début with them in Janáček's *Glagolithic Mass*; Lorin Maazel returned to conduct some highly successful concerts; John Pritchard conducted several events including Rachmaninov's *The Bells*.

An increasingly large number of important occasions were undertaken by the Chorus Master. John Poole was entrusted with the world première of David Bedford's *Twelve Hours of Sunset* in 1975, and in a memorable concert at the Alexandra Palace conducted two symphonies by Havergal Brian with the Choral Society (who had already taken part in the giant *Gothic Symphony* by the same composer in a concert at the Albert Hall). Another first performance, that of Iain Hamilton's *Epitaph for this world and time*, performed before the traditional Beethoven Ninth on the penultimate night of the Proms in 1975, proved one of the most complex undertakings of the Society, for the choir was split into three groups, and positioned around the arena in the Albert Hall. Both this, and another 1975 contemporary work, *Mortales* by Wilfred Josephs, were conducted by John Poole.

In 1976 the work of the BBC's professional choir, the BBC Singers, increased and John Poole gave up his work with the Choral Society in order to concentrate on the Singers' activities. The present Chorus Master, Brian Wright, then took over, and in the following year himself conducted the chorus in public in such works as Duruflé's *Requiem*, Kodály's *Missa Brevis*, and Holst's Choral Symphony. In recognition of its status as a choir appearing in professional concerts under leading conductors, with a repertory second to none, the Choral Society was renamed the BBC Symphony Chorus, and made its first appearance under that name in *A Sea Symphony* by Vaughan Williams on 21 October 1977.

And so the work of the Chorus continues. There are now some 160 members, who re-hearse each week on Friday evening in the Concert Hall of Broadcasting House; along with all the many other calls on their time for final rehearsals, extra sessions, and so on, members found themselves spending (in 1978) eighty-five sessions with the Chorus, rehearsing four-teen different works. New members continue to flow in: as with the auditionees in 1928, some are still discouraged by the sheer hard work and time and breadth of repertoire with which they will be expected to cope. But for those who do join, the rewards appear to be immense. In September and October of 1978 the Chorus travelled to the Flanders Festival, appearing under the baton of the new Chief Conductor of the BBC Symphony Orchestra, Gennadi Rozhdestvensky, as well as that of their Chorus Master Brian Wright. They sang the Mass in F minor and motets by Bruckner, and members regard this as one of the most memorable occasions of the choir's life; one which gives hope for more touring activity in the future. The Chorus gave on 8 April 1979 a performance of Elgar's *The Music Makers* in the Albert Hall to mark the ninetieth birthday of Sir Adrian Boult. To celebrate its fiftieth anniversary, the Chorus gave a concert in the Royal Albert Hall on 10 January 1979, in which it performed Bach's B minor Mass under Brian Wright. And the BBC commissioned a new choral work to mark the anniversary: Alexander Goehr wrote his oratorio *Babylon the Great is Fallen*, which was given its first performance under Michael Gielen at the Royal Festival Hall in December 1979.

General Index

Aberdare 179, 182
Abraham, Professor Gerald 236, 426
ACAS 432, 433
Adam, Kenneth 211
Aeolian Hall 10
Albert Hall, London *see* Royal Albert Hall
Aldeburgh 336
Alexandrov, A. V. 191
Allen, Sir Hugh chairman of Music Advisory Committee (1926) 11; supports appointment of Boult as Director of Music 38; suggested by Walford Davies as 'Chief Musical Adviser' 130; rejects proposal to make Walter Chief Conductor 144, 145; chairs committee on deferment of military service for musicians 171; advises against proposal to make Bliss Director of Music 172; other references 95, 151
Alwyn, William 98, 182, 318; *see also* Index 2
Amis, John 375
Amsterdam 211, 260
Amy, Gilbert 340, 343, 368
Amyot, Étienne 233
Andreae, Volkmar 136
Angel Pavement (Priestley) 50
Annual Register on London Orchestras 8, 116, 183; on Berlin Philharmonic Orchestra 14; on Toscanini 145; on Shostakovich 180; on Festival Hall concerts 339, 354; on 1972 Prom season 384
Ansell, John 10, 46
Ansermet, Ernest conducts BBC SO 59, 60, 74, 79, 80, 96, 117, 131, 135, 213, 292, 316, 516; his influence on Orchestra 60
Antill, John 257
Aprahamian, Felix 74
Aranovich, Yuri 406

Aranyi, Jelly d' 142, 143, 162
Arnold, Malcolm 263, 405; *see also* Index 2
Arrau, Claudio 213, 265
Arts Council of Great Britain 354, 357, 429
Arundel, Dennis 116
Ashkenazy, Vladimir 317
As I Remember (Bliss) 188
Atherton, David 339, 343, 347, 376, 407–9, 421
Atzmon, Moshe 343
Austin, Richard 178, 187
Austral, Florence 71
Austria 388

Bachauer, Gina 265
Backhaus, Wilhelm 61, 84, 151; denounced by Walter 98, 99, 144
Baden-Baden 388
Bailey, Enid 186
Bainbridge, Simon 410
Bainton, Edgar 93
Bantock, Granville 65, 98, 164, 513; *see also* Index 2
Barbican Concert Hall 428
Barbirolli, Sir John 136, 177, 186, 191, 197, 212, 244, 250, 264, 287, 329; considered as successor to Boult 216–18; declines offer 219, 220, 222; tours Eastern Europe with BBC SO 332, 333
Barbirolli, Lady 433
Bardgett, Herbert 287
Barenboim, Daniel 329, 378, 381, 382, 384, 386
Barlow, Harry 46, 53
Barnes, Sir George 151, 201, 206, 233
Barr, Herbert 55
Barrington, Jonah *see* Dalmaine, Cyril
Bartók, Béla 37, 87, 119, 125, 289; *see also* Index 2
Bate, Stanley 148
Baudo, Serge 345, 407
Bax, Sir Arnold 84, 188; *see*

also Index 2
BBC established as Corporation (1 January 27) 11
Music Advisory Committee formed by Reith 11; Boult as member 38, 40; on collaboration with RPS 91, 92; criticism of BBC SO programmes causes resentment 93, 111; and visit of Orchestra to Manchester 103 supports Continental tours 105; dissolution sought by Graves 112; Boult's criticism of in report to Ullswater Committee 112; discusses separation of Directorship of Music and Chief Conductorship 130; formalises post of Assistant Director of Music 129–30; composition enlarged 130; other references 4, 39, 83, 95, 144; Central Music Advisory Committee 290
Music Department (–1952) and Beecham scheme for permanent orchestra 34, 35; and Boult as Director of Music 38–42, 39, 64, 65, 78; and collaboration with Beecham and RPS 89, 91; resentment towards Music Advisory Committee 93, 94, 111; and visit of BBC SO to Manchester 102; and resignation of Clark 125–6; and visit by Toscanini (1937) 127
administration moves to Evesham during War 155; wartime plans for BBC SO 161; moves to Bedford 168, 170; Bliss succeeds Boult as Director of Music 172; forms new branch for music overseas 172; offices in Marylebone High Street 176
and restoration of Orchestra to

pre-war strength 200, 203, 205–6, 214; relations with Chief Conductor 225, 231; relations with Sargent 236, 239, 246–7, 253; other references 15, 99, 181; *see also* BBC: Music Division, music policy, orchestral policy
Music Division (1952–) formation, organisation and personnel 236–8; relations with Sargent 262, 272; resists broadcasting of recorded programmes 277; Glock's reforms 293; other references 309, 314; *see also* BBC: Music Department, music policy, orchestral policy
Music Executive 40, 65
Music Library 78
music policy 3, 110–15, 144–5, 157–8, 160–2, 164, 173–5, 233–6, 277–9, 304–8, 319–21, 355–7, 429–34; *see also* BBC orchestral policy
orchestral policy 5, 7, 8, 10, 12–13, 34–7, 85–92, 103, 105, 110–15, 136, 158–60, 171–2, 185, 193–4, 198–208, 211, 215, 236–8, 247–8, 298–304, 308–14, 336–9, 342, 354–7, 363–5, 367–8, 427–34; *see also* BBC music policy
Premises Broadcasting House 49, 77, 78, 101; No. 10 studio 57–8, 65, 71, 72, 76, 78; Maida Vale studios 101–2, 210, 293, 424, 426; Concert Hall, Broadcasting House 78; Yalding House 240, 424, 425; Marylebone High Street 78, 176
Programme Division 91
Programmes Home Service 160, 185, 230–2; Music Programme 320, 321; Network Three 276, 277, 319; Overseas Service 172, 185; Third Programme inaugurated 201, 210; music policy 210, 211, 231–3; Sargent's concerts 253, 256; presents own concerts 256; records new works 257; 10th anniversary 274, 282, 283; reduced output causes public indignation 276; other references 206, 217, 237, 242, 263, 265, 266, 277, 278, 284, 331; Radio 3 405, 427, 428, 430
Variety Department 168
BBC Bach Orchestra 70
BBC Chorus and Choral Society 140, 146, 147, 513ff.
BBC Light Orchestra 70
BBC Military Band 65, 74
BBC National Chorus 59, 63, 67, 513ff.

BBC Northern Orchestra 102
BBC Quarterly 209, 234, 235
BBC Singers 408
BBC Symphony Chorus 513, 517ff.
BBC Symphony Orchestra first plans for permanent orchestra 8–15; Beecham's proposals 15–23, 27–32; press comments 23–7; Beecham withdraws 32–4; Music Department's plans for organisation 34–8; recruitment of Orchestra 42–6; opposition to BBC policy 46–8 Chief Conductor policy Boult 63–4; Walter 144–5; Barbirolli and Kubelik 215–29; Sargent 238–40, 243–6, 253–5, 261–2, 266, 270–2; Schwarz 279–81, 298–300; 1962–3 season 300–1; Dorati 301–2, 314–15; 1966–7 season 329; C. Davis 327–9, 333–4; Boulez 358, 391–5; Solti 398; Kempe 399–400, 402–3; Rozhdestvensky 411–14; *see also under* individual conductors
orchestral personnel 50–5, 128–9, 203–4, 368, 440–6
Concerts management department 258, 314–15, 393, 423–4
Concert Series
Queen's Hall (1930–1) 49–63; (31–2) 70–7; (32–3) 79–89; (33–4) 93–7; (34–5) 92, 99–101; (35–6) 115–18; (36–7) 131–6; (37–8) 139–47; (38–9) 147–50; (39–40) 151–4
Royal Albert Hall (1944) 187; (45–6) 196–8; (46–7) 209–11; (47–8) 212–13; (48–9) 213–14; (49–50) 214; (50–1) 242; (51–2) 244
Royal Festival Hall (1952–3) 252; (53–4) 256–7; (54–5) 263–7; (55–6) 267; (56–7) 273–4; (57–8) 281–4; (58–9) 287–8; (59–60) 291–5; (60–1) 295; (61–2) 297; (62–3) 308; (63–4) 316; (64–5) 317; (65–6) 329–30; (66–7) 330–2; (67–8) 335; (68–9) 343–5; (69–70) 348–51; (70–1) 352–3; (71–2) 369–70; (72–3) 379–81; (73–4) 381–3; (74–5) 386; (75–6) 403–5; (76–7) 405–6; (77–8) 406–7; (78–9) 418–21; (79–80) 421–4; (80–1) 509–12
Bristol Concerts (1939–41) 158–69
Bedford Concerts (1941–2) 176–81; (42–3) 180–2; (43–4) 186–7, 190–1
Henry Wood Promenade

Concerts (1931) 68; (35) 115; (38) 146; (39) 154; (42) 180; (43) 183; (44) 189; (45) 193; (46) 203; (49) 218; (53) 255; (54) 262; (55) 265; (56) 272–3; (60) 293; (61) 298, 318; (62) 303, 318; (63) 318; (64) 318; (67) 329, 333; (68) 345–7; (69) 345–7; (70) 345–7; (71) 383–4; (72) 368, 384; (73) 385–7; (74) 385, 400; (75) 400–1; (76) 403; (78) 414; (79) 421; (80) 421, 432–4
London Music Festival (1933) 84; (34) 82, 97–9; (35) 92, 105–9; (36: cancelled) 119, 127; (37) 137–9; (38) 145; (39) 147, 150–4
St John's, Smith Square (1971–2) 366–8; (72–3) 377–8; (73–4) 378; (74–5) 378–9; (75–6: in Broadcasting House) 407; (76–7) 408; (77–8) 408; (78–9) 408; (79–80) 408
The Round House, Chalk Farm (1971–2) 370–4; (72–3) 374–5; (73–4) 375–6; (74–5) 376; (75–6) 408; (76–7) 409–10
Studios
'No. 10' Studio (1930–4) 58, 65, 71, 72, 76, 78
Maida Vale Studios (from 1934) 101–4, 210, 293, 424, 426
UK Visits (1934) 102–4; (35–6) 128; (36–7) 136–7; (41–2) 178, 181; (43–4) 184–5; (47–8) 212; (51) 250; (53) 250; (54) 257; (55) 264; (56) 268; (57–8) 284; (58–9) 288; (66) 330; *see also* names of towns
Foreign Tours (1935: Belgium) 104–5; (36: Europe) 118–24; (37: Irish Republic) 137; (47: Europe) 211; (54: Europe) 258–61; (56: Scandinavia) 268–9; (57–8: Irish Republic) 284; (58: Belgium) 284–5; (65: United States) 322–7; (67: Germany) 335; (67: Eastern Europe) 332–3; (68: Germany) 336; (69: Holland) 343; (70: Europe) 348; (71: Germany, Switzerland) 348; (71: Austria) 368–9; (72: France, Switzerland) 370; (74: Europe) 388; (75: Japan) 389–91; (75: Belgium, France) 403; *see also* names of countries and towns
BBC Theatre Orchestra 70, 89, 201, 206, 207
BBC Year Book 68
Beadle, G. C. 160
Bean, Ernest 292
Bean, Hugh 336
Beard, Paul chosen by Boult to

lead BBC SO 128, 129; plays
during air raid 166; retires 303;
other references 55, 131, 152,
162, 181, 211, 249, 281, 284
Beckett, Mrs Gwendolen 65
Beckles, Gordon 83
Bedford   home of BBC SO from
July 41–September 45 170,
176–8, 180–2, 186, 187, 190,
191, 193, 194
Beecham, Sir Thomas involved
in early plans for permanent
orchestra 15–25, 42, 43; his
opposition to broadcasting
music 16, 20, 85; fails to reach
agreement with BBC 26–38,
41, 45, 68; and London
Symphony Orchestra 70, 78;
founds London Philharmonic
Orchestra 79, 80
conducts BBC SO 87, 93,
131, 134, 147, 149, 210, 214,
256, 262, 263, 273; his
proposals for collaboration
between RPS, LPO and BBC
rejected 89–92; and Hallé
Orchestra 102, 113; proposed
by Lady Cunard to succeed
Bliss as BBC Director of
Music 187; conducts
Philharmonia Orchestra,
founds Royal Philharmonic
Orchestra 199, 209; on Royal
Festival Hall 243
other references 50, 52, 55, 57,
70, 100, 151, 165, 199
Beecham Orchestra 52
Beinum, Eduard van 213, 279
Béjart, Maurice 361
Belfast 257, 284
Belfast Philharmonic Orchestra
113, 114
Bellugi, Piero 386
Bender, Charles 54, 129
Benjamin, Arthur 257; see also
Index 2
Bennett, Richard Rodney 318;
see also Index 2
Berberian, Cathy 375
Berg, Alban 66, 97, 119, 132;
see also Index 2
Berio, Luciano 289, 290, 374,
397; see also Index 2
Berkeley, Lennox 182, 433,
515; see also Index 2
Berkeley, Michael 417
Berlin 15, 52, 335
Berlin Philharmonic Orchestra
14, 53, 72, 141
Berlin State Opera 21
Berlioz, Hector centenary, 343;
see also Index 2
Bernard, Anthony 10
Bertini, Gary 331, 340, 411
Bessel, Annamaria 331
'Besses o' th' Barn' band 53

Birmingham 1, 2, 4, 103, 104,
257
Birmingham Post 77, 157
Birmingham Symphony
Orchestra 10
Bishop, Stephen (now Bishop-
Kovacevich) 343
Bitterauf, Richard 96
Blacher, Boris 275; see also
Index 2
Black, Leo 293
Blake, Carice 176
Blech, Harry 54, 129
Bliss, Sir Arthur in charge of
Overseas Music Department
172; appointed Director of
Music 173; supports British
music 175, 182; policies 175–6,
181–2, 185; leaves BBC 187;
other references 98, 150, 180,
188, 343; see also Index 2
Bloch, Ernest 14, 118
Blom, Eric 252
Blyth, Alan 398
Blyth, May 65, 96, 149
Boettcher, Wilfried 403
Bolshoi Theatre 415
Bonavia, Ferruccio 69, 148
Boosey, William 7, 11–13
Bor, Sam 54
Boretz, Benjamin 326
Boston Globe 324
Boston Symphony Orchestra
17, 84
Boughton, Rutland 93, 126
Boulanger, Lili 343
Boulanger, Nadia 134, 148, 343
Boulez, Pierre (Chief Conductor
1971–5, Chief Guest
Conductor 1975–7) conducts
BBC SO 317, 329, 331, 341,
342, 346, 351, 369, 381, 383–5,
387, 398, 404–6, 408, 409, 421,
423; shares conducting with
Dorati on USA tour 322, 325,
326; shares conducting with
Barbirolli on East European
tour 332–3; concert
disrupted at Berlin Festival 335;
invited to be Chief Conductor
345, 361–3; background to
appointment 358–60;
appointed Conductor of New
York Philharmonic 362–3;
negotiations of contract 363;
tours Continent with Orchestra
348; relationship with
Orchestra 360, 391–5; scheme
to reorganise Paris Opéra 360,
361; interviewed by Peter
Heyworth about his plans for
BBC SO 363–5
inaugurates concerts in the
Round House and St John's,
Smith Square 366–7, 370–9;
changes in orchestral planning

367–8; in Graz and Vienna
with Orchestra 368–9; tours
France and Switzerland with
Orchestra 370
final season as Chief Conductor
382, 386; studio work 386,
388; tours Germany, Austria
and Switzerland with
Orchestra 388; tours Japan
with Orchestra 389–91;
assessment 391–5; other
references 238, 290, 340, 353,
354, 357, 396, 397, 400, 403,
433, 516; see also Index 2
Boult, Sir Adrian and City of
Birmingham Orchestra 9, 38,
39; appointed BBC Director of
Music (1930) 39, 40; rejects
collaboration with RPS 41, 42;
and permanent orchestra 43–6,
51; conducts first concerts of
BBC SO 55–7
becomes Chief Conductor of
Orchestra 64; and ISCM
Festival 1931 66, 67; invites
Walter to conduct Orchestra
75, 99, 144, 145; on public
concerts 85, 86, 88, 89, 111,
186; on collaboration with
Beecham and RPS 90–2;
responses to complaints by
Music Advisory Committee
93; on Hallé Orchestra 102,
103; on Glasgow and
Edinburgh 104; and Toscanini
106, 109, 137
report to Ullswater Committee
112–14; tours Europe with
Orchestra (1936) 121–4;
chooses Beard as leader of
Orchestra 128, 129; knighted
134
in Bristol during War
157–68; in Bedford during
War 169–72, 176–9; receives
Gold Medal of RPS 190;
pleads for BBC recognition of
Orchestra's status 192, 193,
199, 202; supports move for
early return of Orchestra to
London 194; on poor standard
of 1946 Proms 204–6; tours
Europe with Orchestra (1947)
211; retirement from BBC
215–17, 220, 222, 223, 226;
farewell concert 240, 241
conducts première of Tippett's
Second Symphony 283, 284;
proposes recording of Proms
during 1980 strike 432;
ninetieth birthday 517; other
references passim
Bournemouth Orchestra 44
Bowen, Meirion 372, 375
Bowles, Ann (Lady Boult) 214
Bradbury, Colin 309, 368

Brahms Centenary Concerts 84
Brain, Aubrey 43, 53, 75, 136, 203
Brecher, Gustav 12
Bridge, Frank 98; *see also* Index 2
Briggs, Asa 110, 156, 232
Briggs, Roger 55
Brighton 407, 420
Brindle, Reginald Smith 318
Brinnen, Gerald 308
Bristol home of BBC SO September 39–July 41 154–69; other references 103, 257, 268
Bristol Choral Society 160, 169
Bristol Evening Post 162
Bristol Evening World 163
Bristol Philharmonic Society 160
British Broadcasting Company 2, 3, 11
British music 94, 175, 176, 279, 353
British National Opera Company 4, 51
British Symphony Orchestra 51
British Women's Symphony Orchestra 9
Britten, Benjamin 260, 275, 516; *see also* Index 2
Broadcasting House *see* BBC
Broadcasting in the Seventies 320, 339, 355, 356, 431
Brosa, Antonia 141
Brown, Iona 420
Brown, Ivor 289
Brussels 104, 211, 260, 403, 419
Brussels Exposition (1958) 284, 285
Brymer, Jack 309
Budapest 15, 122, 123
Buesst, Aylmer 65, 116, 129
Burghauser, Hugo 122
Burgos, Rafael Frühbeck de 403
Burkhard, Willy 146, 147; *see also* Index 2
Burrows, A. R. 2, 3, 4
Burton, Humphrey 340
Busch, Adolf 57, 116, 143
Busch, Fritz 96
Butt, David 309, 368

Cairns, David (music critic, *The Sunday Times*) on Boulez 331; on Rozhdestvensky 418
Calvocoressi, Michel 83, 148
Cambridge 178, 181, 197, 212
Camden, Archie 46, 47, 53, 129
Cameron, Basil 147, 148, 150, 163, 168, 176, 180, 181, 183, 188, 191, 203, 212, 242, 244
Campoli, Alfredo 263
Canterbury Festival 68
Capell, Richard (music critic, *Daily Telegraph*) on BBC SO

80; on Schoenberg 83; on Walton 116; on Stravinsky 118; on Berg 132; on Beecham 134; on Toscanini 138, 152, 153; on Busoni 148
Cardiff 179
Cardus, Neville (music critic, *Manchester Guardian*) on broadcast music 48, 149; on BBC SO 80; on Bartók 87; on Berg 100; on Vaughan Williams 101; on Toscanini 108, 140, 146; on Purcell 117; on Schoenberg 118; on Eugene Goossens 148; on Walter 148–9; on Beecham 149, 150; on Schwarz 299
Carewe, John conducts BBC SO 298, 319, 340, 381
Carner, Mosco 187
Carpendale, Admiral 120–4
Carron, Arthur 210
Carter, Elliott 289
Casals, Pablo 66, 80, 116, 132, 140, 191, 196
Casella, Alfredo 66, 67
Catterall, Arthur (Leader BBC SO 1930–5) background 50, 52; recruited as leader of BBC SO 42, 43, 46; resigns 128; other references 37, 102, 109, 115, 121, 123, 131, 136, 167
Catterall String Quartet 51
Central Hall, Westminster 7, 46
Chamberlain, Neville 140, 154–6
Chappell's 11, 12
Chavez, Carlos 387
Chelmsford 1
Cheltenham Festival 336
Cherkassky, Shura 282
Chester 257
Chesterman, Edward 171
Chisholm, Eric 182
Christoff, Boris 383
Chronicle of My Life (Stravinsky) 125
Churchill, Winston 162, 191, 192
City of Birmingham Orchestra 9, 52, 113, 128, 132
Civil, Alan 368
Clark, Edward (Programme planner 1927–36) background 5, 6; invites Schoenberg to England 14; draws up scheme for permanent orchestra 35, 36; plans programmes 56, 57, 60, 61, 64, 65, 86; advocates contemporary music 66, 77, 96, 103, 115; instigates invitation to Koussevitsky 84; as conductor 88; visits Europe to plan tours 118; attends funeral of Berg 119; resigns from BBC (1936) 124–7; assists Bliss 181

other references 10, 11, 12, 146, 197, 233, 238
Clark, Sir George 121
Clarke, Ralph 309
Clements, Andrew (music critic, *The Financial Times*) on Gielen 422
Clifford, Julian (Conductor) 163, 178, 187
Clive, Sir Sidney 130
Closson, Ernest 104
Coates, Albert (Conductor) 10, 12, 66, 99, 118, 143, 196
Cockerill, Albert 166
Cocteau, Jean 294
Cohen, Harriet 74, 154
Columbia Gramophone Co. 18, 19, 22, 30, 31, 32
Comet, Catherine 370
'Composer Conducts' series 388, 405
Concert Hall (television series) 340
Concerts of British Music 135
Conductor Speaks, The (television programme) 257
Connah, Trevor 308
Connolly, Justin 347, 371; *see also* Index 2
contracts 42, 44–6, 245, 248, 302, 311, 313, 314, 337, 429
Contracts Department 22
Cooke, Arnold 98; *see also* Index 2
Cooke, Deryck 329, 405
Cooper, Martin 379
Copenhagen 268
Copland, Aaron 265; *see also* Index 2
Cortot, Alfred 63, 75, 84
Coulling, John 308
Council for the Encouragement of Music and the Arts (CEMA) 165, 180
Courtauld Concerts 57, 60, 71, 72, 74
Courtauld–Sargent Concerts 79, 116, 134
Covent Garden Opera House 4, 10, 13, 28, 51, 52, 70, 75, 79, 97, 197, 344, 399
Covent Garden Orchestra 12, 53
Cowen, Sir Frederic 93
Cox, David 294
Craig, D. Millar 83
Crawford Committee 11, 16
Craxton, Janet 285, 309
Crichton, Ronald (music critic, *The Financial Times*) on Boulez 341; on Berio 349
Crickmore, Kenneth 217, 219
Croft-Jackson, Harry 238
Crosse, Gordon 375; *see also* Index 2
Crossley, Paul 404

Crossley-Holland, Peter 237
Crowson, Lamar 288
Cruft, Eugene 51, 52
Cruickshank, Enid 72, 74
Crystal Palace 1
Cuénod, Hughes 148
Culshaw, John 340
Cunard, Lady 87, 187
Cundell, Edric 187
Curran, Charles (Director-
General 1969-77) 339, 356,
357, 413
Curzon, Sir Clifford 119, 163,
250, 258-60, 388
Czechoslovakia 332
Czyz, Henryk 332

Daily Chronicle 21, 45
Daily Dispatch 102, 103
Daily Express on first broadcasts
of opera 4; on Beecham and
BBC 26, 29; on first concert of
BBC SO 56; on Orchestra's
concert in Manchester 102; on
Queen's Hall 16; on
Orchestra's concert in
Glasgow 128; on Toscanini 137
Daily Herald 25, 83, 86
Daily Mail promotes music
broadcast 1; on Beecham's
plans for permanent orchestra
19-22; on Beecham and BBC
25; on first concert of BBC SO
56; on Elgar's Third
Symphony 80; on Weingartner
87; on Vaughan Williams 101;
on Toscanini 137
Daily News 25
Daily Telegraph on new music
69; on Walton 73; on
Hindemith 75, 150; on
standard of BBC SO 77; on
Elgar birthday concerts 80; on
Elgar's Third Symphony 81;
on Schoenberg 83; letter from
Moeran 94; on Berg 97, 132
organises competition for
overture 98; letter from Forbes
103; on Koussevitsky 105; on
Toscanini 108, 137, 139, 153;
on length of concerts 115; on
Stravinsky 118; on Beecham
134; on Ireland 135; on
Mahler 141; on Schumann
143; on Busoni 148
on Boult's proposal for 'special
concerts' 162; sponsors
birthday concert for Wood
188; letter from Tertis 209; on
Schwarz 299; on Boulez 331,
341; on Holliger 353; on
Kempe 399; on
Rozhdestvensky 417, 420
Daily Worker 196
Dallapiccola, Luigi 250
Dalmaine, Cyril (alias Jonah

Barrington) 116, 514
Damrosch, Walter 14
Danks, Harry 251, 267, 308,
401
Darnton, Christian 144
Davidson, Belle 308
Davies, Hugh 370
Davies, Meredith 516
Davies, Peter Maxwell 388,
410; see also Index 2
Davies, Tudor 66, 96
Davies, Sir Walford member of
Music Advisory Committee
11; suggests Boult as Director
of Music 38; on visit of BBC
SO to Manchester 103;
suggests Allen as 'Chief
Musical Adviser' 130; on
London Music Festival (1939)
151; other references 65, 112
Davis, Andrew conducts BBC
SO 352, 368, 369, 383, 387,
403, 405, 406; other references
400, 412, 516
Davis, Colin conducts BBC SO
308, 316; offered post of Chief
Conductor 328, 329; becomes
Chief Conductor 333-5;
makes television recordings
336; tours Germany with
Orchestra 336; tries to improve
Orchestra's pay 337, 338;
makes gramophone recording
340; works to improve
standard and build up
repertory of Orchestra 342,
348; offered post of Music
Director at Covent Garden
344; conducts Proms 345-7;
tours on Continent with
Orchestra 348
last season as Chief Conductor
353, 354; conducts concert
during Musicians' Union strike
433; other references 341, 362,
368, 369, 378, 381, 383-6, 394,
403, 405, 406, 408, 516
Davy, Gloria 380
Decker, Franz-Paul 317, 344
Dekany, Bela 336, 368, 417, 423
Delius, Frederick Festival 37;
memorial concert 100; see also
Index 2
Della Casa, Lisa 273
Dello Joio, Norman 267; see
also Index 2
Del Mar, Norman appointed an
assistant conductor of BBC SO
277; other references 283, 308,
316, 319, 329, 332, 336, 340,
343, 347, 384-7, 404-6, 433
Dent, E. J. 66, 146
deputy system 8, 9, 12
Désormière, Roger 190
Dickie, T. J. 10

Dieren, Bernard van 136; see
also Index 2
Dixon, Dean 316
Dobrowen, Issay 242
'Document C' 154
Dohnanyi, Christoph von 329,
331, 344
Dohnanyi, Ernst von 61
Domaine Musical Ensemble
358, 359
Dorati, Antal background 301;
appointed Chief Conductor of
BBC SO 308, 309, 314; works
to improve standard of
Orchestra 315, 316; tours
United States with Orchestra
322-7; final season as Chief
Conductor 328-30; other
references 385, 516; see also
Index 2
Douglas, Keith 151, 165, 179
Downes, Edward 341, 408
Dresden State Opera Orchestra
123, 134
Drew, David 291, 293
Drucker, Gerald 308
Druckman, Jacob 374
Dublin 137, 284
Dundee 104
Du Pré, Jacqueline 323, 333
Düsseldorf 258
Dvořák, Antonin featured in
1954 May festival 255
Dyson, Dr George 130

Eastern Europe 329, 332
Eckersley, Peter 2, 6
Eckersley, Roger (Controller,
Programmes 1924-34;
Controller, Entertainment
1934-5; Assistant Controller,
Programmes 1935-6)
background 6; appointed to
BBC (1924) 6; visits Europe
14, 15; plans permanent
orchestra 16-45; on criticism
of BBC public concerts 85-88;
on collaboration with Beecham
89-92; and Music Advisory
Committee 111-12;
accompanies Orchestra to
Europe 120-24
Edinburgh 136, 137
Edinburgh Festival 213, 217,
265
Edmunds, Chris 182
Edwards, William 258, 335, 425
Elder, Mark 405, 411, 423
Elgar, Sir Edward 75th birthday
concerts 79-81; Third
Symphony commissioned by
BBC 80-2; death 98, 100;
Symphony incomplete 98;
Enigma Variations performed
by Toscanini 108; other
references 7, 39, 241; see also

Index 2
Elizabeth II, Queen 251
Eloy, Jean-Claude 376
Enesco, Georges 242
ENSA 184, 185, 198
Epilogue 58, 59, 166
Epstein, Jacob 57
Erede, Alberto 403, 405
Eschenbach, Christoph 388
Evans, Edwin (music critic) on
  Boult 62; on ISCM Festival
  67; on Schoenberg 73; on Berg
  83, 84; on Vaughan Williams
  101; on Busoni 135; on
  Toscanini 137
Evans, Geraint 433
Eveline, Beatrice 2
Evening Chronicle 103
Evening News 21, 38, 45, 93
Evening Standard on Beecham
  and BBC 26; on first season of
  BBC SO 63; on Walton 73; on
  Weingartner 87; on Ogilvie 145
Evesham home of BBC
  administration during War
  155, 170–2

Fagan, Gideon 187
Falkner, Keith 515
Falla, Manuel de 66; *see also*
  Index 2
Farberman, Harold 386, 404
Felton, Felix 160
Ferber, Albert 190
Ferra, Franco 407
Festival Hall, London *see* Royal
  Festival Hall
Festival of Britain 224, 243, 252
Festival of British Music 95
Feuermann, Emanuel 146
Financial Times, The on Boulez
  331, 341, 345, 371, 373, 376;
  on Carter 349; on Stockhausen
  351; on Kempe 401; on
  Sandström 409; on
  Rozhdestvensky 418; on Gielen
  422; on 50th anniversary of
  BBC SO 435
Finland 269
Firkusny, Rudolf 249
First Flute (Jackson) 129
Fischer, Ivan 405, 408
Fitelberg, Gregor 66, 67, 197,
  198
Fitzwater, William 373
Fjeldstad, Oivin 294
Flagstad, Kirsten 356
Fleming, Amaryllis 287
Flesch, Carl 86, 116
Fogg, Eric 98; *see also* Index 2
Foldes, Andor 282
Foot, R. W. 173
Forbes, R. J. 103
Ford, Christopher 406, 411, 412
Ford, Frank 308
Forsyth, J. A. 83

Foster, Lawrence 351
'Foundations of Music' 65
Fox-Strangways, A. H. 63
France 370
Francis, Alun 402
Freccia, Massimo 292
Freitas Blanco, Pedro de 186,
  273
Frémaux, Louis 369
Fricker, Peter Racine 252; *see
  also* Index 2
Fried, Oskar 63
Friedemann, Samuel 405
Friend, Lionel 411
Friend, Rodney 423
Full Orchestra (Howes) 57
Furtwängler, Wilhelm 14, 72,
  84, 141
Fussell, William 120, 123, 166

Gaetani, Jan de 389
Gaisberg, Fred 82
Gambold, Geoffrey 309
Gardiner, John Eliot 368, 378,
  380, 384, 403, 406
Gauntlett, Ambrose 54, 75, 129
Gellhorn, Peter 387, 515, 516
George V, King 117
George VI, King 137
Gerhard, Roberto 289, 301; *see
  also* Index 2
Germany 336, 348, 388, 406
Gertler, André 264
Gibbs, Cecil Armstrong 182
Gibson, Alexander 397, 400,
  412
Gielen, Michael (Chief Guest
  Conductor 1977–) appointed
  403; compared with Boulez
  403, 422–3; conducts Choral
  Society 517; other references
  297, 308, 349, 373, 405, 406,
  408, 409, 411
Gieseking, Walter 61, 134
Gill, Dominic (music critic, *The
  Financial Times*) on Boulez
  345, 371, 376; on Stockhausen
  351; on Maderna 352–3; on
  Round House concerts 375,
  376; on Balassa 404; on
  Sandström 409
Gillard, Frank (Director of
  Sound Broadcasting 1963–8;
  Managing Director, Radio,
  1969–70) on Music
  Programme 320; on
  Orchestra's tour of United
  States 327; other references
  291, 311, 314, 328
Gillegin, Ernest 129
Giulini, Carlo Mario 318
Glasgow 104, 128
Glasgow Herald 61, 74, 97, 212
Glock, Sir William (Controller,
  Music 1959–72) background
  289–91; early plans 292–5;

297; and Schwarz 298–9;
  chooses Dorati as Chief
  Conductor of Orchestra 301,
  314; rebuilds Orchestra
  302–11; relations with Dorati
  314–16, 328; relations with
  Boulez 317, 333, 341, 395–7
  reforms Proms 318–19, 347–8,
  385, 386; and Music
  Programme 319–21; tours
  United States with Orchestra
  322–6; appoints Davis as
  Chief Conductor 328–30,
  333–4; tries to improve
  Orchestra's pay 338
  chooses Boulez as Chief
  Conductor 344–5, 358–63;
  plans concerts at St John's
  377; at the Round House
  370–5; knighted (1970) 396;
  and Choral Society 515–16;
  other references 125, 237, 332,
  340, 344, 349, 369, 375, 379,
  380
Glyndebourne Opera Company
  210, 318
Godfrey, Dan 7, 10
Goehr, Walter 201, 242, 250,
  251, 256, 257, 264, 267, 293,
  376
Goldberg, Szymon 343
Goldfish Bowl, A (Lutyens) 125
Gomez, Jill 419
Goodall, Reginald 344
Goodman, Lord 354, 433, 434
Goodman Report 354
Goodwin, Noël 287
Goossens, Sir Eugene praised
  by Cardus and Capell 148;
  conducts own Second
  Symphony 210; other
  references 7, 10, 39, 54, 147,
  168, 256, 267, 294; *see also*
  Index 2
Goossens, Sidonie background
  and début in BBC SO 54; in
  Hungary with Orchestra 123;
  with Greenbaum, Rawsthorne,
  and Jessie Hinchliffe in Bristol
  and Bedford during War 159,
  170; on Howgill's retirement
  290–1; fêted at Orchestra's
  50th anniversary concert 434;
  other references 167, 425, 433
Gorell Committee 209
Goren, Eli 336, 368, 401, 423
Graves, Sir Cecil (Controller of
  Programmes 1934–8;
  Director-General 1942–3) as
  Assistant Controller of
  Programmes 41–3, 46; as
  Controller of Programmes 112,
  115; disagrees with Boult on
  broadcasting of concerts 124;
  appointed Director-General
  jointly with R. W. Foot 173;

other references 145, 195
Gray, Harold 187
Graz 368
Greenbaum, Hyam 159, 178
Greenfield, Edward (music critic,
    The Guardian) on Boulez 349;
    on Rozhdestvensky 409
Grenoble 403
Griffiths, Paul (music critic, *The
    Times*) on Boulez's *Rituel*
    382; on Ligeti 404; on Goehr
    423; on BBC SO 50th
    anniversary concert 435
Gromme, E. W. 102
Grove, Freda (Concerts
    Organiser) 258, 425
Groves, Sir Charles tours Japan
    with Orchestra 389; prepares
    Choral Society for Toscanini
    514; other references 140, 265,
    331, 344, 369, 382, 383, 386,
    405, 406, 433
Gruenberg, Erich 420
Guardian, The on Ravel 349; on
    Rands 372; on Kempe 399; on
    Sandström 409; on
    Rozhdestvensky 417, 422; *see
    also Manchester Guardian*
Gui, Vittorio 213, 242, 244, 250
Guildhall School of Music 81

Haendel, Ida 168
Haitink, Bernard 317, 329, 331;
    suggested in press as possible
    Chief Conductor 411
Haley, Olga 100
Haley, William (Director-
    General BBC 1944–52) on
    return of Orchestra to London
    after War 195; on restoration
    of Orchestra to pre-war
    strength 200; on offer to
    Kubelik 225–7; on programme
    planning 231, 232
    talks to Sargent on contract
    239; on Boult's retirement 240;
    receives complaints from
    Sargent 244; retires from BBC
    254; other references 222, 242
Hall, Ernest 43, 53, 75, 123
Hall, Michael 375
Hallé Concerts Society 47, 102,
    103, 219
Hallé Orchestra performs at
    Queen's Hall 13; members
    recruited by BBC 41, 47, 50,
    52, 53; reaction to Manchester
    concert by BBC SO 102;
    reaction to BBC offer to
    Barbirolli 218–19; other
    references 9, 46, 69, 95, 113,
    114
Hamburg 259
Hamilton, Iain 282, 291; *see
    also Index 2*
Handley, Vernon 389

Hanley 136, 212, 257
Harewood, Lord 412
Harper, Heather 323
Harrogate Symphony Orchestra
    129
Hartog, Howard 362
Harty, Sir Hamilton conducts
    concerts at Queen's Hall 13;
    objects to recruiting of Hallé
    Orchestra players by BBC 41,
    46–8, 50–2; attack on BBC SO
    47; other references 7, 9, 12,
    70, 79, 95, 98, 99, 116, 131,
    134, 136, 150, 160, 163, 167
Harvey, Trevor 160
Heath, Kenneth 308
Heifetz, Jascha 101
Helsinki 268, 269
Hely-Hutchinson, Victor
    (Member of Music
    Department 1920–1934;
    Director of Music 1944–6)
    background 65; plans
    'Foundations of Music' 65; as
    conductor 88; appointed
    Director of Music 188;
    arranges return of Orchestra to
    London after War 194–5;
    plans post-war work of
    Orchestra 199–202, 233, 234;
    on restoration of Orchestra to
    pre-war standards 205–6, 208;
    death 214; other references
    192, 209
Henderson, Roy 100
Henriot, Nicole 190
Henry Wood Concert Society
    212
Henry Wood Proms, The (Cox)
    294
Henschel, Sir George 65
Henze, Hans Werner 397; *see
    also Index 2*
Hepton, Albert 55
Herbage, Julian (Programme
    Planner 1927–46) appointed
    Programme Planner 6; devises
    plan for permanent orchestra
    35–6, 57, 64, 65; proposes
    reforms 88; work for
    pre-classical composers
    116–17; arranges BBC concert
    for Barbirolli 177
    plans Orchestra's return to
    London after War 190; on
    Kubelik 197; leaves BBC 212;
    other references 71, 86, 91,
    103, 176, 179, 185, 186, 196
Herbig, Gunter 405
Hess, Dame Myra establishes
    National Gallery Concerts 159,
    162, 182; other references 116,
    131, 167, 180, 282
Heward, Leslie 132, 136, 168,
    177
Heyworth, Peter (music critic,

The Observer) on Walton
    274; on Glock 289; on
    Penderecki 332; on Boulez 341,
    345, 363–5; on Messiaen 403
Hibberd, Stuart 58, 59, 166,
    188
Hill, Lord 339
Hill, Ralph 132, 197
Hinchliffe, Jessie 54, 159, 170
Hindemith, Paul 37, 117, 264,
    289; *see also Index 2*
Hitler, Adolf 144, 154, 155,
    189, 190
HMV Gramophone Company
    28, 30, 42, 199
Hofmann, Josef 116
Holland, James 343, 361, 410
Hollingsworth, John 263, 265,
    319
Hollweg, Ilse 257
Holmboe, Vagn 275
Holst, Gustav 9, 12, 100, 241;
    see also Index 2
Holst, Henry 177, 264
Holt, Harold 78, 111, 177, 190
Home Guard 166
Home Service 160, 185; *see
    also BBC: Programmes*
Home Service Board 160
Honegger, Arthur 12
Hooton, Florence 183
Horenstein, Jascha 279, 282,
    295, 384
Horizons of Immortality
    (Palmstierna) 142
Horsley, Colin 288
Howard, George 434
Howarth, Elgar 347, 376, 386,
    387, 405, 408, 409, 410
Howes, Frank (music critic, *The
    Times*) 14; on first BBC SO
    concerts 57, 262
Howgill, Richard (Assistant
    Controller, Programmes
    1942–5; Controller,
    Entertainment 1945–52;
    Controller, Music 1952–9)
    and return of Orchestra to
    London after War 193–4; and
    restoration of Orchestra to
    pre-war strength 200, 201, 203
    appointed Controller,
    Entertainment 216; and offer
    to Barbirolli 218–19; on offer
    to Kubelik 225, 226; appointed
    Controller, Music 236;
    relations with Sargent 239,
    246–7, 254, 262, 270–2, 277;
    offers post of Chief Conductor
    to Schwarz 280–1; and
    Tippett's Second Symphony
    283, 284; retires and supports
    Glock as his successor 290–1;
    other references 205, 206, 222,
    225, 237, 278
Huband, Paul (General Manager,

BBC Symphony Orchestra)
309–15, 367, 400
Huberman, Bronislaw 82
Huddersfield Choral Society
133
Hughes, Arwel 179
Hurok, Sol 322, 327
Hussey, Dyneley 177, 231
Hylton, Jack 165

Ibert, Jacques 275
Imperial League of Opera 38
Inbal, Eliahu 343, 352
Incorporated Society of
Musicians 68, 110, 112
Incorporated Society of Organists
47
Innsbruck 388
Institut de Recherche et
Coordination Acoustique/
Musique (IRCAM) 395, 403,
406
Institute of Electrical Engineers
5
Instone, Anna 6
International Society for
Contemporary Music (ISCM)
66, 67, 141, 146, 197
international tours see BBC SO,
tours
Into the Wind (Reith) 112
Ireland 284
'Irwell Springs' band 53
Isaacs, Leonard 237, 270, 299
Ismay, Sir George 226, 227

Jackson, Gerald 129
Jacob, Gordon 182; see also
Index 2
Jacob, Sir Ian 255, 267, 271,
272
Jacques, Reginald 214
Japan 389–91
Jarred, Mary 96, 148
Jeffries, Stanton 2, 3, 5
Jewish Chronicle 197
Joachim, Johannes 142, 143
Johnstone, Maurice (Head of
Music Programmes, Radio
1952–60) background and
appointment 237; relations
with Sargent 253; advocates
year's notice for Sargent 261–2,
266, 270; leaves BBC 316
Jones, Parry 96
Joyce, Eileen 186
Joyce, James 72

Karajan, Herbert von 199, 217,
385
Keefe, Bernard 238
Keller, Hans (BBC Music
Division) joins Music
Division 293; on Music
Programme 320; on C. Davis's
repertoire 342; on Boulez 394;

on Postnikova 416
Kelley, Edgar Stillman 10
Kelley, Kneale 5
Kempe, Rudolf conducts BBC
SO 273, 287, 329, 331, 381,
386; background 399;
appointed Chief Conductor
399–400; death 401, 411;
tributes 401–2; other reference
283
Kennedy, Daisy 13
Kennedy, Lauri 37, 43, 51, 129,
138
Kennedy, Michael on Boult 241
Kent, Duke of 152
Kentner, Louis 178, 181, 211
Kersey, Eda 181, 186
Kettering 178
Keynes, Maynard 180
Kitchin, Margaret 351
Klee, Bernhard 352, 386, 389,
403
Klemperer, Otto 267
Klenovsky (pseudonym of Sir
Henry Wood) 75
Kletzki, Paul 256, 279
Knightley, T. F. 49
Knowles, Charles 2
Kodály, Zoltán 79, 210; see also
Index 2
Koechlin, Charles 66; see also
Index 2
Kohler, Irene 257
Kok, Alexander 308
Koussevitsky, Serge conducts
BBC SO on invitation of Clark
84–5, 87; declines to return to
London 127; other references
88, 105, 106, 131
Kreisler, Fritz 71
Kubelik, Rafael conducts BBC
SO 196, 210–11, 242, 255;
background 222; approached
by BBC as successor to Boult
222–27; accepts offer from
Chicago Orchestra and declines
BBC offer 227–8; other
reference 279

Lalandi, Lina 374
Lam, Basil 237
Lambert, Constant (as music
critic, Sunday Referee) on
Schoenberg and Stravinsky 72,
73; on British composers 94,
95; on Mahler 96; conducts
première of own work 117; on
Berg 132; on Toscanini 138;
on Tovey 140; (as conductor)
136, 168, 169, 178, 196, 203;
other references 84, 163, 167,
180; see also Index 2
Lamond, Frederic 84
Landowska, Wanda 59
Langston, Sidney 129
Large, Brian 387

Last Night of Proms 347, 348,
384, 386
Lateiner, Jacob 349
Latham-Koenig, Jan 410
Lauder, Sir Harry 65
Law, Bonar 2
Lawrence, D. H. 3
Lawrence, Marjorie 197, 210
Lea, Lawrie 424
Leavins, Arthur 308
Leeds 136
Leeds Festival 73, 143, 287
Lefebvre, Yvonne 190
Legge, Walter 184, 198, 199
Leibowitz, René 359
Leicester 128, 182, 184, 250,
330, 344
Leinsdorf, Erich 297, 349, 378,
380
Leipzig Opera 12
Leitner, Ferdinand 408
Lemare, Iris 133
Leppard, Raymond 352, 368,
378, 381, 385, 387, 402, 405,
408
Levien, Mewburn 8
Lewin, Ronald 320
Lewis, Sir Anthony 233, 410
Lewis, Cecil 6
Lewis, Idris 179
Lewis, Joseph 10, 46, 57
Lilburn, Douglas 257
Listener, The 98, 143, 355, 356
Liverpool 1, 257
Liverpool Post and Mercury 103
Lockier, Charles 158
London musical life 57, 147,
165, 198, 358; see Queen's
Hall, Royal Albert Hall, Royal
Festival Hall, Queen Elizabeth
Hall, St John's, Smith Square,
The Round House, Royal
College of Music, Royal
Academy of Music, Guildhall
School of Music, Logan Hall
University; see also BBC SO:
Concert Series
London Chamber Orchestra 52
London Flute Quartet 52
London Mercury 135
London Mozart Players 54, 243
London Music Festival 82, 84,
92, 97, 105, 119, 127, 137, 145,
147, 150, 151; see also BBC
Symphony Orchestra: Concert
Series
London Philharmonic Orchestra
planned by Beecham 22;
inauguration 79; Cardus'
opinion of 80; collaboration
with BBC proposed by
Beecham 89–91; Beecham
appeals for funds 165; shares
1942 Proms with BBC SO 180;
other references 116, 129, 134
London Select Choir 67

London Sinfonietta 339, 411
London Station 5, 6
London Symphony Orchestra and Beecham's plans for permanent orchestra 27–30, 34; opposes BBC public concerts 47–8; financial crisis and Beecham's proposals 70, 78 other references 8, 16, 34, 42, 51, 52, 53, 69, 71, 79, 84, 98, 147, 165, 177, 401
London Wind Quintet 52
London Wireless Chorus 6
Lopes-Graça, Fernando 186
Loppert, Max (music critic, *The Financial Times*) on Rozhdestvensky 418; on BBC SO 50th anniversary concert 435
Loughran, James 387, 403, 406
Luker, Norman 227, 228
Luton 178
Lutoslawski, Witold 289, 388, 421; *see also* Index 2
Lutyens, Elisabeth 125, 146, 197; *see also* Index 2
Luxon, Benjamin 382
Lympany, Moura 167, 169, 177

Maastricht 260
Maazel, Lorin first appearance in England 295; conducts BBC SO 308, 317, 345, 380, 385; conducts Choral Society 516
McCormack, John 51, 71
McDonagh, Terence 55, 171, 309
McEwen, Sir John 11, 95, 111, 130
Mackerras, Charles (Chief Guest Conductor 1976–8) conducts BBC SO 368, 387, 408, 421; becomes Chief Guest Conductor 403; tours Continent with Orchestra 406, 407
MacKinnon, Lilias 84
Mackintosh, Jack 55
Maderna, Bruno conducts BBC SO 295, 297, 352, 353, 380; considered as successor to Schwarz 299; death 381; other reference 370; *see also* Index 2
Maguire, Hugh 303, 308, 330, 336
Mahler, Gustav 38, 39, 58; *see also* Index 2
Maida Vale Studios rebuilt as home of BBC Orchestras 101–2; not ready for return of Orchestra after War 193, 194, 196; modernised 426; other references 65, 210, 293, 424; *see also* BBC: Studios
Malcolm, George 263, 293, 368
Malko, Nicolai 74, 136, 143, 210

Malraux, André 360, 361
Manchester early broadcasts from 1, 2, 4; and Hallé Orchestra 9, 50, 52, 53, 79, 95, 129; visit by BBC SO 102–3
Manchester College of Music 102, 103
Manchester Evening Chronicle 102
Manchester Guardian on 1930 Proms 46; on broadcast music 48; on Mossolov 61; on Schoenberg 72, 73; on Stravinsky 73; on BBC SO and Beecham 80; on Hindemith 84; on Bartók 87; on Berg 100; on Toscanini 108, 138, 140; on Beecham 149–50; *see also Guardian*
Manduell, John 238; and foundation of Music Programme 319–21
Mann, William (music critic, *The Times*) on Penderecki 332; on Boulez 341, 371–2; on Musgrave 344; on Round House concerts 371–2; on Stockhausen 380; on Rozhdestvensky 422
Manning, Jane 374
Mansell, Gerard 320, 430
Marchant, Dr Stanley 130
Marconi Company 1
Marconi House 4
Marconi's Wireless Telegraph Company 1
Markevitch, Igor 144
Martin, Colonel 27
Martin, Frank 275
Martinet, Maurice 212
Martinon, Jean 297
Mary, Queen 152
Mase, Owen (Assistant Director of Music 1931–3; Music Executive 1930s) recruits players for Orchestra 42, 43; argues case for public concerts by BBC 85, 86, 93; contacts with Toscanini 106, 127, 128, 137, 139; contacts Walter 144; leaves BBC 145 organises London Festival of Music 150, 151; appointed Concerts Adviser to Festival Hall 243; other references 65, 82, 147
Massine, Leonid 412
Masson, Diego 370, 375, 389, 410
Masur, Kurt 408
Matthews, Denis 266, 285
Matthews, Thomas 169
Maxwell Davies, Peter 388, 410; *see also* Index 2
Mays, Edgar 258
Melba, Dame Nellie 1, 4, 51

Mengelberg, Willem 131, 132, 141, 143
Menges, Herbert 168, 178
Menuhin, Yehudi and Schumann Violin Concerto 142–3; first broadcast 182; performs Bartók's Second Violin Concerto 191, 196; on Rozhdestvensky 416–17; other reference 71
Messiaen, Olivier 238, 403, 404, 407; *see also* Index 2
Mica, Frantisek 211
Milanov, Zinka 146
Miles, Maurice 178
Milford, Robin 182
Milhaud, Darius 77, 118, 351; *see also* Index 2
military service 159, 171, 200, 220
Milne, Hamish 405
Ministry of Information 158
Mitchell, Donald 242, 299
Moeran, E. J. 93, 94
Moiseiwitsch, Benno 59, 160, 163, 177, 292
Molinari, Bernardino 12
Monn, G. M. 116
Mont, Willem de 171
Monte Carlo 118, 119, 144
Monteux, Pierre 10, 257, 268, 275, 297
Monthly Musical Record 63
Moore, Douglas 310
Morgan, Joseph 179
Morning Post on first BBC SO concerts 55, 56; on Poulenc 59; on 1931–2 season 77; on Vaughan Williams 101; on Sibelius 105; on Busoni 135; on Toscanini 138
Moscona, Nicola 146
Munch, Charles 141, 190, 213
Murchie, Robert 52, 129
Murrill, Herbert (Music Programmes Organiser 1942–6; Assistant Director, Music 1946–50; Head of Music 1950–2) appointed Head of Music 235; on broadcast music 235–6; relations with Sargent 245–7, 253; death and memorial concert 251; other references 176, 210, 235
Musgrave, Thea 376, 388
Music Advisory Committee *see* BBC
Music Department (later, Music Division) *see* BBC
Music Ho! (Lambert) 73
Music Journal, The 111
'Music of our Time' 181, 196
Music Programme *see* BBC
Musical Times on Queen's Hall concerts (1928) 14; on London

Music Festival (1934) 97; on Koussevitsky 106; criticises wartime music policy (1939) 157; on Stravinsky 214

Musicians' Union and plans for permanent orchestra 18, 41, 42, 44–5; gains salary increases for BBC SO players 202–3; and payment for rehearsals 208; calls strike over television appearances 267; agrees increase in 'needle time' 321; calls strike over BBC orchestral economies (1980) 424, 432–4; other references 41, 372, 427

My Own Trumpet (Boult) 167, 168

Nation, The 326
National Chorus (BBC) 59, 63, 67, 513
National Gallery Concerts 159, 162, 182
National Orchestra of Wales 71
National Symphony Orchestra 13
Naylor, Bernard 318
Neel, Boyd 168
Nelson, Norman 308
Network Three *see* BBC
Neveu, Ginette 190
Newcastle 4, 5, 212
New English Weekly 96
Newly, Harold 431
Newman, Ernest (music critic, *The Sunday Times*) on deputy system 8; on poor standard of London orchestras 9, 13; on rehearsals 13; on Ravel 38; on Richard Strauss 71–2; on Prokofiev 75; on Schoenberg 83; on Bartók 87; on Benjamin 94; on Shostakovich 118; on Berg 132; on Busoni 135; on Toscanini 138–9, 153, 154; on Walton 141, 177; on BBC music policy 157, 158, 278; on Bax 186
Newport 179, 212
New Queen's Hall Orchestra 53
News Chronicle on Bliss 63; on Schoenberg 83; on Hindemith 84; on Weingartner 87; on Vaughan Williams 134; on successor to Boult 225
New Statesman 61, 94, 162
New Symphony Orchestra 70
Newton, Richard 53, 129
New York 322, 324, 326, 327, 394
New York Herald Tribune 325
New York Philharmonic Orchestra 14, 17, 159, 363
New York Times 325
New York World Telegram 325
Nicolls, Basil (Controller of Programmes, 1938–44; Senior Controller 1944–8; Director of Sound Broadcasting 1948–52) opposes collaboration with Royal Philharmonic Society 92; supports Boult on special wartime concerts 162; on music policy 173, 175; and post-war problems of Orchestra 200, 203, 206, 208 on successor to Boult 216, 217, 220–3, 225, 226; Sargent invited to be Chief Conductor 229; relations with Sargent 239, 245–47, 252; retires 254; other references 119, 158, 161, 167, 194

Nifosi, Alex 54, 60, 76, 106, 392
Nikisch, Artur 8, 39, 53
1975 (1984 minus 9) (Keller) 394
Nissen, Hermann 100
Noble, Jeremy (music critic, *Sunday Telegraph*) on Berio 379
Nono, Luigi 289, 290
Norrington, Roger 384
Northern Orchestra (BBC) 102
Norway 269
Norwich 197, 264
Norwich Festival 63
'No 10' Studio 58, 65, 71, 72, 76, 78; *see also* BBC: Studios
Nottingham 178, 250, 330

Observer, The on Holst 61; on Bliss 63; on Walter 65; on Shostakovich 118; on 1936 Continental tour 124; on Toscanini 153; on number of London orchestras 209; on Sargent 252; on Walton 274; on Glock 289; on Boulez 341, 345, 363–5; on Berio 349; on Messiaen 403; on Rozhdestvensky 416, 419
O'Donnell, Walton 65
Ogdon, John 323
Ogilvie, Frederick W. (Director-General 1938–42) succeeds Reith 145; addresses Orchestra on plans for wartime 154, 155; visits Orchestra in Bristol 158; other reference 172
Olszewska, Maria 63
Orchestral Committee 54, 247
Ormandy, Eugene 264
Orpheus Britannicus (Radio 3 series) 387
Otterloo, Willem van 260
Overseas Service *see* BBC
Ovey, Sir Esmond 104
Oxford 66, 178
Oxford Times 213

Paderewski, Ignacy Jan 71

Page, Philip 26, 73
Palester, Roman 198
Palmer, Felicity 379, 381
Palmer, Rex 5, 6
Palmstierna, Baron Erik 142
Panufnik, Andrzej 275; *see also* Index 2
Paray, Paul 190
Parikian, Manoug 288, 348
Paris 211, 406
Parker, Robert 74
Parminter, Colonel 130
Paston, W. G. 258
Paterson, R. G. 258
Peacock Report 354, 429
Pears, Peter 264, 287
Peatfield, Thomas 55
Penderecki, Krzystof 388; *see also* Index 2
pension scheme (for orchestral players) 44, 245, 311–13
People's Palace 39, 196, 197, 210
Pesko, Zoltan 407
Peterborough 264
Petrassi, Goffredo 275
Petri, Egon 96, 116
Peyer, Gervase de 344
Peyser, Joan 360, 393
Philadelphia Symphony Orchestra 17, 21, 24
Philharmonia 199
Phillips, Montague 182
Piatigorsky, Gregor 274
Pilkington Committee 319
Pitt, Percy (Director of Music, 1924–30) as Music Adviser 4–7; as Director of Music 10–12; plans permanent Orchestra 14; arranges auditions 32; leaves BBC (1929) 38; as conductor 57, 66; death 84; other references 39, 40, 42–4, 51
Plaistow, Stephen 293, 410, 411, 426
Poland 332
Policy Study Group (BBC) 339
Ponsonby, Robert (Controller, Music 1972–) succeeds Glock as Controller, Music 375, 396; plans Round House concerts with Boulez 375; plans St John's concerts 378; plans Festival Hall concerts 381; plans Boulez's final season as Chief Conductor 382; plans 1974 Proms 385, 386; starts 'The Composer Conducts' studio concerts 388; accompanies Orchestra on tour of Japan 389–91; background 396–7; offers post of Chief Conductor to Solti 398; appoints Kempe as Chief Conductor 399–402; tribute to

Kempe 402; seeks successor to Kempe 403, 411; negotiates appointment of Rozhdestvensky as Chief Conductor 412–14; other reference 409
Poole, John   408, 516, 517
Popov, Vladimir   413
Porter, Andrew (music critic, *The Financial Times*) on Boulez 331; on Salzman 372
Postnikova, Victoria   335, 416
Post-Victorian Britain (Seaman) 3
Pougnet, Jean   178
Poulenc, Francis   59, 168
Powell, Lionel   criticises BBC 16; plans permanent orchestra with Beecham 17–19, 27–30, 34, 78; death 70
Pratt, Richard (Orchestral Manager 1930–46)   45, 120, 203
Prausnitz, Frederic   346, 404
Pravda   415
Preger, Leo   148
Prerauer, Kurt   96
Priestley, J. B.   50
Priestman, Brian   386
Primrose, William   242, 256
Pritchard, John (Chief Guest Conductor 1978–)   tours Germany with BBC SO 336; conducts BBC SO 340, 343, 344, 348, 349, 352, 368, 369, 378, 380, 381, 382, 383, 384, 386, 402, 404, 406, 408, 434; and Stockhausen concert 350; appointed Chief Guest Conductor 423; background 423; other references 294, 400, 411, 516
Programme Division (BBC)   91
Prokofiev, Sergey   141
Promenade Concerts   BBC's agreement with Sir Henry Wood 12, 18; (1927) 13; (1928) 20; (1929) 21; (1930) 46; *see also* BBC Symphony Orchestra: *Concert Series*, for seasons from 1931 to 1980; 1980 season affected by strike 432–4
Protheroe, Guy   426
provincial tours   of BBC SO *see* BBC Symphony Orchestra: *UK Tours*
Psychic News   142
Puck, Sir Percy   130
Purcell Room   331

Queen Elizabeth Hall   331, 339
Queen's Hall   BBC public concerts 13, 21; and Beecham's plans for permanent orchestra 19, 20; booked for first concerts of BBC SO 37, 46; description 49, 50; concerts by BBC SO 51, 53–57, 58, 59, 60, 67; destroyed by bombing 170; other references 7, 12, 14, 39 *see* BBC Symphony Orchestra: *Concert Series*, for seasons 1930–40
Queen's Hall Orchestra   9, 13, 21, 51
Quilter, Roger   93; *see also* Index 2

Rachmaninov, Sergei   71; *see also* Index 2
Radio Manufacturers' Association 83
Radio 3   *see* BBC: Programmes
Radio Times   on Concert Hall, Broadcasting House 78; Koussevitsky congratulates BBC 85; as vehicle for publicity 87; on Casals 132; on Newman 157; interview with Bliss 175; criticism of Wilson 214; other references 156, 176
Rainier, Priaulx   318
Rands, Bernard   375, 376
Rankl, Karl   250
Rawsthorne, Alan   159, 164, 167, 178
Raybould, Clarence (Chief Assistant Conductor)   appointed 133; background 133; conducts BBC SO 136, 150, 160, 163, 167, 169, 177, 178, 181, 244, 250, 256, 257, 264; carries out auditions with Boult 200
Red Lion Warehouse   58
Redman, Reginald   164, 187
Reed, W. H.   98
Reeves, Wynn   12
Reger, Max   39, 242
rehearsals   and deputy system 8; inadequacy of 13, 17, 88; for 1930 Proms 46; under Koussevitsky 85; for *Wozzeck* 96; under Toscanini 106–7, 139; under Mengelberg 131; under Beecham 134, 135; policy of Musicians' Union 202, 203, 209, 427; under Schwarz 285; under Rozhdestvensky 419–20; in Maida Vale Studios 426; other references 18, 21, 70, 74, 80, 83, 85, 221, 424
Reid, Charles   245, 269
Reiner, Fritz   136
Reith, Sir John (Director-General 1927–38)   appointed General Manager of British Broadcasting Company 2; appointed Director-General of BBC 11; forms Music Advisory Committee 11; plans permanent orchestra 15–23; relations with Beecham 28–31, 35; removes Pitt 38; relations with Boult 39–41; invites Boult to become permanent conductor of Orchestra 64; disagreement with Royal Philharmonic Society 68; commissions Elgar's Third Symphony 81, 82; on Schoenberg 83; disagreement with Music Advisory Committee 93, 111, 112; leaves BBC (1938) 145; other references 7, 33, 36, 43, 45, 46, 86, 92, 130, 144, 154, 232
Relton, William (Orchestral Manager 1970–5; General Manager Symphony Orchestra 1975–)   background and appointments 367, 424; succeeds Huband 400; and Round House concerts 410; accompanies Ponsonby to Berlin to contact Rozhdestvensky 413; goes to Moscow with Ponsonby 414
Reynolds News   140
Richter, Hans   8
Riddick, Kathleen   187
Riddle, Frederick   178
Rigby, Cormac   428
Robeson, Paul   71
Robinson, Stanford   joins staff at Savoy Hill 6; and BBC National Chorus 59, 513; conducts BBC SO 57, 68, 264, 267, 275, 287; in concert with Sir Harry Lauder 65; and Theatre Orchestra 89, 514; appointed Opera Director and Deputy Conductor of Symphony Orchestra 201; discusses offer to Barbirolli with Crickmore 219; other references 277, 283
Roll, Michael   389
Ronald, Sir Landon   as conductor 7, 9, 12, 14, 59, 79, 80, 93; member of Music Advisory Committee 11, 95, 111, 130; plans permanent orchestra 15; negotiates with Beecham 16, 18, 23, 25, 70; negotiates with Elgar on Third Symphony 81, 82; on Toscanini 108; death 130; other reference 6
Rootham, Cyril B.   116
Rosbaud, Hans   256, 295, 326, 359
Rosen, Charles   383
Rosenthal, Manuel   197
Rossi, Mario   329, 331, 353
Rostal, Max   178
Rostropovich, Mstislav   412

Roswaenge, Helge 146
Round House, Chalk Farm
description and history 366;
BBC concerts of new music
366, 367, 371–2; see also BBC
Symphony Orchestra: Concert
Series
Roussel, Albert 263
Royal Albert Hall acoustics
improved 346; other references
9, 19, 20, 22, 187, 191, 196,
197, 209, 212, 246, 264, 317,
383–5, 387; see also BBC
Symphony Orchestra: Concert
Series
Royal Albert Hall Orchestra 52
Royal College of Music 38,
411–12
Royal Festival Hall description
243; opening celebrations 243,
244; Coronation concerts 251;
small audiences for BBC SO
concerts 292; 'pre-concerts'
367, 369; other references 256,
264, 266, 267, 291, 294, 308,
317, 318, 354, 379, 423; see also
BBC Symphony Orchestra:
Concert Series
Royal Philharmonic Orchestra
52, 53, 209
Royal Philharmonic Society
shortage of funds 8, 9;
involved in discussions on
permanent orchestra 15, 16, 22,
27, 28, 30–2, 34, 37, 41–2;
opposes public concerts by
BBC 48, 68, 110; in
competition with BBC SO 86;
collaboration with BBC SO
proposed by Beecham 90, 92;
provides 1940 Proms in
Queen's Hall 165; forms Royal
Philharmonic Orchestra 209;
other references 43, 70, 79, 81,
100, 134, 147, 151
Rozhdestvensky, Gennadi
conducts BBC SO 344, 352,
416–19, 421, 422, 517; sought
by Ponsonby as Chief
Conductor of BBC SO 412;
offered appointment by
Ponsonby and Relton in Berlin
413; appointment finalised in
Moscow 414; background
414–16; assessments 416; tours
with Orchestra 419; advocates
British music 422, 434;
conducts 50th anniversary
concert 434–5; conducts
Symphony Chorus 517
Rubinstein, Artur 56, 135, 263,
281, 282, 292
Rubinstein, Ida 100
Russia 332, 333

Sacher, Paul 283, 408

Sadie, Stanley (music critic, The
Times) 379
St John's Church, Smith Square
description and history 366;
concerts started by Boulez
366–8, 377–9; see also BBC
Symphony Orchestra: Concert
Series
salaries (of orchestral players)
proposed for permanent
orchestra 19, 22, 42, 44;
Musicians' Union agreement
202, 203; increases needed to
attract players and improve
standards 204, 207, 310, 339,
367, 398, 429; increase
advocated by Davis 337;
proposed increase rejected by
Department of Economic
Affairs 338
Salisbury Cathedral 268
Salter, Lionel 340, 426
Sammons, Albert 32, 61, 74
Samuelson, Christopher 316,
425
Sanderling, Kurt 407, 421
Sanders, Neill 310
Santos, Artur 186
Sanzogno, Nino 287, 288, 294
Sargent, Sir Malcolm conducts
Courtauld concerts 57, 71, 79;
conducts Women's Symphony
Orchestra 133; considered for
appointment as Chief
Conductor of BBC SO 216–18,
223; appointed Chief
Conductor 229–31;
relationship with BBC 236–47;
narrow repertoire 242;
conducts re-auditions 247–9;
criticised by Music
Department 253–5, 261, 262;
takes Orchestra on first tour of
Continent 258–61; takes
Orchestra to Scandinavia
268–9; contract terminated
266, 270–5; death (1967) 333;
memorial concert 335; other
references 9, 73, 136, 141, 163,
177, 188, 250–2, 257, 263–5,
277, 281, 292, 295, 297, 298,
316–18, 327, 329, 331, 335, 515
Saturday Review, The 325
Savoy Hill 5, 6, 7, 57, 77
Scandinavia 268
Scherchen, Hermann 12, 37,
59, 67, 144, 146, 256, 257, 273,
295, 359, 513
Scheveningen 211, 259, 361
Schidlof, Peter 379
Schiff, Dr 120, 123, 124
Schmid, Erich 329, 331, 340,
378, 386, 406, 408
Schmidt-Isserstedt, Hans 251,
267, 268, 281, 287, 332, 380
Schmitt, Florent 9

Schnabel, Artur 79, 84
Schneiderhan, Wolfgang 288
Schoenberg, Arnold comes to
England for première of
Gurrelieder 14; conducts BBC
SO 58, 66, 79, 359; reception
of his music 72–3, 305; death
359; article by Boulez 359;
other references 87, 117
Scholes, Percy 11
Schuman, William 322; see also
Index 2
Schumann, Clara 142
Schumann, Elisabeth 58, 75
Schumann, Eugenie 143
Schumann, Robert 142–3; see
also Index 2
Schwarz, Rudolf background
and wartime experiences
279–80; conducts BBC SO
250, 264, 287, 292, 294, 297,
343, 403; appointed Chief
Conductor of BBC SO 280,
281; style criticised 282,
298–9; defends Orchestra's
performance of Tippett's
Second Symphony 284;
assessment 285–6; offers
resignation 299; contract
expires 300; other references
222, 515
Score, The 289, 326, 359
Scotsman, The 60
Scott, Cyril 93, 97
Scottish National Orchestra 52,
54
Seaman, L. C. B. 3
Searle, Humphrey 291, 333, 344
Selby, Sir Walford 122
Sessions, Roger 289, 404; see
also Index 2
Shaporin, Yuri 100
Shaw, George Bernard 81
Shaw, Dr G. T. 130
Shawe-Taylor, Desmond (music
critic, The Sunday Times) on
Busoni 135; on Crosse 348; on
Rozhdestvensky 420; on 50th
anniversary concert 435
Sherman, Alec 209
Shore, Bernard background 51;
on Koussevitsky 85, 105;
stands in for Tertis 96; on
Toscanini 107, 138; on
Mengelberg 131; on Beecham
134, 135; other references 146,
203, 204, 515
Shostakovich, Dimitri 77, 282
Sibelius, Jean 269
Sibelius Festival 147
Simpson, Robert 237, 270, 331
Singer, Aubrey 432
Slater, Veronica 376, 410
Smalley, Roger 374
Smith, Cyril 177
Smyth, Ethel 12, 53, 93

Snowden, Lady 130
Solomon, Izler 59, 151, 163, 297
Solti, Sir Georg offered post of Chief Conductor of BBC SO 398; declines offer 398–9; other references 318, 334, 344
Somerville, Colonel 130
Sorabji, K. S. 96
Souster, Tim 351, 376
Southampton 136, 184
Southend 257
South Wales 178
Spain 424
Spectator, The 177
Squire, Barry 51
Stadlen, Peter 331, 353
'Stage Revolves, The' 70
Stamp, Jesse 53, 129
Star, The 74, 83, 128
Steidry, Fritz 134
Steinberg, William 264
Stevens, Denis 238, 346
Stockhausen, Karlheinz his music ignored in Britain 238, 290; music advocated by Glock 305, 342; supervises preparations for concert of his music 349–51; *Mixtur* performed at Round House 370; directs performance of *Momente* 379–80; projected performance of *Hymnen* abandoned 409–10; *see also* Index 2
Stockholm 268, 269
Stokowski, Leopold 24, 84, 250, 257, 318, 516
Stone, David 238
Stratford, E. J. 186
Strauss, Johann 76
Strauss, Richard 12, 52, 58, 72, 212; *see also* Index 2
Stravinsky, Igor conducts BBC SO 58, 60, 99, 287, 292, 297; soloist in own Piano Concerto 59; compared with Schoenberg 72; soloist in own *Capriccio* 74; *Oedipus Rex* and Mass praised in press 213–14; illness 273; at Glock's summer school 289; conducts *Oedipus Rex* for Third Programme 294; music performed in Round House concerts 364; other references 117, 366, 369; *see also* Index 2
strikes (by orchestral players) 267, 424, 432, 433
studio audience 58
studio recordings 426, 427
Suggia, Guilhermina 55, 61, 77
Suisse Romande Orchestra 59
Sun, The 83
Sunday Dispatch 140
Sunday Referee 72, 94, 96, 132, 140

Sunday Telegraph 332, 379
Sunday Times, The on deputy system 8; on poor standard of London orchestras 9; on Ravel 38; on first concert of BBC SO 56; on Richard Strauss 71–2; on Wagner concert 74; on Prokofiev 75; on Busoni 135; on Sargent 141; on Malipiero 143; on Toscanini 153, 154; on BBC music policy 157; on Walton 177; on failure to appoint Kubelik 228; on tour of United States 326; on Boulez 331, 370; on Rozhdestvensky 416, 418, 420; on 50th anniversary concert 435
Supervia, Conchita 71
Susskind, Walter 279, 329, 340, 407, 408
Sutcliffe, Sidney 309
Sutherland, Joan 264
Swann, Sir Michael 434
Swansea 128, 179, 268
Sweden 269
Switzerland 348, 370, 388
Szalowski, Antoni 148
Szell, George 322, 359
Szigeti, Josef 61, 74, 116, 148, 151
Szymanowski, Karol 141

Tabachnik, Michel 341
Tapp, Frank 98
Tausky, Vilem 265
television 266, 267, 336, 338, 340, 355, 395, 417
Terry, Sir Richard 97
Tertis, Lionel conducts auditions for permanent orchestra 32; suggests sectional rehearsals 89; 60th birthday 135; letter to *Daily Telegraph* 209; other references 51, 74, 96, 116, 120, 163
Teschemacher, Margarete 71
Teyte, Maggie 66, 75, 181
Thalben-Ball, George 515
Thatcher, Dr Reginald 130, 170, 171, 172
Theodore, David 368
Third Programme Defence Society 276
Thomas, Marjorie 285
Thompson, W. W. (Concerts Manager 1927–54) joins BBC 6, 43, 46; plans Proms 64; duties 65, 120; favours approach to Koussevitsky 84; accompanies Orchestra on Continental tour 123–4; in Bristol with Orchestra during War 158, 168; retires 258; other references 125, 170, 244, 425
Thorborg, Kerstin 146

Three Choirs Festival 80
Thurston, Frederick 52, 213
Time and Tide 62, 73, 83
Times, The on Schoenberg 14; on 'Ideal Orchestra' 23, 24; on first concert of BBC SO 56; on third concert 57; on Boult 61, 62, 63, 67; on Holst 74; on public appearances of Orchestra 75; letter from Shaw 81; on Vaughan Williams 83; letter from Music Advisory Committee 95; on Weingartner 99 letter from Ronald on Elgar 108; on Walton 116; on Stravinsky 118; on Berg 135; on Toscanini 153; on Schumann 143; on music in London 147, 198; letter on fading out of programmes 176; on Orchestra's return to London in 1942 179; on Martinů 211; on Schwarz 299; on successor to Schwarz 300; on Davis 333, 334; on Round House Concerts 371, 372; on Berio 379 letter from Glock 380; on Solti 398; on Rozhdestvensky 422; on Goehr 423; letter from Boult 432; on 50th anniversary concert of BBC SO 435; on National Chorus 513
Tinel, Paul 104
Tippett, Michael conducts première of own *Fantasia Concertante* 255; 50th birthday 264; commissioned to compose Second Symphony 275, 283; correspondence on completion and première of Second Symphony 283–4; première of *Vision of St Augustine* 329; other references 290, 297, 405; *see also* Index 2
Todd, John Douglas 334
Tortelier, Paul 282
Toscanini, Arturo as conductor 53, 84, 90; conducts BBC SO in London Music Festival (1935) 105–109, 114; contacted by Owen Mase in Paris 127, 128; conducts in 1937 London Music Festival 137–40, 514; conducts in 1938 Festival 145; conducts in 1939 Festival 150–4; cancels visit to Royal Festival Hall 243; other references 98, 118, 119, 131, 392
tours – UK and foreign *see* BBC Symphony Orchestra: *UK Tours* and *Foreign Tours*
Tovey, Donald 11, 75, 140; *see also* Index 2

Toye, Francis 77, 101
Toye, Geoffrey 23
Trethowan, Sir Ian 433
Trowell, Brian 355
Tschaikov, Anton 55
Tschaikov, Basil 55
Turner, Eva 163
Turner, Laurance 128, 204
Turner, W. J. 61, 94, 162
2 LO 2
2 LO Wireless Orchestra 7, 54

Ulanova, Galina 415
Ullswater Committee 93, 110, 111, 115, 233
Uminska, Eugenia 198
Unger, Heinz 257
United States 322-7

Variety Department see BBC
Vaughan Williams, Ralph 241, 252
Venice Biennale (1961) 295
Vienna 15, 122, 369
Vienna Philharmonic Orchestra 15, 122
Vienna Symphony Orchestra 134
Vilar, Jean 360, 361
Vogler, Wolfgang 259
Vonk, Hans 405, 408, 421

Waart, Edo de 352
Wade, Frank 255
Wadis, C. J. A. 257
Wagner, Richard 163, 365; see also Index 2
Wagner, Siegfried 12
Wakefield, Jeffrey 308
Walker, Ethel 2
Walker, Sarah 422
Wallace, Ian 412
Wallenstein, Alfred 267
Walsh, Stephen (music critic, The Observer) on Crosse 348; on Carter 349; on Berio 375; on Rozhdestvensky 419
Walter, Bruno as conductor 10, 58, 95; admired by Boult 75; conducts BBC SO at London Music Festival (1934) 97-9; refuses to appear with Backhaus 144, 145; returns (1939) 148, 149; Boult wishes to offer him Chief Conductorship 222, 223; conducts Orchestra in 1955 Festival 265; illness prevents return (1957) 273, 274; other references 39, 53, 95, 122, 131, 147
Walthamstow 212
Walton, Sir William 168, 177, 336
Ward, Barbara 223
Warr, Eric 237, 316

Warrack, John 332, 416
Washbourne, Kathleen 32, 54
Waterhouse, William 309, 310
Watson, Sydney 133
Webern, Anton 66, 126, 146, 359, 377; see also Index 2
Webster, Sir David 344
Weingartner, Felix 75, 87, 88, 97, 99, 101
Wellington, Lindsay (Assistant Controller, Programmes 1936-42; Controller, Programmes 1944-5; Controller, Home Service 1945-52; Director of Sound Broadcasting 1952-63) relations with Sargent 255, 271; on pay of BBC SO 278; sympathetic to Glock's plans 291, 303; other references 206, 230, 282
Welt, Die 259
Western Electric 2
Western Studio Orchestra 71
Westrup, J. A. 108, 141
Whewell, Michael 237
White, Mark 355
Whitehead, James 146
Whitfield, Dr Ernest 207, 208, 221
Whittaker, Alec 46, 52, 55
Whittaker, Douglas 309, 368
Whyte, Ian 181
Widdicombe, Gillian 373, 416
Widdop, Walter 74, 76, 96, 148
Wilbraham, John 368
Willan, Healey 257
Willcocks, Sir David 264, 317, 410
Williams, Elizabeth 425
Williams, Grace 98, 179
Williams, Trevor 336
Williamson, Malcolm 376
Willoughby, George 258, 284, 296, 309
Wilson, Marie 54, 115, 128, 162, 181, 182, 187, 204
Wilson, Sir Steuart (Head of Music 1948-50) appointment and background 214; sues BBC 214; plans replacement for Boult 215-16, 222-3; offers post of Chief Conductor of BBC SO to Barbirolli 217-19; offers post to Kubelik 224-5; fails to procure acceptance by Kubelik 227-8; on music broadcasting policy 234-5, 236; other references 220, 238, 239, 244
Wilson, Thomas 333
Winter Garden Theatre, London 10
Winter Promenade Concerts 84, 135, 250, 385
Wireless Military Band 129

Wireless Players 10
Wireless Quartet 54
Wireless Symphony Orchestra formation 10, 12; collaboration with RPS considered by BBC 15; proposed use at Proms opposed by Wood 20, 21; other references 43-5, 53, 54, 129
Wolf, Endre 273, 294
Wolff, Albert 163, 197, 242
Wolff, Fritz 63
Wolstencroft, Joan 308
Wolverhampton 212
Women's Symphony Orchestra 133
Wood, Dorothy 6, 170, 258
Wood, Ernest 513
Wood, Sir Henry and Proms 6, 12, 18; reforms Queen's Hall Orchestra 9; opposes use of Wireless Orchestra for 1928 Proms 20-1; as conductor 37, 38, 58, 63, 68, 75, 79, 95, 99, 132, 135, 160, 163, 167, 169, 179, 180, 181; and recruitment of permanent orchestra 43, 46; angered by cutting short of broadcast 58-9; dismayed by cancellation of Winter Proms 136
celebrates jubilee as conductor 147, 148; addresses audience at end of 1939 Proms 154; illness 183; gives last BBC SO concert 186; 75th birthday concert 188; Diamond Jubilee celebration of first Proms 262; conducts National Chorus 513; other references 5, 13, 53, 55, 98, 165, 189; see also Klenovsky
Wood, Hugh 373, 375, 376; see also Index 2
Woodgate, Leslie as Chorus Master 514-15; death 515; other references 70, 168, 169, 187
Woodhouse, Charles 42, 43, 46, 129
Woodward, Kerry 388
Woodward, Roger 372
Worthing 316, 317
Wright, Brian 388, 405, 407, 517
Wright, Kenneth (in Music Department 1926-48; Assistant Director of Music 1935-7; Acting Director of Music 1946-8) background 5, 6; on Music Advisory Committee 11; and plan for permanent orchestra 35, 38, 40, 41, 43, 57; in Music Department 64-6, 93; defends BBC policy on British artists 111; defends Clark's visit to

Vienna 119; accompanies
Orchestra to Europe 120, 123;
visits Goebbels 142; and
orchestral players' hours 200,
201; on Continental tour
(1947) 211; Acting Director of
Music (1946) 214; Artists
Manager 215; other references

125, 129, 172, 176
Writtle   1, 2, 6
Wyk, Arnold van   134, 257
Wyss, Sophie   164

Xenakis, Iannis   374

Yalding House   see BBC
Yorkshire Post   60, 94

Young, Filson   23
Young, Joseph   55

Zecchi, Carlo   213
Zender, Hans   378, 387, 410;
   see also Index 2
Zirato, Bruno   127
Zurich   121

Index of Composers and Works

Absil, Jean *Le Zodiaque* 470
Addison, J. *Carte Blanche* 473
Aitken, Robert *Spiral* 486
Allende, Humberto *Tonada* No. 11 468
Alsina, Carlos Roqué *Funktionen* 483; *Schichten* 375, 484
Alwyn, William Concerto Grosso: No. 1 464; No. 2 251; No. 3 473; *Derby Day* 294, 476; Harp Concerto 471; *The Innumerable Dance* 454; Pastoral Fantasia for Viola and String Orchestra 462; Symphonies: No. 1 250; No. 2 256, 470; No. 3 **273, 275**, 473
Amy, Gilbert *Cette étoile enseigne à s'incliner* 482; *Trajectoires* 481; *Triade* **340**, 480
Andreae, Volkmar Rhapsody for violin and orchestra 136
Anson, Hugo Concerto for Two Pianos and Strings 455
Aperghis, George *Il gigante Golia* 410, 486
ApIvor, Denis *Mirror for Witches* 263, 471; *Neumes* **387**, 484; *Yerma* 477
Apostel, Hans Erich *Passacaglia*, Op. 50 484
Arne, Thomas Little Concerto for Piano and String Orchestra 462
Arnell, Richard *Symphonic Portrait: Lord Byron* 256
Arnold, Malcolm Concerto for Two Pianos **347**, 481; *Fantasy for Audience and Orchestra* 482; Harmonica Concerto 263, 471; Sailor's Hornpipe 348; Symphonies: No. 4 **295**, 477; No. 6 352
Auric, Georges Overture 467

Bacewicz, Grażyna Overture for Orchestra 473; Music for Five Trumpets, Percussion and Strings 477
Bach, Johann Sebastian Cantata No. 21 295, 315; Chaconne for Full Orchestra 456; Cello Suite No. 5 293; *Christmas Oratorio* 196; Fugue for organ 75; Goldberg Variations 384; Mass in B minor 75, 105, **143**, 308, 380; Prelude and Fugue in D 452; 'St Anne' Prelude and Fugue 66, 103, 448; *St John Passion* 297, 369; *St Matthew Passion* 129, 168; *Ricercare* from The Musical Offering 317, 453; Suite No. 3 164; Toccata in D minor 75
Bäck, S.-E. *Sinfonia da Camera* 477; Violin Concerto 476
Badings, H. Concerto for Two Violins and Orchestra 476

Bainton, Edgar *Epithalamion* 450
Baird, Tadeusz *Erotics for Soprano and Orchestra* 478; *Espressioni varianti* 352, 481; Four Essays 386
Baker, Allan Hawthorne *Aubade* 464
Balakirev, Mily Alexeievich Piano Concerto No. 2 405; Symphonies: No. 1 249; No. 2 210
Balassa, Sandor *Iris* **404**, 485
Banks, Don Violin Concerto **347**, 480
Bantock, Granville *Five Ghazals of Hafiz* 458; *King Solomon* 457; *Omar Khayyám* 343, 481, 487; *Pagan Symphony, A* 455
Barber, Samuel *Essay for Orchestra* No. 1 461; No. 2 264; *School for Scandal* Overture 178; Symphony No. 1 256, 257
Barbirolli, Sir John *Elizabethan Suite* 186
Barraine, Elsa Symphony No. 2 197, 242, **250**, 466
Barraqué, Jean Clarinet Concerto for Six Instrumental Groups 481
Barraud, Henry *Offrande à une ombre* 473; Piano Concerto 468
Bartók, Béla *Cantata profana* 116, 118, 308, 382, 452, 455; Concerto for Orchestra 197, 198, 242, 379, 390, 465; Divertimento for Strings 181, 462; *Duke Bluebeard's Castle* 267, 352, 404; Four Orchestral Pieces 120; Hungarian Peasant Songs 453; *Miraculous Mandarin Suite* 77, 323, 330, 382, 478; Music for Strings, Percussion and Celesta 164, 340, 381, 458; Piano Concertos: No. 1 37, 287, 323; No. 2 86, 336, 346, 451; No. 3 **211**, 466; Rhapsody for piano and orchestra 58; Sonata for two pianos and percussion 293, 295, 375; Viola Concerto 242; Violin Concerto No. 2 **191**, 196, 464, 465
Bate, Stanley Piano Concerto No. 3 474
Bax, Sir Arnold Edward Trevor *The Bard of the Dimbovitza* 468; Concerto for Orchestra and Piano (left hand) 469; *London Pageantry* 457; *November Woods* 61; *Paean* 459; *Polish Christmas Carols* 464; *Summer Music* 181; Symphonies: No. 1 96, 181, 387; No. 2 85; No. 3 125; No. 4 **79**, 93, 148, 181; No. 5 141; No. 6 116; No. 7 164, 461; *Tintagel* 120; Viola Concerto 9; Violin Concerto 186, 273, 464; *Winter Legends* **74**, 450
Beck, Conrad Clarinet Concerto 485; *Innominata* 454; Serenade for Flute, Clarinet and Strings 458; Symphony No. 4 472
Bedford, David *Twelve Hours of Sunset* 485; *With 100 Kazoos* 372

Beecroft, Norma *Improvisation* No. 2 486
Beethoven, Ludwig van *Archduke* Trio 384;
  Cantata on the Death of the Emperor Joseph II 353,
  408; Choral Fantasia 243; *Coriolan* Overture 138;
  Glorreiche Augenblick 295; *Leonora* Overture
  No. 2 383; Mass in D (Missa Solemnis) 59,
  151, **153**, 182, 264, 295, 297, 317, 329, 330, 383,
  384, 401, 403; Piano Concertos: No. 2 154;
  No. 3 151, 383; No. 4 **61**, 151, 167, 263; No. 5 59,
  75, 151, 245, 259, 260, 324, 329; Serenade, Op. 25
  293; Symphonies No. 1 243; No. 2 260; No. 3
  (Eroica) **61**, 105, 138 141, **152**, 163, 287, 335, 346,
  384, 405; No. 4 **152**; No.5 **99**, 120, 123, 125, **153**,
  160, 179; No. 6 (Pastoral) 128, **138**, **153**; No. 7
  104, 108, **153**, 162, 189, 251, 315; No. 8 62, 119,
  153, 162; No. 9 (Choral) 63, 77, 81, 139, **140**, 147,
  149, **153**, 183, 187, 192, 243, 265, 286, 294, 308,
  316, 331, 344, 353, 380; Violin Concerto **57**, 86,
  151, 346
Bell, W. H.   *The Strain Upraise* 470
Bellini, Vincenzo   Mass in A Minor 481
Ben-Haim, Paul   Symphony No. 1 470
Benjamin, Arthur   *Cotillon* 460; *Jamaican Song and
  Jamaican Rumba* 460; *Prelude to Holiday* 462;
  Symphony 471; Violin Concerto **94**, 450
Benjamin, George   *Ringed by the flat horizon*
  487
Bennett, Richard Rodney   *Actaeon* 486; *Aubade*
  318, 479; *Journal for Orchestra* 477
Bentzon, Nils Viggo   *Symphonic Variations* 288,
  475
Berg, Alban   *Altenburg-Lieder* 406; Chamber
  Concerto 376, 378, 451; *Lulu* **99**, 100, 295, 453;
  Lyric Suite 115, 376, 451, 454; Three Orchestral
  Pieces, Op. 6 346, 387, 459; Violin Concerto **126**,
  131, **132**, 135, 189, 251, 287, 341, 379, 401, 455,
  456; *Der Wein* 452; *Wozzeck* 79, **83**, 86, **96**, 97,
  149, 181, 186, 324, 391, 451, 452
Berger, Arthur   *Rondo Ostinato* 473
Bergman, Valentina Semenovna   *Aubade* 477
Berio, Luciano   *Allelujah II* 388; *Bewegung* 389;
  Chemins IIC 375, 483; *Circles* 375; Concerto for
  Two Pianos 379, 484; *Epifanie* 349, 370, 481;
  Recital 375, 484; *Sinfonia* 347, 481
Berkeley, Lennox   Concerto for Piano and Double
  String Orchestra **288**, 475; Concerto for Two
  Pianos 257; Divertimento for Strings, Op. 18 463;
  Domini est Terra 459; Five pieces for Violin and
  Orchestra 478; Flute Concerto 257, 470; Four
  Ronsard Sonnets for Tenor and Orchestra 478;
  Jonah 455; *Mont Juic* 458; Nocturne for
  Orchestra 466; Suite for Orchestra 252, 470;
  Symphonies: No. 1 464; No. 2 475; *Winter's
  Tale* 477
Berlioz, Hector   *Beatrice and Benedict* Overture
  260, 268, 345; *Benvenuto Cellini* 308, 343; *La
  Damnation de Faust* 244, 249, 251, 282, 317, 343;
  L'Enfance du Christ 148, 251, 295, 385, 408, 421;
  Grande Messe des Morts 12, 345; *Harold in Italy*
  135, 163, 256, 348, 379; *Requiem* 430; *Romeo and
  Juliet* 138, 267, 316, 331, 335, 382, 390;
  Symphonie fantastique 63, **87**, 186, 211, 265, 266;
  Te Deum 297, 329, 381, 384; *Tristia* 421
Berners, Lord   *Luna Park* 449
Besly, Maurice   *Mary's Blue Eyes* 451
Binet, Jean   *Danses pour orchestre* 146

Birtwistle, Harrison   *Fields of Sorrow* 378, 484;
  Imaginary Landscape 353, 369, 482; *Nenia on
  the Death of Orpheus* 387, 389, 391; *Nomos* 343,
  480; *Verses for Ensembles* 348
Bizet, Georges   *Arlésienne Suite* 268; *Jeux
  d'enfants* Suite No. 2 464; Symphony No. 1 454
Blacher, Boris   *Clementi Variations* 479;
  Concertante 268, 324; *Fantasy for Orchestra* 473;
  Orchester-Ornament Op. 44 295; *Study in
  Pianissimo* 473; *Variations* 287
Blake, David   Violin Concerto 485
Bliss, Sir Arthur   *Adam Zero* 466; *Colour
  Symphony* **77**, 93, 178, 257, 450; *Film Music:
  Conquest of the Air* 460; *Lady of Shalott, The* 481;
  Mélée Fantasque 453; *Morning Heroes* 61, **63**, 150,
  187, 448; *Music for Strings* 163, 176, 210, 408;
  Pastoral 294; Piano Concerto 163, 191, 461; *Song
  of Welcome* 471; *Suite from the Film Music: 1935*
  453; *Theme and Cadenza for Violin and
  Orchestra* 465; Violin Concerto **265**, 472
Bloch, Ernest   *Baal Shem Suite* 287; Concerto
  Grosso 249, 251, 470; Israel Symphony 14;
  Proclamation for Trumpet and Orchestra 474;
  Sacred Service 264; *Schelomo* 250; *Sinfonia Breve*
  251, 470; Symphony in C sharp minor 250;
  Three Poems of the Sea 458; Violin Concerto 147
Blomdahl, Karl-Birger   Chamber Concerto 482;
  In the Hall of Mirrors 473
Borodin, Alexander Porfirievich   *Polovtsian Dances*
  179; Symphony No. 2 58, 100, 177
Boughton, Rutland   *The Lady Maid* 214
Boulanger, Lili   Psalm: *Du fond de l'abîme*
  480
Boulez, Pierre   *Doubles* 324, 479; *Éclat* 331, 332,
  352, 370, 480; *Éclat-multiples* **352**, 369, 370, 423,
  482; *e. e. cummings ist der dichter* **369**, 374, 378,
  387, 483; *. . . explosante-fixe . . .* 385, 387, 484;
  Figures/Doubles/Prismes 388; *Improvisation No. 2
  (Mallarmé)* 293; *Le Marteau sans maître* 278, 293,
  341, 346, **359**, 376; *Pli selon pli* 293, 329, 345, 346,
  349, 386, 430, 481; *Rituel: in memoriam Maderna*
  382, 389, 390, 391, 485; *Soleil des eaux* **317**, 406;
  Structures 359
Bowen, York   *Festal Overture* 474; Piano Concerto
  No. 4 457; *Rhapsody* 457
Boyce, William   *The Cambridge Ode* 460; *The
  Power of Music* 456
Bradford, Hugh   *Variations on a Popular Theme*
  449
Brahms, Johannes   *Academic Festival Overture* 158,
  268; Double Concerto 37; *German Requiem* 140,
  267, 274; Horn Trio 378; Piano Concertos: No. 1
  61, 213; No. 2 61, 131; Piano Quartet in G
  minor 386; *Song of Destiny* 149; Symphonies:
  No. 1 138, 253; No. 2 146, 191, 287, 315; No. 4
  46, 55, 103, **106**, 107, 120, 162, 287, 401; Tragic
  Overture 120, 149; Violin Concerto **13**, 182;
  Variations on a theme by Haydn 138
Braithwaite, Sam Hartley   *Crab Apple Fair* 463;
  Suite of 18th-Century Country Dances 462
Brian, Havergal   *Gothic Symphony* 331;
  Symphony No. 9 474
Bridge, Frank   *Oration for Cello and Orchestra* 454;
  Phantasm 94, 451; *Rebus* 461; *Summer* 408, 422
Bridgewater, Leslie   Piano Concerto 466
Bright, Dora   *Theme and Variations* 457

Brindle, Reginald Smith *Apocalypses* 482; *Cosmos for Orchestra* 476; *Creation Epic* 479; *Homage to H. G. Wells* 478

Britten, Benjamin *A Canadian Kermesse* **164**, 461; *Diversions* 417; *Frank Bridge Variations* 190, 315; *Illuminations* **164**, 336, 461; *Mont Juic* 458; *Nocturne* 286, **287**, 296, 474; *Occasional Overture* 210, 466; *Our Hunting Fathers* 136, 324, 455, 479; *Peter Grimes* 210, 401, 465; *Phaedra* 422; Piano Concerto 148, **389**, 459; *Rape of Lucretia* 210; Simple Symphony 315, 390; *Sinfonia da Requiem* 181, 281, 317; *Soirée Musicale* 456; Spring Symphony 252, 308; Violin Concerto **169**, 211, 406, 462; *War Requiem* 478; *Young Person's Guide to the Orchestra* 250, 259, 260, 268, 269

Brookes, H. H. *Three Midsummer Dances* 459

Brott, A. *Royal Tribute* 472

Bruckner, Anton Mass in E minor 378; Mass in F minor 317, 419; Symphonies: No. 4 134, 344; No. 5 384; No. 6 331, 344, 383; No. 7 134, 267, 343, 348, 398; No. 8 344; No. 9 87, 265, 274, 297, 451; *Te Deum* 274

Buesst, Victor Concerto for Three Pianos and Orchestra 459

Buller, John *The Mime of Mick, Nick and the Maggies* 486; *Proença* 423, 486; *Le Terrazze* **409**, 485

Burkhard, Willy *The Hunting Parson* 471; *Vision of Isaiah* 133, **146**, 460

Busch, William Cello Concerto **183**, 463, 464; Piano Concerto 460

Bush, Alan Concerto Suite for Cello and Orchestra 473; Dorian Passacaglia and Fugue 477; Piano Concerto 144; *Piers Plowman's Day* 469; *Resolution* 464; Scherzo for Wind and Percussion **347**, 481

Bush, G. Symphony No. 1 474

Busoni, Ferruccio Benvenuto *Arlecchino* 144, 150; Comedy Overture 77; Concerto for Piano, Male Voice Chorus and Orchestra 96; *Doktor Faust* 103, 120, **129**, **131**, 135, 423, 457; *Fantasia Contrappuntistica* 469; *Indian Fantasy* 454; Piano Concerto 452; *Rondo Arlecchinesco* 138; *Turandot* Suite 77; Violin Concerto 77, 148, 178, **386**, 405, 450

Bussotti, Sylvano Three madrigals 483

Butterworth, George *The Banks of Green Willow* 213

Byrd, William Mass for five voices 380

Callender, Mary *Suite* 455

Campbell, Colin M. *Five Dances for Orchestra* 460; *Thaïs and Talmaae* 456

Campo, Conrado del *El Scherzo del Borriquillo* 455

Cannon, Philip *Spring* 471

Caplet, André *Epiphanie* for Cello and Orchestra 468

Carissimi, Giacomo *Balthazar* 387

Carpenter, John Alden Concertino for Piano and Orchestra 150; *Song of Faith* **169**, 462; Violin Concerto 462

Carr, Howard *Sir Walter Raleigh* 461

Carse, Adam *Romantic Legend, A* 460

Carter, Elliott Concerto for Orchestra **369**, 384, 482, 483; *Holiday Overture* 478; *Mirror on which to dwell* 486; Piano Concerto **349**, 481;

Symphony of Three Orchestras **421**, 487

Casella, Alfredo *Concerto Romano* 460

Casken, John *Kagura* 410

Castelnuovo-Tedesco, Mario Concerto da Camera for Oboe and Strings 469

Castiglioni, Niccolò *Apreludes* 479

Castro, Juan José *Tres Trozos Sinfónicos* 67, 449

Cavalli, Pietro Francesco *Missa Concertata* 378

Charpentier, Marc-Antoine *Te Deum* 287, 474

Chausson, Ernest Symphony 268

Chavez, Carlos *Sinfonia de Antigona* 468, 482; *Sinfonia India* 463

Cherubini, Luigi *Anacreon* Overture 107; *Requiem* 407; *Symphony* 138

Chisholm, Eric Symphony No. 1 460

Chopin, Frédéric Piano Concerto No. 2 317

Clarke, Jeremiah Trumpet Voluntary 169

Clifford, Hubert John *Five English Nursery Tunes* 462

Coates, Eric Concerto in C 456; *Dancing Nights* 450; *The Enchanted Garden* 460; *From Meadow to Mayfair* 448; *Jester at the Wedding* 450; *London Every Day* 450; *Saxo-Rhapsody* 456; *Song of Loyalty* 453; *Springtime* 457; *The Three Elizabeths* 464

Collins, Anthony *Pastoral: Topley Pike* 457

Connolly, Justin *Tetramorph* 370, 482

Constant, Marius 24 *Preludes* 476

Cooke, Arnold Cello Concerto 485; Concert Overture No. 1 452; Piano Concerto 463; *Processional Ode* 467; Symphonies: No. 1 468; No. 4 **383**, 485

Copland, Aaron *Appalacian Spring* 265, 465; *Billy the Kid* **180**, 462; *Dance Symphony* 453; *Lincoln Portrait* **183**, 463; *Music for a Great City* 324; *Music for the Theatre* 454; *Quiet City* 476; *Statements* 352; Symphonies: No. 1 **352**; No. 3 282, 468; *The Tender Land* 476

Cowen, Sir Frederic *Magic Goblet* 452; *Miniature Variations (Humoresque)* 453

Cowie, Edward *Leighton Moss: December Notebook* 376, 485; *Leviathan* 485

Cox, Robert *The Golden Fleece* 458

Creith, G. Violin Concerto 455

Creston, Paul *Poem for Harp and Orchestra* 466; Symphonies: No. 2 **257**, 471; No. 3 471; *Threnody* 481

Crosse, Gordon *Celebrations* **384**, 483; *Ceremony for Cello and Orchestra* 480; *Memories of morning: night* **369**, 482; Violin Concerto No. 2 348, 481

Crossley-Holland, Peter *Chansonnier des Puys d'amore* 474

Crumb, George *Echoes of time and the river* 384, 483; *Star-Child* 487; Variations for Orchestra 485

Curzon, Frederic *Robin Hood* 458

Dalby, Martin Viola Concerto 484

Dale, Benjamin *The Flowing Tide* 463

Dallapiccola, Luigi *Canti di Liberazione* 288, 475; *Marsia* 467, 469; *Il Prigioniero* **256**; *Requiscant* 480; *Sacra Rappresentazione, Job* **294**; *Three questions with two answers* 486; *Tre Laudi* 340, 458; *Variazioni* 476

Darnton, Christian Concerto for Viola and String Orchestra 455; Piano Concerto 241, 454;

Symphony No. 3 465
Davie, Cedric Thorpe *Dirge for Cuthullin* 455
Davies, Peter Maxwell *Blind Man's Buff* **373**, 483;
 Fantasia on an 'In Nomine' of John Taverner 318,
 478; *Leopardi Fragments* 410; *St Thomas Wake*
 406; *Second Fantasia on an 'In Nomine' of John
 Taverner* 423; *Stone Litany* 389, 390, 391;
 Worldes Blis 347, **383**, 481
Debussy, Claude Achille *En Blanc et Noir* 453;
 Ibéria 59, 138; *Images* 293, 317, 324, **360**; *Le Jet
 d'eau* 421; *Jeux* 295, 324, 348, 390, 406; *Martyre
 de Saint-Sébastien* 242, 297, 331, 421; *La Mer*
 96, 108, 243, 317; *Nocturnes* 250, 329, 332, 346;
 Pelléas et Mélisande 66, 448; *Prélude à l'après-
 midi d'un faune* 332; Rhapsody for Saxophone
 134
Delius, Frederick *Brigg Fair* 181; *La Calinda* 260;
 Dance Rhapsody 58, 59, 103; Double Concerto for
 Violin, Viola and Orchestra 453; *Fantastic Dance*
 94, 451; *Fennimore and Gerda* 478; *Idyll* 451; *In a
 Summer Garden* 104, 149; *Irmelin* Prelude 260;
 Life's Dance 387; *Mass of Life* 37, 100, 263; *Paris*
 134, 273; *Sea Drift* 187; *Song Before Sunrise* 182,
 211; *Song of Summer* 449, 450; *Village Romeo
 and Juliet* 450
Dello Joio, Norman *Epigraph* 264; *Variations,
 Chaconne and Finale* 472
Demuth, Norman *Fantasia and Fugue* 465;
 Nachtmusik 453; *Portraits* (1935) 459; *Valses
 graves et gaies* 462
Denisov, Edison Flute Concerto 487; *Pas de
 quatre* 487
Diamond, David *Rounds for Strings* 466
Dickinson, Peter Organ Concerto 405, 486
Dieren, Bernard van *Anjou* Overture 136;
 Overture 454; *Symphony on Chinese texts* 136;
 Symphony Op. 6 455
Dolmetsch, Rudolph *Spring Tidings* 455
Donatoni, Franco *Etwas rühiger im Ausdruck* 481
Dorati, Antal *Madrigal Suite* 330, 480; Symphony
 330, 480
Douglas, Roy *Warra-Wirrawaal* 469
Druckman, Jacob *Incenters* 374, 483
Dukelsky, Vladimir Symphony No. 2 67, 449
Dunhill, Thomas *Dick Whittington* 454;
 Divertimento 462; *May-time* 465; Symphony in A
 Minor 116; *Triptych for Viola and Orchestra* 462;
 Waltz Suite 463
Durko, Zsolt *Turner Illustrations* 411
Duruflé, Maurice *Trois Danses* 467
Dvořák, Antonin *Carnaval* 268; Cello Concerto
 61, 196; *Rusalka* 255; Symphonies: No. 6 315;
 No. 7 197, 259, 260, 315; No. 9 (New World) 386,
 400; Violin Concerto 141
Dyson, George *The Canterbury Pilgrims* 463;
 Motherland 462; Violin Concerto 462

Eberl, Anton Piano Concerto 460
Einem, Gottfried von *Symphonic Scenes* 475
Elgar, Sir Edward *The Apostles* 274, 433; Cello
 Concerto in E minor 191, 324, 333; *Cockaigne*
 Overture 79; *The Dream of Gerontius* 68, 73, 163,
 273, 285; *Enigma Variations* 79, 96, 107, **108**, 158,
 211, 419; *Falstaff* 140, 177, 348; *Introduction and
 Allegro* 79, 120, 137, 336; *Kingdom* 79, 81, 274;
 Land of Hope and Glory 347; *The Music Makers*

160; *Nimrod* 335; *Nursery Suite* 449; *Pomp and
 Circumstance March No. 1* 347; Symphonies:
 No. 1 75, 79, 252, 346, 421; No. 2 **39**, 46, 61, 79,
 336, 353, 418; No. 3 (not completed) 80, 81, 82,
 98; Violin Concerto 61, 79, 132
Eloy, Jean-Claude *Equivalences* 484; *Faisceaux-
 diffractions* 484
Enesco, Georges Overture 251; *Sinfonia
 Concertante* 267; Symphony in E flat, Op. 13 242
Erdmann, Eduard *Serenade* 453
Erlanger, Frédéric d' *Les Cent Baisers* 455;
 Prélude Lyrique 450; Requiem Mass 448; *Sappho*
 458
Evans, D. Moule *Cliff Castle* 461; *Poem for
 Orchestra: September Dusk* 465; *The Spirit of
 London* 464; *Vienna Rhapsody* 464

Falla, Manuel de Harpsichord Concerto 448;
 Master Peter's Puppet Show 66, 448; *Nights in the
 Gardens of Spain* 77, 177; *The Three-Cornered
 Hat* 448
Farberman, Harold *The Losers* 483
Farjeon, Harry *Phantasie Concerto* 452
Fauré, Gabriel Urbain *Pavane* 251; Requiem **134**,
 256, 378
Feldman, Morton *The Rothko Chapel* 378, 484;
 The Viola in My Life No. 4 374, 483
Ferrers, Herbert *Songs of a Roman Legion* 457
Filz, Anton *Bohemian Symphony in A* 461
Fine, Irving *Serious Song for String Orchestra* 482
Finnissy, Michael *Pathway of sun and stars* 485;
 World **410**, 486
Finzi, Gerald *Dies Natalis* 351; *Ode for St
 Cecilia's Day* 467
Fogg, Eric Bassoon Concerto 449
Fortner, Wolfgang *Capriccio and Finale* 268, 472;
 Fantasy on BACH 475
Foss, Lukas Piano Concerto No. 2 **267**, 472
Françaix, Jean *Concertino* 455; *Le Diable boîteux*
 148, 460
Franck, César Auguste *Les Djinns* 263; *Les
 Éolides* 257; *Symphonic Variations* 177;
 Symphony 163
Franckenstein, Clemens von *Praeludium* 458
Frankel, Benjamin *Serenata Concertate*, Op. 37
 477; Symphonies: No. 1 476; No. 2 478; Violin
 Concerto 266, 270
Frazer-Simson, Harold *A Venetian Wedding* 448
Freedman, Harry *Tapestry* 486
Frescobaldi, Girolamo *Toccate* 453
Fricker, Peter Racine *Laudi Concertati* 487;
 Litany for double string orchestra 473; *O longs
 désirs* 479; Piano Concerto 263; Symphonies:
 No. 1 469; No. 2 267, 474; No. 5 405, 485;
 Toccata for Piano and Orchestra 351; *Viola
 Concerto* **256**, 257, 470
Fried, Oskar Concerto for Two Pianos and
 Orchestra 475
Frumerie, Gunnar de Variations and Fugue for
 Piano and Orchestra 464
Fuleihan, Anis *Concerto* 459; *Mediterranean* Suite
 150
Fulton, Norman *Sinfonia Pastorale* 470

Gál, Hans *Concertino* 264; *Idyllikon* 477
Gardner, John Symphony No. 1 251

Geehl, Henry *A Comedy Overture* 458
Geminiani, Francesco Concerto Grosso 108;
 La Follia 138
Gerber, René *Prelude: Stonehenge* 461
Gerhard, Roberto *Albada: Interludi i Dansi* 458;
 Collages 295; Concerto for Orchestra 324, 329,
 335, 336, 479; *Don Quixote* Suite 178, 462;
 The Duenna 477; *Epithalamion* 336, 480;
 Harpsichord Concerto 378; *Metamorphoses* 484;
 Pandora 376; *Pedrelliana* 471; *The Plague* 316,
 479; Symphonies: No. 1 330, 473; No. 2 275,
 292, 389, 476, 484; No. 3 477; No. 4 343, 380,
 481; Violin Concerto 282, 474
German, Edward *A Princess of Kensington* 448
Gershwin, George *An American in Paris* 67;
 Second Rhapsody 453; Symphony No. 3 333
Ghedini, Giorgio Federico *Concerto dell' Albatro*
 469; *Pezzo Concertante* 476
Gibbs, Cecil Armstrong *Concertino for Piano* 463;
 Dance Suite 462; *Fancy Dress* 454; Symphony in
 E 450
Gibson, Paul *La Mer* 104
Gielen, Michael *Four Poems of Stephan George*
 483; *Pentaphonie* 423, 487; *Variations for Forty
 Instruments* 478
Gipps, Ruth *Knight in Armour* 462
Glazunov, Alexander Constantinovich Saxophone
 Concerto 134; Symphony No. 6 249
Glière, Reinhold Concerto for coloratura soprano
 and orchestra 257; *Overture on Slavonic Tunes* 464
Globokar, Vinko *Discours II* 374, 483; *Fluide* 483
Gnattali, Radamés *Braziliana* 468
Godfrey, Dan *Hornpipe* 455; *Torland* 456
Goehr, Alexander *Arden Must Die* 388; *Babylon
 the Great is Fallen* 423, 487; *Chaconne for wind
 instruments* 485; *Hecuba's Lament* 298, 477; *Little
 Symphony* 351; *Naboth's Vineyard* 410; *Pastorals*
 383, 406
Goossens, Sir Eugene *The Apocalypse* 267, 472;
 Fantasy for Piano and Orchestra 468; *Judith* 148;
 Nature Poems 148, 460; Phantasy Concerto 191,
 294, 464, 476; Sinfonietta 93, 468; Symphonies:
 No. 1 464; No. 2 210, 466; Violin Concerto 475
Grayson, Denys *In Linden Time* 454
Greenwood, John *Salute to Gustav Holst* 454;
 Symphonic Movement 458; Viola Concerto 473
Grétry, André *La Rosière Républicaine* 455
Grieg, Edvard Hagerup Four Lyric Pieces 460;
 Holberg Suite 420; Lyric Suite 268; Piano
 Concerto 134; *Recognition of Land* 182
Guarnieri, Camargo Piano Concerto 474
Guridi, Jésus *Una Aventura de Don Quijote* 448
Guy, Barry *D* 376, 485

Haba, Alois *Nova Zeme* 458
Hadley, Patrick *The Hills* 466
Halffter, E. *Sinfonietta* 449
Hall, R. Symphony No. 4 479
Hamilton, Iain *Aurora* 407; *The Bermudas* 275,
 281, 282, 474; *Cantos for Orchestra* 479; *Circus*
 349, 481; Clarinet Concerto 471; *The Death of
 Tamburlaine* 405, 486; *Five Love Songs for
 Tenor and Orchestra* 477; Piano Concerto 482;
 Scena: Cleopatra 407, 486; *Scottish Dances* 294,
 476; Symphonic Variations 473; Violin Concerto
 288, 475

Handel, George Frederick *Acis and Galatea* 100;
 Allegro ed il Penseroso 386; Concerto for String
 Quartet and Orchestra 457; Concerto Grosso 136;
 Elijah 179; *Judas Maccabaeus* 148; *Messiah* 179,
 244, 249, 345, 348; *Music for the Royal Fireworks*
 150, 210; *Perseus and Andromeda from Jupiter in
 Argos* 454; *La Resurrezione* 459
Harris, Roy *Heroic Prelude* 462; Symphony No. 3
 179, 186, 462
Harrison, Julius *Autumn Landscapes for Strings*
 457; *Mass* 249, 264
Hart, Fritz *Cold Blows the Wind* 456
Hartmann, Karl Amadeus *Concerto funèbre* 483;
 Symphonies: No. 3 251, 472; No. 6 288
Harty, Sir Hamilton *Children of Lir* 150, 461;
 Irish Symphony 9; *John Field Suite* (arr. Harty)
 461; Piano Concerto No. 2 134
Harvey, Jonathan *Inner Light III* 404, 485
Haubenstock-Ramati, Roman *Petite musique de
 nuit* 388
Haydn, Franz Joseph Cello Concerto in D major
 80; *Creation* 317, 331, 402, 403; *Harmoniemesse*
 368, 378; *Litany* 474; Mass 297; Organ Concerto
 in C 467; *Return of Tobias* 251; *Seasons* 273, 336,
 343; *The Storm* 474; Symphonies: No. 97 134;
 No. 100 (Military) 259; No. 102 274; No. 104
 (London) 269, 401
Hely-Hutchinson, Victor Symphony for Small
 Orchestra 467
Heming, Michael *Threnody for a Soldier killed in
 Action* 464
Henkemans, Hans Harp Concerto 474
Henman, Geoffrey *High Street* 453; *Olde Wayes*
 460
Henze, Hans Werner *Antifone* 388, 478, 485;
 Ariosi 388; *Being Beauteous* 410; *Los Caprichos*
 388, 485; Chamber Music 293; Concertino 388;
 Five Neapolitan Songs 340; *Nachtstücke und Arien*
 388; *Novae de infinito laudes* 317; *Ode to the West
 Wind* for Cello and Orchestra 473; Piano
 Concerto No. 2 404; *The Raft of the Medusa* 486;
 Symphony No. 5 329, 388; Three Symphonic
 Studies 388; *Der Vorwurf* 388, 485
Herrmann, Hugo *The Devil and Daniel Webster*
 466
Hétu, Jacques Piano Concerto 486
Heward, Leslie *Quodlibet* 450
Hindemith, Paul *Cardillac* 133, 340, 456, 480;
 Concerto, Op. 38 295; *Kammermusik*, Op. 24 No.
 1 451; *Konzertmusik*: Op. 39 65; Op. 48 451; Op.
 49 448; *Konzertmusik* for strings and
 brass 75; *Das Lehrstück* 451; *Mathis der Maler*
 133, 134, 135, 146, 150, 181, 244, 452, 461;
 Nobilissima Visione 461; Philharmonic Concerto
 84, 103, 450; Piano Concerto 468; *Requiem* 264;
 Der Schwanendreher 117; Sinfonietta in E 420;
 Symphonia Serena 401; *Symphonic Dances* 144,
 458; *Symphonic metamorphoses on themes of Weber*
 466; Symphony in E flat 251, 463; *Trauermusik*
 117, 408, 454; *Das Unaufhörliche* ('The
 Perpetual') 79, 82, 84, 97, 451; Viola Concerto
 (*Kammermusik* No. 5) 37; Violin concerto
 (*Kammermusik* No. 4) 456
Hoddinott, Alun Concerto for Clarinet and Strings
 473; Harp Concerto 474; Symphony No. 2 478
Holbrooke, Joseph *Byron* 257; Double Concerto

(*Tannerlane*) 463
Holland, Theodore   *Billingham Marshes* 461
Holliger, Heinz   *Siebengesang* 353, 387, 482
Holloway, Robin   *Domination of Black* 484;
   Evening with Angels 376
Holmboe, Vagn   *Symphonic Metamorphosis:
   Epitaph* 473
Holst, Gustav Theodore   *Beni Mora* 266; Choral
   Symphony 96, 251, 316, 407; Concerto for Two
   Violins 181; *Egdon Heath* 191; Fugal Concerto
   106; *Hammersmith* 74, 449; *Hymn of Jesus* 9, 147,
   149, 256, 351, 382; Lyric Movement for Violin
   and Orchestra 452; *Morning of the Year* 12; *The
   Perfect Fool* 53, 252, 260; *The Planets* 39, 61, 100,
   128, 183, 245, 317, 348, 385; Scherzo 100, 453
Honegger, Arthur   *Chant de Joie* 120; Cello
   Concerto 453; *Christmas Cantata* 292, 476; *Cris
   du Monde* 451; *La Danse des Morts* 467; *Joan of
   Arc at the Stake* 212, 214, 466, 467; *King David*
   oratorio 12, 147, 256; *Monopartita* 470; *Pacific
   231* 12, 256; *Rugby* 37; Symphonic Movement
   No. 3 451; Symphonies: No. 1 77, 450; No. 2
   380; No. 3 (*Liturgique*) 466; No. 4 266; No. 5 251
Howells, Herbert   Concerto for String Orchestra
   148, 460; *Corydon's Dance* 213, 467; *Hymnus
   Paradisi* 469; *A Kent Yeoman's Wooing Song* 257,
   470
Huber, Klaus   *Cujus Legibus Rotantur Poli* 478
Hughes, Robert   *Essay for Orchestra* 472
Humperdinck, Engelbert   *Hansel and Gretel* 4

Ibert, Jacques   *Bacchanale* 473; *Escales* 168;
   Symphonie Concertante 470, 475
Indy, Vincent d'   *Symphonie Montagnarde* 136, 186
Ireland, John   *Legend for Piano and Orchestra* 94,
   181, 452; London Overture 141; *Mai-Dun
   Overture* 250; *Mai-Dun* Rhapsody 103; Piano
   Concerto 135, 167, 177, 263, 265; *Satyricon* 466;
   These things shall be 141, 181, 262, 457
Ivanov-Radkevich, Nikolai Pavlovitch   *Russian
   Overture* 466
Ives, Charles   *The Pond* 482; Symphony No. 4
   351, 369, 406, 466, 480; *Tone Roads* 482

Jacob, Gordon   Cello Concerto 265; Concerto for
   Bassoon, Strings and Percussion 467; Fantasia on
   the Alleluia Hymn 468; Festival March 213, 467;
   Fiddle Concerto 456; *Gallop* 460; *Laudate
   Dominum* 257, 471; Oboe Concerto 116;
   Passacaglia Stereophonica 476; Sinfonietta 463,
   471; Symphonic Suite 469; Symphony No. 2 465;
   Third Suite 281; Variations on an Original
   Theme 457
Janáček, Leoš   *Fiddler's Child, The* 461;
   Glagolithic Mass 352, 453; *Sinfonietta* 14, 196,
   400, 401
Jarnach, Philipp   Prelude 251, 470
Jarré, Maurice   *Mobiles* 478
Johnstone, Maurice   *A Cumbrian Rhapsody: Tarn
   Hows* 469
Jolas, Betsy   *Points d'aube* 483; *Quatre plages* 483
Jolivet, André   *Concertino* 257, 262, 471;
   Concerto for Flute and Strings 476
Jones, Daniel   Concert Overture 264; *Cystuddiau
   Branwen* 468; Five Pieces for Orchestra 469;
   Symphonies: No. 2 251; No. 5 275, 287, 288, 475

Jones, Sidney   *Daddy Longlegs* 448
Jongen, Joseph   Symphony Concertante for Organ
   and Orchestra 470

Kabalevsky, Dmitry   *Colas Breugnon* 183, 463;
   Piano Concerto No. 2 467; Symphony No. 2
   456
Kagel, Maurizio   *Hallelujah II* 374
Kappel, Hermann   Concertino for Strings 474
Kelley, Edgar Stillman   *Pilgrim's Progress* 10
Khachaturian, Aram   *Lezginka* 463; *Ode to Stalin*
   463; Piano Concerto 168, 177; Violin Concerto
   178
Knaifel, Alexander   *The Canterville Ghost* 487
Knipper, Leff   Suite 465; *Suite Lyrique*, Op. 18 449
Knussen, Oliver   Symphony No. 3 487
Kodály, Zoltán   Ballet Music 457; Concerto for
   Orchestra 210, 466; *Dances of Galanta* 164, 452;
   Dances of Marosszek 448; *Háry János* 143; *Missa
   Brevis* 265; *The Peacock* 472; *Psalmus Hungaricus*
   287; *Skékely Fonó* (The Spinning Room) 451;
   Summer Evening 336; *Te Deum* 133, 456; *Theatre
   Overture* 455; Variations for Orchestra 465
Koechlin, Charles   *Les Bandar-Log* 479
Koos, Robert de   Piano Concerto 197
Krein, Julian   Cello Concerto, Op. 25 450
Křenek, Ernst   *Durch die Nacht* 451; *Four plus
   three makes seven* 352; *Perspectives* 352; Piano
   Concerto 459; Three fragments from *Karl V* 352
Kridel, Johann Cristoph   *Cantata No. 4* 457

Ladmirault, Paul   *Tristan et Iseult* 468
Lajtha, László   *In Memoriam* 467; Symphony No.
   7 475
Lamarter, Eric de   *The Betrothal* 471
Lambert, Constant   Concerto for Piano and
   Chamber Ensemble 178, 449; *Formations and
   Transformations* 483; *Horoscope* 459; *Music for
   Orchestra* 67; *Rio Grande* 117, 119, 121, 163;
   Summer's Last Will and Testament 116, 264, 317,
   454
Lancen, Serge   Piano Concerto 475
Larsson, Lars Erik   Concerto for Saxophone and
   Strings 454; *Divertimento* 141; Violin Concerto
   266
Lefanu, Nicola   *The Hidden Landscape* 404, 484,
   485
Lehár, Franz   *The Land of Smiles* 448
Leifs, Jón   *Three Icelandic Folk Dances* 450
Leigh, Walter   *Interlude for Theatre Orchestra* 450
Leighton, Kenneth   *Burlesque* 475; Cello Concerto
   287, 474; *Passacaglia, Chorale and Fugue* 475;
   Primavera Romana 257, 264, 471; Violin Concerto
   471
Liebermann, Rolf   Concerto for Jazz Band 267,
   472
Ligeti, György   *Aventures* 410; *Nouvelles
   Aventures* 410; *Ramifications* 372, **373**, 376, 482;
   Requiem 369, 482; *San Francisco Polyphony* **404**,
   406, 485
Lipkin, Malcolm   Piano Concerto 288, 475
Liszt, Franz   *Cantico del Sole* 265; *Christus* 344;
   Dante Symphony 211, 343; *Faust Symphony* 297;
   Hymne de l'enfant 265; Piano Concerto No. 1 59;
   Psalm 13 265; *Via Crucis* 381
Lloyd, George   Symphony in F 454

Loeffler, Charles *The Dream of Tintagiles* 267, 472

Lokshin, Alexander Lazarevich Symphonies: No. 3 487; No. 5 486.

Lopatnikoff, Nikolai Lvovitch Concerto for Two Pianos and Orchestra 476

Loucheur, Raymond *Nocturne* 198, 466

Lovelock, William Second Suite for Orchestra 456

Lucas, Leighton *Chaconne in C sharp minor* 468; *Litany* 467; *Sinfonia Brevis* 136, 457; *Suite Française* 462

Lumsdaine, David *Hagoromo* 406, 486

Lutoslawski, Witold Cello Concerto 388; Concerto for Orchestra 421, 473; *Les Espaces du Sommeil* 487; Funeral Music (Musique Funèbre) 295, 388, 405, 476; Symphony No. 1 388; *Trois Poèmes d'Henri Michaux* 388

Lutyens, Elisabeth *And suddenly it's evening* 331, 480; *Counting your steps* 373, 483; *De Amore* 484; *Essence of our Happinesses* 482; *Music for Orchestra* 477, 479; *Petite Suite* 467; *Quincunx*, Op. 44 478; *Salute for Orchestra* 464; *Symphonies* 298, 477; Three Symphonic Preludes 197, 466; Viola Concerto 469

Machaut, Guillaume de *Messe de Notre Dame* 293

Maconchy, Elizabeth Concertino for Bassoon and Strings 471; Concerto for Piano and Chamber Orchestra 455; *Great Agrippa* 455; *Proud Thames* 256, 470; *Puck Fair* 464; Symphony 241, 468; Viola Concerto 144, 459

Maderna, Bruno *Amanda* 374, 376, 483; *Aura* 381, 484; *Biogramma* 381; *Juilliard Serenade* 482; Oboe Concerto No. 3 381, 484; *Quadrivium* 352, 482

Mahler, Gustav *Lieder eines fahrenden Gesellen* 63; *Lied von der Erde* 39, 95, 148, 353, 401; Symphonies: No. 1 95, 265; No. 2 95, 295, 329, 331, 384, 386, 468; No. 3 382, 385; No. 4 5, 39, 95, 191, 251, 274, 315, 316, 324, 381, 389, 391, 405; No. 5 287, 341, 346; No. 6 308, 329, 379, 384, 388; No. 7 316, 384; No. 8 38, 95, 141, 212, 384, 480; No. 9 95, 96, 299, 316, 332, 353, 452; No. 10 329, 352

Maklakiewicz, Jan Four Japanese Songs for Voice and Orchestra 449; Symphonic Poem: *Grünwald* 465

Malipiero, Gian Francesco *La Cena* 476; *Filomela e l'Infatuato* 454; *El Mondo Novo* 470; Symphonies: No. 1 453, 480; No. 2 143, 459; No. 3 295; No. 5 469; *Three Preludes to comedies by Goldoni* 454

Mann, R. W. Music for Orchestra 264

Markevitch, Igor *Le Paradis perdu* 454

Martin, Frank *Athalie* 473; Etudes for string orchestra 474; *Golgotha* 257, 266, 472; Harpsichord Concerto 263, 471; *Petite Symphonie Concertante* 263, 408; *Six Monologues for Everyman* 288; Violin Concerto 251, 264, 470

Martinon, Jean *Sinfonietta* 263, 471

Martinů, Bohuslav Cello Concerto 461; *The Epic of Gilgamesh* 475; Fantasia Concertante for Piano and Orchestra 475; *Frescoes of Piero della Francesca* 275; *Lidice Memorial* 464; *Mass for the Field of Battle* 287; Piano Concertos: No. 3 249, 469; No. 4 474; Symphonies: No. 2 465; No. 3

243; No. 4 210, 466; No. 6 265, 472

Mase, Owen *Lights Out* 455

Mathias, William Piano Concerto No. 3 343, 480

Matthews, Edmund *Queen of Ithaca* 469

Maw, Nicholas *Life Studies* 409, 485; *Nocturne* 476; *Scenes and Arias* 318, 335, 478; *Sinfonia* 411; Sonata for two horns and strings 378

May, Frederick *Suite of Irish Airs* 463

Mayerl, Billy *The Millionaire Kid* 448

Mendelssohn, Felix Concerto for Two Pianos 478; Hebrides Overture 62; *Hymn of Praise* 169, 179; Italian Symphony 197; *Midsummer Night's Dream* 108; Violin Concerto 61, 82

Menotti, Gian Carlo *Amelia goes to the Ball* 472

Messiaen, Olivier *Ascension* 257; *Chronochromie* 330, 341, 346, 478; *Couleurs de la Cité Céleste* 351, 374, 411; *Des canyons aux étoiles* 403, 485; *Et exspecto resurrectionem mortuorum* 330, 346, 407, 480; *Hymne au Saint-Sacrement* 407; *Mode de valeurs et d'intensités* 359; *Oiseaux exotiques* 349, 407, 477; *Poèmes pour Mi* 352, 379, 384, 387, 482; *Reveil des oiseaux* 297, 478; *Seven Haikai* 376; *Transfiguration de Notre Seigneur Jésus-Christ* 345, 482; *Turangalîla Symphony* 256, 344

Miaskovsky, Nicolai Symphonies: No. 7 452; No. 14 143, 458

Milford, Robin Sinfonietta for Small Orchestra 463; Violin Concerto 459

Milhaud, Darius *Le Bal Martinique* 469; *Christophe Colomb* 118, 136, 456; Concerto for Percussion and Small Orchestra 475; *La Création du Monde* 77; *Deux Marches* 466; *Fantasie Pastorale* 462; Harp Concerto 472; *Kentuckiana* 468; *Maximilian* 452; *Musique pour l'Indiana* 481; *Saudades de Brasil* 77; *Suite Française* 467; *Suite Provençale* 164, 458; Symphonies: No. 3 469; No. 6 474; No. 10 351, 481; Violin Concerto 77

Milner, Anthony Divertimento 298; *Midway* 389, 485; Symphony 380, 484; *Variations for Orchestra* 476

Moeran, Ernest John Cello Concerto 465; *Farrago* 451; *My Country* 464; Rhapsody No. 3 183, 463; Sinfonietta 191, 242, 465; Symphony in G minor 168; Violin Concerto 263

Mohaupt, Richard *Stadtpfeifermusik* 197; *Town-Piper Music* 466

Mompou, Federico Four Catalan Songs and Dances 457

Monn, Georg Cello Concerto 116, 451

Monteverdi, Claudio *Incoronazione di Poppea* 318; *1610 Vespers* 287, 384

Morris, Reginald Owen Symphony in D 94, 451

Mortari, Virgilio *Rapsodia per Orchestra* 67, 449

Mortet, Cluzeau *Llanuvas* 468

Mossolov, Alexander *Factory: the Music of Machines* 61, 77, 448; Piano Concerto 77, 450; *Three Songs with Orchestra* 453; *Turkmenian Music* 453

Mozart, Wolfgang Amadeus Adagio and Fugue in C minor 317; Bassoon Concerto 129; Clarinet Concerto 169; *Clemenza di Tito* 340, 344; Concerto for Two Pianos 295; *Così fan tutte* 318; *Don Giovanni* 318, 328; *Eine Kleine Nachtmusik* 274; *Idomeneo* 335, 343; *Magic Flute* 4, 274, 317; Masonic Funeral Music 274; Mass in C minor

243, 264, 266, 297, 335, 380; *Nozze di Figaro* 318, 343, 415; Piano Concerto in A major 76, 260; Piano quartet in E flat 386; *Requiem* 147, 148, 265, 295, 308, 318, 343, 384, 423; Rondo in A, K.386, 453; Serenade in C minor 378, 433; *Sinfonia Concertante*, K.364 74; Symphonies: No. 32 417; No. 35 (Haffner) 108; No. 36 (Linz) 96, 274; No. 40 138, 148; No. 41 274; in B flat, K.45 463; Vespers 317, 368

Murrill, Herbert Cello Concerto 455, 469; Country Dances 463; Songs for Tenor and Orchestra 251

Musgrave, Thea Clarinet Concerto 344, 481; Concerto for Orchestra 347; *Five Ages of Man* 388; *Memento Vitae* 387; *Obliques* 388; Viola Concerto 388

Mussorgsky, Modest *Boris Godunov* 383

Nabokoff, Nikolai *Biblical Symphony* 466
Naylor, Edward Cantata: *Sing o my love* 479
Newson, George *Arena* 482
Noble, Harold Mass 471
Nono, Luigi *Canti per 13* 278; *Composizione I* 477; *España nel corazón* 483; *Il canto sospeso* 406, 481; *Intolleranza 1960* 296, 477
Novák, Vítězslav *Triptych on a chorale theme of St Wenceslas* 467
Nystroem, Gösta *Sinfonia Espressiva* 468

Olsen, P. R. Symphonic Variations 474
Orff, Carl *Carmina Burana* 273
Osborne, Nigel Cello Concerto 411, 487

Pakeman, Kenneth *Day that I have loved* 456
Palester, Roman *Muzyka Symfoniczna* 67, 449; Violin Concerto 198, 466
Panufnik, Andrzej Rhapsody 473; *Sinfonia Rustica* 265, 472
Parry, Hubert *Blest Pair of Sirens* 210; *Pied Piper of Hamelin* 182; Symphonic Variations 351
Pärt, Arvo *Cantus to the memory of Benjamin Britten* 420, 487; *Pas de quatre* 487
Partos, Ödön *Sinfonia Concertante* for Viola and Orchestra 315
Patterson, Paul Trumpet Concerto 387; *Wildfire* 485
Pattman, G. T. *Cinderella* 458
Paynter, John *Galaxies for Orchestra and Audience* 486
Penderecki, Krzystof *De natura sonoris* 332, 480; Music from the Psalms of David 340, 480; *St Luke Passion* 332, 333, 480; *Threnody for the victims of Hiroshima* 332; *Tren, for 52 Instruments* 478
Peragallo, Mario Violin Concerto 264, 471
Persichetti, Vincent Symphony No. 4 264, 471
Petrassi, Goffredo Piano Concerto 287, 475
Pfitzner, Hans Erich Cello Concerto 263; Piano Concerto 77 134
Phillips, Montague *Charles II* 456; *Moorland Idyll* 456; *Revelry* 458; *Sinfonietta* 463; *Surrey Suite* 455
Pick-Mangiagalli, Riccardo *Sortilegi* 160
Piston, Walter Symphonies: No. 2 467; No. 4 267, 472

Pizzetti, Ildebrando *Canti della stagione alta* 288; Concerto in C 461; *Rondo Veneziano* 451; Symphony in A 468
Porter, Quincey Viola Concerto 251, 470
Poulenc, Francis *Aubade for Piano and 18 Instruments* 449; *Concert champêtre* 59, 448; Piano Concerto 242, 469
Préger, Léo *Il viendra vers toi* 460
Prokofiev, Serge *Alexander Nevsky* 242, 462; Cello Concertino 386, 482; *Chout* 263, 452; *Hamlet* 408, 487; *The Love for Three Oranges* 453; *Ode to the End of the War* 197, 466, 486; Piano Concertos: No. 1 401; No. 3 75; No. 5 95, 452; *Portraits* 452; *Romeo and Juliet* 141, 459; *Symphonic Suite: Four Portraits* 452; Symphonies: No. 1 (Classical) 141; No. 3 452; No. 5 420; *A Toast to Stalin* 464; Violin Concertos: No. 1 71, 74, 450; No. 2 141, 456, 458; *The White Swan* 487
Puccini, Giacomo *La Bohème* 4
Purcell, Henry *Come ye sons of art away* 348; *Hail, bright Cecilia* 196; *King Arthur* 116, 242, 317; Trumpet Voluntary see Clarke, Jeremiah; *Welcome to all the pleasures* 293

Quilter, Roger *I arise from dreams of thee* 448; *Pastoral Dance* 451; *Song of Freedom, A* 462
Quinet, Fernand *Trois Mouvements Symphoniques* 67, 449

Rachmaninov, Sergei Vassilievich *The Bells* 135, 457; Paganini Rhapsody 116; Piano Concertos: No. 1 191; No. 3 265; Rhapsody 287; Symphonic Dances 471; Symphony No. 1 420
Rainier, Priaulx *Aequora Lunae* 480; Cello Concerto 479
Rameau, Jean-Philippe *Castor et Pollux* 163; *Dardanus* 387
Rands, Bernard *Aum* 382, 484; *Mésalliance* 372, 376, 483; *Wildtrack* 368, 388, 484
Rankl, Karl Symphonies: No. 1 470; No. 4 471
Rathaus, Karol *The Lion in Love* 459; Serenade 456
Ravel, Maurice *Une Barque sur l'océan* 469; *Bolero* 38, 58, 103, 104, 128, 169, 256; *Daphnis and Chloe* 46, 56, 104, 120, 138, 183, 346, 349, 379, 390; *L'Enfant et les Sortilèges* 263, 316, 382, 387; *Le Gibet* 477; *Heure Espagnole* 295, 387; *Pavane* 128; Piano Concerto for the Left Hand 450; *Shéhérazade* 75, 181; *La Valse* 60
Rawsthorne, Alan *Carmen Vitale* 316, 479; Clarinet Concerto 458; Concerto for String Orchestra 468; *Cortèges* Overture 198, 465; *Kubla Khan* 164, 461; *Madame Chrysanthème* 474; *Medieval Diptych for Baritone and Orchestra* 478; Oboe Concerto 467; Piano Concertos: No. 1 181, 191, 211, 242, 387; No. 2 250, 259; Symphonic Studies 164, 178; Symphonies: No. 1 242, 251, 469; No. 3 404; *Three French Nursery Songs* 460; Violin Concerto No. 2 273, 467, 473
Reeve, Stephen *. . . aux régions éthérées . . .* 409, 485
Reizenstein, Franz *Cyrano de Bergerac* 474; Piano Concerto No. 2 477; *Voices of Night* 263
Respighi, Ottorino *Antiche Danze ed Arie* 451; *Church Windows* 14; *Concerto Gregoriano* 249

Rieti, Vittorio   Piano Concerto No. 2 458
Rimsky-Korsakov, Nikolai Andreievich   *Capriccio Espagnol* 268; *Kitezh* 10, 66
Rivier, Jean   Symphony No. 2 459
Roger-Ducasse, Jean Jules   Symphonic poems 250
Roos, Robert de   Piano Concerto 466
Rootham, Cyril B.   Symphonies: No. 1 456; No. 2 461
Roseingrave, Thomas   *Overture in F* 450
Rosenberg, Hilding   Overture 269
Rosenthal, Manuel   *Musique de Table* 481
Rossini, Gioacchino   *Semiramide* Overture 108
Rota, Nino   *Serenata* 461; *Variations on a Gay Tune* 475
Roussel, Albert   *Bacchus et Ariane* 468; *Concert, Op. 34* 450; *Concertino* Op. 57 458; *Padmâvâti* 458; *Petite Suite,* Op. 39 457; Piano Concerto in G 458; *Pour une fête de printemps* 119, 121, 168; *Psalm LXXX* 67, 263, 449; *Sinfonietta for Strings* 461; Symphonies: No. 3 190, 243, 450; No. 4 164, 178, 249, 454
Rowley, Alec   Piano Concerto in D 460; Suite in A 462; Three Idylls for Piano and Orchestra 462
Rozhdestvensky, Gennadi   *Pas de quatre* 487
Rubbra, Edmund Duncan   *Festival Overture* 213; Improvisation for Violin and Orchestra 266, 472; *In Die et Nocte Canticum* 481; Ode to the Queen 252, 470; Piano Concerto 266, 472; *Sinfonia Concertante* 183, 463, 464; Symphonies: No. 1 136, 405, 457; No. 2 148, 263, 460; No. 3 168; No. 4 180, 242, 407, 462; No. 5 213, 250, 467; No. 6 263, 265, 471; No. 7 281; Viola Concerto 287, 470; Violin Concerto 294, 476
Ruggles, Carl   *Portals* 479

Saeverud, Harald   *Siljuslatten* 269, 473
Saint-Saëns, Camille   Cello Concerto 55; Piano Concerto No. 4 63
Sainton, Prosper   *Serenade Fantastique for Oboe and Strings* 469
Salzman, Eric   *Foxes and Hedgehogs* 372, 483
Sandström, David   *Utmost* 409, 485
Satie, Erik   *Jack-in-the-Box,* Suite No. 1 452; *Mercure* 450; *Relâche* 457
Sauguet, Henri   *Sinfonie Expiatoire* 468
Saxton, Robert   *Reflections of Narziss and Goldmund* 486
Schafer, Murray   *Requiem for a party girl* 374, 483; *Son of Heldenleben* 486
Schedrin, Rodion Konstantinovich   Piano Concerto 344, 481
Schelling, Ernest Henry   *Suite fantastique* 177
Scherchen, Tona   *Khouang* 376
Schmidt, Franz   Symphony No. 4 459
Schmitt, Florent   *Le Palais Hanté* 9
Schnittke, Alfred   *Pas de quatre* 487; *St Florian* Symphony 422, 487
Schoeck, Othmar   *Summer Night* 475
Schoenberg, Arnold   Chamber Symphony 10, 297; *Erwartung* 66, 331, 448; Five Orchestral Pieces, Op. 16 72, 189, 249, 323, 341, 391; *Die glückliche Hand* 308, 406, 478; *Gurrelieder* 5, 14, 66, 385; Handel Concerto Grosso 136; *Herzgewächse* 378; *Jacob's Ladder (Jacobsleiter)* 345, 369, 407; *Moses und Aron* 308, 382, 386; *Music for a Film Scene* 66, 341, 448; *Ode to Napoleon Bonaparte*

376; Orchestral Variations 406; *Pelleas und Melisande* 59, 242, 448; Piano Concerto 341, 383, 465; *Pierrot Lunaire* 346, 375; *Prelude to Genesis,* Op. 44 297, 477; Second Quartet 10; *Song of the Wood Dove* 66; Songs, Op. 22 250, 295, 470, 476; *Survivor from Warsaw* 297; Variations for Orchestra, Op. 31 72, 79, 83, 120, 122, 294, 297, 341, 449, 451; *Verklärte Nacht* 12, 72, 73, 297; *Von Heute auf Morgen* 316, 479; Violin Concerto 250, 295, 343, 469
Schreker, Franz   *Birthday of the Infanta* 419, 487
Schubert, Franz Peter   *Divertissement* 461; *Lazarus* 378; Mass in A flat 378; Mass in G 378; *Rosamunde* 66; Symphonies: No. 2 378; No. 3 378; No. 5 274, 317; No. 6 284; No. 7 101, 453, 486; No. 9 75, 273, 286, 292, 384, 385, 387, 406
Schuller, Gunther   Dramatic Overture 324; Sequences from Movements for Flute and Strings 480; *Seven Studies on themes of Paul Klee* 340
Schuman, William   Circus Overture 257; Free Song for Chorus and Orchestra, A 465; Symphony No. 3 183, 463; Violin Concerto 476
Schumann, Robert Alexander   Cello Concerto 191; *Faust* 297, 379, 387; *Overture, Scherzo and Finale* 379; Piano Concerto 335; *Der Rose Pilgerfahrt* 378; Symphony No. 4 61; Violin Concerto 139, 141, 142, 459
Schütz, Heinrich   Christmas Story 182
Scott, Cyril   Overture 98; *Fantasia for Strings* 464; Oboe Concerto 467; *Passacaglia* No. 1 448
Scott, Leonard   *Introduzione, Fugato, Andante* 257; Three Symphonic Studies 264
Scriabin, Alexander Nicolas   *Poem of Ecstasy* 250; *Prometheus* 100, 144
Searle, Humphrey   *Overture to a drama* 468; Piano Concertos: No. 1 465; No. 2 473
Seiber, Matyas   *Cantata Secularis* 264; Four Greek Songs for Soprano and Strings 464; Renaissance Suite 477; Three Pieces for Cello and Orchestra 287, 475; *Ulysses* 241, 256, 281, 468
Seixas, Carlos de   *Suite Ancienne* 473
Sessions, Roger   *The Black Maskers* 452; Concerto for violin, cello and orchestra 405, 485; Piano Concerto 386, 479; Symphonies: No. 2 469; No. 5 483; No. 8 404
Shaporin, Yuri   *On the Field of Kullikorvo* 196; Symphony in C Minor 453
Shaw, Christopher   *Peter and the lame man* 484
Shebalin, Vissarion Yakovlevitch   Overture, Op. 25 463
Shostakovich, Dimitri   Cello Concerto No. 2 480; *Columbus* Overture 421, 487; *Lady Macbeth of Mtsensk* 118, 455; *The Nose* 413, 452; Piano Concerto No. 2 475; *Suite on verses of Michelangelo* 421; Symphonies: No. 1 77, 138, 181, 450, 453; No. 2 348, 481; No. 3 454; No. 4 331, 405, 417, 418; No. 5 263, 405; No. 7 (Leningrad) 179; No. 8 189, 344, 464; No. 9 273, 344; No. 10 265, 324, 472; No. 11 282; No. 12 308; Violin Concerto No. 2 421
Sibelius, Jean   *En Saga* 269; *The Ferryman's Brides* 456; *Finlandia* 269; *Four Legends for Orchestra* 469; *Night Ride and Sunrise* 449; *Oceanides* 450; *Return of Lemminkäinen* 134; *The Swan of Tuonela* 134; Symphonies: No. 1 269; No. 2 105, 146, 264; No. 3 269; No. 4 282; No. 5

284; No. 7 176, 269; *Tapiola* 269; *Three Historical Scenes* 269
Silvestri, Constantin   Three Pieces for String Orchestra 479
Simpson, Robert   Symphonies: No. 1 263, 471; No. 4 383
Sinopoli, Giuseppe   *Drei Stücke aus 'Souvenirs à la mémoire'* 486; *Tombeau d'armor II* 486
Skalkottas, Nikos   *Greek Dances* 257, 470; Piano Concerto No. 2 480; Suite No. 2 480; Violin Concerto 315, 479
Smalley, Roger   Sonata for Strings 374, 484
Sohal, Naresh   *Dhayan I* 376, 485
Sorozabal, Pablo   *Basque Sketch: Mendian* 455
Souster, Tim   *Song of an average city* 376, 484; *Triple Music II* 347, 482
Sowande, Fela   *Africania* 464
Sowerby, Leo   Organ Concerto in C 469
Speer, William   *Impressions* 456
Spisak, Michal   *Concerto Giocoso* 477
Stanford, Sir Charles Villiers   Clarinet Concerto 213; *Requiem* 251; *Songs of the Fleet* 182
Stephen, David   *Coronach* 104
Stevens, James   *Fugal Overture* 467; Symphony No. 1 257; Violin Concerto 465
Still, William Grant   *Afro-American Symphony* 455
Stockhausen, Karlheinz   *Carré* 384, 483; *Drei Lieder* 409; *Formal* 409; *Gruppen* 333, 341, 349, 380, 385; *Harlequin* 409; *Hymnen* 409; *Kontakte* 347, 410; *Kontrapunkte* 378, 388; *Kreuzspiel* 374, 378; *Mixtur* 370, 482; *Momente* 351, 364, 379, 409; Piano Piece No. 10 346; *Punkte* 348, 349, 350, 481; *Setz die Segel* 349, 350, 481; *Spiel* 409; *Telemusik* 349; *Zeitmasse* 278; *Zyklus* 349, 350
Stoll, Denis   *The Blonde Persian* 456; *Princess Margaret Rose* 457
Strauss, Richard   Alpine Symphony 12; *Also sprach Zarathustra* 58, 100; *Don Juan* 71, 243; *Don Quixote* 146; Four Last Songs 273; *Ein Heldenleben* 79, 80, 103, 131, 211, 400; Hölderlin settings, Op. 71 71, 449; *Japanische Festmusik* 476; *Kampf und Sieg* 448; *Macbeth* 71, 449; Oboe Concerto 466; *Der Rosenkavalier* 232; *Salome* 452; *Die schweigsame Frau* 454; Symphony No. 2 in F minor 459; *Till Eulenspiegel* 212; *Tod und Verklärung* 71, 138, 265; Violin Concerto 456
Stravinsky, Igor   *Agon* 287, 297; *Apollo* 59, 251, 287, 308; *Cantata* 293; *Capriccio* 74, 100, 168; *Chant du Rossignol* (Song of the Nightingale) 37, 323, 330, 340, 382; Concerto for two pianos 293; *Dumbarton Oaks* 148, 460; *Duo Concertant* 235; *Eight Easy Pieces* 60, 448; *The Firebird* 60, 100, 176, 178, 287, 316, 346, 390, 406, 425; *Fireworks Fantasia* 100; *The Flood* 316, 480; Four Studies for Orchestra 59, 323, 448; Mass 213, 214, 378, 468; *Mavra* 448, 452; *Monumentum in memoriam Gesualdo* 477; *Movements* for piano and orchestra 295, 477; *Les Noces* 60, 295; *Oedipus Rex* 117, 118, 294, 316, 348; *Orpheus* 213, 468; *Perséphone* 100, 295, 297, 353, 452; *Petrushka* 420; Piano Concerto 59; *Pulcinella* 60, 273; *Renard* 60, 410; *Requiem Canticles* 346, 411, 480; *Rite of Spring* 60, 80, 105, 119, 121, 128, 135, 148, 181, 187, 256, 308, 323, 325, 329, 335, 340, 346, 348; *Le Roi des Etoiles* 346; *A Sermon, a narrative and*

a prayer 369, 411, 478; *Soldier's Tale* 10, 60; Study for Pianola 60; Symphonies of wind instruments 317, 323, 352, 369; Symphony in C 186, 273, 463; Symphony in Three Movements 287; Symphony of Psalms 60, 73, 74, 273, 297, 331, 344, 379; Three Pieces for String Quartet 60; *Threni* 369, 411
Suchon, Eugen   *Metamorfozy* 476
Sullivan, Arthur   *Di Ballo* overture 268
Surinach, Carlos   *Sinfonietta Flamenca* 472
Susskind, Walter   *Nine Slovak Sketches* 474
Svendsen, Johan   *Carnival in Paris* 269
Szabo, Ferencz   *Song of the Wolves* 67
Szymanowski, Karol   Chansons Polonaises 67; *Harnasie* 141, 458; Overture, Op. 12 141, 457; *Sinfonia Concertante* 79, 257, 281, 407; Violin Concertos: No. 1 181; No. 2 141, 457

Tallis, Thomas   *Spem in alium numquam habui* 295
Tansman, Alexander   *The Prophet Isaiah* 473; *Sinfonia Piccola* 470; Violin Concerto 473
Tapp, Frank   *Beachy Head* 460; *Metropolis* 452
Tarp, S. V.   Comedy Overture No. 2 474
Tate, Phyllis   *Elegiac March* 464
Tavener, John   *In alium* 347, 480; *Ultimos Ritos* 386
Tchaikovsky, Peter Ilyich   *The Empress's Shoes* 340; *Manfred* 344; Piano Concerto No. 1 56, 98; *Queen of Spades* 415; *Romeo and Juliet* 169; *Sleeping Beauty* 421; Symphonies: No. 4 58, 420; No. 5 149, 264, 400, 419; No. 6 106, 269; Violin Concerto 100, 168
Tcherepnin, Alexander   Piano Concerto 481; Symphony No. 1 381, 481
Tharichen, Werner   Timpani Concerto 479
Thiman, Eric   *Barbara Allen* 459; *Variations on a Theme of Elgar* 461
Thomson, Virgil   Symphony No. 3 469
Tippett, Michael   *Birthday Suite* 213, 264, 467; *A Child of our Time* 382, 386; Concerto for Double String Orchestra 251, 263, 401; *Divertimento on Sellinger's Round* 297; *Fantasia Concertante on a theme of Corelli* 255, 348, 353, 389, 470; *Fantasia on a theme of Handel* 463; *Midsummer Marriage* 423; Piano Concerto 288, 324, 479; *Preludium* 308, 478; *Ritual Dances* 264; Symphonies: No. 2 275, 281, 283, 284, 335, 336, 422, 474; No. 3 380; *The Vision of St Augustine* 329, 405, 421, 479
Toch, Ernst   *Bunte Suite* 451; Piano Concerto 37; Symphony No. 2 267, 472
Togni, Camillo   *Helian Di Trakl*, Op. 39 478
Tommasini, Vicenzo   *Carneval di Venezia* 138, 457
Toomey, Timothy   *Celtic Tunes for String Orchestra* 454
Tovey, Donald   Cello Concerto 116, 140

Valen, Fartein   *Le Cimetière Marin* 470; Symphony No. 3 294, 476
Van Maldere, Pierre   Symphony in B flat 405
Varèse, Edgard   *Arcana* 341, 346; *Ecuatorial* 480; *Ionisation* 346
Vaughan Williams, Ralph   *Benedicite* 67, 449; Concerto for two pianos 211; *Dona nobis pacem* 133, 266, 456; Fantasia on a Theme of Thomas Tallis 104, 106, 259; *Fantasia on the Old 104th Psalm Tune* 469; *Five Tudor Portraits* 131, 134,

457; *Five Variants on Dives and Lazarus* 159, 461; *Flos Campi* 133; *Job* 266; *Hodie* 264, 471; *The Lark Ascending* 162; Partita for double string orchestra 467; Piano Concerto 79, 82, 181, 451; *The Running Set* 182; *Sancta Civitas* 422; *Serenade to Music* 460; *Sinfonia Antartica* 251; *Six Choral Songs for time of war* 168; Symphonies: No. 1 (Sea) 57, 252; No. 2 (London) 136, 177, 268; No. 3 (Pastoral) 9, 163, 178, 181; No. 4 99, 101, 116, 120, 122, 144, 187, 287, 296, 324, 336, 383, 453; No. 5 186, 187; No. 6 212, 243, 251, 259, 260, 381, 467; No. 8 273; *Thanksgiving for Victory* 465

Veale, John *Kubla Khan* 475; *Panorama* 472
Veerhoff, Carlos *Mirages for Orchestra* 478
Veprik, Alexander *Song of Jubilation* 465
Verde, Giuseppe Four Sacred Pieces 353; *Otello* 318; *Requiem* 139, 146, 197, 244, 251, 264, 294, 315, 345, 353, 405; *Te Deum* 266
Veress, Sándor *Divertimento* 461
Vermeulen, Matthijs *Passacaglia and Cortège* 471
Victoria, Tomás Luis de *Requiem* 293
Villa-Lobos, Heitor *Chôros:* No. 6 467; No. 10 468; Harp Concerto 273, 473; Symphony No. 7 468
Vincent, John Symphony in D 478
Vivaldi, Antonio Concerto 131, 138; Concerto Grosso 256
Vogel, Vladimir *Ritmica Ostinata* 455; *Zwei Etüden für Orchester* 67, 449

Wagner, Richard *Chorus of Gibichungs* 453; *Faust Overture* 108; *The Flying Dutchman* 46, 55, 104; *Götterdämmerung* 107; *Liebesmahl der Apostel* 406; *Meistersinger Overture* 66, 119, 121, 122, 138, 250; *Parsifal* 68, 108, 384; *Ride of the Valkyries* (Die Walküre) 4, 121, 122, 210; *Rienzi Overture* 188; *The Ring* 10, 75, 399; *Siegfried* 74; *Tristan und Isolde* 210, 340, 345, 430
Wallace, William *Sister Helen* 457
Walthew, Richard *Mosaic in ten pieces for Viola and Orchestra* 463
Walton, Sir William *Belshazzar's Feast* 73, 80, 95, 141, 256, 285, 449; *Capriccio burlesca* 344, 481; Cello Concerto 274, 473; *Children's Pieces* 168; *Coronation March: Crown Imperial* 457; *Coronation Te Deum* 256, 470; *Façade* (Second Suite) 460; *Henry V* 465; *In Honour of the City of London* 141; *Johannesburg Festival Overture* 273, 473; *Memorial Fanfare* 465; *Partita* 387, 389; *Portsmouth Point* 85, 281; *Scapino Overture* 177, 181, 462; Symphony No. 1 82, 98, 116, 136, 144, 148, 163, 181, 210, 260, 421, 454; *Troilus and Cressida* 265, 294, 472; Viola Concerto 96, 120, 135, 177, 178, 252; Violin Concerto 176, 177, 211, 287, 382
Warner, H. Waldo *Camera Snaps* 455
Weber, Carl Maria von *Euryanthe* 128, 381; *Oberon Overture* 104, 349; Symphony No. 1 in C 472
Webern, Anton *Das Augenlicht* 146, 459; Cantata, Op. 29 329, 379; Cantata, Op. 31 329,

379; Concerto, Op. 24 278; Five Orchestral Pieces, Op. 10 330; Five Pieces for String Quartet, Op. 5 (Five Movements for String Orchestra) 66, 297, 448; Op. 6 pieces 295, 317, 323; *Passacaglia*, Op. 1 68, 189, 449; *Siegfrieds Schwert* 487; Six Orchestral Pieces 294; Symphony for small orchestra, Op. 21 67, 330, 359, 410, 419, 449; Three Orchestral Studies on a Ground 487; Variations for Orchestra, Op. 30 323, 329, 379
Weigl, Karl Piano Concerto in F Minor 452
Weill, Kurt *The Lindbergh Flight* 345, 353, 482; *The Protagonist* 486; Symphonies 340; *The Tsar has his photograph taken* 486; Violin Concerto 386, 420
Weingartner, Felix *The Spring* 75
Weisgall, Hugo *American Comedy 1943* 463
Whettam, Graham *Dance Concertante* 475; Symphony No. 2 267
White, Felix *Nocturne* 457; *A Revel* 456; *Sinfonietta in C* 459
Whithorne, Emerson Symphony No. 2 150
Whyte, Ian *Festival March* 465
Williams, Grace *Overture* 452; *Rhiannon* 461; *Sinfonia Concertante* 463
Williams, Russell *Symphonic Fantasia* 455
Williamson, Malcolm *Fiesta* 487; *Hammarskjöld Portrait* 484; *Les Olympiques* 487; Organ Concerto 298; Piano Concerto 475; *Santiago de Espada* 474; *The Stone Wall* 384, 482
Wilson, Stanley *Double Concerto* 457
Wolf, Hugo *Italian Serenade* 66
Wolf-Ferrari, Ermanno *Idillio Concertante for Oboe and Orchestra* 451
Wood, Arthur *Strolling Players* 459
Wood, Haydn *Apollo* 453; *Cities of Romance* 458; *A Day in Fairyland* 451; *East of Suez* 461; *Frescoes* 454; *King Orry* 459; *Love and Life* 459; *Manx Overture: The Isle of Mountains and Glens* 456; *Manx Tone Poem: Manin Veg Veen* 451; *Market Day* 452; *Minerva* 462; *Moods* 450; *Phantasy for Strings* 464; *Scherzo in the Olden Style* 450; *Theme and Variations for Cello and Orchestra* 461; Violin Concerto 451
Wood, Hugh Cello Concerto 347, 353, 370, 481; *Song cycle to Poems of Neruda* 376, 484; *Scenes from Comus* 332, 420, 479
Wood, Thomas *Daniel and the Lions* 460
Woodgate, Leslie *Marginale* 455; *A Song of Joys* 459
Wooldridge, David *Five Italian Songs* 487
Wordsworth, William Symphony No. 2 251, 470
Wyk, Arnold van *Saudade* 183, 463

Xenakis, Iannis *Aurora* 483

Zafred, Mario Viola Concerto 477
Zemlinsky, Alexander *Lyric Symphony* 389, 407
Zender, Hans *Muji No Kyo* 486; *Zeitstrome* 486
Zimmermann, Bernd Alois *Canto di Speranza* 483; Concerto for two pianos 411, 487; *Photoptosis* 381, 484; *Stille und Umkehr* 378, 484